THE REBELLION IN WICKLOW 1798

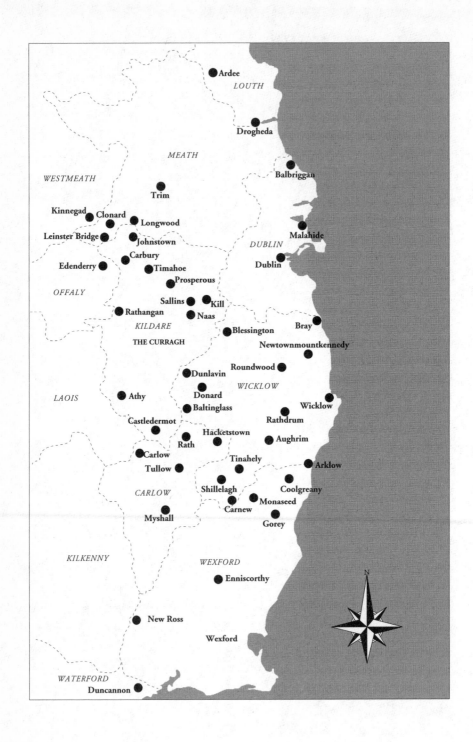

The Rebellion in Wicklow 1798

Ruán O'Donnell

IRISH ACADEMIC PRESS

First published in 1998 by
IRISH ACADEMIC PRESS
44, Northumberland Road, Dublin 4, Ireland
and in North America by
IRISH ACADEMIC PRESS
c/o ISBS, 5804 NE Hassalo Street, Portland, OR 97213
website: http://www.iap.ie

British Library Cataloguing in Publication Data

O'Donnell, Ruán
    The Rebellion in Wicklow, 1798. (New directions in Irish history)
    1. United Irishmen – History   2. Ireland – History – Rebellion of 1798
    3. Wicklow (Ireland) – History
    I. Title
    941.8'85'07

ISBN 0–7165–2659–X Hardback
ISBN 0–7165–2694–8 Paperback
ISSN 1393–5356 New Directions in Irish History

Typeset in 11 pt on 13 pt Sabon
by Carrigboy Typesetting Services, Co. Cork
Printed by ColourBooks Ltd., Dublin

Contents

Acknowledgements

I would like to acknowledge the help extended to me during the research and writing of this book by Kevin Whelan, Pat Power and Thomas Bartlett. Thanks also to Rory Buckley, Stan O'Reilly, Maeve O'Donnell, James Doran, Daire Keogh, Richard Aylmer, Al and June O'Donnell, Bob Reece, Henry Cairns, Michael Kunz, Andrew O'Brien, Barry Doyle, James McGuire, Maurice Kirwan, Jim Dolan, Joan Kavanagh, Ned Travers, Jimmy Kelly, Jim Rees, Kevin Byrne, Tom O'Dwyer, Niamh O'Sullivan, Alastair Smeaton, Peter O'Shaughnessy, Grant Howie, Tom McCaughran, Vincent O'Reilly, Conor O'Brien, Annie and Sean Holt, Tommy Graham.

In memory of James Kirwan and George O'Donnell

List of Illustrations

Introduction

Wicklow, although one of the most neglected areas of the burgeoning historiography of the 1798 rebellion, was one of the most consistently and violently disturbed counties. It suffered greatly in terms of lives lost and property destroyed and at times the course of the fighting within its borders held the key to the success or failure of the insurrection. Wicklowmen fought from the very first night of hostilities on 23 May 1798 to the bitter end in October/November, long after a series of government victories and subsequent amnesties had driven their comrades from the field elsewhere. The county's untypically large loyalist community sustained the second highest amount of damage to their houses, business and farms of any in Ireland, and were obliged to hold the line against their insurgent neighbours for several years after the cataclysm of 1798. They were early adherents of the Orange Order and yet also harboured within their ranks nominal loyalists, men who collaborated with the rebels. Swathes of south and west Wicklow were virtually abandoned by their neutral and pro-government residents for the duration of the rebellion while their combatant elements retreated into the comparative safety of garrison towns.

Rebel losses in Wicklow are incalculable but were certainly very severe. The county was one of the first outside Ulster to be subjected to martial law regulations in late 1797 and by 1803 was the last in which co-ordinated rebellion existed. No county sent more of its inhabitants to the penal colonies of New South Wales in the aftermath of 1798 and it is evident that the per capita involvement of its inhabitants in the struggle was exceptionally high for a sector that was never completely overrun by the insurgents. On the eve of the rebellion, Wicklow's 14,000 United Irishmen had comprised the largest paper force in Leinster and, notwithstanding a series of crushing setbacks, a significant proportion turned out during a gruelling summer-long campaign. The bloody contest for the town of Arklow in the south of the county on 9 June 1798 was arguably the principal turning-point of the rebellion and it was this engagement which most resembled a conventional late eighteenth-century pitched battle.

When the open phase of the rebellion drew to a tentative but permanent close in early July, the rump United Irish forces in Wicklow exploited the county's mountainous topography to wage one of Europe's first guerrilla campaigns. No military strategy succeeded in rooting the rebels out of their highland strongholds and the bitter lessons of successive failed counter-insurgency drives contributed towards the decision to build the arterial Military Road into the heart of the county. The rebels in Wicklow, who numbered small factions from Wexford and other adjacent counties, were the only sizeable body of insurgents under arms when the French invasion fleet arrived off Killala on 22 August 1798 and the violent resurgence sparked by the landings long outlasted the more intense and better known campaign in the west.

The fighting in what might be termed the late rebellion in Wicklow was relatively minor in comparison to the carnage of the early summer, but it was of the first importance in terms of its political and strategic implications. The steady attrition that was both inflicted and endured by the outstanding rebels within twenty miles of the seat of government prevented the normalization of Irish politics in the wake of the conflagrations of May/June 1798 and in the advent of the sensitive preparations for legislative union with Britain. The chronic instability of Wicklow in the autumn and winter of 1798 was even deemed to threaten the operation of the vital clemency programme which had successfully demobilized the vast bulk of active insurgents. Dublin Castle administrators also feared that the hard core in the mountains might function as a cadre around which a second rebellion could be launched. This very nearly became the case in July 1803 when Wicklow United Irishmen played a very prominent part in Robert Emmet's underestimated plot. It was not until December 1803 that the surviving insurgents of Wicklow were forced to call a halt to five years of continuous conflict and it was a tribute to their ability that they did so under the terms of a negotiated peace.

There are many reasons why Wicklow's dynamic role in 1798 has been overshadowed by events in Wexford, Antrim, Down and Mayo, (this is the first full-length interpretation of the rebellion in the county). An important factor was that the Wicklow rising was not as controversial in the early 1800s as the Wexford segment. It consequently escaped the bitter literary debates stimulated the pioneering historical writings which set down popular perceptions of 1798 in south Leinster. Wicklow's engagement in this controversy remained tangential as loyalists found it difficult to sustain their allegations of republican sectarianism in a county in which the most militant rebel commander was a Protestant and there was much less need for a comprehensive refutation. Furthermore, Wicklow was a complex and somewhat unglamorous theatre which proved difficult to document and assess in more temperate times. The confused elements of inter-communal strife, state terrorism, revolutionary and United Irish ideals could not be easily reconciled with traditional denominational and social lines of demarcation. Unlike Wexford, moreover, there was little to guide those seeking information on Wicklow in 1798 as very few participants committed their experiences to print. No record of the government perspective has appeared other than the snippets contained in the memoirs of professional soldiers, such as General Sir John Moore and Private Archibald MacLaren.

The only Wicklow United Irishman to leave an account of his experiences was rebel 'General' Joseph Holt, whose posthumous 1838 autobiography quite possibly hindered the in-depth study of the events described. His two-volumed work was unpopular because of its perceived apologetic tone and overblown style which, unknown to the readers, was the work of its 'editor', Thomas Crofton Croker. Another impediment was the orthodox time frame imposed on the rebellion by nineteenth-century historians which effectively ignored the period after July 1798 in which Wicklow's insurgents were pre-eminent. A tendency to view the rebellion in terms of a variant of the American War of Independence increased the appeal of the more conventional aspects of 1798 and militated against the acknowledgement of the multiple skirmishes, assassinations and prison massacres that characterized the rebellion in Wicklow. This bias exacerbated the trend of wholly subsuming the battles of Arklow, Hacketstown and Ballyellis into an artificially delineated Wexford rebellion, notwithstanding the major and, in some cases the majority, input of their Wicklow comrades in the same events.

When the able propagandists of the Young Ireland and Fenian movements helped re-ignite awareness of 1798 and generate pride in the ideals of the United Irishmen, there was little material available to enable them to promote an historically minded treatment of the insurrection in Wicklow. Other than the disdained Holt memoir and the relevant passages of the Wexford rebel Miles Byrne published in the 1850s, readers were reliant upon snippets of second-hand information in the nationalist and Catholic press and John Thomas Campion's folklore-based work of historical fiction, *Michael Dwyer, or, the insurgent captain of the Wicklow mountains, a tale of the rising in '98*. Campion's novel helped propel Dwyer into the ranks of leading United Irish heroes but his exploits were not accurately portrayed and the book largely ignored the 1798 rebellion. Heroic and tragic individuals and certain notorious incidents were, however, already imprinted on the popular mind by the late 1800s but their proper context had long been obscured with the result that the county's premier rebel songs, 'Dunlavin Green' and 'Billy Byrne of Ballymanus', never resonated with the power of 'Boolavogue'. Knowledge of the Wicklow rebellion was at a low ebb in 1898 when the centenary celebrations were held and the revival of interest within the county between that year and 1905 was not translated into the type of historical research that might have initiated a sustained recovery.

The belated editing and printing of extracts from the Luke Cullen manuscripts in 1938, 1948 and 1959, however, placed a considerable amount of firsthand information at the disposal of modern historians. Cullen, a Bray man, had collected dozens of interviews with rebel veterans between 1815 and his death in 1859 and thus preserved a valuble record that was largely uncontaminated by misremembered and invented folklore. Segments of the MSS are held in the National Library of Ireland, Trinity College Dublin and the National Archives. When allowances are made for its compilers' deeply conservative views, the influence of secondary sources and their geographically uneven scope, the Cullen MSS remain the singlemost useful resource for insurgent Wicklow, 1797–1803. Much of this material was made available to R.R. Madden and William John Fitzpatrick from the 1840s who utilized only a fraction in their possession in their many works on 1798. Wicklow had already been denigrated to the status of a secondary campaign in the broad scheme of the rebellion and Fitzpatrick was struck by the political sensitivity attending the presentation of some of the more sensational items.

An important advance was made in 1944 with the appearance of Dr Charles Dickson's *The life of Michael Dwyer* which drew heavily upon the records left by Luke Cullen and a painstaking survey of the most reliable folk accounts. Dickson also collected much previously unpublished information from local authorities and identified innumerable sites connected with the rebellion. Its impact on rebellion historiography, unfortunately, was limited by the book's poor format, an inadequate index, Dickson's primary interest in historical topography and its concentration on post-1798 events. It is, however, an indispensable and accessible compendium of useful information for the period 1799 to 1803 and helped pave the way for the first phase of a critical re-evaluation of the Wicklow sector in the early 1990s.

This work has drawn extensively on new and hitherto under used primary sources including the vast Rebellion Papers in the National Archives which contains hundreds of relevant documents written by Wicklow magistrates, informers, army officers, loyalist correspondents and Dublin Castle officials, in addition to court martial transcripts and depositions of participants. The associated State of the Country Papers, Official Papers, Fraser Papers and Prisoners Petitions and Cases were also consulted, as were the voluminous Home Office papers in the Public Record Office (England) which detail high level deliberations between Dublin and London. Various public and privately owned estate documents, letters and personal records of leading protagonists, such as those of the Earls Fitzwilliam and Hardwicke as well as the Powerscourt, Stratford, Downshire, Tighe, Archer, Parsons, Coates, La Touche and Proby families, provide revealing insights into neutral and loyalist activity and opinion during the rebellion years. The Kilmainham Papers and lesser military archives held by the National Library of Ireland complemented British Army and Irish Militia material available in the War Office files at the PRO in Kew, London, and were invaluable in reconstructing the nature and course of anti-insurgent operations in Wicklow.

Conservative, liberal and republican newspapers and periodicals spanning the years 1797 and 1803 also proved particularly fertile for charting the progress of the Wicklow United Irishmen and the rebellion they fomented. The county's insurgent history could not be ignored by contemporaries and was frequently, sometimes daily, in the news. Men like Holt and Dwyer were household names in the late 1790s and far better known than many currently famous United Irish leaders whose status was retrospectively conferred in the late 1800s. The level of attention elicited by the Wicklow rebels during and immediately after the rebellion exceeded that devoted to most other counties and this, if any further reason was necessary, makes a strong case for re-assessing the significance of their campaign.

CHAPTER ONE

'O'Byrne's country': Wicklow before the rebellion

The scale and ferocity of the Wicklow rebellion of 1798 largely reflected the issues of settlement and dispossession of the late sixteenth and early seventeenth centuries. This was the period in which the small 'Pale' district extending from the Dublin mountains to Drogheda, where English settlement and crown authority was relatively secure, expanded to encompass every part of Ireland and to impact on all facets of traditional Gaelic society. The Elizabethans deemed Wicklow, known to them as 'O'Byrne's country', a wild and dangerous tract of mountain, forest and highland bog, which was highly unusual given that it was the closest non-Pale territory to the theoretical seat of government. Geography and vigorous native resistance had combined to impede such fundamental processes as the formalization of a county administration in Wicklow. This presented a major challenge to new English colonizers of the 1500s who learned that Wicklow was prone to rebellions of a type that were difficult to suppress. Yet by the early 1700s, 'O'Byrne's Country' had been transformed into the heavily planted county of Wicklow where English customs, fashion and language were irrevocably emplaced.[1]

The roots of this cultural revolution can be traced to the mid-1500s when the rising of 1534–40 and the extension of the Reformation to Ireland from 1536 necessitated a strengthening of the British connection. Henry VIII's agents obliged Gaelic chieftains to symbolically 'surrender' their authority in order to have it restored by the crown in return for undertakings to observe certain laws and regulations which enhanced British security at home and in Ireland. This initiative was a qualified success and laid the basis for realigning the complex web of traditional Irish power structures along English lines.[2]

London's inability to enforce its religious changes in Ireland prevented the Reformation from becoming an explosive issue, yet the instability caused by the vacillations of Edward VI, Mary and Elizabeth gave scope

6

for counter-reformatory organization in Ireland, particularly after 1560 when the Dublin parliament passed the Acts of Uniformity and Supremacy. The threat of Spanish interference in Ireland led to a series of clashes in Munster and Leinster where the steady encroachment of royal power was frequently resented, most notably in 1579–1583. Attempts were made from the 1570s to foster colonies of 'New English' whose ethnic and religious allegiances provided the Pale governors with a bulwark against inimical Irish trends and the structure of a centralized shirred state was developed. Renewed efforts to bring Wicklow into the fold in 1580 galvanized a firm alliance between the Old English and Gaelic Irish against the 'New English' and the Dublin Castle executive. Lord Grey de Wilton's bid to quash the forces of the Old English figure-head James Eustace (Viscount Baltinglass) and Gaelic chieftain Feagh MacHugh O'Byrne ended in disaster in Glenmalure on 25 August 1580. A body of several thousand suffered one of the most serious defeats sustained by English troops in the centuries of Anglo-Irish conflict.[3]

The Baltinglass revolt was partially a display of counter-reformation defiance but it was also a calculated response to perceived crown despotism. Eustace had brokered significant links between his Old English co-conspirators and the O'Byrnes, the Kavanaghs, the O'Connors and the O'Mores, who were amongst the most powerful Gaelic septs in Leinster. Common cause was also made with the defiant Munster-based followers of the Desmondites who had repudiated the Elizabethan agenda. It was apparent by late December 1580, however, that the raids on Pale and midland settlements could not deliver a lethal blow to the Government. O'Byrne was pardoned on the grounds of expediency in September 1580 and Eustace fled to the continent in November 1581 leaving most of his lieutenants to bear the brunt of Grey's reckoning.[4]

The legacy of Glenmalure, reflected in Edmund Spenser's unsettling 'Faerie Queen', haunted Castle strategists for centuries. It also prevented the planned shirring of Wicklow into a county for over twenty years after it was first mooted in 1578 as there were insufficient 'gentlemen' and freeholders in the district to form county offices. O'Byrne remained a thorn in the side of the Palesmen and in 1594 aided the rescue of Red Hugh O'Donnell and Henry and Art O'Neil from Dublin Castle. The hydra head of Feagh McHugh O'Byrne was removed by his summary execution at Ballinacor in May 1597 but the extreme hazards of campaigning against Wicklow insurgents were never again underestimated. Indeed, the military road advocated by Spenser was finally built 200 years later after hard fought rebellions in 1641 and 1798 had underlined its long-term necessity.[5]

The victory of the Ulster leader Hugh O'Neil at Yellow Ford in August 1598 again unsettled Wicklow and in late May 1599 Phelim MacFeagh O'Byrne defeated Sir Henry Harrington and Captain Adam Loftus near Rathdrum. Once again, however, the myriad logistic and strategic difficulties of consolidating isolated insurgent triumphs enabled the authorities to regain the initiative. A punitive expedition by Lord Deputy Mountjoy in 1600 gravely weakened the O'Byrnes and containment of the Spanish expeditionary forces at Kinsale in September 1601 turned the fortunes of the Elizabethans.[6]

In Wicklow Tudor triumph brought dramatic, albeit superficial, change in the form of accelerated anglicization. When the territory was belatedly shirred by Lord Deputy Sir Arthur Chichester in 1606, the last part of Ireland to become a county, Solicitor General Sir John Davies noted with surprise how those entitled to attend the assizes wore English-style clothes. As the nascent potential of Wicklow began to be realized, so did the attractiveness of more comprehensive development. Lord Deputy Falkland attempted to wrest territory from Phelim McFeagh O'Byrne in 1628 and the steady removal of Gaelic title to the O'Toole and O'Byrne lands kept pace with the redistribution of forfeited Baltinglass properties. While Wicklow had been partially 'planted' with English settlers in the 1620s, much of the county remained in Irish hands in the aftermath of the seventeenth-century Williamite and Cromwellian deluges. Settlers were allowed Irish tenants and the planned fuller conquest of the county had to be postponed when the war of 1641 broke out.[7]

English policy in Ireland after 1603 was an uneven mixture of repression and conciliation which pleased no-one. Wicklow was affected by the divisive policies of Lord Deputy Thomas Viscount Wentworth who acquired a 14,000-acre Royal Plantation grant in the county in 1640 to add to his purchase of Shillelagh three years earlier. When the county revolted in November 1641, the administration was concerned that Wicklow's strategic importance and its responsibilities towards its New English settlers would necessitate a hard campaign. Its distance from the principal insurrectionary counties lessened the urgency of taking action even though the O'Byrnes and O'Tooles captured several important castles. The reprisals taken by Sir Charles Coote's forces in 1641–2 made a deep impact on the psyche of the Wicklow people. Not for the last time Wicklow loyalists incurred a disproportionate degree of losses with their claims for compensation ranking the fourth highest of any county in Ireland.[8]

The destructive capacity of the Cromwellians was also applied to Wicklow through which their army blazed a path *en route* to the south in 1649. Cromwell's men swept all before them on their march sacking Killincarrig Castle near Delgany on 27 September 1649 and recapturing Arklow the following day. Mountain-based fighters under Christopher Toole managed to steal Cromwell's horse but no victories of consequence were won and Arklow easily withstood two counterattacks. Scorched earth tactics were then used by Edmund Ludlow and Henry Ireton in their struggle to eradicate the 'tory' guerrillas of the O'Byrnes, O'Kavanaghs and Tooles. Low-level conflict continued into the mid-1650s but the backbone of resistance was broken in August 1652 with the highly effective dual strategy of military superiority and clemency. As early as 1647, one hundred and forty-six O'Byrnes and twenty-four O'Tooles had been indicted as outlaws along with fourteen Archbolds and five Wolverstons from the Old English community.[9]

The legacy of Cromwellian atrocities in Wicklow and the plantations which followed had great bearing on the course of the 1798 rebellion; the perceived injustices of the 1640s were recalled by the United Irishmen and the descendants of the incoming communities who dominated the forces of their loyalist adversaries. In the short-term all remaining O'Byrne lands in Wicklow were confiscated along with that of most surviving major Catholic landowners. The county's native proprietors had retained approximately 20,000 acres of their 75,000-acre pre-Tudor lands until 1641, but had lost it all by 1653. While 35 per cent of Wicklow was expropriated the poor quality of much of the land and settler insecurities ensured that the county had one of the lowest rates of redistribution to immigrants. Only 33 per cent of the seized land was granted to settlers by 1688 in comparison with 60 per cent of Wexford, 76 per cent of Meath and 72 per cent of Carlow. Catholic-owned land, however, was reduced to 14 per cent of the county from about 50 per cent in 1641.[10]

The restoration of the monarchy in 1660 did not greatly ameliorate the discomforture of Wicklow families who had suffered during the previous decade as Charles II subordinated his desire to reward those who had fought for the crown in the 1640s to the necessity of placating Irish-based Cromwellians. The accession of King James in 1685 and his toleration of Catholicism elicited great alarm from Irish Protestants but the defeat of his forces at the Boyne and Aughrim during the Williamite War of 1688–91 ensured that no radical revision of land settlement occurred. Wicklow Jacobites Sir William Talbot and Robert Stewart lost estates totalling 3,000 acres and the new anti-

Catholic 'penal laws' disrupted religious life in the county. An official priest hunt was held in 1712 and the earliest known inmate of Wicklow Gaol, Fr Owen McFee, had fallen foul of High Sheriff Thomas Ryves in October 1714. The penal era denuded Wicklow of its senior Catholic clergymen but the discreet practice of the faith generally met with the tacit approval in the early eighteenth century. The Williamite victory completed the conquest of Wicklow and froze the political and social life of the county until the late eighteenth century.[11]

ORIGINS OF THE UNITED IRISHMEN

The French Revolution of July 1789 had immense repercussions in Ireland and reinvigorated the largely dormant campaign for parliamentary reform. Dublin barrister Theobald Wolfe Tone established contact with Thomas Russell and Samuel Neilson and was introduced to a secret society in Belfast which had grown out of the patriotic Volunteer movement of the 1780s. They discussed the desirability of reconciling the northern Presbyterian dissenters with the disaffected Catholic population for political ends. On 14 July 1791, the second anniversary of the fall of the Bastille, Tone sent the committee a draft document which condemned the Castle Executive as a corrupt and foreign institution and called for an 'equal representation of all the people in Parliament'.[12]

Presbyterian fears that the extension of political rights to Catholics would lead to restitution of forfeited land were allayed by Tone's cogent pamphlet of September 1791 entitled *An Argument on behalf of the Catholics of Ireland*. This paved the way for the founding of The Society of United Irishmen in Belfast on 14 October 1791 and a second club in Dublin on 9 November under the aegis of Napper Tandy. Initially conceived as a debating and lobbying forum pledged to unite 'Catholic, Protestant and Dissenter' in the cause of reform, the aims and methods of the United Irishmen were more radical than any previous reformist agency. They capitalized on a wide range of popular grievances in a period of mounting insecurity and promoted anti-government sentiment by disseminating radical printed propaganda.

A Catholic Convention, so called to invoke the memory of the Volunteer demonstrations of the previous decade, was called for December 1792 to demonstrate solidarity in support of reform. The selection of delegates and employment of parish networks to collect the huge numbers of signatures alarmed political opponents and Protestant extremists. The use of such democratic *modus operandi* to elect an extra-parliamentary assembly was a bold step, as was the ensuing Convention's call for Catholic emancipation in December 1792. A massive petitioning campaign commenced and tens of thousands were engaged in what amounted to their first political act. Unprecedented political consciousness was consequently stirred and vehement conservative reaction aroused.[13]

The discontent of those opposed to the granting of further political and economic concessions to Catholics was exacerbated by the violence of the arms-raiding 'Defenders', a jacobin-style paramilitary body which had spread from Ulster in the early 1790s. The Defender menace was discovered in 1793 to be systematic and resilient to the hitherto effective application of exemplary justice. Scores of death and transportation sentences were handed down at the assizes of Dundalk, Cork, Down, Dublin city, Roscommon and Meath, but in January 1794 the Grand Jury of Dublin County was told that they had 'never before known sedition [to] stalk so publicly and confidently thro[ugh] the country'. Armed confrontations flared between Defenders and the newly embodied militia and the Government suspected that the protests against tithes, taxation and the military shielded a revolutionary agenda.[14] Cork had reverted to being relatively tranquil by April 1794 owing to the 'firm means' employed by the military and an uneasy peace was also restored in Roscommon and Leitrim by early 1796. The counter-insurgency experience gained by the authorities in the mid-1790s and the development of new coercive legislation were of prime importance to the suppression of the United Irishmen from 1797.[15]

The outbreak of war with France in 1793 exposed reform groups to accusations of treason and proscription. The French Directory contemplated using Ireland as a means to attack Britain and sent agents to ascertain how the people would respond to their intervention. The most important was the Revd William Jackson who found Tone receptive to offers of military assistance in April 1794. Many United Irishmen had then resigned themselves to the notion that foreign intervention was necessary to effect their objectives. Jackson's arrest provided the authorities with the pretext to ban the United Irishmen in May 1794, a blow which prompted many of its leaders to flee the country or to withdraw from radical politics. Tone was exiled to America but first visited his principal colleagues in Belfast where he rededicated himself to the furtherance of the United Irish programme on Cave Hill. His departure closely followed the sacking of liberal Viceroy Earl Fitzwilliam who was recalled to London after only two months in office in March 1795.

Fitzwilliam held vast estates in southern Wicklow and dined at Powerscourt in January 1795 with Sir John Parnell and Earl Milltown amidst rumours of a French invasion. The heightened prospect of Catholic advancement, which Fitzwilliam was known to favour, stimulated renewed political activity in the form of petitioning and the revival of the largely dormant Catholic Committee. His recall incensed and demoralized those who looked for wider reform than that delivered by the 1793 Relief Act and was a key incident in fomenting revolution. The United Irishmen reorganized underground along paramilitary lines from May 1795 and their activists stepped up their ongoing efforts to take over the sprawling Defender movement. Thereafter the combined body began to build an oath-bound revolutionary organization to function as auxiliaries to an invading force and concerted efforts were made to extend republican influence into hitherto untouched districts.[16]

Popular outrage stemming from the suppression of the 'Armagh outrages' of the mid-1790s aided the consolidation of the resurgent United Irishmen in consequence of the government's policy of punishing suspected Defenders but not their more culpable Peep O'Day Boys/Orange Order adversaries. The introduction of the draconian Insurrection Act of 1796 heightened tensions still further as mass arrests took place, *habeas corpus* was suspended and thousands were pressed into the royal navy and marines without trial. An exodus of Catholic refugees out of Armagh added to the sense of crisis and helped cast the United Irishmen in the role of a counterweight to ultra-loyalist extremists and the implacable Camden administration.[17]

WICKLOW IN THE LATE EIGHTEENTH CENTURY

Few counties responded to the overtures of United Irish recruiters with greater alacrity than Wicklow in the spring of 1797. Wicklow had a reputation for social stability and had not experienced the agrarian insurgency of the Whiteboys in the mid-1780s or the traumatic Defenderism of the early 1790s endured by neighbouring counties Wexford and Carlow. Yet by May 1798 the county boasted the largest United Irish organization in Leinster and the emergence of violent republicanism requires explanation.

Perhaps the single most important determinant of Wicklow's social character was its mountainous geography which divided the county into several distinct sectors. Most were linked both commercially and socially to neighbouring counties rather than to their own territorial hinterland. This had a profound effect on the manner in which the United Irishmen established a presence in Wicklow in early 1797, as well as how and where they mobilized to fight the following year. Geography, furthermore, fostered the protracted guerrilla war fought in Wicklow from 1798 to 1803, arguably the most intense waged by the British army prior to the Peninsular War of 1808–9.[18]

The county's northernmost barony, Rathdown, and in particular its populated coastal segment, was intimately connected with south county Dublin. The border town of Bray was the main access route between the city and southern Leinster and the travel writer Edward Wakefield found in 1809 that the 'people on the sea coast are either connected by business with Dublin, or reside there occasionally.' Arklow and Shillelagh baronies in south Wicklow similarly gravitated towards their natural hinterlands of north Wexford and eastern Carlow respectively, rather than the interior of their own county. Newtownmountkennedy, Wicklow town and Arklow town in the baronies of Newcastle and Arklow were all situated on or near the coast and straddled the main communication route to the south. Apart from a road leading to the market town of Rathdrum in Ballinacor North, the urban communities of Arklow and Newcastle did not enjoy easy access to central Wicklow. The Croghan/Aghavannagh range greatly hindered contact with the western baronies of Upper and Lower Talbotstown where the major population centres were sited near the county borders facing into contiguous parts of Carlow, Kildare and Dublin.[19]

Cross-border associations were compounded by trade practices, intermarriage, inter-county communications and social events which were all exploited by United Irish agitators in the late 1790s. The result was an extensive, secret, armed force which, although structured in accordance with a democratic constitutional model, was essentially a confederation of allied paramilitary groups. These factions paid allegiance to a national leadership, to which they were connected by tiers of elected controlling committees, and were inspired by their broad republican agenda. The intensity of fighting during the rebellion of 1798, however, indicates the importance, if not primacy, of local stimuli.[20]

To an extent, the phased introduction of martial law reflected the regionalized character of its object and Camden tended to tailor counter-insurgent coercion to specific sectors regardless of whether the affected districts were confined to the borders of a single county or encompassed parts of an adjoining county.

Perhaps the most striking example of United Irish geo-political solidarity was the alliance of the southern Wicklow rebel forces known as the 'Ballymanus Division' with the north Wexford rebel army in June/July 1798. They usually fought together while detached from other active elements of their home counties to which they were structurally linked in the pre-mobilization phase. For this reason United Irish county organizations cannot be equated with the regular army 'county' regiments which their military nomenclature, officer cadre and peacetime regulations implied. Such bodies had arisen owing to the imperatives of building a clandestine mass conspiracy in an organic and democratic format from 10 May 1795. This constitutional model had been designed to facilitate the dissemination of orders, propaganda and weaponry, the collection of funds and reports and ultimately the mobilization to assist French allies.[21]

The inter-denominational and egalitarian ideals of the United Irishmen were embraced with surprising ease in Wicklow in 1797 where religious diversity had not given rise to the violent economic inspired 'sectarian' rivalry witnessed in southern Ulster in the late 1780s. None of the secret societies which had sprung up in the wake of vicious factionalism in that sector had gained recruits in Wicklow. Indeed, the antithetical forces of Republicanism and Orangeism were not formally embodied or widely represented in the county until late 1797. While Wicklow produced several leading Protestant rebels, it also played host to several extremist yeomanry corps whose conduct during and after the rebellion was deemed to be reprehensible by the Government. The insurrection in Wicklow could, therefore, be viewed as an intensified version of a struggle waged elsewhere in Ireland over a ten-year time span.[22]

In 1798 there were approximately 12,000 Protestants, mainly Church of Ireland, and 44,500 Catholics in Wicklow giving the county Ireland's largest rural non-Catholic community outside Ulster. The ratio of Protestants to Catholics at roughly 1:5 compared with Wexford's 1:10 (where 7,800 protestants lived) was also exceptionally high. The Protestant character of the county was further emphasized by the demographic spread of the community which, for the most part, adhered to the estates founded by seventeenth-century settlers that were maintained by leasing arrangements. Castlemacadam parish was consequently roughly 30 per cent Protestant while the village of Delgany was 37 per cent, Rathdrum 25 per cent, Newcastle 20 per cent and Wicklow Town 23 per cent.[23] The predominately Protestant villages of Tinahely, Shillelagh, Coolkenna and Carnew in south Wicklow were close to other similar centres such as Clonegal in Carlow and Gorey in north Wexford to whom they were bound by social and business life. The juxtaposition of southern Wicklow Protestant communities with mainly Catholic parishes created what have been termed 'cultural and settlement frontiers'.[24]

Although Wicklow possessed some of the most fertile land in Leinster, this rich area was confined mostly to the coastal strip running between Bray and Arklow and to the lowlands of the south. The county's inhabitants were concentrated in these lowlying swathes and also in several mountain villages. Most of the county consisted of exposed infertile boggy highland ground which suited only sheep farming and Wicklow's mountain sheep were unique in Ireland for their short wool coats.[25]

In the 1780s, Protestants typically farmed the most productive land which often adjoined less fertile undulating plots occupied by the descendants of those whom their ancestors had displaced. As Ordnance Surveyor Eugene Curry noted: 'the bulk of the tenantry on the Powerscourt estate are Protestants who hold the best part of the lands, the Catholics being principally located on the mountain sides, and in the rugged bottoms of Glencree'.[26] This was the case with prominent Wicklow United Irishman Hugh 'Vesty' Byrne of Kirikee and also with Wexford leaders Edward and John Hay of Ballinkeele and Miles Byrne of Monaseed. Catholic resentment was most forcefully expressed by Miles Byrne who recalled how his father 'had shown me the lands that belonged to our ancestors now in the hands of the sanguinary followers of Cromwell, who preserved their plunder and robberies after the restoration of that scoundrel Charles II'.[27]

The Wicklow gentry who dominated local politics bore a large measure of responsibility for creating the conditions under which the United Irishmen flourished from early 1797 and, perhaps, for the intensity of the fighting which ensued from May 1798. They were an overwhelmingly Protestant class: only one Catholic family possessed sufficient land to qualify for Grand Jury membership in 1812. This circumstance and the exclusively Protestant preserves of militia commissions, the magistracy and other county offices were powerful expressions of 'Protestant Ascendancy'. Ironically, the county's social elite was notably liberal in politics and presented a stark contrast with the aggressive attitude of their peers in Wexford and Carlow on law and order issues. Traditional liberalism, as revealed in their opposition to extending the Insurrection Act to Wicklow in late 1797, effectively ceded control of security initiatives to a conservative clique who supported the uncompromising Castle administration. Furthermore, Government wariness as to the efficacy of the magistracy led to its direct intervention in counter-insurgent operations in September 1797 with the dispatch of the Antrim Militia.[28]

Wicklow's upper nobility was relatively small and lacked political influence in the national context until the 1780s. When the Knights of St Patrick were founded in 1783 not one of the fifteen knights or their forty-seven squires either lived or had been born in Wicklow. As that decade progressed, however, the county quickly gained a high concentration of titled families resulting from the advancement of native gentry and an influx of new residents. This metamorphosis reflected the rapid development of the local economy which, fuelled by the expansion of the cloth trade, underwent an unprecedented period of growth from the early 1780s that continued until the French War heralded a downturn in 1793.[29]

One of the first and foremost migrants was Lieutenant-General Robert Cunningham who purchased an estate at Newtownmount-kennedy in the mid-1770s. Commander-in-Chief of the Irish army from May 1793–5, Cunningham received the Freedom of Dublin City in 1794 and was created Baron Rossmore of Monaghan in October 1796. The prestigious title Viscount Wicklow was first bestowed on Ralph Howard of Shelton Abbey in 1785 who later became Viscount Wicklow and Baron Clonmore of Clonmore Castle (County Carlow).[30] Another figure in the Baltinglass district was Edward Stratford, second Earl Aldborough from 1777, who built the industrial town of Stratford-on-Slaney upon coming into a £50,000 fortune through his marriage to Anne Henniker in 1778. Stratford represented the borough of Baltinglass between 1759–68 while his brother John received the Freedom of Dublin City in October 1786 and was created Lord Viscount Stratford in February 1795, an honour bestowed for 'public services to the Kingdom in general'.[31]

The granting of an Earldom to south Wicklow landowner, John Joshua Proby (Baron Carysfort) in August 1789 advanced another individual destined to play a leading role in national affairs during the rebellion. Carysfort was admitted to the Privy Council two months after his elevation and was related by marriage to the powerful Marquis Buckingham. He was MP for Stamford in England between 1790 and 1801 and, although generally absentee, controlled the borough which bore his name in opposition to Earl Fitzwilliam. Fitzwilliam, William Wentworth, Wicklow's largest magnate and most powerful political force, owned 66,000 acres in Wicklow and 46,000 in the barony of Shillelagh alone.[32] County Down landowner William Hill acquired a 15,000 acre estate at Blessington in 1785 and was promoted Marquis of Downshire four years later. He controlled the two Blessington borough seats in addition to his extensive interests in Down and King's County and influenced Castle policy in Wicklow in early 1798. His Blessington property adjoined that of liberal city brewer Earl Milltown, Joseph Leeson, whose seat of Russborough House was among the most lavish mansions in Ireland.[33]

Lesser but rising figures included veteran parliamentarian Sir Francis Hely-Hutchinson of Ballycullen, proprietor of much of the Imaal valley, a rebel stronghold 1797–1803, who advanced to the baronetcy in October 1782 and was High Sheriff the following year. Peter La Touche of Bellvue, Delgany, represented Leitrim in the House of Commons and was a member of a powerful family headed by his brother David who founded the Bank of Ireland. La Touche supported Catholic emancipation and it was Charles Stanley Monck of Charleville House who functioned as a key ally of Government in the north of the county. Monck inherited his uncle's Charleville estate near Powerscourt in 1772 and was created Baron Monck of Ballytrammon in November 1797. His role as MP for Gorey, County Wexford, between 1790 and 1797 ensured that he was in the thick of that county's political controversies.[34]

Two of the most important resident noblemen in Wicklow were the Earl of Meath, Arthur Brabazon, and Viscount Powerscourt, Richard Wingfield, who both lived in the north of the county. Meath was a well respected figure who did much to encourage local economic growth until his death on his Kilruddery (Bray) estate in January 1790. He was succeeded by his equally moderate son William whose premature death in 1797 from duelling upset the power balance in Rathdown at a critical juncture. The Brabazons were proprietors of the Earl of Meath's Liberty, a district of Dublin's south city that became a stronghold of the Defenders and subsequently United Irishmen in the early 1790s, and owned large estates in the baronies of Rathdown and Ballinacor. Powerscourt was an equally prominent north Wicklow landowner whose support of the Ascendancy did not waver during the crisis years of the 1790s. He entertained the Viceroy at one of his occasional ballet parties on 2 June 1789.[35]

Politically prominent non-native Wicklow residents included Dublin politician Ambrose Leet, a former High Sheriff of Dublin and member of Dublin Corporation, who lived at Carageen near Baltinglass, State Solicitor Thomas Kemmis whose family built Ballinacor House in 1780 and Carnew resident John James whose brother William was High Sheriff and afterwards Lord Mayor of Dublin in 1794. Alderman

Thomas Fleming lived at Diamond Hill near Roundwood and was High Sheriff of Wicklow in 1786, a Police Justice in Dublin in November 1791 and the city's conservative Lord Mayor in 1797–8. Henry de la Poer Beresford (2nd Marquis of Waterford), a member of the extremely powerful political clan which ran foul of Fitzwilliam in 1795, kept a lodge at Hollywood in west Wicklow.[36]

Marriages between Wicklow's leading families and Ireland's upper nobility were common in the 1780s and served to reinforce the county's emergent political influence. A typical marriage was that of Powerscourt to Lady Catherine Meade, second daughter of Earl Clanwilliam, on 1 July 1789 which was performed by the bride's uncle, the Archbishop of Tuam. A less socially prominent match was that of Ms Ambrose Bayly, daughter of Revd Edward Bayly of Lamberton (Arklow), who married James Hewitt, Lord Viscount and Baron Lifford in May 1789.[37]

Protestant tenants in Wicklow received leases of twenty-one years and a life while their Catholic neighbours, although eligible to obtain leases from 1778, remained bound to a thirty-one year limit. This left them without long tenure and subject to frequent rent rises in an expanding economic environment. Most land was apparently relet '3 or 4 deep' by middlemen whose profits were often immense. The Brownrigg family of Wingfield rented part of the Powerscourt estate for forty pounds a year in the late eighteenth century which they relet for £4,000 a year. Good land in the vicinity of the county town was rented in the early 1800s at between £3 and £5 per acre a year but the average countywide rental in 1810 was only 12s per acre. This compared with a much higher average of £1 8s in more fertile Wexford and Kildare.[38]

Young assessed land in northern Wicklow in the 1770s at an average of 15s an acre but high rents were offset by comparatively good wages for skilled labourers, a category into which a high proportion of Wicklow's working population fell. This was the probable cause of the conspicuous absence of agrarian disputes in Wicklow in the 1780s and early 1790s. Rural tranquillity also probably owed much to the structure of the county economy as in the face of a dearth of arable property, alternative cottage industries were developed which were not land intensive. 'Light' farming endeavours, such as shepherding flourished and the construction industry trades of quarrying, masonry, kiln working, carting and brickmaking were also common pursuits in central and north Wicklow. Wicklow's population, therefore, while overwhelmingly rurally located in a county with very little good soil, was not reliant on agricultural pursuits for survival to the same extent as their peers in Munster. Those who farmed, moreover, generally had viable and well maintained holdings.[39]

Irish leasing arrangements were an intensely political issue in that they embodied institutional sectarianism that the United Irishmen wished to abolish. Their religious differentiation both implied and underlined Protestant insecurity. Short leases rendered tenants financially and physically insecure and accentuated the sense of grievance felt by many middle-class Catholic families. Leasing policy, paradoxically, was vital to preserving the county's exceptionally good record of religious tolerance as small Protestant tenants did not feel vulnerable to Catholic encroachment to the extent that they did in southern and central Ulster in the early 1780s. Many Wicklow tenants benefitted from an 'old tenant preference' system that lessened the prospect of dispossession when their leases expired. While economically prudent, this reinforced the status quo of Protestant ascendancy, and transfers in which Catholic tenants displaced Protestants were extremely rare in Wicklow.

Inter-denominational economic competition, so often a variant of inter-communal rivalry, was not sharpened by political concerns and did not result in overt sectarian friction in Wicklow; the 'Peep of Day Boys' found no acolytes among Wicklow's weaving and small farming communities whom they superficially resembled. A buoyant cloth trade in the late 1780s and early 1790s also forestalled the emergence of factional competition and no cycle of violence was set in train until late 1797 when the political landscape was redefined by national issues. The concentration of Wicklow Protestants in heavily planted parishes and villages insulated them from the palpable spectre of Catholic mobilization so prevalent in southern Ulster. The potential for paranoid insecurity was also probably lessened by the passive disposition of the county's small and muted Catholic middle class prior to the 1790s.[40]

The economic and agricultural development of Wicklow in the 1780s could have left few tenants entirely untouched by the forces of change. Advertisements concerning Wicklow properties were distinguished by the emphasis laid on the 'improving' ethic and in 1789 Earl Meath leased nineteen farms totalling 4,500 acres in the Rathdrum district giving preference to existing tenants capable of renewing their leases. Applicants for the Ballard, Ballynaclash and Ballydowling properties auctioned on 25 March 1789 were required to reside and build dwellings on them if none already existed. Also auctioned by Redcross agents Matthew Byrne and Joseph Revell on that occasion was a 118-acre East Acton farm which was leased with a new house, stables and other buildings on 'choicest land'.[41] Subdivision of large estates into smaller holdings leased to resident 'industrious men' was considered progressive, as it minimized the requirement for middlemen who were notoriously inefficient and corrupt.[42]

Cunningham's 10,000-acre Mountkennedy estate was purchased 'in a state of comparable waste' in the 1770s but his adoption of improving techniques and practices dramatically upgraded the quality and productivity of the land.[43] In 1794 the estate town reportedly offered a 'view over a richly cultivated country in which many handsome villas' were situated.[44] A 56-acre farm was let at Bole Island (Drumbawn) in 1793 and in March of that year another 63-acre plot at Ballinroan was made available in the 'highest state of cultivation.' In February 1793 a Miss Byrne of Johnstown, County Wicklow advertised a 90-acre property of 'most excellent ground' near Newtown which was offered for the unusually secure term of three lives at £27 pounds per annum.[45]

This progressiveness was in keeping with the policies advocated by the Dublin Society which had many Wicklow members and correspondents. It also complemented the 'patriotic' Grattanite and Volunteer ideals of self-reliance and independence. Monck, Abraham Mills of Cronebane, Thomas King of Kingston (Rathdrum), Turner Camac of Castlemacadam, William Tighe of Rossana and John Blachford of Powerscourt were all members of the Society's 'Committee of Chemistry and Mineralogy'.[46] In 1779 the Volunteer Colonel Samuel Hayes, MP for Maryborough and one of Ireland's leading arborists, planted a 4,500-acre estate at Avondale near Rathdrum. Hayes, the Commissioner of Stamp Duty from June 1789, reputedly planted 'every foreign and domestic tree suited to the soil and climate' in addition to writing the highly regarded *A Practical Treatise on Planting*.[47]

More and better farms became available in Wicklow throughout the 1780s and 1789 was one of the busiest for the leasing, selling and letting of property in the county. A particularly dense concentration appeared in the Bray/Kilcoole area which was picturesque and convenient to the capital. Colonel Alcock's Templecarrig residence with twenty-five acres was offered to let near Bray in 1789 in addition to a house in the town itself and Thomas Tisdall's demesne. Another twenty-two-acre parcel of land at Ballywaltrin was described as possessing a 'beautiful situation for building' with a view of Bray Head. Several townlands in the Kilcoole district containing a mill, two fair grounds and many houses were also offered for lease in November 1790 by Edward Westby in fulfilment of a Chancery Court decree.[48]

Forestry, supported from 1765 by grants from the Dublin Society and Parliament, was another sector which improved in Wicklow. The county was largely devoid of trees in the 1790s other than the remnants of the ancient oak forests of Shillelagh and small pockets of Dunran wood, Imaal, the Devil's Glen, Glen of the Downs and the Avoca valley. Hutchinson, Aldborough, Tighe, La Touche, Marquis Waterford and other wealthy landlords fostered small plantations, apparently motivated as much by the aesthetic qualities of the endeavour as the need to supply tanning bark and timber markets. Fitzwilliam paid his tenants to cultivate a rood or two 'round their cabins' and such modest efforts were sufficient to change the appearance of much of the county in the lifetime of the rebellion generation.[49]

An even more dramatic testament of change resulted from the upgrading of the county's road system, a herculean task which derived much impetus from the creation of the Irish Post Office in 1784. Two mail routes were inaugurated in the county which required the building and maintenance of new and existing roads. The routes encompassed Bray, Delgany, Newtownmountkennedy, Ashford and Rathdrum in eastern and central Wicklow and Blessington, Tinahely and Carnew in the west and south. Wicklow Town and Baltinglass were linked to these routes by couriers. The original Dublin to Wicklow road left the city environs at Donnybrook and went through Blackrock to Bray following the historic route to Arklow. Another neglected 'great avenue' to the city markets passed inland through Milltown, Dundrum and Enniskerry. After the Road Act of 1760 cess tax-funded roadworks were generally carried out by local labour under the aegis of resident gentry or their agents. Fraud was commonplace and the competition arising from rival bids before the assize Grand Jury led to friction. One dispute allegedly pitted the future rebel General Joseph Holt against the conservative leader Thomas Hugo of Drummin.[50]

County development was driven by the spirit of innovation and modernism that permeated Wicklow society in the 1780s and 1790s and evinced a vigorous and ambitious gentry. Bray innkeeper M.R. Quinn and his brother-in-law Lord Monck were the main supporters of the cultivation of English red wheat in Wicklow in the late 1790s. Sarah Tighe of Rossana, who entertained Methodist leader John Wesley in her home in June 1786, pioneered several ploughing methods on her 300-acre model farm and in 1791 Joseph Pim of Ballymurrin invented a loom capable of weaving three pieces of stuff simultaneously. The most ambitious proposal was that of engineer William Chapman who in 1791 surveyed a canal system intended to facilitate the movement of ore mined in the Avoca valley to Arklow for export as well as the inland transportation of British coal. The unfavourable and erratic national economic climate of the mid-1790s and a mounting political crisis therefore found Wicklow at a moment of vulnerability.[51]

Wicklow had extensive shipping businesses in the late eighteenth century when Arklow supported a large fishing fleet of 400–500 men. The port was shallow and poorly appointed but was used to export ore and cattle as well as the transhipment of cargo along the coast to Dublin and Cork. Prosperous Catholic families with shipping interests and smuggling ventures included the McDaniels of Arklow, the Byrnes of Wicklow Town/Threemilewater and the Murrays of Sheepwalk who were all deeply implicated in the south Wicklow United Irish leadership in 1797–8. Piracy and wrecking had been longstanding features of coastal life in Wicklow, particularly in the Ardainary district, but smuggling and salvaging remained very much in evidence throughout the rebellion era.[52]

The production of low-priced woollen goods, friezes, flannels, textiles and calicoes in Wicklow increased steadily throughout the 1770s. The trade became the mainstay of the county economy after 1783 when the imposition of a 10 per cent tax on imported calicoes coupled with bounties on domestic sales boosted the market. Weaving, a traditional cottage industry among the poorer Protestant families living on infertile mountain plots around Rathdrum, underwent major growth during the textile boom of 1780s bringing a degree of prosperity to hundreds of families. National linen exports similarly rose from fifteen million yards in 1781 to twenty-six million in 1785, reaching a pre-French War peak of forty-five million in 1792. Young ascertained that cottiers paid about half their rent with the proceeds of homespun flannel and friezes. Small farmers generally organized the labour of their cottiers for maximum effect and were encouraged by artificially high wool prices which made sheep farming almost twice as profitable as it was in England.[53]

Stratford-on-Slaney, the largest single linen operation, had been purpose built by its west Wicklow landlord, Edward Stratford and was fully paved and lighted with over 108 houses, an extensive linen and carpet factory complex and other community buildings. The partially built complex was offered for let in September 1787 at which time it included a linen printing factory, a bleach green, a mill, a dye house, a bleaching house, a church and a fourteen-roomed house called

'Amiens Lodge' with a walled garden. John and Henry Orr, entrepreneurs from Hillsborough, County Down, were the sole proprietors of the 140-acre site by 1795 in which they reputedly invested £30,000. Five hundred Wicklowmen, Ulster migrants and a small number of Scottish Presbyterians from Paisley were employed. Imported Scottish yarn was finished in Stratford in the mid-1780s and sold out of a warehouse at 8 Merchants Quay, Dublin. The Orrs were well regarded in Wicklow prior to the rebellion crisis, possibly arising out of their charitable donations such as one of £30 to Revd Dr McDaniel's school attached to St Mary's Abbey Meeting Place in Dublin.[54]

The Stratford workforce provided fertile ground for the United Irish recruiters and numbered men who had been driven out of Ulster in the late 1780s and others who played leading roles in spreading disaffection in west Wicklow. Perhaps the most important was one McCabe, foreman of the weavers and spinners, whose brother, William Putnam McCabe of Belfast, was the leading organizer of Leinster Directory of United Irishmen.[55] In May 1798 the arrest of Stratford's baker James Fox was urged on the grounds that he could divulge details of how northern rebels 'under the protection and influence of the Orrs' had spread sedition to Stratford'.[56] The Orrs were apparently sympathetic towards the United Irishmen if not fully-fledged members and allegedly met members of the National Directory in April 1798, including Samuel Neilson of Belfast. It may be significant that government agent John Hughes reported that Neilson had also visited Wicklow resident Henry Grattan to swear him into the United Irishmen in the spring of 1798 and that Henry Allen, owner of the county's second biggest cloth factory in Greenan, was certainly a United Irishman. It would appear that those with vested interests in the county's linen trade were gravely unsettled in the late 1790s.[57]

RATHDRUM FLANNEL HALL, 1796.
Power Collection

A thriving cottage cloth industry centred on Rathdrum functioned independently of the big operations producing frieze, flannel and other woollen goods which were sold to city merchants at monthly fairs. A fair of 7 December 1789 offered the largest quantity ever assembled in Wicklow but such was the demand that every item was sold. The boom continued throughout 1790 and in October of that year record-breaking business was again transacted in Rathdrum. Even greater increases in trade were anticipated when Fitzwilliam announced the building of a Flannel Hall at a cost of £3,500 and the six years from its opening to the rebellion witnessed steady growth of the industry. The building work was supervised by Fitzwilliam's agent William Wainwright who refused donations from local businessmen and Dublin flannel merchants. The Hall opened to 'unusually brisk' trade on Monday 3 September 1792, notwithstanding the high price of wool at 2s 6d a yard.[58] Fitzwilliam observed ten years later that the Hall fostered 'a most rapid increase of sale from one [weekly] market day to another'. Earl Meath pre-empted this gesture in October 1790 when he built a Market House in Bray at a cost of £400 and the Howards displayed their civic awareness and sense of duty by building a bridge in Wicklow Town in 1787.[59]

Another major employer in Wicklow was the mining industry which worked some the richest mineral deposits in Britain and Ireland. It was primarily located in the Avoca valley with major operations at Ballymurtagh, Tigrony, Upper and Lower Ballgahan and Cronebane where copper, silver, sulpher, lead, gold and other valuble ores were extracted from the 1730s. Eight hundred and forty tonnes of copper worth £1,000 a ton were extracted from the Avoca workings in 1771–8 and the profits of the Duke of Bridgewater's English Mining Company's operations at Ballymurtagh apparently exceeded £80,000 by 1790. The industry's labour-intensive subsidiaries included hauling, smelting and shipping which provided local producers and landlords with considerable custom. New forges and smelting works were established in the 1780s at Ballynaclash, Aughrim, Ballycapple, Furnace, Avonbeg, Moneyteigue and Knocknamohill.[60]

Cronebane's Associated Irish Mining Company commenced work on the south bank of the Avoca River in the favourable economic climate of 1789 and was established amidst backing for the development of an Irish-owned refining and manufacturing capability 'to the credit and advantage of the Nation'. This, it was hoped, would halt the export of crude copper and iron ore to Swansea and to the Netherlands. Dutch ships apparently loaded crude copper and lead ore at Wicklow town, Waterford city and Wexford's port of New Ross which were 'afterwards returned to us in a finished state by those industrious republicans, at a clear profit of twenty-five per cent'. This appeal, echoing the Volunteer values, was well placed and the company's directors, John Camac, Turner Camac and Howard Kyan, signalled their support for such political sentiment by issuing their own coins in 1789.[61]

Kyan, who had owned mines from 1766, had properties at Mount Howard in Wexford and Mount Pleasant and Ballymurtagh in Wicklow and was related to several of the most prominent Catholic families in Leinster. This heritage was indicated by the adorning of the 'Cronebane Halfpenny' with the unmistakably 'patriotic' motif of St. Patrick. This quasi-political stance, as much as the AIMC's allegedly lavish spending, was probably the real reason underlying the attacks on the company by *Faulkner's Dublin Journal*. From June 1787 to October 1790 he was in partnership with William Roe and other Macclesfield businessmen before embarking on the AIMC venture in 1789 with Colonel James Camac and family.[62]

Howard Kyan envisaged direct engagement in parliamentary elections after the Fitzwilliam crisis and was one of many Catholic landlords who engineered the creation of freeholds in order to obtain influence over the new votes their tenants received. His attempted usage of company land for this purpose, however, antagonized the Camacs and hastened the dissolution of their partnership in 1798. A chancery suit remained unresolved in 1856. In the late 1790s the AIMC directors were strongly suspected of being in sympathy with the United Irishmen and Chancellor of the Exchequer, Sir John Parnell, described their 500-strong workforce in 1797 as the 'most dangerous body of men to the peace of the country'. Parnell's judgement was partly vindicated in 1798 when several mine employees emerged as active rebel leaders, including Chief Clerk Thomas Brady of Tigrony.[63]

The 1792 Hearth Tax returns indicate the relative wealth and size of Wicklow's burgeoning Protestant middle class. They show that while there were roughly three times as many homes possessing between seven and nine hearths in more populous Wexford, Wicklow's upper gentry were just as numerous and owned a total of thirty-six houses with ten to forty-four hearths compared to Wexford's thirty-eight. This points to the homes maintained by the large magnates and also the large number of Dublin families with Wicklow residences. Many Wicklow families, such as the Howards, Mannings, Wingfields and Moncks, kept homes in the city.[64]

Gentry self-confidence and wealth was also exhibited by their funding of several church building projects in the 1790s including the building of an Anglican church in Delgany in February 1791 with a substantial grant from Peter La Touche. Rathdrum's Church of Ireland inhabitants petitioned for aid to build a church in the town in 1794 and were granted 100 guineas towards their expenses by Dublin Corporation which also subscribed sums in support of Revd Richard Powell's pioneering Sunday Schools.[65] A benevolent relationship also existed in 1790s-Wicklow between several Protestant magnates and their Catholic tenantry which, if not entirely ecumenical in spirit, was nonetheless enlightened. Fitzwilliam provided the parish priest of Wicklow Town with a residence and Earl Courtown's generosity enabled the construction of Johnstown's Catholic church in addition to a priest's residence in September 1794. A further grant of land and £100 from Carysfort later that year assisted efforts to erect a new Catholic chapel in Arklow. Thomas Atkins chaired a meeting to raise funds for the Arklow project in 1794 and nothing perhaps illustrated the dramatic social changes wrought by the rebellion crisis than the suspicions that yeomen under his command murdered Fr William Ryan in 1798.[66]

Wealth and prosperity was further evidenced by the Eccles family's ornamental gardens at Mount Usher near Glenealy and Peter La Touche's extraordinary tropical greenhouse complex on his Bellvue estate. Edmund Burke was impressed by the greenhouse which was reputedly 'so long as to form a considerable walk furnished with lemon and orange trees, palms and other tropical vegetation'.[67] Such pursuits were the preserve of the wealthy but the country people flocked in great numbers to major social events such as Macreddin's riotous annual fair and the Glendalough's Festival of St Kevin (3 June). In late May 1789 500 tents were erected in Glendalough and 'wines with every other accommodation provided in plenty' in anticipation of the crowds expected to attend the gathering.[68]

The construction of new civic buildings was equally impressive in this period beginning with a new courthouse in Wicklow town in 1785 and work on a new county gaol in May 1790. The need for a new courtroom had been demonstrated in August 1785 when a portion of the roof collapsed on a crowded session and almost resulted in the breakout of the five prisoners on trial. The gaol project dated from the Lent a sizes of 1786 when a subscription was collected to redress 'the insecure and ruinous state of the Gaol'. This had been sensationally demonstrated on Christmas Day 1785 when a group of criminals were narrowly prevented from breaking out. Meath, Powerscourt, Westby and Wicklow contributed £50 each but most county figures donated at least £5.[69]

Investment opportunities in Wicklow abounded in the late 1780s and early 1790s, ranging from tuck mills and shops offered for sale or lease to large scale mining speculation, factories and estates. These ventures testified to Wicklow's sudden attainment of suitable infrastructure and the vitality of the county economy. Newcourt mansion and its 'excellent meadow ground' were on the market in April 1789 and three months later 800 acres of dairy and pasture land at Snugborough near Donard was available. A flour and oat mill in Newtownmountkennedy was offered for sale by a Mr Ready on Cunningham's behalf along with some 'excellent ground' in 1793 and the following year a new woollen factory with a tuck mill was advertised located at Ballinahown near Blessington.[70]

The horse races on the Murragh in Wicklow Town on 8 June 1794 were allegedly the best attended in living memory and were held in a year in which the evolution of Wicklow from backwater to fashionable resort with a nascent tourist industry was affirmed by the publication of McKenzie's *The Beauties of the County of Wicklow*. As travel writing was a relatively new and small genre in Ireland, the production of a dedicated work indicates the county's appeal and popularity in Dublin circles. County landlords consciously promoted Wicklow's image as a serene retreat from city life and one of the more expensive undertakings was carried out by Charles Tottenham who built a carriage way to facilitate access to the rugged Devil's Glen on his Ballycurry property. Viceregal contact with Wicklow notables became increasingly common throughout the 1790s: Downshire played host to the Viceroy for several days in August 1790 when the two shot grouse on his Blessington estate and Rutland shot at the Marquis of Waterford's Hollywood Lodge the following year. Theopolis Jones of Corke Abbey (Bray) entertained the Countess Westmoreland at his residence in June 1791.[71]

Wicklow's image as a liberal bastion was largely created in the 1770s and was undoubtedly boosted in that decade by the enthusiasm with which the Volunteer movement was greeted. The Volunteers numbered many of the county's residents in its national leadership. One of the first units raised anywhere in Ireland had been formed in Wexford in 1776 as an 'independent company' but Wicklow was not far behind. County demographics ensured that it boasted a large population of military age Protestants, many of whom were connected with the textile industry which Westminster was perceived to have hampered with restrictions on exports from Ireland. Wicklow fielded at least fourteen corps by the winter of 1779–80 when the 40,000 Volunteers were the largest armed force in the country. These included two prestigious and costly support units; the Wicklow Artillery and the Aldborough Artillery which were reviewed with their Wicklow comrades at Stephen's Green on 3 June 1782.[72]

The Wicklow corps were represented at the Dungannon Convention on 15 February 1782 by Nicholas Westby of High Park and its resolutions in support of Irish legislative freedom were endorsed at a meeting in their native barony on 7 April 1782. Westby commanded the Talbotstown Invincibles which he had formed in 1780 with fellow liberals Major John Smith and Lieutenant Francis Greene of Greeneville. Another prominent formation was the Wicklow Foresters under the command of Colonel Samuel Hayes, Captain Thomas King and Captain Andrew Price. The medals struck for both corps were unusual examples of the genre in that the Invincibles depicted a sinister 'liberty or death' scene with an Irish harp counterpointed by a skeleton while the Foresters incorporated the harp above an altar/pedestal, the symbol of reformed religion and a favourite masonic emblem.[73]

The Rathdown Association, commanded by Colonel John Edwards of Oldcourt, Bray, was Leinster's most socially elite unit. The Association, together with its dismounted equivalent, the Rathdown Infantry, was reviewed in Dublin by the organization's patron, the Duke of Leinster, in April 1780. It also had the honour of leading the Rotunda Convention procession to College Green in November 1783 by which time it was said that 'noblemen and gentlemen formed its ranks indiscriminately.' Valentine Lawless, the future Lord Cloncurry, was a member, and later one of the most socially privileged United Irishman.[74] On 6 July 1783, Edward Stratford, then a Lieutenant-General of Volunteers, reviewed the Leinster units on the Curragh of Kildare and was present with Westby and Hayes on 9 October at the controversial Royal Exchange demonstration. The Volunteers had then demanded a 'more equal representation of the people in Parliament' and narrowly avoided a potentially momentous decision to explicitly support Catholic Emancipation. In June 1785, when the movement was in terminal decline owing to the divisive Renunciation Act and Catholic question controversies, the Rathdown Carbineers and Rathdown Light Dragoons featured prominently in a city Grand Review.[75]

Leinster Volunteer officer cadres generally prefigured that of the yeomanry of 1796 and many commanders in Wexford, Meath and

Carlow became promoters of the Orange Order. This trend was not replicated in Wicklow where the county's more moderate gentry and parliamentarians resisted pressure to move to the right as the national crisis deepened. Freedom from the internal unrest afflicting neighbouring counties undoubtedly lessened the urgency of establishing counter-insurgent forces. Ultra-loyalist political factions and coercive measures were not required to keep public order in Wicklow until peace was suddenly and irretrievably shattered in the winter months of 1797.[76]

In Borris, county Carlow, Thomas Kavanagh's Independent Volunteers were engaged in suppressing Whiteboyism in June 1780 but no such service was necessary in Wicklow because of the almost complete absence of political or agrarian crime. The Rathdown Association and the 'Ballymore Association', founded by Milltown in December 1785, were instead used in the mid-1780s to deter criminal elements in north Wicklow and south county Dublin.

Milltown and Aldborough offered cash inducements to informers to gain intelligence on the gangs operating in the county, a precedent which was revived just over ten years later by the magistracy to elicit information on the United Irishmen.[77] A 'banditti' based around Merginstown, nevertheless, committed many robberies in late 1786 although a ringleader named Whelan and five of his associates were tried at the Lent assizes of that year. Locals occasionally took matters into their own hands and in October 1787 a group of labourers working near Blessington killed a suspected thief. On the whole, however, the county, had exceptionally little violent criminal activity.[78]

The 1785 land dispute in Humphreystown in which Miles Quinn was killed was devoid of political or agrarian motivation and two murders committed between 1788 and 1791 were isolated incidents. Tithes, while undoubtedly odious to those who had to pay, did not stimulate appreciable acts of violence and Young noted in the 1770s that there were 'no White Boys in Wicklow.' Their non-emergence was perhaps attributable to the availability of non-agricultural employment but a secondary factor may have been the principled anti-tithe stance taken by the county's elected representatives. The most serious manifestation of agrarian disorder occurred over the Carlow border at Clonegal in October 1786 when a party of 'Rightboys' assembled in arms.[79]

Some of the worst pre-rebellion unrest in Wicklow stemmed from the introduction of new spirit licensing laws in 1790–1 which resulted in the revocation of over 50 per cent of existing licences in 1790.

When more stringent regulations came into effect on 29 September 1791, the magistracy oversaw the raising of gentlemen 'associations' to ensure that they were implemented. Monck chaired a series of three meetings which co-ordinated the adoption of new regulations on spirit sales, tree barking and light bread with the aid of four constables.[80] More serious breaches of the peace arose from the Ballinvally 'gold rush' in October 1795 prompted by the discovery of alluvial gold in the streams running off Croghan Mountain. Public disorder arising from work gang rivalry and whiskey booth brawls as well as the Government's desire to protect the gold resources on behalf of the treasury led to the deployment of a detachment of Kildare Militia. Royal assent was granted to operate a gold mine in April 1797 after trials and exploratory surveys by local mineralogists King, Mills and Weaver. The government's takeover aroused considerable animosity which was expressed on the night of 5 August 1797 when large quantities of mining equipment was destroyed at Monyglough. A military camp at the goldmines, moreover, was burned by the Wicklow United Irishmen when the opportunity arose in July 1798.[81]

Wicklow was one of the most politically significant counties in Ireland in the 1790s as its Commons representatives were predominately liberal and remained so as the conservative Dublin Castle administration attempted to rally support in the country. The county's residents included the premier figures of the Opposition, not least Henry Grattan who lived at Tinnehinch near Powerscourt where he was twice visited in early 1798 by Samuel Neilson. Grattan had purchased Tinnehinch with money donated by a grateful patriot parliament in 1782 and died there in 1820. His brother-in-law and near neighbour John Blachford provided a marriage link to the liberal Tighe family of Rossana and, more distantly, to the conservative Wingfields.[82] Grattan considered standing for election in the county in December 1788 but having identified the main political interests as those of Fitzwilliam, Meath, Powerscourt and Cunningham opted for a Dublin city seat. He had been primarily interested in unseating John Stratford and considered replacing Nicholas Westby. George Ponsonby, nominal head of the Opposition in the House of Commons, was politically allied to his relative Earl Fitzwilliam and enjoyed the support of the two MPs returned in the borough attached to the magnate's interest. Ponsonby and Tighe were prominent in voting against the Insurrection Bill in March 1796 while Monck, Powerscourt and the conservative Carysfort/Downshire interests generally voted with the Government in both houses.[83]

The Wicklow election of 1790 in which Fitzwilliamites Nicholas Westby and William Hume of Humewood (Kiltegan) were returned heralded a new period of bitterness in local politics. Their success vested both prestigious county seats in the hands of Whigs, a circumstance which, excepting Antrim, was then without parallel in Ireland. Westby, High Sheriff in 1777, had pointedly renounced 'private interest' and was re-elected to a seat he would hold until his death in 1801.[84] The liberal victory was seconded by the more predictable unopposed return of Edward and William Tighe of Rossana for the Wicklow Town borough on 15 April 1790. Government supporters John Reilly and Sir Richard Johnson were successful in Downshire's pocket borough of Blessington and Carysfort's southern Wicklow borough was secured by his nominees Sir Thomas Osbourne and Charles Osbourne. Wicklow's small pro-Government party was moved to allege spurious charges of electoral irregularities on Hume's part which resulted in a parliamentary enquiry, the second in two elections. Benjamin O'Neil Stratford's assertion that two liberal interests had illegally combined to defeat a third was dismissed as 'frivolous' by the House of Commons' Wicklow Election Committee in March 1791.[85]

It was not until 1792 that Wicklow politicians were forced to address the reform campaign with any degree of urgency in their own locality. Wexford's ultra-loyalist MP George Ogle, a leading member of Earl Ely's conservative faction, then headed the protests in parliament against Edward Byrne's Catholic Committee resolutions. Ogle was also active in his home county where a meeting held on 1 September 1792 at Enniscorthy upheld the desirability of maintaining the 'Protestant Ascendancy.' Conservative mobilization in Wexford at this level necessarily affected Wicklow by drawing those concerned at the pace and direction of reform into its orbit.[86]

Wicklow's conservative High Sheriff, William King of Baltinglass, avoided convening a freeholder meeting until 15 October 1792 when the Catholic Convention was criticized. Two dissenters, however, ensured that Wicklow was one of only two counties to print resolutions which did not dismiss Byrne's arguments out of hand, indicating deep disquiet and division in the county as a whole.[87] Wicklow's Grand Jury had also neglected to publish a notice declaring their unequivocal support of the status quo in August/September 1792 and, from the outset, the county's elected political figures considered the issue with an open mind. Their pragmatic liberalism was to some extent a luxury their hardline Wexford counterparts could ill-afford since they harboured within their borders the Nation's foremost rural pro-reform bloc. Wexford's Catholic middle-class, while a distinct minority, still dwarfed that of Wicklow, and combined with their liberal Protestant allies, numbered many of Leinster's most senior United Irishmen. The Wexford Catholic Committee included Edward Hay, Matthew Keogh, James Devereaux, Nicholas Gray, Beauchamp Bagenal Harvey and Edward Sweetman, most of whom were or became United Irishmen. Their efforts led to the collection of over 20,000 signatures by September 1792.[88]

The Wexfordians were joined by a handful of Wicklow radicals, most notably Esmond Kyan, fourth son of AIMC director Howard Kyan, a man known for his 'high ascendancy polemics and politics'. The younger Kyan's profile in Wexford derived not only from his residence in the northern part of that county near Monomoling but also from the absence of a comparable forum in his native county.[89] Esmond Kyan was given to discussing his 'popular opinions' with Ballinacor's small farmers and demonstrated his egalitarian principles by marrying a country girl shortly before the rebellion.[90]

Catholic Committee financial accounts for the spring of 1793 list £27 raised by Wicklow subscribers in addition to £38 in Arklow. Arklow donations were the fourth highest collected in any town in Ireland and confirmed its position at the forefront of reform politics. Wicklow was represented on the Committee by United Irishman Walter Byrne of Abbey Street, a merchant whose family owned a property at Killoughter (Rathnew) from the 1700s. He was related to the Byrnes of Ballymanus and in 1795 was appointed trustee of the settlement agreed between Garret Byrne and his estranged wife Mary Byrne née Sparling of Hacketstown. Charles Fitzsimmons was another politically active Wicklow reformer who added his name to an address to the Viceroy dated 27 December 1791 seeking Catholic emancipation.[91]

The atmosphere attending constitutional debates in Wicklow could not have been unaffected by the serious violence which occurred across the Wexford border in 1793, even though the bloodshed at Templescoby and Wexford Town presented a very different state of affairs to the characteristic passivity of Wicklow. The lack of overt anti-Militia Bill defiance in Wicklow highlights the virtual absence or extreme weakness of the Defender organization in the county and an indisposition towards Defenderism. It may not have been coincidental that Wicklow's cloth industry workers were in the midst of a period of expansion and there was consequently no compelling economic spur to make them receptive to revolutionary politics. Faith in the ability of parliamentarians to deliver social change probably delayed the emergence of the county's disaffected middle-class element as a distinct pressure group.[92]

It is also clearly significant that Wicklow's small county militia levy was largely, if not entirely, met by volunteers which obviated the need for large-scale impressment of conscripts and the resentment that such a measure would have entailed. The ballot was fixed at a mere 366 men in May 1793 compared with Wexford's 560 and the Wicklow formation was so small that it was technically a battalion rather than a regiment. A compelling indication that the county's martial resources had not been overly taxed by the levy was the fact that John Stratford enjoyed considerable success that month in recruiting for two regiments in Arklow and Bray.[93]

The Wicklow Militia boasted such a high Protestant complement for a Leinster unit that disaffected Catholic recruits were limited to the rank-and-file where they could exert little influence. They were first reviewed by Lieutenant-General Eyre Massey on 5 November 1793 at the Lamberton (Arklow) home of magistrate Rev. Edward Bayly who may have been involved in administering the intake of volunteers. Massey then commented on the 'regularity of their manoeuvres [and] the exactness of their firing' which was impressive for a regiment that was only four months old. Captain-Lieutenant John Hoey, the adjutant, was singled out for special praise and the occasion was marked by the presenting of their colours by their Colonel, Robert Howard. They marched through Dublin in March 1794 en route for Tyrone and in September 1794 had three companies based at Strabane and one at Omagh.[94]

The uncomplicated manifestation of the militia was undoubtedly a major reason why the county assizes of July 1793 were 'maiden', an extraordinary circumstance given the turbulence experienced else-where in Leinster. The Grand Jury issued a proclamation on 20 July 1793 trumpeting the county's 'peaceable and loyal conduct' and its resolution to obviate the emergence of the forces of discord. The document bore the imprint of High Sheriff Thomas King who was to become one of the most effective anti-insurgents in 1797–1803.[95] King's 'integrity and firmness' were extolled by the Grand Jury of the 1794 spring assizes and a declaration to that effect was published. His conduct was sufficiently noteworthy in a year of ferment to attract the critical attention of the *Morning Post* whose proprietor, Peter Cooney, was sent to Newgate for six months for libelling him on 23 August 1793. That Cooney also libelled Dublin High Sheriff John Giffard and John Lees, two of the most powerful and active Government supporters, suggests that King had been attacked on account of his politics, quite possibly for using the powers of his office to limit or prevent freeholder meetings that might have embarrassed the Government.[96]

Giffard's son, Counsellor Ambrose Harding Giffard, was engaged in another political controversy which was settled in Wicklow in the traditional manner of duelling. Beauchamp Bagenal Harvey, seconded by his fellow top-ranking United Irishman Thomas Addis Emmet, fought him at the Scalp, near Enniskerry in May 1794 where Giffard was shot and seriously wounded for alleging 'that the Society of United Irishmen were the instigators of the insurgents in Armagh'.[97]

While Wicklow's conservative gentry did not feel the need to form an 'Association' in 1793, Powerscourt, Monck, Cunningham, Nicholas Stratford, John Moreton and Annesley Brownrigg attended meetings of the Wexford unit on 16 July and 1 August 1793. The 1794 anniversary of the Battle of the Boyne on 12 July was, however, celebrated in Wicklow by a new loyalist body called the 'Friendly Brothers' at Bates' Inn in Rathdrum. After a meal in the inn the 'Brothers', who were probably freemasons, watched forty members of the 'original volunteers' fire twenty rounds, a gesture which revealed the associations between the conservative lesser gentry and those bodies.[98]

The creation of such loyalist cadres was an emergent pattern of vital importance to the subsequent spread of the Orange Order to Wicklow, Wexford, Carlow and Meath in 1797. The Rathdrum display was well organized and extended to the decoration of houses with orange lilies. The event probably derived much of its dynamism from Lord Howe's recent victory over a French convoy at the battle of 'The Glorious First of June' and it amounted to the most conspicuous display of loyalty in Wicklow since the ascension of George III to the throne seven years earlier. A city paper claimed that 'never was this day more joyfully commemorated in any town in Ireland', reportage which indicates that the rally had been carefully staged, possibly with a view to challenging local liberal opponents.[99]

The Rathdrum rally constituted the first physical expression of the creation of a loyalist faction in Wicklow and when it was repeated the following year friction arising from the recall crisis almost sparked a violent confrontation with the forewarned local Fitzwilliamites. The driving force behind the inaugural Rathdrum event was Thomas King who, when High Sheriff, had deliberately promoted such displays by calling for co-operation 'in support of the laws'.[100] His central role is further evidenced by the 1794 involvement of former Volunteers who were very probably known to him from his officership of the Wicklow

Foresters. Another officer in the unit, Andrew Price of Mullinaveigue (Roundwood), was one of Wicklow's first gentleman orangemen. When King attended the 1795 demonstration his reputation as an 'active magistrate' and as a leader of central Wicklow conservatism was well established.[101]

The shockwaves of the Fitzwilliam recall reverberated throughout the country in 1795 but were felt with particular keenness in Wicklow where many of the Earl's tenants and political supporters resided. One resignation attributed to the crisis, perhaps wrongly, was that of General Cunningham who retired as commander-in-chief. More certain is that a sizeable proportion of Wicklow's liberal gentry threw their weight behind the petitions of protest which were addressed to the King and helped select delegates for their delivery. Petitioning implied a rebuke of constitutional forms and competency in bypassing the office of the Viceroy and served to further polarize the political factions.[102]

Wexford freeholders deputed Thomas Knox Grogan, Edward Hay and Beauchamp Bagenal Harvey in March 1795 to deliver a petition of 22,521 signatures, including those of 'the most independent and respectable gentlemen'. James Devereaux and Hay presented it to the King on 22 April 1795 in St. James' Palace. The delegates chosen by the Wicklow's freeholders were the AIMC's John Camac and Milltown's nephew John Leeson who were both later denounced as United Irishmen. They left for England on 11 March 1795 with an unknown number of signatures and the deep resentment of the county's pro-Government lobby. The Fitzwilliam incident agitated many who had remained aloof from similar Catholic Committee agitation and laid the seeds for Republican proselytization in 1797. In practical terms the popular campaigns advanced the development of the techniques of lobbying, propaganda and debate and brought radical leaders, most of whom were United Irishmen, into collaboration with the 'men of no property' Tone wished to conscript. The recall also precipitated the emergence of a government party in Wicklow which, within the space of two years, had shattered the unity of the magistracy.[103]

The sense of crisis was probably exacerbated by the May 1795 decision to form a major army camp just outside Bray on the Dublin side of the Wicklow border at Loughlinstown, some fourteen miles from Dublin city. Loughlinstown Camp was the principal base of the army reserves which would be used to deter French landings in the Dublin Bay area and to contest any which occurred. Three to five regiments were generally encamped on the site which cast a shadow over north Wicklow county politics. In June 1795 the Roscommon

Militia were reported to be at 'Loughlinstown camping ground' where 5,000 soldiers were expected within a month.[104]

On the eve of the rebellion crisis Wicklow residents could reflect on almost two decades of extraordinary growth and investment in the county economy that generated profitable employment for quarrymen, road builders, surveyors, masons, labourers, carpenters, miners, carters and agricultural producers. Workers who experienced a measure of prosperity and security hitherto denied to them had their expectations raised in a way that lent itself to political disaffection when matters took a turn for the worse.

Wicklow's woollen industry was vulnerable to the impact of the French war and foreign competition on Irish exports which plummeted from a high in 1785 to well below their pre-protection quantities in the mid to late 1790s. The county was not heavily dependent on cereal crops to sustain its local economy but the fluctuating prices had an immediate effect on the population. The price of wheat reached an all-time high of £1 9s 3d per barrel in the turbulent years of 1793–4, rising annually until 1796 when prices fell slightly to £1 5s 6d in 1797–8. Flour prices were less erratic but experienced a sharp rise in 1796–7. Barley, similarly rose from 10s 9d in 1785 to a short term peak of £1 0s 4d per unit in 1795–6 while oats reached a pre-rebellion high of 11s 4d in the same season.[105]

Rising costs of consumption were accompanied by the decreasing profitability of grain production. Among the families likely to have suffered from the recession were the Grahams of Arklow who were among the main wheat, oats and potato producers in southern Wicklow. They were related to the Byrnes of Ballymanus and closely connected to Wexford United Irishmen whose brewing interests suffered on account of the depressed state of the barley trade. Their hardship was intensified in 1796 when the abolition of transportation bounties to Dublin markets made the trade unprofitable overnight. Prominent Wicklow United Irish families like the Beakeys of Ballysallagh, Toners of Knockroe (Kilcoole), Brophys of Rathmoon and Shorts of Keelogue would have incurred losses at this time.[106] One of Wicklow's pioneering United Irishmen, Richard O'Reilly of Newtownmountkennedy, was an 'extensive' corn mill owner and several others maintained commercial links with the capital. It is apparent that a combination of economic and political factors arose in the late 1790s which disposed wealthy and rising Catholics and liberal Protestants to oversee the extension of the United Irish movement into Wicklow in the spring of 1797.[107]

CHAPTER TWO

'Contagion': the Wicklow United Irishmen, 1796–97[1]

Before 1795 the United Irishmen had been largely content to raise their reform agenda from within surrogate bodies but the futility of further involvement in constitutional politics was underscored by the recall of Fitzwilliam and other parliamentary reverses. This hastened United Irish plans to negotiate an invasion force from France and in May 1795 they began to build a secret oath-bound organization. By then the initial promise of the Catholic Committee had run its course and all constitutional avenues appeared stalled well short of the cherished objectives of a wide franchise in conjunction with catholic representation. Trenchant, partisan and threatening loyalist reaction to the reform campaign, moreover, had exposed the most abhorrent aspects of the Irish establishment and thereby highlighted the urgent need for change.[2]

The goal of effecting revolution with foreign aid necessitated control over a large and secret paramilitary auxiliary force and this led to the strengthening of links with the Defenders. The Defenders were an eminently suitable grouping by 1795 and proved receptive to the merger proposal put to them by prominent United Irishmen with whom they were associated. The alliance was broached during the summer of 1795 by Samuel Neilson and Luke and Charles Teeling assisted by James Hope of Templepatrick and William Putnam McCabe of Belfast. Their lodges were soon integrated into the newly created United Irish structure which was delineated in the 'constitution' adopted by the society on 10 May 1795. It consisted of societies of thirty-six men linked by elected higher committees at parish, barony, county and ultimately provincial and national level.[3] The cellular organization was built around the pre-existing Defender core although the United Irishmen quickly expanded into areas which had been unaffected by defenderism. Only three months later 8,000 Ulster United Irishmen elected

PARISHES AND BARONIES OF WICKLOW
1798

RATHDOWN

TALBOTSTOWN
LOWER

BALLINACOR
NORTH

NEWCASTLE

TALBOTSTOWN
UPPER

BALLINACOR SOUTH

ARKLOW

N

SHILLELAGH

1 Aghowle	16 Crecrin	30 Hollywood	44 Moyacomb
2 Ardoyne	17 Crehelp	31 Inch	45 Moyne
3 Arklow	18 Crosspatrick	32 Kilbride	46 Mullinacuff
4 Ballinacor	19 Delgany	33 Kilcommon	47 Newcastle Lower
5 Ballintemple	20 Derrylossary	34 Kilcoole	48 Newcastle Upper
6 Ballykine	21 Donaghmore	35 Killahurler	49 Powerscourt
7 Ballynure	22 Donard	36 Killiskey	50 Preban
8 Baltinglass	23 Drumkay	37 Kilmacanoge	51 Rathbran
9 Blessington	24 Dunganstown	38 Kilpipe	52 Rathdrum
10 Boystown	25 Dunlavin	39 Kilpoole	53 Rathnew
11 Bray	26 Ennereilly	40 Kilranelagh	54 Rathsallagh
12 Burgage	27 Freynestown	41 Kiltegan	55 Rathcoole
13 Calary	28 Glenealy	42 Knockrath	56 Redcross
14 Carnew	29 Hacketstown	43 Liscolman	57 Tober
15 Castlemacadam			

their first provincial committee and commenced a massive recruitment programme.[4]

The oath generally sworn by new members was as follows:

'I, A.B., in the presence of God, do pledge myself to my country that I will use all my abilities and influence in the attainment of an adequate and impartial representation of the Irish nation in Parliament, and as a means of absolute and immediate necessity in the attainment of this chief good of Ireland, I will endeavour as much as lies in my ability, to forward a brotherhood of affection, an identity of interests, a communion of rights, and an union of power among Irishmen of all religious persuasions [to effect] . . . the freedom of this country'.[5]

New recruits were required to be proposed, seconded and unanimously approved by the members of the cell they were joining.[6] A basic or simple society initially consisted of up to thirty-six men who, on attainment of that number, would 'split' or 'divide by lot or most convenient way' with half the membership forming a distinct society. All societies elected a secretary and a treasurer, ostensibly 'men of good moral character, sober, steady, & active'. These posts were contested every three months at the first meeting in November, February, May and August.[7] A document addressed to the 'United Men of Ireland' warned that members arrested for arms raiding would not be defended by hired lawyers at the assizes or paid compensation by the society. This firm discipline was widely observed; Lord Ashtown recalled years later that owing to the society's influence in the pre-rebellion period 'drunkenness was almost unknown and private quarrels extremely rare'.[8]

Societies could also form a 'committee of finance' to help the treasurer collect weekly and monthly dues which generally consisted of six and a half pence with occasional extraordinary payments. In order to safeguard the security of the cellular societies, members of other groups could only attend if in possession of sealed accreditation from their home branch. A further precaution was the discouragement of written communications which minimized the risk of physical evidence of the conspiracy falling into the hands of the authorities.[9] When more than three societies were formed in any one barony or district, three members of each were obliged to form a governing baronial committee elected every three months. If eight or more existed, a second or 'upper baronial committee' had to be created. These upper baronial committees, if two or more were convened, were required to send two members each to a county committee which was supposed to meet at least once a month on or before the 25th. In theory, two or more county committees could send three delegates to a provincial committee but in practice only Ulster and Leinster attained this level of organization.[10]

The provincial committees were themselves subordinate to a National Committee composed of five members from each and also to a non-elected Supreme Directory consisting of longstanding adherents of proven commitment and ability.[11] Oliver Bond, Samuel Neilson and Dr William James McNeven were members of this supreme body which was also known as the 'Head or Select Committee'. It does not seem that a national committee was formed conforming to this model and power within the United Irish movement rested with the members of the provincial committees of Ulster and Leinster and the unelected 'directory'. This sophisticated hierarchy enabled the United Irishmen to develop and manage a huge conspiracy whilst honouring their democratic principles and maintaining a relatively high degree of security.[12]

While the Ulster Defenders were not completely subsumed by the United Irishmen in 1795–6 and reputedly displayed signs of their autonomy during several battles in June 1798, many if not all Defenders swore the United Irish oath and accepted their plans and leadership. Government spy William Bird reported in the summer of 1796 that 'there had been a junction between the leaders of the United Irishmen and the Defenders . . . there was a complete union between the Defenders and the United Irishmen'.[13] The re-emergence of Catholic 'Defenders' in Ulster in 1799, while outwardly indicative of a somewhat luke warm incorporation, was primarily a tactical response to ultra-loyalist misrepresentations of the southern United Irishmen as sectarian-minded. This, added to Protestant apprehensions of the mooted Act of Union, turned northern presbyterians away from paramilitary republicanism.[14] Outside Ulster, however, where Protestant input was necessarily limited by demographics and the potential for rupture consequently minimal, the transition from Defender lodges to United Irish societies was a total and irreversible process.

The key stimulus to mass radical organization was the invasion crisis of December 1796 when a large French fleet under General Lazare Hoche broke through a British naval squadron blockading Brest and sailed for Ireland to assist the United Irish effort. Thirty-five ships carrying at least half the 12,000 troops embarked at Brest anchored in Bantry Bay off County Cork on 21 December where the absence of their commander and poor weather conditions prevented landings. Matters had not improved before the fleet was scattered by

The destruction of the French invaders in BANTRY BAY *by a storm.*

a severe storm and a tantalizing opportunity was lost. This narrow reprieve stunned the Government which then set about tackling the nascent insurgent army with an urgency born of the realization that the French were intent on invading Ireland and could return in better weather. The proactive policies adopted in consequence of Castle nervounsness put the country on course for an insurrection.[15]

The only part of Ireland where the United Irishmen were strongly embodied and armed in late 1796 was in the north-eastern counties of Ulster where Lieutenant-General Gerard Lake was ordered to take 'the most immediate and decisive measures' to disarm them. It was felt that a severe internal upheaval had only been averted by the arrival of the French off Cork rather than the coast of Antrim where their presence was awaited by thousands of sworn auxiliaries. The Chief Secretary took pains to impress Lake with the urgency of the situation and invited extreme measures by assuring the General in a covering letter that his authority was 'full and without limitations, excepting what your own discretion may suggest'.[16] Lake's troops, aided by a massive, albeit untried, yeomanry corps which had been raised from October 1796 to augment the military forces, badly disrupted the northern United Irishmen in a campaign characterized by unusual brutality.[17] Yet coercion in Ulster ultimately failed to prevent the rebels of Antrim and Down rising in June 1798 and the crackdown encouraged the United Irish leadership to redouble their efforts to

LIEUTENANT-GENERAL
GERARD LAKE by

E.L. Lightfoot. *Power Collection*

organize a mass movement in Leinster where the bulk of the fighting of the rebellion was to take place.[18]

The failure of the Bantry Bay expedition also alerted the United Irishmen to the heightened prospect of combat on Irish soil. They reacted by attempting to render their movement more adaptable for military purposes, reconstituting the organization to facilitate mobilization during the next French effort.[19] In August 1797 the Dublin County Committee instructed its members to become 'new modelled immediately' by which it meant that existing simple societies were to be limited to twelve members of whom only one, instead of three, could attend lower baronial meetings. These in turn could only represent a maximum of ten simple societies. This reduction in the size of the standard society, whose leader approximated in rank to a sergeant, made each group more manageable and secure. One 'captain' from each group of more than 120 men was then elected to the baronials while upper baronial or district committees were only created if there were more than ten lower committees in the sector. It is uncertain whether Wicklow, Wexford and other counties organized after the Spring of 1797 by the Dublin based leaders ever possessed upper baronials. The removal of this cumbersome tier of representation could only have accelerated the spread of the conspiracy in Leinster.[20]

The revised constitution stipulated that four baronial committees, rather than three, could form the county level body. Only two members from each could be advanced, a rule which was perhaps intended to encourage emergent United counties to fully develop the conspiracy at local level before aspiring to county level authority. This restructuring increased the number of men under the command of a 'colonel' from 960 to 1,200 which was then comparable in size to a regular army infantry regiment. Each baronial/district committee could send two colonels to the county committee although it is unclear whether all members of this body were automatically deemed to be colonels or if a distinct civil wing was maintained. Counties were also instructed to forward a list of three nominees for the position of adjutant-general to the provincial committee from which one man would be selected to 'receive and communicate all military orders from the Executive'.[21] Very few, if any, were chosen in Leinster prior to May 1798 and their role was fulfilled by colonels in an 'acting' capacity.[22]

A further important innovation was the appointment of a military committee in February 1798. It was formed to develop plans to act in concert with French expeditionary forces as well as alternate contingencies of insurrection without foreign assistance.[23] This body was clearly under the control of Lord Edward Fitzgerald whose charisma, military aptitude and social connections made him an exceptional asset of the movement. He was also the de facto 'General' of the shadow army that was taking shape in Leinster and Ulster, who, like several of those earmarked for high commands, stood apart from the elected structures. A meeting of the Leinster provincial committee on 26 February 1798 requested that the acting adjutant-generals inform report on the 'numbers, strength & arms of the regiments under their command' and the military experience of the officers.[24] Veterans of the continental armies such as Philip Hay, William Barker and Esmonde Kyan of Wexford and Malachy Delaney of Kildare commanded greater influence in the mobilized rebel forces than their ranks suggested. Fitzgerald needed information on such persons to realistically assess the potential of the forces at his disposal.

Those who overcame loyalist suspicions and joined the yeomanry, generally those raised by liberal Protestants, were also extremely prominent in the fighting rebel officer cadre. The Wicklow sectors' personalities included Anthony Perry of Inch (Second Lieutenant of the Coolgreany Cavalry), Edward Roche of Garrylough, Felix Rourke of Rathcoole, William Byrne of Ballymanus (Wicklow Town Cavalry), William Michael Byrne of Parkhill (Newtownmountkennedy Cavalry), Charles Byrne of Ballyrogan (Castlemacadam Cavalry) and Thomas Kavanagh of Talbotstown (Baltinglass Cavalry). Their infiltration served many useful purposes, not least the opportunity to become familiar with army dispositions, infrastructure and methodology. Furthermore, it could be assumed that the rebel yeomen would be privy to sensitive intelligence during the very periods of crisis when such details would be at a premium. Those wearing yeomanry uniforms also enjoyed a degree of protection from loyalist scrutiny which several exploited.

Charles Ormsby, commander of the Rathcoole unit in which rebel leaders Felix and Charles Rourke served, was amazed by 'the astonishing art of those fellows, their apparent loyalty as yeomen, at the very time when they were organizing the whole county around them.'[25]

Details were also sought in February 1798 regarding the type and condition of roads within the county zones, the location and number of mills, the extent of flour stocks and the identification of sites where rivers could be forded. Logistic and topographical knowledge of this kind was essential to an army of irregulars anticipating a possibly lengthy campaign. Responses were required on other key themes such as the numerical strength of local crown forces and the location of their bases, both of which had great bearing on the selection of places that were deemed suitable for battle and for mobilization. Questions of this nature served to concentrate the minds of the county officers on the issues that would determine the fate of the entire United Irish project. Their mere articulation and the thought processes elicited would, no doubt, have encouraged an appropriate tone of seriousness while there was still time to consider such matters. The Leinster officers and Fitzgerald's clique simultaneously took stock of the physical state of the army in waiting and, by implication, the success or failure of prior initiatives. Accurate figures were requested, therefore, for the percentage of men who had weapons together with a breakdown of the type of material in their possession. Contingent orders were also issued directing commanders on how to act in the event of allies appearing on the coast. They were to 'collect their force and march forward with as many of the yeomanry and militia as possible', commandeered horses and 'three days subsistence'.[26]

Comprehensive instructions were issued by the military committee in April 1798 when the information submitted by the county committees had been assessed. The instructions specified how each county was to be organized for war. Unfortunately for the Leinster United Irishmen, the circulation of this document coincided with the marked intensification of coercion in the Spring of 1798 which gravely weakened the offensive capacity of the organization but the guidelines were a pragmatic effort to prepare the rebels for battle. They revealed the type of campaign envisaged by the United leadership and demonstrated that their adherence to military forms had a genuine tactical dimension. A recommendation that standards be procured was practical, as they not only provided focal points for rallying untrained irregulars, but were good for morale and greatly prized. The symbolic link that such banners provided with the respected Volunteering tradition may have been one that was consciously forged. A suggestion that distracting colours be used to confuse cavalry, on the other hand, was impractical and was probably intended to quell the justifiable fears entertained by those anticipating combat. Obtaining a bugle for each projected corps, moreover, was neither simple nor inconspicuous and while their utility in gathering combat forces was undeniable, they were rarely employed by the rebels in 1798.[27]

The strong emphasis placed on unit self-sufficiency suggests that the provincial committee did not expect to be in a position to replenish the munitions of the county bodies once the rebellion had broken out. It was inherently unwise for them to encourage the large scale stock piling of centralized stores and no attempt was made to do so. That Fitzgerald did not rely upon the French to satisfy their supply deficiencies, however, was more noteworthy but the down playing of what was expected from them was prudent lest it encourage complacency and inaction amongst the United Irish forces. This approach was in keeping with the tacit policy of fostering a proactive spirit in the Dublin sector.

The frequent use of the qualifying 'if possible' is also telling, as it implies that the committee recognized the limited capabilities of the movement, even in its intended role of auxiliaries to trained professionals. The United Irishmen, therefore, did not relish the prospect of contesting British troops without the assistance of foreign regulars and their military preparations must be assessed with this in mind. By mid-March 1798 the intense pressure brought to bear on the organization by the actual and anticipated workings of martial law, however, had strengthened the arguments of those who called for domestic uprising. The ultimate decision to mount a unilateral uprising was by no means inevitable and was not undertaken lightly.

The spread of the United Irishmen was managed by emissaries who sought out disaffected radicals and helped them to found and regulate new societies. They also carried messages and orders from higher committees and helped disburse or collect funds. One highly placed informer revealed the existence of 'inspectors . . . leading members who go around the Provinces & see that the state of things corresponds with the reports'.[28]

Emissaries distributed a wide variety of printed propaganda ranging in sophistication from crudely printed hand bills to radical newspapers such as Neilson's *Northern Star* and Walter Cox's *Union Star*. Republican tracts were also pinned up in public places and distributed at fairs. Sir John Beresford complained that United Irish 'public prints are of the most seditious and inflammatory species. . . . They have songs and prophecies, just written, stating all late events and what is to happen, as if made several years ago'.[29]

Popular culture of all forms was exploited by the United Irishmen with ballads, catechisms and poems proving an extremely efficient way to impart propaganda to illiterate sectors of the population.[30] Entire song books were produced even though their recitation was a potentially transportable offence under the 'idle and disorderly' clause of the Insurrection Act. Republican martyrs like William Orr, Laurence O'Connor and William Byrne of Ballymanus were all commemorated in song shortly after their executions and long before popular outrage had subsided.[31] Prophecies of victory following foreign intervention and social upheaval addressed the darker side of popular superstition and in particular the millenarianism prevalent towards the close of the eighteenth century. A notable militia deserter named 'Antrim' John and some of his comrades reputedly timed their defection to the Wicklow rebels in accordance with prophesied signals. In the summer of 1803 Michael Dwyer revived the confidence-building tactic by making a series of widely reported prophecies of an imminent United Irish victory based on his knowledge of and involvement in Robert Emmet's coup attempt.[32]

Great efforts were made to suborn the military whose allegiance to the United Irishman offered them trained, equipped and well-motivated recruits while weakening Government forces to the same degree. Concerned loyalists flooded Dublin Castle with dire warnings of the extent of military disaffection which peaked in mid-1797. In May 1797 Camden reported to London that 'every attempt is made to corrupt and to alienate the military'.[33] The knowledge that agents of the United Irishman were in their midst produced many reported sightings, many of which were undoubtedly spurious and derived from the presence of citymen and strangers in rural areas. One travelling geography tutor in Wexford was allegedly found to be in possession of a copy of Paine's *Rights of Man*. More doubtful was the May 1797 story that the nephew of a Dublin pawnbroker had been observed distributing propaganda at the gates of Boolavogue chapel in north Wexford.[34]

General social and economic conditions in the 1790s gave rise to unrest in many parts of Ireland which left a substantial proportion of the population receptive to involvement in the United Irishmen. The motivation of this burgeoning disaffected element was also influenced by factors peculiar to particular regions and localities such as the decline of the linen industry in Wicklow and the difficulties afflicting the brewing trade in Wexford.[35] In east Leinster in 1797 perceptions of the threat posed by the emergent Orange Order to Catholic families and their prospects of political advancement were viewed against the backdrop of the social upheaval and atrocities of the Armagh troubles.[36] The United Irishmen proved very adept at exploiting this potent issue and in predominantly Catholic parishes the fear and unease aroused by loyalist extremism was fanned by agitators. The United movement was, to some extent, responsible for heightening tensions in culturally mixed borderland areas of north Wexford and south Wicklow with tragic results during the rebellion. They evidently exaggerated the prevalence and nature of Orange Order in the counties adjoining Dublin so as to terrify Catholics into welcoming United Irish protection.

The process was generally crude but extremely effective. In Wicklow Dunlavin distiller Richard Fowler was condemned in the pages of the *Union Star* of November 1797 as 'a notorious informer and one of those principled murderers, orangemen'.[37] While Fowler was an extremist and may have been an orangeman there is no tradition of a lodge in Dunlavin at that time, although the linking of the town with that organization would, nevertheless, have excited alarm. Camden wrote to London that month to detail the 'infinite pains' which had been taken by the United Irishmen 'to raise a religious jealousy and to impress upon the catholics that their oppression is one of the favourite measures of Government'. He claimed that the United Irishmen had distributed 'garbled extracts . . . of the orangemen's oath distinguished from that of the United Irishmen in the former they endeavour to impress that the object of the orangemen is to eradicate the catholics in the latter that the object is brotherly love'.[38] One of the main inspirations for the sophisticated oath hoax was evidently a 1797 publication entitled *A view of the present state of Ireland* which was suspected of have been written by the militant Arthur O'Connor.[39]

While it is impossible to gauge accurately to what extent such black propaganda motivated those who turned out to fight in 1798, it led to several dramatic episodes in the advent of the rebellion. Hundreds of 'deluded persons' in Wicklow apparently slept outdoors one night in the winter of 1797 on being told that 'the orangemen were to march'. Word spread from mouth to mouth creating panic and confusion. Camden's sources informed him that the 'alarm of the designs of the orangemen' had been the work of local United Irishmen who had sought to exploit the assemblies. He conceded, however, that the fear had been 'really created in some parts'.[40]

Wicklow was amongst the worst affected sectors, possibly in view of the plausibility of an orange atrocity occurring in a county with such a large loyalist community. There were, furthermore, a number of Orange Lodges in Shillelagh in 1797 and many adherents elsewhere, while the well publicized 12 July demonstrations in Rathdrum may have lent credibility to rumours in the north of the county. The reports were often highly specific and made allegations that could not be easily checked. A man named Collins was tried at the Spring assizes of 1798 for exciting unrest on 11 October 1797 with a rumour that the French were off Bantry Bay and 'that the yeoman or orangemen . . . were to march to resist the invasion; and that it was designed by them previously to commit a massacre upon the catholics.' This incident allegedly induced 'every person from Bray to Arklow' to sleep outdoors to avoid being murdered in their homes.[41] It was estimated that 3,700 men, women and children abandoned their homes that night and the phenomenon was raised in the House of Commons by the ultra-loyalist Patrick Duigenan during a debate to which Wicklow member Edward Tighe contributed. Few Wicklow Catholics would have heeded the protestations of the Grand Orange Lodge in Dublin that their motives had been 'maligned' or their repudiation of 'all idea of injuring any person on account of his religion'.[42]

There was, in fact, no evidence that Protestant extremists conducted sectarian attacks on Catholics in Leinster or had planned to do so before the rebellion. Admittedly, anti-Catholic violence surfaced in the county after the Rebellion but this had largely receded by 1802. Yet the activities of certain 'active' magistrates and yeomanries in the Wicklow/Wexford border area gave Catholics cause for concern and these fears were deliberately exacerbated by the rebels. Miles Byrne of Monaseed and other energetic north Wexford United Irishmen attempted to discourage unsanctioned arms raids by propagating the unfounded rumour 'that the Orangemen were seizing the arms in order to throw suspicion on the poor people'.[43] In one elaborate ploy, Byrne's men rode through their home district shouting out the names of Gorey yeomen as if to each other. Similar tactics were certainly utilized by the closely aligned Wicklow United Irishmen. In late 1797 John Mulligan of Paddock was accosted by George Coleman, secretary of the local society, 'on the night that the report was spread that the orangemen were out'. Coleman's greeting to him was the unequivocal warning that 'the Orangemen were to massacre all the Roman Catholics'. Mulligan allegedly then saw the logic of swearing the United Irishman's oath in order to gain their protection and promptly received it from Coleman.[44]

Such negative and divisive recruiting techniques were balanced by a range of positive inducements, albeit of questionable authenticity. An apparently major draw was the prospect of land redistribution after victory, which was cited in the statements of many compromized rebels as an element of the overtures made by their recruiters. Mulligan expected that when the French landed, the United Irishmen as a reward for their activity 'should have their lands cheap & free to the French'.[45] A rebel miner at Ballymurtagh, in a similar vein, told his workmate Hugh Woolaghan that there were 'acres enough in the Kingdom for every man if they would choose to take them up, to assist the French'.[46] This theme of justice and material reward must have been a compelling one for landless miners, many of whom would have had no roots within the local community and little or no prospect of obtaining property by the conventional means of purchase and inheritance. Pat Byrne of Kilmacoe understood 'that every poor man who took the oath and became united would get four of five acres of land, and that higher people would get more in proportion to their consequence'.[47]

In this instance, the quantity of land to be awarded was directly linked to one's position in a hierarchy that was constructed, at least ostensibly, by democratic means. An added attraction was that the recruiters presumably claimed that the land in question would be obtained by attainder from defeated loyalist landlords. Such persons were very often conservative yeomanry officers whose social status, politics and coercive role epitomized many of the injustices which the United Irishmen wished to redress. The result of such recruiting techniques was that, by skilful manipulation and a well-crafted structure, the United Irishmen of Wicklow grew to be the largest county army in Leinster by February 1798.

While this expansion was underway, many Wicklow Protestants who opposed reform became convinced that the nature of the sedition known to be gathering pace around them derived from Catholic sectarianism as well as the misguided liberalism of their own co-religionists. With these ill-conceived premises in mind the emergent ultra-loyalists insisted on such provocative measures as the 'Test oath' in early 1798, which affronted pro-government catholics enrolled in the yeomanry. Those who supported such initiatives became increasingly disaffected as they mistrusted the motives of the liberal county establishment and doubted their ability to do what was required to defeat republicanism. Inevitably, United Irish organization in Wicklow raised the spectre of 1641, however misunderstood in Protestant folk memory. It was probably this legacy as much as yeomanry associations that prompted the evacuation of isolated Protestant communities during the rebellion of 1798. An in depth knowledge of the real character of the United Irishmen might have reassured such persons, particularly neutrals and those without active links to extremists, but such information remained privileged and was often misrepresented by those who had stepped forward to defend crown interests.[48]

The United Irishman were an oath-bound society at a time when high illiteracy rates gave oaths heightened significance. Their administration was often conducted in a ritualistic manner with formalities differing according to the policy of the recruiter. Oath givers frequently placed a bible or the *Book of Common Prayer* on the ground and required the recruit to pick it up before proceeding to recite a printed formula.

The first overture to a prospective rebel was usually an offer to give the oath of secrecy which reduced the likelihood of outright betrayal by loose talk while bringing new members into the movement progressively. A second 'military oath' was also given in Wicklow from late 1797 which included an explicit undertaking to assist allied French invaders and obey the orders of men of superior rank. Christopher Byrne of Ferrybank (Arklow) allegedly met John Mernagh around this time who 'brought him into a field . . . and there administered to him the oath to keep the secrets of the United Irishmen and also to be ready to join them when called'.[49] The secrecy oath was highly regarded by the rebels who in some instances during the rebellion freed captive loyalist suspects who had been sworn. Those deemed to have taken the full military or 'second oath', however, were sometimes compelled to fight with the rebels.[50]

Secluded locations were not a prerequisite for initiation; homes and workplaces were commonly used as congregating would have aroused less suspicion. John Tyson of Cronebane was taken to the mines stampyard by a disaffected workmate where Samuel Judd had him lay his hand on *The Book of Common Prayer* and repeat an oath 'to keep the secrets of the United Irishmen and not to prosecute them'. He was then told that another oath would have to be sworn which could only be given by 'the man who had authority'.[51] On the following day, Tyson was brought to Tigrony Hill to meet Thomas

Brady of that place who administered the military oath that made him a fully fledged United Irishmen. Brady was clearly the captain of the local rebel company and a figure of natural authority in the district owing to his position as chief clerk of the mines. Thomas Barry of Rochestown, similarly, obliged Pat Byrne of Kilmacoe to pick a prayer book from the ground and told him that the oath 'would be his protection when the French arrived'.[52]

It seems that entreaties were generally made by people known to either the sponsor or the administrator, usually close friends and relatives. Not all overtures were accepted, however, as Michael Dwyer of Imaal discovered in late 1797 when he approached a distant relative named Roche who had a further large circle of male relatives. Roche had been expected to join the United Irishmen and then exert his influence over other family members but he rebuffed Dwyer's repeated overtures owing to his proclaimed aversion to the 'atheism of France'.[53] It must be presumed that many catholics genuinely resented French maltreatment of clergymen and were also unwilling to risk their properties, businesses and families in a revolution. Joseph Harding of Tomriland (Roundwood) was threatened and then assaulted by his erstwhile friends, Neil Devitt of Scar mountain and Edward Brady of Ballinacorbeg, for refusing to join in December 1797. Harding later aligned himself with the loyalist faction and had his home destroyed during the insurrection by a rebel party which included his former companions. The refusal of one of the Hanbidges of Tinnehinch (Imaal) to join when approached by his neighbour, Tom Hayden, steeled the latter to return the following day to demand the repayment of an old debt. The same man advised him in the spring of 1798 to stop planting potatoes as 'no one would ever dig them'.[54]

The key members of Dwyer's group from 1798 to 1803 were all closely related and Dwyer, Hugh 'Vesty' Byrne of Kirikee and Arthur Devlin of Cronybyrne were all cousins. The Devitts of Scar mountain, the Healys and Andrew Thompson of Annamoe were also closely related.[55] Indeed, an extensive network of allied families dominated the pre-rebellion leadership of the United Irishman in Wicklow. The county delegate, William Michael Byrne of Parkhill, was a cousin of at least two other committee members, Richard O'Reilly of Newtownmountkennedy and Garret Byrne of Ballymanus. Brothers Garret and William 'Billy' Byrne of Ballymanus, who played such an important part in the rebellion, were related to John Loftus of Annacurra, 'a poor fellow', who hosted the inaugural meeting of the county committee and many subsequent assemblies.[56] The Byrnes of Ballymanus were also cousins of the prominent Arklow United Irishmen the Murrays of Sheepwalk and more distantly related to the Grahams of Arklow Town, the Shillelagh county committee representative John Waters of Johnstown Aghowle and Wexford leaders Esmond Kyan and Edward Fitzgerald of Newpark.[57]

The Byrnes of Ballymanus were also connected by marriage to many other middle and low level United Irish families in Wicklow including the 'Kittagh' Byrnes of Seven Churches. Edward 'Ned' Byrne, brother to Garret and William, married the sister of Edward Byrne of Rathdrum, a prosperous shopkeeper and 'very disaffected man'.[58] Another sister of Byrne of Rathdrum married Edward Byrne of Liscolman who led the rebel forces at the first battle of Hacketstown on 25 May 1798. According to Thomas King, Byrne of Rathdrum was 'nearly connected' to Bryan Byrne of the town who employed the future rebel general Holt of Mullinaveigue as a 'care keeper'. Bryan's sister Catherine, moreover, was married to Roundwood's leading United Irishman and publican, James Kavanagh, who claimed to have initiated Holt. Catherine Kavanagh had held the licence before her marriage and was closely related to the notoriously violent rebel Harmans of Killafeen.[59]

This powerful and intricate alliance was matched by similar groups in Wexford and Kildare where many of the principal Catholic landed families had family ties. Blood and marriage networks extended through all ranks of the United Irishmen, reflecting recruiting policy and the common aspirations and grievances of the rebels. Miles Byrne of Monaseed and Thomas Cloney of Moneyhore were both working with life-long friends and relatives holding comparable ranks; Byrne's ties spanning the Wicklow border and Cloney's the Carlow side. The existence of these systems would probably have bolstered solidarity among the rebel cadres and perhaps lessened tensions at command level where the failure to establish an authoritative supreme leader allowed an unfortunate latitude for dissension in Leinster.[60]

Membership of the United Irishmen entailed paying monthly dues of six and a half pence towards the expenses of the higher committees and the provision of weaponry. From late 1797 an additional sum of a penny a month was levied to hire lawyers to defend United Irish prisoners at assizes. The welfare of their families was also a concern and the contribution was made weekly prior to the rebellion. These payments were evidently not strictly enforced and it does not seem that failure to pay resulted in expulsion. It may, however, have rendered the individual ineligible to stand in elections or to receive legal aid if arrested. These sanctions were not entirely enforced. One Newcastle barony treasurer claimed to have received dues from half of those within his circle.[61] Some probably resented the subscription or were unable to pay but the donations were a practical demonstration of the democratic principles advocated by the society. That everyone paid the same amount and received the same entitlements could only have promoted a sense of common cause and spirit of comradeship that the United Irishmen relied upon. Morale-boosting satisfaction may have been derived from the acquittal of comrades who had been represented by such well-known lawyers as John Philpot Curran, Matthew Dowling and Leonard McNally. More tangible returns in the form of pikes and other weaponry must also have been appreciated. At grass-roots level the treasurers who handled the money were elected and were consequently made accountable for any impropriety or incompetence which may have arisen.

Although it was not until the spring of 1797 that Dublin-based emissaries succeeded in creating a United Irish mass movement in Wicklow, radicals had taken an interest in extending their influence to the county from the earliest days of the organization.[62] The extent of these early overtures is unknown but the seemingly instantaneous emergence of the prominent the Byrnes of Ballymanus and Parkhill, the Grahams and the O'Neils of Arklow, the Murrays of Sheepwalk and allied families at the head of the conspiracy in mid-1797 is indicative of early adherence to the United Irishmen. The reputed close links between the Orrs of Stratford-on-Slaney, John Dwyer of Seskin, John Lynch of Roundwood and Richard O'Reilly of Newtownmountkennedy with important city United Irishmen is also indicative of such contacts.[63] There was, however, no attempt to prepare a substantial paramilitary force in the county until the spring of 1797 when, with French intervention and the weakening of the Ulstermen in mind, the United Irishmen sought to expand into southern Leinster. Unlike Louth, Meath, Dublin city and other parts of Leinster where defenderism had flourished from 1793, the labourers and artisans of Wicklow remained aloof from the movement and the county was untroubled by the violent political protests it inspired elsewhere. Indeed, Wicklow was so law abiding that 'maiden' assizes which closed without convictions were not infrequent.[64]

The theory that there were Defenders in the Ballymurtagh/Cronebane mining district based around a cadre of Louth refugees of 1792 is not entirely improbable as the mines drew a large workforce from all parts of Ireland. Musgrave's informant on this subject was clearly Thomas

King whose political opposition to the Camac family is indicated by the less probable 1801 implication that they had actively encouraged defenderism in Ballymurtagh.[65] The Cavan Militia were a more credible source of disaffection and had been stationed in Wicklow and Wexford in late 1793. They had a reputation for defenderism and were known to have proselytized in other postings. Their presence may have fostered an early south Leinster recourse to organized sedition amongst the communities who had survived or had been radicalized by Wexford's fatal anti-militia riots earlier that year. There is extremely little overt evidence, however, of any success in this regard in Wicklow.[66]

In the late summer of 1796, when the Dublin cells had been all but absorbed by the United Irish superstructure, a fresh wave of Defender-type agitation unsettled southern and eastern Leinster.[67] The earliest reports of seditious meetings and transactions in Wicklow date from this period, including one concerning a group 'supposed to be defenders' who met regularly at Maurice McCue's sheebeen at Curtlestown near Powerscourt. McCue, who had apparently been identified by Patrick Macken of Glencullen, was unmasked as the secretary of a United Irish society in 1798 which would have been amongst the first in Wicklow if the Curtlestown report was accurate. Aldborough, writing in more general terms from Belan on 9 August 1796, informed Cooke that there were agitators on the Kildare/Wicklow border and Kildare, with its early adoption of defenderism and United Irish organization, continued to influence the pace of events in west Wicklow.[68]

Another concerned loyalist Castle correspondent was William Nixon, a south Wicklow magistrate, who in December 1796 interviewed a prominent Defender who had been arrested and lodged in Wicklow gaol. Michael Campbell divulged significant information concerning the strengthening of links between the Dublin and Ulster republicans but revealed nothing of his associations with Wicklow.[69] While individual Defender figures like Campbell and Richard Dry of Dublin city undoubtedly passed through the county and probably enjoyed the support of sympathizers, it is apparent from the total absence of arms raiding that no independent structure had been created. The use of the term in connection with Wicklow from 1796 was in almost all cases meant for United Irishman which in terms of objectives and personnel was by then virtually synonymous with Defender.[70]

Although the revelations concerning the existence of illegal societies in Wicklow were not greatly alarming in the context of the times, they alerted the county's loyalists to the fact that they were no longer

JAMES HOPE
(1764–1847) by
William Charles Nixon

*Courtesy of the Ulster
Museum*

immune to seditious activity and that steps would have to be taken to
contain its spread. Nixon's letter preceded an important meeting at
Rathdrum on 30 December 1796 convened by the High Sheriff
Thomas Hugo of Drummin. This session marked the first anti-insurgent
initiative of the county's loyalist establishment and was undoubtedly
a response to the menace presented by the French invasion fleet in
Bantry Bay. The magistrates and gentry who met at Rathdrum declared
their 'determined resolution . . . at this alarming crisis to pursue such
measures as will most effectually tend to evince our steady attachment to our King'. This amounted to a more vigorous posture than
that adopted during the annual Battle of the Boyne celebrations in
Rathdrum since 1794.[71]

It is likely that contacts between Wicklow residents and the wider
United Irish movement prior to mid-1796 were the work of individuals who had been sworn in the city and who, upon returning to their
native county, attempted to interest their friends. A far more serious
and thorough attempt, however, was made sometime in late 1796 or
early 1797 when Richard Turner of Earl Street, Dublin, met James
Hope of Templepatrick, the emissary of the Antrim United Irishman,
when visiting his father in Arklow. Turner, a United Irishman and silk

weaver, had previously met Hope and another Ulster emissary William Metcalfe in company with senior city rebels in 1796 when they had conferred on opening a formal channel of communication between Dublin and Belfast. The project may also have occasioned the presence of the mysterious Michael Campbell in Wicklow.[72] Hope claimed that he and Metcalfe had conferred with senior Dublin United Irishmen in the spring of 1796 when, having overcome initial distrust, inter-provincial links were first effected.[73]

Writing in 1847 Hope recalled operating in north Leinster and southern Ulster in 1797 with William Putnam McCabe and visiting Stratford-on-Slaney and the Wicklow mountains at that time. Both men were then assisting the fledgling Leinster provincial committee expand its authority into Meath and Kildare and then Wicklow, Carlow and Wexford. When Turner met Hope in Arklow, which may have been as early as 1796, the Ulsterman 'wanted to introduce the business' there and sought his assistance. Turner claimed, when a prisoner in the city in July 1798, that poor health and a spell in prison for stealing a set of regimental colours on Essex bridge had dissuaded him from working with Hope. The northerner allegedly told Turner that he was 'a coward & ought to be shot' and left Arklow the following day.[74] Yet, as Turner went on to fight in the Wicklow campaign in the rebellion and was a radical of proven mettle it is very likely that his meeting with Hope formed part of the deliberate effort to organize that part of Wicklow from Dublin. Hope evidently wanted to establish contact with disaffected northerners living in the Arklow district whose politics, if not their persons, were known to him and perhaps also to Campbell. The fact that Wicklow's first United Irish representatives were Ulsterborn residents of Arklow Town, Arklow barony and Talbotstown points to the success of Hope's mission.

This *modus operandi* also indicates that the close-knit and somewhat paranoid coterie who comprised the Leinster leadership had decided that a province-wide organization would be imposed from above in strategically vital counties if there was insufficient time to await its independent development from below. At very least, therefore, the Dubliners would have access to trusted United Irishmen whose local contacts and premises could be used to accelerate the development of the organic mass movement. Moreover, it may not be coincidental that the two sectors prioritized in 1796, Talbotstown and Arklow, comprised Wicklow's vital mobilization interface with the Kildare stronghold and radical north Wexford. The central figure on the Wexford side of south Wicklow border was veteran United Irishman Anthony Perry of Inch, a native of Down and long-term Wexford resident.

The first signs of widespread disaffection in Wicklow did not became apparent until May 1797 when Camden informed London that the rebel emissaries were 'very active in Dublin and in various parts of the country'. The Viceroy's inclusion of Wicklow was confirmed by a separate report from Leonard McNally, the United Irish lawyer and Government spy.[75] The key inroads were made in the Dunlavin district of west Wicklow in the last days of April when rebel organizers moved across the border from east Kildare. The principal agents were Malachy Delaney and Hope's associate William Metcalfe who reputedly used their 'utmost endeavours to spread the flame of Rebellion' and 'plant the *Tree* of *Liberty* in defiance of the yeomanry'.[76] Delaney hailed from the Ballitore district on the Kildare side of the Wicklow border and had seen service as an officer in the Austrian army. His former landlord, Colonel Keating, claimed that he had escaped punishment for a murder he committed on his land around 1790.[77]

Metcalfe had clearly been engaged in the same task as his colleague in Kildare where the conspiracy was already highly developed before moving into Talbotstown barony in Wicklow. Fostering cross-border networks was absolutely vital to United Irish war plans as they formed natural military zones that were threatened by communication weakness arising from the practice of constructing complementary but distinct county organizations. Contacts between leading activists had to be forged across notional boundaries to ensure that proper co-operation was readily forthcoming at the moment of truth. This was likely to flow from prior social, business and political links between the various leadership echelons but could not be left to chance.

The personalized nature of much of the most important planning was evident during the summer of 1803 when Hope, Delaney and Metcalfe returned to the district to rally support for Robert Emmet's coup attempt where they no doubt rekindled earlier associations. Delaney, furthermore, possessed 'a long extended connexion of brothers and brothers-in-law' in and around Dunlavin and Blessington whom he must have drawn upon for support. Metcalfe, an experienced emissary from the north, was well placed to liaise with the sizeable population of Ulster settlers in Talbotstown and he may even have been related to the Dunlavin family bearing his name. Their work did not go unreported and government agent John Smith learned in June 1797 that 'Men from Dublin or the north' had attended fairs at Ballymore-Eustace, Dunlavin, Donard and Hollywood to proselytize and had frequented unlicensed whiskey shops.[78] Metcalfe preceded his more famous Belfast comrade William Putnam McCabe who visited the Ulster residents of Stratford and travelled extensively throughout the county in the late Spring and Autumn of 1797.[79]

Most of the lesser emissaries who followed the Kildare mission came directly from Dublin city and it seems that their presence, in conjunction with the senior activists of the Provincial committee, constituted a co-ordinated attempt to comprehensively organize west Wicklow. Smith, whose sojourn in Wicklow in May/June 1797 was financed by secret service funds, reported the presence of United Irish agents at Hollywood, Baltiboys and Lockstown and noted their preparations to organize in the mountains. On 15 May Smith was astounded when Hollywood innkeeper Patrick Burke publically declared himself '*to be up*' (i.e. a United Irishman) and that 'every person from there to Galway was *up*'.[80] If Smith's account is accurate, it would appear that the emissaries managed to convince their recruits that the United system was far more extensive that it actually was, a stratagem that may have been intended to instill confidence in those contemplating involvement.

One Donovan pointedly claimed to have been 'a delegate employed to distribute papers etc' and 'been thro[ugh] the counties of Kildare, Wicklow, Wexford and Carlow doing so'. He may have emphasized these travels and produced a letter attributed to Lord Edward Fitzgerald to impress recruits. He further claimed to have received 'a large purse of gold and silver . . . from [the] United [Irish] Treasury in Dublin'. In June 1797 Donovan told one rebel that the French would arrive during the winter and that 'two thirds of the army and militia were united and would join them'. Further indications of United Irish power were his assurances that a Carlow magistrate was disaffected and that another, Robert Cornwall, would be assassinated for prosecuting United Irishmen.[81]

Scaremongering was definitely employed as a recruiting technique as James Duff was confined to Wicklow gaol in May 1797 for creating a 'very disagreeable effect' with reports that 70,000 French troops had landed in Ireland. This was not an isolated boast as Nixon jailed one Grumbly the following month for claiming there were 5,000 French troops at Bantry. One of the more ominous contentions reported by Smith was that many of Captain William Ryves' Dunlavin yeoman cavalry were United Irishmen although he could only name one named Noble. While this was too, in all probability, merely a ploy designed to alleviate the fears of prospective recruits by playing down the threat posed by their local enemies, such propaganda was to generate great fears amongst loyalists of a fifth column. This had terrible consequences in Dunlavin in May 1798.[82]

Smith also learned that a Dublin-based tradesman was in the Wicklow Town area with 'books to swear U.[nited] I.[rish] M.[en]'. This man's name was Byrne, a carpenter who generally worked in Dublin, but given his surname and mission it is likely that he was a native of Wicklow dispatched to 'unite' his home area.[83] Another important west Wicklowman with Dublin connections was Matthew Nowlan of Barraderry who, upon returning from a trip to the city in May 1797, was observed hiding documents and a prayer book in his thatch by Eleanor Ryan, a nurse in his employ. Groups of men called to his house at night shortly afterwards, 'thirteen or fourteen at a time', who addressed him as 'captain.' Nowlan apparently formed the nucleus of a United Irish society very quickly although one of his visitors, William McGuinness of Baltinglass, was a yeoman whose politics wavered. He was killed by Dwyer's men on 8 December 1798.[84]

Nowlan's industry exposed him to danger and he was arrested when Dunlavin resident James Byrne claimed that he had sworn him and 'all the country [people]' around Hacketstown.[85] The seizure of Patrick Hackett of Carnew in Baltinglass, 'a very noted defender [sic]', was regarded by Benjamin O'Neil Stratford as something of a coup as he had distributed seditious papers brought from Dublin at the town's fair on 12 May. The documents had created a sensation in loyalist circles as their content indicated that the United Irish menace to Wicklow was far more sophisticated than hitherto suspected.[86] Stratford correctly ascertained from the incident that 'the contagion of the county Kildare' had reached west Wicklow and he responded by instituting regular yeomanry patrols, perhaps the first in the county.[87]

The purpose of this flurry of recruiting and emissary traffic was to bring Wicklow's small farmers, labourers, townspeople, artisans and all those who comprised what was known as the 'lower orders' into the movement and establish a foothold in every parish. Once this had been achieved the society was encouraged to develop organically using local networks in accordance with United Irish constitutional guidelines. Supervision was provided by provincial organizers like McCabe who does not seem to have been present in the county until the late Spring at which time the newly formed societies were attempting to create baronial structures through elections and required his expertize.

ARKLOW

Members of some of the most prosperous families in Arklow barony emerged as leaders of the United Irishman in mid-1797 and the organization seems to have encompassed much of Arklow town's Catholic middle class. The town was deemed 'a considerable place' in the 1790s and prospered from the business derived from its status as the home port of a large fishing fleet.[88] Arklow also boasted one of the two permanent purpose-built barracks in the county which was generally garrisoned by a company strength formation. A company of the 22th Infantry had been stationed there in March 1793 but it was an uncomfortable posting in a building with just eleven overcrowded rooms and no water supply. Fresh water had to be drawn a mile away as the adjacent river Avon was 'strongly impregnated with copper' from Cronebane mines and unfit for human consumption.[89]

On 30 October 1794 Miles O'Neil, Richard Graham, John Doran, Thomas Murray and Fr William Ryan formed a committee to raise funds to build a new chapel in Arklow Town.[90] They were then acknowledged as representing the 'principal [Catholic] inhabitants of Arklow' and as such it is significant that members of all four families emerged as the leaders of the local United Irishmen.[91] This transition, however, does not seem to have occurred until late 1797 and seditious affairs were conducted in the interim by the Ulster connections of James Hope. The pioneering northerners, Sternes, Philpot and the Coulson brothers, represented the Arklow sector United Irishmen until October 1797 at meetings of the provincial committee in Dublin. Philpot was a shipowner who also owned a property in Arklow Town where his associate Sternes kept a pub. Peter Coulson farmed near Arklow while his brother John was a publican at Ardanairy on the coast between the town and county town. Both men hailed from Belfast and were very probably the first men contacted by Hope in 1796.[92]

Once the movement expanded to the point that higher committees and electoral procedures were required, the leading Catholic trading families of Arklow assumed control of the baronial organization. Richard Graham was described by the astute Thomas King as a man of 'very considerable property' whose son, Garret, was an early United Irishman.[93] In January 1789 William Graham oversaw the shipment of 606 stones of malt grown in Arklow by his relative Richard Graham which was carried to Dublin by John Coughlan. A further batch of 354 stone was sent later that month.[94] Philip O'Neil's father, Miles, was in Major Hardy's estimation 'a biggoted [sic] catholic shopkeeper of considerable oppulence [sic]' and transacted business with city based merchants.[95] The younger O'Neil was treasurer of Arklow barony, a member of the county committee and, from mid-March 1798, one of the two provincial delegates. Miles Byrne of Monaseed, who knew the Arklow leadership and numbered Graham and O'Neil among his friends, affirmed that they were 'very active and well known to the principle men in Dublin'.[96]

While it appears that John Doran was not directly associated with any rebel committee, he was strongly suspected of sedition and was detained in Wicklow gaol from May to November 1798 along with members of the Graham, O'Neil and Murray families.[97] His dealings with Anthony Perry who lived at Inch may have been very significant in cementing cross-border communications. Perry was the key United Irish organizer in north-eastern Wexford and probably the military commander of the strong forces organized along the borderlands from the coast to Monaseed inland. Doran knew Perry in the 1790s and shortly before the rebellion had mortgaged one of his Ballyoake properties on 19 January 1796, a deal witnessed by Matthew Dowling.

John Lacey of Wicklow Town, a tobacconist 'of some consequence' and county treasurer, was another influential figure who commanded much respect in the northern part of the barony.[98] Among Lacey's close associates were several members of the Arklow McDaniels who were very disaffected and became involved in Robert Emmet's plot with him in 1803. Sixty-one-year old Joseph McDaniel, perhaps the head of the family, was arrested by the Arklow cavalry in early 1798 and placed on the tender *John and Esther* where he remained untried in September of that year.[99] While the McDaniels do not feature in the elected Arklow leadership coterie, their gunrunning for the United Irishmen in March 1798, long term militancy and smuggling enterprises in partnership with the disaffected Murrays of Sheepwalk and Byrnes of Ennisboyne in the late 1790s and early 1800s suggest that they were deeply engaged in sedition.[100]

Perhaps the most important United organizer to emerge from Arklow barony was Matthew Doyle of Polahoney (Glenart), a wealthy cattle and horse dealer who at around forty years of age in 1798 was one of the more mature conspirators. He was reputedly 'a man of very great stature and amazing strength' and joined his eight brothers in the movement. The nature of his business required trips to rural markets and travel to Dublin which enabled him to operate for a time without arousing suspicion and most of his efforts were apparently employed outside his home area.[101] Doyle, along with William Putnam McCabe and William Young of Ballinacor, was instrumental in effecting the adoption of the military system in Wicklow in late 1797 and in promoting the conspiracy in north Wexford. Towards the close of 1797 Miles Byrne recalled that Doyle 'was appointed by the provincial chiefs to travel through the adjacent counties, to give instructions to the societies, and to report on their progress'.[102] Byrne met Doyle and McCabe in Monaseed in company with Nick Murphy in the summer of 1797 and the Wicklowman also conferred with Perry at Thomas Howlett's in Inch where he 'proposed to organize the county of Wexford in the same manner as the county Wicklow'.[103]

The prominence of both Perry and Murphy in north Wexford points to the importance of Doyle's input in the region as a whole. Doyle did not apparently hold senior rank in the pre-rebellion organization but was a captain and once the fighting had commenced his prestige was such that he raised an ad hoc company of up to 200 men based around a core of Arklow fishermen. He had worked with such men in 1797 when he had taken delivery of illegally imported gunpowder. Only a minority of the fishermen participated in the rebellion but those under Doyle's command distinguished themselves at Arklow and Mountpleasant Hill. A veteran of the unit, John Carthy, claimed that the corps was called the 'Arklow northshire' which was also the name given to one of the town's two yeoman cavalry corps. Doyle's rank approximated to that of a colonel and he was acknowledged as holding that position when second-in-command to Holt.[104]

In May 1797 Garret Graham initiated his friend Thomas Murray Jr of Sheepwalk who immediately began forming cells in the area lying between Arklow town and the Wicklow mountains. The Murrays were relatively affluent and in a position to send Thomas' younger brother Daniel to Salamanca in 1784 for clerical instruction. The Peter Murray detained in Wicklow Gaol until November 1798 was another brother and the Richard Murray in whose forge pikes were made prior to the rebellion may have been a member of the family.[105] Thomas Murray became one of the first elected captains in Arklow barony and regularly sent messages to his subordinates via servants. He was described as a 'person of some consideration' and his identity was withheld from the Chief Secretary Castlereagh as a security precaution in May 1798 when Murray made a comprehensive confession to Arklow's 'committee for receiving information'.[106] Murray told them that initially '175 men were enrolled in parties of 36' which were then subdivided 'into parties of 12' in October 1797 on the direction of McCabe. This process marked the first stage of the adoption of military structures in accordance with the revised United Irish constitution of August 1797. This was effected relatively early in Wicklow and enabled the county to quickly bring its organization up to par with those of Kildare and Carlow. McCabe did not fulfil the same task in Westmeath until April 1798.[107]

Simon Beakey of Ballysallagh, sworn in the summer of 1797, rose quickly through the movement to the post of treasurer and captain. His family were substantial wheat producers in the early 1790s and would have suffered from the discontinuance of lucrative bounties in 1796–7.[108] Beakey was initiated by John Kavanagh at Johnstown and was chosen at a meeting at Pennycomequick to obtain instructions from John Lacey in Wicklow Town. Beakey and his brother Christopher attended parish-level meetings at David Gilbert's of Arklow in the winter of 1797 and passed subscriptions on to Murray of Sheepwalk. By his own admission he became a captain, apparently succession to Murray, in April 1798 at Miles Darcy's in Arklow. The electors, all secretarys, included Christopher Beakey, Patrick Malone, Con Hopkins and one Kavanagh, probably Denis of Johnstown. The following month he informed Revd Edward Bayly that 'from Ballinacor round to Pennycom[e]quick and from that to Arklow there were about 10 or 11 societies' but 'they were not all full'. These were clearly the constituent societies of his command and, even if Beakey made other no longer extant statements detailing the composition of their leadership, it is not surprising that most of the Arklowmen, having been so compromised, failed to act at the critical moment on 23/4 May 1798.[109]

In his statement Murray claimed that he stood down being 'disgusted at the business getting into very low hands' but his continued contact with the O'Neils and activity on the periphery suggests that he was being evasive even if genuinely troubled by the type of recruits who were entering the movement. Shortly before the election of Murray, which in all probability occurred in the winter of 1797, Beakey was given an important document by Matthew Doyle which he had obtained from McCabe. It contained instructions 'for each company to collect pikes' and had been issued by the military committee attached to the provincial executive in Dublin.[110] Beakey briefed Murray who understood that the dispatch had come from Dublin via Phil O'Neil. O'Neil's links with the capital were clearly strong even before he was promoted onto the provincial committee after 12 March 1798 arrests at Oliver Bond's. The 'secretaries of 12ves' were ordered to 'prepare arms and to regulate matters according to the directions'.[111]

On 23 May 1798, the day upon which the rebellion commenced, a self-confessed United Irishman told Revd Bayly that he had overheard Christopher and Thomas Beakey 'whispering to each other that they believed the whole business would be discovered and the discovery would come to young Thomas Murray and they then would get at the heads'. This suggests that Murray had remained a respected and important figure in the barony until the rebellion and that the Beakeys were concerned that his cousins, Garret, Ned and William Byrne of Ballymanus, would be implicated.[112] Murray prudently denied acting in 'any official capacity' after his resignation but admitted that he 'still continued of the body and was made acquainted with the subsequent proceedings'.[113] Given that his name features so prominently in the depositions of low-and-middle ranking United Irishmen, it is clear that had played a dynamic role in spreading the movement. He was known to the Ballymurtagh United Irishmen in the neighbouring parish of Castlemacadam where John Tyson, sworn in July 1797 by Thomas Brady of Tigrony, estimated that Murray was over 140 men, very close to the figure of 120 men stipulated for a company under a captain.[114]

The mining district adjacent to Sheepwalk attracted thousands of workers from all over Ireland and proved a particularly fertile recruiting ground for United Irish agitators.[115] The three yeomanry corps raised in the locality in October 1796 drew the bulk of their members from the mining population and were captained by James Camac (Castlemacadam Cavalry), Turner Camac (Castlemacadam Infantry) and Abraham Mills (Cronebane Infantry).[116] These corps attracted the interest of the United Irishmen and were thoroughly infiltrated in late 1797 and early 1798 just as Sir John Parnell had predicted in September 1796.[117] The liberal politics of the Camac brothers and Howard Kyan laid them bare to accusations of connivance in this process but the full extent of their culpability was probably nothing more than their broad enlistment criteria. This was a risk run by any commander of a yeomanry corps that recruited from a large industrial workforce rather than from intimate tenant families. Mining communities were inherently unstable with considerable numbers of part-time and temporary employees coming and going. Avoca was by no means unique, one of the main United Irish activists in Glenmalure was a man named Boyd from Newtownards, County Down, who worked in the valley's lead mines from 1798 to 1802.[118]

The detailed knowledge of the mines yeomanry gained by the authorities in the winter of 1797 put the innocence of the Camacs and Kyan beyond reasonable doubt. Indeed, Camac was sufficiently reliable to give evidence for the prosecution at the trial of William Michael Byrne of Parkhill in July 1798 even after he had endured the ignominy of having his corps disbanded.[119] Musgrave's claim that the rebel emissary Fr.John Martin had been arrested when attempting to contact Camac on seditious business in June 1798 rested on weak circumstantial evidence that was belied by more reliable sources.[120] The Castle was apprized that the infiltration of the mines yeomanry had actually been masterminded at the home of William Kavanagh who, in August 1797, was alleged to have hosted seditious meetings when the 'whole' district was uniting.[121] One of Kavanagh's close associates was Charles Byrne of Ballyrogan who, in addition to being a private in the Castlemacadam Cavalry, was elected captain of the Redcross United Irishmen. Byrne was consequently almost certainly the driving force behind the plot along with Thomas Brady. The Ballyrogan man was described by fellow rebel officer James Doyle of Ballinacor as one of the 'wealthy farmers' of the coastal area involved in the society and was one of the few to successfully mobilize and fight during the Rebellion.[122]

Hugh Woolaghan, a mason employed at Ballymurtagh, was sworn in Arklow Town on 1 October 1797 by George and William Tracey who were both privates in the mines yeomanry. Having received the oath of secrecy Woolaghan was encouraged to enlist and was told that Camac's corps already had twenty-six rebels in their ranks.[123] John Tyson also revealed the extent of the conspiracy to Tom King in January 1798 by naming thirty-eight co-workers as United Irishmen, including many who had not been implicated by Woolaghan. This level of infiltration led to the dismissal of both Castlemacadam corps and the reorganization of Mills' infantry on 17 March 1798.[124] King learned from Woolaghan, that the Cronebane corps were 'almost all united and particularly named W[illia]m Holt, mason' who was also mentioned by Tyson. This was the older brother of Joseph Holt who lived at Ballymoneen above Castlemacadam and worked locally as 'an architect' or a mason.[125] Many of the Cronebane corps were related to the Holts who evidently played an active role in recruiting for the local United Irishmen. In August 1798 the re-organized Cronebane yeomen attempted to murder William Holt.[126]

TALBOTSTOWN

The barony of Talbotstown with a paper strength of 3,680 men in January 1798 was the most intensively organized in Wicklow with a structure then reflecting the administrative partition of the barony into upper (2974 men) and lower (706 men) segments.[127] Each half-barony advanced individual returns to the county committee from the beginning of 1798 which suggests that there were two baronial committees, one of which convened in Stratford-on-Slaney. The initial impetus behind the movement in this district in May 1797 has already been examined but it seems that the Orr family of Stratford had a role to play in the vicinity of the town.[128]

In April 1798 a Dublin-based informer alleged that John Orr had met with Samuel Neilson in company with socially prominent United Irishmen Lord Gormanstown and Hamden Evans.[129] If this report was well founded it would suggest that the Orr family were indeed highly disaffected and known to influential figures in the movement. O'Neil Stratford, a bitter opponent, was one loyalist commentator who suspected as much. In July 1799 he successfully defended himself against 'several charges' brought against him by the Orrs arising out of his conduct towards them and their property during the rebellion. Another regular reporter of information on the family was the zealous Revd Charles Robinson of Knockrigg who in 1789 had been appointed the first Presbyterian curate in Stratford when the church was opened by Archbishop Richard Robinson of Armagh.[130]

The Orrs were the most successful members of a large community of northeners living in the Stratford area. Economic migrants to the textile industry and supporting trades was supplemented in the late 1790s by refugees fleeing the military crackdowns in Ulster against the Defenders and then the United Irishmen. Many of those who relocated as part of this wave were United Irishmen whose political and personal experiences at the sharp end of government policy would have yielded compelling insights to local Wicklow sympathizers. The Castle authorities were well aware of this situation and were informed in May 1798 that many Stratford inhabitants 'were fugitives from the county Antrim . . . who had been obliged to fly from there for rebellious practices, and were intimately acquainted with many of the Antrim militia'.[131] Perhaps the most notable individual was the foreman over the spinners and weavers at the Orr's factory, the brother of the 'provincial delegate' William Putnam McCabe. This contact could only have boosted the links available to the northern emissary when operating in the county.[132]

McCabe was one of the most effective and indefatigable United organizers and was aptly described by Thomas Judkin Fitzgerald, High Sheriff of Tipperary, as 'the right arm of sedition'.[133] Before reaching Wicklow in the late spring of 1797 McCabe and Hope had organized much of Down and Antrim in late 1796 and the hazardous months of early 1797. McCabe apparently initiated 200 men in one night. Both men adopted disguises, such as that of an evangelical preacher, and utilized masonic networks to gain access to potential recruits. They also collaborated from the winter of 1796 in establishing links between the Ulster and Leinster provincial committees and McCabe became a close colleague of Lord Edward Fitzgerald while helping to spread the movement into the counties adjoining Dublin. He also organized in Leitrim and Roscommon with Hope's assistance in mid-1797 and then in Wicklow and Wexford with Matthew Doyle.[134]

The Belfastman's role encompassed all levels of the conspiracy from grassroots level to the implementation of high strategy, and in Wicklow he co-ordinated the emergence of the movement on a county-wide basis from its earliest phase to its attainment of proper representation on the provincial committee. A knowledgeable loyalist credited him with the introduction of the approved United Irish system in Stratford and Luke Cullen's sources affirmed that nearby Imaal had received several visits from McCabe in the 'latter end of '97 and first of 98 . . . to encourage them to war'. McCabe's main concern at that time was the adoption of the military structure as it is clear that the society pre-dated his visits to the county.[135]

James Fox, a baker, was one of the key figures in the Stratford area and in May 1798 his arrest was advocated on the grounds that he was a 'committee man', 'a secretary' and 'one of the first who swore united men in the county of Wicklow'. Fox reputedly knew how 'the fugitive rebels from Belfast, Lisburn, Hillsborough etc under the protection and influence of the Orrs first introduced uniting in Stratford and spread it through all parts of the adjacent townlands.'[136] Fox may have had business contacts with one Dempsey, 'a baker from Dublin', who in August 1797 was believed to be 'a principal agent' in Stratford along with a tailor named Doyle who was involved in swearing recruits in the mountains. Tyrone-born blacksmith Roger McGuire, allegedly a fugitive from the dragooning of Ulster, was denounced alongside Fox as being 'one of the first and most active citizens . . . [who] had sworn more men and probably made more pikes than any other smith in the county Wicklow'.[137]

A direct consequence of the presence these Ulster born rebels in west Wicklow and Arklow was the thorough infiltration of the Antrim Militia garrisons stationed in those districts in the late Autumn of 1797. Thomas Murray claimed that a militiaman named Ferris in the

Arklow Town detachment told him that 'many of the regiment were so dissatisfied and kept up a communication with McCabe in Belfast'.[138] Ferris also allegedly met McCabe in December 1797 at which time he informed him that the regimental artillery housed at Arklow would be made available to the United Irishmen in the event of a rising. The militiamen were not only receptive to radical politics but on occasion took the initiative in swearing adherents. In July 1797 Antrim militia-man Gabriel Holles met an Antrim-born teacher in James Street, Dublin to whom he administered the oath of the United Irishmen.[139] The great 'sympathy' between this regiment and the Wicklow rebels was an important factor contributing to the success of Holt's campaign in the Autumn of 1798. At least twenty-eight of the forty-four men who deserted from the Antrims during the rebellion fought with Holt and many sympathizers who did not defect provided the rebels with munitions. There was particularly close liaison with the Antrim dissenters in the garrisons of Arklow and Baltinglass which was com-pounded by the unwitting recruitment of local United Irishmen.[140]

Wicklow-born Pierse Hayden of Ballyhook was another 'officer of considerable rank' in the Talbotstown organization and 'secretary to several parishes'. He was assisted by Laurence Doyle of Dunlavin who was arrested with him in April 1798 and then shot the following month in Dunlavin. Hayden made a full confession to Major Hardy in late May 1798 and thereby survived the rebellion.[141] The precise identity of one 'Colgan' eluded the Stratford informer but it may well have been a misrendering of Coogan. Two men of that surname from Horseshoe near Blessington attended a series of United Irish meetings on Dorset Street in November 1797. These 'respectable farmers' were described by the Castle informer as 'the principal committee men in that Quarter' which would have necessitated their presence in Stratford on occasion.[142] An intelligence report of February 1799, furthermore, indicated that four chests of pikes had been concealed under a bush in 'Cughan's meadows' near Tally Hill, Wicklow. This cache may have belonged to rebels under their influence or command.[143]

The parish of Baltinglass was reputedly the most heavily organized in the county where it was alleged that 500 of the 8,000 pikes believed to have been manufactured in Wicklow were hidden.[144] The Glen of Imaal furnished the United Irishmen with many resolute insurgents, including Michael Dwyer of Camera and Martin Burke of Donough-more. Cullen was informed that it was in the 'Spring of 1797 that the men in the Glen of Imaile began to take the oath', sworn by a Protestant of that place named Hawkins 'who for some time [had] been residing

in Dublin and on his returning to Imaile initiated some of his friends.'
This was a typical pattern of small scale recruitment which seems
credible in this instance in view of the fact that Hawkins' brother-in-law
was 'intimate' with Dwyer and his circle.[145] Dwyer was literate and
apparently politically aware, having attended the Ballyhubbock school
run by Peter Burr, a Protestant graduate of Trinity College Dublin.
Burr's liberal and progressive tendencies attracted many Catholic
students from Imaal who, like Dwyer, were destined to battle with
former schoolmates turned yeomen in 1798.[146]

The main recruiting push in Imaal came almost simultaneously
when United Irishmen 'from the vicinity of Belfast . . . employed at
Stratford-on-Slaney' systematically spread their activity into the nearby
valley.[147] Several well-attended meetings were addressed by McCabe
who may have feigned employment at Stratford to cover his northern
origins or have accompanied men like his brother, Fox and McGuire
who really did. Dwyer became acquainted with McCabe and once
initiated was allegedly 'indefatigable in the organisation'.[148] One of
those sworn by him at a wedding function was Larry Byrne who then
'united' associates as far afield as Blackrock, Aghavannagh, Glenmalure
and Seven Churches (Glendalough).[149]

The tradition that Dwyer had been 'voted to the office of lower
baronial delegate' is highly unlikely and confusion may have arisen
between John Dwyer of Camera (father of Michael) and the younger
man's cousin or uncle, John Dwyer of Seskin, Imaal.[150] Dwyer of
Seskin was 'a wealthy man for a catholic' who visited the capital on
business, a profile common to many senior Wicklow rebels, and was
shot in the Dunlavin massacre on 24 May 1798. Had Michael Dwyer
been sufficiently prominent in the movement to attend baronial
meetings in Stratford he would have almost certainly fallen under
suspicion in April 1798 when informers in the town implicated many
leading activists. This was not the case. The seniority of John Dwyer
is also indicated by an entry in the Rathdrum parish register which
recorded that at Ballyboy, near Seskin, 'in a hollow of the road John
Dwyer of Imaal swore in the rebels in '98'.[151] Moreover, James Doyle
of Ballinacor claimed, and was in a position to know, that the 'Imale
district and that bordering on the Co[unty] Kildare was represented
by one of the O'Dwyers and a young man named [Peter] Hayden'
who were both killed in Dunlavin. These men were rebel officials and
Hayden had, in fact, defeated Michael Dwyer in an election to the
post of captain prior to the insurrection, probably in November
1797. The second defeated candidate in what must have been a hard-

fought session was Dwyer's childhood teacher Peter Burr.[152] Dwyer of Seskin was clearly the baronial delegate who accompanied Thomas Kavanagh of Talbotstown to a meeting of the county committee in Annacurra. His identity escaped the informer Thomas Murray other than a reference to the delegate as being 'a lame man'.[153]

SHILLELAGH

Little is known of the rebel organization in the barony of Shillelagh even though it one of the most disturbed areas in Wicklow in the pre-rebellion period. Few depositions are extant and if this can be taken as in some way indicative of Castle intelligence on the profile of the local rebels the authorities were surprisingly ill-informed. An important exception is John Waters of Johnstown, later Baltinglass, who was one of the baronial delegates and described his own status as 'Grand secretary for the half barony of Shillela[g]h'. His claim to have 'never acted' was untrue as he was capable of informing on the proceedings of rebel committees in Dublin from December 1797. That Waters was the 'intimate friend' and kinsman of Garret Byrne of Ballymanus further suggests deep involvement. Their long-term relationship survived the rebellion and in 1803 Waters managed Byrne's chaotic finances in Ireland while the latter was in the midst of negotiations to return from exile.[154]

Waters was a weak-willed character and was given recognition by loyalists for his 'very strenuous' efforts to curtail the effectiveness of his own organization once the rebellion had commenced. This position was similar to Murray's and may have arisen from an early flirtation with radical politics leading to prominence in a sector where the lesser gentry were unusually conservative. It seems likely that Waters had viewed the evolving objectives of the leadership as it progressed towards a policy of attempting revolution without foreign aid with some disquiet. His disengagement from this dangerous course was secured with the aid of the Orange Order enthusiast Revd James M'Ghee of Clonmore (Hacketstown) who in July 1798 obtained Waters' promise to 'prosecute [Garret Byrne] whenever he shall be called upon'. M'Ghee also then obtained sufficiently incriminating details of William Byrne of Ballymanus to request his arrest on murder charges.[155]

The other delegate to the county committee from Shillelagh was the mysterious 'Mr. Byrne of Tinahely' who was implicated by Rathdown delegate Thomas Miller during the trial of William Michael Byrne in

July 1798.[156] While this may have been an allusion to Garret Byrne of Ballymanus who lived less than three miles from Tinahely, albeit in the barony of Ballinacor South, it was probably a more obscure and inactive figure. Byrne's younger brother Edward 'Ned' Byrne is perhaps the most likely alternative given that he remained a committed United Irishman into the 1800s and owned a business in Tinahely which was burned by loyalist extremists prior to the rebellion. The loss of this premises and the threat it presented in one of the county's orange strongholds evidently prompted Byrne to move to Dublin city, a relocation which would explain his very low profile in Wicklow during the rebellion.[157]

In early 1798 Byrne of Tinahely attended two meetings of the Wicklow county committee held in Dublin in Francis and Cuffe streets but was absent from the inaugural meeting at Annacurra. This corroborates Murray's claim that only one Shillelagh delegate attended at Annacurra whom he did not recognize but was clearly Waters. As the Francis street meeting was held in the Sun Inn 'to complete the county committee' and this was Byrne's first appearance it would appear that Shillelagh was the barony which had to be brought up to par to forward its second delegate. This further suggests that the baronial organization was inefficient and lagging behind those of other sectors.[158]

Shillelagh was the smallest barony in the county excepting Rathdown but in January 1798 could only muster 1,080 men in comparison with the other barony's 2,000.[159] This relatively poor performance was probably due in no small part to the considerable organized loyalist presence in the form of orange lodges and yeomanry units in the towns of Shillelagh, Carnew, Tinahely, Coolattin and Coolkenna and an aggressive magistracy with extremist tendencies. Another factor was the numerous 'outrages' committed in the barony during the winter of 1797/1798 which had galvanized anti-United Irish elements and exposed rank-and-file republicans to the threat of informers. This led to the disruption of the movement by mass arrests before the society reached its peak recruitment. As early as November 1797 William Wainwright of the Shillelagh yeoman cavalry reported that Burton of Killinure had 'sent a great many of his labourers etc to gaol'.[160]

Arms raiding was symptomatic of poor discipline and impatience on the part of the Shillelagh United Irishmen and perhaps, given their peculiarly hostile environs, a high level of militancy.[161] Shillelagh men were well-represented in the ranks of those transported to New South Wales and while this may have been partially the result of an unsympathetic magistracy, it also points to a fanatical strain evidenced in their executions of 'orange' prisoners and burning of loyalist property during the rebellion.[162] The 1797 raids were carried out by rebels to secure the weaponry that their leadership was unable to supply at the time, a practice which caused Major Hardy to comment in November 1797 on the 'alarming state of Shillela[gh]'. Determined efforts were made by the loyalists to contain the conspirators at Carnew town on its Wexford border which became a flash point in May 1798.[163]

The village of Carnew and the townlands surrounding it was home to many United Irishmen who played prominent roles in the rebellion. Patrick and John Murray of Carnew were distinguished for burning the premises of Ralph Blayney for whom they worked as chandlers. Their motive was probably Blayney's position as Second-Lieutenant of the Carnew yeoman infantry although he was on good terms with Fitzwilliam. The Carnew-born informer and prosecutrix Bridget 'Croppy Biddy' Dolan identified Patrick Stafford as the treasurer or secretary to Carnew's United Irishmen in the pre-rebellion period and Tom Cooke as the main rebel organizer. Another important Shillelagh activist was John Fowler who worked as a rent collector for the Symes family of Ballybeg and fought as a captain in southern Wicklow and north Wexford. Fowler also acted as an agent for Joseph Chamney of Ballyrahan in the early 1790s and was acquainted with many other prominent south Wicklow families.[164]

BALLINACOR

The mountainous barony of Ballinacor was divided into upper/north and lower/south administrative sections which the United Irishmen adhered to up to a point in their organization. Ballinacor North, closest to Dublin, had an estimated 1,800 men sworn in January 1798 while the lower barony had 840 which gave the largest geographic district in the county the second highest nominal total of members.[165] The combined barony was represented on the county committee by John Lynch from Dublin who 'had a county seat in the vicinity of Round-wood' and William Young of Ballinacor.[166] Thomas Murray of Arklow was under the impression that William Young 'organised the Barony of Ballinacor' and attended the county committee meeting at Annacurra as a representative for the barony.[167] Tom King concurred in his view of Young's importance and when he was captured in May 1798 he recommended that the rebel's removal to a Dublin prison from Wicklow

Gaol 'would terrify and keep quiet a dangerous knot who are in his power', presumably out of fear that he had become an informer.[168] The statement of James Doyle of Ballinacor that Young was deputed by Garret Byrne in late 1797 to 'to make cap[tai]ns or see them made', however, raises the question of the respective positions of Young and Byrne in the baronial leadership cadre.[169]

It is unclear when Garret Byrne became a United Irishman but a mid-1790s induction is not unlikely given his social prominence, family connections and subsequent authority in the county organization. He was visited in Ballymanus House in the 'early part of [17]97' by John Lynch and William Michael Byrne, Wicklow's two representatives on the provincial committee in March 1798, who even then probably had seditious business in mind.[170] Garret Byrne was said to have 'frequently visited Dublin' and, if stimulated by the same motives which steered many of his Wexford peers towards radical politics, could have previously joined a city society.

Once involved, however, Byrne was reputedly highly active in organising the county and seems to have concentrated his efforts in perfecting the military aspect of the force. It is far from certain that Byrne was elected to the county committee which convened at Annacurra in December 1797.[171] If returned Byrne would logically have represented his home district of Ballinacor but his name is not linked with that post or any other in any extant documents. This indicates that, notwithstanding his acknowledged dynamism, he had either been defeated in the election, or, more probably, had not stood at all. Young, a highly regarded activist in a democratically structured organization, could not have been instructed by Byrne on any matter unless he held a comparable or more senior rank.[172] Cullen, drawing on James Doyle's account of his experiences in Ballinacor, maintained that twenty-four captains had elected Byrne adjutant general of the county 'with acclamation' in late 1797.[173] In actuality, Byrne could only have been elected to the position of colonel as the post of adjutant was only obtainable by appointment of the Leinster provincial committee who never filled the positions.[174]

As the 2,640 men of the combined barony of Ballinacor warranted twenty-six captains who could have elected two colonels, there is little doubt but that this was what Doyle had related.[175] However, as each county was theoretically supposed to have an adjutant-general, one man in each was deemed to hold the position in an acting capacity pending the formal appointments. Byrne was clearly Wicklow's designated man given his documented efforts to develop the military structure and strategy in Wicklow. His being returned a colonel is also significant as candidature theoretically necessitated being voted onto baronial level office. Byrne may well have held a seat on a lower baronial committee and it is quite possible that he replaced Young on the county committee when the latter was arrested in March 1798 on charges of 'swearing and exercising U[nited] I[rishmen]'.[176] His real authority derived from his evident contacts with the military committee of the provincial committee, his social status and his anticipated instatement as adjutant-general for Wicklow.

Nationalist historians and folklorists have given too much credence to the arguments advanced by William Byrne of Ballymanus when on trial for murder in July 1799 that he had only belatedly and reluctantly joined the rebel forces. The main reasons cited to support this claim are his inaction during the first days of the rebellion, his brief membership of the Wicklow town yeoman cavalry, his alleged belief that the planned insurrection would fail and reputed abhorrence of French atheism, all of which supposedly steeled him to spurn the overtures of his rebel brother and friends.[177] Charles Dickson concluded that there was 'nothing improbable' in Byrne's statement at his trial 'that he never was a United Irishman, that his participation was forced upon him and that he never held a titular command'.[178] There is, however, a 'Captain William Byrne, of Ballymanus' listed on a United Irish document dating from 1797 which is virtually irrefutable proof that he was indeed a rebel officer.[179]

It is also beyond question that, regardless of his constitutional position in the United Irishmen, Byrne commanded the Wicklow rebels at the battle of Arklow on 9 June and only relinquished the task to his brother after the battle of Vinegar Hill on 21 June. Clearly, in the confused and difficult circumstances under which the Wicklowmen had taken to the field, the prestige arising from Byrne's social status entitled him to a position of leadership out of proportion to his actual rank, which was at least that of captain. Byrne's defence at his courtmartial was dependent on establishing that he had not served as a rebel officer or in a position of influence over the Wicklow rebels and had been in their company against his will and better judgement. His patently false protestations to this effect have been seized upon by those eager to highlight the tragedy of his fate and to stigmatize those responsible for his execution.[180]

The social prominence of the Byrnes of Ballymanus involved them with leading Protestant families destined to play a part in their downfall in 1797–1799. Intermarriage by the Byrnes and the Coates family of Clone, which numbered more than one mixed marriage before the 1760s, was highly likely and would explain why William Byrne received shelter in Clone House when a fugitive in early June 1798. A less beneficial relationship was evidently formed with the Hugos of Drummin who were leading pro-government agents in central Wicklow from the mid-1790s. In 1747 Garret Byrne senior, the father of rebel leaders William and Garret of Ballymanus, had obtained a judgement from the Court of Exchequer which forced Thomas Sherwood to sell his interest in properties at Glendalough and Drummin to Thomas Byrne of Laragh. The executor of Thomas Byrne's will a few years later was his Protestant nephew Thomas Hugo senior who took possession of Drummin. Hugo's eponymous son was the notorious High Sheriff, magistrate and yeoman during the rebellion period who, for a time, served alongside William Byrne in the Wicklow Town Cavalry.[181] The president of the courtmartial which tried Byrne in 1799, Lieutenant-Colonel John Caldwell, ascertained that William Byrne had become estranged from his brother Garret in 1795 and had taken 'refuge at the house of Thomas Hugo, Esq., who received and entertained him' until May 1798.[182] Nationalist sources put the relationship as one between peers and stressed that it was Hugo who 'professed a great deal of friendship for Mr Byrne' from whom he borrowed £100 and wanted to marry his daughter.[183]

The Glenmalure district forming the baronial boundary between Ballinacor North and Ballinacor South, more populous than in modern times, was thoroughly organized by the winter of 1797. Towards the end of that year James Doyle met the well travelled William Young at Bartholomew Kavanagh's home in the townland of Ballinacor near Greenan. Kavanagh must have been a well-trusted and active man to host the meeting at which the military command of the area was decided upon. Doyle was elected captain of his native Ballinacor townland district that night while a near neighbour of his from the opposite bank of the Avonbeg river, Patrick Grant of Kirikee, was returned for Ballintombay. At a subsequent pre-rebellion election the officers chosen to represent the overlapping 'parish and district' of Rathdrum were James Doyle and Darby Healy.[184]

Lower-level United Irish organisers included Peter McCabe who was a schoolmaster at Glendasan near Glendalough and Michael Byrne who was also a teacher in the Ballynockan area.[185] Terence 'Kittagh' Byrne of Moneystown was reputedly 'early a United Irishman and made no secret of it', as was his father Owen.[186] In the northern extremity of the barony, innkeeper James Kavanagh of Roundwood was one of the United Irishman's 'leading men in that quarter' and was credited with initiating Joseph Holt who lived near the village at Mullinaveigue.[187] Holt's autobiographical account of when and why he became involved in the United Irishmen is unreliable and was geared towards rehabilitating his reputation among loyalists following his return to Ireland from thirteen years exile in New South Wales.[188] He was not, as he claimed, a 'forced rebel' obliged to take refuge with the United Irishman having aroused the suspicions of the ultra loyalist ex-High Sheriff Thomas Hugo but was rather a high-ranking recruiter and emissary from 1797.[189]

It may be significant that one of Holt's employers was Bryan Byrne of Rathdrum who was deemed 'very disaffected' and had a brother who had married into the Byrnes of Ballymanus.[190] A further link between Holt and William Byrne of Ballymanus was their mutual acquaintance Thomas Hugo with whom Holt had been involved in road construction projects and a resultant financial dispute. Hugo's association with two of the county's three most active rebel leaders in 1798 was a remarkable coincidence which illustrated how even the most conservative and most radical elements could co-exist in Wicklow prior to the political crisis. If Holt and Byrne did not encounter each other in Drummin, they may well have met at the Chritchley household at Ballyboy which was also frequented by both men, Byrne apparently to visit Betty Chritchley and Holt to confer with her father on legal business.[191]

Mixing in such circles could have resulted in Holt's early initiation and at least three of his four brothers were rebels, one of whom, Jonathan, was killed in a skirmish in October 1798.[192] As a small farmer, baronial sub-constable, building contractor and cloth assessor Holt was well placed to fulfil a similar role to that of his friend Matthew Doyle and he cultivated links with the important Francis and Thomas Street United Irish committees in Dublin through Fr John Martin, McCabe and others who worked for them.[193] Such details were obscured by Holt who must also, at some point, have been part of a formal society given that he was returned as a captain before the close of 1797 and was listed as such on a document recovered after the recapture of Wexford town in late June 1798.[194] Holt emerged as an aggressive leader of the movement in north Wicklow in June 1798 and, following his battlefield promotion to general in July 1798, became the last commander-in-chief of the United Irishmen.

RATHDOWN

William Michael Byrne of Parkhill was appointed by the provincial committee in the latter half of 1797 'to regulate the half barony of Rathdown' where he lived in the Glen of the Downs.[195] Byrne was one of the first leading catholics in Wicklow to become a United Irishman and his competence and the esteem in which he was held is reflected by his formal appointment as provincial delegate for Wicklow in December 1797.[196] An assertion by the generally reliable Murray of Sheepwalk that 'W[illiam Michael] Byrne opened a communication between the [Leinster] Directory and the committee at Cork' places Byrne in the first echelon of agents of the provincial committee along with McCabe with whom he often appeared in Wicklow at United meetings. The extent of his sedition certainly surprised Camden who described him as 'a young gentlemen of very ancient family in Wicklow'.[197] The proximity of Rathdown to Dublin city and Byrne's activities led to a mass recruiting effort in the barony from April 1797. Powerscourt schoolteacher John Ryan was sworn into the conspiracy that month and became highly active, probably in conjunction with Patrick Nugent, the teacher from the adjacent village of Enniskerry.[198]

The rapidity and depth of the spread may have been facilitated by the ascendancy of liberal-minded gentry and magistracy in the barony who were slow to respond to the threat posed by the United Irishmen and reluctant to take the extreme measures used to contain them elsewhere in Wicklow. This tardiness was not remedied until late in the year when Monck, Powerscourt and William Colthurst began to consolidate the conservative elements of the magistracy. Two of the earliest suspected United Irish emissaries were Enniskerry residents Captain Flood and 'Count' O'Flanagan. Their importance was evidently overstated by the informer as the pair were clearly either just nominal adherents or men deemed sympathetic towards radical politics.[199]

The main drive to adopt military structures and form higher committees seems to have occurred in August 1797 which coincided with the dissemination of the new constitution dated the 27th of that month. Byrne was assisted in this task by his Protestant friend Thomas Miller of Powerscourt whom he instructed to compile a list of 120 men 'to be under a captain' during the harvest of 1797. In Rathdown, therefore, the evolution from 'civil' to 'military' organization was essentially a matter of assuming the appropriate titles.[200] Castlereagh was informed the following year that the military system had indeed been 'as near

A VIEW OF BRAY, *c.* 1800 N.L.I., TA 1808

as could be engrafted on the civil'.[201] Miller delegated the task of appointing captains to James Ryan and showed him how the list was to be structured at a special meeting in Castletown (Curtlestown).[202]

The Powerscourt district was intensively organized with about thirty-one societies. By November/December 1797 they had developed their organization to the point that higher committees were elected to sit at Castletown where a colonel was probably appointed.[203] George Coleman of Long Hill was secretary to a society which included the industrious John Mulligan of Paddock and Roger Coleman of Ballinteskin. Mulligan had been recruited by Coleman who had himself been sworn by 'one Burke, a schoolmaster upon the commons of the long hill [i.e. Long Hill Commons]' in November 1797.[204] This man recruited extensively in the parish of Kilmacanoge close to William Michael Byrne's home and was widely regarded as 'a united man and capable of swearing'. His prominence resulted in his arrest and execution on Bray Sea Commons in April 1798, the month in which his colleague Nugent of Enniskerry was also killed.[205] Paul Murray of Kilmurry emerged as a captain, during the rebellion and Mulligan of Paddock named 'Mr. Bryans son-in-law to Mr. Hoey of Hoeyfield (Hollybrook) was to be their cap[tai]n'.[206] There were many Bryans in north-eastern Wicklow but the man alluded to by Mulligan was very probably Charles Bryan of Bray who in June 1798 commanded a corps on the hills overlooking New Ross. That William Michael Byrne was married to a Rosanna Hoey may also indicate that he was related to Bryan.[207]

Other Rathdown captains were Thomas Miller, who may well have held the rank of colonel, William Mooney, Jeremiah Delamere and Charles Gallagher (aka Calligan).[208] Delamere had been elected in December 1797 having been sworn by Gallagher in Thomas Street and was, like Miller, a member of the Church of Ireland.[209] This Thomas Street connection suggests that the United Irish structures built around William Michael Byrne enjoyed close links with Dublin's militant Workhouse Division committee and may well have derived its initial impetus to spread the conspiracy in north Wicklow from it. It seems that on the eve of the rebellion the Workhouse Division assumed became the supreme authority in the national organization as the long established leadership was in disarray after the arrests of Fitzgerald, Neilson and other capable activists.[210]

As in Castlemacadam, the Bray yeoman infantry was full of disaffected members for which it elicited much loyalist criticism in the advent of the Rebellion.[211] The corps was raised in early 1797 by Captain John Edwards of Oldcourt who had commanded the Volunteer Rathdown Cavalry Association in the 1780s and remained a man of liberal politics. He had hoped and applied to raise a cavalry corps in November 1797 but had to withdrew his offer in deference to the rival bid of Earl of Meath.[212] Bray, unlike Arklow, had insufficient human and financial resources to support two mounted units. The infantry corps was one of the largest in the county with over sixty members of whom about half were Catholic and roughly two-thirds United Irishmen by 1798.[213] It is likely that the permanent sergeant of the formation, Thomas Ledwidge, who farmed on Edwards' Oldcourt estate, was one of the main instigators of this plot and he was obliged to flee the town in March 1798. Ledwidge and fellow yeoman Richard Kennedy were arrested on a packet at the Pigeon House and brought back to Bray for courtmartial and execution. Arrested with them were John Murray, John Sullivan and Terence Lawlor of Little Cork, Loughlinstown who were all probably compromised United Irishmen.[214]

The United Irishmen in the Bray district undoubtedly attempted to subvert the militia regiments stationed very close to the village but just over the county border at Lehaunstown Camp (Loughlinstown). This force, together with the units encamped at Blaris outside Belfast, comprised the strategic reserves from the summer of 1795 until the rebellion and were vital to the Government plans to protect the capital.

Considerable success was enjoyed by the Wicklow and south Dublin United Irishmen in recruiting cells within the King's County Militia in late 1797 and the regiment was ultimately removed from Wicklow on account of its unacceptably high level of fraternization with rebels. At least forty-one King's Countymen made good on their seditious oaths and deserted between April and September 1798. A high proportion of these men demonstrated that they were not just evading draconian military discipline by risking their lives with the Wicklow rebels. The locally based 5th Royal Irish Dragoons also proved to be very disaffected, so much so that the unit was demobilized in 1799.[215]

NEWCASTLE

Luke Cullen was informed that one Johnson, a Protestant carpenter in the employ of General Cunningham (then Lord Rossmore) 'was the first man to introduce the system of United Irishmen' in the barony of Newcastle.[216] He frequently worked in Dublin and was probably been sworn there in early 1797. In view of the unusual manner in which Johnson was alleged to have operated in Wicklow it is quite possible that he was acting on his own initiative rather than on behalf of the city leadership. This was perfectly legitimate as any ordinary United Irishman could administer the oath of secrecy if certain precautions were taken. Johnson reputedly only recruited people 'of his own religious creed' for some time which is unusual in the context of a society devoted to breaking down religious barriers but this could simply mean he first approached his extended family members. Cullen maintained that Johnson became nervous of his activities when the rebellion began and in order to gain favour with Rossmore planted ammunition on an innocent man named Turpin who was executed by the Newtownmountkennedy yeomen.[217]

When the movement took root in the barony, the prosperous mill owner Richard O'Reilly of Newtownmountkennedy emerged as its leading figure. His father, also Richard O'Reilly, had been a lieutenant in the Wicklow Militia at the time of his death in 1795 when stationed with the regiment at Strabane, County Tyrone. The militia commission indicated that the family were very prominent for Catholics in the social as well as the commercial life of the county.[218] O'Reilly junior enjoyed a high profile in the Wicklow United Irishmen up until his arrest on 24 March 1798 when on a mission to meet Philip O'Neil in Arklow and then Beauchamp Bagenal Harvey in Wexford. The Harvey connection may indicate that O'Reilly had been involved in the duel fought between the Wexford United Irish leader and Ambrose Harding Giffard at the Scalp, Enniskerry, 18 May 1794. Such an early association with Harvey and Thomas Addis Emmet would largely account for O'Reilly's prominence in the Wicklow organization in 1797–8. He also lived near William Michael Byrne's home and operated very closely with him in late 1797.[219]

John Murphy of Knockrobbin claimed that he had received a communication from O'Reilly on 1 November 1797 ordering him to 'ascertain the number of United Irishmen in his district' which at that time amounted to 160. He was then summoned to attend a meeting at John Brett's of Ballinalea on 8 November 'for the purpose of electing a secretary to the committee of said county, & a delegate for the barony of Newcastle.' John Byrne of Cronroe was elected delegate and O'Reilly secretary by a baronial assembly which attracted John Lynch as an observer from Ballinacor, William Michael Byrne from Rathdown and William Putnam McCabe from Dublin. The presence of so many notable conspirators and the forced pace of events denotes an sense of urgency that had very probably arisen from the need to formalize the county committee. The secretaries and electors present were Terence Byrne of Blackbull, Charles McDaniel of Ballymacahara, Cornelius Byrne of Ballynagran, Michael Dempsey of Ballymole, Kirwan of Kilcoole, Gregory Conyan of Ballycullen, Francis Reynolds of Upper Ballinahinch and John Dorney of Tiglin who chaired. As secretary to the parish of Killiskey, Murphy periodically advanced funds to O'Reilly and worked on behalf of the baronial committee.[220]

A typical but important middle-level rebel in the barony was Michael Neil or Niall of Upper Newcastle whose father was a 'highly respectable and extensive landowner'. Richard Neil was a sufficiently prominent member of the community in April 1796 to dispossess himself of a weapon in accordance with advertised instructions from a Kilcoole magistrates session.[221] It was said that 'no man in the county was better versed in the secrets' of the United Irishman than Michael Neil who was almost certainly an elected captain. The political activism of the family is also indicated by the inclusion of Neil's brother James on the Fugitive Act of August 1798.[222] At the battle of Newtownmount-kennedy on 30 May 1798 the McGuire brothers of Ballydonough, 'a superior class of farmer', emerged as the commanders of the men from the coastal parts of Newcastle. They had Protestant yeomen relatives who were well disposed towards them and must have held either high rank in the baronial organization or commanded the allegiance of the local United Irishmen on social grounds.[223]

THE COUNTY COMMITTEE

The first meeting between a provincial level committee in Dublin and delegates of the Wicklow United Irishmen took place in mid to late October 1797 at McVeagh's Inn on Dorset Street opposite Granby Row.[224] It seems that the county was then represented by men from only two baronies, Talbotstown and Arklow, both of which had been visited by Ulster emissaries the previous spring. The importance of the northern connection is borne out by the composition of the delegation which included Peter and John Coulson, Philpot and Sternes. The farming Coogan brothers of Horseshoe, near Blessington, represented Talbotstown and were recognized as being 'the principal committee men in that Quarter'.[225] This delegation did not constitute the Wicklow county committee but was rather an interim body intended to liaise with the emergent provincial committee until the electoral system in all six baronial sectors was sufficiently developed to create an official committee.

The delegates informed the Dubliners that number of United Irishmen in Wicklow was 'daily increasing' and delivered about £30 each to the treasurer, Pat Byrne of Britain Street, a grocer, who handled the finances of the Rotunda Division as well as to 'certain county committees.'[226] Byrne was soon afterwards removed from office for corruption and was probably the man who had failed to advance funds to James Hope in 1797. Hope was obliged to go to Stratford-on-Slaney in order to raise money from the sale of a horse McCabe had left with his brother.[227] Byrne's position in October 1797 and the siting of the meeting in the north of the city suggests that the impetus to form the committee came from the district committee of the Rotunda Division. This body may have fielded emissaries in Wicklow independently of the geographically closer Workhouse division which quickly superseded them in this role. The Dorset Street United Irishmen had contacts which extended north of Dublin including a delegate named Murphy in Mayo from whom 'good news' was anticipated. The Thomas and Francis street committees in the Workhouse division orientated towards south and west Leinster.

The delegates at McVeagh's were told that an agent would be sent 'to inform them how they are to act', probably an allusion to McCabe or one of his circle. A second meeting apparently took place on or around 16 November 1797 at the same venue following by another on the 30th when twenty-five of 'the same delegates' from Wicklow, Wexford, Meath and north county Dublin reassembled in McVeaghs.[228]

This meeting was addressed by Watty Cox of Abbey Street, gunsmith and proprietor of the *Union Star*, who requested the names of 'whatever persons they disliked' for inclusion in the propaganda broadsheet.[229] The paper was widely circulated in Wicklow and one informer understood that 'every person therein described was to be murdered.'[230] Cox protested that his objective was to foster an 'empire of universal benevolence and fraternity from Wicklow Hill to Belfast'.[231]

The Wicklow delegation lost its authority at the end of November 1797 when, with McCabe's assistance, baronial elections were held in every parish in the county formalizing the Wicklow organization. Newcastle elected its baronial committee on 8 November at which time Rathdown and Ballinacor already possessed recognized leaders in William Michael Byrne and John Lynch which implied that they had previously formed a baronial committee.[232] The Ballinalea meeting was convened specifically to return delegates to the Wicklow county committee which held its inaugural meeting 'in or about December' at Annacurra. Significantly, representatives from all six baronial sectors attended even though the United Irish constitution permitted the formation of a committee from only four baronies in a county. That Wicklow was capable of attaining full organization within seven months of the first mass recruiting drive indicates the extent of the conspiracy in the county and also perhaps that it was quite evenly spread. This apparently uniform progress of the movement resulted in the near simultaneous emergence of higher committees under McCabe's co-ordination. It seems that every barony had returned a committee by the end of November 1797 and that they immediately set about attaining a county committee. As this timescale corresponds with the last meeting of the Wicklow delegates in McVeagh's on 30 November, it is evident that the new county committee did not represent a distinct United structure but was rather a perfected version of the existing one.[233]

The venue for the meeting was John Loftus' whiskey house at Annacurra near Aughrim, a relatively secluded location which was connected by road routes to all other Wicklow centres.[234] Loftus was a cousin of the Byrnes of Ballymanus, a United Irishman and someone who could be relied upon to be discreet about what was transacted in the house.[235] He was probably the same John Loftus who was killed at the battle of Vinegar Hill. Arklow barony was represented by the inveterate John Lacey but the baronial treasurer Philip O'Neil apparently 'did not attend'. William Michael Byrne and Thomas Miller were forwarded by the many Rathdown societies and rode to

Annacurra together from Newtownmountkennedy.[236] Newcastle was represented by Richard O'Reilly and John Byrne of Cronroe while the strategically important combined barony of Ballinacor was entrusted to William Young and John Lynch of Roundwood. The sole delegate who attended for Shillelagh was almost certainly John Waters and of the two Talbotstown men one was Thomas Kavanagh of Baltinglass, 'a yeoman in uniform', who may have been newly appointed, given that Young made a point of introducing him to the other delegates. The other Talbotstown man was John Dwyer of Seskin whose identity was also unknown to those who later divulged details of the session.[237]

The first task and main purpose of the meeting, according to Thomas Murray of Sheepwalk who attended as an observer with McCabe and others, was to appoint two delegates to represent the county on the Leinster provincial committee. William Michael Byrne was chosen as the head delegate and O'Reilly as the secretary.[238] O'Reilly was then paid subscriptions amounting from £30 to £40 from several baronies to be advanced to the provincial committee, in addition to ten guineas to support Wicklow United Irishmen who had been arrested and their dependents. McCabe, whose presence in Wicklow at committees of every level points to his status as a key advisor, recommended that 'pikes be procured' and military preparations intensified.[239]

Thomas Miller, however, claimed that no business was done in Annacurra pending a meeting at the Sun Inn on Francis Street where the Wicklow county committee reconvened the following Sunday, although it is clear that some progress had been made.[240] The Sun Inn session was ostensibly held to 'complete the county committee' and, as both Phil O'Neil and Byrne of Tinahely were present on this occasion, it appears that the main impediment to finalizing policy at Loftus' had been their absence. The delegates at the Sun Inn meeting had focused their attention on the growth of the organization in Wicklow and urged that Arklow barony's was to 'be forwarded as soon as possible'. This evidently occurred.[241] Miller recalled that there was 'a controversy' concerning whether or not they should 'go on of themselves, or wait for the French', a debate which divided the United Irish executive into rival factions but one on which the Wicklowmen were at least ostensibly united in their militancy.[242] Murray was apparently disturbed by the French debate and implausibly claimed that 'when he joined first, he had no conception that there was any intention of joining the French. But about January [1798] last it appeared, and was full publicly known, by the whole party, that it was intended to assist the French on their landing and this information was communicated to the lowest ranks'. His May defection suggests that the real source of his anxiety was the wide dissemination of such sensational news.[243]

A second meeting of the Wicklow county committee took place a month later in early to mid-January 1798 in Cuffe Street of which few details are extant.[244] This preceded a provincial gathering in the city which was attended by William Michael Byrne, O'Reilly and also apparently John Lacey who would have had no voting rights. Another county session was then held in Annacurra, no doubt to discuss latest information obtained in Dublin. It was not as well attended as the inaugural gathering and Bridget Loftus claimed that it involved only 'some of the persons who were at the first'. This suggests that the marked intensification in counter-insurgency in Wicklow in January 1798, including the torturing of United Irish suspects that month in Carnew and Dunlavin, had forced the elected delegates to restrict access to their deliberations. Loyalist scrutiny may have also hindered their own ability to travel in safety to Annacurra.[245] The meeting of 22 January 1798 authorized the issuing of a detailed report to their 'constituents', or at least those privy to baronial level committee business.[246]

The document revealed mounting tensions within the organization in connection with military preparations and reflected the growing effectiveness of the tactics employed by Major Hardy and his loyalist allies. According to the baronial returns there were 12,794 sworn United Irishmen in Wicklow in January 1798 who advanced a total of £162 to the county committee but while the individual baronial strengths were in proportion to the size and population of the territory the financial burden was not evenly spread. Arklow, perhaps the most affluent part of Wicklow, had 2,400 members who donated £59 compared with densely organized Rathdown's return of only £17 for its 2,000 men. The contrast with Shillelagh is even more dramatic where 1,080 men only paid in £7 19s 3d nineteen shillings and three pence, a figure which may have resulted from the difficulty experienced by the rebel infrastructure fulfilling its duties in its hostile loyalist environs.[247]

Talbotstown, moreover, after enduring two months of martial law, still managed to deliver a total of £40 from its baronial committees and with 3,680 men remained the largest rebel force in the county. In the report the figure is given as £20 3s 4d for the upper barony with 2,974 members and exactly the same amount for the lower barony's 706 men. This implies that even though two baronial committees had been formed in Talbotstown, their structures were so interlinked that the total sum of subscriptions raised in the barony was paid into one fund and merely halved for accounting purposes. By contrast, the upper and lower baronial committees of Ballinacor advanced separate returns and may have refined their organization to a greater extent.

The report acknowledged that the forty-five United Irishmen imprisoned in Wicklow were in need of 'common necessaries' and a lawyer to defend them at the Spring Assizes by which time the committee must have envisaged many more facing trial.[248] The crux of the problem was that considerable numbers refused to pay the extra subscription of a penny a month to support the prisoners in addition to their six-and-a-half pence dues. County treasurer John Lacey was obliged to advance £10 for the purpose out of his own pocket.[249] Part of the urgency attending this issue was the belief that none of the prisoners had betrayed 'the trust reposed in them' and it was extremely important that their resolve was rewarded before they lost faith in their comrades and became informers.

The rebels were exhorted to ignore the 'idle reports' disseminated by their opponents and were told that 'very flattering' accounts had been received from abroad, an overture perhaps intended to bolster wavering morale and allay nervousness at grass roots level. It amounted to a fairly explicit statement that a French invasion was in the offing.[250] The county committee also urged the completion of all due elections before 15 February 1798 to ward off the stagnation which was slowing the growth of the United Irishmen elsewhere and to ensure readiness for the anticipated revolt. This process, if carried out, should have led to the appointment of colonels. With an invasion predicted 'about the 17 March' the Wicklowmen began forming 'regiments of 10 companies of 120 each' to be under a colonel. This was a relatively straightforward procedure but one which, in the case of Rathdown at least, involved a partial restructuring of societies which had originally consisted of regiments of only eight companies.[251]

In this context the complaints of Newcastle barony 'not being as yet fully supplied with arms' were of serious concern and was addressed by the promise of 'p[ike]s . . . ready for delivery' and advice on how to manufacture them within their area of responsibility.[252] The progression towards hostilities was noted by the Government and as the severity of coercion increased, the United Irishman as a whole became less and less disposed to await French troops. A provincial meeting on 26 February 1798 acknowledged the 'manly offer of emancipation directly' by Wicklow and other counties but were requested to 'bear the shackles of tyranny a little longer until the whole kingdom be in such a state of organisation'.[253]

The elections intervening the county ballot on and around 15 February and the provincial meeting on the 26th led to a rare voluntary change in Wicklow's representation at the city meetings. William Michael Byrne and John Lynch were deputed to attend the fateful meeting held at Oliver Bond's on 12 March 1798 and Lynch, therefore, must have defeated O'Reilly for the position of secretary for the first time since December 1797.

O'Reilly was perhaps fortunate as the provincial meeting was raided and all the delegates present seized due to the treachery of Kildareman Thomas Reynolds.[254] Byrne and Lynch had been unable to destroy or secrete what was described by Attorney-General Arthur Wolfe as 'a very treasonable printed paper, importing to be an address from the county of Wicklow delegate, and a return in manuscript of the force of Wicklow'.[255] The loss of the two men had a powerful impact on all United Irishmen and those in Wicklow were angered to the point that they reputedly resolved 'that even if the French did not come it was intended to rise and risk everything to prevent the execution of Bond and the other prisoners in Dublin'.[256] This sentiment, however, had probably more to do with the identification of the Wicklow leaders with the militarists in the executive than their concern for Byrne and Lynch.

March 1798 brought a host of other more immediate difficulties for the Wicklow United Irishmen, not least the task of replacing the arrested delegates. In mid-May 1798 Murray divulged that '[Phil] O'Neil was latterly a provincial committee man and expected to be appointed cornel [sic]' which reveals that while the Arklowman had succeeded William Michael Byrne, the important elections to the post of colonel had not then taken place in the barony. Murray insisted, moreover, that 'none was appointed for Arklow', a remarkable admission of organizational backwardness in such a numerically strong and otherwise highly developed barony.[257] Another Arklow captain, John Murray of Magheramore, corroborated the assertions of his Sheepwalk colleague informing Town Major Henry Charles Sirr that 'he never was at the appointment of a military commander above his own rank.'[258] There is little doubt but that the sudden impasse reached by the Arklow leadership was directly attributable to the efforts of the military to weaken or destroy Wicklow's rebel networks as rebellion neared.

CHAPTER THREE

'Measures of Rigour': sedition, counter-insurgency and martial law in Wicklow, April 1797–May 1798[1]

In the late summer and autumn of 1797 armed confrontations became increasingly common in Leinster and Munster as newly organized cells of United Irishmen raided the homes of yeomen and magistrates to obtain firearms. The Leinster executive of the United Irishmen repeatedly discouraged the practice as they were 'unwilling to raise alarm in their adversaries, or let the members of their body acquire habits of plunder, and be confounded with robbers'.[2] The raids continued, however, and the growing militancy and confidence of the grass roots manifested itself in other forms which attracted the attention of the authorities. The trend towards open hostilities was signalled by the intimidation and killing of state witnesses and jurors, the felling of trees to obtain wood for pike handles and the holding of seditious meetings convened for ostensibly innocuous purposes. Paramilitary displays were held in Dublin at the funerals of United Irishmen and in Wexford one of the first intimations to the magistracy that the people were acting strangely arose out of a burial organized by Toole of Annagh who marshalled a huge crowd 'into sections and marching order'.[3] Similar events were held in Wicklow and in the Powerscourt area in late 1797 a large meeting took place 'on the night of the funeral'.[4]

The Wicklow United Irish leaders had no overriding policy regarding the arming of the rank-and-file and little in the way of uniformity attended the progression to combat preparedness. The standard weapon, the pike, was provided to most recruits by the early months of 1798 when the military aspect of the organization was perfected.

Firearms were the preferred armament but were expensive, required training that could not be carried out in secret and were difficult to procure in the quantities needed. Pikes were the only weapons that met the criteria of the United Irishmen whose options were narrowed in the necessity of planning for a unilateral rising if the French did not arrive. Major Hardy was shocked by the sight of some of the first pike blades recovered in Wicklow which he described as being 'from 18 inches to 2 feet long, with two wings about 10 inches long, reversed in a bow for cutting bridle reins, and they and pikes as sharp as razors.' Blacksmiths came to be recognized as the weak link in United Irish organization and were frequently interrogated in April/May 1798 to discover how many blades had been made and to whom they had been delivered. They were also sometimes required to obtain licences from the magistracy to operate forges and to give guarantees that they would not produce pikes. Many rebels only received a pike head from sympathetic blacksmiths and were responsible for obtaining their own shafts. Carpenters provided minimal amounts of suitable poles but most engaged in the ill-advised devastation of loyalist-owned plantations, many of which had been created in the 1770s and 1780s with the aid of Dublin Society and Parliamentary grants.[5]

Complete pikes and pike heads were transferred from barony to barony and also over county borders. This was a practical arrangement which transcended the theoretical impediments of structure and organization as laid down in the movement's constitution. John Mernagh of Arklow barony sent pikes to his more famous eponymous cousin who lived at Ballinaskea (Glenmalure) in Ballinacor.[6] Two blacksmiths in Ballykillageer and Ballycoog near Woodenbridge, moreover, reputedly supplied at least seven townlands with 300–400 pikes, including the United Irishmen of Croghan, Ballyfad and Newtown in county Wexford.[7] This instance of mass production contrasts with the experience of Rathdown rebel Garret Quinn whose cell cut down just thirteen small trees at Seskin 'for the purpose of making pike handles.' Blacksmith John Hall of Ballynakeen claimed, somewhat implausibly, to have only forged two pike blades of which one was for his own use. Thomas Murray's assertion that there were only 200 pikes in the barony of Arklow in January 1798 also seems low and may represent the figure for Arklow Town alone. The overall picture suggests that the movement armed itself in fits and starts and was heavily dependent on the initiative and social contacts of their leading activists.[8]

Quantities of firearms were obtained from house raids which supplemented small numbers purchased from sympathetic or unsuspecting gunsmiths in Dublin. James Hanlon, a Narraghmore yeoman and United Irishman, was found in possession of three guns and twenty-two unmounted barrels in March 1798 for which he was making stocks. Wicklow's United Irish county committee estimated that over 1,000 firearms were stockpiled in January 1798, many hundreds of which were subsequently surrendered to the authorities after the declaration of martial law in March. The demonstrable failure of such weapons to affect the course of the Wicklow rebellion indicates that many of those retained were inoperative. Repairing guns was highly skilled work which was carried out in 1800 by an Imaal blacksmith who maintained the weapons of two distinct factions, those led by Michael Dwyer and Michael Dalton.[9]

Firepower in 1798 generally only ever told in the hands of practised marksmen such as Wexford's Shelmalier riflemen and individual sharpshooters. Indeed, the procurement of such limited numbers of guns for the use of untrained amateurs was probably only useful in that it tended to instill confidence in the majority armed with pikes. The several hundred rebels who attacked Stratford-on-Slaney on 24 May 1798 included men armed with muskets who failed to inflict a single fatality on their adversaries despite closing to within point-blank range. No insurgent victories of note hinged on the deployment of musketeers while acute shortages of ammunition and powder occasioned a series of disastrous assaults on fortified positions which further wasted resources and dictated poor strategy. Had the French succeeded in supplying large quantities of firearms to the United Irishmen, the course of the insurrection may well have been quite different. In practice, the Wicklow rebels were obliged to entrust muskets only to those deemed capable of using them properly. A cache of guns hidden near Arklow was consequently earmarked for the use of United Irishmen dismissed from three yeomanry corps in the Avoca area in March 1798. It may be assumed that obtaining weapons and training in their use were among the main reasons for infiltrating the yeomanry and militia in the first place.[10]

According to a statement attributed to Michael Dwyer, the Wicklow rebels were armed with just 1,200 guns when the insurrection began and possessed only four cartridges and seventeen musket balls per man. The Wexfordmen he knew and fought with reputedly 'had twice as much guns' having escaped the full weight of martial law.[11] The Wexfordians also enjoyed access to stocks captured from the depots they had overrun and from defeated enemies after 26–7 May 1798. Dwyer, when in captivity in 1804, was disdainful of the pike which he claimed was never effective 'except against a prisoner', although this was clearly in reference to the type of long-range skirmishing in mountainous terrain that his faction engaged in after 1798.[12]

That Arklow was the centre for importing arms and gunpowder into Wicklow it not surprising given that the close-knit families who dominated the United Irish leadership there had shipping interests, access to capital and valuble experience of smuggling contraband. The principal agent was a local cattle exporter, John Byrne of Three-milewater (Ennisboyne), who owned a share in the forty ton *Golden Pillar*. The vessel generally carried cattle to Wales but on at least one trip returned with 8 hundredweight of gunpowder which was divided between the United Irishmen of Arklow and Newcastle baronies. Thomas Murray of Sheepwalk claimed that the powder was packed in casks and was handed over to Phil O'Neil, Richard O'Reilly and John Lacey.[13] Byrne was arrested in Dublin in April 1798 while preparing to emigrate to America and remained an untried prisoner in mid-1799 when the Grahams, Beakeys, McDaniels and other families with United Irish links supported his petition for release. His father Loughlin farmed a sizeable property at Threemilewater, near John Lacey's home, until in was burned by the military in 1798 and the family as a whole were stated to have been 'reduced by smuggling and the rebellion'. This was clearly a reprisal for their involvement in a series of well-organized landings of illegal munitions for the United Irishmen.[14]

In January 1798, Major Hardy and Tom King conferred in Wicklow Town about the political prisoners being held there and decided to investigate the reported presence in Arklow of two suspected members of the Wicklow county committee. One of the jailed United Irishmen had evidently implicated John Lacey and one of the McDaniels who was discovered to be staying with him in Miles O'Neil's house where Phil O'Neil also lived. It was afterwards ascertained that their meeting had been occasioned by the arrival of a large consignment of weapons which the Arklow yeomanry had inadvertently allowed proceed to O'Neil's. King, writing of the event five years later, misdated it as having occurred 'about March 1798' and recalled following the tracks of the cart believed to have conveyed the guns the home, as did Hardy. They learned that the arms had lain on Arklow strand for a night or two concealed by upturned fishing boats before being brought into the town and distributed to the delegates. Lacey and McDaniel were challenged to explain their business that night but could not be implicated as no trace of the shipment remained in the house. Richard O'Reilly was arrested by King's Rathdrum cavalry en route to O'Neil's on 24 March 1798 and, as Murray independently named both men as recipients of smuggled munitions, it is likely that their meeting concerned another batch brought in by the *Golden Pillar*. The seizure of O'Reilly probably precipitated Byrne's flight to the city where he was apprehended the following month.[15]

Fishermen operating out of the port reportedly conveyed munitions to dumps along the coast and large quantities of guns and ammunition were thought to have been buried in sandbanks between Kilpatrick and Arklow. Revd Bayly was convinced of their role and in late 1797 asserted that 200–300 Arklow fishermen were disaffected. The Major requested the imposition of a navy-enforced embargo on all sea traffic off Arklow in order to impede such activity. This was an unacceptable initiative in relation to the county's busiest harbour and his repeated suggestions to that end went unheeded. It far from certain that the United Irishmen were in a position to recover these weapons when the rebellion began and King was of the opinion they remained where they had been hidden. Many fishermen Arklow fishing crews reputedly fled to Wales with their boats when the rebellion began and while some certainly stayed to fight with Matthew Doyle the precise location of arms dumps may well have been obscured by this exodus. The vagueness of Joseph Holt's assertion in November 1798 that there was a keg of powder 'somewhere in Barnesky . . . near Arklow' (Ballynabarny) suggests that this was the case.[16]

In the early summer of 1797, Wicklow magistrates tended to treat minor political offences, such as illegal tree felling, as ordinary criminal crimes against property and did not invoke the draconian anti-Defender and Whiteboy powers at their disposal. It is also possible that the magistracy genuinely believed that the wood was required for innocent purposes as no finished pikes were recovered in the county prior to November 1797. Some United Irish societies were aware of the need for subtlety lest the magistracy discern their real motives and the recruitment of Holt reputedly hinged on gaining influence over his 'inseparable friend' who worked as a steward to Thomas Hugo of Drumeen. The Roundwood men wanted the young ash trees in the charge of the steward for pike handles without alerting his employer.[17] At the Newcastle sessions of April 1797 Patrick Keenan was merely fined £5 by G. B. Hoey for having removed an ash tree from Bally-donna, a crime for which he could have been transported. Three months later Charles Coates of Clone offered Andrew Butler of Bahana the choice of the same fine or three months imprisonment for an identical offence. That neither Keenan nor Butler were even remanded until the county assizes indicates that their crimes had been deemed relatively trivial. Harsher sanctions were not imposed on such men until the winter of 1797 when the unmistakably political crime of arms raiding became prevalent. Once the purpose of tree felling was widely known it became a warning signal to magistrates that disaffection was abroad in their jurisdictions. Tree stealing near Dunlavin in December 1798 convinced one loyalist that 'every preparation in on foot for a general rising'.[18]

One of the first and most serious seditious incidents to occur in Wicklow took place in Blessington on 8 August 1797, when a crowd of 200–300 local men rushed into the town brandishing pikes and muskets. They surrounded the house of William McCormick, a prosecution witness due to appear at the county assizes, and quickly gained entry. McCormick was alleged to have posed as a radical in order to identify Blessington United Irishmen whom he then betrayed to the authorities. The yeomen and constables guarding him were clearly terrified by the unexpected tenacity of the mob and proved incapable of saving McCormick's life. His body was then severely mutilated, allegedly by decapitation and the severance of his nose, ears and limbs.[19] The Defender/Whiteboy-style punishment inflicted on McCormick's corpse had been unknown in eighteenth-century Wicklow and would not be repeated until the rebellion when loyalist elements began dismembering the bodies of fallen rebels. The impact of this extraordinary and horrific attack was exacerbated when the insurgents decided to demonstrate their defiance of authority still further by vandalizing the home of magistrate Revd Hill Benson. Benson, the inefficient manager of Earl Downshire's extensive Blessington estate, was involved in intelligence work until 1803 and had evidently aroused the anger of the locals by issuing warrants against suspected United Irishmen on the strength of McCormick's disclosures. Clerical magistrates like Benson, Bayly and Revd Charles Cope were deeply unpopular with the United Irishmen as they tended to be sectarian extremists.[20]

News of the Blessington incident was received with great concern in Wicklow's landed circles and was deliberated upon by the Privy Council, possibly at the behest of its Wicklow member Lord Rossmore. A proclamation was issued by the Council on 18 August 1797 which offered a substantial £100 reward for each of the first three persons arrested in connection with the killing.[21] The suddenness and violence of the murder shocked local loyalists and the extremely poor showing of the town's yeomanry could not have allayed their fears. They responded by creating an additional reward fund to which concerned gentry and magistrates could subscribe. The largest single donation was that of £113 from the arch conservative Downshire who was probably McCormick's landlord while Lord Waterford, Aldborough, Powerscourt, Fitzwilliam, Rossmore and High Sheriff Peter La Touche each donated between £22 and £43. Non-local subscribers such as hardline magistrates Tom King, James Chritchley, William Colthurst, William Eccles and Thomas Archer showed their solidarity with their west Wicklow peers by paying £5 each.[22]

The killing of McCormick emboldened the United Irishmen of the Blessington district and gave their anti-informer threats real potency. Castle agent John Smith was clearly perturbed that his landlady's son knew him to be a spy and had promised to 'have him fixed' in September 1797.[23] The area had previously been regarded as something of a safe haven for active loyalists from other parts of the country and in June 1797 Smith had met five men from the Belfast area who had moved to Wicklow on being 'driven from home by the U[nited]. I[rish]. M.[en]'.[24] This was almost certainly the same group identified by local men as 'Ulster informers who . . . had finished their work at the Castle of Dublin [and] were sent out of the way to the neighbourhood of Blessington'. Late in the rebellion Jonathan Eves of Blessington was killed having been confused with Benjamin Eves, one of Smith's harbourers in the autumn of 1797.[25]

Few details are extant of the Wicklow Summer Assizes held on 16 August before Justices Baron Carleton and Thomas Kelly. It seems, however, that the presence of the United Irishmen and the ineffectiveness of the authorities to contain them was clearly shown by the acquittal of at least one prisoner McCormick had been expected to prosecute. One Clark had been accused of administering an illegal oath to McCormick but was freed when it was discovered that the latter had deserted from the 94th Foot, a revelation that invalidated his testimony. There were no capital convictions at the Wicklow assizes compared to the fifty-one handed down to 'traitors' on the north eastern circuit alone.[26] Indeed, the sentencing of William McDaniel of Cronroe to six months imprisonment for spreading seditious propaganda only served to emphasize the poor showing of the county's magistracy. McDaniel had on 7 August 1797 declared in Humewood and elsewhere in west Wicklow that the Lower Talbotstown yeomanry were plotting to burn down the houses of Catholics. The corps only boasted one Catholic member but was by no means extremist. While Kildare was more disturbed than Wicklow, its forces of law and order had apprehended a disproportionately high number of suspects giving them the dubious honour of hosting the largest assizes in Ireland. The Kildare magistracy was, nevertheless, deemed unduly lenient and negligent by Government organs.[27]

The case which apparently attracted the most interest at the Wicklow assizes was that of Robert Gore of Newtownmountkennedy, who was tried for the murder of the Earl of Meath during a duel. Gore had been High Sheriff of Wicklow in 1795 and became captain of the Newtowmountkennedy yeoman cavalry when the unit was formed in October 1796. Meath's wound was not initially deemed serious, and in March 1797 he was reported to be recovering on his Kilruddery estate but it proved mortal. Gore was evidently a popular as well as prominent man and his acquittal was said to have been cheered by a 'vast number of the country people'.[28]

Many United Irishmen in western and southern Wicklow armed themselves in the early autumn of 1797 by calling under cover of darkness to the homes of loyalists known to possess weaponry and forcing the occupants to hand them over. This provocative activity contributed to the sharpening of tensions within the Wicklow magistracy and was used by the emergent conservative 'Castle Party' to disparage the efficiency and political reliability of the county's traditionally liberal magistrates. The new faction was centred on the anti-reform lesser gentry and minor nobility who were disproportionally prominent in the increasingly powerful magistracy and yeomanry.[29]

The return of liberal Wicklow MP Nicholas Westby to Parliament for the third consecutive time in August 1797 may have spurred political enemies like Benjamin O'Neil Stratford to discredit him and the Opposition's moderate policy on coercion by highlighting the crisis in Wicklow. Westby had pointedly stressed that he was 'uninfluenced by any private interest', unlike the pro-Government borough MPs of Blessington, who comprised the interest of the absentee local magnate Lord Downshire. Blessington was described in 1784 as 'a corrupt, venal and rotten borough, at the absolute command of its patron Lord Hillsborough [Downshire]'. The other pro-Government elements in 1790s Wicklow were the absentee Earl Carysfort in the southern baronies and his young son Lord Proby.[30] The emergence of such factions had been anticipated and perhaps encouraged by Camden in the aftermath of the Bantry Bay crisis of December 1796. In January 1797 the Viceroy expressed his confidence 'that a party is likely to come forward in support of government'.[31]

O'Neil Stratford was one of the most prolific hardline correspondents in west Wicklow who frequently criticized liberal county MP and magistrate William Hume of Humewood. One important clash arose from an encounter between three Carnew yeomen and a group of United Irishmen who had accosted them in the mountains near Kiltegan on 12 September 1797. One account mistakenly claimed that they were members of the Shillelagh yeomanry, an error which may have arisen from the shortlived practice of describing the Coolattin, Tinahely, Coolkenna and Carnew yeomanries as constituent companies of the Shillelagh Legion rather than independent units. The involvement of Captain Thomas Swan and Second-Lieutenant Robert Blayney of the Carnew infantry puts the issue beyond doubt. The accosted yeomen had prudently allowed themselves be sworn in as United Irishmen and, on being threatened with McCormick's fate if they informed, were given the names of contacts in their home area. This threat must have carried some weight after the recent Blessington killing but was not likely to coerce loyalists who lived so far to the south.[32]

Extremist Shillelagh and Ballinacor South magistrates Revd Charles Cope and Henry Moreton seized upon the fact that one of the United Irishmen implicated in the Humewood incident was an employee of Hume's and had not been called to account for his actions. Cope and Moreton were quick to exploit the controversy and attempted to undermine Hume's authority by sending two yeoman officers to Humewood to execute a warrant for the man's arrest. They arrested one suspect on the estate who was sent to Wicklow gaol and several others were later apprehended by the Rathdrum yeoman cavalry.[33] The involvement of Tom King's Rathdrum corps in lieu of a local Talbotstown formation and the conspicuous role of the south Wicklowmen points to a carefully contrived plan by conservative magistrates to embarrass their liberal opponents. King's role in the affair was highlighted by *Faulkner's Dublin Journal*, a paper with strong links to the Wicklow extremists, while Hume was referred to cryptically as a gentleman of 'very high rank'. This is further suggested by Stratford's raising the incident when pressing for the dispatch of a 'confidential person' from Dublin Castle to examine the state of affairs in Wicklow. The request implied that the Government could not place its confidence in the county's leading political representatives and should intervene. This was a very serious imputation which was probably instrumental in securing the dispatch of the military to Wicklow on 27 September.[34]

O'Neil Stratford claimed that Hume had been unwilling 'to appear in the business' of arresting the suspects and had contemplated using troops from Hacketstown to carry it out while he was absent. Hume's critics regarded this as an improper evasion of responsibility. O'Neil Stratford, moreover, confessed to having been tricked by a United Irishman posing as a 4th Dragoon who had almost succeeded in convincing him to denude Baltinglass of its infantry garrison. This stratagem was interpreted as a ruse to facilitate an arms raid on the Aldborough and Saundersgrove yeomanry corps and, like the spurious plot to burn the town of Stratford-on-Slaney he had reported in early August, seems highly improbable. Yet, by counterpointing Hume's weakness and the mounting threat posed by subversives, Stratford may have strengthened his argument for the direct intervention of the Government in Wicklow.[35]

A significant escalation in seditious activity had indeed became apparent towards the end of September 1797 when 'arms for about 50 men' had been stolen from loyalists in virtually every townland in the parish of Baltinglass.[36] William Cooke of Ballilea had his house 'robbed of arms & burned' while others had their cattle maimed and iron gates or ash trees taken away for the manufacture of pikes. Mary Leadbeater of Ballitore on the Kildare side of the border recorded that the attack of Cooke was one of the first acts of violence to occur in her home district and that the townspeople 'saw with dread the approaching flames of discord'. A possibly forewarned Cooke, aided by several friends, had fired at least fifty shots into the crowd besieging his home but ultimately failed to prevent them from burning the building when he refused to hand over his weapons. The attack was the only incidence of Wicklow arms raiding to receive much publicity, probably in consequence of Cooke's social status, the fact that he had been wounded repelling the raiders and that his home was burned, an extremely rare loss in Wicklow at that time. His relocation to Baltinglass would have underlined the sense of vulnerability felt by well affected west Wicklow families.[37]

United Irish determination to confront their perceived enemies did not auger well for the loyalist community and led to nightly yeomanry patrols in the worst affected areas around Baltinglass and Dunlavin. An anonymous Castle correspondent, very probably the Revd Charles Robinson of Knockrigg, Chaplain to the Aldborough cavalry, sent a heavily annotated map of the parish detailing United activity. In the last week of September 1797 yeomanry issue and privately held weapons were stolen from Ambrose Leet of Carrageen, James Wilson of Cardiff, Andrew Morris of Griffinstown, Cooke of Ballilea, Patrick Whelan of Porterside, Gilthrop, Wilson and others of Baronstown,

Crampton of Ballitore, Martin Sraith and James Harrowe of Rathtoole. Losses were also suffered by magistrates Walter Bagnell Carroll, who became High Sheriff of Wicklow in 1798, as well as Henry Harrington of Grangecon and his loyalist tenantry.[38] Such widespread activity gave rise to rumours in Dublin that Wicklow 'swarms with United Irishmen' and their total disregard of authority demanded action. Smith even reported from Blessington that the United Irishmen were as numerous in Wicklow as in the north of Ireland.[39]

It was reported on 30 September 1797 that Upper and Lower Talbotstown had been proclaimed 'under the provisions of the Insurrection Act'. Martial law was not, in fact, declared in the barony until 10 November 1797 but the Antrim militia had been sent to the county to augment the civil authorities.[40] A Baltinglass correspondent wrote on 30 September:

> 'This being the day appointed to take into consideration the *alarming* state of the barony of Talbotstown, in consequence of it being a very wet morning, but few justices, and only those of the neighbourhood attended-though their number amounted only to *ten*, they undertook the burthen [sic] of not only declaring that barony to be in as state of insurrection, but also, included the adjacent barony [Lower Talbotstown], and the several parishes adjoining those two baronies; in consequence of which I suppose, we shall have a chain of barracks, or military outposts, from Dublin to Hacketstown, through Blessington, Ballimore [sic] Eustace, Dunlavin, Stratford-on-Slaney, Baltinglass, Tullow etc etc . . . '

The ten magistrates evidently made a formal request for troops to be quartered in the affected district.[41]

The development was unusual as Wicklow, prior to September, had not been particularly disturbed and was less so than Kildare, Meath, Cork and other counties where militia garrisons had already been emplaced. By May 1797 the Wicklow Militia, stationed in Edenderry (King's County), had established a reputation for extreme loyalty which manifested itself in several incidences of brutal conduct. The notorious 'walking gallows' of folk memory, Lieutenant Edward Hepenstall of Newcastle, was credited with killing 'two ruffians with his own hand' on 6 May 1797 during a clash between the militia and 250 United Irishmen at Carbury (Kildare).[42] That Wicklow was one of the first counties outside of Ulster to receive troops indicated that the Castle had been persuaded that its resident forces were either unable or unwilling to take the steps necessary to contain the United Irishmen. This was largely the work of O'Neil Stratford who, if not highly regarded in the Castle, was championed by the capital's loyalist establishment. He was given the freedom of the city on 18 October 1797 in recognition of 'his active exertions in apprehending and bringing to justice numbers of persons for administering unlawful oaths under the denomination of United Irishmen'. The previous recipient for coercion was no less a person than General Carhampton in 1795. Militarization was undoubtedly a rebuke to Wicklow's liberal establishment but the policy change also represented a prudent attempt to forestall further outrages in a strategically vital sector.[43]

It is significant that no such measures were deemed necessary in Wexford where evidence of United Irish activity was then apparent if less confrontational in nature. As early as 22 May 1797 concerned magistrates had met in Enniscorthy to discuss the appearance of 'seditious handbills . . . lately circulated'.[44] The decision not to send troops to Wexford at that time reflected not only the absence of regular outrages but also Camden's confidence in the county's politicians to whom he was ideologically far closer than their Wicklow counterparts. They had also proven their mettle in July 1793 by killing eighty anti-militia rioters outside the county town.[45] A further Enniscorthy meeting of twenty-six magistrates on 16 October 1797 voted their 'thanks' to High Sheriff James Boyd as well as to Archibald Hamilton Jacob, Hawtrey White and the 13th Regiment for their 'zeal and activity in apprehending . . . sundry persons charged with administering and taking unlawful oaths'. Also present was John Hunter Gowan of Mount Nebo, who, together with the named yeomanry officers, could already be identified as the driving force behind counter-insurgent operations in northern Wexford. Security issues remained in their uncompromising hands and the notorious North Cork Militia were not dispatched to augment the small garrisons of Gorey, Enniscorthy and Wexford town until 18 April 1798.[46]

The arrival of the Antrim Militia in Wicklow some seven months earlier did not herald the first dispatch of troops to the county. It was, rather, the first initiative to militarize and centralize the command of anti-United Irish effort in the county with a view to combating its spread. Local ultra loyalists, while less numerous and less socially prominent than their counterparts in Wexford and Carlow, retained a key role in the programme but they operated within a framework imposed by the Castle. Elements of the North Cork Militia had been present in west Wicklow since mid-September 1797 at the latest and had been actively involved in the Humewood arrests on 25th of that month. They were probably based at that time in Kildare or at Hacketstown and may have been the regiment's light company under the command of Captain Edward Heard which had relocated to Shillelagh in December 1797. Other detachments were in Ballitore and probably also Narraghmore and Ballymore-Eustace on the borders of Wicklow.[47]

The ramifications of republican organization in Wicklow presented Dublin Castle with an untypical range of political and military concerns. These complications ensured that the decision to deploy troops in the county and the extent and nature of that course of action demanded particularly close liaison between the Castle and the military. Army chiefs Earl Carhampton and Sir Ralph Abercromby conferred at some length on the subject in the autumn of 1797 with key civilian administrators Edward Cooke and William Elliott, the Undersecretary for Military Affairs. Counter-insurgent duties in Wicklow were regarded by them from the outset as a 'special service' for which Major Joseph Hardy was deemed uniquely qualified owing to his acknowledged zeal, intelligence and intimate local links. Hardy was so suitable, in fact, that he was appointed to a command befitting a Brigadier-General notwithstanding his considerably more junior substantive rank and from March 1798 he was granted the pay and entitlements of a general. This process was so unorthodox that its details were largely unofficial and verbal, a factor which greatly hindered Hardy's post-rebellion efforts to obtain back pay for 1797–8.[48]

Hardy's dispatch to Wicklow on 27 September 1797 with 'a flying camp of 300 men' of the Antrim Militia signalled the first comprehensive attempt of the Castle to exert direct control of counter-insurgency in a politically sensitive and strategically vital sector.[49] Hardy's most important previous assignment had been in December 1797 when he had the distinction of commanding the militia's elite flank battalion on its march from Dublin to contain the threatened French invasion at Bantry Bay. *Faulkner's Dublin Journal* of 26 January 1797 printed the 'thanks' of Hardy and Lord Granard to the Mayor and citizens of Clonmel for their hospitality after the 'long and fatiguing march in a most inclement season'. Hardy had first seen service in the American War of Independence twenty years before and had risen through the ranks from that of private to obtain a commission at the battle of Bunker Hill.[50] His understanding of the Wicklow posting was that it had arisen 'in consequence of the insurgents burning the houses and houghing the cattle of some yeomen near Dunlavin without provocation'. Upon arrival he immediately distributed his troops in small garrisons from Blessington to Enniscorthy providing symbolic if not effective reinforcement to the yeomanry.[51]

Army chain of command devolved from commander-in-chief Lieutenant-General Sir Ralph Abercromby to Major-General Sir Peter Craig who commanded the Eastern District. Hardy's immediate superiors were Major-Generals William Loftus and Francis Needham who commanded at Lehaunstown camp towards the end of 1797. Camp General Orders of 17 December 1797 specified that Loftus and Nugent were to attend Loughlinstown and 'take charge of the troops in Wicklow, Wexford and the rest of the district', a task entrusted to Needham alone the following week. Hardy, however, retained operational control of all Wicklow forces and answered directly to the Castle. Available to Hardy in an emergency were Colonel Cholmely Dering's New Romney (or the Duke of York's Own) Fencible Dragoon Cavalry, the Cavan Militia, the 6th Regiment of Foot and the 1st Flank Battalion at Lehaunstown. The Flank Battalions consisted of the detached light and grenadier companies from militia, fencible and sometimes regular infantry regiments which were generally the only elements trained in skirmishing and open-order tactics.[52]

The Castle adopted a very similar strategy to that of Wicklow in the worst-affected districts of eastern Carlow in November 1797 when the Ninth Dragoons were sent to the county. Their commander, Colonel, later General, Brydges Trecothic Henniker, was Aldborough's brother-in-law and as such might have been expected to benefit from the introductions flowing from the Earl's social prominence, even if this connection was fraught with potential for political embarrassment owing to Aldborough's antipathy towards aspects of Government policy. The unwelcome prospect of Henniker's becoming embroiled in jurisdictional clashes with unco-operative magistrates was obviated by his appointment to a civil commission of the peace, what was coyly termed 'a *pacifying* commission'. Joint civil and martial powers were comparatively rare and yet Henniker's status and his recourse to a 'flying camp' mirrored precisely the commands held in adjacent parts of southern Leinster by Hardy and Lord Blayney.[53]

It could not have escaped the notice of informed contemporaries that Blayney and Henniker had been sent to Leinster fresh from the controversial and brutal dragooning of Ulster. A clear strategy then, if not an overt agenda, was being pursued by the Executive. The flying columns of Blayney and Henniker had comprised two of the leading instruments of coercion in the proclaimed districts of Antrim, Down and Armagh, a circumstance which would have been familiar to many southern United Irishmen from the pages of the *Press* and other anti-Government organs. House burnings, transportation to the

fleet without trial, mass floggings and summary executions had carved
a swathe through the east and mid-Ulster Republican organization in
1797 with serious consequences for the stability of the region. The
conduct of the columns in southern Leinster might well have been
identical to that of their northern operations had the appropriate
combination of political, legal and seditious conditions coalesced.[54]

This, as matters transpired, was not forthcoming until the early
months of 1798 when the Ancient Britons, Northumberland fencibles,
Tyrone Militia and other experienced veterans of the Ulster programme
were redeployed to the eastern province. Yet, the provision for dragooning in the autumn of 1797 ensured that the state's ultimate contingency
hung over the succession of more moderate initiatives several months
before the prerequisite licence of martial law was granted by the
Castle.[55] In Wicklow, in the interim, Major Hardy's commission of
the peace gave him useful civil powers which, combined with his
military rank, stood him in good stead in his dealings with those
conservatively minded magistrates whom the Government wished to
organize. He also held a commission for county Carlow from 1797,
the year in which his brother Thomas and Revd James McGhee also
became magistrates. The arrangement had been experimented with by
Rossmore during the Defender unrest of 1795 when he, as commander-
in-chief, had approved the granting of commissions of the peace for
two senior officers in Fermanagh and north Leinster. The commission
advocated for a major in the Breadalbine fencibles was intended to
cover both Meath and Cavan and dual jurisdictions were also a
feature of the south Leinster strategy in 1797–8.[56]

Hardy brought a rare perspective to his task having spent part of
his youth at Hilbrook in southern Wicklow where his aunt Mrs
Symes lived. He enjoyed a very cordial relationship with the local
conservative magistrates and yeomanry officers who felt secure in the
knowledge that his 'sentiments . . . agreed with our own' and they
evidently respected his judgement on politically sensitive matters. His
familiarity with the local terrain was to have a bearing on General
Lake's preparations to recapture Wexford in June 1798. Writing
many years after the rebellion, Revd Henry Lambart Bayly of Arklow
recalled Hardy's local knowledge and intimacy with the Wicklow
gentry and claimed that the county was 'particularly indebted to his
vigilance and talents'.[57] A further local connection was provided by
Hardy's younger and only brother, Thomas, who lived at Hacketstown
on the Wicklow/Carlow border and raised a yeoman infantry corps
in that town; 'the last, but one of the best'. Such extra-professional con-

tacts could only have improved Hardy's relations with the dynamic forces of Carlow loyalism and he may well have gleaned an otherwise unobtainable degree of insight into their thinking from his brother. Liaisons of this nature were of particular importance prior to the declaration of martial law when the army required at least the tacit co-operation of the civil powers.[58]

By January 1798 Hardy had taken stock of his mission and in the course of that month recalled the small detachments he had sent into adjacent parts of Kildare, Wexford and Carlow. It is unclear, however, for how long and what proportion of his force had been deployed outside Wicklow and their release to his principal theatre may have been reliant on the prior arrival of replacements.[59] He claimed in retrospect that even though his powers were 'unlimited' he had managed to pacify the county 'without murder, or torture, or even free quarters with one militia regiment and detachments of 300 men.'[60] That October 1797 was relatively free from violent incidents in Wicklow may indicate that the United Irishmen had become more wary of raiding for arms in areas where the militia were present. The lull could also have resulted from the imposition of greater control on raiding parties by their governing committees. Camden confidently asserted that 'the march of the military' into the county had quelled unrest in the barony of Newcastle around Rossmore's Newtownmountkennedy estate, as well as on the coast. The Viceroy's impressions were apparently influenced by accounts which reached him of a single major incident in Newtown as well as by a catalogue of minor largely unreported episodes.[61]

Newcastle loyalists were astounded on the night of 11 October 1797 when hundreds of country people from the coastal district suddenly appeared in the fields around the village of Newtown-mountkennedy. One account estimated that the crowd consisted of '700' people who reputedly 'paraded' through the town, evidently without opposition from surprised and unmobilized local yeomanry forces. The demonstration was attributed to a United Irishman named James McQuillan, a Louth-born mine worker at Cronebane, and had ostensibly been contrived to facilitate paramilitary manoeuvres. A very similar episode had taken place in August 1797 when William McDaniels spread false claims about the intentions of the Humewood yeomanry had excited widespread panic.[62] McQuillan had allegedly impersonated a member of the Rathdrum cavalry the previous day and ridden around north Wicklow issuing warnings that the corps, who were falsely stated to be all orangemen, were planning to attack Catholics on the night of the 11th. He impersonated James Collins, who belonged to a family with several Rathdrum yeomanry members, and returned to his Ballymurtagh home by a different route to maximize the extent of the warning. The subsequent gathering may have been inspired by fears elicited by this report although the fact that the village of Newtownmountkennedy was overrun and the behaviour of the crowd when there implied a deeper motive. The occasion was certainly exploited by United Irish recruiters and Musgrave's loyalist sources informed him that McQuillan's role was simply to summon the previously briefed Newcastle United Irishmen to turn out.[63]

The general demeanour of the people was not that of nervous fugitives but rather of well-organized protestors who had been allegedly 'headed by their captains and variously armed'.[64] This was a salient feature of the demonstration and one which indicated an eagerness of the participants to show defiance in the face of a perceived orange threat, if not against the Government. The incident made a deep impression on the Lord Lieutenant who was inclined to accept the more innocent premise of the event and was, perhaps, all the more struck by the phenomenon having spent the night of 10 October as a guest in Rossmore's Mountkennedy home. The Viceroy's presence in the district may, in fact, have inspired the local United Irishmen to stage the event as a form of protest. The mansion was then only lightly guarded as Rossmore, who had first seen service as a boy volunteer at Culloden in 1746, rising to become C.I.C. of the Irish army in May 1793, was a popular and progressive landlord. He had been elevated to the peerage on his retirement in late 1796 and was not been deemed to be at great risk from the United Irishmen. It is highly doubtful that the October gathering could have taken place if the 5th Royal Irish (or Rossmore's) Dragoons had been stationed in the their usual quarters of Newtownmountkennedy. Camden recounted the following month how the 'ignorant and deluded persons left their houses and lay in the fields and at last assembled in large numbers for their own protection'.[65] An immediate outcome of the meeting was a tightening of security with the reinforcement of Rossmore's military guard but its most serious effect may have been to predispose the Viceroy to doubt the ability of Wicklow's resident forces to contain the United Irish threat. This very probably hastened the introduction of martial law when the crisis perceptibly deepened in the course of November.[66]

Trouble had also flared in the northwest of the county in October between soldiers and some of the Earl of Milltown's tenants in Blessington who had 'set their faces ag[ain]st the [military] party there'. Downshire's advisor William Patrickson, the High Sheriff in 1790, complained that the people 'were inclined to starve them and would not bring in their turf as they had usually done', a circumstance highlighting the depths of local opposition to the role of the military in parts of Talbotstown.[67] Hardy personally investigated the incident to ascertain whether his troops had transgressed when requisitioning supplies and twice conferred with the active Patrickson. Conservative ill-will towards John Leeson, who had accompanied Camac to London in 1795 to protest the recall of Fitzwilliam, failed to prevent his December 1797 appointment to oversee a munitions depot earmarked for Blessington. This relatively minor problem was engendered with a degree of importance as the aggrieved tenants were Milltown's, whose political sympathies were deeply distrusted by loyalists and government agents. Castle spy John Smith claimed to be 'certain' that the Earl's nephews, Joseph and John Leeson, 'were the chief agitators that first seduced from their allegiance the peasantry of the county of Wicklow, bordering on their uncles estates'.[68]

Smith was well placed to evaluate the Leesons on behalf of Cooke and State Solicitor Thomas Kemmis as he was based in Blessington when the incident took place, probably in the home of either Benjamin Eves or Mrs Morris who were both compensated out of secret service funds in December 1798 for Smith's expenses. That monies were advanced to him by Patrickson suggests he was the source of his information on this matter.[69] The reputations of the Leesons became so tarnished in Dublin conservative circles that Lord Shannon privately declared Milltown to be 'an *amicus*' of the United Irishmen and dismissed out of hand rumours that Russborough House had been destroyed by the rebels in September 1798.[70] Three months earlier John Patrickson claimed that a rebel prisoner had told him 'John Leeson is one of the most implicated in giving support and encouragement to the rebels'.[71]

Such opinions may have been first articulated when John Leeson, who held a commission of the peace, had formally complained about soldiers straying onto the Milltown estate from the neighbouring Downshire property where they had permission to forage. The Earl also raised the matter himself in Dublin, presumably with Camden or other senior members of the Executive. As with the Hume/Cope dispute, the incident may have been contrived to test the attitude of Wicklow liberals in a period of mounting crisis and it was certainly raised in attempts to diminish the standing of the Leesons. However, whereas Hume, Westby, Morley Saunders, Henry Harrington and other moderates in the west of the county were merely accused of incompetence or misguided liberalism, the Leesons were charged, at least privately, with overt United Irish tendencies. This theoretically placed them in the same bracket as Lord Edward Fitzgerald in Kildare and may explain why the Earl saw fit to embark on a lengthy tour of Europe as Ireland's political situation continued to deteriorate.[72]

The strength of Patrickson's enmity may be gauged from the fact that he persisted in his attempts to inculpate the Leesons as late as February 1799 when he surmised that 'Mr J[ohn] Leeson's conduct . . . [had] protected' Russborough while the homes and estates of Blessington loyalists had been devastated by the rebels.[73] Russborough had, in fact, suffered considerable damage, but at the hands of the Duke of York's Highlanders who had occupied it as an auxiliary barracks in 1798. The Highlanders had evidently deemed Milltown's absence in Italy as suspicious and avenged this affront to their patriotism by looting his celebrated wine cellars and vandalizing portions of the mansion's interior.[74]

Of more consequence than the appearance of menacing crowds and the vilification of liberal gentry were the series of violent attacks on yeoman families which flared in November 1797 in the barony of Shillelagh, then a sector where very few militiamen had been stationed. One raid claimed the life of the elderly Richard Nixon of Killinure on 7 November and set in train a succession of events which moved the county inexorably towards a state of crisis. Hitherto the 'loyalty and spirit' of the Shillelagh yeomanry had been praised for ensuring tranquillity in the barony but Nixon's death exposed the fragility of this level of security.[75] Nixon, 'an infirm man' of eighty, had been mortally wounded when remonstrating with a gang of arms raiders who had demanded his weapons while holding a lighted wisp to his thatch. Although a relative of Coolkenna yeoman Captain Abraham Nixon, the Killinure man was probably not the victim of a premeditated assassination plot given that the raiders did not harm any of the other loyalists intimidated by them that night. Fr Purcell of Clonegal, who described Nixon 'as one of the most inoffensive men in the world', ascertained that he had been shot when his deafness had prevented his compliance with an order to remain in the house.[76] The raiders proceeded to attack the homes of three yeoman households of the Tomkins family where firearms were obtained without further acts of violence. On 10 November two more provocative raids were mounted on the homes of Thomas Whelan at Ballyconnell and the Symes of Hilbrook but in both cases the defenders, no doubt alert to the threat and fearful of Nixon's fate, offered successful resistance.[77]

Several Catholic families with yeomanry members were also beset on the night of the 10th on the Carlow side of the border adding to the climate of fear and sense of emergency. Yet, despite the clearly unsectarian nature of the raids, Fitzwilliam's agent William Wainwright expressed the opinion that the United Irishmen planned to 'massacre the whole race of those professing the protestant religion whenever an opportunity offers'. Protestant tenants on the Fitzwilliam estate around Shillelagh were reputedly afraid to sleep in their beds and many passed the nights in yeomanry uniform. While the fears of Fitzwilliam's tenants were undoubtedly genuine, the sectarian theory advanced by pro-Government extremists in early 1798 as the justification for their own illegal and atrocious conduct was not borne out by events. It was also belied by the type of precautions which had been taken by loyalists against rebel attacks.[78]

The placing of a military guard on William Burton's residence indicates that the Shillelagh loyalists regarded the threat as having a specific political dimension.[79] Burton was captain of the Carlow Infantry and one of the first loyalists in Wicklow or Carlow to preside over mass arrests. His actions were in keeping with the determination of Shillelagh's pro-Government faction to take decisive anti-insurgent steps. Perhaps the first such arrests had taken place at Clonegal and Newtownbarry in late September 1797.[80] He had every reason to apprehend retaliatory actions from the many enemies such hard line practices must have generated. Indeed, the attacks on the Symes, Nixons and Whelans, families with strong yeomanry associations, revealed that the United Irishmen were willing to confront their ideological and most immediate enemies in Wicklow's loyalist heartland. This circumstance entailed a far graver threat than an ephemeral bout of sectarianism. Thomas Whelan was prominent in barony politics, one of the first signatories of a loyal address presented to Fitzwilliam upon his arrival as Viceroy in January 1795 and probably the man of that name who lodged a claim for a house destroyed by the rebels in 1798 at Lower Munny. He or one of his relatives was a magistrate in Coolkenna.[81] Revd James Symes' ministry (from which he was removed in 1802 for inattendence) was at Kilmallock and Castle Ellis in Wexford but he had been deeply involved in raising yeomanry corps in Ballinacor South in November/December 1796.[82]

Similar attacks on loyalist figures in Carlow, such as an attempt to kill Lieutenant John Butler of the Carlow cavalry in early November, had spurred that county's politically dominant hardline magistrates to press for the imposition of martial law. *Faulkner's Dublin Journal* of 7 November 1797 highlighted the 'alarming reports' emanating from Carlow where 'emissaries of the North have so far succeeded as to have set nocturnal meetings and robberies in a train of regular organization.' The paper further claimed that 400–500 United Irishmen had taken over an inn at Leighlin-Bridge, consumed a cask of ale and fired on yeomen before dispersing. Initial speculation, later dismissed, had attributed Nixon's death to United Irishmen from the Carlow side of the border and the raiders certainly operated in both counties.[83]

It was in this tense atmosphere that a special meeting of Shillelagh barony magistrates was convened in Coolattin courthouse on 9 November under the chairmanship of Revd Charles Cope. The resolutions arising from the meeting stated that it was 'absolutely necessary' to quarter twenty-five soldiers in the villages of Shillelagh, Carnew and Tinahely and that the barony should be proclaimed to be in a state of rebellion, in other words, subject to martial law. An important initiative was the establishment of a fund to reward those who informed on United Irish activity to which almost £400 was immediately pledged or subscribed by twenty-nine loyalists. This was a long-term strategy which ultimately vested the most useful intelligence on seditionists in the hands of extremists, but the clamour for action was met by the inauguration of nightly yeomanry patrols.[84]

The patrolling initiative fell just short of 'permanent', or full-time, duty required of corps operating within proclaimed sectors but was significant in that the burden of financing the effort consequently remained with local loyalists rather than with the Castle. Much of the costs were met by Fitzwilliam, whose trenchant opposition to martial law was a critical factor in any discussion of the measure in southern Wicklow. Pressure to progress to more arbitrary legal initiatives may have been alleviated when the strategy of increased yeomanry activity quickly bore fruit. One of two Baltinglass men apprehended in Shillelagh on 11 November was found to be in possession of a stolen yeomanry pistol and was suspected of having burned a house near Dunlavin. A third prisoner from Baltinglass had been arrested by Wainwright's corps on 1 November and sent under guard to Rathdrum.[85]

As the Coolatin session took place just one day before the barony of Talbotstown was proclaimed to be in a state of insurrection, it seems likely that it had been intended to also have Shillelagh placed under martial law. Extant documents indicate that this would have occurred had not Wainwright reconsidered his position on the issue, quite possibly in consequence of instructions from his employer. It is probably not a coincidence that an important meeting of the Carlow magistracy had taken place on 2 November which had been followed a week later with a request that the entire county be proclaimed. This suggests that the allied conservative elements of Wicklow and Carlow had considered the simultaneous proclamation of their respective districts arising out of consultative sessions at Coolattin, Baltinglass and in east Carlow. In the event, the Carlow loyalists opted for an amnesty-backed ultimatum to the United Irishmen, counterpointed with the threat of martial law, rather than its immediate imposition, while the Shillelagh magistrates followed Wainwright's lead and stopped short of proclaiming. The tide of events was moving against those who argued for restraint in the district and the Carlow baronies of Idrone, Rathvilly, Forth and St Mullins were all proclaimed on 15 November 1797.[86]

When Wainwright had left for Baltinglass sessions on 14 November to present them with the Coolattin resolutions, he claimed to have been 'undetermined' whether or not to support the recommendations on martial law. Consultation with Hardy on the matter was also a consideration in the light of the proclamation of Upper and Lower Talbotstown on 10 November, a development which may also have encouraged the Carlow magistrates to hesitate until the measure had been observed in action. Talbotstown was the first part of Ireland to be placed under martial law since May 1797. Selective proclaiming of parishes was the preferred option of the Castle prior to the spiralling crisis of March 1798 in counties where the unequivocal support of magnates was not forthcoming and where seditious unrest had co-existed with doubts as to the reliability of the resident political authorities. Talbotstown was a case in point in that the killing of Lorenzo Nixon in southern Wicklow was deemed to necessitate action in the troubled west of the county where the incident threatened to embolden radicals into perpetrating more widespread and frequent outrages.[87] O'Neil Stratford argued that the United Irishmen had become 'more desperate' in the face of perceived government reluctance to proclaim Wicklow and anticipated its 'most salutary effect'.[88]

Whereas the government could rely on the strong loyalist interest at grass roots level in east Carlow, north Wexford and south Wicklow, doubts were growing concerning the commitment of the Fitzwilliamite MPs and magistrates in their stronghold of west Wicklow. Criticism of those suspected of misguided leniency, magisterial inaction or United Irish sympathies were persistent and increasingly harsh in tone. The 9th Dragoons, sent to Carlow in mid-October 1797, were by early 1798 also stationed further north on the Kildare/Wicklow border, an area which was generally considered one operational district by the government. Mass arrests soon followed the deployment and rebel suspects were said to be 'rotting in gaols, or packed up like cargoes of negroes'.[89] Hardy must have been closely consulted on the decision to proclaim Talbotstown as unrest in the barony had occasioned his presence in September and it remained the principal resort of his troops. He would, no doubt, have been concerned about the efforts to suborn his soldiers, the most serious case of which had just come to light in Baltinglass on 11 November.[90]

Antrim Militia private Webb had drunk 'raw whiskey' on 9 November with twenty other men in the home of Michael Kean in Baltinglass when seditious toasts were made, probably to test his reaction in advance of more serious overture. One toast with republican and enlightenment themes was as follows:

> May the King's skin be a paraplue to save the United Irishmen from rain, may Pitt's skin be converted into drumheads to beat the United Irishmen to arms, may the stars that shine over America shine over France and illuminate the whole world.

Webb was taken to Peter Lennon's house outside Baltinglass where he received the oath of the United Irishmen from Edward Kenny. He was told to desert at a particular time and place where he was told he would be met and sent 'to a little village not far off to their friends where he would be taken great care of'. Information divulged by Webb led to the arrests of thirteen men by the Antrim Militia, Stratford's Baltinglass Cavalry and Cornet Love of the 9th Dragoons who were sent to Wicklow goal. Stratford was amused by the claim advanced by Kean's daughter that a bullet mould found in their house was 'a thing for curling her hair' but the incident was worrying as it revealed the determination of the United Irishmen to gain influence over the militia even after the much publicized trial and execution of William Orr of Carrickfergus for the same crime.[91]

Camden, when outlining his reasons for extending the Insurrection Act to Wicklow to the Duke of Portland, specified that 'the exertions' of the county's resident gentry had 'not reached the evil.' With renewed efforts being made by Dublin based agitators to build up the United Irishmen in Wicklow and the growing sense of foreboding nationally, the Viceroy felt compelled to respond positively 'to the reiterated requests and entreaties of the magistrates'.[92] Wainwright, as Fitzwilliam's representative in Wicklow, enjoyed political influence far above his status as a magistrate and yeomanry officer and his judgement on such an important matter evidently carried enough weight to override, or at least influence, the vociferous loyalist minor gentry of Shillelagh and Ballinacor South. The Earl's opposition to martial law and later the tactic of 'freequarters' affected both the nature and pace of implementation of coercion in Wicklow.

A similar role to Wainwright's was played by the Burtons in Carlow who prevented the extension of a military regime like that of Hardy's in Forth barony into their home barony of Carlow. Hardy was deeply impressed by Wainwright's accounts of the 'alarming state' of Shillelagh and devised a programme of anti-insurgent tactics which offered an alternative to proclaiming the barony. The crux of the policy was the hope that the moral and practical effect of martial law in Talbotstown, as well as the increased militarization in Carlow and southern Wicklow, would be sufficient to deter further outrages in Shillelagh. While Henniker's dragoons in Carlow may not have been guilty of 'extermination', as the United Irish paper *Press* alleged, the harsh sanction of house burning had commenced in Leighlin bridge.[93] One hundred extra troops were earmarked for service in Shillelagh barony to add weight to the threat in south Wicklow and ten were immediately provided to guard Fitzwilliam's mansion at Malton. Another small party was sent from Hacketstown to Hilbrook to protect Hardy's loyalist relatives, the Symes family. Hardy expressed his confidence that the county would 'tranquillize without much coercion' if the French did not invade and that the best solution was offered by 'constant residence, & active exertions of the principal gentry, magistrates [and] yeomanry'.[94] He placed much store in mixing yeoman personnel with his precious regular units which theoretically maximized the fighting strength and morale of the loyalist amateurs while placing their local knowledge of terrain and people at the direct disposal of his scarce troops.[95]

The major's interpretation of the powers of the Insurrection Act were of vital importance in determining the level of coercion adopted by his forces in Wicklow, which might easily have amounted to dragooning as experienced in parts of Ulster in 1797. In one incident in July 1797 the Ancient British Light Fencible Dragoons had burned thirty homes in Ballinahinch, Dromore and Hillsborough, County Down.[96] One measure applicable in Talbotstown after proclamation, but opposed by Hardy, was the forced billeting of troops in private homes without compensation. This became known as 'free quarters' and was intended to force the return of illegally held weapons by inflicting hardship on disaffected communities. Hardy's moderation on this issue was due in no small part to his desire to avoid the negative impact of free quarters on army discipline and it was one which entailed logistic problems. It was unusually difficult to deploy large numbers of troops in Wicklow, as the county was virtually devoid of military infrastructure in 1797–8 and had only two permanent barracks in Bray and Arklow. This circumstance was exacerbated by the Quarter Master-General's financial objections to erecting temporary barracks in 'towns of little note' which would be immediately vacated in the event of a rising or invasion.[97] Hardy was consequently reliant upon the voluntary assistance of landlords to house the bulk of his men and profited in this regard from his good relations with Wainwright. The Light Company of the North Cork Militia were accommodated by Wainwright in Shillelagh in December 1797 and on the commencement of the rebellion in May 1798 he made the Rathdrum Flannel Hall available to the military.[98]

Hardy mounted a 'general search' in late November 1797 to seize the initiative from the arms raiders. It was intended to deny the United Irishmen the premise of their action by confiscating as many as possible of the large numbers of weapons that were traditionally held by the Protestant community. The first patrols failed to find a single pike of which Hardy was certain 'many [had been] made but hid'.[99] Over 500 weapons were collected in Wicklow and adjacent parts of Kildare and Carlow 'without any distinction as to persons or religion' which effectively deprived loyalists of the means of defending themselves. This drastic and unprecedented step was palliated with assurances that the arms would be held under guard in local depots and reissued to loyalists in an emergency. It was not universally popular and undoubtedly increased the sense of threat perceived by loyalists. Wainwright claimed that the search had been undertaken 'without any legal authority (by the advice of major Hardy)' but remained convinced that the decision not to proclaim Shillelagh was correct. Two weeks later he admitted that he did not think 'any of the arms surrendered and taken up were procured for the purpose of insurrection as very few of them were found in the hands of Catholics'.[100]

The evidence for this was contained in a report dated 20 November 1797 which Hardy lodged with the Castle detailing the various armaments recovered in Wicklow and the proclaimed parts of Carlow. The first fruits of martial law and its threat yielded a superficially impressive final total of 555 firearms of all descriptions which had been collected by nine yeomanry corps operating in the militarized parts of Hardy's jurisdiction. Details of 173 extra firearms which had been surrendered to his depots in Baltinglass, Hacketstown and Tullow were also supplied with a note that the figure was an underestimate which did not include weapons deposited in Dunlavin or Coolatin. That a mere nineteen (3.4 per cent) of the weapons were described as 'pikes' indicates that the Wicklow United Irishmen had not commenced their mass production. Much, if not most of the war material recovered, including a four-pounder cannon obtained by Captain William Ryves of Dunlavin, had never been in republican hands. Significantly, most of the pikes had been obtained in Talbotstown by units whose questionable political reliability had not impeded their effectiveness in the role; William Hume's corps delivered five, Aldborough's men found four and Morley Saunders' produced seven. The only conservative commander to uncover a pike was Benjamin O'Neil Stratford whose Baltinglass Cavalry collected three. Ryves (Dunlavin Cavalry), George Heighington (Donard Infantry), Edward Eustace (Tullow Cavalry) and Richard Hornidge (Lower Talbotstown Cavalry) failed to take possession of anything fitting the description of pikes or 'scythes on shafts'. Wainwright's Shillelagh Cavalry and Infantry were also empty-handed.[101]

The results were first examined by Lieutenant-General Carhampton and then passed by Chief Secretary Thomas Pelham to Camden whose 'approbation' was immediately forthcoming. So impressed were the Castle with the efficacy of the Wicklow yeomanry that Hardy was given special dispensation to disregard the standing orders requiring the lodgement of all captured weaponry with the Board of Ordnance. Instead Hardy was authorized to disperse the firearms to local loyalists who required them, and his presence was requested in Dublin to discuss the security situation. A committee to regulate their dispersal held its first meeting in Baltinglass on 23 December 1797. Pelham promised to supply ammunition to this otherwise self-sufficient project which was financed by local patronage. Members were drawn from the affected parts of Talbotstown, Shillelagh, the parishes of Hacketstown, Kilpipe and Kilcomer in Ballinacor South, the parishes of Killelan, Hughestown, Carrageen and Graney in Kildare and the barony of Rathvilly in Carlow.[102]

That liberal magistrates Hume, Leeson, Saunders and Francis Greene of Greenville were represented on the governing committee is indicative of the eagerness of the Fitzwilliamites to support security measures that fell short of martial law while the presence of Hardy, O'Neil Stratford and William King of Baltinglass, the treasurer, ensured that control of the depots could be closely monitored by the conservatives. The region was divided into ten districts with a central arms depot in each under the control of local yeomen officers and magistrates. It was envisaged that depots would be located in Dunlavin, Blessington, Tullow, Baltinglass, Belan, Hacketstown, Coolkenna, Coolattin, Tinahely and Carnew. In the event of the military being called away 'well disposed' men previously sworn as supplementary yeomen were to rally at their local depot to receive the arms and defend them from rebels. It is likely that the scheme accounted for the relatively large number of supplementary yeomanry units in Wicklow and it may also have given a boost to the Orange Order.[103] Yet despite an initially positive response, Brigadier-General Sir Charles Asgill directed Hardy to empty the depots in February 1798 and convey the weapons for safekeeping to Waterford's Duncannon Fort. The major's professed 'attachment to the inhabitants' moved him to disregard the order at some professional peril and he began re-distributing the arms to their owners in March 1798. A serious command crisis was averted midway through this process when Pelham finally decided that the issue should be resolved in that manner, perhaps in recognition of Hardy's dilemma and the need to maintain his authority ahead of the full extension of martial law to the county.[104]

Hardy's erratic and often insubordinate behaviour testified to the great affinity between him and the conservative magistrates. Their influence was also apparent in the arguments advanced by him in favour of the retention of the arms, reasoning that encompassed an incongruous sectarian dimension. He claimed that Lieutenant-General Sir Ralph Abercromby's objections to the manning of small depots on the grounds that they were insecure were not valid in Wicklow owing to alleged intensity of the 'religious war between protestant & papist'. This was a surprising assertion in relation to a county renowned for its excellent communal relations in the early 1790s and reflects the rapid growth of ultra-loyalism. He further stated that the 'loyal armed protestant . . . would keep the country in check', a telling comment that implied distrust of the county's liberal Protestants and certainly of the Catholic majority. The major's reassurances also served to remind his superiors that the county's demography ensured that Wicklow population contained a far higher proportion of ostensibly trust-worthy Protestants that any other strategic Leinster sector.

In his efforts to persuade the unbigoted Fitzwilliam of the United Irish threat, Hardy was unequivocal in stating his belief that 'the mass' of Catholics 'even despairing of foreign aid . . . look for nothing else but insurrection, . . . are strengthening themselves by pikes and concealed arms.' He also echoed the paranoia and sectarianism of several clerical magistrates by asserting that 'their priests do not sufficiently discourage them.'[105] This was despite the fact that several had taken the oath of allegiance before Wainwright in November 1797 and had 'exhorted their flocks' to eschew sedition. Fr James Purcell of Clonegal, parish priest of Moyacomb and Barragh on the Carlow/Wicklow border, almost certainly took the oath in November around the time that he issued a loyal address deprecating the 'united devils'. He specifically condemned their practice of attributing 'to priests . . . the same ferocious principles' as themselves.[106]

MARTIAL LAW IN WICKLOW

In December 1797 a curfew was imposed in the Hollywood area of Lower Talbotstown to deter 'nocturnal enormities' and to hamper the movement of emissaries between Dublin and Wicklow. This would have met with the approbation of local landlord Earl Downshire who favoured rigorous approaches to sedition. In keeping with Hardy's discriminating approach to coercion, no other part of Wicklow was obliged to observe the stipulation that inhabitants had to display their names on their doors. Under the terms of the Insurrection Act all arms had to be registered and could be collected by the army, but Hardy's November arms drive had removed most of those in circulation. Curfews and searches were legalized in December and could be undertaken by magistrates without warrants. This enabled patrolling militia and yeomen to ascertain whether persons encountered during their nightly house searches were on lawful business.[107]

Hardy presumably intended that this measure would emulate the success of the 'salutary operations of the Insurrection Law' in Carlow and forestall the mounting unrest present in Kildare.[108] In early November 1797 Carlow and neighbouring parts of Wicklow and Wexford were reputedly 'scoured every night by the military in search of United Irishmen'. However, as pikes were not recovered in Hollywood until late February 1798, it can be assumed that previous searches had not been prosecuted with thoroughness and were not guided by local informers. It is also apparent that the drive to mass produce weapons rather than stealing or buying them in small quantities gathered pace in the advent of the rebellion. Lack of troops may also have hindered Hardy's efforts in Talbotstown but the importance of intelligence in counter-insurgency and that of the resolute magistrates who generally obtained it was demonstrated by investigations into Nixon's killing in Shillelagh.[109]

In the first week of December 1797 information was received from a Shillelagh resident, John Cooper (aka Morgan) of Umrygar, which implicated four men in the Nixon raid and named three others as United Irishmen. Cooper was allegedly a former English convict named Morgan who had worked in Avoca coppermines before becoming a gelder and was 'adept at every kind of villainy'.[110] His statements about 'many others' caused widespread unrest in the barony which was manifested in the refusal of tenants to pay their rent, after one week spent collecting rent Wainwright had received only 2,600 guineas of the 7,000 due.[111] Arrests followed notwithstanding doubts as to Cooper's reliability and some accurate details of United Irish activity were revealed.[112] Cooper, or someone he implicated, probably informed Wainwright of a meeting of Wicklow United Irish delegates in Dublin and as the details were few and vague it is evident that the original source had not been a participant. William Young, the most senior activist compromised by Cooper, was almost certainly privy to such information and may have mentioned the Dorset Street meeting of 30 November 1797 to the Shillelagh men he drilled. That this disclosure had come from outside Young's native Ballinacor and concerned military preparations indicates his major role in creating an armed force of United Irishmen in southern Wicklow. It may also reflect the need to discipline those whose arms-raiding had elicited unwanted government scrutiny and to give them a structured outlet for their aggressive spirit.[113]

The Shillelagh breakthrough and the allegations of several other Ballinacor informants obliged High Sheriff Peter La Touche to convene a meeting of magistrates on 9 January 1798. No record of the resolutions is extant but they probably called for extra troops and possibly the declaration of martial law in Shillelagh. Camden deferred judgement on their demands pending additional consultation with Hardy relating to the implications of Cooper's testimony. It seems that the uncertainty arising from Cooper's defection had obliged Shillelagh's United Irishmen to redouble their efforts to perfect their organization and probably encouraged the less committed members to fall out. The report of the Wicklow county committee in January 1798 claimed that eight Shillelagh United Irishmen were in jail, but this may only have represented the number of fully-fledged members they were prepared to support rather than the total number of suspects held for seditious practices from the barony. Other Shillelagh insurgents were probably held in Carlow gaols.[114]

The tougher security policies adopted in the west of the county did not cow elements of the Ballinacor United Irishmen. In one highly provocative raid in December 1797 Laurence McGuirke of Balinalea and Patrick Staunton of Ballinahinch raided the Tighe family's home at Rossana (Ashford). William Tighe was a Fitzwilliamite MP for the county and his home, while frequently menaced by the rebels during the rebellion, was never badly damaged. The group to which Staunton and McGuirke belonged made off with a quantity of lead for use in the manufacture of musket balls and may not have directly con-fronted the Rossana occupants. It was, nevertheless, an incident that underscored the vulnerability of the Wicklow gentry. Both men were prosecuted by a Wicklow courtmartial and sent to New Geneva from which Staunton was liberated upon appeal after the rebellion.[115]

The emergence of informers within the ranks of the Wicklow United Irishmen from January 1798 onwards gave their loyalist opponents unprecedented insight into the extent and workings of the conspiracy. Particularly useful knowledge was gained of the Ballinacor and Arklow sectors where arms-raiding had been uncommon and rebel strength underestimated as a consequence. The lengthy depositions of Hugh Woolaghan, John Kavanagh and John Tyson startled the investigating magistrates, Tom King and Abraham Mills as the revelations regard-ing yeomanry infiltration, initiation procedures and United Irish numerical strength confirmed their worst fears. Writing to Cooke in January 1798, Hardy mentioned that 'Latouche has informed you of much of the Camacks [sic] corps being United [Irishmen]' implying that the subject of the infiltrated Castlemacadam yeomanry had been discussed on 9 January.[116] Tyson of Cronebane had named over thirty-eight men he claimed were United Irishmen, some of whom probably divulged more information when approached by the authorities. Indeed, the allegations in January 1798 of John Kavanagh of Knockaurea against Thomas Murray of Sheepwalk laid the basis of the later's damaging revelations on the eve of rebellion. Physical evidence of rebel organization in the form of captured weapons, documentation and crowded prisons also gave the cumulative impres-sion that the county was in a state of crisis. The unexpected extent of the conspiracy served to instill a greater sense of threat which widened the breach between conservative and liberal factions within the county establishment.[117]

The most dramatic proof of seditious encroachment was the dis-covery on the Arklow/Wicklow road near Dunganstown of the report of the Wicklow county committee of United Irishmen of 22 January

1798. It included a comprehensive breakdown of the county's 12,794 members as well as their finances and weaponry. A more detailed copy of the same report was found on the person of John Lynch when he was arrested at Oliver Bond's in March 1798 and it was admitted as evidence at the trial of William Michael Byrne two months later. That Lynch's copy was deemed 'very important' by the Attorney General three months after the first one had been recovered points to the sensation aroused by the Wicklow find which was not fully authenticated until May 1798.[118] It did, however, fit the trend of mounting tensions across Ireland which saw county after county being proclaimed and brazen paramilitary displays proceed without opposition. In late October 1797 five yeomen of Dublin's Liberty Rangers were courtmartialled for taking part in a disloyal demonstration outside Napper Tandy's house where bands played the jacobin airs 'Ca-Ira' and 'Erin go bragh'. Three months later it was reported that the United Irishmen 'grow every day more insolent' and had assembled in large bodies on successive Sundays in the city. The predictable response of Hardy and his loyalist supporters was to step up their anti-insurgent programme.[119]

THE ORANGE ORDER

Camden's endorsement of extra-parliamentary loyalist organizations such as the yeomanry and, in particular, the Orange Order, ensured that sectarian politics, abhorrent to the bulk of Wicklow's tolerant gentry in times of peace and social stability, had a bearing on the form of the county's anti-republican effort in early 1798. It was noted in Down in September 1796 that in order to 'stem the tide of United Irishmen, government seem[s] to encourage the Orange party'.[120] Protestantism and the willingness to employ severe coercion became the key determinants of loyalty in Wicklow despite their limited validity in view of the county's denominational diversity and the nature of United Irish philosophy. Proclaiming and the religious composition of the county's yeomanries consequently emerged as the main bones of contention between the competing factions of the county gentry. Given that about one fifth of Wicklow's population were Protestant and that the magistracy in the southern baronies was dominated by extremists, it is not surprising that the Orange Order extended its influence into the county in the advent of the rebellion. Orange lodges were established in late 1797 or early 1798 at Tinahely, Carnew and Coolkenna, presumably under the auspices of Hunter Gowan whose own lodge at Mount Nebo was one of the first outside Ulster. Clonegal in Carlow and Camolin in Wexford may also have had lodges and there was perhaps another in Newtownmountkennedy.[121]

The impetus to found lodges may have come from Major Hardy as their establishment coincided with his arrival in the county and he showed a marked willingness to employ loyalist auxiliaries. Just one week after his posting to Wicklow Arthur O'Connor's *Press* reported the following:

> A very wicked attempt has been made in several counties, and so near us as the county Wicklow, to form associations under the appellation of Orange-men, by which the parties bind themselves to each other by a most atrocious oath . . . This is said to have had the countenance of men high in rank and office.

The order was inherently conservative and pro-Government and exactly the type of agency Hardy required in Wicklow to support coercion and counteract the influence of the liberals.[122] It is possible that Captain Heard's company of North Cork Militia stationed in Shillelagh in late December 1797 contained a lodge as the regiment to which it belonged was one of the most notoriously orange formations in Ireland. Hardy considered them 'well adapted to the service and country, young & active' and given the general character of the regiment small scale proselytization cannot be discounted. Their commander, Earl Kingsborough, was Ireland's most prominent orangemen and had belonged to several proto-orange societies in Cork such as the Hanover Association which opposed catholic emancipation.[123]

The military were far from agreed as to the propriety of encouraging or even tolerating orange societies in the ranks. Major George Mathews of the Downshire Militia opposed them on the grounds that 'there is nothing surer than that orangemen . . . will be the means of making United Men', the converse of the argument often advanced in their favour. Elements within the North Corks, by contrast, actively promoted orangeism and fostered lodges in Wexford from April 1798 and may have done so earlier in Wicklow. They were one of relatively few units to defy the orders of Generals Abercromby and Asgill prohibiting the display of sectarian emblems on their uniforms. Their arrival in Wexford on 21 April 1798, when the divide between insurrectionists and loyalists was most pronounced, encouraged some influential local acolytes to express their politics through association with the Order, particularly in the Ferns/Enniscorthy area.[124]

Wexford's James Boyd, Hawtrey White and Archibald Hamilton Jacob and the three yeomanry corps they commanded were foremost among those who embraced orangeism. It is clear that a similar if less documented process was also experienced in south Wicklow. White's Ballaghkeen yeomanry were amongst the foremost chapel burners and murderers in north Wexford in the aftermath of the rebellion and were described by Bishop Caulfield as an 'orange incendiary party'.[125] The Order was also relatively strong in Meath, Queen's County, Westmeath and especially so in Carlow where the staunchly loyalist Rochforts played a notable role in the establishment of ten lodges. By November 1797 lodges were allegedly established in the 'principal inns' of Mullingar, 'sanctioned and attended by some of the leading gentry of the country'. It is no coincidence that all these counties had sizeable United Irish organizations and were strategically important on account of their proximity to the capital. Their role in inciting rebellion, however, is much less certain and they had no major effect on the timing of the Wicklow outbreak.[126] As the Orange Order drew heavily on the forms, nomenclature and personnel of the freemasons it is possible that this also occurred in Wicklow even though the craft was apparently not very strong in the county. The Bray lodge 324, to which John Quinn of that town's innkeeping family belonged in January 1801, was comparatively prominent and a stone of Wicklow Town's Church of Ireland parish church bore an old masonic symbol until it was accidentally erased by workmen in 1904.[127]

In addition to formally organized lodges there were orange enthusiasts in Wicklow in Coolattin, Shillelagh, Donard, Dunlavin, Bray and Hacketstown in 1797. Moreover, the Stratford family of Baltinglass had two members in John Verner's lodge in Dublin, a constituent of the prestigious Grand Lodge which was created in the capital in April 1798.[128] The Verners were instrumental in promoting the Order from the 1790s until the mid-1800s and with men of the stature of Benjamin O'Neil Stratford joining in Wicklow its spread may have been very extensive, although deliberate efforts were made after the rebellion to obscure its influence. O'Neil Stratford was an associate of leading city orangeman Dr Patrick Duigenan as far back as 1783 and could well have been brought into the society through his influence in the late 1790s or made amenable to its aims. Duigenan, in his legal capacity, had represented O'Neil Stratford during a bitter parliamentary enquiry into election fraud in Baltinglass. He joined Lodge 176 in early 1798 which formed the nucleus of Dublin's Grand Lodge. Another Wicklow family with strong orange links were the Derenzys who, although agents for Aldborough in Wicklow and Kildare, also owned property in Carlow where they presided over a Clonegal lodge. The prevalence of orangemen in the yeomanry gave the Wicklow corps a well-deserved reputation for extremism and militated against the enrolment of Catholic members who were still technically entitled to join or be nominated.[129]

Individual or informal groupings of orangemen were probably what Hardy had in mind when he referred to active supporters as 'well disposed men' and 'loyal armed protestants'. The latter phrase was often applied to supplementary yeomen such as those who helped orangeman Revd James McGhee defend Hacketstown from rebel attack on 25 June 1798 and it would appear that entire lodges were sworn as supplementaries, as was frequently the case in Ulster.[130] McGhee's orangeism may have resulted from familial and social links with the Order in the north of Ireland where he resided for a period in mid-1800 when his wife was seriously ill. There was also a quasi-orange organization in Tinahely boasting 151 members who styled themselves the 'True Blues' from which a large supplementary yeomanry corps was raised under the command of local zealot Henry Moreton. This formation was similar in nature to Hunter Gowan's 'Black Mob' which allegedly comprised 'thirty or forty low Orangemen' and had a reputation for ferocity. Moreton's 'True Blues' were also apparently a separate body from the gazetted Tinahely Infantry commanded by his brother James.[131] In 1801 Gowan was accused of having put 'men, women and children to death in cold blood . . . his principal object was enriching himself by the property of the publick [sic] and in taking the rings from off the women's fingers. [It was] often said he w[oul]d cut them off if they defied him and [that he] made some of the women drink the Blood of their husbands which they were after Butchering'. The Tinahely loyalists also gained a reputation for ferocity which resulted in the destruction of the village in June 1798.[132]

In Wicklow and north Wexford, however, the main showing of the Orange Order did not occur until 1799 and 1800 when it spearheaded a 'white terror' which countered both the military and civil policy of the Cornwallis administration. While orangeism had only gained a foothold in Wicklow and Wexford by mid-1798 and probably had little impact on bringing about rebellion in southern Ireland its members may well have masterminded the 'test oath' controversy which polarized the yeomanry in February 1798 leaving an almost exclusively Protestant force. The United Irishmen, nevertheless, blamed the Order for loyalist atrocities committed just before and immediately after the outbreak of rebellion, excesses similar in nature to those which their recruiting propaganda had predicted. They tended, in consequence, to treat loyalist prisoners suspected of orange affiliations very harshly in May/July 1798.[133] Few details have survived of loyalist anti-insurgent excesses in Wicklow in early 1798 but Hardy's decision to confine and report Lieutenant Hogg of his own regiment for flogging prisoners at Dunlavin in January 1798 suggests that ill-treatment of suspects was sufficiently widespread to require decisive action. The extremely high rate of defections to the United Irishmen from the Antrim Militia in late 1798 was not in keeping with the regiment's general reliability. Antrim men were notably willing to prosecute United Irishmen who had attempted to suborn them and their role in the massacre of rebel prisoners at Carnew in May 1798 and staunch performances in the battles of Newtownbarry, Arklow and Hacketstown puts their overall political allegiance beyond doubt.[134]

One of those known to have fallen foul of the loyalists was Carnew man Patrick Doyle who was arrested by soldiers for using 'improper words' when drunk in early January and confined in the guardhouse. He was visited by two of the town's yeomen, William McCormick and perhaps one of the Blaneys or Bookeys who, having failed to recruit him as an informer, twice 'suspended [him] from a penny cord' until the rope broke under his weight. This was a variant of the interrogation procedure known as 'half hanging' which was designed to cause partial strangulation. The practice may well have been introduced to Shillelagh by Heard's North Cork militiamen who were veterans of counter-insurgency having suppressed the Roscommon Defenders in May 1795. The North Corks are credited with instigating pitchcapping when based in north Wexford in May 1798 which involved setting fire to a piece of coarse linen or paper smeared with pitch which had been stuck to the top of the victim's head. If the crackdown was intended to terrorize local United Irishmen it was only a qualified success as on 12 April 1798 they burned down the Carnew premises of chandler Ralph Blaney whose brother was Second Lieutenant of the town's yeoman cavalry.[135]

Doyle's ordeal allegedly drove him insane and it was one of the earliest recorded incidences of torture to occur in east Leinster in 1798. A specific reason for maltreating Doyle may have been the urgent need to corroborate Cooper's allegations in advance of the March assizes. It was not an isolated incident, however, as half hanging was also inflicted on Michael Egan of Dunlavin in February whose father suffered several broken bones when attacked by a militia officer and loyalists including one Fowler, a reputed orangeman. Egan was half hanged three times and detained with his father in the village's Market House for six days before being transferred to Wicklow gaol where he was held 'in a dismal cell, loaded with very heavy irons'. Like Doyle he was accused of having spoken seditious words but freed on bail of £500. He was acquitted, nevertheless, at Baltinglass sessions on 19 February and Fowler subjected to a bail until a case against him was heard at Wicklow assizes in March.[136]

Edward Hay, the first and one of the best nationalist historians of the rebellion, wrote in 1801 of a 'private memoranda' in his possession concerning the fate of fourteen men who had been flogged and pitchcapped in the town of Carnew before the insurrection. This, in all probability, had taken place between January and April 1798 and was one of a series of atrocious incidents which culminated in the summary execution of fifty or so rebel prisoners in Carnew gaol when the rebellion began.[137] Soldiers were also responsible for a 'terrible' atrocity which occurred at Aughrim in January 1798 and greatly frightened the locals. Whether the incident involved drunken soldiers attacking locals or an unsanctioned bout of torture is now unknown although, judging from the lack of extant material relating to it, it was probably not deemed as serious as the murderous conduct of the Ancient Britons when at Newtownmountkennedy in April.[138]

While Hardy discouraged extreme coercion he bore some responsibility for the excesses committed by the loyalist party attached to him by not promoting moderate alternatives. It does not seem, for instance, that Hardy placed any faith in the practice of offering conditional pardons to repentant United Irishmen willing to swear the oath of allegiance. He was not, furthermore, impressed by the loyal addresses volunteered by Catholic congregations, such as that organized by Fr Purcell at his Clonegal chapel on 31 December 1797. Purcell's collection of 1,561 signatures was some achievement given that he had to contend with United Irish sponsored rumours which accused the orangemen of stealing a chalice from a Carlow chapel. Similar stories were then prevalent in Stradbally, Athy and Baltinglass and could only have frustrated attempts by priests to maintain public order in their parishes.[139]

There were no equivalents in Wicklow to mass oath-taking meetings which occurred in Waterford's proclaimed Glenahiry on 22 December 1797 or at Monaseed in north Wexford on 10 January 1798. At the Waterford meeting Lord Donoughmore personally administered an oath which he had composed himself to a 'great number' at Four

Mile Water. The oath was translated into Gaelic for those who did not speak English and 'its import and tendency commented upon very forcibly'. As Donoughmore was the nephew of the murdered Shillelagh loyalist Nixon it can be assumed that the logic and mechanics of the policy were discussed in Wicklow. Nixon informed Wainwright in early December that Donoughmore was using 'every effort to suppress' the United Irishmen on his Waterford estates having received word that they would destroy his residence if he interfered with their nocturnal meetings.[140]

Between Monaseed and the coast, a hotbed of United Irish activity, over 400 'respectable tenantry' took the oath between 8 and 10 January 1798 before Thomas Knox Grogan, in addition to many more of 'inferior note'. Grogan was captain of the Castletown Cavalry from which most Catholic members resigned when asked to swear the test oath. The driving force behind the loyal address petitions and oaths of allegiance in northern Wexford from November 1797 was Lord Mountnorris who in the months preceding the rebellion organized the collection of signatures from nineteen parish priests.[141] Progress of this kind confused the Castle who remained unsure of Wexford's level of United Irish organization in January 1798 and sent Judge Robert Johnson on a tour of Wexford, Waterford and Cork 'to examine into all the informations and commitments made by magistrates . . . of defenders [sic], and make report to Government.' Such practices were apparently deemed unworkable in Wicklow because the Hardy clique believed that the county's notoriously large rebel force would not respond to moderation and they were deeply distrusting of Catholic clergymen.[142]

The only sector where oaths were deemed useful by Wicklow loyalists was in the yeomanry corps where the selective application of the 'test oath' to units with Catholic members revealed it to be a sectarian ploy. The oath issue tended to embarrass liberal corps commanders who had not restricted membership along religious lines and were generally opposed its application. If, as it seems, the ascendant hardliners clamoured for martial law style coercion whether or not the county was officially proclaimed, it was necessary to marginalize liberal opponents before getting to grips with the republican menace.

On 19 January 1798 Hardy wrote an important letter to Undersecretary Cooke in which he delineated his strategy in Wicklow and on its borders. For the first time his assertions concerning United Irish strength and their command by 'a wealthy description of catholics' were not pure supposition but grounded in reliable intelligence. This may have been why Hardy chose this moment to enlist Cooke's assistance to reform the magistracy whom he admitted were generally inexperienced 'at united work'. He advocated extending the powers of the active and 'highly laudable' Hunter Gowan into Wicklow and dismissing the ineffective Thomas Bolger of St Austins. Gowan had operated in Wicklow before when a baronial constable and in May 1793 arrested three men in Rathdrum suspected of murdering Samuel Waddy of Janesville, Wexford.[143] Hardy's endorsement of Gowan signals the type of coercion he wished to introduce in Wicklow but his orange credentials must have impressed likeminded magistrates and yeomanry officers who founded lodges in southern Wicklow in late 1797 and 1798. When the rebels engulfed Gowan's home district he took up residence in Wicklow and operated in the Aughrim area with his supplementary yeomen until the Autumn of 1798. His status made him uniquely qualified to ally the north Wexford ultra-loyalists with their Wicklow neighbours and, as such, it is not surprising that Hardy was anxious to facilitate him with a commission.[144]

The advancement of favoured magistrates was used to compensate for those who had been discredited by inaction or liberalism, particularly in border areas where their exertions could be nullified through the limits of jurisdiction. Lord Monck, a key loyalist figure in northern Wicklow who in November 1797 was created Baron Monck of Ballytrammin, claimed that 'conciliatory measures' had endangered his life when recommending that William Colthurst be granted a commission of the peace for County Dublin in addition to the one he held for Wicklow.[145] Monck, who had seen service with the 14th Light Dragoons at Carrick-on-Suir when suppressing the Rightboy movement in 1782, was awarded a medal by those who served under him in the Powerscourt yeomanry in 1797. His support for Colthurst was successful and boosted the effectiveness of an 'uncommonly active' magistrate.[146] Similarly, Thomas Hugo, who had been High Sheriff in 1796 and an important member of the nascent Government party in Wicklow, was credited by Hardy as having 'greatly aided the King's service' and was nominated by him for a commission of the peace even after the rebellion had begun. As Hugo had already been active against the United Irishmen at that time his appointment was a formality, perhaps intended to shield him from prosecution for his actions.[147]

The second strand of Hardy's letter concerned action against three suspected yeomanry corps, specifically Grogan's Castletown Cavalry of which Gowan had obtained 'positive proof' of disloyalty. Also discussed were the two Castlemacadam corps which Tyson, Woolaghan and Kavanagh had implicated. The Grogans had identified themselves with the liberal interests in north Wexford and, along with United Irishmen Edward Hay and Bagenal Harvey, had presented a petition of 22,521 names to Fitzwilliam upon his recall from the county free-holders. Cornelius Grogan of Johnstown Castle became a rebel leader and was executed in the aftermath of Vinegar Hill. The yeomanry issue was closely related to divisions in the magistracy who dominated its officer cadre in that suspicions were focused, with some justification, on the reliability of Catholic members. As Catholics generally only gained admission to corps commanded by liberals the matter was sharpened by both ideological and sectarian factors and Hardy's raising of it amounted to the first salvo of the test oath confrontation.[148]

Fitzwilliam's donation of £500 to the various Shillelagh yeomanry corps was linked to his insistence that Catholics be enrolled but this had elicited a defensive response from the captain of the Coolkenna Infantry who claimed that fifteen of its forty or so members when first embodied in December 1796 were non-Protestants. This corps would have been one of the exceptions in southern Wicklow where Protestant extremism militated against integrated units. Major Hardy's brother Thomas commanded just five Catholics in his fifty-seven strong Hacketstown Infantry and it is likely that the corps raised in Shillelagh, Carnew and Tinahely had none whatsoever.[149] Indeed, the low level of Catholic recruitment was so striking that it was speculated in 1803 that Dublin based radicals, evidently members of the Catholic Committee who later became United Irishmen, had used their influence to dissuade Catholic Wicklowmen from joining the yeomanry. The shortfall of personnel from the majority segment of the population, according to Plowden, obliged the Wicklow commanders to enrol 'the lowest cast of protestants' who later 'made a very bad use of their arms and of their powers'.[150] A more likely explanation was the disproportionate number of conservative gentry at the head of yeomanries, men who like Baltinglass' Revd Robinson, absolutely opposed the admission of 'poisoned papists'. Such officers were quick to criticize corps commanded by liberals once evidence of United Irish infiltration came to light.[151]

Hardy's attention was also focused on the March assizes which promised to be the first real test of Wicklow's counter-insurgent effort. In a bid to ensure results from Cooper's defection Hardy proposed transferring William Young to a Dublin prison where, if he did not become an informer, doubts about his intentions might 'terrify and keep quiet a dangerous knot who are in his power'. Pressure was also brought in to bear in February on another high ranking United Irish suspect, Garret Byrne of Ballymanus, who had troops stationed 'under his nose' at Aughrim. Byrne and Thomas Murray junior of Sheepwalk were clearly two of the wealthy Catholics to whom Hardy had alluded.[152] Hardy informed Cooke two weeks later that in consequence of the presence of the troops 'Mr B[yrne] of Ballymanus has fled' his home leaving his affairs in the hands of an attorney. The major conjectured that Byrne had gone to England but it was only to Dublin where he resided with the widow Caulfield in Booterstown. That doubts were held as to Byrne's role in the organization is indicated by Hardy's remark to Cooke 'you see I was not mistaken in my information about him.'[153]

In the first days of February Hardy's forces dealt effectively with a group of 'armed mountain insurgents' who had raided homes on the Wicklow/Carlow border around Hacketstown. On 1 February 1798 three rich farmers were robbed of seventy-four guineas but in a follow-up search by Captain Thomas Hardy's Hacketstown Infantry, the Antrim Militia and William Hume's Upper Talbotstown Cavalry, two men were arrested and a quantity of silver recovered. In return for offering one prisoner immunity from prosecution, Major Hardy managed to apprehend six of the eight-man gang by 5 February. As the thieves were security conscious and had lived in pairs two miles from each other in the Wicklow mountains, the benefit of tempering coercion with conciliation was not lost on Hardy. He was to use this pragmatic approach more frequently as the crisis deepened.[154]

Peter La Touche convened a special session of the peace in the county town on 2 February which was attended by most of Wicklow's increasingly coherent right-wing faction. Monck, Colthurst, James McClatchy and Thomas Archer of Mount John (Newtownmount-kennedy) attended from Rathdown and Newcastle who, together with Lord Powerscourt, comprised the most active supporters of Government in the north of the county. Rathdrum's Tom King was present in company with lesser central Wicklow magistrates Abraham Coates, Thomas Acton and William Eccles of Cronroe. The southern baronies were strongly represented by Alexander Carroll, Revd Bayly, Revd Symes, Wainwright and Thomas Jones Atkins. Revd Cope, Henry Moreton and James Chritchley were absent but shared their uncompromising politics.[155] The presence of Viscount Wicklow, who headed the general liberally inclined Howard family and captained the Arklow Northshire Cavalry, and that of Sir Robert Hodson was untypical and may have arisen from the siting of the meeting in their locality more than any close affinity with the political leanings of the other participants.[156] The only significant loyalist absentees were west Wicklow's O'Neil Stratford and George Heighington of Donard while Thomas Hugo, not then holding a commission, was precluded from attending in an active capacity. It was from these men that the 'secret committee for receiving information' was formed which played a vital role in identifying Wicklow's United Irish leaders and implementing the Government's coercion policy. The committee was apparently granted £4,000 by the Government to pay informers, agents and other expenses.[157]

Whereas a previous session on 9 January 1798 had merely called attention to the unsatisfactory state of the Castlemacadam Cavalry and Infantry, the meeting of 6 February petitioned the Government to disarm and dismiss the units. This did not occur until the following month but any hope of reformation was dashed by the harshness of the magistracy's claim that the corps were 'almost entirely composed of seditious and disaffected persons' and, in a pointed phrase directed at the Camac family, 'unattended by their officers'.[158] Controversy had dogged the Castlemacadam corps from the outset on account of the type of men recruited and the politics of their officers. On 23 November 1796 Revd Symes had relinquished the chair of a meeting of the newly formed Castlemacadam Cavalry at Newbridge (Avoca) when Major Lane and other interested parties objected to the fact that he had 'taken [it] upon himself' to nominate to Government officers to command the corps. With the conservative representatives outvoted, Lane had proposed liberals John Camac, Burgess Camac and Benjamin Coates which, while agreed to by the majority of those present, led to the resignation of thirty-five men on 14 December 1797. Those who withdrew apparently joined corps commanded by hard liners and they included members of the loyalist Leeson, Tuke, Gill and Chritchley families.[159]

Having delivered a blow to Wicklow's liberal Protestants the Wicklow meeting seconded their assault by recommending that other yeomanry corps swear the new 'test oath' which compelled the taker to disavow United Irish membership and anti-government sentiments. The reputed text was:

> I ____ do, in the presence of my neighbours, solemnly swear by the contents of this book, containing the Holy Gospels of Christ, that I have not joined, nor in any manner entered into any society or association of persons styling themselves 'United Irishmen', or any

other seditious society or association whatsoever, or taken any oath to keep the secrets of any such society, or taken any oath to the prejudice of his Majesty King George the Third, or contrary to the existing laws or constitution of this kingdom of Ireland; and all this I do freely and voluntarily swear, without any mental evasion or secret reservation whatsoever. So help me God'.[160]

The compilation with a view to publication of a list of those who had taken the oath and thereby proven 'their innocence' negated its supposed voluntary nature resulting in the resignation of many Catholic yeomen who viewed it as an affront.[161]

The oath was put to several corps in Wicklow and north Wexford as well as units in Dublin and Carlow before a response was received from the government and, as no decision had been communicated to the magistrates by 20 February when the session reconvened, it was resolved to postpone publishing the list.[162] The effects of its dissemination had a marked impact on the membership of the yeomanry in the three months prior to the outbreak of rebellion. The Ballyellis Infantry captained by Jervis White were disbanded and their arms placed under guard in Carnew while Knox Grogan's Castletown corps and John Beaumann's Coolgreany corps were both considerably reduced in numbers by the mass resignation of Catholics.[163] An obvious shortcoming of this de facto sectarian policy was that Protestant United Irishmen of the stature of Anthony Perry, Second Lieutenant of the Coolgreany Cavalry from November 1796, were not scrutinized to the point that they felt obliged to refuse the test on principle. Few problems were encountered with most of Wicklow's overwhelmingly Protestant corps such as Captain Robert Gore's Newtownmountkennedy Cavalry which had only one or two Catholics of its approximately forty men. Rossmore was the corps patron and, like Fitzwilliam, was personally liberal but incapable of imposing his moderation on the force. William Michael Byrne was probably only admitted due to his social status. The zealous Corporal George Kennedy was the only Catholic to serve in the corps during the rebellion and the notorious killer Hugh Woolaghan transferred to it from the disgraced Castlemacadam Cavalry. Forty-four of Captain Mills' Cronebane Infantry refused the test and were expelled, as were fourteen of the Coolgreany corps.[164]

As early as October 1797 William Michael Byrne was forced to resign from the corps for refusing to swear an earlier loyalty oath. It was also rejected by his protestant friend and fellow yeoman, Dr Samuel Paisley, on the grounds that 'the lower part of the people held orange men in such detestation' that taking the oath would have jeopardized his practice. This implies that those who took the oath and remained in the corps were regarded by the community as either being members of the Orange Order or sympathetic towards their politics.[165] Another important United Irishman, William Byrne of Ballymanus, was expelled from the Wicklow Town Cavalry along with four others in February 1798 for refusing the test and it seems that few Catholics could have avoided the issue given Captain John Edwards' assertion that 'almost every corps in the county . . . [had] voluntarily taken a test' by March.[166] William Byrne had joined the county town corps somewhat belatedly in September 1797 and requested a few days to consider his position. His declining the oath when reapplied to resulted in his immediate ejection, notwithstanding his apparent friendship with loyalist member Thomas Hugo junior.[167] He did, however, apply to join Hume's Upper Talbotstown Cavalry just prior to the insurrection when he had good reason to assume that he was suspected of disaffection. Hume turned down the offer claiming that there were no vacancies but Byrne's application to him indicates that the Humewood corps, as they were known, had not taken the oath. This principled stand may have been one of the reasons why Hume was so bitterly criticised in May 1798 for 'screening the disaffected' around Baltinglass. It may also be pertinent that the corps had only one catholic member which would explain why Hume was not subjected to intolerable pressure.[168]

The most protracted test controversy centred on the Bray Infantry whose commander, John Edwards of Oldcourt, had been one of the province's leading Volunteers in the 1780s and he remained a committed liberal in the more troubled decade which ensued. Lord Charlemont, Ireland's leading Whig, was apparently his 'dear and valuble friend' and he was related to the Attorney General, Arthur Wolfe, later Viscount Kilwarden. Edwards was the most credible and high profile liberal in the north east of the county and as such was probably the figurehead of the pro-reform gentry. This had probably frustrated his efforts to gain command of a cavalry unit in late 1796 when the apparently unexpected materialization of a rival bid by the young Earl Meath had quashed his claim. In marked contrast to the Volunteer period all Rathdown cavalry units were dominated by conservative gentry, a circumstance that indicates the existence of an understanding between local government supporters and the Castle. Rebuffed but undeterred, Edwards had raised a much less prestigious dismounted corps which numbered around twenty Catholic yeomen out of its sixty men.[169] This was considered a high proportion and left the unit vulnerable to criticism on the test oath, particularly given the determination of the Hardy faction to exploit the issue in their dealings with political opponents. The committee of twenty-eight magistrates expressed their belief at the March 1798 assizes that thirty-three Bray infantrymen were 'strongly suspected of being United Irishmen' owing to their refusal to take the test oath.[170]

Luke Cullen, citing a pamphlet written by Edwards in 1814, claimed that there were actually at least forty United Irishmen in the corps but that only the Catholics suspects were expelled leaving vacancies that were filled by 'the refuse of Protestants'. The remark was meant to convey the lowly class origins of the new recruits rather than sectarian hostility and Cullen elsewhere castigated the corps for 'fostering in its bosom a den of robbers' led by one Wakely who was executed for robbing Revd Dr Whitelaw of Delgany in early 1798.[171] It is apparent that Edwards had initially trusted in his reputation and patronage in his efforts to resist pressure to dismiss those who would not take the oath. He correctly argued that the Government did not require such a loyal declaration and that there was no legal provision to insist on compliance. This, however, was a somewhat naive position to adopt in the context a county in which extreme measures were gaining currency and his stance was gravely weakened when a mere seventeen yeomen consented to the test. Most surprising was the refusal of Second Lieutenant Isaac Litton to follow his lead, a betrayal which moved Edwards to disclaim him on the grounds that he had only been appointed by the men and was someone who could not 'keep himself sober even when on guard duty or parade'. When forced to expel several men in the wake of the assize censure he remained convinced of their reliability and felt vindicated when the ejected members voluntarily swore the oath after their dismissal. It is also likely that the outright refusal of the predominately, if not exclusively, Protestant Bray Cavalry had bolstered the resolve of the infantry.[172]

Events elsewhere in Wicklow did nothing to alleviate the difficulties endured by Edwards and other liberal officers. Hardy had received authorization on or before 15 March to disarm the Castlemacadam Cavalry and Infantry despite the patriotic gesture which had been made by the mounted yeomen that month in donating two months pay towards the defence of the kingdom. By then several members of the corps were facing prosecution for sedition at the spring assizes and Hardy's suspicions of the institution was such that he raided a yeoman's house near Peter La Touche's Luggela Lodge between 11 and 19 March in expectation of finding the fugitive Lord Edward Fitzgerald. The decision to act against the mines units was probably inspired in part by the arrest of former yeoman William Michael Byrne at Oliver Bond's house on 12 March, an event which lent credence to the reports of United Irish strength emanating from the county. An attempt to deflect loyalist attention was also made by the Aughrim yeomanry, a supplementary corps, who paid £41 into the defense fund in comparison to the £180 donated by the various Rathdown corps. As the Aughrim unit did not feature in the rebellion it may have been either reduced or amalgamated into the Rathdrum corps.[173]

Yet another problem with disaffected yeomen came to light during this period in the west of the county where John Curran, Charles Behan, Oliver Corey, Patrick Hoare, John Howlett and James Muldoon were accused of planning to assassinate Captain Paul Stratford of the Stratford-on-Slaney Infantry. Howlett, for one, was a Stratford yeoman and had aided his confederates digging graves to intimidate Stratford and his steward. This was an old Whiteboy tactic but the revelation of that the Stratford corps was heavily infiltrated alarmed loyalists. Their concerns were compounded by the discovery that the same men had attempted to suborn members of the Wicklow Militia and had felled trees for pike handles. According to Revd Robinson a similar plot against the life of Captain Morley Saunders, which also involved six men, was discovered in the Saundersgrove Infantry in May 1798.[174]

After the March 1798 reductions and purgings the only Wicklow corps rated as 'bad' by Major Hardy were Earl Aldborough's Cavalry, the Bray Infantry and the Stratford Infantry. The Saundersgrove Infantry, destined for tragedy at Dunlavin on 24 May, were deemed 'middling', as, more surprisingly, were the undoubtedly loyalist Baltinglass Cavalry, Lower Talbotstown Cavalry and Wicklow Town Infantry. Political criteria were evidently not the only factors addressed by Hardy, however, as the performances of the various Arklow units and those of the extremist Donard and Newtownmountkennedy garrisons did not merit his most fullsome praise.[175]

Matters had taken a turn for the worse in the county as a whole in the late winter and early spring. Newcastle gentlemen in mid-February were allegedly dining with their pistols and carbines within easy reach on their tables. One of them, John Craven, had been obliged to drive a United Irish party away from his home with a signal pistol lest they injure the informer under his protection. Republican attempts to kill prosecution witnesses and informers had intensified in early 1798 and *Faulkner's Dublin Journal* found it necessary on 18 February to refute rumours of the assassination of Smith, aka Bird, a former journalist of theirs who had spied in Wicklow.[176] When a quantity of pikes and guns were found concealed in the Talbotstown village of Hollywood on 25 February Hardy became convinced that it was 'unsafe to leave that county longer without military'. He moved a small detachment of militia comprising twelve men and a sergeant and some Donard yeomanry into a house belonging to Lord Waterford near the village and made preparations to recall his overstretched troops from Wexford, Carlow and Kildare. Lieutenant Gardiner's Antrim Militia company left Newtownbarry (Bunclody) on 8 February and relocated to Hacketstown.[177]

On the night of 12 March 1798, just one week before the assizes were due to begin in Wicklow, a daring attack was made on the Sherwood farm at Tomacork within a mile of Carnew. Its owner, John Sherwood, was Second Lieutenant of the Arklow Southshire Cavalry, well connected with government and very probably one of the district's leading orangemen. He was certainly intimate with the city orange figure John Giffard and around the time of the Rebellion had demonstrated his contempt for catholic sensibilities by removing the last traces of the ruined Arklow Abbey in order to build a store house. Sherwood's orange credentials were also suggested by his links with Musgrave to whom he gave a bizarre sectarian document attributed to a Catholic priest which he had found in Gorey on 19 June 1798.[178] The March raid claimed Sherwood's farmhouse, one of the most extensive in the county, and all the outlying buildings. Seven horses and up to twenty head of black cattle perished in the blaze which prompted an alert in Carnew where the flames were clearly visible. The attack on such a prominent loyalist figure so close to Carnew was probably a calculated act of defiance by the United Irishmen who had displayed uncommon vindictiveness in breaking a plough and causing the deaths of livestock. They may have been seeking to avenge a specific act by Sherwood or his corps and the incident was cited by Camden when justifying his decision to extend the Insurrection Act to all Wicklow.[179]

News of the incident was closely followed by word of the deaths of two men in the Blessington area and a near fatal assault on a yeoman going from that town to attend the assizes. Outrages continued on 19 March with an arms raid on Revd William Porter at Hollywood during which shots were fired before three guns were handed over. Loyalist concerns could not have been allayed by the knowledge that two prominent Wicklowmen, William Michael Byrne and John Lynch, had been arrested at a meeting of the Leinster Provincial Directory on

12 March. Given this unprecedented intensity of rebel attacks it is not surprising that the Wicklow assizes commenced on 19 March 1798 with a unanimous declaration from the twenty-eight magistrates in attendance that every part of the county 'was in an actual state of disturbance or likely to be so.'[180] Monck chaired this pivotal meeting which had evidently been timed to precede the tenure of the incoming liberal High Sheriff, Walter Bagnal Carroll, who may not have been trusted to handle matters to the liking of the conservatives. Carroll's exceptionally minor role in the 1798 rebellion had much to do with the fact that he was an alienated liberal closely related to other dis-liked moderates such as Colonel Keating of Narraghmore, the Bagnals of Kildare and Harrington and Wall of west Wicklow. Furthermore, one of his family had married the Catholic farmer and United Irish captain John North of Nurney (Kildare), a relationship of sufficient interest to loyalists to warrant emphasis in the tense post-rebellion political climate.[181]

While the magistracy awaited the response of the Castle the general business of the assize got underway. The Wicklow United Irishmen put their weekly subscriptions to good use at the assizes in hiring the illustrious John Philpot Curran and Matthew Dowling to defend upwards of ninety prisoners who were brought to trial, many of whom had been implicated by Cooper.[182] Wicklowmen were also tried that spring at both the Carlow and Kildare assizes for such diverse crimes such as taking illegal oaths, arms raiding and threatening the life of Paul Stratford. The six men accused of the Stratford plot all received death sentences at Carlow assizes which was commuted to transportation for life in two cases. Major Hardy was closely involved in the trials and alleged that a priest had prevented the brother of one of those capitally convicted from striking a deal in return for clemency. Much to his disappointment and that of the Wicklow magistrates, the vast bulk of the political defendants in the Wicklow jurisdiction were acquitted by Judge Baron Yelverton when the uncorroborated testi-mony of Cooper, the main prosecution witness, failed to withstand cross-examination by Curran.[183]

This check had been anticipated by Hardy and Wainwright who had feared that the gambit of using Cooper without supporting evi-dence would harm the credibility of the prosecution and undermine respect for the law. The release of William Young, of whom Curran had reputedly spoke 'feelingly of', was the most galling as he repre-sented a very dangerous class of subversive being Protestant, well estab-lished and hitherto upstanding. The south Wicklow loyalists would have noted the addition of Young's signature to a public welcome to Earl Fitzwilliam in January 1795, a document perhaps also endorsed by his March 1798 co-accused, Richard Byrne of Colvinstown.[184] Cooper's scheduled appearance at the Wexford assizes was cancelled in consequence of his poor performance in Wicklow and several men he had sworn against were bailed. Popular resentment at his actions ran very high and Cooper's guards were obliged to take cover from a barrage of stones when his carriage was attacked by an angry mob as it passed through Bray. Such was the antipathy towards him that Hardy sought permission from General Craig to allow Cooper to live in the Provost prison or some other secure place until he and his family could emigrate. William Hume, foreman of the Grand Jury, was moved to petition the Government on his behalf to provide more than the £50 granted to enable Cooper and his six children to go abroad.[185]

Convictions for seditious crimes were, however, secured against Thomas Brady of Tigrony Hill, John Dorney, a slatier from Tighlin, Richard Byrne, a Glenmalure-born bricklayer who lived at Colvinstown on the Wicklow/Kildare border, and Wicklow Town plasterer Michael Mulhall. All four received sentences of transportation for life and following imprisonment in Dublin's Newgate prison and on hulks moored in Dublin Bay were shipped out to New South Wales on the *Minerva* and *Anne* between 1799 and 1801.[186] Brady was deeply implicated in the infiltration of the mines yeomanry corps and such was the detailed evidence against him that his conviction could not have been in doubt. Dorney was a leading member of the Newcastle baronial committee and had chaired the meeting on 1 November 1797 which had elected John Byrne of Cronroe and Richard O'Reilly to represent the sector on the county committee. The branding and two months imprisonment imposed on Terence Doyle and Michael Sheil for criminal manslaughter was of little consequence in comparison with the four minor victories.[187]

These token convictions did not, as Hardy put it, dispel the 'bad effects, felt by the return of so many scoundrels' to their families which gave 'great courage to the disaffected'. Hardy apportioned much blame to the magistrates who, against his advice, had committed large numbers of suspects to prison on slender grounds. Minor offenders and innocent men crowded the guardhouses that required protection out of Hardy's meagre troop resources. That justice was seen to be done and the guilty punished, however, was a very important aspect of holding assizes. The steps taken to preserve the efficacy of exemplary justice in the summer of 1797 had resulted in a prison tour by the respected Kerryman Judge Robert Day. Kildare gaols and those of other counties with problematic assizes had been visited by Day who discharged those against whom charges were unlikely to be sustained at the assizes.[188]

The poor showing of the Wicklow prosecution contrasted with the sessions in Carlow, Maryborough (Portlaoise), Athlone and Down, districts with lesser or comparable levels of disturbance to Wicklow, where scores of death sentences had been handed down and a 'multitude' sentenced to transportation. At Tipperary's Clonmel assizes an insecure but extremist magistracy proclaimed its loyalty by imposing capital convictions on all those found guilty of seditious crimes, a gesture their Wicklow counterparts would no doubt have relished.[189] Despite allegations of jury intimidation and, in the case of Kildare, impropriety on their part, the general consensus was that the spring assizes had proven successful. State Solicitor Thomas Kemmis, whose family owned Ballinacor House near Glenmalure, was satisfied that Wicklow's jurymen had acted properly which was a further indictment on the quality of the county's prosecution effort. Kemmis utilized the services of the spy Smith and may have had other motives for enquiring into the management of the assizes in that it had been ascertained that George Howell, a clerk to Justice Wilson, had boasted of securing the release of Wicklow United Irishmen and swearing in recruits.[190]

A serious blow was struck against the upper echelon of the Wicklow United Irishmen on 24 March when county committee member Richard O'Reilly was arrested on suspicion of having 'seditious purposes' by a patrol of the Rathdrum Cavalry. O'Reilly unwisely volunteered that he had intended spending the night with Phil O'Neill in Arklow whom Hardy knew to be disaffected and was proceeding to meet Bagenal Harvey in Wexford. The precise purpose of these consultations was not revealed but probably concerned the implications of the Bond arrests.[191] He was escorted to the city on the 27 March by the Bray Cavalry and questioned the following day in the Bermingham Tower, Dublin Castle, where important prisoners were generally interviewed. O'Reilly was accompanied to Dublin by Kemmis' associate and King's Messenger Mr Dawes, who liaised with Smith and whose presence raises the possibility that the Wicklowman had been under surveillance. Thomas King's Rathdrum men may have chosen to intercept O'Reilly when a pretext was offered by his travelling a secluded mountain road at night. His arrest brought to three the number of committee men neutralized in the space of two weeks, not counting the enforced absence of Garret Byrne.[192]

Troops continued to arrive in Wicklow to reinforce Hardy's militia-men and on or around 20 March 1798 a detachment of seventy Ancient British Dragoons reached Bray where they instituted a reign of terror. They were a Welsh regiment hardened by a year's duty in Antrim and Down where they had indulged in house-burning, torture and murder. Their first victim in Bray, ironically, was reputedly an orangeman named Moore whose house was vandalized when he un-wisely objected to the troopers interfering with his garden.[193] A delft shop owner named Doran was also attacked being 'cut and knocked about the street, whipt [sic] and dragged to prison, his furniture smashed and burned in the street'. He had been named as a United Irishman by a soldier who had been flogged for theft. The sudden introduction of such decisive and often atrocious methods profoundly shocked those who witnessed it in 1798.[194]

From 24 March 1798, however, it became more difficult to protest against such brutality as Hardy's authority in the county was strength-ened by his formal appointment to the acting rank of Brigadier-General with the benefits apparently backdated to 27 September 1797. This was in recognition of his good services and followed extensive discussions on the matter between Pelham and Castlereagh, as well as a personal message of thanks from Camden who followed Hardy's subsequent career with interest for many years. The result was that Hardy obtained undisputed operational control of the Wicklow district just as the pace of counter-insurgency was being stepped up and was its sole military strategist when the rebellion broke out.[195] By the end of March 1798 Hardy commanded 700 Antrim Militia, 200 militiamen drawn from various Light Companies, 40 Ninth Dragoons and 70 Ancient Britons. These 1,010 professionals were supported by approximately 590 mounted yeomen organized into fourteen reliable corps and 660 yeo-man infantry in eleven corps, excluding the two disgraced Castle-macadam units. Also available were at least 250 armed loyalists formed into several ah hoc supplementary units which by May 1798 included Morton's Tinahely True Blues, Revd McGhee's Hacketstown orangemen and the Newtownmountkennedy Infantry.[196]

The mere presence of the military had long ceased to cow the Wicklow United Irishmen and the clamour of the conservative magis-tracy for effective action increased in volume. On Sunday 25 March about sixty rebels called to the Ballyboy home of county treasurer Abraham Chritchley near Rathdrum and demanded his firearms. Chritchley, who had just returned from the assizes, refused and in the ensuing confrontation part of his house was burned down and several raiders were shot and wounded. A garbled and incorrect report reached Rathdrum that the insurgents were approaching the town which caused thirty of the town's yeoman cavalry and self-declared 'loyal citizens' to turn out and gather outside Bates' Inn, the traditional focal point of mid-Wicklow loyalty. They remained ready for action until the recently purged Cronebane Infantry under Captain Abraham Mills arrived who exacerbated the sense of emergency by ordering the extinguishment of the town's lights. Their presence, nevertheless, freed the mounted yeomen to proceed towards Ballyboy where it was discovered that the raiders had retreated to the mountains killing two soldiers stationed in Carlow *en route*.[197] Chritchley's 'spirited' actions were singled out for praise by the magistrates who met on 3 April to call for yet more troops against the backdrop of further 'acts of outrage'.[198] The Blessington area had again become disturbed and several arms raids were carried out around Bray and Powerscourt. Hardy determined that the time had come for 'strong & vigorous measures' to deter the United Irishmen from rising, which he feared they intended even without French assistance.[199]

The deteriorating situation in Wicklow underscored the assize resolutions of the previous week and resulted in the extension of martial law to all parts of Wicklow on 26 March 1798. In the event the proclamation of the county predated by only four days the imposition of the Insurrection Act on all counties where it was not already in effect. Camden had noted the spread of disturbances to previously peaceable counties and had resigned himself to the likelihood of a popular revolt. On 3 April he thought it 'extremely probable that these insurrections will be very general' and considered the large-scale hiring of German and Swiss mercenaries to aid the Irish army. While rebellion was then seen as being almost inevitable it was expected under the more favourable circumstances of occurring without foreign intervention. The implication of this was that the army would not necessarily be forced to abandon the defence of the county to the yeomanry alone and could engage the rebels themselves. Rebellion, therefore, could not present an insuperable challenge to the government so long as the United Irishmen were deprived of the means to fight. The policy of disarming, considered a success in Ulster in 1797, consequently began in earnest in Leinster and Munster.[200]

Castlereagh's orders to Lieutenant-General Abercromby, Commander-in-Chief of the Irish army from December 1797 until the end of April 1798, were 'to act without waiting for directions from the civil magistrates in dispersing any tumultuous assemblies of persons threatening the peace of the realm [and] . . . to crush the Rebellion in whatever shape it shall show itself by the most summary military measures, and that you do employ similar means effectively to disarm the rebels.'[201] The liberally inclined and professionally minded Abercromby was far from pleased with having to commit his forces to what he perceived to be a provocative and violent police action but had no choice but to follow the instructions of the Executive. Martial law freed the army from the constraints of the civil authority and suspended habeas corpus. It was hailed by ultra-loyalists as a charter for 'disarming and punishing' the rebellious and resulted in an explosion of atrocious behaviour.[202]

The primary method used to compel the return of stolen and illegal weaponry was for the commander of a district to stipulate a period of grace during which time the rebels could divest themselves of war material with impunity and swear an oath of allegiance before a magistrate or army officer. A certificate of protection that indemnified the named bearer from prosecution was granted in return. If the response of the district was deemed unsatisfactory, troops were sent into the targeted locality to live off the population without reimbursement or legal redress. This plan was devised by Abercromby who wished to avoid the arbitrary severities inflicted on the population of Ulster by Lake's men in 1797. Entire communities were punishable for the crimes of their recalcitrant elements. Brigadier-General Sir Charles Asgill managed the scheme to great effect in Queen's County as did Major-General John Moore in Cork who later became one of Britain's foremost military heroes for service during the Peninsular War. Whereas a mere 33 pikes had been surrendered in Queen's County, King's County and Kildare during the last week of March 1798 over 300 were delivered up in Queen's County alone within one week of free quarters being declared. Dramatic results of this order were achieved when disciplined troops were directed by informers to suspected sections of the community but the tendency of individual officers to tolerate excessive conduct, such as house burnings, wholescale pillaging and assaults, was ultimately counter-productive.[203]

The return of arms did not equate to a rejection of sedition by the United Irishmen and the numbers handed over were a relatively small proportion of those manufactured. Limerick magistrate John Massey castigated the 'cursed defenders' for sending old and inoperable firearms and claimed he had been obliged 'to burn some houses of notorious vagabonds by which [means] alone we get information.'[204] Generally, freequarters was ruinous to army discipline as it encouraged laziness and boorishness while generating 'fresh enemies to Government' as predicted by Asgill.[205] Lord Shannon, who did not shirk from strong measures, commented on the uncommon severity of flogging being practised along with the 'plunder and waste of provision' which he feared could result in famine. Ill-discipline and casual violence by the military certainly increased under the freequarters scheme and in one incident in Drogheda in April 1798 several Fermanagh Militia and Suffolk Fencibles privates were killed in a dispute over carts. The line between murderous conduct and 'exemplary firmness' was very thin and was often blurred by the Ancient Britons or Durham Fencibles when stationed in Down and Louth.[206]

A printed statement circulated in Wicklow on 3 April 1798 explained the reasoning of the county magistracy in seeking martial law and their alleged reluctance to take the step. It stressed the temporary nature of the 'measures of rigour' and implored the United Irishmen to hand over their weapons. It had been composed at a meeting of mainly north Wicklow magistrates from Rathdown and Newcastle who had evidently met in Bray under the chairmanship of Powerscourt and then William Hoey. It was also apparently indebted to the 'spirited and loyal address' of Arklow's Revd Bayly who had travelled north to show his solidarity. Although similar to notices posted up in Kildare, King's County and Queen's County, the Wicklow proclamation differed in that freequarters was not explicitly threatened for non-compliance. The declaration signed by Clerk of the Peace James McClatchly simply implored the disaffected to 'awake, ere yet too late, from this fatal delusion; withdraw from this infamous conspiracy; prove your repentance by surrendering illegal arms, and refraining from seditious meetings: Act thus, and fear not the laws.'[207]

That freequarters was not envisaged in Wicklow in the spring of 1798 owed much to the absolute opposition of the parliamentary Fitzwilliamites, as well as to Hardy's personal aversion to the practice. Hardy was an experienced and well-trained soldier whose primary concern was the ill-effects of freequartering on the discipline of his forces. After the rebellion he recalled with pride his opposition to 'the exercise of torture or fire, and even . . . the introduction of free quarters'. His viewpoint was supported by most of Wicklow's extreme loyalists who feared that it would render their tenants incapable of paying rent and it is clear that the county's new conservative consensus did not extend to levels of coercion that jeopardized the local economy.[208]

Preparations to enforce the blunt warning of the magistracy were being contemplated at the time it was issued, which closely corresponded with the movement of the King's County Militia from Lehaunstown to garrisons in Wicklow and bordering parts of Wexford and Kildare.[209] This and the sense of the ultimatum did not meet with the approval of the discredited liberals and, while Edwards automatically registered his opposition to the imminent introduction of extra troops on 2 April, the faction he represented had been totally outmanoeuvered. Hardy no longer required his co-operation at any level and privately derided him as a 'man who shuts himself up in a cloister' in Bray.[210] Edwards was just one of many liberal magistrates subjected to constant scrutiny and invective by loyalists in their handling of issuing 'protections' and receiving weapons. County MP William Hume was not above criticism and was reproached for being prone to liberate rebel prisoners as well as for drawing 'no distinction between the protestant & the papist'.[211]

Many of Hardy's alternative initiatives to the pressure tactic of freequarters were highly eccentric and could only have been legally tolerated under military government. One of the most striking measures was his April detention in Wicklow goal without charge of four sons of 'the principal inhabitants' of Arklow who were explicitly referred to as 'as hostages for the good behaviour of their parents and friends'. The first four were Garret Graham, John Doran, Thomas Murray junior and Phil O'Neil but more of their family members were subsequently added, including Murray's brother Peter. That the group were effectively interned for the duration of the rebellion greatly hindered the mobilization of the local forces in what should have been a stronghold.[212] Edward Hay recalled that in April/May 1798 'there had been [Wicklow United Irish] leaders (afterwards imprisoned) who made discoveries which led the public to believe that all idea of a rising was at that time given up'.[213] The fact that they consented to detention is indicative of a lack of commitment and radicalism even if their actions were coerced by Hardy's threat to destroy the property of their wealthy parents. Co-operation with the authorities ensured that the families involved recovered quickly under the Cornwallis administration from their years of disaffection. The government did not attempt to hinder Fr Daniel Murray's spectacular clerical career, despite the activities of his brothers, and in late June 1800 James O'Neill of Arklow was appointed an attorney to the Court of Common Pleas, a classic example of the emergent Catholic middle-class professional. John Doran, William Graham and Richard Graham of Arklow, moreover, registered the 117-ton coaster *Catherine* in 1799.[214]

Martial law necessitated the full mobilization of the Wicklow yeomanry who were placed on 'permanent duty' and quartered in barracks
where they were better situated to operate with regular and fencible
dragoons. Daily musters were held in Bray which became the centre of
yeomanry operations in north Wicklow just as Arklow's small parade
ground adjacent to its barracks was used for yeoman assemblies and
roll calls. Government pay and equipment was distributed to the
various corps and twice weekly parades of Rathdown units were held
on Bray's Sea Common.[215] William Hume and Lord Powerscourt both
permitted the yeomanries they commanded and other armed loyalists
to camp on their estates and Powerscourt House, or at least a portion
of it, was reputedly 'nearly . . . converted into a barrack'.[216] In the west
of the county William Ryves of the Dunlavin Cavalry fortified his
Rathsallagh property, 'a large old mansion' in which a militia guard
was accommodated and sent all the female members of his family away
during the rebellion.[217] Marlsfield House, built by the La Touches at
Monamuck, was also occupied by a yeomanry or dragoon detachment
during the rebellion period. It would have functioned as a forward base
of the Russborough garrison four miles away and as a buffer between
the dangerous Ballynockan and Black Ditches area and the isolated
gentry homes at Tulfarris (Hornidge) and Baltyboys (Smith). As with
other temporary yeomanry and army bases, Marlsfield House was a
site associated with floggings and the maltreatment of prisoners.[218]

The meeting of magistrates on 3 April seized the opportunity offered
by the arms proclamation and their numbers to request 'a large reinforcement of dragoons for Newtownmountkennedy'. Newcastle loyalists apparently had the Ancient Britons quartered at Bray in mind
and probably felt that they needed a cadre of dragoons to conduct
effective arms searches. Apart from the pretext offered by the dramatic
United Irish demonstrations of October 1797, active magistrate
Thomas Archer of Mount John had arrested a wealthy Mayoman
named Taaffe in Newtownmountkennedy as recently as 28 March
who was suspected of treasonable practices. Taaffe was escorted to
Dublin for questioning by the Bray Cavalry and the New Romney
Fencible Light Dragoons, another regiment which had just appeared
in the county where they were to become notorious for their brutality.
The New Romneys had been based in Lehaunstown camp in October
1797 and by April 1798 were assisting the Ancient Britons in bringing
suspects into Bray's makeshift guardhouse. The two regiments
wrought mayhem during April as the searches which followed the
expiration of the arms ultimatum resulted in unprecedented violence.[219]

Strangers in rural areas where the communities were close-knit and relatively static were likely to be challenged by yeomen in this period. King's Rathdrum Cavalry arrested Englishmen Charles Power of Bristol and William Johnson of Norfolk in the Wicklow mountains in late April whom they conveyed to Wicklow Goal on the mistaken assumption that they were deserters from a British regiment. There is little doubt but that emissarial traffic between Dublin United Irishmen and their Wicklow comrades was indeed taking place in the run up to the rebellion. John Duff, when confined to the county gaol in late April, made a detailed statement concerning United Irish activity in Milltown and Clonskeagh (County Dublin) which suggests that while he had been primarily active in that area he had been sent to Wicklow on seditious business.[220]

Some idea of the terror evoked by the Britons was conveyed to Luke Cullen around 1840 by a woman named Mrs Dowling who had been a young girl in 1798 but clearly recalled the deeds of the 'Welsh horse'. She had tended the family's cattle on their Kilcoole farm as 'no one but a child dare go [out]'. She was, nevertheless, slightly wounded by a cavalry patrol who called to the property and, in one of the first incidents of its kind in Wicklow, burned their farmhouse.[221] Dowling's father had probably been named as a United Irishman and he only escaped arrest at the forfeit of his home. If apprehended he may not have survived long enough to be committed to prison given that a patrol commanded by Lieutenant Blaney Winslow of the Fermanagh Militia murdered at least one Wicklow rebel suspect in their custody in April 1798. Winslow initially absconded to avoid trial but when apprehended and courtmartialled in Dublin on the 16th was only reprimanded for being drunk on duty. Blaney's 'wanton cruelty' towards an inoffensive man was mentioned in General Orders was evidently the full extent of his punishment. Edward Doherty, but this a resident of the Bahana area, was also brutally maltreated during this period by being pitchcapped and having his ears severed.[222]

On 8 April 1798, Easter Sunday, Captain John Burganey's troop of Ancient Britons arrived in Newtownmountkennedy from Bray to the rousing welcome of the town's loyalists. Burganey may well have been known to the Wicklow readers of the *Press* which in October 1797 had printed an account of how he and Major Gwilliam Wardle of the same regiment had destroyed several homes in Newry which had not complied with their instructions to illuminate lights in honour of the British naval victory at Camperdown. Burganey had then allegedly threatened to decapitate one remonstrating victim if he continued to protest. Once the Welshmen had taken up quarters in Newtownmountkennedy floggings, half-hanging and picketing commenced in the district surrounding the town eliciting a 'sullen silence' from the terrified locals.[223]

The worst single incident occurred on 11 April 1798, the town's annual fair day, when the Britons were plied with drink by approving loyalists who afterwards identified suspected rebels as they called to the town. Sir Lawrence Parsons, an MP for King's County and commander of the county's militia regiment, received a vivid account of the ensuing massacre from his brother Thomas who was an eyewitness.[224] According to Thomas Parsons:

> six of the inhabitants [were] selected indifferently from those they met in the street & without any trial whatsoever or previous suspicion of guilt, hung them because the[y] w[oul]d not make such discoveries as they were required to make . . . others were half strangled others beat & wounded & all filled with horror & consternation . . . none are allowed to stir out of their houses in the morn[in]g till the trumpet sounds none to have lights after night fall & the soldiers pleasure is the only law.[225]

Women whose apparel included pieces of green cloth were also viciously assaulted as such clothes were interpreted by the Britons as indicative of radical sympathies. The scene was also observed by the future rebel leader Joseph Holt who recalled with horror the Britons 'cutting the haunches and the thighs of the young women . . . for wearing green stuff petticoats'.[226]

This brutal but non-fatal attack on the women at Newtown fair has eclipsed the summary execution of six men in both folk and historical accounts. Edwards was appalled by news of the incident and queried 'where is the man whose blood will not boil with revenge who sees the petticoat of his wife or sister cut off her back by the sabre of a dragoon, merely for the crime of being green, a colour certainly with them innocent of disaffection?'[227] This statement was undoubtedly well-intentioned but was somewhat naive given that the wearing of green cloth very often signified political allegiance in the late 1790s and was used for identification purposes just as orange was by loyalists. According to one nationalist source even the United Irish prisoners of Carrickfergus gaol in late 1797 wore green silk handkerchiefs 'about their necks', including the ill-fated William Orr. Once the rebellion commenced Mary Leadbeater in Ballitore was applied to by a Kildare rebel with whom she was not acquainted for 'anything of a green colour' and was relieved that the man did not requisition her table-cloth.[228]

The Newtownmountkennedy incident instilled the United Irishmen with a deep hatred for this regiment above all others in Wicklow, a circumstance which did much to ensure that the Britons and 5th Dragoons ambushed at Ballyellis on 30 June 1798 were given no quarter. Dublin spymaster Samuel Sproule wrote from Shangannagh near Bray in June 1798 to report that 'the fury of the [Wicklow] rebels was and is directed against the Ancient British for their conduct when first sent to Newtownmountkennedy'.[229] Holt referred to the Britons on a number of occasions in his memoirs and recalled how 'after taking what cash they could get from individuals, would then shoot them at their doors.'[230] Plunder and rapine were certainly widespread in counties where soldiers had been garrisoned in April/May 1798 under martial law. Sarah Tighe of Rossana, whose husband William was a Wicklow MP, noted with evident relief on 21 April that the soldiers sent to protect the county town and its locality were 'well behaved' and that the magistrates were 'all mild and sensible', comments which implied knowledge of less idyllic circumstances. She also pointedly commended their commander for being 'a very peaceable man', who was probably either an Antrim or King's County officer.[231]

Further north on the coast, however, Bray guardhouse became packed with prisoners and reportedly 'echoed with the groans of men flogging', many of whom were members of the King's County Militia suspected of sedition. A courtmartial of a large group of King's Countymen in early May 1798 convicted just one man of sedition who received sentence of 1,000 lashes but little pretext was required to administer corporal punishment under martial law.[232] The ferocity of the Britons reputedly inspired the local loyalists and yeomen who executed two leading United Irish members of the Bray Infantry; Sergeant Thomas Ledwidge of Bog Hall road, Oldcourt, and Corporal Richard Kennedy of Bray. The pair had been arrested on a packet at the Pigeon House in Dublin while trying to escape abroad and were brought back to Bray where a distiller named Sutherland had them hanged outside Cooper's pub in Little Bray. Edwards attempted to secure mitigation of their sentences but could do little in the time span allotted to the condemned men. There is a tradition that he avenged their loss by having a senior excise surveyor, a relative, examine the affairs of Sutherland to the detriment of his business. Also arrested with Ledwidge and Kennedy on the packet but apparently not executed were John Murray, John Sullivan and Terence Lawlor of Little

Cork, Loughlinstown who were probably transported.[233] At least two other United Irishmen were shot by the Bray Infantry on their Sea Common parade ground in this period, a choice of site perhaps inspired by the fact that the victims had been implicated in suborning the corps. Tom White, Ledwidge's brother-in-law, was executed in April along with Patrick Burke, the Long Hill schoolmaster and United Irish organizer who had operated in the barony and may well have intrigued with the Bray yeomanry.[234]

Despite the flogging of suspects, however, the loyalists were unable to procure physical or confessional evidence against the bulk of their prisoners. They consequently cleared the cells early one April morning by marching the prisoners to Dublin for pressed service in the British army or Royal Navy. Many of the men had been pitchcapped prior to their dispatch and Enniskerry teacher Pat Nugent was apparently shot and mortally wounded by Darby Mackey of Little Bray for falling out of line without permission. Another man named Devlin was also reputedly shot dead outside Bray around this time when being taken to Wicklow gaol. This mode of prisoner disposal was by no means uncommon and in February 1798 seventeen prisoners who had languished in Carlow gaol for three months were 'transported one morning' without the benefit of any trial proceedings.[235] Indeed, many hundreds, if not thousands, of Defender and United Irish prisoners had been pressed into the Royal Navy, marines and infantry regiments posted overseas in the mid-to late 1790s. Lord Blayney even suggested raising a regiment solely recruited from 'persons taken up in Ireland under the Insurrection Act, together with deserters from the army in general'.[236]

The Act provided for the summary transportation of suspects to the military or to New South Wales without trial if any two magistrates concurred on the matter. The Bray deportations would have been justified under this provision but hard-line magistrates in central and southern Wicklow were also quick to employ the powers. Revd Cope, singly, or with the assistance of Hunter Gowan, committed pikemaker Edward Nowlan, Philip Kearney, Hugh Toole, James Kavanagh, William Kealy, Edward Murphy, Patrick Carroll, Timothy Byrne, Gregory Donnelly, John Toole and two men named Patrick Carroll to the tenders under the Insurrection Act in the pre-rebellion period. Many others were sent by 'active' magistrates Alexander Carroll, Thomas King, Henry Moreton and Benjamin O'Neil Stratford. There is no evidence, however, that any other Wicklow magistrate employed the legislation at their disposal and the whigs were patently opposed to invoking the catch-all 'idle and disorderly' clause.[237] While few details remain of 'uncommonly active' William Colthurst's magisterial experience in north Wicklow in late 1797 and early 1798, it is likely that he accounted for many of those confined in Bray guardhouse and transported under the Insurrection Act.[238]

Around 20 April 1798 a captain of the Britons led a patrol to the home of the Long family near Delgany whom he suspected of con-ealing pikes and munitions. When the Longs were deemed unco-operative one of them was subjected to the torture known as

> 'picketing' until he revealed the location of hidden pikes and musket balls. The picket was described as 'a spike of wood or iron, twelve or eighteen inches long, fastened upright in the floor; the victim was put with one foot on the point of it, and, by a rope fastened overhead, so that the weight was divided between the fulcrum and the pulley, and then wheeled round on it as long as it afforded pastime to the torturers'.

It was generally carried out in the seclusion of a barracks but on this occasion the Britons either brought the equipment with them or improvised a set on the spot.[239] This practice was dismissed as a 'slight punishment' by *Saunder's Newsletter* from which *Faulkner's Dublin Journal* republished the account on 21 April and such activity was apparently widespread in Wicklow from late March 1798. Torture was also meted out in the west of the county in late April 1798 and over fifty men were reputedly flogged at Dunlavin guardhouse in early May. They were whipped at a rate of four or five a day by the detached Light Infantry company of the Wicklow Militia under Captain Edward Richardson, notwithstanding the protests of the local protestant minister, Revd Morgan whose courageous interjections fell on deaf ears.[240] Moderation may not have been a likely proposition in view of the regiments brutal actions in Westmeath and it may also be significant that Richardson's company lieutenant in Dunlavin was Francis Derenzy while Benjamin Derenzy was a junior officer in another company. This family's connections with the Orange Order and their property interests in west Wicklow gave them a degree of local insight and political extremism which may have militated against restraint.[241]

The Dunlavin punishments may have been carried out in retaliation for an attack on a local loyalist named Fowler whose house had been burned by United Irish raiders. Pat Fahey, a United Irish captain from Ballymore-Eustace, and local man Billy Power of Dunlavin made strenuous efforts to dissuade their men from carrying out such attacks. Fowler had been described in the *Union Star* of November 1797 as 'a notorious informer' and 'orangemen' was evidently a local hate figure in United Irish circles.[242] He had played a 'principal' role along with some Dunlavin yeomen in inflicting severe injuries on Michael and Thomas Egan in February 1798 when the militiamen in his company had refused to participate in the brutal interrogation. One of those burned out by the army in Talbotstown in late April was the prominent county committee member John Dwyer of Seskin (Imaal) who had been under close surveillance by the yeomanry and was arrested in April by the Donard Infantry. He had apparently been followed to Dublin by one Fenton on the day of his arrest, possibly First Lieutenant Michael Fenton of the Upper Talbotstown Cavalry, but had not been observed conducting seditious business. Dwyer was committed to Dunlavin goal and shot there with other inmates on the commencement of the rebellion in late May.[243]

Coercion intended to exert pressure on the United Irish infrastructure necessarily impacted on the wider community and spurred several clergymen to intervene. Little information on Catholic clergy in Wicklow during the rebellion period is available as there was no equivalent to Wexford's Bishop Caulfield of Ferns who sent numerous letters to Troy on the political allegiances of his clergy. Wicklow also lacked a Mountnorris figure to co-ordinate mass displays of loyalty through the media of petitions and addresses and Major Hardy evinced little support for such activity. Fr John Meagher of Rathdrum was one parish priest who advised his parishioners to take the oath of allegiance when the April 1798 arms searches began. This was apparently 'implicitly obeyed', albeit without an obvious amelioration of conditions.[244]

In the south of the county Fr William Ryan of Arklow and Kilgorman parishes added his name on 18 April 1798 to a loyal address signed by Fr John Murphy of Boolavogue and other Wexford priests who were to side with the United Irishmen when rebellion broke out. Fr Murphy was one of the most ardent opponents of the United Irishmen and Caulfield recalled that 'Gen[era]l [John] Murphy . . . [was] often reproached, reprimanded and threatened. He refused sacraments to all United Irishmen who refused to abjure their oath and business the Easter immediately before the Rebellion-poor giddy mortal'. Fr Daniel Murray, curate to Fr Andrew O'Toole in Wicklow Town, was also acknowledged as having striven to preserve tranquillity in the district surrounding the county town had sworn an oath of allegiance himself before Revd Bayly on 27 May. Bayly's acceptance of Murray's declaration indicates that he did not share the politics of his United Irish brothers then in prison.[245]

In Powerscourt and Bray Fr Christopher Callaghan was credited with being 'a great anti-republican' having ran afoul of the jacobins during the French Revolution. This was not appreciated by the Bray loyalists who burned his six-year-old Old Connaught chapel when the rebellion commenced obliging him to take refuge on Meath's Kilruddery estate where he celebrated Mass. Many of those who had attended Mass at Old Connaught were soldiers from nearby Loughlinstown camp who were given permission to do so in June 1796. In Wexford younger priests who had been in France during the Revolution tended to be foremost among the radicals. Fr Mogue Kearns of Kiltealy reputedly survived hanging at the hands of a jacobin mob in 1789 but went on to become one of Leinster's greatest field leaders.[246] There is no evidence, furthermore, that the common cause effected between lesser clergy and the rebels in parts of Wexford was paralleled in Wicklow. There was certainly no equivalent to Blackwater's Fr Thomas Dixon in the pre-rebellion period and while several Wicklow priests fraternized with the rebels during the insurrection the county failed to produce a single clerical fighting leader.[247]

Fr Edward Synnott and Fr Thomas Dixon had both died before the rebellion but were acknowledged by their bishop as having been 'notorious agitators' whom he censured for doing 'much mischief'.[248] Very little such information is extant relating to Wicklow-based priests, notwithstanding the watchful eyes of the county's Protestant clerical magistrates and an ultimately broad base of informants. John Smith alleged that Fr Maguire, curate to Fr Connolly at Blackrock, County Dublin, had been 'very active in the county Wicklow, and had put a great many up' but this concerned a visitor rather than a resident priest. Musgrave's claim that an Arklow rebel had confessed to having been initiated by his priest is inherently implausible as it is unsubstantiated and implicates either the aged Fr Toole or the loyal Fr Murray. Indeed, Musgrave found it very difficult to reconcile his theory of the Catholic nature of the rebellion with the lack of sectarian incidents in Wicklow in 1798 and the total absence of priest leaders.[249]

The county's most likely candidate for the role of clerical activist was Fr William Travers, parish priest of Baltinglass from 1768, who was much criticized by his Presbyterian counterpart Revd Robinson for his meagre efforts in recovering only one or two pikes. His conspicuous lack of enthusiasm for the task bolstered suspicions that he was a United Irishman and specific information to this end was evidently received by the authorities which resulted in Travers being twice courtmartialled in the spring and early summer of 1798. He was probably confined in either Baltinglass or Carlow Town when the rebellion broke out and any prospect of him emulating Fr John Murphy was lost. His two sentences of transportation, however, were overturned by the intercession of sympathetic local gentry and the crisis-stricken Stratford family in particular. Thus exposed he narrowly emerged unscathed from an attempt on his life after the Battle of Stratford-on-Slaney on 24 May 1798 when the ailing Lady Aldborough reputedly 'threw herself' between him and a group of angry yeomen intent of killing him. Travers was also deemed fortunate to survive ill-treatment at the hands of his jailers in Carlow Town gaol where he apparently suffered a nervous breakdown and shocked his fellow political prisoners by shouting out his republican opinions. When released from prison in late 1798 or early 1799 Travers fled to Ballyadams for safety from whence he did not return.[250]

Holt considered Fr Christopher 'Wiggy' Lowe of Derrylossary parish and two other unnamed Wicklow priests as 'very good men' in a context that implied that they were United Irishmen. Lowe's successful attempt to prevent rebels burning houses in the Roundwood/Glendalough area on the night of 13/14 June 1798 was interpreted by loyalists as a sign that he held influence over them and his church at Annamoe was burned in revenge. Quite apart from Holt's allegations and the concerted efforts of loyalists to attack Lowe, rebel connections were further indicated by United Irish emissary Fr John Martin of Drogheda who obtained a letter of introduction to him and one Gilligan from Rathfarnham's disaffected Fr William Ledwich in early June 1798. This came to light on 14 June 1798 when Martin was captured attempting to co-ordinate an attack on Dublin city and made a series of statements when interrogated in Rathdrum.[251] The elderly Fr Lowe was the victim of three separate assassination bids by members of the Wicklow Town Cavalry who hailed from his home parish in Glendalough as well as their comrades from the county town. Another priest Holt may have been alluding to was Fr Patrick Donnellan of Blackditches with whom he breakfasted before leading his men into the midlands in July 1798. Blackditches, even towards the end of the nineteenth century, was considered 'the Siberia of the diocese' and Donnellan's posting may have resulted from some political or personal infraction.[252]

While harsh measures turned up accurate information on senior rebels and led to many arrests, very few weapons were recovered in Wicklow before freequarters began in Kildare and Queen's County. The programme was announced on 21 April 1798 and its introduction was paralleled in Wicklow by a marked increase in coércion. John Patterson reported from Blessington that day that no arms had come in under Abercromby's earlier policy but that the state of Wicklow was 'very bad' and that 'Kildare and other parts will be loaded with troops next week'.[253] General Dundas reported to the Castle that insignificant numbers of arms had been obtained in south Leinster and would have concurred with Robert Ross' view that the United Irishmen 'go on as much as ever'.[254] The government's more robust program was signalled by Castlereagh on 25 April when he announced the new 'vigorous and effectual measures for enforcing the speedy surrender of arms'. This was deemed preferable to lengthy bouts of freequarters alone which affected the interests of propertied loyalists to an intolerable degree and produced mixed results.[255]

Under the direction of extremists such as Lord Waterford freequarters had degenerated into the dragooning and brutalization which Abercromby had striven to obviate and this informed his decision to resign as Commander-in-Chief. Loyalist figures had expected Abercromby to employ severe coercion as soon as martial law had been declared and were incredulous when he prefaced freequarters with a period of grace to enable the surrender of arms. It was insinuated that he was friendly with Lord Edward Fitzgerald and Lord Moira whose anti-coercion speeches in the House of Lords incensed the Downshire faction and other influential hardliners. He was replaced by Lieutenant-General Gerard Lake who considered himself to have acted 'with propriety and humanity' during the notorious dragooning of Ulster. Lake promised in April 1798 to spare 'no exertion . . . to protect Ireland against foreign or domestic foes'.[256]

The Quaker community in the south Kildare border town of Ballitore were among the first to experience the new policy and were terrorized in early May when a detachment of the Tyrone Militia replaced the tolerant King's Countymen. Many of the newcomers were held to be 'professed orangemen, wearing the ribbon of their party' who considered the Quakers to be of suspect loyalty for their refusal to swear the oath of allegiance. On 1 May 1798, Lieutenant-Colonel Colin Campbell of the 6th Dragoons dispatched elements of the dreaded Britons to the town supported by a detachment of Suffolk Fencible Infantry. They seized the local blacksmith, William Brennan, as well as his apprentices and their tools and took them to Naas gaol while at least ten others were sent to Athy for interrogation.[257]

Over the course of the next few days large numbers of Kildare rebels fled into the nearby Wicklow mountains fearing that information extracted in the jails and on the flogging triangles in Athy would led to their arrest. Robinson noted that farmers along the Kildare border had begun moving livestock into the Baltinglass district from whence the 'more active rebels' had fled. Flogging triangles were previously used in Dundalk by the Lord Roden's fencibles and it is likely the Britons introduced the practice to Kildare. Campbell's harshness bore fruit and many pikes were surrendered in a heavily organised area that had initially resisted lesser coercion. *Faulkner's Dublin Journal* of 8 May 1798 claimed that over 2,000 pikes had been recovered in Kildare and that three United Irish colonels were compromised, one of whom allegedly became an informer.[258] This level of tension and commotion inevitably unsettled adjacent parts of Wicklow, just as Hardy had hoped and in Baltinglass Revd Robinson advocated the introduction of Kildare-style coercion to his locality and urged that 'no measures can be too strong'.[259]

Random floggings were carried out in Baltinglass but not on the scale practised in Athy under the direction of Captain Erskine and Cornet Love whom Hardy acclaimed as 'useful men' who had 'instilled the United Irishmen with a sense of their guilt & danger.'[260] One of those severely flogged in Wicklow was Brian Coogan of Redwells whose brother Laurence was shot while a third brother was forced into exile. These were sons of a 'comfortable farmer' and were related to the Coogans of Horseshoe who had been pioneers of the Lower Talbots-town United Irishmen. One of them, a rebel captain misidentified as 'Crogan of the Horse Shoe', was transferred from a Wicklow jail to Naas in late May.[261] At least two men were summarily executed in Baltinglass around this time; Pat Brophy, a wealthy farmer from Rathmoon and one McCormick who had allegedly uttered a seditious phrase. A traditional account revealed that Brophy was 'hung from a beam between the houses of Mr John Hourihan and Mr Bailey'. The Brophys of Rathmoon had been identified as United Irish figures by Robinson on 7 May 1798 who also named Anthony Allen of Deerpark and James Doyle of The Barrow (Stratford). In early May the 9th Dragoons also burned the home of the Widow Kearns who had fallen under suspicion for reasons now obscure. While many victims of the military were probably innocents caught in Athy-like trawling operations, families of known radical sympathies presumably bore the brunt of army excesses.[262]

That the Insurrection Act was more frequently resorted after the arms proclamation may be inferred from the arrests of twelve Ballinacor men on 26 April. Matthew McDaniel and eleven others had reputedly

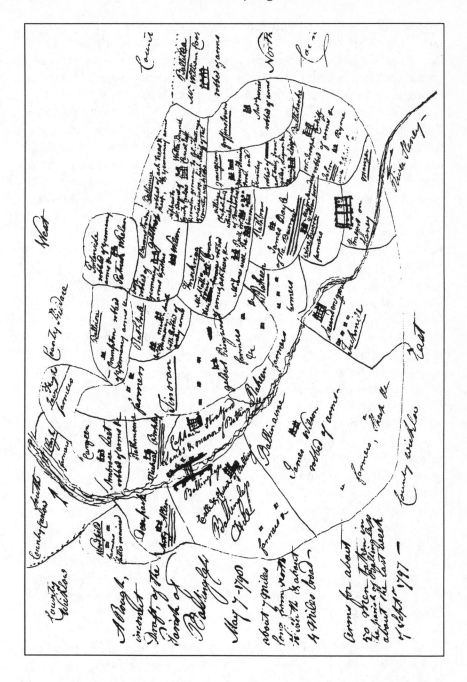

MS MAP OF WEST WICKLOW. *Courtesy of the National Archives*

been seized when out of doors at 'unlawful hours', although this may have been simply a device by their captors to facilitate the arrest and deportation of identified suspects. All twelve were summarily sentenced to transportation under the Act by Thomas King and one other magistrate in Rathdrum, probably Mills, and obliged to enlist.[263] Hardy's main initiative in west Wicklow was to send troops from Baltinglass into the Imaal valley where they built a temporary camp at Knockanarrigan in early May. Troops could be spared for this as he had the bulk of the Antrim, King's County and Fermanagh Militia regiments at his disposal in addition to sizeable contingents of the Ancient Britons, New Romney fencibles, Ninth Dragoons and other mounted forces. Just across from Baltinglass on the Kildare side of the border there were also Tyrone Militia, Suffolk and Warwickshire fencibles in Ballitore, Timolin and Castledermot and a strong garrison at Naas.[264]

Soldiers from Knockanarrigan camp took proactive steps to get to grips with the valley's reputedly large United Irish community; Patrick Byrne and Joseph Toole were severely flogged while Thomas Toole of Imaal and one Murphy of Merginstown were pitchcapped. Imaal farmers were directed 'in the most absolute manner to send in their meal, potatoes, bacon, butter and turf' and also to display lists of occupants. Locals were also conscripted to carry out manual labour on behalf of the army, which was greatly resented. One hundred cart loads of provisions were gathered in the surrounding countryside by such means and brought to Ballitore for distribution amongst the troops. The forced-labour policy may have been the root cause of the difficulty faced by the army in 1801 in hiring men at reasonable rates to work on the construction of the Military Road.[265] The circumstances of this arrangement were tantamount to free quarters and were pursued with identical objectives, although it appears that no provisions were made to enable the rebels in the area to abandon munitions in safety. John Patrickson was unequivocal in stating on 7 May that as very few weapons had been recovered 'troops begin to live at freequarters this day in the neighbourhood of Blessington.' Downshire may have given permission to Colonel Campbell or to Hardy, whose jurisdictions overlapped and whose troops operated together, to employ the measure on his estates.[266]

There does not seem to have been a coherent anti-insurgent policy in Wicklow other than the general purpose of intimidating the rebels with the 'examples of severity' which Hardy had endorsed. These including house burning, torture and transportation and, for a brief period, parts of Wicklow were subjected to coercion as harsh as had been experienced anywhere in Ireland.[267] Edwards opposed such methods and when defending his handling of the issuing protections he pointedly remarked that he had 'not yet burnt houses nor strangled their owners', implying that such practices were being carried out elsewhere in Wicklow. He would not have approved of the tyrannical conduct of the Newtownmountkennedy yeomen who dragged from their horses the retarded Coughlan of Delgany, an employee of the Ludlow family, on a circuit to Willow Grove where he was shot but then rescued by the innkeeping Booths. Freequarters were also not officially used in Carlow although mass arrests had been a feature of the counter-insurgent effort from early 1798.[268]

Well-known Wicklow United Irishmen like Dwyer of Seskin, the Byrnes of Ballymanus and Tinahely, the Coogans of Horseshoe, Holt of Mullinaveigue and Matthew Doyle of Polahoney were singled out for pre-emptive attacks as more and more detail of the rebel organization came to light. Holt's farm at Mullinaveigue was burned down by a party of the Roundwood-based Fermanagh Militia on 10 May 1798 at which time he was already in hiding. Hardy, no doubt mindful of Holt's post-rebellion notoriety, claimed that he had 'burnt his house the only one I sanctioned the destruction of' upon learning of the Wicklowman's attempts to suborn a party of Antrim militiamen guarding the nearby home of magistrate Andrew Price. The fugitive Holt, who had hidden his valuables and recovered his firearms in advance of his flight, was soon followed to the mountains by Michael Dwyer, Thomas Miller, Matthew Doyle and other leading United Irishmen who feared arrest.[269]

Camden informed Portland on 11 May 1798 that he had authorized the troops sent into Wicklow to employ 'every means' in recovering arms owing to the particular danger posed by the proximity of the county and its mountainous terrain to the capital.[270] On that day Lieutenant-General Peter Craig, Commander of the Eastern District, signed an ultimatum which differed in some important respects to those issued in other counties. Craig's 'final warning' threatened treatment of the 'utmost severity' to those who did not hand over offensive weapons but made no mention of the semi-official freequarters which was already in effect around Blessington. The General warned of 'calamities which will attend the obstinately disaffected who are well known' but set no specific time limit for repentant United Irishmen to deliver their material to the nominated depots at Bray, Dunlavin, Newtownmountkennedy, Hacketstown, Baltinglass and Blessington.[271] The success of the whole scheme was jeopardized from the outset by

Hardy who mounted a concerted drive to uncover arms caches before the proclamation had been widely circulated. Indeed, far from offering the typical seven to ten days truce, Hardy had merely suspended his activity in consequence of the proclamation until the evening of 14 May. He also threatened to recommence the search 'with increas[e]d assiduity and where necessary with rigid severity' just two days later if it elicited an unsatisfactory response.[272]

Hardy was perhaps somewhat dismissive of Craig's orders as he was preoccupied from 10 May with the management of an overture from rebels in the Baltinglass area which had been received against a background of horror just over the border in eastern Kildare. At this stage the main thrust of the general search had not begun but roving parties of militia and yeomen, such as those which burned Holt's farm that day and sacked Ballymanus House on 8 May, were out in force. Most magistrates in west Wicklow at that time had issued certificates of protection without receiving either arms or full confessions and William Hume, Henry Harrington, Morley Saunders and High Sheriff Walter Bagnal Carroll were strongly criticised for such leniency and 'whiggism'.[273] Hardy, after consultation with O'Neil Stratford, and backed by their extremist allies Revd Robinson and Captain Ryves, had determined that all surrendering rebels must answer questions regarding their outstanding comrades and confess their seditious activities. House burners and killers would not be considered under any circumstances by O'Neil Stratford's clique even though General Craig's public notice had been deliberately vague on such categories of crime.[274]

It was possibly information imparted by suspects in the hands of conservative magistrates that prompted Ryves to move against senior United Irishmen in Stratford-on-Slaney on 15 May when he arrested James Fox, Roger McGuire and Laurence Doyle from whom more 'good information' was obtained.[275] All three had been identified along with Pierse Hayden, James Doyle and other prominent rebels in the Stratford/Ballitore as early as 9 May but action against them may have been deferred until Craig's anticipated ultimatum had expired and more rigorous treatment could be meted out legally. The seizures were certainly well planned and were carried out by the politically reliable Dunlavin yeomen in preference to the distrusted local units. Hayden of Ballyhooke was also arrested in mid-May and during an interview with Hardy admitted being 'secretary to several parishes and an officer of considerable rank', claims which indicated that he was a baronial committeeman and an elected colonel.[276]

The loss of the baronial-level United Irish officers was a serious blow to the Talbotstown organization which evidently unsettled some of the rank and file. Pikes were suddenly abandoned in unprecedented quantities. Weapons were left anonymously during the night at Robinson's residence in Knockrigg, around 200 more were left in the Grange Con garden of the moderate Harrington and a further 300 were found in the Baltinglass area. The dumping of so many weapons without detection by an alerted military would have required careful planning which points to the existence of a localized, if not a unit policy, to react to the arrests in this manner. The militancy of the Talbotstown rebels, however, had only been temporarily deflated as their actions were to show only two weeks later when the rebellion broke out. Hardy had made considerable progress in recovering arms but was denied a mass surrender and could not have granted many protections.[277]

Pressure was also being felt by the United Irishmen of north-east Wicklow who had to contend with the murderous activities of the Ancient Britons and Romney Horse. Edwards was contacted on 15 May by men who claiming to represent the Powerscourt United Irishmen who asserted that they were 'ready to surrender'. This development pertained to the district under the jurisdiction of Monck and Colthurst although Hardy, with characteristic implacability, refused to allow a twenty-four hour truce to effect the disarming. By that date news of the house-burning and dragooning of the previous day in Newcastle and Arklow would have spread across most of Wicklow unnerving many United Irishmen who were not in a position to properly evaluate the level of threat. The 'general resolution to surrender' of the Powerscourt United Irishmen was conditional on an understanding that the applicants would not be compelled to give information and would receive pardons. Hardy's obstinacy was disregarded by Edwards who, accompanied only by his son, First Lieutenant in his reorganized corps, went into the mountains and distributed fifty protections regardless of whether arms were given up. Edwards had, no doubt, been chosen by the Rathdown rebels as the most suitable magistrate to approach as neither Monck nor Powerscourt would have countenanced such terms. Many of the United Irishmen did surrender weapons and Edwards was satisfied, perhaps naively, that the remainder 'never had any'.[278]

His actions were governed by principle and interpretation of the law and not from weakness. This is suggested by his refusal of protections to rebel officers whom he deemed to have 'brought this misery upon the ignorant peasantry'. This defiance infuriated Hardy who invoked his powers under the Insurrection Act to temporarily remove the Bray Infantry from permanent duty while instructing Captain John Armstrong of the King's County Militia to supersede Edwards' authority in civil affairs in Bray. Yet, the fifty United Irishmen who had sought terms comprised the largest group of its kind to come forward in Wicklow and their overture was symptomatic of the partial breakdown of the conspiracy in that sector.[279] While Hardy quibbled over 'two or three temporising magistrates' who had granted protections without receiving arms, his troops were, in many cases, running amok. The unchallenged primacy of the army, scattered as it was in small mixed detachments across the country, militated against the practice of restraint and conciliation when they were faced with armed insurgents. The junior officers and non-commissioned officers who generally commanded in isolated communities fulfilled what they perceived as their duty in the knowledge that results and not methods would be examined.[280]

Loyalist writers and historians subsequently attempted to suppress details of pro-government atrocities in Wicklow and elsewhere. Henry Lambart Bayly, whose father was an 'active' magistrate in 1798, insisted that no 'unnecessary or wanton severity' had occurred in the Arklow area and that 'no instance of provoked or aggravated oppression or torture was practised by the magistrates'. This was not the case and Bayly used this dishonest premise to support the weak argument that such moderation had deterred all but a 'few' Arklowmen from insurgent activity.[281] In fact, the strategic importance of Arklow was obvious to the loyalists well before Anthony Perry of Inch, described by Arklow postmaster John Kidd as 'the King of the [Gorey] United Men', was compelled under torture to reveal details of the close liaison between the town and the north-Wexford rebels. Perry was arrested on 21 May and forced to implicate Matthew Doyle and other important Wicklow rebels just prior to the insurrection.[282] The southern route to Dublin was accordingly safeguarded by particularly strong exertions of loyalists who applied themselves with zeal in the stronghold of the Orange Order. Indeed, in May 1798 Hardy had found it necessary to replace Captain William West of the Wicklow Infantry with First Lieutenant Thomas Keogh on account of his 'cruelty and torture'.[283]

Miles Byrne recalled that the rebel families in the Arklow area had 'suffered the most cruel tortures and persecutions' which had began in earnest in early May 1798 and intensified until the rebellion commenced.[284] On 7 May the enterprising Revd McGhee set in train one incident with far reaching repercussions when he accompanied a patrol of Antrim militiamen from Hacketstown to the house of a man suspected of conducting a 'treasonable correspondence' with Garret Byrne of Ballymanus. Papers were found which revealed Byrne's secret lodgings to be with the widow Caulfield in Booterstown and the find was undoubtedly the premise used by the Tinahely yeomen to raid Ballymanus House the following day.[285] The mansion was badly vandalized during the search by the yeomen who earned the enmity of the Wicklow rebels for their action and in so doing contributed towards the sacking of their home town by the rebels the following month. A few days later James Moreton, Captain of Tinahely Infantry, had two villagers 'flogged' with 'the others looking on' until they led him to where their weapons were hidden and made statements implicating pike makers and rebel organizers. Weapons were uncovered in Coolkenna, Carnew and Coolattin by such means and the people appeared to Moreton as 'the most humble creatures alive'.[286]

Captain Alexander Carroll of the Wicklow Town Cavalry and Cornet Archibald Paxton of the Ancient Britons also practised discriminate severity by burning several houses at Munduffe (Ballydonnell) on 14 May when a proclamation had expired without the desired effect. A claim by Carroll's niece that 'thousands' of pikes and firearms had been brought in before the following evening was an exaggeration, but the recourse to coercion of this nature was a watershed for the United Irishmen who were forced to concede part of their equipment.[287] Charles Byrne of Ballyrogan, who captained the United Irishmen of the parish of Redcross where the burnings had taken place, personally delivered 400 cartridges to Carroll. He recognized the need to alleviate pressure on the republicans and claimed when on trial for his life that 'numbers were in the utmost danger and terror of death both from the army and the United Irishmen'.[288] One of those made an example of at Munduffe was a man named McKitt who was also sentenced to transportation under the Insurrection Act. Luke Kelly and William Pluck of Ballycullen (Rathnew) were also burned out in Newcastle on the same day, probably by a different party responding to the same proclamation, and such activity is likely to have occurred on a small scale in every parish in Wicklow. Pluck was probably the rebel officer of that name who fought with Holt in the autumn of 1798 and a member of the family who gave their name to Ballycullen's 'Pluck's field'.[289]

House-burning was not as prevalent before the rebellion as popularly believed but it was deemed both justifiable and a highly effective tactic by most army commanders. Hardy certainly opposed burning houses for what he considered vindictive or reprisal purposes, but there is no evidence that he took pains to prevent his officers enforcing government directives by such means. In Athy Colonel Campbell was very satisfied with the results of 'burning a few houses' coupled with bouts of 'moderate flogging' in the Athy district.[290] Large numbers of suspects, generally rank-and-file rebels, were arrested in early May and James Moreton's brother William observed with satisfaction that all but two of the men tried and acquitted at the March assizes on the information of Cooper were known to be rebels by 22 May. William Wainwright was shocked on returning from Dublin on 26 May to discover that Moreton and Cope had dispatched twenty-one black-smiths and rebel 'principals' to New Geneva barracks in Waterford for transportation to New South Wales. All were detained in Carnew goal as the outbreak of rebellion prevented their safe passage to the convict depot through Wexford.[291]

They joined the 'many more' prisoners crowded into the village's guardhouse and brutal counter-insurgent tactics were carried out throughout southern Wicklow.[292] Shannon heard that in Wicklow 'in cases where the man of the house has fled, they whip the children and the ladies on their naked posteriors, and this *mild* punishment has pro-duced more pikes *etc* than any other expedient yet put in practice'.[293] Matthew Doyle's family were reputedly subjected to ill-treatment after he was forced into hiding and Miles Byrne maintained that the Wicklowman's home was 'one of the first in the county where the soldiers were let loose on free quarters'.[294] One of those re-arrested in mid-May was William Young of Ballinacor while Arklow's Thomas Murray of Sheepwalk had pre-empted this fate on the 21st by volun-teering a detailed statement of the utmost importance to Revd Bayly, Thomas Atkins and Thomas King. The trio were the leading members of an intelligence committee which received a series of depositions from high ranking United Irish officers, including Captains Simon Beakey of Ballysallagh and John Murray of Maghermore. Murray and Beakey threw much light on rebel organization in Arklow barony and Wicklow Town between 21 and 25 May 1798 and the content and style of the confessions differs greatly to the remainder of the depositions taken by Bayly alone. This reflects not only the calibre of the deponents but also perhaps the sectarian vision of Bayly.[295]

The arrest of key personnel severely retarded the ability of the United Irishmen to function in accordance with their constitutional regulations. It also demoralized those who had elected them to office and it appears that 'vast multitudes' took the oath of allegiance in the Arklow area in the week preceding the insurrection.[296] The appearance of disintegration in the United Irish leadership in the county was probably heightened by the mysterious absence of Garret Byrne of Ballymanus who had fled to Dublin in early February. This was premature as it was only on the very eve of the insurrection that Hardy obtained positive proof that he was 'deeply implicated'.[297] The holding of elections to fill leadership vacancies was complicated by the tense climate of security. That Murray of Sheepwalk was elected captain by only four sergeants signifies that coercion had rendered the society incapable to honouring its democratic principles.[298]

By 31 May, Hardy variously estimated that he had collected between 700 and 1,300 firearms and 4,000–4,500 pikes of the 8,000 believed to have been made in Wicklow. The figure of 1,300 guns almost certainly included those taken from loyalists and compares with an estimated 4,000 pikes and 3,000 guns recovered in Kildare by General Dundas. Wickham inferred by such positive reports that the 'deluded persons are delivering up their captains and colonels' in Wicklow, Kildare and Tipperary.[299] According to Hardy, information was being received in Wicklow 'faster than the magistrates can take it down' and the haemorrhaging of letters to the Castle, sometimes more than one per day from the same correspondent, attests to widespread recognition that a breakthrough had been achieved.[300] The intelligence obtained by Hardy convinced him that 'all hope is fled' from the conspirators and that their leaders were fleeing their homes to avoid arrest. With whole units, 'partys [sic] of 12', allegedly bringing in their pikes, and blacksmiths naming those for whom they had made weapons, Hardy had reason to be optimistic.[301] There is no doubt but that the United Irishmen in Wicklow suffered a serious setback in April/May 1798 under the weight of martial law but those who believed the 'United business' was 'at an end' were to receive a rude shock.[302]

A statement of the Rathdown defector James Ryan gave a very different impression as to the state of United Irish morale. Ryan had been a major figure in the creation of military structures in late 1797, but on 20 May 1798 he sent an intermediary to Lord Powerscourt to enquire as to what terms of capitulation were available to him as the rebels in his area were apparently 'bent on turning out' and he was 'afraid to fight'.[303] This was the same district in which Edwards had issued over fifty protections the previous week, a circumstance which indicates that the resolve of many Rathdown United Irishmen had not actually diminished. None of the eighty-five pikes possessed by Thomas Miller's Powerscourt company were surrendered prior to the rebellion and many Rathdown men who rallied at Blackmore Hill camp in late May had allegedly 'given up their pikes and arms before'. Consequently, the equation made by the magistracy between weapons surrendered and the operational strength of the insurgents was invalid and under-estimated the resilience of the organisation.[304] When addressing a House of Lords secret committee into the origins of the rebellion in 1799, Thomas Addis Emmet referred to the tensions caused in the Leinster United Irish forces by 'the free quarters, the house burnings, the tortures and the military executions' in Wicklow, Kildare and Carlow. Repression intimidated some but steeled the most extreme and dedicated elements to strike back.[305]

Moreover, arms-raiding continued throughout the crackdown and on 18 May a large group of United Irishmen besieged the home of one Finnamore of Ballyward near Blessington for four hours until he handed over two guns. He was a large cattle farmer who in July 1798 lost almost eighty head to Holt's rebels. The same group behind the May attack had the audacity to break into Downshire's mansion some time after two in the morning while its resident guard were absent drinking in Blessington. Tokens of repentance were only that and did not result from any re-evaluation of ideology. Byrne of Ballyrogan, whose presentation to Carroll of a large quantity of munitions must have been viewed by loyalists as a signal success, rallied his men the following week and fought at their head throughout the campaign in north Wexford.[306]

Loyalist fears of the pervasiveness of sedition in the yeomanry appeared to be realized in early May when long held suspicions about several corps in west Wicklow and east Kildare with significant Catholic personnel were proven correct. Informers in Stratford named Dr Johnson of Ballitore, a constable and member of Aldborough yeomanry as 'the *father* of the United men of Ballitore' and neighbouring parts of Wicklow.[307] In the first week of May the Castledermot yeomanry were 'completely scattered' when twelve men were arrested for seditious activity and another twelve fled from justice.[308] Dozens of men who had enrolled in the Aldborough corps and Colonel Keating's Narraghmore Cavalry were taken into custody and imprisoned in Dunlavin and Naas. Both corps were disarmed and disbanded with the Narraghmore prisoners being escorted to Naas gaol by the Wicklow Militia who whipped them upon arrival. Mary Leadbeater saw six members of the Narraghmore corps being taken to Dunlavin 'with their coats turned inside out' as a mark of disgrace.[309] Those in Dunlavin were joined on 22 May by over twenty members of Morley Saunders' Ballynacrow and Tuckmill (Saundersgrove) infantry who, according to one loyalist commentator, comprised a 'hellish group of Republican assassins' and had plotted to kill their captain.[310]

On 20 May Saunders had caved in to pressure from Robinson, Hardy and other hardliners who suspected that his corps was disaffected by imploring the infiltrators to come forward and receive protections. That no response was received was attributed to the work of Corporal James Dunne, a rebel organizer, who had allegedly discouraged confessions. Dunne, however, had drawn attention to himself and when arrested the following day by the Wicklow Militia implicated four men. During a second parade on 22 May a further twenty yeomen were either bluffed into admissions of disaffection or resolved to do so and were conveyed to Dunlavin gaol by the Wicklow Militia, Baltinglass Cavalry and a troop of the New Romney fencibles whose presence indicates that arrests had been anticipated. That O'Neil Stratford had previously informed Saunders that most of his men and servants were disaffected suggests reliable information had been obtained in the wake of the first parade.[311]

The likely source of this intelligence was Dunne who, on or before 9 May, had apparently given Saunders 'the first information' of William Putnam McCabe's activities in the Stratford district. The cumulative weight of information regarding the infiltration of the Saundersgrove corps was considerable and evidently included disclosures by Dunne, George Wright, Joe Hawkins and Pat Moran.[312] Dunne clearly betrayed those he had suborned or knew to be United Irishmen and the fact that he escaped the fate of his erstwhile comrades points to co-operation. He certainly aroused the anger of the rebel forces attached to Captain James Doyle of Ballinacor who burned his home during the rebellion. Ryves sentenced Dunne to transportation under the Insurrection Act for illegal possession of firearms and had him re-arrested when he was released under the Amnesty Act in late 1798. Dunne was consequently sent out to New South Wales on the *Anne* in 1801 where he spent the remainder of his life.[313] The materialization of such an extensive fifth column in Dunlavin after the mass dismissal of Catholic yeomen and dismissal of several corps must have fuelled the paranoia and extremism that informed many decisions taken by government forces in Wicklow at the end of May. One of the most tragic resolutions was the order to massacre the inmates of Dunlavin guardhouse on 24 May, none of whom had engaged in armed subversion.[314]

In January 1798 the numerical strength of the Wicklow United Irishmen was 12,800 which, when broken down to baronial level, was expressed in rounded figures divisible by 120. A delegate of the Dublin leadership was sent into Wicklow and Wexford that month to meet the county committee men and to obtain reliable returns of their men. He reported the figure 9,666 for Wicklow which had evidently increased by the time the county committee prepared formal returns for the Leinster committee. The only part of the county not composed of the 120-man units was the barony of Talbotstown, then the only sector under martial law, which had evidently had not completed restructuring its societies in the military format. By May 1798, however, there were 14,000 rebels in Wicklow which gave the county the largest total of any in Leinster even though it amounted to only a small increase on the pre-martial law figure.[315] This small accretion supports Thomas Murray's claim that 'very few' had been enrolled in Arklow barony after January 1798 and that not all of them were armed. Yet if the figure of 14,000 was accurately reported it must have been close to the maximum feasible strength of the county force when military age, infirmity and a relatively large resident loyalist community were accounted for. A force of this size should have warranted 120 captains and 12 colonels and in some documents these theoretical totals are included.[316] Arklow's Captain John Murray of Magheramore estimated there were 12,000 rebels in the county on the eve of rebellion of whom 'most had arms', notwithstanding the ferocity of Hardy's endeavour to disarm the movement.[317]

The full effect of coercion on Wicklow's fighting strength is impossible to gauge and there were certainly not 14,000 United Irishmen ready for action in late May 1798. Few units could have remained totally undisturbed by martial law and every baronial sector lost one or more of their county committee representatives, as well as part of their junior officer cadre and large quantities of munitions. Quite apart from the paralyzing effect of the arrest or defection of key leaders, many otherwise intact companies were deprived of their officers who had gone into hiding during the very week in which orders had come from Dublin to rise. The cell structure, which held up reasonably well to coercion due to its inherently secretive nature, was not well suited to re-establishing a chain of command. Communications with other disrupted units was, therefore, often difficult and this resulted in mobilization problems in late May.[318]

While not an elected officer, Michael Dwyer was an important pre-rebellion organizer whose identity would have been widely known as a consequence in parts of Talbotstown and Ballinacor North. The arrests of Imaal leaders Peter Hayden of Boleycarrigeen, Peter Burr and John Dwyer of Seskin and the co-operation with the authorities by James Fox and perhaps other Stratford committee men destroyed the hub of the baronial network. Michael Dwyer was not arrested with them in April/May 1798 as his relatively junior position had shielded him from the magistracy and it was not until the week preceding the rebellion that he was forced to go into hiding on Lugnaquillia mountain. Martin Burke of Donoughmore, another important rebel from Imaal, also remained at large and took part in the battle of Stratford on 24 May. Dwyer, isolated at Lugnaquillia, seemed unaware that rebel camps were being formed along the borders of Wicklow, Kildare and Dublin when he began his trek to Wexford on 29 May.[319]

Reports in Dublin of the ongoing military operations in Leinster convinced the city's leadership that it was necessary to bolster the resolve of their rural comrades lest irreversible damage be inflicted on the organization. Emissaries were dispatched in late May who argued that 'surrendering the arms will not gain a man protection, and only expose him'. Preliminary instructions on the codes and signals for mobilization were probably also imparted together with general orders.[320] There were grounds for supporting assertions of bad faith on the part of the authorities. Sixty-year-old Dennis Farrell of Redcross handed over his pike on 16 May only to be arrested three days later and imprisoned in Wicklow gaol. Two members of the McDonald family of Lemonstown near Dunlavin fared much worse and were shot dead by a party of Ancient Britons who elected to ignore the protections issued to them by Captain Ryves. These incidents can only have undermined confidence in the conditional pardons and discouraged the surrender of weapons. In the autumn of 1798 hundreds of men who had retired from the United Irishmen returned to fight in the mountains when persecuted.[321] Miles Byrne recalled that, in mid-May 1798, owing to the terrors and strain of coercion, 'everyone considered himself as walking on a mine ready to be blown up, and all sighed for orders to begin'.[322] The Wicklowmen were reputedly 'much disheartened by [the] loss of arms but desperate by this loss and by disappointment' would rise as planned.[323]

The prospect of mass defections from sympathetic militiamen was probably an important factor in disposing the United Irishmen to attempt a revolt. According to Thomas Murray, the Wicklow insurgents approached rebellion confident in the knowledge that a 'great part of the army [was] dissatisfied' and upon their defection to the United Irishmen would face 'little opposition'. Some militia regiments were expected to defect *en masse* and while no whole formations went over to the rebels in 1798, hundreds of individuals and small groups did so. This danger had been foreseen by the government in 1797 when militia regiments were forbidden to recruit in the counties in which they were stationed, an embargo which was disregarded by the Antrim and King's County Militia in Wicklow.[324] Defender and then United Irish cells within the militia had been cultivated from the early 1790s and by 1798 they were viewed as an alternative to French troops. The location of Lehaunstown Camp on Wicklow's borders from May 1795 ensured that the matter of republican soldiers was highly pertinent. The first serious problems had come to light in June 1797 when two members of the Kildare Militia based in the camp were taken to the Phoenix Park, Dublin, for execution in front of the entire Lehaunstown reserve. A city yeomanry patrol later disturbed a 'patriotic wake' for one of the men in Mary's Lane held by the Dublin United Irishmen.[325]

There was a great deal of contact between soldiers and the inhabitants of the surrounding towns and 163 children born to soldiers based in Lehaunstown were baptized in Bray between 1795 and 1798. Social interaction was also fostered by the market held in the camp every Monday which must have facilitated seditious activity. In October 1797 sentries were given 'strictest orders . . . not on any account to permit any pedlars or beggars to enter the gates of the encampment'.[326] In summer the market and the spectacle of the vast camp attracted visitors from Dublin who thronged the Bray road every Sunday, among them people described as:

> the lowest of the *Bourgeois* from the purlieus of Thomas-street, Smithfield, and Stony-batter, trundled hither on coal-porters' cars, half roasted with the heat of the day, and almost smothered in clouds of dust . . . every hack horse, mule, or ass, that could be procured for hire, joined in the cavalcade.[327]

The camp was visited by senior Dublin United Irishmen Valentine Lawless and William Sampson who allegedly handed out 'a quantity of ultra-nationalist ballads, tracts, and essays amongst the soldiery'. The first meeting between Sampson and Kildare rebel leader William Aylmer had taken place at Lehaunstown during this visit where Aylmer was stationed as a lieutenant of the Kildare Militia. Lawless, who had served as a member of the Rathdown Association with Edwards of Bray, drew back from the conspiracy and was created Lord Cloncurry.[328] Not only did rebels seek out converts in the camp but regiments such as the Clare Militia were deemed to have 'promoted sedition to a great degree' in the locality. Three quarters of the Donegal regiment were suspected of sympathizing with the United Irishmen, as were twelve of the sixty Devonshire Fencibles who passed through the county.[329]

The likelihood of defections on the scale envisaged by the United Irishmen had, however, disappeared by 1798 with the sustained crack-down on subversion within the armed forces the previous year. Disaffection in the summer of 1797 had been rife and resulted in the critical mutinies in the Royal Navy's fleets at Spithead and the Nore in which United Irish agents had played a part. Blaris camp outside Belfast was targeted for intrigue by the Ulster committee of United Irishmen and an alliance was forged with existing Defender cells among the 4,000 troops at the camp. Disaffection, real or alleged, affected all parts of Ireland and was not confined to regiments composed of Irishmen. The Scottish Breadalbane fencibles were accused of training the United Irishmen of Ballinahinch in the use of firearms in April 1797. The socially prominent Captain John St Leger of the 24th Dragoons was a senior United Irishman in Armagh and was supported by rebel subscriptions when imprisoned in May 1797. He was transported to New South Wales in 1799.[330]

In May 1797 carefully contrived investigations and court martials had all but eliminated the threat by executing the ringleaders of the Monaghan Militia and flogging seventy of their converts. By the time the Monaghans were stationed in Wicklow in 1799, one of their principal officers was known as 'Orange Col[onel John] Kerr', a reputation redeemed in part by the role of the Monaghans in the destruction of the *Northern Star* presses.[331] Similar measures country-wide removed the likelihood of widespread mutiny and it is ironic that the executions of the four men at Blaris, which signalled the demise of mass sedition, served as recruiting propaganda in Wicklow for the rebels that the militia would forsake.[332] The delusion that a latent reserve existed probably sustained many Wicklow rebels shaken by Hardy's repression and encouraged perseverance in a time of despair. The United Irish executive in Dublin, dominated by Lord Edward Fitzgerald after the Bond arrests in March, and Samuel Neilson after Fitzgerald's arrest on 19 May, became convinced that the militia pro-vided the means to attempt an insurrection. Time was of the essence as the military capacity of the movement was threatened with severe damage by coercion. The date for the rising in Leinster and Munster was accordingly fixed for 23 May 1798, although it seems that at one point it was planned for Ulster to revolt two days earlier to force the government to commit its reserves. An Ulster feint would have left only those troops in the vicinity of Dublin capable of rapidly counter-attacking rebel-held areas. Tying these troops down was the probably the responsibility of the Wicklowmen and their comrades in Kildare and Meath.[333]

The Wicklow United Irishmen entertained great hopes of the King's County Militia who were deemed particularly amenable to their politics. The regiment was the focus of the plan developed by Cork-born barristers Henry and John Sheares, who were closely associated with, if not members of, the movement's executive after the Bond arrests. On 10 May 1798 John Sheares made an ill-advised approach to Captain John Warneford Armstrong of the King's County Militia whom he had mistaken for a radical. Armstrong, it was hoped, would use his position to foster an even greater United Irish influence in his regiment and the camp as a whole. He claimed at the trial of the Sheares that he was entreated 'for the purpose of bringing about the soldiers . . . to endeavour to practice upon the non-commissioned officers and privates who were of the Roman Catholic religion, as they were most likely to think themselves aggrieved'. They also discussed the strength and disposition of the troops at Lehaunstown and whether or not the camp could be captured internally or by an external assault.[334]

The defection of the militia coupled with the seizure of artillery at Chapelizod barracks was deemed sufficient to bring about the fall of Dublin. The Sheares brothers were so confident of support within the militia that they believed the defectors could capture Dublin city without assistance from the capital's sizeable force of United Irishmen.[335] A spy at a rebel meeting at Lucan on 20 May 1798 learned that

> a plan was fixed upon for an insurrection [in] the course of a few days [and] that the camp at Loughlinstown was to be first attacked in the night that half an hour afterwards the artillery was to be attacked at Chapelizod when the parties were to march to town & the general attack on the castle & city were to take place. That they were to be joined by the King's county regiment at the [Loughlinstown] camp.[336]

However, the arrest of the Sheares brothers on 21 May could only have discouraged the remaining leaders from implementing their plan and it seems that the Corkonians' influence in the movement had already waned.[337]

The basic and most obvious plan was for the counties adjoining Dublin city to mobilize on 23 May in support of a revolt in the city itself and spymaster Samuel Sproule reported accurately to Dublin Castle on 17 May that the rising was planned for the 23/24 May. He alleged it was to 'begin in the North 2 days previous in order to draw off the forces from Dublin the horse particularly. That done Wicklow join in 14 thousand men, Kildare 11, county of Dublin about 10 city the same in all 45 thousand. The city is the object and the cash in the bank chiefly'.[338] The Leinster men and whatever sympathetic militia were available were to prevent the city being reinforced by the army reserves until it was completely controlled by internal rebels. Messages would then be sent to the United Irishmen of other parts of Ireland. A numerically strong organization existed in Cork and other parts of Munster in which John Sheares played a role in preparations for the rising, as did William Michael Byrne and Richard Dry.[339]

It was evident to all informed observers in the days preceding the 23rd that the tempo of coercion and sedition was accelerating towards a crescendo. On 19 May Sproule reported that the Leinster delegates had just received 'full instructions' for the rising and estimated that three emissaries a day were travelling through Wicklow urging the rebels to resist martial law.[340] The need to bolster wavering rebel leaders and their forces was most evident in the days and hours preceding the outbreak of hostilities. On 23 May Neilson was proclaimed a fugitive and was arrested later that night while attempting to rescue Lord Edward Fitzgerald from Newgate. The militant Kildare Colonel Michael Reynolds of Naas was also proclaimed, as was Edward Rattigan, an associate of Fitzgerald's and a United Irish colonel.[341] News of this kind raised the spectre of imminent collapse and underlined the usefulness of the efforts of city emissaries to shore up the resolve and confidence of cadres in the crucial counties adjacent to Dublin. Their task was growing more difficult with every passing day and on the morning of 23 May, four Wicklow United Irish captains, including Jeremiah Delamere and James Ryan of Powerscourt, were brought to Dublin as prisoners.[342] O'Neil Stratford also noted that day that men whom he suspected to be members of the Wicklow county committee were absent in the city attending the 'day expected for rising there' clearly oblivious of the fact that he was writing on that very day.[343]

Earlier on the 23rd at least two heavily armed Dublin emissaries had travelled through Wicklow and Kildare issuing orders for the United Irishmen to rise 'immediately'.[344] The government only received a few hours warning of the imminence of insurrection and that the detention of the mail coaches had been settled upon as the signal to rise in those rural areas which had not been contacted by couriers. It was consequently impossible for Camden to apprize all the garrisons in Kildare, Meath and Wicklow that attacks were to be anticipated and neither Hardy nor Campbell seem to have been aware of the danger. Hardy, in fact, had not been disabused of his conviction that his arms drives had crippled the Wicklow organization until the first assaults had been repulsed from his outposts.[345] City dwellers were less convinced and for some nights prior to 23 May 1798 had been disturbed by the mysterious fires in the Dublin mountains, most of which had probably been set by fugitives from the martial law.[346] Just prior to the insurrection it was discovered that a Newmarket brewer had been sending munitions to the Rathfarnham United Irishmen concealed in ale casks and on the night of the rising two cart loads of pikes were distributed. There were other indications that something was afoot and orangeman James Verner was convinced that on the night of 19/20 May that 'not less than 15,000 persons from Kildare & Wicklow' were concealed in Dublin. Although mistaken, Verner's assertion anticipated the actual plan of the Leinster rebels and as such was probably derived from a genuine instruction issued by a United Irish emissary.[347]

The first genuine threat to the capital occurred on the night of 23 May 1798 when around 500 United Irishmen gathered above Rathfarnham in the foothills of the Dublin mountains. They were led by two United Irish members of the Rathfarnham Cavalry, Ledwich and Wade, and comprised one of several bodies which assembled in Tallaght, Rathcoole, Dalkey and elsewhere. They initially held themselves in readiness to interact with the city rebels and most dispersed without incident when it became clear that matters had not gone according to plan in the capital.[348] Thomas Foy, who lived at Grange near Rathfarnham village, claimed in 1799 that on 23 May 1798 he had gone

> . . . out with a large party [of rebels] about 1600 towards Crumlin to beset Dublin and left 1800 to beset Laughlinstown [sic] camp . . . his party met a few of the 5th dragoons on whom they fired and not hearing of the party having succeeded at Laughlinstown pris[one]r and his party march[e]d towards Clonee [sic] they were there met by some of the Bloody Fermanagh [Militia] and went towards Taragh [sic] Hill [County Meath].

If Foy's recollections were accurate it would appear that the Rathfarnham rebels knew of an intended attempt on Lehaunstown and that both attacks had faltered due to the inactivity of their Dublin comrades whose support was deemed essential to act elsewhere.[349]

The city of Dublin men were prevented from mobilizing by the yeomanry who had turned out in force and at short notice to occupy every suitable site.[350] Watty Cox recalled that around nine o'clock on the night of 23 May 'a very busy and extensive range of preparation took place in Dublin and its vicinity', including a briefing by senior figures to their men in Abbey Street.[351] Samuel Neilson had given final instructions to his subordinates in a meeting at Church Lane. They subsequently gathered their forces, retrieved their weapons from hides and moved towards pre-arranged objectives and mobilization points. It had been intended to mount a wave of attacks at ten o'clock but this was hastily cancelled when it was discovered that the yeomanry, at one or two hours notice from an informer, were in possession of the predesignated rallying sites.[352] Unable to mass in numbers sufficient to overcome an alerted garrison, thousands of city rebels abandoned their weapons in the streets and returned home. One city correspondent claimed that '10,000 stand of arms' were recovered on the morning of the 24th and that some 500 pikes had been found in Bridgefoot Street alone. The United Irish plan for a general rising centred on Dublin was necessarily postponed but it was not altogether abandoned. Numerous attempts were made during the summer and autumn of 1798 to implement versions of the May strategy even though the rebellion had nonetheless begun in Kildare and had taken an unpredictable course.[353]

The Rathfarnham rebels were ignorant of the fatal setback which had befallen the city plans and had moved tentatively towards the alerted garrison of Clondalkin expecting to encounter other groups of comrades. It became apparent upon reaching the outskirts of Clondalkin that the city had not risen and a decision was taken to disperse in two bodies. One was attacked at Fox and Geese when falling back on the mountains by Lord Roden at the head of a force of Rathfarnham yeomen cavalry and 5th Dragoons. The ad hoc patrol included Colonel Richard Puleston of the Ancient Britons and did not totally defeat their opponents. Roden was fortunate to survive a pistol shot to the head which penetrated his helmet without injuring him. Ledwich and Wade were captured, one of whom courageously volunteered 'false information' which confused the dragoons and possibly inhibited them from pursuing the rebels with greater vigour.[354]

The rebels suffered the loss of several men and prisoners but most managed to effect their escape to the comparative safety of the mountains while the second column, which included a small group of Wicklowmen from Ballinacor, moved on towards Meath.[355]

The detention of the Munster mail near Naas alerted insurgents along its route to the south that the anticipated order to turn out had been given. Mary Leadbeater recalled that the detention of the mail coach in Naas and its failure to arrive in Ballitore 'persuaded the people that the day was their own. They threw off the appearance of loyalty and rose in avowed rebellion.' Pakenham has shown that the timing and location of the insurrection was directly linked to the non-arrival of the mail.[356] They may also have been encouraged by the premature circulation of a proclamation prepared by the Sheares brothers announcing the fall of Dublin which was intended to bolster the rebels outside the capital in the event of an early success. It is clear, however, that the thousands of Kildaremen who rose were unaware that the Dubliners had failed to strike, that the Ulster leadership were prevaricating and that the interception of the vital Limerick and Cork mails had been bungled. They surged into Prosperous, Clane and Old Kilcullen and inflicted many casualties on their garrisons but the key objective of Naas town did not fall when attacked by 3,000 rebels under Michael Reynolds and Michael Murphy.[357]

Lieutenant-General Sir Ralph Dundas was disconcerted by the ferocity of the attacks which had mauled his smaller outposts and while checking their advance towards Dublin at Kilcullen Bridge ordered the county garrisons to fall back on Naas. This ceded both territory and initiative to the rebels and the Tyrone Militia detachment which abandoned Ballitore was ambushed on the Narraghmore road. Malachy Delaney, one of the principal agents of the Leinster directory in southern Kildare and west Wicklow, made his appearance soon afterwards at the head of 300 rebels on a white horse. Ballitore, Narraghmore and Kilcullen fell into rebels hands on 24 May and the Wicklow rebels along the border were reputedly 'caught up [in] the enthusiasm' of their comrades in Kildare. On the night of 23 May and the early hours of 24 May insurrection took hold in Wicklow.

CHAPTER FOUR

'Liberty or death': Ballymore-Eustace to Ballygullen, 24 May–4 July 1798

During the early hours of 24 May 1798 the billets of Lieutenant John Beavor's garrison at Ballymore-Eustace were quietly infiltrated by scores of local United Irishmen. Beavor had arrived in the village on 10 May 1798 with 160 Armagh, Antrim and Tyrone Militia as well as a party of Ninth Dragoons to carry out a programme of freequarters. When 3,000 weapons had been collected, all but forty Tyrone Militia and dragoons were sent away although this small force was later supplemented by a party of Ancient Britons. When attacked seven troopers of the Ninth Dragoons were surprised and killed in their quarters and another five were wounded before the alarm was raised. The commotion in the streets alerted the remainder of the soldiery to the threat of annihilation who, once rallied, succeeding in driving the insurgents from the village with some difficulty. Five Tyrone militiamen were killed in the desperate fighting which ensued, including Lieutenant McFarland who had commanded the Ballymore detachment. The shocked survivors in the garrison took swift revenge by summarily executing twelve rebel prisoners, men who were presumably counted among the 'many' reportedly killed by the troops during their 'gallant stand'.[1]

According to Revd Charles Robinson the rebellion commenced in the borderland countryside around Dunlavin, Ballitore, Baltinglass, Stratford-on-Slaney and Castledermot at nine o'clock on the morning of 24 May. Robinson was horrified to witness 'men, women and children' appearing in arms and singing 'horrible' republican songs which threatened the loyalist community.[2] He had been attending Castledermot fair that morning when the crowds suddenly dispersed on hearing unfounded rumours that the insurgents had risen and taken Naas, Ballymore-Eustace and Dublin. Naas and Clane had withstood concerted assaults but Prosperous had fallen with the loss of about forty Ancient Britons and North Cork militiamen. On returning in haste to his Knockrigg residence the clergyman found it occupied by a 'vast number' of Wicklow rebels who had probably gathered to kill him or to retrieve the arms that they had surrendered to him in the course of the previous weeks. The rectory was already ablaze when Robinson appeared and he and his wife, who had been slightly wounded in the affray, were obliged to flee the site on horseback. On sighting the hated Robinson the local insurgents had immediately turned their attention towards him and pursued the mounted couple as far as the relative safety of Dunlavin. They were fired on four times during their flight.[3]

The rumours of victory in the capital and elsewhere in Leinster had strengthened the resolve of the United Irishmen in west Wicklow who began to congregate in several places. They collected whatever weapons were available in accordance with orders received from Dublin the previous week and in response to the incontrovertible evidence that the much anticipated rising had finally begun. Confusion and panic gripped the ill-informed rural loyalist population whose anxiety and sense of vulnerability could not have been allayed by the non-appearance of government forces in the first hours of the rebellion. The majority of mobilized yeomen and soldiers in the sector had then remained very close to, if not inside, the urban centres which they required for protection and had been ordered to hold. Loyalist discomfort may well have been misinterpreted by the insurgents as further evidence that the rising which had been predicted by the emissaries of the Dublin leadership had indeed occurred.

By midday on 24 May at least 400–500 insurgents had assembled in the vicinity of Stratford-on-Slaney and were biding their time to attack the town. Stratford had not been deemed a post of major strategic importance by the authorities and was lightly defended by thirty Antrim militiamen under Lieutenant Macauley, twenty Ninth Dragoons under the notorious Cornet Love and the town's locally recruited yeomanry. The rebels marched along the Baltinglass/Stratford road and were intercepted on the outskirts of the settlement by Love's troopers. The Stratford yeomanry reputedly lacked gun cotton and were forced to give ground until horse hair was substituted.[4] The disorganized and seemingly complacent insurgents could not exploit their numerical advantage owing to the confines of the narrow road and found it impossible to offer effective resistance against the highly motivated and well-armed cavalry regulars. Their headlong advance was abruptly halted outside Stratford, where they probably sustained their first casualties, and quickly became a panicked retreat towards Baltinglass. It was then that the already unsettled insurgents were attacked from the rear and routed with some loss by Captain O'Neil Stratford's corps. As the pro-government forces were numerically weak and did not have cannon at their disposal, it is unlikely that they inflicted more than a hundred fatalities, although non-combatants were among the dead. O'Neil Stratford and twenty of his men were wounded in the short clash but no loyalist fatalities were sustained.[5]

Traditional accounts typically viewed Stratford-on-Slaney as a 'wild and ill-conceived plan without leaders, order, or determination', an impression borne out to an extent by fact that the insurgents only managed to wound their assailants. Moreover, local rebels of the stature of Michael Dwyer were apparently unaware of the plan. Yet there were several rebel officers present whose primary failure was in properly deploying their relatively small number of men. Their plan of capturing Stratford was essentially logical in that success would have brought the surrounding district under rebel control and enabled a fuller mobilization of the rebels. Martin Burke, a close friend of Dwyer's and a leading rebel, fought his first engagement at Stratford as did Thomas Kavanagh of Talbotstown, one of the few original members of the Wicklow county committee of United Irishmen still at large. Kavanagh was also a member of the Baltinglass Cavalry with whom he served on the morning of the battle before defecting to the insurgents he was supposed to have led during the attack on Stratford. Kavanagh was arrested after the battle in the home of William and Rachael Valentine of Manger and summarily executed in Baltinglass. This led to reprisal attacks on the Valentines culminating in the murder of Rachael on 10 February 1799 and the burning of the house by Captain James Hughes' men.[6]

While many had been 'cut down without mercy' during the one-sided contest on the Baltinglass road, other compromised survivors managed to obtain generous terms of amnesty once the outcome had been settled. Hugh McClane lost his wife and brother-in-law in the mêlée and was captured, as was Valentine Case who received a shoulder wound but was afterwards liberated on the intercession of his employer Francis Greene of Greenville. The rebels were completely inexperienced on the 24th and had been deprived by martial law of many of their most active and capable leaders. They had approached Stratford buoyed by unsubstantiated reports of successes by their comrades in Dublin and Kildare which may have instilled an element of recklessness in their poorly executed attack.[7]

The garrison of Dunlavin, a few miles north of the fighting, stood ready on the morning of the 24th having gleaned that something untoward had taken place. The first inklings of danger had come early in the morning when Charles Doyle of Merginstown had arrived 'in a great fright' with the first reliable account of the previous night's attack on Ballymore-Eustace in which he had participated. This greatly alarmed Captains Saunders, Ryves and Richardson, who were then isolated in their village stronghold and incapable of assessing the extent of the threat they faced. Large bodies of rebels were sighted at a distance moving through the fields and hillsides around the town and the flames of what were presumed to be loyalist households they had burned were clearly visible. When a party of Ancient Britons arrived from Ballymore-Eustace with confirmation of the crisis and news of the deaths of many of their comrades it was decided to execute the prisoners confined in the guardhouse. The Welshmen probably belonged to the troop which had summarily executed a batch of rebel prisoners after the attempt on their garrison and had demonstrated their aggression by killing three members of the McDonald family at Lemonstown.[8]

At least seventeen disaffected Saundersgrove yeomen, fourteen Narraghmore men, four senior rebel prisoners and at about eight others were taken from the Market House prison, bound together on Dunlavin fair green and shot dead. An account by the daughter of Daniel Prendergast, the only man to survive, asserted:

> The unfortunates were marched from the market house to the fair green, on the rising ground above the little town. In a hollow on the north side, near the gate of the Roman Catholic chapel the victims were ranged, while a platoon of the Ancient Britons stood on the high ground on the south side of the green. They fired with fatal effect on the thirty-six men. All fell-dead and dying-amid the shrieks and groans of the bystanders, among whom were their widows and relatives.

In actuality, at least forty-three men were killed in Dunlavin on 24 May, including several who were executed in the Market House earlier in the day.[9]

The principal responsibility for the atrocity seems have lain with the extremist Captain Ryves whose assent would certainly have been required rather than that of Morley Saunders who commanded very little influence. Ryves had reputedly survived an assassination attempt on Uske Hill on the 23rd and on the morning of the massacre had led

MARKET-HOUSE OF DUNLAVIN,
COUNTY OF WICKLOW.

DUNLAVIN MARKET HOUSE *from Dublin Penny Journal, 26/12/1835*

a patrol to reconnoitre the 'numerous and desperate' rebels moving freely through the neighbourhood. He had apparently gained the impression that his hopelessly outnumbered garrison was vulnerable to internal attack from the prisoners even though none had previously managed to escape. Specific information had been obtained that Dunlavin was to be assaulted on the 24th, which must have seemed plausible in the light of that morning's attempt on Baltinglass only four miles distant. It was in this context that a consensus was reached to execute the prisoners by a group of officers who belonged to units that had been the foremost practitioners of torture and state terrorism in Wicklow for two months.[10]

The real purpose of the killings was apparently to avenge the friendly losses sustained at Ballymore-Eustace and to deter local republicans from attacking Dunlavin by a show of force. The reprisal mentality was already in evidence during the morning when four or more prisoners were hanged in the Market House and many others whipped. Captured rebel John Martin and the much persecuted smith Thomas Egan had extremely narrow escapes from the makeshift gallows. That twelve Aldborough or Narraghmore yeomanry prisoners were released ahead of the fairgreen shootings further suggests that

Ryves and his officers had agreed a policy on the 24th and were perhaps striving to create the sense of terror of which Hardy had approved in Kildare and west Wicklow the previous week. The cold-blooded and methodical manner with which the executions were carried out were certainly not the actions of a panic-stricken garrison. Whatever the initial motivation of the killings, the incident typified the callousness and inflexibility of the yeomanry who when invested with the power to police and coerce their communities proved in general to be incapable of practising the restraint necessary to defuse tension.[11]

The repercussions of the drastic decision were far-reaching and contributed to galvanizing the insurgent effort in north Wexford. The incident was mentioned as one of the justifications for the aberrant republican atrocity of Scullabogue where considerable numbers of loyalist prisoners were killed on 5 June. Of the local men shot, John Dwyer of Seskin, Peter Hayden of Killabeg and Laurence Doyle of Dunlavin were all high-ranking United Irishmen whose proselytizing and office would have made them known to a great many rebels in the barony of Talbotstown. Michael Dwyer, nephew to Dwyer of Seskin, was deeply affected by the killings which served to instill a desire for revenge which he had not satisfied in 1803.[12] Dunlavin was menaced later in the day of the massacre by 200–300 rebels who fled to the mountains when challenged by Captain Richardson's Light Company of the Wicklow Militia and the combined yeomanry of Baltinglass, Dunlavin and Hacketstown. In contrast to the senseless killings earlier in the day, many rebels were issued with certificates of protection. This moderation addressed the urgent need of the loyalists to reduce the numbers of active rebels even if the amount involved was insignificant and their sincerity doubtful.[13]

The first major battle fought in the west Wicklow region took place at Hacketstown on 25 May and while primarily the initiative of Carlow rebels was probably not without input from a Shillelagh contingent. Edward Byrne of Liscolman, a close relative of the Wicklow Byrnes of Parkhill and Ballymanus, led a force of 3,000–4,000 insurgents against the border town. He was a member of the Tullow yeomanry and later claimed to have fallen in with the rebel force 'on their march to Hacketstown'. His assertion to have joined them under duress is almost certainly false in view of the fact that he did not retire from the field until after 21 July 1798.[14] Lieutenant Gardiner of the Antrim Militia and Captain Thomas Hardy's Hacketstown yeoman infantry reconnoitered the rebels advancing towards their base and when the column drew near, launched a feint from a small hill to confuse them and slow their march. The soldiers then retreated to the relative safety of the town's stone barracks while Captain William Hoare Hume at the head of thirty of his Humewood Cavalry charged the thwarted rebels who broke and withdrew.[15]

Revd McGhee, orangeman and vicar of Clonmore, noted that a general pursuit ensued in which '300 of the miscreants' were killed, a wild overestimate that revealed more about the agitated state of mind of the loyalist forces than their performance against the rebels. McGhee's estimate must be compared with that of Lieutenant-Colonel Longfield of the Royal Cork Militia who on 29 May claimed that his forces, supported by cannon and regular dragoons, had killed fifty to sixty rebels at the battle of Rathangan and total rebel losses between 23 and 25 May were put at 450–500 men by the government. Edward Byrne was not among the fallen and having effected his escape received a protection from Hume, a magnanimous gesture that exposed the MP to much criticism from his peers.[16] The attempt on Hacketstown demonstrated the inability of the insurgents to capture fortified positions without cannon even when they greatly outnumbered lightly armed defenders. A medal was struck in commemoration of the battle for presentation to the Antrim Militia. The obverse was inscribed 'Protectors of Hacketstown, May 25th, 1798' and the reverse, 'King and Country. Suppressors of Rebellion'.[17]

THE MOBILIZATION OF THE WICKLOW REBELS

Although repulsed at Naas and Kilcullen Green, the Kildare rebels established three camps at strategic points in their county; at Knockallen Hill near Kilcullen, the Gibbet Rath on the Curragh, and at Timahoe on the edge of the Bog of Allen. A fourth camp was pitched at Blackmore Hill in the Wicklow mountains near Blessington where hundreds of Rathdown rebels also rallied. Reynolds, a named fugitive since 23 May was mentioned two days later in General Lake's bulletin on the battle of Naas, at which time he was posted on Blackmore with the forces of fellow Kildare leader Michael Murphy. It was alleged that only nine or ten rebels were killed during the assault on Naas but in the four hours after the attack faltered 'fifty-seven . . . were killed, many of them coming out of their doors when their huts were set on fire, and others taken out of their houses, or from their gardens [and] . . . hanged in the street'.[18]

The rebellion had collapsed in much of Kildare when it became obvious that the general rising had failed to materialize and this evidently prompted the surrender of 3,000 rebels at Knockallen to Lieutenant-General Sir Ralph Dundas on 30 May.[19] Other camps would probably have followed suit had not 520 troops under the command of General Sir James Duff, which had just arrived from Limerick, massacred 350 unarmed rebels attempting to surrender at the Gibbet Rath.[20] The killings seems to have resulted from a mis-understanding which prompted Duff's men to slaughter the unarmed and surrendering United Irishmen on 29 May 1798. No provocation was apparently offered to the South Cork and Dublin City Militia and Roden's Fencible Cavalry other than the discharge by one man of his weapon in the air. The Castle were anxious to represent the massacre as a conventional battle maintaining that when Duff's forces were fired upon 'the attack began [and] the rebels routed with the loss of 400'.[21] Duff's forces had reluctantly left the Limerick area on 27 May where it was deemed that 'the far greater part of the inhabitants were sworn United Irishmen' to reinforce the Dublin area from rebel encroachment.[22] Their brutal conduct in Kildare was technically legal as orders issued to senior officers were to 'disarm all those persons who may be still in possession of arms and ammunition. Lieutenant-General Lake's orders are to take no prisoners should the rebels be found in arms or acting against the peace of the country'.[23] The Blackmore Hill group were under the influence of militant leaders and no doubt aggrieved by the fate of their comrades at the Gibbet Rath talked of 'paying' Dublin 'a visit'. This was evidently the purpose of founding the camp at a convenient staging point for such an attack.[24]

Hundreds of Wicklow rebels from Rathdown and some from Lower Talbotstown quickly trekked to Blackmore Hill camp to assist in the proposed assault. None had then been formed deeper in their native mountains and it is clear that Blackmore was one of the locations United Irish officers had been instructed to select in February 1798. Many Wicklow United Irishmen were specifically directed to join the camp where they were formed into fighting units upon arrival that re-created, as near as practicable, the pre-rebellion corps to which they had belonged. John Boothman of Blessington was ordered to Blackmore on 27 May where he claimed to have interceded on behalf of the Finucanes and other loyalist prisoners held by the rebels.[25] Charles Gallagher, Thomas Miller and Charles Bryan were just three Rathdown officers who arrived in Blackmore to organize the men under their authority who probably numbered between 180 and 360. There were at least 1,000 and possibly as many as 4,000 rebels massed at the camp by the end of May which differed in some respects to many of those later formed in Wexford, such as the one on Kilthomas Hill, in that it was clearly an insurgent base rather than a place of refuge for non-combatants. One loyalist maintained that some of the 4,000 rebels who had received terms of surrender on the Curragh 'proceeded (as might be expected) to join the party on Blackamoor [sic] Hill by whom Blessington was burned'.[26]

The rebels dispatched foraging parties to supply the camp with provisions and also to mete out retribution on local loyalists and their property. Many United Irishmen from the Blessington district had endured martial law and were eager to avenge their losses and degradation. George Parvisol lost his horses, carts and cattle to one raiding party which also burned the houses of two of his tenants. Parvisol had evidently rendered himself obnoxious to some local rebels as they attacked his house again on 14 September firing shots through the windows and breaking down his door.[27] The most prominent loyalist victim in late May was the Marquis of Downshire whose Blessington mansion, on which £7,000 had been lavished in 1797, was 'burned and almost levelled', never to be rebuilt.[28] Downshire's agent informed him that the house 'and all its appendages and everything appertaining (except the church) are completely destroyed' and that 'Hornidges, Hemsworths, in short the *protestants*, seem to have been the victims'. This was not entirely accurate as Hornidge and Hemsworth were both active magistrates and yeomanry officers who were absent serving with the Blessington Cavalry under Lake at the Curragh.[29]

Major William Walsh of the Wicklow Militia was also singled out by the rebels who destroyed his home near the town on 30 May, possibly on account of the reputation of his regiment rather than for any specific grievance held against him. It was first stripped of useful items and produce which was conveyed to Blackmore.[30] The rebellion crisis and the depth of the liberal-conservative divide in that part of Wicklow ensured that there were very few neutral families. Writing of Blessington on 5 June William Patrickson asserted that 'few of the tenants, if any, remain to occupy the ground-all gone to the wars . . . I am told that Blessington is completely destroyed – not a vestige remains, except the church and one or two old houses occupied by papists'. The temporary attachment of the Blessington Cavalry to Lake's forces and the village's partial evacuation by loyalist families had left it open to rebel raids.[31]

The threatening presence of Blackmore Hill camp on the outskirts of south county Dublin and the costly depredations carried out by raiders based there made its eradication a priority for the army. It was belatedly attacked on 31 May by which time the rebels had decided to relocate to a more inaccessible part of the mountains. This had been decided on or before 27 May when the failure of the Rebellion to excite massive popular unrest had become evident. The planned city attack was consequently postponed until circumstances became more favourable and this resolution explains why the insurgents displayed no inclination to contest the high ground, so advantageous in defence, from the attacking infantry on the 31st. The army's hesitation in mounting the assault probably owed something to their recent experience at Rathangan (Kildare) in relation to which R. Marshall commented:

> I am afraid we have done something wrong in charging pikemen with our cavalry – in the first attack upon Rathangan . . . we lost 20 men killed and wounded, of the 7th dragoons . . . However, you need not mention this disaster – we did not make any bulletin of it.[32]

Duff's efforts were not as vital to the defence of Dublin as he believed but, in the light of Rathangan and Oulart Hill (Wexford) just five days previously, extreme caution was required. The cumbersome and slow task of siting cannon in such soft and inaccessible terrain was completed before the Dublin City Militia and 6th Dragoons were ordered to approach the camp. Against all expectations the rebels immediately retreated into the mountains towards Whelp Rock abandoning much of the livestock and baggage they had collected. Lord Roden's light dragoons were amongst the first to reach the objective where he killed what he presumed to be a rebel lookout. The insurgent withdrawal had been well executed and they had moved at short notice leaving 'their pots boiling . . . and a quantity of livestock miserably houghed'.[33] Cannon fire killed fifteen or so insurgents but the rebel mainforce remained largely intact as no provision had been made to cut off their line of retreat. Pursuit was impractical and highly dangerous in the surrounding terrain and Duff's inability to neutralize the rebels at Blackmore inhibited the deployment of government forces in the region for several days.[34]

It was felt 'unwise' to march through the area while rebel dispositions and intentions were unknown. On the day of the Blackmore Hill assault Lieutenant-Colonel Blayney of the 89th regiment had written from Newtownmountkennedy to state his objections to marching his men towards Blessington and Luggelaw. His preference was to draw the rebels onto low ground where he could engage them more safely and on 2 June Camden still had 'no particulars' of the rebels who had left Blackmore.[35] Charles Gallagher of Castletown was one of the few unfortunate men captured while moving through the mountains away from the camp. He was seized by the Powerscourt yeomanry who shot him on the Enniskerry estate which also served as their base of operations. Gallagher was reputedly 'half strangled across a large rock of granite . . . then marched to Powerscourt house and without trial was shot within a few yards of the hall door.' Rathdown county committee member Thomas Miller witnessed Gallagher's arrest and determined to avoid his fate by becoming an informer and state's witness.[36] Many Kildare rebels at Blackmore evidently returned to their homes, although a contingent of some hundreds made the dangerous trip south to Wexford where the rebellion was raging after a slow start.[37]

Hundreds more rebels had also assembled in the central and coastal parts of Wicklow during the first days of rebellion, many of whom evidently rallied around officers who had been fugitives in the mountains for up to two weeks. Major Hardy was informed on 29 May that a large party of rebels had assembled near Roundwood, probably under Joseph Holt, who were suspected of planning to destroy loyalist property. Lieutenant John Edwards led half of Captain Thomas Boycott's troop of Ancient Britons and a party of the Newtownmountkennedy Cavalry under Lieutenant Graves Archer into the district to investigate conditions on the ground. They passed through the Devil's Glen where the rebels were supposed to be 'in vast numbers' and soon fell in with sizeable pockets of armed insurgents.[38] Ten years before a travel writer had found that the right-hand side of the Glen 'clothed from bottom to top, to the height of 500 feet, with a thick covering of wood, among which the oak predominates . . . [the] opposite mountain is almost entirely bare of plantation, rough with gloomy coloured rock, and rugged even to rudeness.' It was an ideal place for the insurgents to congregate and they had converged on the place from miles around in late May.[39]

Over 300 rebels were also encountered by the patrol near Roundwood and about twenty-four were killed. Edwards then rushed to Drummin, Annamoe, where they located yet another large group of rebels laying seige to the home of the deeply unpopular magistrate and landlord Thomas Hugo. Holt described Hugo as 'a cruel and inhuman tyrant . . . the first man who commenced burning houses in that part of the country', holding him personally responsible for burning his Mullinaveigue home and for the death of Patrick Merrigan of Clohogue.[40] Hugo's son William and Tomriland constable John

Beaghan were forced to hand over several weapons before the Britons and yeomen arrived and drove the insurgents towards the small mountain settlement of Clohogue from whence many of the participants had come. Its inhabitants, who lived on land which had recently been leased by Hugo to the La Touches, were described during an 1801 court martial as being 'generally considered as disloyal'.[41] At Hugo's behest the cluster's fifteen houses were 'laid waste' by burning and several of its inhabitants were put to death. While it was not apparent at the time, this series of skirmishes in the Roundwood/Annamoe area effectively dispersed one of several large groups of rebels that had been massing to attack Newtownmountkennedy. Others had assembled elsewhere in the mountains, the Devil's Glen and in woods surrounding Dunran on 29–30 May. Holt had spent three weeks with the Devil's Glen faction before leaving to offer leadership to the rebels in his home area of Roundwood on the eve of the battle. He had led the attack on Hugo's house and later boasted that he had 'made good' his promise to avenge the magistrate's misdeeds.[42]

The convergence of so many rebels in the Devil's Glen had panicked local loyalist families causing 'consternation and alarm'. The Tottenhams were not alone in considering going to Wicklow Town until the emergency had passed and were fortunate to receive the protection of a sergeant's guard of Dunbartonshire fencibles who had halted for their night at Newrath Bridge on their march to Wexford. A substantial quantity of arms held by Ambrose Eccles at Glynmouth was distributed to 'protestant servants' in the Ashford area who acted as guards over the mansions of their employers. Surplus weapons were escorted to the comparative safety of the county town lest they fall into insurgent hands. Gentry insecurity was greatly exacerbated in the last days of May by the revelation of previously unsuspected political allegiances. Ann Tottenham was aghast to learn that local man John Bryan of Chraston was a rebel captain and that the sons of her trusted Ballycurry tenants Larry Bryan and Darby Standon were United Irishmen.[43]

THE BATTLE OF NEWTOWNMOUNTKENNEDY

The battle of Newtownmountkennedy was the only major engagement fought in the month of May to the south and within a day's march of the capital. Had the rebels been victorious, the garrisons of Bray, Rathdrum and Wicklow Town would have been extremely difficult to maintain and, with the greater part of the Kildare and Wexford rebels still in arms and few troops available for redeployment, it is highly doubtful whether the garrison of Arklow could have prevented the powerful south Leinstermen from surging northwards to Dublin. Apart from the strategic importance of the town, the local rebels possessed ample emotional motivation to mount an attack on the site of some of the worst pre-rebellion excesses in Wicklow. That such heavy-handed conduct had continued is indicated by a tradition that a 'simple minded poor man' was shot dead on the morning of the battle by one Keogh who had fired from a room within Armstrong's hotel.[44]

Between 1.00 a.m. and 2.00 a.m. on 30 May, at least 1,000 rebels attacked Newtownmountkennedy from both ends of the linear town. The initial main thrust came from the northern end and encountered vigorous opposition from an alerted and tough garrison. The rebels who mounted the first-phase attack were apparently led by one Manren who was captured in the aftermath of the battle and hanged in Wicklow Town. They rushed into the town 'shouting and huzzaing for Napper Tandy', and were possessed of sufficient momentum to fire the empty cavalry stables before attempting to burn the barracks. This onslaught was somewhat premature as the bulk of the Newcastle men had not then arrived from the coastal districts and most of Holt's anticipated 600 strong Ballinacor contingent may not have rallied at all owing to the confusion of the previous day.[45]

The insurgents who entered the town were opposed by forty of Captain Burganey's Britons, around twenty Antrim Militia grenadiers under Lieutenant Ferguson, forty Newtownmountkennedy Cavalry under Captain Robert Gore and a further forty supplementary (dismounted) yeomen who had only been armed the previous day with weapons recovered from the rebels. Burganey ordered the firing of several loyalist-owned buildings to create a smoke screen which he hoped would disconcert the attackers and impede their approach to the town's defensive positions. The houses burnt included those belonging to loyalists Widow Partland and James Johnston but the heaviest losses were incurred by hotelier John Armstrong who lost his premises. Armstrong's Hotel had been used as the headquarters of the small garrison and when rebuilt was the venue for the town's orange lodge. Its destruction undoubtedly aggrieved William Armstrong, permanent sergeant of the Newtownmountkennedy Infantry, and indicated the seriousness of the garrison's predicament.[46] In the confusion which ensued Patrick Byrne and several other prisoners confined in the guardhouse made their escape but George Doyle of the Glen of the Downs and James Toner of Kilcoole were incapacitated by the severe floggings they had received from Burganey's drummer. Doyle, a shopkeeper and publican, had been arrested on 26 May by a party of the town's cavalry under Lieutenant George Andurin of East Hill. The yeomen had ransacked his business and subjected him to grave ill-treatment in their barracks. Toner and Doyle were both put to death after the battle.[47]

Burganey had received sufficient notice of the assault to mount his troopers who were collected and given the order to charge once the insurgents threatened the security of the town's magazine. The captain led from the front and drove his dragoons straight into the massed pikemen where he fell, mortally wounded, 'covered with shot and with pike wounds'. Gore and Lieutenant Graves Archer were both also unhorsed and severely wounded by the rebels and many of the Britons suffered life-threatening injuries. Their desperate counter-attack succeeded in its objective of breaking the impetus of the rebel effort. The United Irishmen began to collect their wounded and fall back.[48]

While the struggle for the magazine was in progress, Thomas Maguire of Ballydonagh and his three brothers arrived at the head of the Newcastle rebels who closed on the town from the Kilcoole side. As they approached the scene of the fighting, a yeoman dispatch rider named Snell was intercepted on the road leading to Wicklow and promptly killed by one Keogh. The bloodied message he was bearing was nevertheless handed to Lord Rossmore by an escorting Briton who managed to evade the insurgents in his path. Maguire's 'seaside men' had arrived too late to swing the tide of battle but they possessed the energy and commitment to hold off the cavalry while their wounded comrades were collected, hidden and carried to safety by the retreating main force. It is a testament to the skill and determination of the Wicklowmen at Newtownmoutkennedy that Hardy considered the town to have been 'retaken' rather than simply held.[49] Initial estimates of rebel losses were as low as thirty and forty but the figure rose sharply in the follow-up operation which Hardy reputedly directed 'with much slaughter'.[50] Lord Shannon calculated government fatalities at ten men which tallied with traditional sources that claimed the fallen loyalists had been buried in the ruins of the coach house. The dead rebels were unceremoniously tossed into a gravel pit at Warble Bank outside the town. The Antrim Militia, which Hardy believed saved the post, lost at least two dead and the garrison at Bray was apprized that 'an officer and some privates' had fallen. The remaining losses were evidently suffered by the yeomen.[51]

The increased death toll incurred by the United Irishmen was undoubtedly boosted by the availability at Bray of reinforcements which were bound for Wexford, including Colonel Scott's Dunbartonshire fencible infantry, fifty Fifth Dragoon Guards and Lord Kingsborough of the North Cork Militia who were instructed to 'make examples'.[52] These forces, together with the yeoman cavalry and infantry of Wicklow Town, were used against the rebels who had retreated to Dunran woods and the Devil's Glen, the camps from which they had marched to attack Newtownmountkennedy. These fresh troops and part of the Newtown garrison formed a cordon around the Devil's Glen in which Sergeant Archibald McLaren of the Dunbartons believed eighty 'skulking' rebels were killed.[53] Most of those who died had been wounded at Newtown and in recent north Wicklow engagements and perished when Sir Francis Hutchinson's plantation on the south slope of the glen was burned. The Tottenham family owned the unwooded slope of the glen and were told that Hutchinson's woods had been burned to force the fugitives 'out of their cover', an explanation which obscured the brutal reality of the action. The woods were said to have been 'entirely destroyed' although the more barren Ballycurry side did not take fire.[54] Dunran was also cleared of rebels and from all accounts no

DUNRAN, *c.* 1795 N.L.I., TB 1835

prisoners were taken. On 1 June Camden reported General Loftus' observations that 'the county round Rathdrum and Arklow are quiet, but alarmed, and that fifty rebels have been pursued and killed in the woods'.[55]

The depredations of the Britons and Newtownmountkennedy yeomen continued in a systematic fashion for two days after the battle. Some of the worst atrocities of the rebellion were committed by them immediately after Burganey's funeral on 31 May when they embarked on a rampage through the townlands of Callowhill and Ballyduff, killing suspected rebels and their families. At least five persons were put to death in Callowhill and a group of rebels incapacitated by their wounds were burned in the furze thicket in which they had taken refuge at Monalern. Edward Halpin was shot together with his wife and child at Callowhill, as were weavers George Jones, Edward Ford and William Gaskin. Daniel Cullen, a strong farmer, was killed and his house burned by a group of Newtownmountkennedy yeomen led by Moses Fox which included Sam Livesley of Ballyphilip, Mark Wickham and William Armstrong. James Byrne, who was reputedly mentally ill, was gravely injured by Livesley and yeoman Griffin Jones of Newcastle killed the wounded miller Wafer and several comrades when he fired the Monalin thicket.[56]

Local magistrate and future High Sheriff Captain Thomas Archer of Mount John, who succeeded the badly injured Gore as commander of the Newtownmountkennedy Cavalry, was almost certainly the main director of the operations as he had supervised the issuing of protections in the Ballyduff district and would have been familiar with identities of suspected United Irishmen. Every house at Ballyduff was burned and at least five of their owners, Coady, Smith, Turner, Mooney and one Lawrence were executed.[57] Owen Rourke, a seventy-year-old blind man, and ninety-year-old Laurence Cooney were murdered as it was believed that their absent sons were rebels; Cooney's throat was reputedly slashed with his own knife which was left embedded in the wound. Fourteen-year-old John Dempsey was then killed on being summoned by Archer from the potato field in which he worked. Terence Reilly and eight men who had tried to escape across the fields were cut down by the cavalry, as was Arthur Flaherty, a wealthy farmer from Killiskey. The death toll would almost certainly have been higher had not most of Killiskey's inhabitants already fled the neighbourhood. Two other victims were the Doyle brothers of Quill near the Glen of the Downs who were killed in their homes while a father and son named

Turpin of Newtown were put to death when ammunition was discovered in their possession and one of them was found to be wounded.[58]

Michael Neil of Grange, Upper Newcastle, had a more prolonged ordeal, being dragged by yeomanry horses to Newtownmountkennedy where he was executed after severe maltreatment at the hands of the Britons in the guardhouse. His family home had been burned and Richard Neil, who headed the family, was injured by yeomen led by Archer. Seventeen-year-old Patrick Neil was saved from the fate of his elder brother by a group of 'protestant women' headed by a Mrs Jones who apparently threw stones at the yeomen as they passed Newcastle village and successfully implored them to release the teenager. She was probably related to the ultra-violent Griffin Jones, the reputed killer of the elderly Cooney and Rourke, who was also believed to have shortly afterwards killed a seventy-year-old Neil or Neil of Newcastle.[59] Michael Neil had been a very prominent rebel in the barony of Newcastle, as were Terence Byrne of Blackbull and Gregory Conyan of Ballycullen who also died and it is likely that the majority of those massacred were known to have been United Irishmen suspected of involvement in the battle. Conyan's farm had been burned by Wicklow Town yeomen in late May who on leaving Ballycullen encountered William Conyan whom they reputedly half-hanged, burned straw under and shot down his throat in a bid to extract information.[60]

The decisive check at Newtownmountkennedy was compounded by the disruption of Blackmore Hill camp the following day and obliged the north Wicklow leaders to put off any attempt to attack the capital. Some of the more militant leaders became convinced that the best short-term prospect of success lay with making the trek to Wexford where matters were known to have taken a more favourable course. One large group of Wicklowmen headed by a Captain Murphy was intercepted in woods near Brusselstown while on the move to Wexford by a joint force of yeomen and militia stationed at Humewood and Hacketstown. Murphy, 'a most active able officer', was seized and many of his men killed or captured after a pursuit. One of the participants, William Steel of Colvinstown, a member of the Upper Talbotstown Cavalry, had received a warning that 'large parties of rebels were making their way along the mountains of the co[unty] of Wicklow (in the neighbourhood of Humewood) to Vinegar Hill in the co[unty] of Wexford their grand place of rendezvous'. Murphy and the Powerscourt Captain Charles Gallagher were unlucky and most factions reached the mobilizing camps of the Wexfordmen without incident. [61]

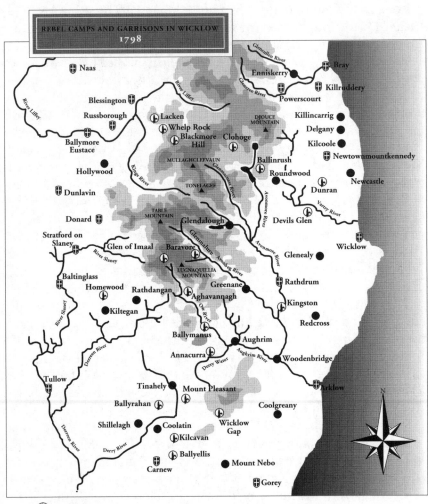

REBEL CAMPS AND GARRISONS IN WICKLOW
1798

Naas

Bray

Gleacullen River

Enniskerry

Killruddery

River Liffey

River Liffey

Blessington

Powerscourt

Russborough

Glencree River

Lacken

Whelp Rock

DJOUCE MOUNTAIN

Killincarrig

Ballymore
Eustace

Blackmore
Hill

Clohoge

Delgany

Kilcoole

Newtownmountkennedy

MULLAGHCLEEVAUN

Ballinrush

Glenimmans River

Hollywood

Kings River

Roundwood

Newcastle

Dunlavin

TONELAGEE

Dunran

Varty River

Donard

TABLE
MOUNTAIN

Glendalough

Avonmore River

Devils Glen

Wicklow

Stratford on
Slaney

Glen of Imaal

Glenmalure

Baravore

Avonbeg River

Avonmore River

Glenealy

River Slaney

LUGNAQUILLIA
MOUNTAIN

Greenane

Rathdrum

Baltinglass

Homewood

Rathdangan

Aghavannagh

Kingston

River Slaney

Kiltegan

Ow River

Redcross

Ballymanus

Aughrim

Woodenbridge

Tullow

Annacurra

Derreen River

Derry Water

Aughrim River

Tinahely

Mount Pleasant

Arklow

Ballyrahan

Coolgreany

N

Shillelagh

Coolatin

Wicklow
Gap

Kilcavan

Derreen River

Ballyellis

Derry River

Carnew

Mount Nebo

Gorey

🜋 **REBEL CAMP**

🛡 **GARRISON**

Newtownmountkennedy was the closest the Wicklow rebels came to a significant victory in May 1798 and the severity of the military in its aftermath may have deterred attacks on Rathdrum, Bray and Wicklow Town. They were among the few garrisons in east Leinster not to be attacked in the insurrection but this security was not taken for granted in June 1798. Captain John Edwards in Bray and his 'much chang[e]d' infantry corps expected an attack in late May and performed guard duty every night. The Rathdrum garrison was far from confident that their town would escape an onslaught and on 31 May Captain Abraham Mills of the Rathdrum (Cronebane) Infantry led a patrol to the site of the gold workings on Ballinavally where they collected several cartloads of materials which were 'of infinite service in fitting up the [Rathdrum] Flannel Hall' as a barrack.[62]

The outbreak of rebellion caused the suspension of mining operations by the Associated Irish Mining Company on the 31st which did not recommence until 30 September. The ninety-strong Cronebane corps, unusually large and well-equipped and swollen by unemployed loyalist volunteers, relocated to Rathdrum where they remained on permanent duty for the duration of the rebellion under Mills, Lieutenant Weaver and Second-Lieutenant Blood.[63] The materials recovered by Mills complemented a grant of £500 from the Barrack Board for fitting the hall up as a barrack for 400 men and fifty officers. In 1799 it remained the 'only building' in Rathdrum suitable for housing large bodies of troops.[64] Rathdrum was substantially reinforced within a few days of the clash at Newtownmountkennedy when 220 Dublin City Militia under Captain John Giffard were detached from Duff's force at Baltinglass after the Blackmore assault and sent through the mountains to Major Hardy's command at Rathdrum. They were accompanied by Captain Dunne of the 7th Dragoons and the sense of crisis felt at the time was expressed by Giffard in 1799 when he described the mission as 'the proudest event' of his life. Giffard also claimed to have 'fortified [Rathdrum] in a manner much approved by every officer who saw it, and thus covered Dublin, and prevented the enemy from turning the left of our wing'.[65]

By 1 June Hardy and Duff had effectively stabilized the Dublin-Wicklow border while the joint efforts of Colonel Campbell and Duff had reversed rebel footholds along the Carlow-Kildare border. The densely populated districts of northern and western Wicklow were temporarily removed from the equation as potential launching pads for an attempt on the capital. The Wexford frontier, however, had degenerated into a critical state as the steady advance of the insurgents in that county threatened to encroach upon Wicklow, Carlow and Kilkenny.[66]

THE REBELLION IN SOUTH WICKLOW AND NORTH WEXFORD

The leadership of the United Irishmen in Wexford was largely unknown to the authorities until 26 May when Anthony Perry of Inch was forced to divulge what names he knew. As a result, far fewer rebel officers had been compromised before the insurrection began and they were consequently able to muster their Companies and regiments to a degree impossible in Wicklow. Mobilization of rebel units was conducted in an orderly fashion between 26 and 28 May in North Wexford. Edward Roche of Garrylough, George Sparks of Blackwater and others together with rebel corps from Monaseed, Ballycanew and some from the barony of Bantry converged on pre-arranged rallying sites such as Castlellis. Elected leaders or popularly acclaimed substitutes like Fr John Murphy of Boolavogue caught the authorities off guard and collected their forces and equipment with little opposition.[67]

The order to rise was to have come from Arklow but the mission undertaken by Miles Byrne of Monaseed which brought him into south Wicklow and east Carlow suggests that the disarray of that town's organization on the eve of the rebellion prevented the communication. News of the Dunlavin massacre reached the Gorey area by 26 May where the severe and worsening violence of government agents had forced many people to abandon their homes.[68] Great importance was attached to the well-being of prisoners in the region whom Fr Murphy is reputed to have called 'the best and the most beloved of our inhabitants' and the Dunlavin incident aroused anger and fear. Two camps of refugees and rebels were hastily formed at Oulart Hill and Kilthomas Hill and skirmishing with the yeomanry and loyalists began.[69]

On the night of 26 May Captain Robert Rowan left Carnew with sixty of his Antrim Militia and Tinahely Infantry supported by the Shillelagh and Carnew Cavalry. They crossed into Wexford to confront a crowd said to have been 'burning the houses of protestant inhabitants' on the Fitzwilliam estate.[70] Major Hardy was more discriminate in his description of rebel actions which he claimed amounted to the destruction of 'every yeoman's property' but the sectarian interpretation is significant as it may well have coloured loyalist perceptions of their adversaries.[71] Captain Wainwright of the Shillelagh corps later recalled that Rowan's patrol had encountered a force of Newtownbarry yeomen on reaching Slieveboy mountain who were retreating from the rebels and had 'burned the houses of those they suspected to be disaffected'. Perhaps as many as 100 were fired by the Carnew-based government forces that night and the summer's night sky must have flickered with the flames of burning cottages on the 26th. Far from intimidating and punishing, the actions of the military exacerbating the widespread chaos, tension and unrequited grievance which attended the early days of the rebellion.[72]

Rowan's Carnewmen spearheaded the attack on Kilthomas Hill where a mixed body of rebels and fearful refugees had gathered. The inexperienced insurgents were probably disconcerted by their first exposure to trained musketmen and were drawn from the height by a well-executed feint. As many as 150 people were killed in the offensive which ensued and the only four prisoners taken were shot the following day in Carnew. Many of the victims hailed from Kiltilly in the parish of Kilrush near Carnew and had been sleeping out of doors for several nights in fear of the yeomen.[73] Hay claimed that: 'The rising of the people in the county of Wexford took place in the direction from Carnew to Oulart, for fear, as they alleged, of being whipped, burned, or exterminated by the Orangemen; hearing of the numbers of the people that were put to death'. These non-combatants were well-represented in the death toll and had been killed in conditions that bore more relation to a massacre than to a battle although the government, who viewed the action as an ordinary 'engagement', may have had genuine difficulty discerning rebel combatants from civilians. The losses served to reinforce the fears of the country people that they were in danger of being exterminated as United Irish propaganda had predicted. This spurred many to take their chances as active rebels.[74]

Oulart camp was attacked with much less success on 27 May by Colonel Richard Foote whose grenadier company of North Cork Militia were virtually annihilated with the loss of 109 men. The incompetence of his second-in-command, Major Lombard, was clearly a factor and the determination of the rebels settled the issue. The scale of the victory over such a hated enemy had a profound effect on the morale of both rebel and government forces. Enniscorthy quickly fell to the buoyant rebels and Gorey was temporarily abandoned by its shocked garrison. They fled to Arklow at 5.00 a.m. on 28 May ahead of unsuspecting rebels obliging Hardy to 'reason' with them.[75] The Gorey refugees were not welcome in Arklow, not least because their flight made the Wicklow border town a potential short term objective of the insurgents. Most were denied admittance to the garrison and one man was shot when he refused to surrender his weapon to the town's guard. When order was restored in Arklow, Lieutenant Swayne of the North Corks and the combined yeomanries of Ballaghkeen, Coolgreany, Coolattin, Tinahely and Wingfield were sent back to

CARNEW CASTLE, 1792, by J.G. Brien N.L.I., TB 1817

re-occupy Gorey with an additional reinforcement of thirty Antrim Militia under Lieutenant Elliot. Skirmishing ensued in the Ballycanew/ Ballymore area on 29 May in which the army claimed to have killed 'above one hundred' insurgents.[76] Yet the situation in Wexford remained volatile and when a relief force dispatched under General Sir William Fawcett lost its howitzers to the insurgents at Three Rock mountain the county town was evacuated by its garrison. Fawcett, an unaggressive commander who feared a 'formidable visit' from the rebels on his Duncannon Fort base, believed that 'to march out against them with a view of defeating them would be madness.'[77]

The first rebel leader in Wexford to attempt breaking into an adjacent county was Fr Moses 'Mogue' Kearns who on 1 June led 2,500 insurgents to assault Colonel L'Estrange's garrison at Newtownbarry (Bunclody) on the Carlow border. Kearns was from Kiltealy, Co. Wexford, and had been sacked from his curate's position at Clonard in Meath by Bishop Delaney on suspicion of complicity with the Defenders.[78] If Kearns had prevailed, he was to have opened communications with his comrades in Carlow and Wicklow and freed the rebels to attack Dunlavin and Carnew. The two villages were of minor strategic importance but had become notorious for ill-treatment of captured United Irishmen. L'Estrange's 230 King's County militiamen faltered under the weight of Kearns' attack and were driven out of their positions on the outskirts of Newtownbarry.[79] An important victory was denied to the rebel army, however, by their inability to exploit the opportunity offered by the retreat of the militia. A critical factor may have been Kearns' lack of a properly trained mounted element which would have been required to convert L'Estrange's withdrawal into a rout. Once regrouped and steadied, L'Estrange ordered his men straight back into the sector of Newtownbarry they had just abandoned. This had not been anticipated by the rebels who proved incapable of holding their ground. They were repulsed from their foothold in the town 'with great slaughter' and consequently squandered the great potential of what might easily have been a decisive encounter.[80] The garrison claimed to have 'killed above 500' and while this is not credible, they certainly deterred rebel attempts to threaten the south Wicklow border.[81]

During or shortly after the Battle of Newtownbarry, Second-Lieutenant Patten of the Antrim regiment took the drastic step of ordering the execution of forty-one of the sixty-one prisoners held in Carnew guardhouse. Wainwright, who related the only extant firsthand account of the Carnew executions to Earl Fitzwilliam in 1800, he had returned from Dublin to Carnew on 26 May 1798 to find 'many' rebel prisoners in the guardhouse. On 28 May the three or four prisoners taken by Rowan's patrol in the Kilthomas Hill/Ferns area the previous night were put to death in the village's ball alley together with 'three or four others under a rule of transportation'. It is likely that William Young of Ballinacor was shot with this batch along with leading Carnew United Irishman Patrick Stafford. This was the first of the Carnew massacres but not the notorious incident related in most nationalist accounts of the rebellion.[82]

According to Wainwright the victims of the major massacre were mainly untried prisoners who had been shot 'to prevent their interference if the town should be attacked'. Kearns' designs on Newtownbarry on 1 June, therefore, was probably the prime factor in the timing of the massacre which followed closely upon similar incidents in Dunlavin, Ballymore-Eustace, Newtownmountkennedy and Carnew itself the previous week. Yet the fact that an obscure and very junior officer had been permitted to issue such an order points to responsiveness of the detachment's leadership cadre to the measure and the willingness of their men to carry them out. This guardhouse executions of 1 June were apparently those later associated with the town's ball alley probably the alley within Carnew Castle. While it is possible that twenty-eight men had indeed been shot in the alley on or around 25

May, as Hay contended, it is evident that the bulk of the deaths, considerably more than allowed for by any authority, had occurred on 1 June. That eighteen of the forty-one shot were married would have ensured that a large network of United Irish families were closely connected to the losses.[83]

Patten's role in the massacre implied Captain Rowan's absence from Carnew on the 1st but the more senior officer's presence would probably have made little difference given the brutality which had permeated his leadership in north Wexford in the late May. Carnew's militia garrison, unlike their comrades in most other Wicklow towns, had been inculcated with a sense of extremism arising from their anti-insurgent activities in north Wexford the previous week and in the advent of the rebellion. They probably influenced south Wicklow loyalists who earned a reputation for atrocious conduct in the first days and weeks of the rebellion that led to many insurgent acts of retaliations later in the summer including the burning of Carnew and Tinahely. That the garrison genuinely feared a prison break is dubious in view of the relative security of the guardhouse but they had certainly been unsettled by events at Newtownbarry. The partially destroyed village was 'still smoking' from the battle on 2 June when Colonel Ancram's relief force of Midlothian Fencibles arrived. Ancram's presence was greeted with great relief by the garrison and residents 'who were in expectation of a second attack from the enemy', an apprehension which undoubtedly affected their loyalist colleagues in nearby Carnew.[84]

The enervating fluidity of the strategic picture in south Wicklow/ north Wexford was illustrated just three days after L'Estrange's triumph at Newtownbarry by a costly reverse at Tubberneering. The disaster of 4 June had its roots on 29 May when Major-General William Loftus had left Dublin with orders to contain the Wexford insurgents and recapture the county when the strength of his forces permitted. He had left Dublin with just 250 men and reported from Wicklow Town on 1 June that the Rathdrum-Arklow area was undisturbed following the battle of Newtownmountkennedy. Loftus was reinforced on his arrival in Arklow with 400 troops under Lieutenant-Colonel Lambart Walpole, Camden's *aide-de-camp*, who reached Gorey on 3 June. The insurgents were then known to be encamped at Ballymore below Carrigrew Hill and were deemed to present a threat to Gorey and its considerable loyalist-owned interests. Loftus planned to safe-guard the district by surrounding the camp with troops from Carnew, Newtownbarry and Gorey on 4 June. Under his rapidly swelling command were elements of over ten regiments which he ordered to engage the rebels simultaneously for maximum effect.[85]

Walpole recklessly disregarded Loftus' instructions and committed his force prematurely at Tuberneering where he unexpectedly ran into a 2,000-strong rebel forward position. It was assumed in Dublin that Walpole 'wanted . . . to do something brilliant'.[86] The insurgents ambushed the soldiers in difficult terrain and forced them towards Clough where Captain McManus and 100 grenadiers of the Antrim Militia were unable to mount an effective rearguard. Their comrades attempted to extricate themselves from the battle but the effort quickly lost whatever cohesion it possessed at the outset.[87] Walpole was shot dead early in the retreat and his troops panicked when the nervous Captain-Lieutenant Jones 'quitted his detachment entirely and suffered them to act for themselves'. Little should have been expected from Jones who had 'complained of a pain in his thigh' at the Battle of Kilcullen two weeks before. Three six-pounder cannons and their crews were overrun and captured by the rebels who also killed or seized fifty-four soldiers. Initial reports of the defeat mentioned that Walpole's men had retreated to Arklow and Loftus to Carnew whereas both bodies pulled back even further.[88]

Only a holding action by Colonel Cope's Armagh Militia and Colonel Sir Watkin Williams Wynne's Ancient Britons had averted even heavier losses as the troops fled in disorder to Gorey. A fifteen-strong group of survivors were led to safety by Henry Tighe of the Wicklow Cavalry having first cut their way 'through half a mile of pike men and back again' to reach Rathdrum for the loss of several men.[89] Several isolated Britons made for Newtownbarry lending credence to the impression that a complete breakdown of discipline had occurred in which the troops had fled in small groups in all directions. Ancram of the Midlothians alluded to this when he noted 'the disorderly conduct of the militia'.[90] Many government casualties were probably incurred during this rout phase when the north Wexford irregulars had scented victory. Sergeant McLaren of the Dunbartons was shocked on viewing the scene of Walpole's defeat and recalled that it 'was covered with the bodies of the slain, some of whom had the marks of twenty pikes in their faces, legs and breasts'.[91]

The repercussions of the defeat rebounded immediately on Loftus' column of Dunbartons and Fifth Dragoons which had been rendered insecure by the sudden emergence of a threat to their flank. He was obliged to not only postpone the attempt to relieve Wexford but to retreat as quickly as possible to Carnew lest the insurgents attempt to exploit their psychological and tactical ascendancy. This was accomplished with some difficulty even though his dispositions were unknown to the rebels yet it merely preceded a further withdrawal to Tullow. The troops remained vulnerable even in Carlow for a while owing to their separation from the bulk of their ammunition supplies which had been stockpiled at Gorey in anticipation of further thrusts into Wexford.[92] The majority of the survivors of Walpole's command had fled to Gorey which was immediately abandoned to the pursuing rebels in favour of the more fortified garrison town of Arklow. The insurgents were motivated not only by the flush of victory in the field but by a determination to prevent their defeated foes taking vengeance on the rebel prisoners crowded into the town's Market House. The bitter legacies of Carnew and Dunlavin were already being felt. Upon reaching Arklow Wynne decided that it too was undefendable under the circumstances and ordered its garrison to evacuate the vital town at 2.00 am on 5 June. This left only the inconsequential strong points of Wicklow Town and Bray in the city-bound path of a victorious rebel army.[93]

The seriousness of the disaster was accentuated by the fact that Walpole's column contained the Antrim Militia units which ordinarily comprised the resident garrisons of both Arklow and Rathdrum. The casualties they had endured in terms of men lost to wounds and captivity, as well as the partial dispersal of their surviving comrades, was guaranteed to unsettle those obliged to defend the two most strategically important posts in Wicklow. General Loftus wrote to Hardy en route from Carnew to Tullow on the evening of 4 June to warn him to 'take care' of himself in Wicklow Town in the light of Walpole's 'scrape'. Of more use was Loftus' decision to send Captain Rowan's Carnew based detachment of Antrim Militia to reinforce Arklow, although, as matters transpired, the soldiers reached Hardy in Wicklow Town before the letter.[94] Rowan's men were shadowed if not actively pursued by the rebels across the enclosed and undulating countryside intervening Carnew and Arklow where the absence of loyalist control was very evident. This experience clearly preyed on the nerves of the militiamen who, on finding their supposed port stronghold abandoned to the enemy, took fright and dropped all their baggage to hasten their onward march to Wicklow Town. Their anxiety may have been exacerbated by whatever garbled news of Tubberneering they had received from the troops with Loftus and also perhaps their anticipation of the reception they might expect from the insurgents just days after the Carnew prison massacres.[95]

The disquieting, albeit unreliable, assertion that the Antrims had been followed by the rebels as far north as Wicklow Town was communicated by Hardy to General Lake at 7.00 a.m. on 5 June. Hardy was then busy overseeing the preparation of defensive positions outside the county town from which the exhausted, barefoot and starving remnants of Walpole's force were expected to face the 10,000–20,000 strong Gorey army once again. He had been aghast when apprized of Wynne's drastic step in Arklow which had been taken 'without knowledge or consent'. The agitated state of Walpole's survivors and that of Rowan's reinforcement prompted Hardy to keep them out of the settlement lest it be sacked. They were instead permitted to entrench on the outskirts of the town pending the allocation of billets.[96] Five hours after Rowan's arrival Hardy sent a second despatch to Lake reflecting on the magnitude of the strategic blunder at Arklow and castigating the retreat as 'the most shameful I ever knew'. He then hinted, with appropriate decorum, that Wynne's command of the forces formerly led by Walpole was causing operational friction and requested the services of a more senior officer. A more obvious problem was the presence of three colonels under the nominal command of a man with the substantive rank of major. Hardy's parting declaration to the commander-in-chief was the dramatic news that he had sent orders to Rathdrum for its garrison to maintain their post 'to the *last*'.[97]

On 4 June, Hardy, anticipating his replacement by Major-General Needham, wrote to Castlereagh to summarize his achievements in the county and to outline the state of affairs:

> The troops in this county have behaved uncommonly well, especially the yeomen of this town. The Shillelagh troops also acquitted themselves nobly in beating back the Wexford rebels. Our yeomen have been now sixteen days on hard duty, and the last ten nights constantly up: their hours of rest from three or four in the morning till ten or eleven. The rebels are numerous in our woods and mountains, but from the great exertions made to get up the arms before the rebellion broke out, and the unremitting assiduity exerted since to prevent any falling into their hands, they have been prevented from acting with the same effect as their associates in Wexford. There have been five engagements at different times in this county, and I do believe we have killed about 700 hundred rebels.[98]

The United Irishmen of Wicklow's southern baronies of Shillelagh, Ballinacor South and Arklow were unable to emulate the success of their comrades in north Wexford and made no attempt to do so. The comparative inaction of the Wicklowman probably owed much to the loss of virtually all their upper leadership and much of the junior officer cadre in the months of coercion. Some of the most damaging losses and defections had occurred on the eve of the rebellion leaving insufficient time for the remainder to devise contingencies. Many key personnel charged with disseminating orders and organizing rallying points had been imprisoned or forced into hiding. Miles Byrne was surprised when visiting Arklow in late May to learn from his kinsman Garret Graham that Phil O'Neil had surrendered.[99]

Insurgent difficulties were exacerbated by the fact that the resident loyalist element was very numerous in the borderlands and backed by a considerable leavening of capable soldiers. South Wicklow was host to nine official yeomanry corps as well as several active supplementary units which enjoyed the support and patronage of the major landowners and magistrates.[100] The inauspicious prospects for rebel mobilization were further affected by the circumstances through which pro-government forces in the Carnew district received notice of the outbreak of rebellion before the local United Irishmen and they were certainly the first to respond. Captain Rowan and others had made strenuous efforts to obviate the threat of a popular uprising by aggressive patrolling. A comprehensive turn out was consequently denied the United Irishmen and no forces succeeded in coalescing with sufficient speed and numerical strength to contemplate assaults on alerted garrisoned towns.[101]

While no immediate challenge to authority emerged on the Arklow to Carnew line numerous small groups of Wicklow rebels assembled in the mountains and woods of the district. They generally made their way to the highground camps across the Wexford border where a succession of insurgent victories had made large concentrations viable.[102] Miles Byrne paid tribute in his memoir to the 'brave Wicklow men' who had marched by night 'in groups of twelves, to join the camp at Vinegar Hill', an account that indicates orderly mobilization.[103] In the first days of June Byrne acknowledged that southern Wicklow had 'furnished our army with the most determined fine, brave fellows, and all to a man priding themselves on being United Irishmen. They had all, either personally, or some members of their families, suffered the most cruel tortures and persecutions'. Byrne, in hindsight, was somewhat critical of their presence in Wexford and felt that their manpower would have been better employed deep in the Wicklow mountains as a focus for later mobilization to aid the French. This viewpoint did not take into account the desire of the Wicklowmen to play an active role in the fighting and their ignorance of French intentions.[104] On 26–27 May the rebel effort in east Kildare had all but collapsed and those wishing to fight on were known to have 'joined the Wexford party'.[105]

News of Oulart had penetrated as far as Lugnaquilla in Ballinacor North by 30 May where Michael Dwyer of Imaal was in hiding. Dwyer travelled alone to Limerick Hill camp, four miles north of Gorey, and joined his fellow Wicklowmen preparing to launch an attack on Arklow. A more senior Wicklow United Irishman, Matthew Doyle of Polahoney, crossed into north Wexford on 29 May where he immediately took command of a squad of pikemen composed of Arklow sailors and townspeople whom he drilled in pike-handling and tactics. Patrick Harold and other members of John Carroll's section of the 'Redcross' company entered Gorey Hill camp on 6 June. They were overtaken en route by their elected captain, Charles Byrne of Ballyrogan, and were one of the few units to mobilize the active element of their pre-rebellion corps. The Redcross men were greeted near the camp by Captain James Doyle of Ballinacor who had divided the sixty or so men under his command into two files.[106]

Doyle of Ballinacor had taken part in the Battle of Tubberneering on the 4th having reached Wexford some days earlier via Mount Pleasant camp, south east of Tinahely. Many Wicklow rebels had rallied at Mount Pleasant in the first days of June and some, like Dwyer, were re-directed there upon arriving in Wexford in a bid to maintain unit and county cohesion. Dwyer attached himself to Doyle's corps and functioned as its 'Lieutenant' for the duration of the Wexford campaign. Bridget Dolan of Carnew claimed at the courtmartial of William Byrne of Ballymanus in 1799 that there were 'two officers and a captain to every [rebel] corps' which would explain the surplus of leaders in the Redcross and Ballinacor units. There was, however, only one 'captain' per corps who was its undisputed commander and who, as Dolan further testified, had generally been 'elected a considerable time before the rebellion'.[107] Given the conditions militating against rebel victories in southern Wicklow, the junior leaders who organized their corps at Mount Pleasant elected to commit themselves to the struggle in Wexford which, if successful, augured well for their native county. The sizeable Wicklow contingent which fought there called themselves the 'Ballymanus Division' in honour of their absent leader, Garret Byrne, and his brother William who commanded in his place from 8 to 21 June.[108]

The rebels encamped at Gorey Hill on 5 June did not realize that Arklow had been abandoned and made belated attempts to ascertain the dispositions of government forces by sending out reconnaissance patrols. Miles Byrne was so engaged on 6 June when he fell in with a column of rebels who were going to attack Loftus and his garrison at Carnew. It was then discovered that the troops and resident garrisons of Carnew, Tinahely and Shillelagh had all retreated to Tullow in Carlow and that the villages were undefended. Fr John Murphy had hoped to fight and defeat Loftus' column on 7 June before attacking Arklow but as that strategic objective could not be fulfilled, the rebels were satisfied to exact retribution on loyalist property for the perceived misdeeds of its owners.[109]

Castletown yeoman and orangeman James Wheatly and a mail courier named Moses from the Tinahely area were piked shortly after crossing the path of the rebels and at least two other yeomen taken prisoner were later executed. Moses was reputedly piked by Lawrence Dowling, a junior officer and standard-bearer of the Redcross company while Wheatly reputedly faced death declaring 'he was an orangeman and w[oul]d die one'. Also killed at this time on or near Gorey Hill were one Rogan of the Arklow yeomanry and Isaac Langrell who had all been captured after 4 June.[110] Richard Cooke of Carnew was seized by the rebels on 4 June 1798 on the Arklow road while fleeing Gorey with his family and after a short period of confinement in Gorey guardhouse he and Roger Pierse of Ballythomas were put to death on Limerick Hill. Cooke was considered a prominent loyalist and had the misfortune to encounter his near neighbour, insurgent Captain John Fowler, outside Gorey. Fowler had lodgings with Mrs Bryan of Gorey but had previously worked as a steward for the James family of Carnew and Ballyconran and also for the Symes of Ballybeg. Fowler was probably Protestant and so close were his links with the south Wicklow loyalists that his landlady asserted 'many of the people except those who knew him best thought he was a loyalist'. His true politics were revealed when he left Gorey before the town's loyalists deemed it necessary to evacuate.[111]

'Unpleasant' accounts of rebel actions in Wexford reached Castlereagh who was informed that they 'put to death all persons who refuse to join them and . . . massacre the protestant inhabitants'.[112] Both assertions were false and possibly circulated with malicious intent but there was sufficient loss of life to lend credence to the wildest rumours. There was also a great deal of destruction of property, mostly that owned by loyalists. Many of those who had fired houses around Slieveboy Mountain on 26 May had their own homes looted and burned. Carnew was reputedly 'burnt to ashes' and was certainly badly damaged by United Irish arsonists, although the fact that it was re-occupied within days by the army indicates that most of its stone structures had not been completely destroyed.[113] Its population had all fled in the preceding days, probably on the evening of 4 June when Loftus had ignored the pleadings of its garrison to make a stand in the village. The Buckstown residence of Carnew loyalist Ralph Blayney was spared by a written order of Anthony Perry which was brought to the attention of John Fowler's men as they prepared to fire the house.[114]

Whatever satisfaction was derived from the morale-building reprisal against the Carnew loyalists was increased when the rebels retired to the makeshift Kilcavan camp, north east of Carnew, where they were joined by the respected William Byrne of Ballymanus.[115] Byrne had apparently seized the opportunity to quit his short-term hiding-place with the Coates family of Clone on 8 June and immediately assumed the position in the rebel army earmarked for his brother. He had previously headed a group of Wicklow rebels attached to the southern Wexford forces of Bagenal Harvey and had made his way north-eastwards from the New Ross area on 4 or 5 June. This would explain how the sup-posedly inactive Byrne was in a position to bring 300 Wicklow recruits with him to the 'Ballymanus Division' on the 8th. Martin Roche of Ballymanus swore in 1799 that Byrne had ridden off towards Arklow on 8 June on his bay mare which was looked after by one Neil, 'considered the greatest rebel in Ballymanus'. Byrne allegedly told Roche that he had been chased that morning by the yeomen through Killacloran to Aughrim and had been forced to conceal himself in a water cut in Ballymanus to avoid capture.[116]

Kilcavan, considered a temporary camp rather than a base of oper-ations, was abandoned later in the day and Byrne led the Wicklow rebels back to Gorey Hill to organize the planned attack on Arklow where they arrived around midday. They learned on arrival of the failure of Bagenal Harvey to overcome the government forces at New Ross on 5 June, a costly defeat which prevented the Wexfordians from moving westward into Kilkenny and the midlands. Yet the increasing confidence of the rebels in north Wexford and the tantalizing options thrown up by the tactical withdrawal conducted by the army ensured that debates and disagreements revealed the weakness of the United Irishmen at command level.[117]

As the interior of the Wicklow mountains was accessible after 4 June it would have been relatively simple to bypass the garrison at Rathdrum and reach the Dublin border, quite possibly without detec-tion. While this manoeuvre would have been highly dangerous for a formally constituted army given that undefeated garrisons menaced both flanks, such considerations should not have hindered the insurgents. The irregulars had no supply lines to forfeit and very little heavy baggage to transport. Weighed against the possible risk of interception was the great potential of a forced march on the city. It might well have revitalized United Irish efforts in north Wicklow and maximized the chances of ultimate victory by giving the Dublin rebels the external assistance they had repeatedly sought. Moreover, Holt proved in the course of the summer of 1798 that it was possible to avoid battle on disadvantageous terms in the mountains and it is unlikely that the government could have prevented the rebels entering County Dublin. Another strategy might have been to leave a strong body blocking the Dublin/Arklow road on the city side which would have complicated any attempt of the town's forces to closing with the rear of the rebel mainforce as it approached the capital.[118]

Valuable time was wasted in a disordered debate in which the relative merits of striking at the earliest opportunity were considered in the context of logistical arguments which highlighted ammunition shortages. One definite proposal concerned the dispatch of 6,000–8,000 rebels through Tinahely to Rathdrum in order to cut the Dublin road but this plan was abandoned when it became known that Arklow had been re-occupied and its defences strengthened. Ex-artillery man Esmond Kyan and former (French) Irish Brigade John Hay of Ballinkeel had strongly advocated taking Arklow when it was vulnerable after Tubberneering but had been overruled for reasons now obscure. The lack of an effective commander-in-chief, the interminable wrangling over ammunition and powder deficiencies and ignorance of Loftus' intentions evidently contributed to the most serious blunder of the Wexford rebels.[119]

Command difficulties had also stymied Harvey's efforts to take New Ross on 5 June. He had left Three Rock camp outside Wexford Town and collected the rebels at Carrickbyrne Hill before taking up positions overlooking New Ross at Corbet Hill on the 4th. There was evidently a great deal of tension in the ranks of the military at this time as a detachment of Meath and Donegal Militia en route to New Ross from Kilkenny accidentally fired upon some Midlothian Dragoons whom they mistook for rebels.[120] Dissension within the rebel leadership at Corbet Hill resulted in John Colclough removing his men from the camp where Harvey seemed incapable of asserting his authority as supreme leader. The Wexford commander Thomas Cloney of Moneyhore considered Harvey's 'ignorance of military affairs, with a weak frame and delicate constitution, rendered him unfit for so arduous and perilous a situation'.[121] Three columns of insurgents had been intended to assault Major-General Henry Johnson's garrison but the Bantry rebels under John Kelly of Killan and Cloney bore the brunt of the fighting when they were prematurely committed without available support.[122]

Only a fraction of Harvey's 15,000-strong force participated in the battle and there was little co-ordination with the Kilkenny rebels.[123] The towns outer defences were breached by the skilful deployment of pike and gunsmen but the battalion guns of the Donegal Militia inflicted heavy casualties on the Bantrymen. Grape shot and disciplined musket fire stemmed the onslaught and encouraged the 5th Dragoons to charge but instead of breaking under the cavalry attack as might have been expected, the imperilled rebels rallied and routed the dragoons. This reverse and the death of the popular Lord Mountjoy of the Dublin City Militia disheartened the defenders who began to retreat across the river Barrow into Kilkenny.[124] Johnson succeeded in re-imposing control over his troops and launched a counter-attack which took the weary and unsuspecting rebels by surprise. The general had a narrow escape when his horse was shot from under him trapping his leg and he had to be rescued by the dragoons. Captain Charles Tottenham of the New Ross Cavalry wrote that prisoners were taken 'in great numbers' and as many as 2,500 insurgents killed. Half that figure was probably more accurate but ninety government troops were killed and a further eighty-one missing of whom a small number had defected.[125] A dragoon who brought the news of the victory to Dublin was heard to exclaim 'we have knocked them all to hell'.[126] Camden was relieved that this 'critical' battle had been won but observed: 'An enemy that only yielded after a struggle of twelve hours is not contemptible'.[127]

The showing of the rebels at Ross did not augur well for the garrison at Arklow who anticipated an attack by the 'Gorey army'. Yet the courage of the insurgents was undermined by Harvey's failure to commit the bulk of his forces and to learn from Fr Kearns' errors at Newtownbarry. He resigned his largely honourary position of commander-in-chief as the survivors fell back on Lacken Hill and was succeeded by Revd Philip Roche. Hundreds of wounded rebels had to be abandoned on the battlefield at New Ross and in its environs, most of whom were massacred. This atrocity contributed to the subsequent killing of scores of loyalist prisoners at Scullabogue, as did government actions at Carnew and Dunlavin.[128]

BATTLE OF NEW ROSS. *The Kings troops attacking the Rebels in the Town of New Ross in the county of Wexford.*

A list kept by John Brennan of Castlehaystown (Taghmon), a former High Sheriff of Wexford turned commissary of the Ross army, throws light on the extent of Wicklow involvement in the theatre. Several Wicklow officers were numbered among the forty-seven persons whom Brennan had supplied with provisions at Corbet Hill. Esmond Kyan and Revd Roche are listed as generals, which accurately reflected their high status in the rebel forces, while the four colonels were Edward Fitzgerald of Newpark, Southwell McClune of Dublin, 'Byrne of Ballymanus' and Joseph Holt of 'Wicklow'. This establishes that Holt had made his way to Wexford with a body of north Wicklow rebels and was exercising command at a time when he claimed to have been hiding in the Devil's Glen.[129]

The reference to a Byrne of Ballymanus is also problematic as Garret Byrne was then apparently trapped in Dublin city until late June 1798 and his brother William's whereabouts are unknown until he reached Kilcavan Hill camp on 8 June.[130] Yet William Byrne could easily have entered Kilcavan directly from New Ross and, while there is no tradition of his presence in Wexford that early, this almost certainly accounts for the 300 men he had amassed by the 8th. While Brennan specified that both Byrne and Holt had been 'supplyed [sic] . . . at Corbet Hill' it is clear that they had not been committed to the battle of Ross and may have withdrawn with Colclough's forces on 4 June. Another Wicklowman named was Charles Bryan of Bray who had probably first joined fellow Rathdown rebel officers in Blackmore Hill camp in late May and then moved south with the Kildare contingent after the 31st when General Duff's assault dispersed the camp.[131] This scenario is further suggested by the presence at Corbet Hill of Dublin officers Felix Rourke of Rathcoole and Colonel McClune who had probably come via Blackmore and were both later concerned in the fighting in the Wicklow mountains with Holt.[132]

It is inherently likely that small numbers of non-Wexford rebel forces became attached to the camps formed in the western part of that county in late May and early June just as they did in the eastern Gorey area. Those who had been at Blackmore Hill may even have entered Wexford before Gorey Hill camp had been established or widely known about and, if they had then travelled towards Enniscorthy and Wexford Town, could well have fallen in with the insurgents later committed to the attack on New Ross. Whatever contact the Wicklow leaders had with Brennan occurred in Wexford before 5 June and involved the transfer of supplies to rebel units. Sproule informed his contacts in early June that the 'late successes' of the rebels were drawing 'the wavering [of Dublin] to join them . . . Kelly is gone.'[133] This supports Miles Byrne's contention that in mid-June 'three men from the city of Dublin, who had escaped with difficulty through the Wicklow mountains joined us'. As they were known to Daniel Kirwan, second-in-command of the Ballymanus Division, they were evidently senior figures.[134]

New Ross may have thrown rebel strategy into disarray but it did not reassure Wexford and Wicklow loyalists. The uneven performance of government forces there and at Newtownbarry and Newtownmountkennedy had done little to instill confidence in the pro-government communities of southern Wicklow. Over 1,000 displaced loyalists had moved into Wicklow Town after the abandonment of Gorey and Arklow to the rebels and 1,070 reputedly stayed in tents pitched on Wicklow strand for a month.[135] Many of the more prosperous left the country altogether for the duration of the rebellion preferring the absolute security of Wales and Liverpool to the risks attending residence in any part of Ireland. Marquis Buckingham wrote: 'the private accounts from Ireland of the horrors in the county of Wicklow are disastrous in the extreme . . . every one is flying from thence to Wales'.[136] Rumours of sectarian massacres apparently fuelled the exodus and heightened tensions. Even the habitually astute and generally well-informed Sarah Tighe of Rossana became convinced that 'the tragedy of 1641 is acting over again'. Her brother, Harry Tighe of the Wicklow Town yeomanry, saw fit to escort her to the county town on 31 May which was then crowded with refugees and wounded soldiers.[137]

Adult males living in areas of Wicklow under government control who had not enrolled in yeomanry corps made strenuous efforts to display their loyalty in June 1798. Bray men reportedly carried arms as they went about their business while 'the lower order, though drest [sic] in their ordinary garb, had pieces of blue or red rags prefixed to the front of their hats as badges of their loyalty'. The situation was the reverse in the Wexford urban centres which had been occupied by the rebels where those who did not endorse the methods and objectives of the United Irishmen were understandably discomfited. Nervous Protestants and loyalists occasionally brandished republican symbols and, in some cases, converted to Catholicism in the belief that it would shield them from rebel violence.[138] Such actions were not always undertaken out of mortal fear as the rebels rarely harmed the families of loyalists but frequently requisitioned their goods. The wife of Imaal yeoman John Hanbidge of Tinnehinch was obliged to cook one of her pigs for a passing group of insurgents who later burned her curing sheds and drove off her sheep. In Bray the crisis completed the marginalization of Edwards who was 'superseded in every duty as magistrate and commander' by Captain Armstrong of the King's County regiment. This prompted him to threaten resignation of his corps and to enlist as a private in a city one. Edwards pointedly identified his 'crime' as pursuing a policy of 'lenity and protection'.[139]

Lord Powerscourt was one of the few major landlords to remain on his estate for the entire insurrection and his mansion became the headquarters to the local yeomanry, many of whom were his own tenants. William Hume similarly armed loyalists in the vicinity of his Humewood estate in June 1798 and allowed them live on his grounds while the young Earl of Meath used his Kilruddery home as a base for the Bray Cavalry.[140] Hume's friend William Steel recalled how the MP in June 1798 had

> for the safety of his protestant tenantry and others of that persuasion in his neighbourhood appropriated his dwelling house and offices (which were very extensive) to their use and for their protection, form[e]d a garrison of near two hundred protestants and was furnished with arms for them by order of his Excellency Lord Cornwallis.[141]

The long-serving and ailing Wicklow liberal MP, Nicholas Westby of Highpark did not follow suit but was reportedly warned by friendly United Irishmen that his home would be attacked. The raiders, who may not have been rebels, apparently killed Westby's butler and stole a large quantity of silver which was not recovered at the time of their arrest in Hacketstown.[142]

Absentees were vulnerable to raids on their properties and Lord Waterford's Hollywood lodge was plundered in early June as soon as Hardy removed its guard post. Earl Milltown, in contrast, left Ireland on an extended tour of Europe, probably to avoid the problems posed by the rebellion for the liberally inclined Leeson family. This resulted in the commandeering of Russborough House as a temporary barracks and guardhouse by the Duke of York's Highlanders who inflicted far more damage on the building than the rebels. That Holt had striven to preserve the mansion before it was pressed into service lent credence to conjecture that the Leesons were unduly sympathetic towards the United Irishmen if not themselves members.[143]

Many Wicklow loyalists were exposed by Hardy's unavoidable decision to 'contract' his force on 30 May, a development which entailed the abandonment of army camps in isolated areas such as the Goldmines and Seven Churches. Although militarily necessary to concentrate available forces in the strategic garrison towns, it was, nonetheless, a redeployment which came at a price. A much greater proportion of patrolling duties devolved on the yeomanry who proved incapable of preventing communication between the rebels of Wicklow and Wexford, much less defeating their enemies. Moreover, the pitting of loyalists tasked with defending their own neighbourhoods against marauding bands of rebels imbued their actions with an element of bitter fanaticism which exacerbated inter-communal strife. The fragility of loyalist ascendancy in Wicklow was further exemplified by the rapidity with which insurgent arsonists encroached on military camps and posts evacuated by the regulars and militia.[144]

Given the harsh realities of the rebellion in Wicklow, the rout of Walpole raised the prospect of imminent attacks on Arklow and Wicklow Town. General Lake perceived the gravity of the situation and stripped the capital of all but 1,500 troops which were sent to Wicklow and placed under the temporary command of Major-General Sir Francis Needham. Camden expressed his 'hope' on 5 June that Needham's dispatch to Arklow the following day 'would prevent the county of Wicklow being entered from Gorey'. The Viceroy must have been concerned at the rumours in Dublin on the 6th which claimed that Arklow had fallen and his persistent requests for additional troops from Britain took on a fresh urgency.[145] On 8 June there were 3,000 infantry and 1,000 cavalry bound for Ireland which was deemed insufficient by Wickham who pressed for an additional 5,000 troops. Castlereagh wrote to London on that day:

> I understand from Marshall you are rather inclined to hold the insurrection cheap. Rely upon it there never was in any country so formidable an effort on the part of the people. It may not disclose itself to the full extent of its preparation if it is early met with vigour and success; but our force cannot cope in a variety of distant points with an enemy that can elude an attack where it is inexpedient to risk a contest.[146]

Military forces in Wicklow amounted to a considerable portion of the troops available to the Castle in Leinster. Hardy had 300 infantry at Baltinglass on 6 June drawn from the Dublin City and Wicklow Militia supported by sixty troopers of the Ancient Britons and 9th Dragoons. Captain Armstrong commanded at least one company of King's County Militia in Bray and the garrison at Rathdrum had Lieutenant Macauley's Antrim men in addition to a detachment of Captain John Paradine's 54th Infantry. Roundwood was defended by one or two companies of Fermanagh Militia and there were parts of the Antrim regiment at both Hacketstown and Newtownmountkennedy. The troop of Britons formerly commanded by Captain Burganey remained to bolster the garrison of Newtownmountkennedy along with elements of the 89th fencible infantry. General Needham was posted in Wicklow Town on 6 June having arrived the day before from Lehaunstown Camp where he had collected 362 Cavan Militia under Colonel Maxwell and a company of Reay Highland Infantry. The Reays were left in position to form a reserve when Needham, Hardy and Wynne took their combined forces forward to re-occupy Arklow on the 6th thereby denying the insurgents any hope of an uncontested route to Dublin. From that day the attention of both government and insurgent forces was focused on Arklow where a battle of the utmost importance was in the offing.[147]

Needham commanded 1,360 infantry and 164 cavalry in Arklow on 9 June supported by the town's two corps of yeoman cavalry as well as the Camolin, Coolgreany, Castletown and Gorey corps from north Wexford. The military were divided into four divisions: Colonel Wynne; elements of the 4th and 5th Royal Irish Dragoon Guards and Ancient Britons, Lieutenant-Colonel Cope; elements of the Armagh, Tyrone, North Cork and Cavan Militia and Suffolk Fencibles, Colonel Maxwell; elements of Antrim and Derry Militia and Colonel Skerret; Durham and Dunbarton Fencibles. Castlereagh put Needham's force at 1,600 men and anticipated Dundas entering Carnew in the days following 8 June with 2,400. General Champagne in Newtownbarry had 900 men and Johnson at New Ross commanded 2,000, exclusive of yeomanry. The yeomanry at Arklow were commanded by Captains Lord Wicklow (Arklow Northshire), Atkins (Arklow Southshire), Mountnorris (Camolin), Beaumann (Coolgreany) and Grogan (Castletown) and amounted to 260 mounted and 77 dismounted men.[148]

Needham's task was greatly facilitated by apparent dissipation of the insurgent effort in north Wicklow after 31 May and its failure to take hold in the southern baronies. As the Dublin road had not been overrun, his passage towards Wexford had been unopposed and he received the valuble reinforcements in the hours before the battle of Arklow on 9 June. Press reports of Wicklow being 'nearly tranquillized' and the rebels around Arklow being 'surrounded in such a manner that a single rebel cannot escape' did not reflect the reality of the situation on the ground.[149] The mood was quite different in private loyalist circles where it was rumoured 'a large body of yeomen' had been 'cut off' and defeated in Wicklow.[150] Castlereagh considered the rebels to be 'well organized' and to consist of virtually the entire male population of Wexford supported by strong bodies from Wicklow, Carlow, Kildare and Kilkenny.[151]

Arklow lacked sufficient sources of supply and services for so many soldiers whose requirements rapidly exerted extreme pressure on local creameries and blacksmiths. The troops were also prone to plundering the local inhabitants in Arklow, Glenart, Curranstown and the surrounding district. Local yeomen also burned many houses which they found empty on the reasonable presumption that their occupants were absent with the rebels. A town premises owned by the shipowner Philpot near Doyle's Lane was requisitioned as a hospital by the soldiers, a choice perhaps suggested by the knowledge that its landlord had pioneered United Irish networks in the barony in late 1797. The Protestant church on the main street was also pressed into service as an auxiliary barracks for a detachment of Gordon Highlanders who cleaned their weapons and kit in the adjacent graveyard. Needham established his command post in front of the town's small permanent barracks but had no time to properly level the banks lying close by.[152]

Arklow was the scene of feverish activity in the three days before the rebels attacked; firing platforms or banquettes were built by the army using wood ripped from houses in the town, fences were destroyed to give the defenders clear fields of fire and trenches were dug at strategic points. Lieutenant Owen Fawcett of the Durhams, later Inspector of Works at Gorey, was charged with organizing the preparation of infantry positions around the field encampment adjacent to the town and deliberately used materials taken from the homes of local United Irishmen for which he was arrested on charges of vandalism after the rebellion. Ship's carpenters were also conscripted to erect a sturdy wooden platform within the barrack walls which gave the cannon mounted on it increased range from the elevation as well as a commanding view of rebels approaching from the Coolgreany road.[153] As the preparations continued apace, specific information was received from Thomas Edwards of Kilpipe who had crossed the mountains from Hacketstown upon learning from three indiscreet 'rebel chiefs' that the anticipated assault on Arklow was imminent. This was only one of many warnings received on 9 June which alerted the army and lessened still further rebel chances of achieving what had promised to be their greatest triumph. Rebel suspects within the garrison were secured and it was falsely rumoured in Dublin that the imprisoned Arklow United Irishman Phil O'Neil had been hanged and his house robbed of 145 guineas. O'Neil was actually safe in Wicklow Town jail but Musgrave's sources informed him that the army 'took as hostages, a great number of . . . [Arklow's] principal disaffected inhabitants'.[154]

Needham's forces was insufficient to protect the entire perimeter of Arklow so he selected only the most strategic locations and the best fighting positions. The Avoca river afforded the Dublin side of the town natural protection as the ground between it and the banks was too marshy and vegetated to facilitate a massed attack. The barracks and the Coolgreany road barricade which blocked access to the main street were both defended by the Antrim Militia under Captain Rowan and Lieutenant Colonel O'Hara respectively. Rowan's men included the unreliable survivors of Tubberneering and were joined on the firing platforms lining the exterior wall by supplementary yeomen. The military encampment in the fields extending from close to the barracks towards, but not reaching, the Yellow Lane ring road were defended by the experienced and well-trained Dunbarton and Durham fencibles under Skerret. The Durhams had taken part in the dragooning of Down in 1797 and had survived a poorly executed ambush at Balbriggan on their march to Dublin in early June. Four cannon were sited within their lines, two of which could cover the approaches to the barricade. The opposite side of the camp was guarded by the elite light companies of the Suffolk and Tyrone regiments under Cope who took advantage of dense hedgerows to shield their English and Scottish comrades as well as access to the centre portions of the linear town. They were also posted with yeomen in

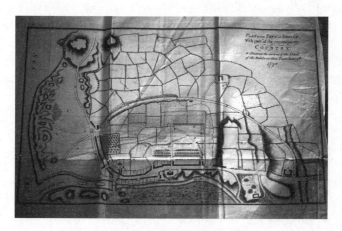

PLAN OF THE TOWN OF ARKLOW.
From Sir Richard Musgrave's *Memoirs of the different Rebellions*, 1801

several buildings at the southern end of the town which effectively sealed the lower part of the street on which the barracks stood. Their positions also offered some protection to the vital Avoca River bridge and the road to Dublin which was also covered by Maxwell's troops and a barricade blocking access from the largely exposed fishery. The bridge itself and its Dublin bank (Ferrybank) were the starting positions of Wynne's cavalry which were held in reserve on the most sensitive portion of Arklow's defences.[155]

Gorey Hill camp on the evening of 8 June 1798 was also seething with as many as 20,000 men, women and children. Rebel officers, distinguished from the men by badges, green sashes or pieces of bear skins on their hats, assembled their units from the masses of rebels and camp followers and practised marching and battle tactics. Maurice Darkie saw Patrick Carroll of the Redcross corps wearing 'a green spencer, with an officer['s] hat with a brush over it, and a black cockade, and a green one over it'. Darkie noted that 'those who were named officers were better dressed and had nicer [fire]arms than the common men. Some officers had not a distinguishing badge except that they were better clothed.' Their advance to Arklow was, unsurprisingly, characterized by ill-discipline and over-confidence and could have been nothing else in view of the massive size of the force which thronged the road. The Ballymanus Division had the honour of forming the vanguard and led the column to Anthony Perry's home village of Inch where it was decided to rest for an hour before proceeding to Coolgreany.[156]

This stop and the general confusion attending the slow advance on Arklow was subsequently criticized by prominent participants; Michael Dwyer reputedly said that the battle was lost at Coolgreany 'by drunkenness and insubordination'. The proportion of incapacitated and inebriated rebels, however, could not have been very great given the huge numbers of men involved and the brevity of the halt.[157] Fr John Murphy, among the most charismatic and respected rebel commanders, withdrew from the rebel column as it passed Castletown, possibly in protest at the decision to detour to Coolgreany rather than march directly for Arklow. That Fr Michael Murphy of Ballycanew also pulled back indicates that the tactical disagreements had created damaging command fissures at a time when unity of purpose was essential. A more immediate problem was the unwieldy size of the force which posed a great impediment to mobility, deployment and supply. When the march recommenced, William Byrne attempted to reach the head of the rebels to restore order and unit cohesion, but was thrown from his horse and was obliged to abandon the effort.[158]

Another reason for the Coolgreany visit was probably the need to obtain food and a local rebel named Byrne was apparently applied to by a hungry officer. The discovery of a large quantity of bread being baked by the Flight family at Cullanogus near Gorey had probably helped raise the spirits of many. The Flights were one of many loyalist families helping supply the Arklow garrison where two of their members were enrolled as supplementary yeomen. They were forced to abandon their home when a patrol of the Arklow Infantry warned them of the imminent approach of the rebels. The bread and stores of fresh milk were hastily consumed by the insurgents who burned the property before recommencing their march.[159] A further moment of paralysis was experienced at Curranstown within two miles of Arklow when Esmond Kyan received a message purporting to come from some of the Antrim Militia in the garrison. The communication urged him to postpone the attack for a day to enable the United Irish sympathizers and members within the regiment to defect. The subsequent rate of desertion from this regiment and high level of rebel infiltration indicates that this overture was probably not a ruse but it came too late to be acted upon. Kyan's personal dilemma may have been

GENERAL JOSEPH HOLT, 1798,
Power Collection.

WILLIAM MICHAEL BYRNE,
*c. 1798, Presidential Collection,
Aras An Uachtarainn.*

EDWARD COOKE.
Power Collection.

MICHAEL DWYER, based on
portrait by George Petrie, *c.* 1804.
Power Collection.

MYLES BYRNE in old age.
Power Collection.

LORD CORNWALLIS.
Power Collection.

LORD CASTLEREAGH.
Power Collection.

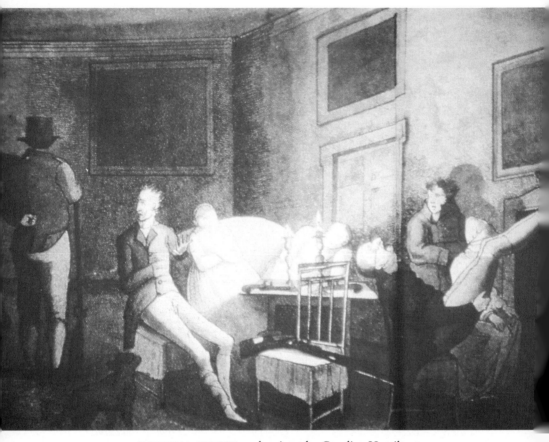

ROSSANA HOUSE under siege, by Caroline Hamilton,
Private Collection.

KINGSTON, HOME OF THOMAS KING, detail of painting
by Thomas Sautell Roberts, 1804. *National Gallery*.

LUGGELA, N.L.I.

CROSS BELT BADGE OF THE RATHDRUM CAVALRY,
courtesy of the Kilmainham Collection, photographed by
Alastair Smeaton.

THE SCALP, 1796, by Thomas Macklin, N.L.I.

CRONEBANE FORT (detail) by Thomas Sautell Roberts, 1804.
National Gallery.

EARL ALDBOROUGH'S SEAT AT BELAN, Kildare.
Power Collection.

THE BATTLE OF ARKLOW,
(detail) by Captain Holmes.

MOUNT KENNEDY HOUSE,
home of Lord Rossmore, N.L.I.

RUSSBOROUGH HOUSE, *c.* 1826,
by J. P. Neale, N.L.I.

KILRUDDERY HOUSE, January 1793,
by J. P. Neale, N.L.I.

THE MEETING OF THE WATERS, 1804,
by Thomas Sautell Roberts, N.L.I.

considerable given that he, according to Luke Cullen's sources, had 'certainly had some previous knowledge of the disposition of these men, and . . . had personal communication with them in Arklow'.[160]

The rebel officers were then busy attempting to regroup the corps which had been partially dispersed since leaving Gorey Hill and made final preparations to deploy the force in three distinct columns. One was instructed to attack the Arklow fishery district from the east and accordingly cut across from McGrath's Cross to the coast road to approach that part of the town through Arklow Rocks. Another strong body, which later coalesced with the Rocks force, progressed a little further along the Coolgreany road as far as the Yellow Lane intersection and then followed the course of its long arc towards its termination on the outskirts of the fishery. The third and probably largest element proceeded along the Coolgreany road which led directly into the town in order to confront the army's blocking positions. These difficult manoeuvres and the siting of at least two captured cannons may have taken over two hours and it is likely that the sheer numbers of insurgents precluded the committal of many units to the battle.[161]

Matters were not alleviated by the unpredictable behaviour of several rebel factions such as the one composed of Wicklowmen which left the Coolgreany road to sack and then burn the Lambarton home of Revd Edward Bayly. Although a man of sixty plus years he had become notorious arising from his pre-rebellion conduct as a magistrate and would probably have been killed if encountered. Henry Bayly's yeoman duties were also resented and it is clear that the family's servant Manifold had no chance of preventing the destruction of Lamberton.[162] Revd Bayly was one of many local figures who had deemed it prudent to sail to Dublin from Arklow on the day of the battle and when explaining why he left the town in its hour of crisis maintained that 'the horror and agony of mrs Bayly was such that I could not resist . . . the men said they saw numbers coming over the rock of Arklow; they were perhaps, like ourselves desolate fugitives, but they might be a party of rebels pushed on that back way'.[163] Lieutenant-Colonel John Caldwell ascertained from an 'undoubted authority' that Lamberton had been burned on William Byrne's orders as 'Bayley [sic] had some years ago purchased part of the estate of Byrne's father under a decree of the Court of Chancery and because of the zeal and activity of Mr. Bayley [sic]'. No such personal animus was necessary, however, as the targeting of the Baylys mirrored the actions of the Wexford rebels on 6 June 1798 who had burned Hunter Gowan's Mount Nebo property.[164]

The army outpost at Charterhouse (Charter School) was engulfed shortly after the ill-disciplined diversion to Lamberton and its occupants soon withdrew down the road towards the barricade. Byrne reputedly shot or stabbed their officer, apparently Lieutenant Elliott of the Antrims, but not fatally. A forward cavalry patrol had also been posted at the Coolgreany/Woodenbridge crossroads which immediately retreated behind the infantry trench lines upon sighting the encroaching insurgents. A Welsh dragoon later told Sarah Tighe that 'the appearance the enemy made was astonishing, they seemed to cover the face of the earth [and] . . . advanced in most regular order each parish by itself and headed by its priest'.[165] Needham also gained the impression that the rebel officers appeared to be all mounted 'priests and farmers', one of whom wore a white uniform and was observed to shoot at several men 'for not coming on in the action'.[166]

Efforts to maintain the physical integrity of fighting units, essential for the smooth dissemination of and efficient response to verbal orders, was bolstered by the practice of each corps carrying its own standard or 'colours'. One of the banners had a white cross superimposed on a green background and another reputedly bore the legend 'Liberty or Death'. They provided focal points during the natural confusion of battle and also fostered camaraderie and fighting spirit. Morale and organization was also promoted by officers who were known to have reassembled partially dispersed corps at Arklow by shouting out the names of their places of origin.[167] While the corps system was a visually impressive manifestation of United Irish solidarity and determination, many professional soldiers viewed their comparative irregularity with disdain. Professional soldiers were accustomed to facing trained infantry and obliged to fight in rigidly co-ordinated ranks, files and squares. The only troops who generally skirmished were the grenadier and light infantry companies which constituted the flank elements of a battalion, several companies of which were present in Arklow.[168]

Cannon within the positions of the Durham fencibles, who had only arrived in Arklow on commandeered carts that morning, swept the road and field approaches with grape and round shot which forced the insurgents to enter the contiguous fields for shelter. Fighting began at around 4.00 p.m. and raged until almost 9.00 p.m. During three frontal charges on the fencibles' position the cannon fire reputedly 'tumbled them by twenties' and made large gaps in the rebel lines which 'were as quickly filled up'. Arklow yeoman Henry Bayly noted that the initial discharge of the cannon 'awakened them from the seeming astonishment into which our appearance had thrown them for a few moments – not having expected to find us prepared. They then rushed on like madmen'. To mount an attack on the camp area the rebels had to leave fields which were shielded by hedges and ridges from enemy musketry, cross a stream bed and negotiate the embankments, trenches and hedges which protected the military opponents. This took time during which they were exposed to the withering firepower of the camp defenders.[169]

Mangled bodies quickly filled the lanes and approaches to the army's entrenchments which impeded subsequent attempts by the rebels to close with their adversaries. The insurgent musketeers had no choice but to persevere and reputedly plied the Durhams with 'a hot but irregular fire' from close range while mounted rebel officers courageously rode into the cannon positions to discharge their pistols at the gun-layers. The cool-headed Colonel John Skerret, a veteran of the West Indies, forced the fencibles to observe strict fire discipline in the face of these harassing forays and claimed to have lost twenty men in the process. Iron discipline was essential if the vastly outnumbered soldiers were to maintain their rate of musket fire. Each man discharged three to four aimed rounds per minute and when organized into co-ordinated firing and reloading ranks this produced an almost contin-uous wall of fire. The protective earthworks and hedgerows fronting the British troops ensured that the insurgents had to get to within point-blank range if their own much weaker firepower was to tell and their pikemen brought to bear.[170]

Control of the two or three rebel-held cannon was initially left to their trained captive Antrim Militia and Royal Irish Artillery crews who apparently endeavoured to save the lives of their comrades and waste ammunition by deliberately overshooting. One was pulled down the Yellow Lane and sited on a hillock, and while overlooking the Durham/Dunbarton positions it had little effect on the course of the battle owing to its distance from the defenders and mishandling. A piece which had been taken from the Derry Militia was placed under the control of an Antrim Militia serjeant who was obliged to correct its aim. One overcorrected shot reputedly tore through a tightly packet knot of pikemen killing many. When much of the scarce round shot had been expended without effect, ex-artillery officer Esmond Kyan and Dick Monk took over the cannon which had been dragged into fields from the Coolgreany road and directed its fire with great effect.[171]

Their most destructive shot scored a direct hit on a British ammu-nition cart which exploded killing thirteen gunners and fencibles while another excellently aimed ball immobilized a Durham operated

gun-carriage by wrecking its wheel. A less accurate cannon ball narrowly missed the barracks and travelled on to demolish the corner Charles Sternes's house, a post master and Carysfort's agent for Arklow Town. Miles Byrne maintained that Kyan's efforts temporarily forced the bulk of the targeted soldiers out of their positions and had brought an insurgent victory within reach. They certainly discomfited the British infantry enabling the insurgents to form up for what transpired to be a failed assault on the Durham and Dunbarton lines. The good run came to an abrupt halt when what remained of Kyan's partially amputated arm was carried off by a British cannon ball and their own ammunition supplies dwindled to negligible levels.[172]

The attack on the fishery by the Arklow Rocks column and the Yellow Lane group commenced before the costly attempts on the Coolgreany road positions but made very little headway against their entrenched and barricaded enemies. A potentially critical situation had been averted, however, when a counter-attack by Wynne's Ancient Britons, aided by the 4th and 5th Dragoons and the yeomanry, was repulsed. The troopers and yeomen had moved off the bridge and crossed from Ferrybank in an attempt to stall if not reverse the rebel advances. Their charge could not have been mounted with great vigour or with any real expectation of sparking a rout in view of the overwhelming numerical strength of the rebels whose stand was, nevertheless, a considerable achievement for what was an essentially untrained guerrilla army. The rebels, in fact, had inflicted several casualties on the cavalrymen and forced them to extricate themselves from a potentially lethal envelopment.[173]

The Yellow Lane rebels were apparently responsible for the burning of the fishery in the hope of creating a smoke-screen under which they could close with their adversaries but their incendiaries were not totally indiscriminate; a row of wooden cabins was preserved when one of them was found to contain a dying man. This stratagem was probably suggested by the absence of nearly all the district's inhabitants in Welsh ports, the insurgent camps and elsewhere. Those who had remained in the town on the morning of the battle had been warned by an English soldier to get out of harm's way. The Kearons and many of the fishery's Protestant inhabitants apparently took to the sea in their boats for the several critical days in which the fate of Arklow lay in the balance. They remained offshore during the hours of daylight and returned once darkness fell to spend the night ashore at Seabank, two miles north of the town in the parish of Kilbride. Virtually all of the highly combustible cabins in which they lived were consumed during the conflagration of 9 June but were quickly rebuilt.[174] The initial benefit of the smoke-screen was reversed when the wind changed direction and blew it back into the faces of the insurgents, although it probably caused the deaths of Captain Thomas Knox Grogan and two Castletown yeomen who inadvertently rode into the path of 'friendly' cannon fire late in the battle.[175]

The insurgents in the fishery maintained their positions for two-and-a-half hours in the face of stiff infantry opposition until a concerted counter-attack by the Cavan Militia forced them to pull back from their objective, the bridge leading to Dublin. Captain Moore of the 5th Dragoons noted that the rebels had 'advanced in an irregular manner and extended themselves for the purpose of turning our left flank . . . rushed into the lower fishery . . . [and were] completely routed'.[176] This was an oversimplification as the insurgents had only reluctantly withdrawn along the coast road leaving the battlefield strewn with bodies and in flames. They were not pursued at this moment of extreme vulnerability, however, as the cavalry were unwilling to risk charging over the boggy terrain and had received a blow to their morale during their first attempt.[177]

The bloody failure of the second Coolgreany road assault encouraged Byrne and Perry to implement a bold initiative which promised to preserve lives and possibly turn the tide of the battle. Pikemen were sent down towards the town through the long sloping parkland which extended from Lamberton along the course of the narrow Avoca river bank. Little or no action had hitherto taken place on this unsuitable ground and a probe of Needham's positions there held out the prospect of outflanking the barracks and thus opening an alternate route to the main street if the defences were found to be weak. The tactic failed almost at the outset when the vigilant soldiers in the barracks noticed the insurgents forming up in the exposed parkland at some distance and diverted a detachment of Dunbartons to cover the territory with their concentrated musketry. They may also have been fired upon by the gun sited in the barracks even though its ammunition was being fast expended. The Scotsmen inflicted many casualties on their adversaries, whom, being armed only with pikes and ultimately incapable of closing with the troops, were virtually defenceless. Perry's ardour in this phase of the battle had also been somewhat cooled when his horse was shot and killed as he rode down the incline, probably throwing him to the ground heavily.[178]

The arrival of Fr Michael Murphy of Ballycanew brandishing a 'liberty or death' standard on the far side of the town occasioned the third and final pike charge on the exposed terrain around the Coolgreany road. He had belatedly followed the main force from Coolgreany and had been surprised to encounter insurgents retreating from what he knew to be a decisive battle upon which all United Irish plans were contingent. When attempting to stem the tide of defeatism, Murphy allegedly produced his handkerchief and 'declared he would shake off the Orange-mens [musket] balls' as he had at Gorey by which he implied that they were invulnerable.[179] William Byrne, who had led from the front with his sword in his hand had already lost many insurgents prior to the priest's arrival and his second-in-command, Daniel Kirwan of Ballymanus, had also impressed his men with his 'coolness and bravery'. Kirwan and Byrne survived the earlier bloody attacks unscathed but a well-directed brace of canister shot felled the dynamic Fr Murphy very close to the barracks. Rebel ranks which had been 'absolutely mowed down . . . three times' finally gave way.[180]

Skerret, responsible for the critical camp sector, claimed that the insurgent . . .

column was restored by their best troops and commanded by their favourite priest Murphy who fell on their third attack. At this a general dismay took place and they flew in every direction. We availed ourselves of it. I ordered Sir W[atkin] Williams [Wynne] with his cavalry to charge. The carnage was astonishing.

He estimated rebel losses at 1,800. The near suicidal heroism displayed by the rebels during their repeated assaults on the Durham guns also surprised Needham. His six pounders had fired grape shot as quickly as they could be reloaded for three-and-a-half hours into the massed ranks of the pikemen who had advanced on several occasions to within point-blank range. The General claimed that 200–300 'fell at the muzzle of them'.[181] Byrne of Ballymanus attempted to rally his demoralized retreating riflemen, who alone could have bolstered the massed pikemen with their supporting fire, but they possessed neither the ammunition nor the willpower for a fourth assault. There were, significantly, 'very few guns' in the Ballymanus Division which was detached from the main body of Wexford riflemen commanded by Edward Fitzgerald of Newpark. With light fading the dejected rebels fell back on Gorey Hill where they regrouped their forces and took stock of their defeat. The strategic initiative passed once again to the government after a battle that was probably the most crucial of the rebellion. The retreat to Gorey Hill was as orderly as could have been expected from an exhausted and disappointed force of its size. Needham was informed by prisoners or defectors that this had occurred 'about ten [o'clock]' and that the withdrawal was covered by 2,000 men who would have been alert to the threat of dragoon attack.[182]

Rebel casualties undoubtedly ran into several hundreds killed and may well have exceeded 1,000 fatalities with many hundreds wounded. The death toll would have almost certainly have reached unprecedented levels for 1798 had Needham ordered the cavalry to charge his defeated enemy. His aide-de-camp, Captain Moore, explained to an exasperated General Lake that the failure to inflict a decisive defeat on the 'Gorey' army had hinged on advice that the surrounding countryside was 'too much enclosed' for the horses.[183] Hundreds of wounded rebels were located and carried to safety on carts but those who had to be left behind were reportedly 'hanged out of the protestant churchyard trees' in accordance with the brutal practices of eighteenth-century regulars. Drumhead court martials of those captured on the field continued for several days after the battle, most of whom were also hanged, although at least one condemned man was dispatched by the extremist Lieutenant Sherwood.[184]

While several commentators have argued that the retreat from Arklow was premature and that Needham was on the point of pulling out, it is apparent that the orders given by the commander late in the battle addressed the consolidation of positions rather than their evacuation. Small groups of yeomen and soldiers had given ground when pressed but the bulk of the forces at Arklow clearly did not, despite having expended nearly all their ammunition preventing the rebels seizing the town. Ammunition was a major factor in the inability of the insurgents to win the day and was also the most critical weakness of Arklow's garrison.[185] Needham's failure to disperse the insurgents obliged him to maintain a state of defence for several days as the possibility of a second attempt had not been ruled out. His exhausted men maintained a state of readiness until 4.00 p.m. on 10 June and were roused a few hours later at dawn to face what they anticipated to be an even stronger rebel army. Dublin loyalist Robert Johnson was far from impressed by the handling of the battle and informed Downshire that 'the glorious victory (as it is called in the papers) of Arklow was nothing more than that troops *were able to maintain their post*, though attacked with great vigour, but could not prevent a great part of the town from being burnt'. Johnson had brought ammunition to Arklow from Dublin on the 10th in response to an urgent express and was aghast to discover that the town could have been lost had the rebels recommenced their attack as the defending troops possessed only eight rounds each and 'not a case of canister or grape shot'.[186]

One of the most controversial episodes of the battle for Arklow was the alleged dismemberment and dishonouring of Fr Murphy's body. Henry Bayly recalled that the priest's body was discovered on 10 June and although beheaded was not otherwise maltreated before being thrown into a burning house with those of other dead rebels. His corpse was clearly identifiable, notwithstanding its extensive disfiguring wounds, as Colonel Maxwell and several members of the government forces knew him 'personally'.[187] Bayly's claim that charred insurgent bodies were afterwards buried in a ditch supports the story that Murphy's head and arm had been severed on the orders of Lord Mountnorris for symbolic purposes. What remained of Murphy's corpse and that of his nephew was reputedly secretly recovered by his sister for a Christian burial on the night of 11 June. It seems highly unlikely, however, that the priest's heart had been removed by the Ancient Britons, as alleged by Revd Gordon, and used to grease their boots. Colonel Wynne dismissed this in December 1801 as 'a gross calumny, totally destitute of any foundation'.[188]

Major Hardy had been leading a yeomanry patrol on Croghan mountain at 6.30 p.m. on 9 June when he heard the sounds of battle emanating from Arklow. When a yeoman ascertained that Needham urgently required extra ammunition, Hardy notified Camden of the development and then went to Rathdrum, from whence he had probably come, to organize a relief force. 100 Antrims and 56 7th Dragoons were hastily dispatched to Arklow from Rathdrum and a temporary camp near Aughrim with all the munitions he could spare but they did not arrive until shortly after the battle. It is unclear whether Captain Maitland's 'earnest request' for a howitzer and a cart-load of canister and shot was met, but 6,000 rounds of ammunition was sent from stores at Lehaunstown Camp and Bray.[189] The reinforcement from Rathdrum returned to its post late on 10 June when it became obvious that the rebels at Gorey Hill had no intention of resuming the offensive against Arklow in the short term. News of the victory was then sent by yeomen and dragoons to Wicklow, Bray, Newtownmount-kennedy, Loughlinstown and Dublin where it altered the timetable for the proposed relief of Wexford.[190] The deployment of the 800-strong regular forces under General Ralph Dundas in Baltinglass on 10 June was also materially affected by the perceived impasse at Arklow. Dundas had intended moving forward to Hacketstown on the 10th but the distinct possibility of an insurgent victory at Arklow obliged him to remain in west Wicklow lest his troops be required to intercept a rebel column *en route* to Dublin. He requested clarification of the strategic picture from the city that day and also from Hardy in Rathdrum who informed him via an express rider that Arklow was secure.[191]

The scale of the carnage at Arklow was considerable and a serious health hazard to residents of the district in the heat of summer. Bodies of those slain at the battle, or at least those killed in the fishery assaults, were laid out at by the sea front at Togher and buried in slit trenches by conscripted labour. Human bones were found in the sand banks for many years after the rebellion. Inland, around Bayly's torched Lamberton home, some of the locals adopted a more sanguine approach. On 10 June fourteen-year-old milkmaid Mary Byrne walked past Lamberton where she observed 'dead bodies . . . lying on the road and the pigs tearing them like anything, all blood from their mouths and flys [sic]. The bodies were thrown on the [Ferrybank] sands and the farmers took them for manure until Lord Wicklow stopped it.' A Gordon Highlander who visited Arklow several days after the battle confirmed that many bodies remained unburied in the parts of the town where fighting had occurred. Some lay in ditches where pigs gorged themselves on their shattered bodies.[192]

Defeat at Arklow was a major blow to the Dublin city rebels and the Leinster leadership who had expected the Wexford and Wicklowmen to 'carry all before them and march down to Dublin'.[193] This view was clearly shared by the rebel leaders at Arklow and was expressed in a letter attributed to Fr Michael Murphy which was addressed to Thomas Houston of the Thomas Street United Irishmen just before the Battle of Arklow. It declared 'great events are ripening. In a few days we shall meet [in Dublin] . . . We shall have an army of brave republicans, one hundred thousand [strong], with fourteen pieces of cannon, on Tuesday before Dublin . . . You will rise with a proportionate force.' The figure 100,000 is of interest as it is much higher than that generally ascribed to the insurgent army at Arklow and certainly more than had been amassed. It could signify that once victorious at Arklow the rebels anticipated a large reinforcement from Wicklow and elsewhere.[194]

The Thomas Street committee had sent Fr John Martin of Drogheda, a disaffected Augustinian priest, into the Wicklow mountains to 'hasten this march' to Dublin which they hoped would be assaulted on 12 June. Martin was a highly experienced United Irish recruiter and propagandist whose activities were facilitated by his clerical status. The men who entrusted him with the post-Arklow strategy had specifically instructed him to have the Wicklowmen 'cooperate at a fixed time-and to excite the people to act'.[195] Martin was probably one of several emissaries charged with this vital task and it is likely the Bray innkeeper arrested on 8 June for 'acting as a spy for the Anarchists of his acquaintance' had come into contact with someone bearing news of the impending Arklow/Dublin assaults. Three city officers who visited the Wicklow rebel forces at Mount Pleasant camp on 17 June bore similar information which affected the decisions of rebel leaders.[196] Martin's communication envisaged co-operation extended from Dublin to Dunboyne in Meath and other districts outlying Dublin where he had preached in late May and early June 1798 and established contact with rebel leaders. He had also spread his message in Manor Kilbride, Wicklow, at this time urging the people to persevere in the face of rebel defeats. The plan went wrong when the vigilant Rathdrum yeomanry arrested Martin at Cronebane on 11 June as he was travelling towards Arklow. He immediately confessed to having been through the mountain communities around Roundwood as well as the villages 'round the coast'.[197]

Martin's excursion had commenced at Rathfarnham in south
County Dublin, a traditional access point to the Dublin and Wicklow
mountains, in the first week in June where he received directions to
meet rebel officers encamped above the town in the Dublin mountains.
Joseph Holt was one of the first to meet the emissary when they
conferred in a shebeen near the Ballynascorney home of the Wicklowman's brother Thomas, sometime between 6 and 8 June at which time
Holt had an estimated 300 rebels under his command whom he
offered to show to Martin. Also in the Bohernabreena/Ballynascorney
area were two other insurgent groups under Dubliners Nugent and
Doyle who comprised part of the command of that county's popular
Colonel Francis McMahon of Aungier Street, Dublin. There was also
a Captain John Doyle of Kilbride who was in contact with Michael
Mahon of Dublin, Arthur Quinn of Rathmore, John Sheridan of
Ballinascorney, the Lawlors of Ballinascorney and other rebel officers
in the Dublin mountains. Nugent was probably the man of that name
who headed a United Irish committee which met at Blake's on Thomas
Street and Doyle was perhaps the Lusk man who kept a hospital for
insurgents wounded in the fighting in Wexford.[198]

On returning from Corbet Hill in early June Holt had 'proceeded
promiscuously through the mountains' until he encountered seventy
rebels led by the former city attorney McMahon. He may have been
led to this group by the Dublin officers with whom he had associated
near New Ross if not before. A veteran of the skirmish at Fox and
Geese on 23 May, the militant McMahon had entered the mountains
two days later in a fruitless bid to encourage the Wicklow rebels to
follow through with the plan to attack the capital.[199] His faction had
not gone to Wexford and was one of several which had formed camps
in the mountains behind Rathfarnham. A castle spy ascertained on
5 June that the 'late successes' in Wexford had 'drawn the wavering
to join them' in the mountains, a development which convinced Camden
that a city revolt was being planned in early June. This factor prevented
the reinforcement of the Wicklow sector until the much anticipated
100th regiment had arrived from Britain and explains why Hardy
was so keen to protect Rathdrum on 10 June.[200]

There was a degree of animosity between Holt and McMahon
which seems to have arisen in consequence of the Dubliner's practice
of distributing requisitioned cash to his men for the support of their
families. Holt, a former subconstable, condemned McMahon's 'bur-
glarious designs' and was clearly unimpressed by arguments that the
citymen required cash to aid relatives in their absence whereas the

Wicklowmen had easy access to loyalist-owned livestock and crops. McMahon palliated his actions by issuing dockets for some of the goods he seized redeemable in the event of a rebel victory.[201] Holt stayed in McMahon's camp from 'Thursday till Saturday evening' (7 to 9 June) before suggesting, with characteristic pragmatism, that it be relocated to a more elevated part of the country. This elicited an unfavourable response from McMahon who was evidently dejected by the terrible news from Arklow, not least in that it nullified the plan which Fr Martin had just outlined to his subordinates. McMahon's faction established a camp at Whelp Rock near Blessington around this time while the Wicklowmen moved to Clohogue in the mountains above Roundwood where many of them had lived.[202]

The presence of large roving concentrations of rebels and their constant subsistence requirements destroyed whatever normality had survived the early weeks of the rebellion in Wicklow. On 4 June 1798 Fr Roger Miley, parish priest of Blessington, informed Archbishop Troy:

> For some days past we are totally convulsed both here and in the neighbouring parishes, every moral and religious sentiment has quit the country our chapels are forsaken by the flock and nothing but anarchy, confusion, rapine, plunder and burning introduced . . . the cottages of the poor and the habitations of many of the middling class have shared the same fate.[203]

This chaos had not been sought by the Dublin leadership who had attempted to steer if not impose a regional strategy on the south Leinster rebellion. Martin's mission was an important element of this co-ordination but it was contingent on the fall of Arklow and the failure of the rebels to prevail there all but invalidated his efforts. A new master plan was consequently sought by those leaders with channels of communication to the Thomas Street clique. An undated spy report from this period stated that 'Holt has sent [word] to Dublin to say that he will not act without orders from the executive.' Clarification of short-term United Irish objectives was then essential but Holt's immediate response to the set-back was to shift the thrust of his operations deeper into the mountains.[204]

In the early hours of 14 June rebels attached to Holt's force at Clohogue descended from their stronghold and attacked the loyalist properties which skirted the mountains from Derrybawn near Laragh to Ballinastow. Captain John Giffard of the Dublin City Militia stationed at Rathdrum 'beat to arms' on sighting the flames and reported that the rebels had burned 'the dwellings of every protestant'.[205] Giffard had spent four days in Rathdrum and his sectarian interpretation was probably influenced by the fact that he was an orangeman, given that the victims of the rebel blitz were almost all prominent loyalists who had been singled out with a discrimination borne of intimate local knowledge. He had also endured the tragedy of the loss of his teenaged son, Lieutenant William Giffard, at the hands of the rebels in the first days of the rebellion while his nephew, Captain Ryan, had sustained a mortal wound when arresting Lord Edward Fitzgerald.[206] When referring to the raid Sarah Tighe simply stated that 'several houses belonging to gentlemen near the Seven Churches were burnt a few nights ago' but the underlying seriousness of the event earned it national attention.[207]

Thomas Hugo's house and outoffices at Drummin were razed while John Chritchley of Laragh, Abraham Chritchley of Derrybawn and William Weekes of Annamoe all lost homes. The Chritchley's homes were reputedly 'totally burned and destroyed' on account of their 'signal loyalty [which had] . . . rendered them very early obnoxious to traitors of every description'.[208] Five to seven loyalists were burned out in Tomriland, five in Ballinastow and three in Castlekevin. The Diamond Hill home owned by the Lord Mayor of Dublin (Thomas Fleming), for whom Holt had once worked, was vandalized and Lady Frances Beresford of the powerful loyalist clan lost her Ballinastow residence. The innocuous Revd Ambrose Weekes, however, was merely robbed of his weapons while the homes belonging to moderate, non-yeomen local magistrates Peter La Touche and Andrew Price were not destroyed. Four 'active' magistrates were among those who suffered heavily, most notably Hugo whose Glendalough House was burned in the second attack on it in two weeks. John Beaghan of Tomriland, the sub-constable wounded in the first attack on Hugo's residence on 29 May by an eighteen-year-old local rebel, John Harman of Killafeen (Laragh), was burned out on 14 June but was not 'murdered in cold blood' as Musgrave claimed. One of Hugo's servants, James Irvine, joined the rebels and went with them to Scarr mountain.[209]

A more wide-ranging attack may have been planned but it was curtailed when Fr Christopher 'Wiggy' Lowe of Derrylossary implored the rebels to desist and managed to save a number of residences they had earmarked for destruction. The success of Lowe's remonstrance may have been due to his involvement with the United Irishmen and he was certainly unpopular in the loyalist community, elements of which burned his Annamoe chapel and attempted to assassinate him on several occasion in 1798–9.[210] They had learned on 11 June that Fr Martin had received a letter of introduction to Lowe from Fr Ledwich of Rathfarnham and that he was sympathetic towards the United Irishman if not a member. The first attempt on Lowe was carried out shortly afterwards by a group of Wicklow Town Cavalry headed by William Hugo whose father's home had been destroyed on 14 June. Richard Cotter was shown to Lowe's bedroom on some pretext where the priest lay ill and made several attempts to discharge his misfiring pistol. Having assured Lowe that he was not serious, Cotter was seen to the door, mounted his horse and fired a shot which passed through the door inflicting a slight injury on the elderly priest. Yeoman James Weekes was also present whose father, Revd Ambrose Weekes, had also suffered at rebel hands.[211]

The official response to the Holt raid was the attack on the house burners mounted by Captain Thomas King and sixteen of his Rathdrum Cavalry. They sallied out to confront the raiders and claimed to have killed 'many' of those they encountered for no losses. One of those taken prisoner was Patrick White of Castle Ellis, Wexford, a member of the famed 'Shelmalier' corps of insurgent riflemen, who claimed to have been visiting relatives near Rathdrum. White may have come from Lacken Hill camp in Wexford where the remnants of the 'Ross' army recuperated after the battle of New Ross on 5 June. His claim to have been visiting his wife is implausible and he was probably one of the many couriers employed by the rebels to maintain contact with various factions. It may be significant that Garret Byrne of Ballymanus made his debut in the insurrection of 21 June with the Shelmaliers under Edward Roche of Garrylough.[212] The raid of 14 June was the first major offensive action undertaken by the rebels in north Wicklow since the battle of Newtownmountkennedy and targeted loyalists who had hitherto been relatively unscathed by the rebellion. The Fermanagh Militia at Roundwood were the only government troops in the path taken by the rebels but were probably absent as they did not intervene. Their absence and the lack of a resident yeomanry corps in Roundwood may have encouraged the raid in an area which afforded immediate access to the mountains.[213]

The Roundwood/Glendalough raid may also have given vent to the frustration felt by the Wicklow rebels at the defeat and near total dissipation of the rebellion in Ulster, although it is unclear to what extent they were informed of developments in the north. The United Irishmen of Antrim and Down had been strongly embodied and reasonably well armed on the eve of the rebellion but, owing to the confusion surrounding its outbreak in Leinster on 23 May and the critical failure to mobilize in Dublin, their leaders prevaricated. Northern Presbyterians were also perturbed and confused by the reputed sectarian conduct of the mainly Catholic rebels in Leinster; stories of sectarian massacres and rebel oaths binding them to kill 'heretics' were readily disseminated by southern-based loyalists.[214]

On 6 June, tired of waiting for the French to land or for a decisive rebel victory in the south-east, veteran United Irishman Henry Joy McCracken ordered the Antrim rebels under his influence to turn out and fight. In the course of the following day engagements were fought at Antrim Town, Randalstown, Ballymena and Carrickfergus with mixed results but few strategic dividends. The battle of Antrim was similar in nature and result to that of New Ross several days earlier in that the initial success of the rebels was reversed by government counter-attack. Belfast, Blaris camp, Newry and other important centres where insurgent victories might have transformed the rebellion were neither threatened nor isolated which had serious repercussions for the insurgents when Major-General Nugent attempted to regain the initiative.[215] Down rebels inflicted a defeat on government forces at Saintfield on 9 June and the following day congregated in great numbers under Henry Munro of Lisburn at Ballinahinch. The Antrim rebel columns debated whether it was better to join their comrades at the camp in Down to decide the issue in Ulster or to march southwards through Newry to open a new front north of Dublin. The matter was resolved on 12 June when the Ballinahinch rebels were defeated and dispersed by Nugent in a lengthy contest with forces converging from Belfast and Downpatrick.[216]

The Ulstermen had failed to consolidate their positions in time to effect a juncture with other rebel bodies in the north and southern Leinster and were comprehensively defeated as a consequence. They were, however, hampered not only by the logistic and tactical challenges facing any group of inexperienced rebels but also by the army's possession of sensitive intelligence as to their intentions. The unexpected arrival of British reinforcements from Scotland increased the myriad difficulties facing McCracken and Munro. Nicholas Magin of Saintfield, a United Irish colonel, informed Dublin Castle of the deliberations of the Ulster Directory and forewarned them of the emergence of a new militant clique on 29 May determined to revolt. The outcome of this long-dreaded rising in the north pleased the government as much as it disheartened the rebels although the possibility of a renewed effort by the Ulstermen remained the object of speculation in both camps.[217]

MOUNT PLEASANT TO VINEGAR HILL

The rebels at Gorey Hill waited for stragglers for two days after the battle of Arklow before abandoning the camp. A small force of 100 men kept a look out on Ark Hill but withdrew when a yeomanry patrol noted their position on 10 or 11 June. The main force moved to the more elevated and defendable Limerick Hill three miles further north of Gorey Hill and within a mile of the strategic Wicklow Gap. These movements kept the army off guard and uncertain of rebel intentions. The Ballymanus Division and some Wexfordians went to Mount Pleasant near Tinahely on 14 June where most of the remainder at Limerick Hill had followed them by the 17th. The rebels at Mount Pleasant enjoyed a clear view of the mountains and routes through which any enemy would have to pass and were posted on a vantage protected by streams and broken ground. It was here that the Ballymanus Division reached its peak strength of at least 1,000 men and possibly as many as 1,800.[218]

Training exercises were carried out by the Wicklow leaders to occupy their men and improve their military potential. Charles Byrne of Ballyrogan drilled his Redcross company while Patrick Grant of Kirikee handled the recently arrived Glenmalure men. Other officers in the division at that time included Daniel Kirwan, Michael Dwyer, John Carroll, James Devitt, John Fowler, Mathew Doyle and James Doyle. News of Napoleon Bonaparte's association with the proposed Irish invasion reached Mount Pleasant which compensated to some degree for the revelation that the United Irish effort had all but collapsed elsewhere. Word of these development had been conveyed by three Dublin city insurgent officers known to Daniel Kirwan and quickly sparked a keen debate among the rebel commanders. One clique argued that they should maintain an intact rebel army on the defensive in the mountains until the French landed while their detractors opined that inflicting a defeat on the military would guarantee the survival of the rebel effort until foreign aid was forthcoming.[219]

The brutality shown to rebel prisoners and civilians by the army and yeomanry as well as those who had been left wounded on the battlefields of New Ross and Arklow imperilled the lives of pro-government forces encountered by the rebels. Dozens of loyalist prisoners were killed in retaliation for such atrocities and it was the general practice of the rebels to execute those perceived to be yeomen, informers and orangemen. Suspected ultra loyalists were generally 'tried' by a panel of rebels who determined their guilt and punishment;

Patrick Doyle and Joseph Codd were reputedly two of the judges at Vinegar Hill in late June.[220] William Byrne had great difficulty saving the life of his friend Thomas Dowse who had been seized near Little Limerick on the 15th and brought into Mount Pleasant as a prisoner by a rebel patrol. Dowse was a respected figure and big employer who was valued by some Wicklow insurgents for his potential as a hostage. Perry, Kyan and Edward Fitzgerald of Newpark were indifferent if not hostile towards Dowse and matters came to a head on 19 June when a group of rebel officers argued that he should be executed. Byrne obviated this by helping Dowse escape during the march of the insurgents to Wexford earning him a 1799 acknowledgement that 'he would have been killed at Camolin had it not been for the prisoner's [Byrne] interference'.[221]

Two Carnew yeomen captured at Tomacork, John Hope and John Brady, were less fortunate and after being brought through the various rebel camps from 10 June were either piked at Vinegar Hill or shot at Toome churchyard. On 17 June at Mount Pleasant and 18 June at Kilcavan Hill the rebels executed John Foster, John Walker, Thomas Braddell, Joshua Scott and Matthew Dowse who were all from the Tinahely/Kilpipe area. These were very probably the men who Miles Byrne claimed had been tried for 'persecuting the people' but the settling of personal scores may also have played a part in ensuring that they were not spared.[222] Executed with Foster was a local man named Free who was killed in retaliation for atrocities committed by the army near Mount Pleasant while one Berry died 'for being an Orangeman'. Matthew Davis of Ballinanty claimed that three men had been brought into the camp and 'shot as being orangemen by captain [Michael] Dwyer; but none of the head leaders were present.' James Doyle was actually absent with Dwyer in Ballinacor when this occurred and the Imaalman was furious to learn upon his return that his prisoners had been put to death without his permission. It is highly doubtful that Dwyer's influence would have been capable of opposing the popular will in this instance.[223] Several elderly and young prisoners belonging to loyalist families were released unharmed from Mount Pleasant although a group of Wexfordmen at Kilcavan Hill whose relatives had been massacred were less reserved and executed John Tomkins of Ballygullen, Hunter Gowan's brother-in-law and the father of two notorious yeomen.[224]

While the rebels reorganized their scattered groupings in the Mount Pleasant area and meted out revenge on loyalist elements within their remit, the government continued its comprehensive preparations to recapture County Wexford. The massing of troops for the campaign was delayed by the late arrival of reinforcements from Britain to protect the capital as well as the reluctance of Major-General Sir James Stewart to release soldiers from his largely passive Munster command where he was convince the insurrection wold take yet hold. On 15 June a large cavalry patrol of Ancient Britons, 5th Dragoons, Camolin and Arklow Cavalry reconnoitred from the gold mines to Aughrim and found the country 'quite destitute of inhabitants, and supposed them to have joined the main body of the rebels' at Mount Pleasant and Ballymanus. The build-up continued without rebel interference and by the 16th Loftus had re-occupied Tinahely from Tullow, Lake's forces were positioned in Carnew and Dundas had moved his troops into Hacketstown from Baltinglass as a prelude to an attempt on Enniscorthy.[225]

Advance parties of British cavalry skirmished with rebel patrols in the Carnew district on the 16th where the insurgents were keen to give battle. Troops operating from Tinahely cautiously probed the rebel positions on Mount Pleasant on 17 June but retreated when challenged by the well-prepared Wicklow pikemen. Matthew Doyle, stripped to the waist and brandishing a sword, manoeuvred his 200 men in the face of the troops in an attempt to provoke them into an ill-advised charge and when this was refused they pursued the withdrawing soldiers towards Tinahely. The military were surprised by this turn of events and hastily abandoned the village with all its military baggage and supplies to the pursuing rebels. Just such a scenario had been envisaged by Lake's advisors who had dispatched a sizeable reinforcement under Lord Roden which arrived too late to forestall the reverse.[226]

Tinahely was reputedly 'doomed in the hearts of the people around it on account of the virulence of the low set of yeomen belonging to it' and was promptly sacked and burned. One rebel veteran claimed 'as soon as we could we set fire to the town and paid but little attention to commanders'.[227] The extreme hostility towards the yeomen derived in part from claims that they were Foundling Hospital orphans who had been nursed and then adopted by Protestant families of the Carnew district. This allegation was backed by the Presbyterian United Irishman James Hope who theorized that having settled in Wicklow 'without any natural ties of blood or kindred, [and] prejudiced by their education against the Roman Catholics [they were] . . . regularly employed either as yeomen or spies'. A more compelling motive for the burning of Tinahely was the fact that its yeomen and 'True Blues' had looted Ballymanus House earlier that month and had acted with great brutality during the rebellion. Tensions would have mounted since the winter of 1797 to 1798 when arms-raiding and a security backlash had gripped the sector. Burning loyalist property, moreover, was the most practical and cogent means through which the insurgents could strike back against their opponents, almost all of whom were absent on yeomanry duty or had taken refuge in more secure garrisons.[228]

One of the most prominent local victims was the Coates family of Clone whose home was burned on 15/16 June even though it had apparently sheltered William Byrne of Ballymanus the previous week. No villagers were killed by the rebels during their brief occupation of Tinahely and it is clear that very few were prepared to risk living there in early June. At least three of the five loyalists captured in the area, however, were later put to death at Kilcavan Hill and Thomas Paslow, an aged man taken in Tinahely, claimed that he was almost piked for being an 'orangeman and [a] heretic' but had been protected by Byrne and Perry. Thomas Dowse, who then remained a prisoner with the rebels, claimed that 'after the town was set on fire, and while it continued burning one father [Andrew] Toole a Popish Priest celebrated Mass to the rebel army, then in sight of the burning town'. This unusual event may have been a calculated response to a pre-rebellion incident, or series of incidents, in which local orangemen had attempted to humiliate a Catholic priest by forcing him and his parishioners to walk under an Orange Order banner placed on the bridge leading from Tinahely to Crossbridge Chapel.[229]

The minor victory at Tinahely strengthened the hand of those who advocated waging a guerrilla war in the Wicklow mountains but they lacked the numbers to prevail against the majority Wexford-orientated bloc. The rebel army consequently returned to Kilcavan Hill on 18 June where they rejoined the main force encamped there and prepared to resist the anticipated army counter-attack. Kilcavan was reconnoitred later that day by General Lake who had just arrived in Carnew from Hacketstown to command the Wexford campaign. The army had not expected to find the rebels at Kilcavan and were diverted to it from their march to Vinegar Hill where they had learned that rebel forces were congregating. Lake's immediate objective was to prevent the rebels approaching Dublin and he had no intention of leaving such a large force to threaten his supply lines and communications. Major Hardy, who was very familiar with the geography of the district, accompanied Lake in his new capacity as acting Quarter-Master-General and advised him against a frontal attack on the position. The rebel camp was situated just above the farms belonging to Hardy's grandfather and uncle and he recommended that it be attacked from the rear. Thomas Hardy of the Hacketstown Infantry escorted Lake to view the approaches but these were also found to be 'too hazardous'.[230]

Musket and some cannon fire was traded by the opposing forces for several hours although no attempt was made to break each other's lines by assault and close combat. Colonel Ancram recalled that 'on firing the first [cannon] shot the whole of the rebel army gave three cheers, or rather yells, waving their hats on the points of their pikes, and their colours of which they had a considerable number.' A large body of cavalry under the normally aggressive Lord Roden approached the hill but were forced to fall back when 'fired upon pretty earnestly by musquetry [sic] behind the walls and hedges'.[231] All efforts to lure the rebels from the heights by means of harassing cannon and cavalry sorties were abandoned when it became clear that a risky infantry operation offered the only chance of clearing the hill. Lake reported that he had found the insurgents in 'great force' on Kilcavan and explained his failure by noting that they 'had taken every precaution to resist an attack'. His refusal of battle reflected the healthy respect of the army for the fighting ability of the rebels when in possession of high ground. The military retired for the night to the largely destroyed town of Carnew where, fearing attack, they remained on alert and shot two men as insurgent spies.[232]

The question of contesting Kilcavan was settled on 19 June by Revd Philip Roche who directed that the rebels fall back on Vinegar Hill, overlooking Enniscorthy, for the decisive encounter that was in the offing. Perry and most of the north Wexford and Wicklow leaders favoured striking through the mountains at Rathdrum to menace Lake's communications but they were overruled by Roche's supporters. This strategy had been foreseen by the military and in mid-June Captain Giffard in Rathdrum believed that 'if any reverse of fortune should befall the King's Army [in Wexford] this place will very probably be surrounded being the very centre of the rebels and a great object to Mr Billy Byrne of Ballymanus who is a chief leader and near neighbour to this town'. Many senior rebel officers, however, evidently viewed Vinegar Hill as another Oulart Hill on a much larger scale, a victory that held out the prospect of re-igniting the rebellion. Shadowed at a distance by two columns of Lake's troops, they marched through Camolin and Carrigrew Hill to Vinegar Hill arriving on 20 June.[233]

It was discovered at Vinegar Hill that Roche's 'Ross' division had failed to arrive and rebel officers found themselves in command of far fewer men than anticipated armed with just 4,000 poorly maintained muskets and a few cannon. Roche's army had been attacked by General John Moore's column at Foulksmill on 20 June and defeated after a short and closely fought battle. This defeat and the subsequent decision not to defend Wexford Town threw rebel strategy into disarray and facilitated the reoccupation of the county town on 22 June. This mysterious shortfall resulted in the dispatch towards Wexford town of a contingent under Edward Roche of Garrylough on a fruitless mission to regroup the Shelmalier corps and round up reinforcements.[234]

On 21 June Lake ordered the convergence of over 10,000 soldiers against Vinegar Hill camp and Enniscorthy under Generals Dundas, Duff, Johnson and Loftus. Needham's men had been ordered to advance through the countryside from Arklow to Oulart in order to cut off a natural line of retreat for the rebels but he mistimed the march and took no part in the battle. Arklow was left in the hands of one company of Durham fencibles under Captain Holmes supported by the Arklow Infantry, Loyal Mountnorris Infantry and the bulk of the cavalry units. It was planned that the army commanders would arrive at the battle scene more or less simultaneously to force the insurgents to stand and fight in a battle where they would be decidedly outgunned. Lake's troops accordingly moved out of their forward positions around six o'clock in the morning Lake's and commenced an attack on the right front of the camp with the light infantry of Dundas' brigade. Loftus attacked the centre of the camp and Duff the left while Johnson's men attempted to recapture Enniscorthy.[235]

The United Irishmen, disappointed by news of Moore's victory over Roche at Foulksmill and the non-arrival of fresh recruits from southern Wexford, offered vigorous opposition to the approaching troops. Several Wicklow yeomanry corps were part of Dundas' First Brigade, including the Dunlavin Cavalry, who had one of their number wounded in the attack. Insurgent musketeers held off Dundas' infantrymen from behind hedges and in ditches enduring twenty minutes of bombardment from the army's new explosive howitzer shells. The use of fused shells ensured that the defenders received their first exposure to shrapnel in the course of the most important battle that had been fought to date. Their misery was compounded by the operation of twelve conventional six-pounders which blasted other parts of the exposed rebel positions with grape shot with 'formidable effect'. Rebel cannon included three captured six-pounders and two howitzers but their insufficient ammunition supplies and inexpert handling yielded a poor rate of fire and effectiveness. Captain Robert Crawford of the Royal Irish Artillery recovered just seventeen rounds for the rebel-operated six-pounders and eleven for their howitzers. Outgoing cannon fire, however, may have steadied the nerves of those facing the terrifying firepower of the army.[236]

Enniscorthy was the scene of some of the first and most bitter fighting of the day where Johnson's troops supported by cannon attempted to drive the rebels under William Barker out of the town. Even before the shelling of Vinegar Hill had commenced in earnest, it had become evident that Barker's men required reinforcement. One of the principal units committed to the task was the Ballymanus Division which endured the majority of its casualties of 21 June contesting the vital Slaney bridge which stood between the army and Vinegar Hill. The sector was also of great importance owing to the access it offered to Darby's Gap, the logical and possibly predesignated avenue of retreat for the insurgents if their positions became untenable.[237]

Much confusion surrounded the deployment of the Wicklowmen on the morning of the battle as it was incorrectly rumoured that Garret Byrne of Ballymanus had entered the camp in the course of the previous night and was holding a council of war with other leaders. As Byrne joined the rebels some hours after the battle, apparently for the first time, it is likely that news of his presence in the locality had reached the camp although no Wicklow veterans saw him at Vinegar Hill. The rumour excited interest in the Wicklow ranks and a minority element apparently declined to be led by his brother William until it was positively ascertained that Garret was not in the camp. The Wicklowmen had resolved the issue and taken up positions in Enniscorthy before Lake's bombardment of the hill had become regular.[238]

They met with resolute opposition from Johnson's infantry whose effective range and field of fire covered the Slaney bridge. A group of Wexfordmen under Barker attempted a crossing but 'staggered and reeled from the stream of musket balls that were pouring over the bridge'.[239] Covered by their own riflemen, William Byrne led the Wicklow pikemen across the river losing his second-in-command Daniel Kirwan, another officer named Loftus and many others in the process. Kirwan's death was a severe loss from which the rebels 'could not easily be roused' and it was at this critical juncture that they exhausted their limited stocks of musket ammunition.[240] Doyle of Ballinacor recalled that . . .

> although the men were falling like leaves in October, they still pressed forward, and our pikemen grappled with their muskets. At this moment we, the Wicklows, came to the bridge. There was a bold and vigorous

cheer in our rear as about fifty of us passed over and that cheer was responded to by a deafening one on Vinegar Hill.

Inability to respond to the deadly blanket fire of Johnson's men prompted a fighting retreat to Vinegar Hill in which Barker and Fr Kearns were severely wounded.[241]

The relentless bombardment of Vinegar Hill and the determination of the soldiers to press home the attack convinced the surviving rebel leaders that defeat and annihilation was almost inevitable. Fortunately for them, Lake's cordon around Vinegar Hill was only partially effective due to the late arrival of Needham, which enabled the defeated insurgents to retreat towards Wexford Town. The absence of his column was particularly beneficial for the rebels as it contained the 5th and 9th Dragoons, Ancient Britons and elements of seven yeomanry cavalry corps which posed a grave threat to retreating irregulars. Matters were extremely serious as few prisoners were taken by the army and the numbers of their dead comrades was sufficiently large for the hill to reek from their half-buried corpses for many weeks.[242] Even Lake was forced to acknowledge that while the troops had behaved 'excessively well in action . . . their determination to destroy everyone they think a rebel is beyond description, and wants much correction.' One of the worst atrocities of 1798 occurred in Enniscorthy after the battle when the insurgent hospital was burned along with fifty-seven of its helpless patients.[243]

The retreating rebels were met at Darby's Gap by Garret Byrne in company with Edward Roche's force of 5,000 men, which included the bulk of the rebel riflemen who had been sorely missed in Enniscorthy. These relatively fresh men covered the withdrawal to Three Rocks camp where the rebel leadership discussed their predicament and waited as long as was prudent for stragglers. It was decided that the best prospect of reviving rebel fortunes lay with a division of forces which took place on the night of 21 June. The majority of the Wicklow and North Wexford men went north to Peppard's Castle *en route* to Gorey and ultimately into the Wicklow mountains while those from southern Wexford made for the barony of Forth under Fr John Murphy and Revd Roche.[244]

Negotiations had been entered into with Lake for the surrender of Wexford town with a view to securing the release of rebel prisoners and safeguarding civilians. Events overtook the issue on 22 June when General Moore's column entered the town without meeting significant opposition having easily defeated a rebel blocking force at

Taghmon. Roche, who favoured concluding a treaty with Lake, relinquished his command to the more militant Fr Murphy and was hanged upon entering the town to seek terms.[245] The government's successes in Wexford in late June undoubtedly dealt a grave blow to the United Irish cause and inflicted crippling damage on their offensive capacity but the insurgents were not easily defeated. A less obvious consequence of the campaign was the injection of fresh grievances to both pro- and anti-government camps which later frustrated attempts to bring the rebellion to a conclusion even after the prospect of an insurgent victory had been greatly reduced.

Amidst the exaggerated rumours of rebel atrocities emanating from Wexford were unsettling stories from authorative persons which detailed loyalist casualties and experiences. One which reached Rathdrum shortly after 21 June described how an unidentified woman, who had been released that week from Captain Dixon's prison ship in Wexford Harbour, had set off home on a two-mile journey from the county town where she was 'near tumbling over two dead bodies which lay in the street almost naked covered with blood'. Food was scarce and upon venturing under rebel escort towards the outskirts of the town the woman was appalled to see an insurgent column coming towards her with prisoners and the caps, side arms and two cannon taken from defeated troops. She conjectured that the equipment had been looted from soldiers 'slaughtered at Enniscorthy' and while 'almost overpowered' by the implications of the sight the woman felt obliged to call out 'brave work boys' and 'success to you my fine stout woman' to conceal her obvious shock and dismay. On reaching home she found that her mansion had been plundered on the day after the fall of Wexford Town to the rebels, 'principally by our own neighbours headed by a man who had been many years steward'. The rebellion in Wexford had been all but settled by the first days of July but the threat to the lives and properties of Wicklow's remaining resident gentry, if not its refugees, had not passed.[246]

After Vinegar Hill, command of the rebel division at Peppard's Castle was exercised by Edward Fitzgerald of Newpark with Garret Byrne, Perry, Kyan and Edward Roche and numbered most of the Ballymanus contingent. William Byrne seized the opportunity offered by the belated presence of his brother to step down from his leadership of the Ballymanus Division and went into hiding until he received a certificate of pardon from the pragmatic and humane Brigade-Major Fitzgerald in Blackwater, Co. Wexford. He then he lived openly in Dublin until his arrest in early 1799.[247] Many Wicklow men became detached from their comrades in the confusion of the retreat from Vinegar Hill and found themselves in Murphy's division. They included Doyle of Ballinacor and Miles Byrne who commanded the displaced Wicklow and North Wexford men in the faction. Murphy's division went from Sleedagh through Carlow into Kilkenny in a desperate effort to spread the insurrection in that sector while Fitzgerald's group detoured from their march to Wicklow and entered Gorey, incensed by news of fresh government atrocities in the Gorey/Coolgreany/ Aughrim area where many of the insurgents lived.[248]

In the aftermath the victorious troops ran amok killing suspected rebels and attacking non-combatants. The yeomen in north Wexford who had been forced to abandon their property and, in some cases, their families, to rebel occupation exacted revenge in the belief that the rebellion had been crushed. News of their depredations, perhaps exaggerated, greatly angered Fitzgerald's men who reputedly swore that 'with or without their leaders they would go [to Gorey] and take vengeance for the blood of their relatives'.[249] When they entered Gorey they were confronted with bodies of civilians strewn in the streets and Fitzgerald, whose own home and stores had been razed, had difficulty restraining those rebels who wanted to retaliate by burning the town and killing loyalist families. He harangued them from horseback urging the preservation of their anger for the actual perpetrators of the atrocities and permitted a party to pursue the fleeing yeomen as far as Coolgreany where several were killed.[250]

Among the dead were about nine women who had been murdered at Ballaghkeen by the Hompesch Dragoons, three women and twelve men killed at Enniscorthy, sixteen men, nine women and six children killed by yeomen between Vinegar Hill and Gorey and four women killed by supplementary yeomanry between Gorey and Arklow. Nine men were killed by yeomen on 21/22 June at Newtownbarry while thirteen more were put to death by the army in the vicinity of Limerick Hill.[251] Many of the victims had evidently been simply cut down by rampaging troopers and yeomen. Loyalist Mrs Newton Lett lamented that:

> government left us three weeks and three days in the hands of a merciless rabble . . . [then the army arrived] who were as merciless as the rebels they came to subdue who fired indiscriminately upon unoffending women and killed the suffering loyalists who escaped the other party.[252]

Misconduct of the yeomanry had been a matter of concern for the military and on 16 June Charles Underwood, Wexford's outgoing yeomanry Brigade-Major, threatened his men with 'most exemplary' punishment if they continued to conduct themselves 'in a manner inconsistent with their duty as soldiers'. The censure proved ineffective and on 25 June Needham insisted that 'the strictest discipline' be observed by cavalry patrols.[253] As late as 4 July, however, General Moore was moved to condemn General Eustace's 'extremely criminal' practice of dispatching patrols from New Ross to 'burn and destroy' and Moore personally warned north Wexford yeomen to eschew revenge attacks.[254]

The insurgents moved on to White Heaps on the southern slope of Croghan mountain for the night where Garret Byrne, being on home territory, received the largely honourary position of chief commander. Their presence alarmed the garrison at Arklow who expected to be attacked on 22 June although it does not seem that such a plan was under consideration. A Castletown yeoman who had fallen into the hands of the rebels on the 22nd was stripped of his regimentals but not otherwise molested, probably in view of the fact that he was known to Perry. He was taken to Woodburnes near Mount Nebo where, having been fed, he managed to escape as the rebels ascended Croghan. Arklow was not as heavily guarded as before but remained the base of operations for the two Arklow cavalry corps in addition to those raised in Castletown, Coolgreany and Wingfield although the Gorey corps had returned to their home town.[255]

It was, however, again proposed to attack Rathdrum on 23 June when the bodies of twenty-seven non-combatants where found on the road near Aughrim, persons correctly presumed to have been killed by the town's yeomen.[256] One rebel recalled that:

> on their march to the lead mines in Glenmalure they met with many revolting sights, particularly in the vicinity of Ballymanus. The village of Aughrim was deserted and numbers of the inhabitants killed.

Also killed around this time were James Murphy, Thomas Doyle, Matthew Cullen, Maurice Crane and Patrick Magrath of Ballycullen who were all betrayed by Hugh Magrath of that place, possibly the same man whom Major Sirr had used as a prosecution witness at the March 1798 assizes.[257] The insurgents probably hoped to find whatever lead and blasting powder in Glenmalure that had not been removed for safekeeping to Rathdrum although. It is doubtful that much remained; Captain Giffard, when requesting artillery and munitions in mid-June, claimed to have 'plenty of powder and lead brought in from the neighbouring mines'. The plan to attack Rathdrum was prudently postponed but the Aughrim atrocities sealed the fate of several yeomen whom they subsequently captured. Rathdrum was then garrisoned by detachments of the Dublin City Militia and Reay Highlanders numbering 220 men who were strongly posted in the town's Flannel Hall and other stone buildings with a three-pounder cannon.[258]

The rebels spent the night of 23 June encamped on Byrne's Ballymanus estate where they burned quantities of hay to prevent its use by the yeomanry. Many saw for the first time how the formerly fine Ballymanus House was 'desolate and in an almost ruined state' having been ransacked by the Tinahely yeomanry and it was completely destroyed by them along with an extensive corn haggard on 26 or 27 June.[259] In April 1799 Byrne referred to the 'almost total destruction of our property during the rebellion by being burned and taken away, the property of many of our tenants being likewise destroyed'.[260] As always, the severe ammunition shortage was the most pressing concern of the insurgents and on 24 June Byrne decided to attack Hacketstown in expectation of overwhelming the garrison and gaining control of its magazine. Hacketstown was superficially a far less formidable post than Rathdrum and a potentially much better source of munitions than Glenmalure. They moved from Ballymanus through the mountains and valleys extending towards Hacketstown on 24 June and massed that evening on the hills surrounding the town on the Wicklow side of the Carlow border. One group moved off towards Imaal and fell in with the north Wicklow and Dublin men under Holt and McMahon who had left the Seven Churches to assist in the attack.[261]

The rebels in the northern baronies of Wicklow under Holt's command were present in some numbers at Clohogue on Duff Hill by 13 June. They dispatched foraging parties to raid loyalist farms for goods and prisoners and generally menaced pro-government interests from their strongholds in the interior of the county. Matthew Byrne rounded up four sheep belonging to John Fitzsimons at Loughpark, a calf and an iron gate which was probably wanted for its metal to make pike blades. Captain 'Black' Paddy Murray of Castlekevin, a local man who had lost thirty barrels of potatoes, forty sheep and ten hundredweight of meal when his farm was burned by the military, led twenty rebels to the home of Mary Rochfort of Tomriland in search of her husband John whom he called 'an Orange dog'. Rochfort was absent when the rebels called to his farm but was robbed of his meal and potato stocks. He was evidently not in dire danger as he was released unharmed by the rebels in July 1798 when accosted at Annamoe.[262]

Other absentee loyalist figures within reach of Clohogue, Henry Harding, Andrew Price and Thomas Hugo, were robbed of cattle and pigs which were driven back to the rebel camp to be butchered. These attacks were highly discriminate and illustrated the intimate nature of the Wicklow rebellion in the politically polarized Roundwood district. James Casey was court-martialled in 1799 for stealing two bullocks worth £17 from Andrew Price on 16 June 1798, one of which been personally reared by Holt for Price, his landlord. In 1794 Harding's application for an inn licence had been backed by Edward Brady of Ballinacorbeg who in 1798 was a prominent rebel. Harding's other supporter was Roger Mahon of Moneystown who was forced at gunpoint in mid-June 1798 to drive his animals to the rebel camp where many of his neighbours and life-long associates were under arms. Joseph Harding had exchanged blows with erstwhile United Irish friends Brady and Neil Devitt in December 1797 when he had refused their overtures to join the society but he did not betray them to the authorities and they had no intention of offering violence to him when the opportunity arose the following year.[263]

Some pro-government inhabitants of the mountain clusters and villages were less fortunate. Joseph Thompson, wood ranger to Francis Synge, was seized in a Roundwood Inn on 17 or 18 June and taken to Clohogue with about eight others. They found that their captors possessed a large store of meat but no alcohol or shelter. Thompson claimed to have been 'try[e]d [sic] by a court martial . . . of about 10 members for being an Orangeman'.[264] Holt knew Thompson well and claimed in his memoirs that nothing other than 'negligence of duty' was held against him as he had been sworn a United Irishman, a detail omitted by Thompson in his statements. It is clear that many of those forced to go to the rebel camps were men who had not honoured their oaths when the rebellion commenced. That Richard Barry, who was proven 'to have taken the oath of secrecy', was liberated whereas Thompson was obliged to remain with the rebels suggests that Holt's group only insisted that fully-fledged United Irishmen who had sworn the military oath were compelled to become active.[265]

On 17 June the insurgents moved to Glendasan near Seven Churches where another 300 rebels from other parts of north Wicklow joined them bringing their combined strength to at least 500. Two days later Holt learned that the yeomen were 'burning the adjacent neighbourhood', possibly to avenge his attacks on loyalists, and decided to give battle.[266] Thompson claimed that the rebels had heard that the army was 'coming to meet them' and moved towards Annamoe where Holt ordered the prisoners to be taken back to the Seven Churches. Once fighting began, not far from the temporarily abandoned Clohogue camp, the rebel guards were instructed to take the prisoners across the mountains to McMahon's camp at Whelp Rock near Blessington where the main body intended to follow.[267]

A force of Reay Highlanders under Lieutenant McLaren and Captain Gore's Newtownmountkennedy Cavalry were sighted on the Ballinrush side of Sleamaine Hill (Ballinvalla Hill) whereupon Holt tried to commit his pikemen while his marksmen distracted the soldiers. McLaren claimed to have encountered 300 rebels near Ballinrush on coming from Fancy Hill during a patrol of the Clohogue-Luggelaw area from Roundwood. The rebels had 'formed a regular front' when confronted by his soldiers and dismounted about fifty of their horsemen. As both sides were either unwilling or unable to approach the other the skirmish was fought at some distance and was relatively unbloody. After twenty minutes or so of firing, the rebels apparently pulled back leaving up to twenty men dead on the mountain for no government losses.[268] Holt, who read the official account of the engagement, refuted the assertion that they had sheltered behind a hedge claiming there had never been one on the mountain 'since the birth of Christ' and countered that his men had 'ran after the enemy till quite out of breath'. They were in possession of an easily defendable positions and McLaren may not have enjoyed such a clear-cut victory given his commanding officer's subsequent requests for reinforcements before undertaking to clear the rebels out of the mountains around Glendalough. Shortly after the skirmish, known as 'the battle of Ballinrush' in rebel circles, one of the yeomen with McLaren shot and killed a blacksmith named Phelim Sally at Annamoe who was probably suspected of supplying the rebels with pike blades.[269]

Holt's force remained intact and marched that night to Whelp Rock where 200 of McMahon's Dubliners were encamped, arriving in the early hours of 20 June. A Blessington loyalist heard that 'all the rebels had collected that could assemble at Whelp Rock, two miles and a half from Blackamore [sic] Hill' on the Downshire estate. While doubting rumours that their numbers were 10,000–15,000, Patrickson held them responsible for robbing the mails at Kill on 23 June, stealing large quantities of flour and cattle and, by their presence, driving many of the estates 'best protestants' from their homes. The quickest and easiest route of Holt's march would have been through the Sally Gap to the area around Sorrel Hill where Whelp Rock was situated. Also then present at Whelp Rock was a small group of Kildare rebels under Captain Michael Murphy who had taken part in the abortive attack on Naas on 23 May.[270]

As gunpowder was in short supply, Holt instructed the assembled officers on a method for manufacturing a crude substitute from heather, sulphur and saltpetre. Thompson saw horsemen gathering 'heath coal' for the process and was told by insurgent musketmen that the 'new powder . . . was very good'. Poor granulation was the most serious drawback of the powder but this may have been rectified when the Dublin United Irish figure Surgeon Thomas Wright supplied McMahon with suitable equipment and thus made the rebels in the mountains virtually self-sufficient in the commodity. It became known in some quarters as 'Holt's mixture'.[271] Ammunition and military-grade powder was also procured for the rebels by a woman known as the 'Moving Magazine' who visited army camps to collect small quantities of munitions from sympathetic militiamen and yeomen.[272] On 23 June most, if not all, of the rebels at Whelp Rock returned to the Seven Churches where they were joined by three large groups of their comrades from Dublin, Kildare and Wexford. The Wexfordians were part of Garret Byrne's column which was then camped at Ballymanus and they had entered Seven Churches driving a herd of black cattle and sheep before them. It seems that news of the impending attack on Hacketstown had preceded them occasioning the unprecedented build-up in Glendalough where their strength was 'hourly' augmented until it reached around 10,000.[273]

The Wexfordians in Glendalough exhibited a harsh attitude to the loyalist prisoners being held in an old yard and advocated the immediate execution of those deemed to be 'Orangemen'. Their intense hatred of orangemen was shared by some Wicklow leaders; Captain Murray claimed in August 1799 that 'the Roman Catholicks [sic] were solemnly assured that the protestants had entered into a Federal Union [i.e. the Orange Order] the main object of which was the intended alleged extermination of the Roman Catholicks [sic]'. The conduct of the soldiery in the aftermath of Vinegar Hill would not have contradicted this misconception which had been encouraged by the United Irishmen in 1797 as a recruiting ploy. When Mary Rochfort asked Murray in June 1798 if he intended to shoot her he allegedly replied: 'not yet, but as soon as the other party begin to shoot women he would do so'.[274]

Some of the Wexfordmen had been incensed by the sight of the bodies of those who had been massacred in Aughrim by yeomen operating out of Rathdrum and tensions were high in consequence. The extremists were opposed by several Wicklowmen attached to Holt's group who interceded for lifelong friends and neighbours who had ended up on the opposite side of the political divide. When David and William Edge were stripped to be piked William Lennon objected by declaring that their blood 'should not be spilt on that bless[e]d ground'.[275] Another loyalist prisoner in jeopardy, Isaac Sutton, later praised Lennon's delaying tactics which enabled McMahon to intervene and order the trial of the prisoners to ascertain if they were 'Orangemen'.[276] This stratagem and other persuasive arguments ensured that McMahon and Holt were alerted to what was taking place and were able to impose their authority before any executions were carried out. Holt implied that there may have been an element of settling scores in the treatment of the Edges and loyalist captives in general when he stated: 'The two Edges were accused to be Orange Men but on strict examination [the accusations were found to be] nothing but bare accusation'. Most of the eight or ten prisoners were compelled to join the rebels but the Edge brothers were released and promptly enlisted in the Powerscourt yeomanry.[277]

In general, the Wicklow rebels tended to attack the property rather than the person of their enemies unless the owners had been particularly noted for tyrannical conduct. The tight-knit nature of the mountain communities afforded ample opportunities to assassinate loyalists but relatively few were killed. Even prominent figures in the yeomanry and magistracy were only rarely attacked in cold blood. Very few prisoners, moreover, were killed in Wicklow without some form of trial, albeit, often of a cursory variety, and the intercession of friendly voices from the rebel ranks was frequently sufficient to secure their release. Some rebels protected the interests of their loyalist landlords and employers and the Tighe family of Rossana considered themselves indebted for the preservation of their mansion to their 'rebel acquaintances and the Roman Catholics'. Of paramount significance was that the Tighes, like the Leesons of Russborough, were politically liberal and the politicized Wicklowmen had no reason to strike at their interests. Wexfordmen in Wicklow were apparently more ruthless than the locals, possibly in view of their lack of communal and personal associations with loyalist captives and their immunity from direct retaliation against their families.[278]

THE SECOND BATTLE OF HACKETSTOWN

On the morning of 24 June the combined rebel force descended to Glenmalure where they halted for three hours on learning that the army had visited Seven Churches shortly after their departure. An ambush was laid with forty or fifty men who ruined the initiative by opening fire prematurely on the advance parties of the following troops. No other resistance was offered to insurgents on their march to Hacketstown and they camped that night with the battle-hardened remnants of the Ballymanus Division and the north Wexford insurgents under Byrne and Fitzgerald. News of their presence evidently prompted some loyalists to leave the safety of the garrison in search of their wives and several of those intercepted by the rebels were put to death. Hardy's wife, Chamney's wife and two of his daughters had fallen into rebel hands but were conveyed to a place of safety on the orders of Perry and McMahon. Word was also sent to surrounding garrison towns and Hacketstown's forty-six yeoman infantry were reinforced while their enemies slept by fifty Antrim Militia under Captain Rowan and Lieutenant Gardiner whom Major Hardy had dispatched from Wexford. Hacketstown was entered early on the morning of the battle by Captain Joseph Chamney with thirty Coolattin Infantry, Captain William Hume with fifty Upper Talbotstown Cavalry and Second-Lieutenant Joseph Braddell with twenty-four Shillelagh Cavalry, presumably from the direction of Rathvilly.[279]

The rebels had taken up positions on the heights which surrounded Hacketstown on all sides other than the western approach where the Dereen river flowed. Michael Dwyer's company took post on Kilmacart Hill which left the heavily outnumbered garrison with Carlow as their only open line of retreat. He had been formally appointed a captain in command of his own company on the 24th at which time he drew his men off from the main body and spent the night at High Park before moving into position on Kilmacart Hill on the morning of the 25th. The large rebel army of at least 10,000 included 1,000 horsemen and 500–1,500 gunsmen and moved towards the forward emplacements of the Antrim Militia around 9.00 a.m. on the morning of 25 June 1798.[280] Despite his overwhelming numerical superiority and favourable deployment it does not seem that Byrne attempted to attack the town in more than one place simultaneously, an omission perhaps indicative of overconfidence. The insurgents simply descended from their bivouacs and marched straight for the Dereen bridge which was defended by entrenched infantrymen. Once the insurgents had neared the bridge the Talbotstown and Shillelagh Cavalry went forward to meet them, no doubt hoping to disperse the rebels as they had done in the first battle of Hacketstown on 25 May.[281]

Michael Reynolds of Naas led his Kildare corps through fields adjacent to the road on which the oncoming cavalry approached while Dwyer's men advanced on the opposite side. Cattle was driven along the road in front of the rebel main body which prevented the yeomen from making a charge. Indeed, the loyalists quickly found themselves in some difficulty as reorienting their horses away from the cattle was dangerous and access to the surrounding fields was impeded by piles of drying turf. Hume and Braddell were obliged to give way to avoid being outflanked by Reynolds and Dwyer and were fired on as they withdrew by rebels sheltering behind the turf clumps. At such short range the insurgent fire was deadly, killing Dwyer's Humewood friends Thomas and Joseph Jackson and two other cavalrymen. Several others were wounded and heavier losses were only averted by a rapid retreat which saw the yeomen cut across to the Clonmore road and fall back behind Eagle Hill south of the town. They took no further part in the battle and probably withdrew altogether from the scene of the contest.[282]

The approaches to the bridge defences were then clear and were attacked by a cadre of Dublin insurgents led by John Mathews of Tallaght Hill who lost twelve men in the process. On viewing this setback Fitzgerald directed Perry to support the Dubliners with the Shelmalier riflemen whose excellent shooting suppressed the defensive fire to an extent that permitted the crossing of the Dereen. Captain Thomas Hardy's position quickly became untenable. His Hacketstown yeomen infantry covered the retreat of the Antrim company once the bridge became congested with advancing insurgents and prepared to pull out. While the retreat to the town's barracks was in progress, Reynolds and Murphy of Kildare forded the river and enfiladed Hardy's yeomen killing four privates and wounding six others. Hardy was then fatally piked at Bridge Lane in the fighting withdrawal from the trenches as the rebels poured into town but his holding action had been crucial as it had enabled the Antrims to gain the barracks without significant loss.[283]

Revd James McGhee with nine orangemen offered strong resistance to rebels who approached the otherwise vulnerable rear wall of the barracks. Among those who had taken refuge in his fortified house was Garret Byrne's estranged wife whom Musgrave alleged he 'wished to get rid of' and a contingent of Donoughmore (Imaal) loyalists who

ATTACK ON MCGHEE'S HOUSE, HACKETSTOWN. *G. Cruickshank, 1845*

found themselves pitted against many of their Republican neighbours from behind the protection of the stone walls of fortified houses.[284] The Imaal loyalists were very probably supplementary yeoman, given that the majority of military age male Protestant farmers of the valley had enlisted, a commitment which obliged them to evacuate their homes with their families for the comparative safety of Hacketstown and Donard on the onset of rebellion. Some of their peers even left the garrisoned Baltinglass in June in favour of the slightly less threatened sector of Ballitore in Kildare. The Imaal women in McGhee's house procured ammunition and loaded the weapons while their husbands, who included members of the Fenton, Hanbidge and Finlay families, monitored and fired upon the rebels surging around the front of the auxiliary barracks. Finlay was credited with discharging a blunderbuss at close range which 'cut a lane' through attackers who had been advancing under the cover of featherbeds. Moderate clerical magistrates Revd Brownrigg and Revd Blake were praised for their conduct in the battle and were probably with McGhee's group.[285]

The bulk of the militia occupied the barracks in which a firing platform had been raised to increase command of the streets. They were joined by Chamney's infantry. A small group of soldiers had also taken refuge in the adjacent malt house which jutted onto the main street and the combination of positions afforded Hacketstown's defenders with a wide field of fire. The rebels attempted to counteract this exposure by setting fire to the town in several places. If the defenders could not be burned out of their buildings, the smoke haze created by the fires would reduce their visibility. Over seventy-six houses were destroyed during the battle, at least sixteen of which belonged to yeomen. Blinded by the smoke the militia and yeomen were subjected to the 'incessant fire' of the rebels but retained control of all key strongholds other than the malt house which had to be abandoned when its thatched roof went up in flames. Infantry fire from the roof of the barracks was countered by a section of the Shelmaliers who ultimately obliged its defenders to take cover.[286]

Efforts at co-ordinating the attack were not always so effective and, while Garret Byrne was apparently the main commander, Fitzgerald retained operational control of the Wexford men and galloped about the town giving orders. McMahon, who had two horses shot under him during the battle, reputedly held 'equal command' with Holt but his relationship with Felix Rourke's faction of Dublin rebels is unknown. Dublinmen from the city, Rathcoole, Tallaght and Rathfarnham played a prominent part and were led by Colonel Edward Rattigan, a former associate of Lord Edward Fitzgerald, another colonel named Burke who was a leading committee member in October 1798 and Colonel Felix Rourke.[287] Rourke's brother Charles, who came from Rathcoole, County Dublin, was a captain as were Matthews of Tallaght, O'Neil of Francis St, one Lyons and a man named Fitzpatrick who had 'organised the company of men' under McMahon in Dublin city. As McMahon and Rattigan were both assisted by Dillon of Donnybrook and Fitzpatrick and McMahon were independently aided by Surgeon Wright, it is likely that close links existed between most of the city and county militants before they entered Wicklow and Wexford. They were certainly in evidence once the rebellion commenced.[288]

Without cannon the insurgents were obliged to resort to furtive attempts to fire the barracks and McGhee's post, attacks which exposed them to defensive fire at point blank range. One of those killed in the assault was a young man named Murphy of Ballinoulard (Wexford) who had reputedly performed 'daring feats of valour' at Hacketstown and in other battles. He had intended following his brother Fr Michael Murphy of Ballycanew into the priesthood and was the third member of the family killed in less than a month.[289] Reynolds was severely wounded in one effort which entailed approaching the occupied buildings under cover of carts which had been filled with hay. Others

BULLETIN

FROM THE

LONDON GAZETTE

MY LORD,   *Dublin Castle, June* 25, 1798.
I HAVE the Honour to acquaint your Grace
that this Day Advices were received from Lieut.
Gardner of the Antrim Militia, dated from Baltin-
glas the 26th Inſtant, which ſtate, that early in the
Morning of the 25th, a very large Body of Rebels
attacked his Poſt at Hacketſtown.   They were in
Number many Thouſands.   Lieutenant Gardner's
Force conſiſted of 50 Upper Talbotſtown, and 24
Shebagh Cavalry, 50 of the Antrim Regiment, 46
Hacketſtown, and 30 Coolattin Yeoman Infantry.
He at firſt took an advantageous Situation in Front
to defend the Barracks. A Conteſt took Place in the
Midſt of Flames for near Nine Hours, for the Rebels ſet Fire to the Town.   They were at laſt re-
pulſed with conſiderable Loſs ;   many dead were
found in the Streets and Ditches, and 30 Car Loads
of Killed and Wounded were carried off in their Retreat.

Lieutenant Gardner ſpeaks in the higheſt Terms
of the Gallantry of his whole Detachment.   He
particularly praiſes Lieutenant Rowen of the An-
trim, Captain Hume of the Upper Talbotſtown
Cavalry, Captain and Lieutenant Charnley of the
Coolattin, Lieutenants Saul and Thomas of the
Hacketſtown Cavalry, and Lieutenants Braddell and
Taylor of the Shebagh Cavalry; and he ſtrongly
mentions the good Conduct of Serjeant Nixon of the
Antrim Regiment.

He ſeverely laments the Loſs of a good Officer,
Captain Hardy of the Hacketſtown Yeomen Infantry, who fell early in the Action.   His other
Loſs conſiſts of 10 Privates killed, and of 1 Serjeant
and 19 Privates wounded.

I incloſe to your Grace a further Account of the
Action near Goreſbridge, and a Return of Killed
and Wounded, which has been received from Major-
General Sir Charles Aſgill.
               I have the Honor to be, &c.   &c.
                    CORNWALLIS.

HACKETSTOWN BULLETIN

attempted to shield themselves with commandeered mattresses which, like the hay, were to be used for their incendiary properties once the open ground had been crossed. McGhee saw Reynolds fall from a shot fired by his men at an 'incredible distance' and, believing him to have been killed, claimed the £300 bounty offered by government for him in May 1798. Dwyer and two men named Laffan from Kilmuckridge distinguished themselves when they tried to enter the barracks by using scaling ladders but were repelled by the militia.[290]

Insurgent losses increased when the burnt-out shells of the houses collapsed and a high wind dispelled the protective smoke screen which had been billowing out of their smouldering ruins. McGhee's party could then clearly discern their enemies and began to exact a heavy toll of the Rathfarnham rebels assaulting the rear of the barracks. Unable to dislodge the militiamen in the barracks, Byrne was forced to call off the attack when his musketmen had expended their ammunition. His options narrowed when the pikemen 'positively refused' to go on unsupported.[291] They had killed about nine loyalists and injured a further twenty-two in nine hours of fighting. The wounded included five Antrims, eight Coolattin yeoman and two of McGhee's men. The Hacketstown Infantry suffered the heaviest losses with five men dead and six wounded while the Humewood Cavalry lost four killed and one wounded. Rebel casualties were considered extremely high for an action in which neither cannon nor cavalry had been effectively deployed and may have totalled a few hundred with estimates ranging from a mere twelve to a much inflated eight hundred. Many of those killed and wounded were evacuated to safety on carts. The rebel dead were loaded onto carts which had been procured at Humewood and transported to a sand pit at the top of Church Hill where they were covered with earth from a nearby embankment.[292]

Some thirty cart-loads of insurgent wounded were hauled away by their comrades while the equally exhausted garrison, being critically short of ammunition, seized the opportunity to pull out of the town and fall back on Tullow. The insurgents were credited with drawing off their forces 'slowly and deliberately, carrying off their dead and wounded and leaving behind a complete wreck'. The abandonment of Hacketstown gave the insurgents what might have been described as a pyrrhic victory of which they were oblivious. They headed into the Blessington area, although some, probably the Dublin city men and Kildaremen, split off at Donard and approached the east Kildare and south Dublin borders. The most severely wounded rebels were taken to nearby Imaal where rudimentary medical treatment was administered and protection offered against the vengeful yeomanry. James Dempsey of Carnew was brought to the house of Mary Scott at Monamuck, Imaal on the morning of 26 June where his injured hand was dressed by Charles Kealy who cauterised the wound with whiskey.[293]

The presence of several thousand Leinster rebels in the Hacketstown district intimidated many non-aligned Protestant families along the borderlands who had not previously felt the need to relocate to garrison towns. One group of insurgents which fell back from Hacketstown on 25 June temporarily took over the hastily abandoned Plant household near Imaal. Its owner, 'Black Jem' Plant and his friend William Hanbidge of Tinnehinch were uncertain of what treatment they might have received from such visitors and had taken the precaution of hiding near the banks of the Slaney. This may have been prudent given that many of Hanbidge's family were yeoman and that his uncle was shot dead in Black Ditches shortly after being taken prisoner by rebels in Ballymore Eustace. The threat in late June may have been magnified by the proximity of United Irishmen from other parts of Wicklow, Wexford and elsewhere who would have been unfamiliar with the political demographics of Imaal and might have been in ill-humour after their failure to prevail at Hacketstown. The immediate source of danger for the harried neutrals, however, quickly reverted to loyalist agents. Yeomen made a relatively rare appearance in Imaal shortly after the battle to burn many suspected rebel-owned houses. The militarily valid task of seeking out United Irish stragglers may on this occasion have offered the pretext to avenge the deaths of the popular Jacksons and Captain Hardy.[294]

The insurgents falling back from Hacketstown were fortunate not to have encountered a sizeable force of militia and yeomen which Camden had sent into the county on 24 June. The Viceroy had bowed to the pressure of 'repeated representations' from the garrisons of Rathdrum and Newtownmountkennedy who had become greatly alarmed by the movements of huge bodies of rebels in the Wicklow mountains. Robert Ross, writing in the city on the 24th stated:

> An alarm was spread very early this morning that the rebels were in force near Lord Powerscourt's, and that Powerscourt House was burnt to the ground. This came in about one o'clock. [Major] General [William] Myers, who commands the yeomanry, immediately beat to arms and selected as many as he could, and marched immediately with two pieces of cannon and some infantry, yeomen and regulars, and all the cavalry he could collect.[295]

News that the rebels had gathered in large numbers at Enniskerry and were preparing to attack the city could not be ignored and Dublin was thrown 'into some consternation' when the unfounded report was confirmed by another express on the night of 24 June.[296]

At 2.00 a.m. on 24 June 700 yeomen of the Lawyers and Attorney's, Loyal Dublin and Rotunda Cavalry and yeoman infantry of the Merchants, St Stephen's Green, Lawyers and Attorney's and College corps were assembled at St Stephen's Green under Major-General Myers. Each unit was required to send at least fifty men to the muster which was augmented by a hundred-strong company of the Fermanagh Militia with two cannon and three days provisions. Myers's column moved out through Rathfarnham and Stepaside towards Enniskerry taking 'every military precaution' to avoid ambush when traversing the narrow glacial valley of the Scalp. At Enniskerry they learned that while Powerscourt had not been burned, 10,000 rebels had been spotted in the Seven Churches. Myers halted to rest his men and to take stock of the situation and was reinforced by 200 more mounted Dublin yeomen who had left the city at 8.00. a.m. The column left Enniskerry for Roundwood after a short rest and were met on the road by a troop of Powerscourt Cavalry who briefed them on the latest developments. They had ascertained that the insurgents had moved away from the city and deeper into the mountains but it was not then realized that Holt and McMahon had relocated in order to participate in the Battle of Hacketstown. Myers and his men camped for the night on the townland of Ballinastow near Roundwood where they remained on high alert against the possibility of a night attack from the mountains.[297]

This caution negated any chance of closing with the rebels as they moved towards Hacketstown although Myers' primary mission was to prevent them approaching the capital. Once news of the destruction of Hacketstown reached Dublin on the night of 25 June, orders were issued for the recall of the city yeomen as it was felt that the garrison could not be weakened at that time. A large proportion of the army was still committed to Wexford and there was no way of knowing whether the rebels might enter Blessington and approach the capital. Word of the battle did not arrive in Ballinastow, however, until the early hours of the 26th, causing Myers to shift part of his force to Rathdrum the following morning. On the march to Rathdrum Myers encountered Captains Giffard and King with elements of the Dublin City Militia and Rathdrum Cavalry who told him that their patrols had spotted about 5,000 rebels moving towards the border with Carlow and Kildare the previous day. They also confirmed that he was to return to the capital where exaggerated rumours of a rebel attack on Rathfarnham and large-scale concentrations in west Wicklow had heightened anxiety.

Another factor behind the recall of Myers was that the new Viceroy, Lord Cornwallis, was 'extremely angry' that he had not been consulted on the operation and opposed the use of city yeomanry outside the capital.[298] Only one house had in fact been burned in Rathfarnham but, in the context of the determined attempt on Hacketstown and Castle intelligence on rebel objectives, the recall was prudent. Post Office spy John Lees received a report from his chief agent which stated that: 'different partys of the rebels are to collect & form on the borders of the county of Dublin – this side [of] Bray [and] above Rathfarnham, Blessington, Clondalkin, Swords etc and to show themselves *on one day* (the end of this week) . . . [and] attack the city, the Castle particularly for arms & the bank for money.'[299]

After Hacketstown the bulk of the rebels bypassed the lightly defended village of Donard and climbed to Whelp Rock camp where a council of war was held on 26 June to decide future strategy. During the discussions Byrne, Fitzgerald and several other senior figures agreed on a plan to return towards Wexford with about 8,000 men to attack Carnew and to ascertain how Fr Murphy's division had fared in Kilkenny. The Dubliners under McMahon and Rourke declined to accompany the main body on this march as did most of the remaining Kildaremen. The Wexfordians, however, were optimistic that Murphy would join them with a 'great flock of men', not suspecting that the foray into Kilkenny had been a disastrous ordeal for their much depleted comrades.[300] Holt's men attached themselves to Byrne's command preserving the union of the north and south Wicklow insurgent army and accompanied them as they retraced their route through Hollywood Glen to Donard. A well-known informer was found hiding in a potato patch and having received 'immediate sentence' was shot in a field beside the Donard/Baltinglass road. Holt, Byrne and Perry were provided with wine by the servants of Justice Hynes' home in Donard whose resident yeomanry had left the area.[301]

The insurgents reached Ballymanus that evening where Edward Roche was encamped with a small group of Wexford rebels. Holt apparently then formalized his position within the rebel army, a matter which may have been pressed owing to the increased likelihood of dissension at command level arising from the continued co-operation of geographically distinct units from Wicklow. It was only then that Holt acknowledged that he had been given 'the title of colonel' with

'960 men', the precise number a rebel colonel was supposed to command under the original military system of the pre-rebellion United Irishmen.[302] In September 1798 a Castle spy within the Dublin contingent claimed that 'Holt had no commission nor ever had' whereas McMahon had been formally returned a colonel, a comment which suggests that the animosity between the two factions was mutual. Holt, for his part, readily denied military rank in his disingenuous auto-biography as it was necessary to obscure his pre-rebellion prominence in the organization to support the fiction of his being a 'forced rebel'.[303]

On 27 June the insurgents ascended Roddenagh Hill and observed 200 troops coming towards them through Aughrim on the Rathdrum road, probably the route which skirted Cushbawn mountain.

According to Holt, Roche and Garret Byrne spoiled a plan he had devised to encircle the army with three columns and were accused of cowardice by some of the men when they fell back after a few cannon rounds had been fired at them. The army were probably too weak to press home their attack and the rebels consequently returned unhindered to their camps.[304] They were joined on Roddenagh by a small group of survivors from Murphy's division who, having penetrated Kilkenny as far as Castlecomer, had been obliged to retrace their steps to Wexford when their march failed to generate new recruits. They had been harried on the retreat by Asgill's troops who attacked them at Kilconnel Hill and pursued them to Scullogue Gap where some hundreds of rebels and innocents were killed on the 26th. Colonel Howard of the Wicklow Militia was one of those singled out for praise by Asgill for his role at Kilconnel Hill.[305]

Fr Murphy was separated from his men in the confusion of the retreat from Kilkenny and was captured and executed in Tullow. Many Wexford and Wicklow men remained absent with the shattered rump of his forces in Killaughrim woods and elsewhere, some of whom managed to link up with the men led by Fitzgerald and Byrne in the course of the following weeks. The slightly augmented main force went on 30 June through Tinahely and Wingfield destroying loyalist property en route to Wicklow Gap where they turned south into Wexford and marched to Monaseed. *En route* to Monaseed they burned Sir John Jervis White's 'old mansion' at Wingfield and it was further alleged that on 28 June they had 'plundered and destroyed 13 houses, belonging to Protestants, 11 of whom were of the yeomanry'.[306]

THE BATTLE OF BALLYELLIS

Needham's troops at Gorey Hill had observed the rebel concentrations in the Croghan Mountain – Camolin area in the last days of June 1798 and had taken the precaution of remobilizing the district's hitherto stood down yeomanry corps. Hunter Gowan with part of his Wingfield cavalry reconnoitred the countryside between Gorey and Monaseed early on the morning of 30 June and discovered that the rebels were present 'in great force'. His men had probably been responsible for killing eight or ten rebels led by Johnny Doyle of Monaseed who had been sent out to forage on behalf of the rebel mainforce. One Edge of Craan was later said to have killed Doyle Gowan's intelligence was received by Needham at 10.00 a.m. at Gorey Hill who correctly surmised that the insurgents intended to attack the re-garrisoned Carnew once again. The general decided to neutralize the threat to one of the region's most important loyalist outposts by dispatching a strong cavalry patrol of almost 200 troopers.[307]

The patrol consisted of a sizeable body of Ancient Britons under Lieutenant-Colonel Richard Puleston, some 5th Dragoon Guards and the Ballaghkeen, Gorey and Wingfield yeomanry corps with whom they often operated. The 4th Dragoon Guards may also have formed part of the patrol but did not accompany their comrades as far as Ballyellis. On reaching Monaseed about a half-hour behind the rebels, Puleston was assured by a lady publican named Moore, a cousin of the Grogans of Castletown, that they were very fatigued and short of ammunition. This increased his confidence leading him to dismiss the large body of infantry which had accompanied but slowed the patrol. Puleston evidently envisaged charging the rear of the column and 'swore he would cut them to pieces'.[308] This transpired to be a grave error and at Ballyellis, one mile from Carnew on the Monaseed side of the Gorey road, the troopers evidently sensed that something was awry and halted again to enquire of the rebels. They were told by an elderly woman that their quarry was already some miles ahead 'although they were in ambush on their right and left'. Ballyellis was an excellent site for an ambush as the right-hand side of the road was then bordered by a ruined deer park wall which ran for half-a-mile and the other side was lined by a dense thorn bush which stood behind a five-foot-deep drainage ditch. Behind the bush was a bog or waterlogged field and the ground on the far side rose sharply towards Kilcavan Gap.[309]

The rebels had realized earlier in the day that the army were in close pursuit. The failure of Johnny Doyle's foraging patrol to rejoin their ranks may have sparked an alert and it seems probable that the yeomanry outriders of Puleston's column had been spotted traversing the hill sides south of Carnew in advance of the military column. On Holt's direction the rebels decided to make their stand at Ballyellis and hastily prepared an ideal ambush site for the pursuing cavalry. Seven or eight carts being used to carry their baggage and wounded were cleared and pressed into service as a makeshift barricade.[310] Most were placed on the road a short distance from a bend and some were used to block the ancillary Drummond Lane which could have afforded the cavalry a convenient avenue of retreat. A hundred musketmen took up positions behind the still limbered carts while up to 500 others concealed themselves behind the deer park wall fronting the roadside. A body of pikemen remained on the road in front of the concealed barricades to induce the cavalry to approach but they had cleared rough access passages through the thorn hedges to facilitate their escape from the road at the appropriate time. When the troopers caught sight of what appeared to be a confused mass of pikemen on the road ahead they spurred their horses on and were astonished to see most of their enemies pass through the dense hedgerows just before the distance was closed. The leading horses and their riders came to an abrupt stop when confronted by the carts against which the troopers became immediately compressed and entangled. One loyalist recalled catching sight of the pikemen and then charging 'with great impetuosity'. On getting within a short distance of their enemy the insurgents apparently 'leaped over the hedges at each side, on which the horses in front were entangled in the cars'.[311]

Some pikemen were caught in the path of the horsemen and had to stand and fight while their comrades, protected by the surrounding ditches, hedges and walls, 'opened a heavy fire' on the patrol. Once the head of the column had been ensnared in the barricades, the rear was attacked by a large force of pikemen who corralled the startled horses to such a degree that their riders found it exceptional difficulty to manoeuvre. The majority of the troopers were incapable of using their sabres for fear of injuring each other and, for once, the tactical advantage afforded by being mounted became a serious liability.[312] Elements of all six troops of the Ancient British regiment suffered what amounted to their highest losses of the rebellion in a single action. Lieutenant-Adjutant Adolphus Giffard, a French-born nobleman and expert swordsman, was killed with five others in Puleston's troop; Major Gwilliam Lloyd Wardle's troop lost two corporals and four other ranks; Captain Thomas Boycott's lost another corporal and two men; Captain

THE BATTLE OF BALLYELLIS by W. Sadler, 1879. *Power Collection*

William Wynne's lost three men; Captain Sir Henry Goodricke lost five troopers and the attached Quarter-Master John Davies while a further two members of Colonel Wynne's troop were killed.[313]

Edward Roche personally accounted for some of the British fatalities and such was the intensity of the attack that he nearly severed the hand of a rebel named Kenna of Stratford while making a back-handed sword cut. Many horses were piked in order to dismount their riders including that of Puleston who hastily remounted another on which he eventually escaped the carnage. The 5th Dragoon Guards, who had evidently ridden into the ambush behind the Britons, managed at length to force their way into a field, although at least eleven of their men were killed in the process. Byrne or Fitzgerald noted the development and ordered a group of Shelmaliers to cut off the retreat of the troopers whereupon Holt organized the pursuit of their hated foes.[314] The Britons and yeomen who gained the roadside fields found themselves in the midst of a considerable body of rebels who were eager to pursue and kill them. No quarter was shown to the compromised dragoons and some were taunted with references to the cruelties which had been committed by their regiment in Newtownmountkennedy. Dwyer, having initially fought alongside Roche on the road, found himself face to face with a terrified Welsh trooper in a ruined cabin and 'clove his head nearly in two' with a captured sword.[315]

Anthony King, a black drummer, hacked at the pike shafts of his pursuers when his horse failed to negotiate the boggy ground but succumbed at length and, in Holt's words, 'took more piking than five white men.' Holt also remarked that King, who he thought was a trumpeter, had called out 'the passwords of a United Irishman' but was piked nonetheless.[316] King's fate had reputedly been sealed as 'the remembrance of his floggings was too fresh' which is plausible given that he belonged to one of the troops stationed in Newtown and that drummers often acted as floggers. His body was thrown into a part of the hedgerow later dubbed 'drummer's corner' where it remained until it disintegrated.[317] Thirty-five guineas was discovered on the body of another Briton by Gough of Clone which had apparently been plundered by the regiment the previous day. The conduct of the Britons in Wicklow before the Rebellion and during its early weeks was deemed to be the principal reason for the slaughter of virtually every member who fell into the hands of the rebels. Edward Deery heard that the rebels had 'smashed a power of Britons & killed above 60' which indicates the degree to which Ballyellis was viewed by nationalists as a success against the Welsh regiment alone.[318]

Two or three Britons got as far as Henry Stones's potato field where they were trapped and killed by John Doyle and three other insurgents. The body of yeoman John Godkin was later found at the site with multiple head and pike wounds while that of William Inman was located in a shallow grave nearby where a local farmer had hidden the body in a bid to avoid reprisals.[319] The most reliable figure for government casualties at Ballyellis is forty-nine fatalities and an unknown number of wounded, some of whom later died. Missing from the parade muster at Gorey the following day were twenty-five Ancient Britons, eleven 5th Dragoon Guards, six Gorey and two Ballaghkeen yeomen 'besides a number wounded'.[320] At least one more Briton had been killed, however, along with about four more loyalists or supplementary yeomen, probably Carnewmen who had sallied out in a short lived attempt to assist the patrol but were pursued back into the town. That the death toll mounted from mortal wounds is indicated by loyalist sources which gave a figure of two officers and sixty privates killed while the government organ the *Annual Register* acknowledged that 'more than eighty of the King's troops fell'.[321]

As the yeomen suffered relatively few losses in the battle it seems likely that most of those who had acted as scouts and outriders did not rush to assist their comrades when the ambush was sprung. Loyalists maintained that Gowan's dismounted yeomanry had engaged the rebels and 'killed a number' as their nondescript apparel, a black armband being the only distinguishing feature to mark them as yeomen, had allegedly enabled them to close with the insurgents unnoticed. This is implausible given that the notorious 'Black mob' were well known in the area around Monaseed and apparently suffered no losses.[322] That only Adjutant Parsons, Inman, Godkin and five others from the Ballaghkeen and Gorey corps were killed supports the contention that the bulk of the yeomanry had ascended Kilcavan Hill and abandoned the dragoons on the road to their fate. While this was prudent and justifiable under the circumstances, it did much to dispel rebel fears of the yeomanry and exposed the hated 'Orange faction' and 'cruel Ascendancy' to ridicule. The rebels were in exultant mood after the clash and trumpeter Harry Neil, a Naas Cavalry defector, sounded several calls after the battle which confused the trained horses, more for the spectacle than for any practical purpose.[323]

Large quantities of cavalry equipment and many unwounded horses fell into the hands of the rebels and their morale received a timely boost and, according to Miles Byrne, no other battle made 'so great a sensation in the country' in 1798.[324] Sabres, carbines, saddles, pistols, ammunition, uniforms and other booty was readily collected. James Cullen was reputed to have ridden around wearing a scarlet cloak taken from a dead Ancient Briton while waving 'a pair of leather breeches much stained with blood'. Ballyellis was the first insurgent victory of note since Tubberneering and was perhaps was the only battle of the rebellion in which they had suffered no fatalities.[325] While Ballyellis posed no strategic problems for the government the unusually high losses had not been anticipated after 21 June and proved controversial. Government forces at Vinegar Hill, where a vastly superior force had been deployed, endured fatalities of just four officers and eighteen other ranks while a mere two soldiers had been killed at Kilconnell Hill on 26 June. The scale and nature of the rebel victory worried local residents and Sarah Erraghty was one of many with rebel affiliations who left their homes for the night fearing loyalist reprisals. Her husband Michael was an ex-member of the Ballyellis Infantry and had served as a commissary for the rebels.[326]

The garrison in Rathdrum learned of what had occurred from Abraham Manning, who had returned from delivering despatches to Gorey on Sunday, 1 July. Manning ascertained in Gorey that the Puleston's patrol had been ambushed 'beyond Carnew' by . . .

rebels who hid until the cavalry had gone a considerable distance before they saw the main body when they [i.e. the cavalry] began to retreat. Within an ins[tan]t the rebels then began their fire from behind the ditches & had stopped the road with carts so that (report says) 20 were killed of the German [sic] and Antient Brittans [sic].[327]

The gunfire and sounds of battle at Ballyellis had been audible on Gorey Hill and a concerned General Needham personally led another patrol towards Carnew where he met two survivors who related the 'melancholy tidings'. He then decided to pull back to protect Gorey leaving Carnew to its fate but dispatched an overdue relief force of twenty Camolin Cavalry under Lieutenant Smith and 'a strong party of infantry'. They took the Monaseed road towards Ballyellis but were recalled when the first remnants of the ambushed patrol reached Gorey having taken the indirect route through Carnew. Puleston's men had eventually succeeded in forcing the barricades which blocked their path and had arrived in Gorey 'in a shattered condition' at 2.00 a.m. Their yeomen colleagues had fared little better and were scattered all over the surrounding area. Neither Needham nor Puleston took steps necessary to prevent a rebel attack on Carnew which apparently took place in the interval between the general's first visit to the town and the arrival of Smith's reinforcements.[328]

James Kelly, an Irish-born Ancient Briton, had brought the first news of the ambush to Carnew earlier that day when his horse cleared the roadside hedges after receiving a stab wound in the haunches.[329] Captain Thomas Swan of the Carnew Infantry and his men hastily barricaded themselves into the malt house premises of Robert Blaney, Second-Lieutenant of the corps. Blayney's brother Ralph was 'a zealous loyalist' and probably an orangeman whose chandling house had been burned on 18 April 1798 by United Irishmen in his workforce but the malt house had been left intact when the rebels fired most of the town in early June on account of Robert Blayney's moderate character. The imprudence of this sentimental gesture was revealed on the 30th by which time it had been transformed into 'a formidable and well fortified barrack'.[330] The stone walls and slated roof of the malt house proved invulnerable to rebel small-arms fire during repeated attacks by Holt and Garret Byrne. The same ploys which had failed to burn the barracks at Hacketstown failed again in Carnew and at least nineteen rebels were killed for very few loyalist casualties. The building would not take fire but the rebels razed whatever partially burned or intact buildings had survived previous attacks and thereby 'destroyed' the town. A feigned retreat momentarily drew the yeomen out of their stronghold which was quickly reoccupied when the ruse was discovered. Fitzgerald, anticipating an attack on his men by Needham, was unwilling to remain in the town until nightfall when it would have been easier to approach the malt house and called a halt to the effort.[331]

The insurgents withdrew to Kilcavan Hill where Holt and the north Wicklowmen made a decision to return to their home district. They were opposed to entering war-ravaged Wexford where food was in short supply and their enemies numerous and were much less familiar with the district than their predominately south Wicklow comrades of the original Ballymanus Division. They returned through Wicklow Gap and spent the night in or near Annacurra moving on 1 July through Ballymanus, Ballycurragh and on to Aghavannagh. After a short rest on the slopes of Aghavannagh, Holt led his men across the bridle paths leading into Glenmalure from whence they crossed over Table Mountain to Knockalt. The final leg to Whelp Rock was completed before darkness fell and saw the north Wicklowmen back on very familiar ground. Holt's men were reasonably well supplied with munitions and carbines taken at Ballyellis which encouraged him to lead twenty-four mounted raiders towards Kilcullen on 3 July where they rounded up cattle for their camp.[332]

A reconnaissance patrol from Rathdrum on 2 July reported that 'many' insurgent stragglers were passing through Ballymanus and one group of 100 rebels was sighted moving into the Rathdrum district from the direction of south Wicklow. Another 400-strong party, presumed to be under the command of Garret Byrne, reportedly returned through Ballymanus on the same day and passed over the mountains towards Imaal at 4.00 p.m. This was probably Holt's force. The Rathdrum garrison were then aware that elements of the Wicklow and Wexford forces had parted company and wrongly speculated that the cause of this was 'G[arret] Byrnes being angry as [to] their burning houses'.[333] Byrne's column were far from moderate and killed several loyalists on their march towards Tinahely on 2 July. William Waters of Cronelea was piked in cold blood at his home place on the Shillelagh road 'for being an orangeman' by Morgan Summers and others but the rebels also killed Robert Stephens and John Restly of Coolatin, George Driver of Tinahely and Joseph and William Halfpenny of Coolkenna that day, some of whom had probably fallen at the Battle of Ballyrahan despite loyalist claims to the contrary.[334]

When nearing Tinahely on the Shillelagh road on 2 July, Fitzgerald and Byrne encountered a large yeomanry force and promptly ascended Ballyrahan Hill lest their partially mounted opponents cut them off from the high ground. The 'greater spirit' displayed by the loyalists was apparent and led to speculation that they were attempting to redeem their honour tarnished at Ballyellis. The yeomen had been in search of the rebels and numbered at least 120 – Joseph Chamney's Coolattin, James Moreton's Tinahely and Abraham Nixon's Coolkenna Infantry supported by the Wingfield and Shillelagh Cavalry.[335] The patrol was led by Captain Abraham Nixon sr of Munny, who although in command of an infantry unit, was mounted as an officer. He had led them that morning down from Laragh near Kilquiggan to Stranakelly at Tallon's Crossroads where they found several unarmed fugitives hiding in a house. They shot and mortally wounded one Garret before continuing on the road leading towards Chamney's large house on Ballyrahan. On nearing this building their attention was drawn to the sight of what appeared to be small numbers of insurgents running up the hill ahead of them which lulled them into a false sense of security. The consequences of their complacency became apparent immediately

ATTACK ON CHAMNEY'S HOUSE AT BALLYRAHAN. G. Cruickshank, 1845

afterwards when concealed rebel riflemen opened fire at close range and large numbers of pikemen appeared along the hedgerows skirting the road. The rebels may have been attempting to repeat the tactics of Ballyellis but had no time to prepare a similar ambush site.[336]

The two cavalry corps turned and fled back down the hill upon the first fire of the rebels while the infantry had little option but to take refuge in Chamney's fortified house or be engulfed on even less advantageous terms as they attempted to escape on foot. The Tinahely yeomanry apparently managed to pull back before they had to fight for their lives and suffered very few casualties on 2 July. The abandonment of their comrades from Coolkenna and Coolattin was allegedly prompted by their belief that they would receive 'but little mercy . . . on account of their ferocity at the commencement of hostilities'.[337] The two isolated infantry corps lost their captains and most of the seventeen other ranks killed that day in a brief but ferocious encounter while the survivors fought their way into Chamney's mansion on the hill. Chamney's death, and that of his nephew Joseph, did not result from personal animosity against the family as he was a moderate magistrate on friendly terms prior to the rebellion with both Garret Byrne and Holt. Lieutenant Thomas Chamney of the Coolattin Infantry found himself in charge of up to 200 yeomen, loyalists and terrified locals crammed into the building as it was surrounded by thousands of highly motivated rebels.[338]

The retreating cavalry had been momentarily shielded from the insurgent's line of sight as they passed back along the road through Stranakelly but were again exposed on the climb towards Tallon's Cross. Lieutenant Abraham Nixon jr's horse was shot dead but he managed to grasp the stirrup of a comrade named Wall as the yeomen gained the crossroads. The retreat was disorganized and some of those who lost their mounts were forced to make their way through the fields as best they could when abandoned. The intensity of the rebel gunfire evidently prompted the yeomen to veer left towards Ballynultagh Hill, which while opposite Ballyrahan, afforded the protection of an intervening high hedgerow. A man named Garret, brother of the man killed that morning, reputedly used a three-pronged fork to crush the skull of a Coolkenna yeoman named Lennon whom he encountered on Ballynultagh.[339]

While this was in progress, the neighbouring house to Chamney's which belonged to the notorious Henry Morton was burned by the rebels. This transpired to be a tactical error as the flames illuminated the insurgents once darkness fell, to the benefit of the defenders who were attempting to shoot otherwise invisible opponents. The rebels could not force an entry into the mansion and were repulsed with relatively heavy losses; one was shot dead through a feather mattress as he tried to break open the hall door and others died trying to set fire the house. The skeletal remains of one insurgent killed in the attack was found to have ten Cronebane halfpennies resting on a thighbone, metal which may well have been shot into him when the defenders in Chamney's had run short of ammunition. Garret Byrne had some difficulty convincing his men to relinquish their hopeless task but succeeded at length and led them to White Heaps on the southern side of Croghan mountain for the night.[340]

They were joined at Croghan the following day by a small group of men from Murphy's division who had been sheltering in Killaughrim Woods along with the wounded Fr Kearns but were greatly disappointed by their numerical weakness. The insurgents were further augmented at Ballyfad by others who had ventured into Kilkenny with Murphy on 22 June and they began to form a detailed picture of the strategic situation in which they operated. An expedition was sent to the gold mines to burn the wooden barracks abandoned by Hardy before the battle of Arklow which then returned to Croghan where the rebels were encamped.[341]

Needham assembled a strong force on the night of 4 July to assault White Heaps camp at first light and, no doubt, hoped to achieve the decisive victory which had eluded the government at Vinegar Hill largely due to his incompetence. A similar operation had taken place on 3 July but had failed to locate the constantly moving rebels. Duff with troops collected in Carnew led a column towards White Heaps on the 4th while the Marquis of Huntley brought his 89th Highlanders over Croghan from Arklow to cut off their lines of retreat. It was discovered at dawn on 5 July that the rebel camp had been abandoned by the insurgents who were ascertained to be moving through heavy fog towards the Wicklow Gap. Duff's cavalry established contact with them at Wicklow Gap when the fog abated and the insurgents fell back in anticipation of a heavy attack, apparently believing that the troopers were 'breathing revenge and destruction on them for the defeat of their brothers in arms at Ballyellis'.[342] As Needham had yet again misjudged his march, however, he was unable to modify his battle plans in time to bring his infantry to bear against the rebels during a twelve-mile pursuit. Unable to elude Duff's cavalry and anxious to give battle before Needham managed to synchronize his efforts, the rebels turned back towards Wexford and fought their way through the pursuing horsemen. The cavalry were surprised by this courageous and somewhat desperate manoeuvre and reputedly lost many casualties in the hand-to-hand fighting which ensued before the rebels made headway and pushed towards Ballygullen near Craanford.[343]

The insurgents left the Ballygullen road and faced the Louth and Leitrim Militia with the 89th regiment and the combined cavalry of Needham and Duff. They drove the Leitrims from their four six-pounder battalion guns more than once but, lacking ammunition, were unable to resist the counter-attacks of Lord Roden's 1st Fencible Dragoons and the Highlanders. In the light of their experiences at Hacketstown, Carnew and Ballyrahan Perry, Byrne and Fitzgerald were very eager to capture artillery but could not prevail against their mounted foes and the defensive fire of Lieutenant Hemmings' small battery. Few losses were incurred by the rebels in the action and those of the army were minimized by the inability of the pikemen to get to grips with their adversaries. When it became clear that the government forces were too strong and well-equipped to be defeated, a retreat was made to Carrigrew Hill while a small column went directly to the Wicklow mountains as far as Glenmalure.[344]

Ballygullen transpired to be the last major battle fought in Wexford in the rebellion of 1798 but it was by no means the final action of the insurgents from the county. While the majority left Carrigrew to accept the amnesty terms offered by Lord Cornwallis in Arklow, Gorey and other garrisons, some thousands made their way to the Wicklow mountains to fight on. They evidently hoped to add their forces to those of Kildare leader William Aylmer in Timahoe Bog and to hold out until the French invaded. The militants, however, were very much a minority as the new amnesty terms being promulgated made it possible for most United Irishmen to retire from hostilities with their lives if not their honour. Brigadier-General Francis Grose had received the surrender of 'near 1600' at Enniscorthy by 8 July and mopping-up operations sent a steady stream of prisoners to the south Leinster guardhouses and the prison tenders in Dublin Bay.[345]

CHAPTER FIVE

Late rebellion to 'Brigand war': July–November 1798[1]

In the days following the battle of Ballygullen small groups of rebels made their way through the mountains towards Whelp Rock camp near Blessington. One group killed several loyalists whom they encountered *en route* just as they had on 2 July when marching to Ballyrahan. Edward Neil of Carnew was leading several mounted rebels on the Kilpipe road on 6 July when they unexpectedly met George Hepenstall of Rosnastraw in company with John Myers and George Twamley of Coolsaney. Twamley's teenaged son Robert and brother Richard also formed part of the company and were taken by the rebels to Aghavannagh camp. The loyalists had sensed the danger of their predicament which spurred George Twamley to make good his escape when confronted by Neil's patrol. The others were brought to Aghavannagh where 200–300 rebels attached to Anthony Perry had collected. The mood in the camp was dark following the privations and losses of the Wexford campaign and Hepenstall and Richard Twamley were promptly piked as 'Orangemen'. Garret 'Banogue' Kavanagh, however, managed to prevent the execution of young Robert Twamley before Perry's intervention put a stop to the blood-letting. This intercession was not without hazard for Kavanagh who braved threats from Neil before Perry reprieved the surviving prisoners. Perry lacked writing materials to issue safe conduct passes which forced the men to remain with the insurgents and accompany them into Meath the next week. There were '40 holes in the shirt of Rich[ar]d Twamley' when his body was recovered.[2]

Another group of Ballygullen stragglers on the trek into Wicklow was reputedly starving and 'hastening to join their General *Holt* and his party at the *Seven Churches*, on their way to *Blackmore Hill*'. They were met by three soldier's wives who, to shield themselves from possible harm, pretended that they were seeking their Kildare rebel husbands. The women later reported to Rathdrum that all the rebels were mounted . . .

> and more than one third wounded. The wounded rode, each supported between two men on the same horse, and were every moment dropping down upon the road, they had with them one man, who for having worn an orange ribbon, they were preparing to murder. They were in a state of absolute famine, devouring the offal and carrion which they frequently met upon the road.[3]

Holt, who was actually based at Whelp Rock, had received notice that the rebels he had parted from in Wexford had been 'fiercely attacked' at Ballygullen and was told to expect 11,000 survivors at his camp. This figure was probably a considerable overestimate but he prepared for the arrival of a huge force by removing two metal boilers from a factory owned by a man named Radcliffe, probably Lieutenant-Colonel William Radcliffe of the Wicklow Militia. The requisitioned containers were used to cook seventy-nine head of cattle stolen from Finnamore of Ballyward near Kilbride who had previously incurred losses during the first days of the Rebellion when the rebels were based at Blackmore Hill. Holt recalled that men who reached his camp were in 'languid spirits' and with 'hungered stomachs'.[4]

A concerted effort was made by the insurgent officers at Whelp Rock and nearby camps to increase their numbers to a level sufficient to undertake offensive action. After Ballygullen no effort was made by the rebels to voluntarily fight superior government forces in the open field, where the prospect of success had virtually disappeared with the disembarkation of thousands of troops from Britain in late June. Between 13 and 25 June 1798 the Berwickshire, Dumfriesshire, Lancashire and Durham (Princess Charlotte of Wales') Fencible Cavalry arrived in Ireland. They were supported by the Loyal Cheshire, Glengarry (British Highlanders) and Loyal Nottingham Fencible Infantry regiments and the regular 2nd (Queen's), 29th and 100th regiments who all arrived in June.[5] The Irish administration, having prevailed in Ulster and Leinster, was then free to deploy more units against a greatly diminished rebel army which lacked the munitions to win battles and were, by July 1798, incapable of committing pikemen *en masse*. Government artillery and cavalry were almost invincible when supported with the strong bodies of infantry available at that time. With the lowlands untenable, the insurgents had no alternative but to remain in the mountainous parts of Wicklow where the terrain reduced the threat of encirclement and nullified the threat of cavalry.

The lack of roads, furthermore, militated against the transportation and deployment of cannon. The other tenable position was the bog lands of Kildare where William Aylmer's rump of that county's forces gained a respite from the rigours of successive defeats.[6]

The government realized that Wicklow was not a suitable county for waging a war of containment. *Saunder's Newsletter* of 13 July 1798 reported: 'The whole country from Ballymore-Eustace and Blessington, to Glendalough and Rathdrum, is at present covered by numerous though scattered parties of rebels, amounting in the whole to a very formidable force, but unfurnished with provisions, ammunition or artillery, except that of the latter they have two old iron ship guns (sixteen pounders) and such provisions and ammunition as can be privately conveyed from this city, or plundered by their marauding parties on the mountains. Strange to tell the tract of county now occupied by the rebels, though little more than from ten to twenty miles distant form this city, has long been, and still continues to be as little known to us as any of the wildest parts of America; a rude and barren extent of heath, moor, bog and mountain, it has been hitherto considered as scarcely penetrable by the most adventurous sportsman.' The county had not been well mapped but the timely reissue of Bernard Scale's ten year old 'Hibernian Atlas' in 1798 provided the military with an inch to six mile scale sheet for the county. Other references were the good 1778 road map produced by George Taylor and Andrew Skinner which remained the best available as Arthur Richard Nevill's 1798 'Map of said county of Wicklow, taken from actual surveys' did not appear until some years later.[7]

The occupation of the highlands could not in itself conclude the rebellion to the satisfaction of the insurgents and their presence there was consequently nothing more than a holding action. They were still apparently confident that an attack on Dublin city could transform the insurrection into a general uprising and held out renewed hopes of assistance from France. Emissaries were sent from the city in early July 'with promise and assurance' that a French invasion was planned for 24–5 July, a report which may have encouraged three King's County Militia and four Royal Irish Dragoons to desert from Lehaunstown camp with their arms and ammunition.[8] These defectors drilled the Whelp Rock rebels and 'encouraged them by saying that soon they would have the world to themselves & that they would soon have more of the soldiers.'[9] Other intelligence sources indicated that many more defections were anticipated and when they occurred the insurgents would 'pour into Dublin'.[10] The reserve camp featured strongly in the planned resurgence and on 18 July seven dragoons were sentenced to death for 'exciting a man to desert and for conspiracy to murder the troops at Laughlinstown [sic]'. Ten new recruits to the 5th Royal Irish Dragoons had also been implicated in a conspiracy to burn the camp. This activity resembled the Sheares brothers plan of mid-May 1798 and the July crackdown had direct parallels with the staged executions of 1797 which weakened the United Irish grip on disaffected soldiers.[11]

Fears were also entertained by the establishment of the reliability of untested small garrisons far from the scenes of fighting in the early summer. Even the staunchly loyal North Cork Militia came under suspicion when a sergeant and fifteen privates were brought into Dublin on 11 July from Carrick-on-Shannon and 'confessed themselves United Irishmen'.[12] Another factor in favour of continued resistance in the Wicklow mountains was optimistic, albeit false, reports of the rebellion in Ulster which hitherto had disappointed expectations. In the relative security of the Wicklow interior, the rebels awaited further developments and prepared to prosecute the rebellion under the mistaken impression that the northern rebels, the French and legions of sworn militiamen were at last to commit themselves to the struggle in force.[13]

In early July the interception of rebel agents conveying ammunition to the Wicklow mountains became more frequent and it was evident to city loyalists that a significant build-up was underway. Dublin United Irishmen were deeply involved in stimulating this revival and on 8 July two women were arrested in Camden Street bringing gunpowder and musket balls to the rebels. The munitions had been concealed in salt sacks that were still being sold in the city under licence, a security lapse which gave city republicans the opportunity to assist their comrades in the mountains. A 'committee' of twenty-four men arrested at Summerhill in early July were deemed to have been planning to liaise with the Wicklow/Dublin and mountain rebels. The purpose of these preparations was indicated by the heavy toll taken by the rebels on livestock and property in the vicinity of Whelp Rock and many influential loyalists were convinced that large numbers of insurgents intended assaulting the capital.[14]

The precise timing of the mooted attack could not be discerned but the intensification of United Irish activity in the second week of July suggested that it could well be imminent. Rebel 'express boys' were then known to be moving freely between the city and the mountains guiding recruits and fugitives to the main force.[15] Writing of the night of 10 July Dublin loyalist William Hartigan noted 'almost all the labourers in the environs of Dublin, and a great number of servants, absented themselves the night before last, in consequence of a requisition to join the rebel camp.' This was a menacing development which coincided with Major Sirr's discovery of a huge cache of pikes in a dung hill on Arbour Hill and in Back Lane. All the signs pointed to the mounting of an external attack from the mountains linking the Blessington and Rathfarnham districts either triggered by or in support of an internal rising. By 10 July new or reoccupied camps had been established at Castlekelly, near Raheen, at Ballynahowa and on Sorrel Hill which were evidently staging points for Whelp Rock as well as forward bases from which an attack on Dublin could be launched. Wicklow garrisons were also threatened by the presence of rebel forces close to their communication routes with the capital and while Newtownmountkennedy was cited as a possible target of attack, the yeomanry base of Powerscourt was considered for a large scale-raid.[16]

Richard Turner, a veteran radical who had evidently played a role in establishing the United Irish organization in south Wicklow in early 1797, left the city with a rebel emissary who took him to Francis McMahon's camp at Castlekelly. He met on arrival Dublin Colonels Felix Rourke, Edward Rattigan, Southwell McClune and one Thompson in company with Holt, all of whom had earned reputations as capable and militant leaders. The following day Turner accompanied up to fifty men on the climb to Whelp Rock from whence Holt had probably come to organize or order the move. He found 500 rebels there in the first week in July, the boilers Holt had requisitioned and quantities of 'beef, mutton & veal' but little salt and bread and 'no drink except water'.[17]

Ballybrack mason Bartholomew Connolly, as well as twenty-five others, was also summoned to the mountains that week by Edward Donnellan from Milltown and found himself in the midst of feverish activity. Connolly apparently did not ascend as far as Whelp Rock where he heard that 4,000–5,000 Wexfordmen were encamped under Garret Byrne and Holt. It was rumoured that the Wicklowmen and Wexfordians had 'quarel[le]d very much about plundering', a dispute which had probably centred on which farms were suitable for requisitioning supplies. Many, if not most, of the new arrivals were unarmed and there was consequently a shortage of pikes in Castlekelly. No less than three blacksmiths were attempting to rectify this dearth with the aid of a forge, bellows and other metal-working equipment.[18] Mobilization evidently occurred at the same time and in an identical fashion on both sides of the north Wicklow border. John Farrell of the Glen of the Downs, an employee of Peter La Touche of Bellvue, had called to Loughlinstown in early July and ordered local men to go to Whelp Rock the next day. Edward McLaughlin was one of those who complied with Farrell's instructions and went to the camp via Castlekelly where he found '150' men, mostly from the Glen of the Downs and Killincarrig near Delgany. The Delgany area men proceeded to Whelp Rock on the 11th but McLaughlin was sent back to his locality with a list of rebel secretaries whom he was to order 'to bring all their people to the camp without delay'.[19]

This systematic augmentation drew both new and previously retired recruits from Palmerstown, Tallaght, Kilgobbin and many other parishes in south and west County Dublin and probably some from north Dublin. Much to the dismay of the authorities and satisfaction of ultra-loyalists who opposed Cornwallis' amnesty programme, some of those who entered the mountains were formerly active insurgents who had received certificates of pardon from government. Sir John Beresford, who led a faction supporting Camden's hard-line approach, believed that 'no pardon or concession will bind them one moment beyond what they think to their advantage.'[20] This was undoubtedly true of the hard core rebels but it appears that some rebel recruiters compelled men to join them by invoking the counter proclamations issued by their leaders 'threatening death' to those who accepted terms. Richard Turner told his interrogators on 9 July that a 'great number' of rebels at Whelp Rock wished to seek terms but the vigilance of their comrades and the tyrannical conduct of the yeomen dissuaded them from attempting to surrender.[21]

Loyalist apprehension concerning the rebel forces on the fringes of the Dublin mountains were accentuated by a widely reported incident on 9 July when a rebel party bearing munitions to the mountains was intercepted near Rathfarnham. The patrol was commanded by Captain John Beresford jr, who led the first troop of the Dublin County Cavalry, and George La Touche, the *de facto* leader of the Rathfarnham Cavalry of which he was technically second-in-command to the Earl of Ely. Shannon, who had detailed knowledge of the incident informed his son:

> 14 fellows left this town [Dublin] yesterday with arms and ammunition, to go and join the camp above Rathfarnham. Appious's [i.e. Beresford's] corps had intelligence, and posted a party where they were to pass. They were, on being discovered, fired at, but they shot 3 of the rebels, hung 4 and brought 5 in, who I hear were hung today . . . people have no doubt of an attack here on the trials.[22]

Five of those seized were found to have the 'protections' issued in return for surrendering weapons and taking the oath of allegiance confirming suspicions as to the efficacy of the amnesty program.[23]

John Edwards in Bray viewed the situation from a different perspective having heard rumours that the yeomanry intended exacting revenge upon protectioned rebels and that this had obliged many to go into hiding or remain in arms. Captain Morrison of the Reay regiment in Newtownmountkennedy gave a degree of credence to the story by harassing a group of labourers on Sugarloaf mountain who worked for the liberal Peter La Touche. Edwards maintained that this over zealousness and 'some late instances' had given 'too much colour of credibility' to the massacre rumours and had resulted in men taking to the mountains. It is probable, however, that at least some of those he believed to be in hiding, also natives of the Downs area, were the men whom Edward McLaughlin had met at Castlekelly and that the rebels had again propagated massacre rumours to 'increase their forces'.[24]

The July treason trials of the Sheares brothers, William Michael Byrne and the other State prisoners aroused tension in the capital even without the renewed fears of militia disaffection and apparent resurgence of the so-called 'Irish and Catholic Army'.[25] The coincidence of these factors created what Cooke termed a 'state of alarm' but one which he reasoned, on the basis of information gleaned by his intelligence network, that was not as dire as Camden's circle represented.[26] The fighting strength of the rebels in July 1798 was estimated by loyalists observers at between a mere 2,000 and an alarmist 30,000 and by the insurgents themselves at 11,000–20,000. Even if the rebels numbered 15,000, which seems doubtful, there were not enough to undertake an attempt on an alert city garrison and the prospects of localized recruitment outpacing the workings of the amnesty seemed remote. This became apparent to the rebel commanders who in the continued absence of French aid adopted a fresh approach to stimulate new and maximize existing support. This entailed reprising Fr John Murphy's hitherto unsuccessful revivalist strategy of spreading the rebellion from partially mobilized active areas to peaceable districts.[27]

What really troubled informed government figures was the credible prospect of the rump of the rebel forces engaging in a costly 'brigand war' with its attendant political instability and destruction of the rural economy.[28] The disastrous potential of such a campaign was indicated by the devastation of loyalist farms in the vicinity of rebel camps, attacks on the mail coaches and murders of suspected 'orangemen' on the outskirts of Dublin. One incident which typified rebel activity at this time was the seizure of Ponsonby Pillsworth and James Hayden on 4 July while riding towards Dublin on the Baltinglass road. Pillsworth was apparently connected to the loyalist Pillsworths of Graney near Baltinglass and Hayden was deemed to be 'in some measure the cause of the massacre in Carlow [on 24 May 1798]'. After much deliberation and disagreement among the rebel officers Pillsworth was released and the condemned Hayden escaped.[29] General Lake attempted to forestall such activities by moving large numbers of troops into Wicklow with orders to 'act offensively'. General Moore, who had relieved the ailing Duff of responsibility for his brigade and the troops at Arklow and Wicklow Town, was ordered to enter Glenmalure where it was erroneously believed that the rebels were encamped. Needham retained control of the stationary garrisons of Rathdrum and Gorey while Lake at Arklow directed the operation.[30]

Moore rendezvoused with the Meath and Dublin City militiamen at Taghmon on the night of 7 July and brought the Meathmen with his command to Enniscorthy on the morning of the 8th. These were detached to cover the Scarawalsh and Ballycarney bridges on 10 July while the Fourth Flank Battalion under Lord Blayney was left at Ferns. The placement of troops along the Wexford border was intended to prevent the escape of the rebel army into that county and all strategic passes and bridges from Wicklow were well guarded. Moore's column marched through Carnew and Tinahely to Hacketstown on 11 July where several extra regiments had been assembled for the operation. Hacketstown was the staging area of the 22nd Light Brigade who had expected their general some days earlier. With no further time to lose, the army marched towards Ballinabarny Gap beyond Rathdangan under Ballineddan Mountain where they pitched camp in anticipation of a dawn attack on nearby Imaal where it was thought the insurgents were located. Colonel Campbell of the 89th regiment with the First Flank Battalion and the Fermanaghs moved at the same time through Donard to Ballinaclea on the opposite site of the Imaal valley adding their forces to the Dunbarton fencibles and the Fifth Battalion of the 60th Foot (Hesse-Darmstadt Legion) under Moore.

A plan was devised to co-ordinate a night attack on rebel positions in Glenmalure and the Seven Churches when intelligence was received that the rebels had relocated there from Imaal. Four columns were directed to starting positions around Glenmalure from which they were to descend into the valley and Seven Churches at 4.00 a.m. on the 12th. General Lake and Colonel Forster were to enter Glenmalure from the Rathdrum side and marched on the night of the 11th from

Rathdangan to Greenan, a trek which probably took them through the rebel haunt of Aghavannagh. Marquis Huntley's 450 Gordon Highlanders were to move from Aughrim and drive north into Rathdrum and Campbell was to retrace his steps through Donard and approach Wicklow Gap near the Seven Churches from Blessington. Moore's own column went from Ballinaclea and climbed towards the head of Glenmalure where they arrived in the early hours of 12 July on the side of Table Mountain. Great difficulty was experienced moving his detachment's two six-pounder cannon and baggage and at 6.00 p.m. they entered the valley and spent five hours on a fruitless search for the rebels.[31]

Huntley's column arrived in Rathdrum at midnight on 11/12 July and added their men to a 1,400-strong force in the town. The Flannel Hall was then crammed with far more men than it had been adapted to accommodate and many households were obliged to billet three or more Leitrim militiamen on hay-covered floors. Huntley's Highlanders moved out of Rathdrum the following morning and crossed into the Seven Churches in a bid to trap the elusive insurgents between his column and Campbell's which was moving from Wicklow Gap. Rathdrum loyalists had expressed hopes on the morning of the 12th that the Friendly Brothers would hold their annual dinner as usual with Revd Powell, with the popular young Huntley, son of the Duke of Gordon, as their guest of honour. It is unclear if the event passed off as Rathdrum was in a state of ferment with nearly 2,000 militia, fencibles and regulars preparing for the pre-emptive attack on Glenmalure. The town's gaol was also full of rebel suspects, including Fr Byrne, the Greenan-based curate to Fr Meagher, who had been confined for 'some days' by 12 July 1798 when Fr Conroy was also brought as a prisoner into Rathdrum.[32]

The much delayed offensive of 12 July proved to be an anticlimax for the military, as neither the Highlanders nor any of the other columns encountered any real opposition. Two shots fired on Moore's men were probably the only ones discharged in anger and the soldiers, who had not brought their tents in the interests of mobility, suffered from the unseasonal heavy rain and coldness in boggy terrain. Moore conferred with Huntley and Campbell in the Seven Churches on the 13th and decided to go to Blessington as the rebels were reportedly encamped once again on Blackmore Hill and at Whelp Rock. He collected his own forces in Glenmalure and left for Blessington at 2.00 p.m. having sent his cumbersome cannon and baggage ahead by road to Lake. The recombined and fatigued brigade, however, went no further than

Imaal where they passed the night, moving the following day through Donard and Hollywood. Although a veteran of the hard-fought Wexford campaign, Moore was surprised at the outward signs of fear displayed by the inhabitants towards his troops and found the sight of the burned villages 'a melancholy spectacle'. The comforts of Lord Waterford's lodge provided Moore with a brief respite from his rigorous mission although he made a point of spending the night of 14 July in the troop bivouacs.

The general berated the 'dreadful' conduct of his troops during the operation and was unsympathetic when three Hessian soldiers of Major Von Verna's 5th Battalion were killed on straying from Hollywood to pillage. The incident was seized upon by Moore to rein the men in and to discourage them from ill-disciplined raids on the country people. Sergeant McLaren of the Dunbartons was amazed to see a Hessian tear down a cabin for firewood in order to cook plundered meat.[33] Having searched the woods on Milltown's estate, Moore withdrew to Blessington on the 15th where Lake informed him that the insurgents had left the Blackmore Hill area and were believed to have gone towards county Meath. The failure of the sweep came as no surprise to Cooke who had learned on 12 July that a dispatch detailing Lake's plan had fallen into the hands of the insurgents, although there is no evidence that this reached the rebels at Whelp Rock or influenced their decision to leave Wicklow. William Pole heard that the rebels had left Wicklow upon intercepting one of Lake's messengers and had been 'entirely driven' out of the county. His sources echoed Moore's perceptions of the enterprise and speculated that 'from the manner in which they have been harassed, they are driven to the last extremity, and their numbers much reduced.'[34]

THE MEATH EXPEDITION

The primary reason for Moore's inability to find the main rebel force had arisen from a 'council of war' at Whelp Rock on 7 or 8 July when the rebel officers met to debate strategy in the light of recent experience and national developments. Contributors to the discussion weighed up the relative merits of mounting a risky expedition to the midlands and the more passive alternative of maintaining a presence in the mountains to await the French. While an attack on Dublin city remained their ultimate objective, several officers believed that their numbers and munitions were insufficient in the short term and un-likely to increase without fresh initiatives.[35]

Holt was one of those who spoke against leaving the mountains and argued that an attack on the weak garrison of Newtownmount-kennedy would glean two cannon which could be used to bolster an attempt on Dublin. News that such a plan was in contemplation may have been leaked causing the alert in the town on night of 8 or 9 July. Fr Kearns, however, argued that a thrust into the midlands would facilitate the seizure of the arms and munitions which were believed to have been stored in Clonard. Kearns had served as a curate in the village some time before the insurrection and may have received specific information from old comrades on the garrison's dispositions. This proposal was ultimately adopted by a small majority when put to a vote and, having manufactured a supply of cartridges and powder, the rebels formed themselves into companies on the night of 8 July and marched toward Kildare.[36]

Rathcoole rebel leader Felix Rourke understood that they intended to march 'through the various counties in order to raise them – to avoid fighting as much as possible, but to harass small parties' of pro-government forces. It was hoped that their numbers would be sub-stantially increased by the anticipated joining of forces with the rebels under William Aylmer of Painstown and Bryan McDermott who were situated at Timahoe on the edge of the Bog of Allen in Kildare. McDermott and Aylmer had fought a guerrilla campaign but unknown to the insurgents in Wicklow were endeavouring to surrender in early July.[37] At least two groups of rebels remained in Wicklow, one of which was commanded by Dublin's Francis McMahon who had probably opposed the plan. His faction stayed at Whelp Rock and its locality and probably carried out a series of robberies in the Kilgobbin/Rath-farnham area in early July. On 10 July the garrison of Rathfarnham turned out and prepared to meet an attack which did not materialize from rebels assembling in the mountains. The Whelp Rock men were well-armed and were believed to have obtained 'a great quantity of saltpetre' which they used to manufacture gunpowder. Another group under Miles Byrne of Monaseed and Michael Dwyer camped in Glenmalure with their wounded. Dwyer had also refused to coun-tenance the midlands strategy and would rarely again venture beyond the fastnesses of Ballinacor and Talbotstown.[38]

The main insurgent force went through Blessington and Kilcullen pressing into Kildare as far as Robertstown. The route and pace adopted by the rebels indicated a determination to retain the element of surprise and they requisitioned a large number of horses to increase their mobility. At Newbridge a small body of soldiers was deprived of a quantity of gunpowder and a yeomanry corps which attempted to shadow them was driven off by an aggressive rear guard. Fatigue and poor morale took its toll and Holt claimed that one in seven of the insurgents who had left the mountains deserted on their march to Prosperous. On 10 July the rebels destroyed the Dublin mails at Kill before establishing contact with elements of Aylmer's group near Prosperous. This proved to be a bitterly disappointing encounter as the Kildare men were far fewer than expected and a section of his force were unwilling to accompany the rebel column to Clonard the following day.[39] The Kildare forces had suffered defeats at Ovidstown on 18 June and Fox's Hill on 30 June.

Little resistance had been anticipated from the small garrison in Clonard which was approached by two columns but Holt asserted that the rebels 'received a warm reception' from yeomen covering the bridge crossing into the town.[40] Two houses on the outskirts of the settlement were fired to generate a smoke-screen and its barracks was gutted when its roof was prised off with pikes and burning straw thrown into its interior. Rourke claimed that the county and city of Dublin rebels spearheaded the attack but his boast that 'not one soldier escaped the flames' in the barracks was incorrect. In fact, the shaken defenders escaped the conflagration and continued to mount an effective resistance from adjacent fortified houses.[41] Lieutenant John Tyrell's twenty-seven yeomen reputedly expended over 1,300 rounds on their assailants at Leinster Bridge and probably accounted for many of the sixty or so rebels killed in the six-hour attack for three yeoman fatalities. Tyrell was related to Thomas Tyrell of Kilreny, a High Sheriff of Kildare in the 1790s, whose home was converted into a 'virtual fortress' to guard against his many Defender and United Irish enemies. The Kilreny residence and George Tyrell's Ballinderry house were both destroyed by the rebels.[42]

The fate of Clonard and rebel efforts to reduce its garrison was sealed upon the arrival of Colonel Blake with fifty Northumberland fencibles and fifty yeomen cavalry from Mullingar and Kinnegad. They were further supported by Lieutenant Houghton with fourteen Kinnegad Infantry. Blake had brought two cannon which immediately 'commenced a dreadful fire of grape and round shot' upon the exposed rebels.[43] Holt noted that one shot killed eight rebels who had taken refuge behind a wall, an incident which served to convince the survivors that further heavy losses were inevitable in what increasingly appeared to be a futile attempt. The Kinnegad reinforcement enabled a party of Tyrell's yeomen to leave their stronghold and attempt to clear the

ATTACKS ON TYRELL'S HOUSE near Clonard. G. Cruickshank, 1845

enclosed garden of their enemies. Six yeomen were badly wounded, one mortally, in driving the insurgents out of a fir tree plantation and from behind the protection of a privet hedge. The rebels reluctantly withdrew to conserve their strength and fast dwindling ammunition stocks and fell back on Carbury Hill for the night. 'Sharp words' were exchanged on the hill concerning the somewhat ignominious defeat which resulted in a number of aggrieved Wicklow and Wexfordmen returning towards the mountains from which they had marched. The implications of defeat at Clonard were very serious for the expedition and level- headed discussion of this was probably not helped by the breaking open of Lord Harberton's well-stocked wine cellar at Newbury Hall.[44]

On 12 July the initiative passed once more to the army when Lieutenant-Colonel George Gough received word at Edenderry that the insurgents at Carbury Hill intended to attack his garrison. To obviate this development Gough took 207 dragoons, Major John Ormsby's Limerick City Militia and a body of yeomen to launch a pre-emptive strike on the rebel camp, but on arrival at Carbury discovered that the insurgents had destroyed Johnstown. Gough attempted to regain contact with the marauding rebels and quickly discovered that around 4,000 were posted on nearby Rynville Hill. Reconnaissance informed Gough that the insurgents appeared to be prepared to give battle on the high ground and were reputedly yelling 'most horribly'.[45] This shout was very probably one of alarm as the rebels were not in fact expecting an attack from such a strong force and many of their well-armed mounted element were absent foraging for supplies. An even more serious deficiency was that the Rynville musketmen had very little ammunition and expended much of their reserves by opening fire on Gough's men from cornfields at the bottom of the hill. Scenes of chaos ensued on the approach of the troops to close quarters and many insurgents in the camp were effectively incapacitated by intoxication, fatigue and wounds. Moreover, a large proportion of the able-bodied men attempted to make good their escape from the battlefield rather than reap the potential benefits of defending an elevated position against assault.[46]

As the terrain around Rynville was generally more open and firm than that of either north Wexford or Wicklow the disorganized rebels were vulnerable to the dragoons who comprised the bulk of Gough's force. All who could be revived and transported hastily evacuated the camp while Holt, assisted by west Wicklowman Michael Dalton, tried to improvise a rearguard to ward off the deadly cavalry. Holt ordered the burning of houses adjoining the road-side in a bid to obscure their movements by a smoke-screen as they dispersed in all directions. He was thrown from his horse and concussed while crossing a hedge in Longwood Bog and awoke to find that he had been left for dead with his line of retreat cut off by the soldiers. He consequently lost contact with his group and was obliged to feign death to avoid summary execution, a ruse facilitated by the bloody but minor wounds he had sustained to his head and arm.[47] The majority of the rebels, about 1,500 men, fled northwards towards Garristown and quarrelled during the retreat causing further factionalism and divisions. Most of the Kildaremen returned with Edward Fitzgerald to Timahoe to seek terms, which were being negotiated between Aylmer and General Wilford while the Dubliners, of whom no further mention is to be found in extant documents dealing with the expedition to Meath, probably returned to Whelp Rock. They may have hoped to rejoin their comrades who had remained under McMahon but many evidently retired to the city. Other smaller groups embarked on the perilous trek to Glenmalure where Dwyer and Miles Byrne were encamped.[48]

By 14 July the Meath incursion had proved a disastrous undertaking which, far from bolstering the strength of the rebel army, had split the largest and most militant body in the country into several disillusioned factions. Very few recruits had joined the effort and it is highly unlikely that their numbers exceeded those who deserted. Reports of the ill-fated rebel activity in Meath contrasted sharply with the pro-government 'happy accounts' emanating from Kilkenny, Queen's County, Carlow and Wexford where the 'deluded people' were flocking to accept the amnesty terms. One body of almost 1,000 former rebels had received protections at this time in Abbeyleix; a similar number surrendered in Kilcullen and some 4,000 pardons were distributed in Arklow.[49] That neither Kildare nor Meath had displayed any signs of revolting was undoubtedly galling to the unreconciled cadre and the prospects of risings further afield could not have been increased by the very poor showing of the insurgents at Clonard and Rynville.

Captain George Lambart of Drogheda learned that 'some Garristown & Dunboyne folk' had joined 'Gen[era]l Holt' but his comments probably pertained to Holt's men with Garret Byrne as the rebels arrested by Lambart's yeomen were north Wicklowmen who would have been separated from Holt at Rynville.[50] It was believed in Dublin Castle that the Meath people were unsympathetic towards the insurgents and that those living on the borders of Louth were 'bringing in the stragglers'. Cooke was informed that the rebels expected 'a general insurrection' in the Dublin area and were surprised that 'very few' joined them from this area. Indeed, as government forces gathered in mid-July to engage the weak and poorly armed rebels, the midlands venture was in danger of degenerating into a massacre.[51]

These reverses exacerbated tensions within the command structure of the insurgent army giving rise to paralyzing recrimination, dissension and defeatism. Command difficulties were probably worsened by the unusual prevalence of senior leaders without a recognized commander-in-chief. Stephen Murray of Gorey believed that the commander was Esmond Kyan with Holt, Garret Byrne, Kearns and Fitzgerald under him, which was in agreement with Daniel Doyne's opinion.[52] Another participant claimed that the rebels were 'commanded by Garret Byrne and Jos[eph] Holt' which makes Holt's absence from a list of rebel leaders compiled by Felix Rourke remarkable, although it may be that Holt was out of favour with all Dublin commanders and not just McMahon.[53] Kyan acted 'as general' according to Rourke but his position was clearly honourary as he had been badly wounded at Arklow and his name has not been associated with any action on the expedition. If Kyan did wield supreme command, he was unable to prevent the fragmentation of his force and order Rourke's men to remain with the rump of Wicklowmen and Wexfordians.[54] The formerly aggressive and spirited Anthony Perry was dismayed by the performance of the exhausted insurgents and reportedly told a yeoman prisoner that '100 soldiers were enough to beat them.'[55]

Brigadier-General Meyrick used Lieutenant-Colonel Orde's Durham Light Fencible Cavalry to harry rebel stragglers at Longwood and Kilmullen of whom forty or fifty were killed. Meyrick was in aggressive mood and ordered Colonel Gordon's Duke of York's Highlanders 'not to lose sight' of the insurgents as he was determined to prevent them returning to Wicklow. The Wicklow mountains were not the immediate objective of all remaining rebel forces; Garret Byrne and those who intended to fight on kept moving in the opposite direction and reached Garristown Hill where they gained a short respite during the hours of darkness. They moved the following morning to Blacklion, crossed the River Boyne at Stackallen later that evening and proceeded to Knightstown Bog on 14 July where they elected to stand their ground. The coincidence of exhaustion with access to slightly more favourable terrain for defence had probably dictated this course of action.[56]

Major-Generals Weyms and Meyrick had moved from their respective positions at Drogheda and Tara Hill to meet at Blacklion on the 13th and followed the rebels across the Boyne at Stackallen. At 11 a.m. on 14 July their forward cavalry patrols established contact with the insurgents in Knightstown Bog which they quickly began to surround. Weyms, whose Northumberland Highlanders played an leading part in the fighting, claimed that the rebels were 'very strongly posted behind a defile between two bogs'. After the bulk of the infantry had arrived to man a loose cordon, the battalion guns of the Northumberlands targeted the identified insurgent strongpoints. The brief but intense bombardment drove the defenders from their positions whereupon they were attacked. Weyms noted: 'the Highlanders got into the bog and killed all that were in it. Those who got out on the opposite side were met by the cavalry'. Despite this rout a 'great many' desperate rebels broke through gaps in the army's line and escaped in the direction of Garristown.[57]

The remnants under Byrne had extricated themselves from Knightstown Bog with some difficulty and then retreated southwards towards Wicklow while a small number of Wexfordians who doubted the possibility of reaching home headed into the Ardee area. In the days following 14 July scores of insurgents were found hiding in cornfields north of the Boyne and elsewhere in Meath by the soldiers and yeomen scouring the countryside. Many were shot out-of-hand and dozens of others were only taken prisoner to be courtmartialled for the capital crime of 'waging war against our sovereign Lord the King'.[58] In practice execution rarely followed conviction, and Daniel Fogarty of Tinahely, a fifty-five-year old father of eleven, was one of those who eventually obtained his liberty. John Byrne of Redcross and Thomas Dogherty of Killincarrig were court-martialled at Slane by the Cavan Militia on 18 July 1798 along with fourteen other Wicklowmen with whom they had probably been captured. Most of the prisoners encountered by constable Johnson had fought at Hacketstown and Vinegar Hill and were deemed 'very harden[e]d' men.[59]

The small column under Garret Byrne which had evaded the troops on the 14th forded the Boyne once again at Dowth and after resting and regrouping were finally routed at Ballyboughill west of Lusk after a ten-mile pursuit by Captain Archibald Gordon's Dumfries dragoons. The rebels had offered a 'feeble' resistance to the Scots and no longer constituted a credible threat to the government's will. Only fourteen or fifteen had been killed in the skirmish but their dispersion was almost complete and their 'military titles were all gone'. Survivors made their way as best could they singly or in small groups to Dublin city and the Wicklow mountains where local government forces awaited their return.[60]

The midlands campaign left fugitive rebel leaders scattered all over Meath, Kildare and north county Dublin. Anthony Perry and Fr Kearns fared the worst and were arrested by yeomen named Ridgeway and Robinson near Edenderry (King's County), tried by courtmartial and executed on the 21st. The highly regarded Esmond Kyan was equally unfortunate despite regaining the Wicklow mountains. He had refused all requests to rejoin the rump rebel forces and was captured in north Wexford on 20 July before he could make terms with the military. His execution followed a perfunctory courtmartial which, like that of Kearns and Perry, was probably intended by loyalists to forestall attempts to admit him to 'State Prisoner' status.[61]

Aylmer, Byrne and Fitzgerald entered into formal negotiations with General Dundas and were at length awarded terms by Cornwallis. The government was anxious to end all vestiges of rebellion and to this end was prepared to adopt a conciliatory attitude towards senior rebels who were technically ineligible for clemency. Cornwallis' personal inclination to permit such pacts was in this instance endorsed by Sir Fenton Aylmer and the powerful former Viceroy Marquis of Buckingham, who had interested themselves on William Aylmer's behalf. The terms granted guaranteed only that their lives would be spared but this was tantamount to an arrangement of self-exile. It was understood that the leaders would bring influence to bear on their adherents and encourage them to obtain protections.[62] Cooke, writing on the eve of the surrender specified that 'Aylmer, Fitzgerald & others submit & promise for their people.'[63] Four days later the Undersecretary reiterated that even though the compact had

> . . . not given much satisfaction . . . it has shortened the rebellion, which is of more consequence. Some small parties are plundering in the Wicklow mountains still, but we trust they will be rooted out in a day or two. The people are endeavouring to obtain protections, and I believe are in general heartily tired.[64]

General Wilford, however, had almost precipitated a major crisis when he met a rebel delegation at Sallins on 18 July and concluded an armistice with Fitzgerald, who falsely claimed that he had been authorized to seek terms by the entire leadership of the Wicklow, Wexford and Kildare insurgents. Cornwallis was aghast that Wilford had signed an unapproved treaty with 'rebels in arms' who then flaunted the gesture by failing to surrender within the stipulated period.[65] The Viceroy was undoubtedly mindful of the acrimony in parliament and in public which had been aroused by similar dealings with the Kildare rebels by Dundas on 24 May. He promptly cancelled the treaty, reduced the concessions to sparing the lives of the leaders and offered substantial bounties for their capture if they refused to comply. This had the desired effect and on 21 July, fifteen Kildare, Wexford and Wicklow rebel officers surrendered at Sallins and were that evening 'dirtying' Cooke's parlour in Dublin.[66] This pragmatic and magnanimous gesture was received with disdain and hostility by the conservative establishment who found it difficult to countenance the 'greatest and most cruel scoundrels' being banished rather than executed.[67]

Holt reached Whelp Rock after a series of narrow escapes on or shortly after 16 July but immediately pressed on to Glenmalure where he was told there were many wounded without medical care. Another reason for not remaining at Whelp Rock may have been that it was then occupied by his enemy, McMahon. A small force of rebels under Dwyer and Miles Byrne had protected the wounded in Glenmalure against yeoman incursions and moved them temporarily to Seven Churches on 12 July when General Moore's column had entered the glen. James Chritchley received intelligence in Rathdrum that '[Miles] Byrne from ye county Wexford' had commanded in Glenmalure and that it was the destination of 'straggling parties' dispersed at the

Boyne in late July.[68] The Glenmalure group and McMahon's 200–strong faction at Whelp Rock were indeed augmented daily by men who had broken through the necessarily cursory cordon manned around the city and its environs. Dublin magistrate William James reported that several hundred dejected rebels had passed unopposed through the city into the mountains and Holt recalled receiving as many as thirty to forty a night. They reputedly entered the city 'in groups of three and four – all unarmed and appear like savages with long beards, little clothes and appeared half starved.' In their absence, however, the nature of the warfare in Wicklow had changed.[69]

From mid-July 1798 the execution of loyalist prisoners became common in Wicklow as veterans of the Wexford campaign, where such killings were a more frequent feature of the insurrection, returned to their native county and displayed less mercy to captives than earlier in the struggle. While the main rebel force was engaged in Meath, elements of Patrick Grant's 'Glenmalure company' had seized local men Samuel Langrell of Ballynabarney and William Carter of Ballintombay on Carriglineen Mountain. Grant's men disbelieved the claims advanced by their loyalist prisoners that they had been looking for horses and after a short discussion piked Langrell and shot Carter near Pierse Harney's Baravore home. Carter apparently received the quicker death as he was 'not considered so blameable'.[70] Henry Wybrants alleged at a 1799 courtmartial that Dwyer had suggested that Carter be spared piking on account of his Catholicism although Musgrave considered the victim a Protestant and the Imaal leader was not known for sectarian conduct. The men were accused of apprehending two Wexford insurgents who were shot by the Antrim Militia but it is more likely that they had delivered two rebels into the hands of the Ancient Britons after the battle of Newtownmountkennedy when the dragoons were stationed at a camp near Ballynabarney. The Britons had apparently flogged the pair before shooting them, actions which were also avenged later in the rebellion by burning out a yeoman named Chritchley.[71]

These cold-blooded killings were not an isolated incident but one in a series of multiple executions of marked men. Also killed by the rebels at the time of the Glenmalure deaths were Joseph Ellison and John Bolton of Clara and John Goggin of Balleese who were seized together in Acton's Wood near Clarabridge. The three loyalists were probably either recovering cattle driven off by the insurgents or stealing herds belonging to local men. A more pertinent factor may have been their membership of the extremist Rathdrum yeomen infantry and it seems they were captured near Ballinacor House by men attached to

Dwyer's Glenmalure associate John Mernagh. Their deaths would have aroused widespread attention as Bolton was wood ranger to local landowner Thomas Acton and Ellison worked in the same job for Earl Fitzwilliam.[72]

Some rebel leaders in Glenmalure had qualms about killing the prisoners despite the fact they were deemed to be committed loyalists and a meeting was held in Edward Kelly's home to determine their fate on 18 July. Edward's son Richard was regarded as the 'most active and dangerous' rebel in the valley and the house was frequently used for insurgent conferences.[73] Michael Malone of Ballintombay resigned his captaincy in protest at the majority resolution to execute the loyalists at the Strand, Glenmalure. Grant was also disappointed at the executions as he had hoped to exchange the prisoners for his brother-in-law and others held by the army in Rathdrum but it is highly unlikely that such a deal would have been countenanced. A more cogent argument had been made at the meeting by the popular Antrim Militia defector known as 'Antrim John' who stated: 'it was a rebellion & no war & there was no way of keeping pris[one]r[s].'[74] Glenealy cobbler Edward Dockerill also fell foul of this new ruthlessness when he tried to intervene on behalf of the captives and was also piked. This probably arose on account of his own yeomanry membership and his presence in the camp was clearly involuntary. In a macabre twist a suspected spy named Patrick Farrell was obliged to pike the bodies to ensure that they had died.[75]

Despite this implacable attitude, the respected Captain James Doyle of Ballinacor managed to free his captive loyalist friend Robert Hughes of Ballinaclash, although it is likely that this was facilitated by the fact that Hughes was apparently not a yeomen or suspected of anti-republican atrocities. Another survivor was John Ellis who was seized at Ballinacor by Dwyer's men on suspicion of being 'an orangeman'. Ellis testified at the 1799 trial of Michael Malone and Patrick Grant that both men had interceded on his behalf and secured his release. On the same evening that Doyle had saved Hughes from being shot by Dalton of Ballycoog, Dwyer's men captured one of the Chritchleys of Ballyboy with four of his workmen. Dwyer, perhaps fearing that the five would be killed if taken to Glenmalure, decided to commandeer their firearms but release them unharmed. This aroused considerable surprise, if not indignation, in the camp as Chritchley had recently shot a man named Toomey in Greenan.[76]

There were at least 300–400 insurgents in Glenmalure when Holt became their commander-in-chief on his arrival from Meath. Holt claimed that on the day after he reached Pierse Harney's house in Glenmalure, 300 men came to Baravore of whom 150 had returned from the Boyne and 'the majority' had lost their homes. He was the only senior Wicklow rebel willing to fight on and having acquitted himself well at Ballyellis, Carnew and Rynville was immediately accepted as their leader. However, Holt took command at a time when every other leading contender was either dead or attempting to surrender.[77] The most important rebel officers then in Glenmalure or associated with Holt at that time were Dwyer, Martin Burke, Patrick Grant, Miles Byrne of Monaseed, Murtough Byrne of Aughrim, James Doyle of Ballinacor, William Casey of Glenmalure (who succeeded Malone of Ballintombay), Michael Dalton, James Ryder, James Hughes, Andrew Hackett, Michael Neil, Paul Murray of Kilmurray, 'Antrim John' Mooney and one Pluck, probably William Pluck of Ballycotton.[78]

GLENMALURE, April 1793, by J. Fisher. N.L.I., TB 1872

In 1794 a travel writer described Glenmalure as

> . . . a valley of considerable length and great depth, rude and uncultivated to the last degree, except a little rich lawn thro[ugh] which the river meanders, and which, tho[ugh] very narrow, forms by its verdure and its flatness, a beautiful and romantic contrast to the stupendous broken rocks and steep craggy mountains that environ it. In some places these actually overhang, and being covered with short smooth grass, cattle grazing too near the edge, have frequently slipped down the precipice, and been killed by the fall . . .[79]

It looked very much as it had in 1580 when the insurgents of the Elizabethan era had inflicted their famous victory on Lord Grey de Wilton. To make Glenmalure more inaccessible to the army in 1798 the rebels destroyed the bridge over the River Avonbeg which flowed through the valley and trenched nearby roads. The following week Captain Stratford reported that the rebels had 'cut trenches across the road & cover[e]d the same with slight sticks & rushes & grounded it over in order to deceive the cavalry or cannoniers [sic]'.[80]

Between 20 and 24 July the insurgents were joined by twenty-four Antrim militiamen who defected in two batches from the garrison at Arklow bringing both weapons and training skills. Two more followed their comrades before the end of the month verifying Holt's claim that '28 of the Antrim militia' joined him 'in a short time'.[81] Nineteen of these men had enlisted in the county in April 1798 which suggests that the Wicklow United Irishmen had infiltrated the regiment with proselytization and the obtaining of equipment in mind, including the famous Samuel McAllister who, despite northern origins, signed on in Wicklow on 1 April 1798. It is possible that he was then re-enlisting but the prevalence of men who were certainly from Wicklow in the group he deserted with suggests that he may have been a member of the community of Antrim people who had settled in Wicklow before the rebellion. Felix McGuinness, shot dead in Arklow on 24 July, was presumably either a loyal soldier killed resisting the defectors or a conspirator who fell in the attempt.[82] As deserters were rarely treated leniently if captured they generally proved highly motivated recruits reputedly sworn to a 'compact of death'.[83] Holt exploited his deserter contingent to the full and claimed 'about 120 soldiers from 13 reg[imen]ts of militia' by the late autumn who comprised the backbone of his force.[84]

The defectors fought together with their own weapons as an elite corps and were distinguished from their comrades by their uniforms, better equipment and junior officers. Perhaps the most influential deserter leader was 'Antrim John' Mooney who had defected from Captain William Moore's company during the battle of New Ross on 5 June 1798 and was presumed dead. Many deserters named John from the Antrim regiment were called 'Antrim John' or 'Antrim Jack' but the man Holt consistently referred to in his memoir by that title was Mooney.[85] Miles Byrne described two Antrim Johns in his narrative of the Wicklow campaign but concentrated on a northern Presbyterian whereas Mooney was described 'a staunch Catholic'.[86] Holt used Mooney and other prominent defectors to drill his men and was one of the few rebel commanders to conduct large-scale manoeuvres to practise the tactics he devised and on 14 July. Byrne saw Antrim John 'marching and drilling platoons of our men in the meadows on the riverside.'[87] Laurence Mulligan took part in 'a sham battle in Glenmalure where Holt acted as Gener[a]l' and Patrick Grant and 'Antrim John' as captains of 300 men divided into pike and gun units. These exercises no doubt fostered camaraderie and confidence among rebels of disparate backgrounds and may well have improved their ability to respond to orders. Closing with the enemy was exceptionally difficult in the exposed mountainous terrain of Wicklow and retreating in good order was an essential skill.[88]

It came to the attention of the rebels in late July that Henry Allen of Greenan intended offering his spacious cloth-manufacturing factory to the military for use as a barrack. Holt, after consultation with his officers in Harney's, determined that such strongpoints should be denied the government as experience at Clonard and before had shown that loyalist retention of redoubts had thwarted rebel designs and caused heavy casualties. In July 1798 the need for the rebels to minimize the number of fortified positions available to their enemies was acute, as their strength had waned to a point that even slated farmhouses were virtually impregnable if resolutely defended. Holt consequently ordered the destruction of all such dwellings which in general belonged to prosperous Protestant farmers and middlemen.[89] Miles Byrne wrote that the destruction of stone buildings was 'a cruel alternative' but necessary, and Allen's factory, strategically located on the Rathdrum road, became a prime target in the last week of July.[90] A secondary reason for attacking Allen was the fact that he was a United Irishman 'early in the business' who had refused to take part in the rebellion.[91] It emerged at a 1799 courtmartial that 'Allen was a United man but would not assist and therefore they would burn his house'.[92]

About a week before the factory was burned Holt dispatched Doyle of Ballinacor and Mooney at the head of a raiding party to ascertain details of the defences protecting Allen's residence. Doyle gleaned most of the information from Allen's employee, Pat Toole, and on a second visit shortly afterwards seized a yeoman named William Snell of Templelyon who was released unharmed but without his equipment. On the morning of the Greenan raid the insurgents formed into their respective companies, including one which had joined them from Imaal, and moved towards the village.[93] A detachment remained to monitor the crossroads on the Ballinacor side of the Avonbeg river while the main body moved forward towards Allen's home and factory. John and Samuel Wheeler were at work in Allen's garden when they approached and unsuccessfully attempted to hide from the raiders. John Wheeler had evidently anticipated the subsequent accusations that he was 'an orangeman' and when noticed made an attempt to escape to Greenan but was struck with a bottle, seized and taken back to the crossroads. Antrim defector John McVeigh shot Wheeler in the shoulder and chest whereupon he was repeatedly piked and was thrown dead or mortally wounded into the Avonbeg River. In an inexplicable and unusually brutal act his fourteen-year-old son Samuel was also put to death.[94]

No resistance was offered to the rebels as they entered Greenan and broke into the factory complex. These buildings and several houses belonging to workmen were set on fire but Allen's premises did not burn easily. Patrick Grant's company were obliged to return to the village and relight the blaze, where many of them had worked prior to the rebellion. At least £500 worth of cloth was plundered along with 'several horse loads' of goods which were of great use in Glenmalure. One group of rebels retreated through Macreddin village near Cushbawn Mountain where they forced some of the inhabitants to accompany them to Aghavannagh, and in all about 300 returned to Glenmalure. The losses were avenged that night by the Rathdrum yeomanry who burned Greenan chapel and 'several' houses of suspected local rebels, including that of the local curate, Fr Byrne who was already in custody.[95]

Towards the end of July the insurgents began to cross more frequently into Imaal and to Whelp Rock, possibly on account of the renewed efforts of the authorities to crack down on their activities in Glenmalure. On 22 July rebels based in or near Whelp Rock attacked soldiers near Blessington who were escorting prisoners to Dublin and were only driven off when a second party of the military came to their aid. This aggressiveness was demonstrated again on the night of 25–26

July when mounted raiders sallied out from Imaal and burned loyalist houses at Clonmore and Ballyconnell near Hacketstown. They were intercepted when returning towards the mountains by eighty-six yeomen from Baltinglass, Hacketstown and Upper Talbotstown supported by forty Antrim Militia under Lieutenant Gardiner. A separate detachment of Sligo Militia and Tullow Cavalry under Captain Ormsby also made contact with the retreating rebels and inflicted several more casualties which were thought to include an insurgent captain. Benjamin O'Neil Stratford claimed that the Wicklow-based units had killed about thirty raiders in all and that horses stolen from members of the Humewood corps had been recovered. Government losses were very slight in the skirmishing although at least one Talbotstown yeoman was wounded and his horse killed.[96]

The deaths suffered by the rebels evidently steeled them to mount a second attack later that night or on the following one. About fifty mounted rebels launched a daring attack on the Humewood yeomanry base in which they burned 'almost every house' on the estate. They were preparing to set fire to the mansion when the resident cavalry returned from their patrol.[97] Captain Hume's yeomen and a small force of Antrim and Derry Militia soon gained the upper hand in the fighting that ensued driving the retreating rebels to a nearby bog in which they were forced to dismount. After a sharp exchange of fire the rebels managed to elude their pursuers and escaped with the relatively small loss of eight men. That they were credited with being 'extremely well armed . . . which they appeared to know well the use of [and] fought with great bravery for some time' suggests that Holt's defector faction had been involved in the raid. Yeomen losses were put at one dead and three or four badly wounded.[98]

These raiding parties generally conducted themselves in a humane fashion taking only clothes, food, weapons, money and other items necessary for subsistence in the mountains. One of Holt's patrols went as far as Ballitore in Kildare to levy their 'blackmail' from the vulnerable villagers who were otherwise unharmed.[99] Criminals and renegade insurgents often took advantage of the rebellion to extort goods and money by invoking the authority of rebel commanders to requisition supplies. This practice led to violent feuds between criminal and rebel factions and Holt and others made repeated attempts to curb criminal agents associated with their forces.[100] An attempt to pre-empt such raids from Imaal was made in late July in which three yeomanry corps operating from Hacketstown penetrated the rebel stronghold. The yeomen were unwise to confront their insurgent foes on their home territory and came off the worst in a brief engagement. Despite holding their own in Imaal, the insurgents moved briefly to Whelp Rock camp and then back to Glenmalure by the end of July. They learned in Glenmalure that it was the intention of the army to invade the valley in strength from 'every direction'.[101]

Shortly before the anticipated army offensive took place a party of mounted rebels attacked off-duty yeomen at work ploughing Robert Freeman's potato fields in Tomriland near Roundwood. Thomas Hatton escaped across terrain suitable for concealment but his comrades Freeman and John Burbidge were immediately killed. Two other yeomen, Henry Marks and James Flynn, were taken prisoner to Holt who had located his men in the Three Crosses/Drumgoff area. Flynn either escaped or was released in the Seven Churches but Marks, who was known to have attempted to arrest Holt on 12 May 1798, was executed once the military were perceived approaching them. John Healy of Drummin allegedly declared 'this is the best time to kill the bloody orange rogue or he will be rescued by the army and we will not get him again'.[102] Thomas King believed that Holt had ordered his execution but Marks was apparently held responsible for the death of Dick Byrne of Glenealy and it was chiefly on this account that the formidable John Harman insisted on putting the prisoner to death.[103]

The killings predictably resulted in a spate of house-burning by their enraged yeoman colleagues within a few days. Major Hardy recalled that the men were buried three days after their deaths and that yeomen returning from the funerals 'set fire to every catholic house' they came upon. Hardy accosted the arsonists and forced them to extinguish as many of the fires as possible.[104] The intimate and violent nature of the fighting in Wicklow in the late summer and autumn gave rise to a reprisal mentality which further heightened inter communal tensions. The actions of the yeomanry seemed 'ferocious' to Cornwallis who, while recognizing their role in defeating the rebellion, lamented that they had taken 'the lead in rapine and murder and every kind of atrocity'. The Viceroy considered the efforts of the rebels as 'feeble outrages, burnings and murders which . . . serve to keep up the sanguinary disposition on our side' and as long as they continued he could 'see no prospect of amendment' of the behaviour of Government troops. Cornwallis clearly had Wicklow in mind when he recorded his sentiments on the yeomanry as he had just returned from visiting the charred ruins of Blessington on 24 July.[105] It seems likely that Cornwallis had then conferred with officers and yeomen on the ground in advance of dispatching General Moore and Marquis

Huntley to pacify Wicklow in the last days of July. The Viceroy selected the tolerant and effective Moore and his troops in counter-insurgent drives in preference to locally based yeomen and Irish militia whom he deemed 'contemptible before the enemy'.[106]

Moore met Cornwallis in Dublin the previous week and was informed that his reinforced brigade was to be composed of reliable troops who could be rushed to any sector where unrest had flared. Their primary role, once the wet weather subsided and his regiments were rested, was to keep the Wicklow and Dublin mountains clear of rebels. According to Moore:

> Had it been favourable I should have sent detachments into the mountains, but have given them directions not to treat as enemies any parties they might see, but to endeavour to communicate with them, inform them of the [amnesty] proclamation and offer them protection . . . Above 1200 have already surrendered their arms and received 'protections' and numbers are crowding in every hour.[107]

An incredulous William Hartigan met a man who had come from Blessington on 22 July where 'a little army under . . . General Moore' was stationed with 'express orders not to act against the rebels'.[108] Moore's Highlanders, many of whom were Catholic and Gaelic-speaking, were temperamentally and physically suited to the task of operating in Wicklow. Cornwallis thought them men 'that can be depended upon to try either to subdue . . . or invite them [i.e. the rebels] to surrender' in marked contrast to the troops of the Irish establishment who were 'more likely to provoke rebellion than to suppress it'.[109]

The key to Cornwallis' pacification strategy was the wide and liberal dissemination of the amnesty which he believed would neutralize outstanding rebel groups and marginalize the die-hard element. The success of this policy was to a large degree dependent on winning the trust of the remaining rebels for which Moore was made responsible. If clemency failed, however, Moore's strong brigade, which consisted of the First and Second Flank Battalions, 60th, 89th and 100th regiments and a detachment of Hompesch dragoons, was more than a match for any existing rebel opposition.[110] Amnesty proclamations were not widely disseminated in Wicklow in July 1798, perhaps owing to the difficulty of contacting fugitives in the places they frequented. Colonel Walter Jones of the Leitrim Militia discovered on arriving with his regiment in Rathdrum on 17 July that instructions had not been received, let alone acted upon, by his predecessors.[111] This should have happened in early July when senior officers were advised by the

Castle that the 'full benefit' of the amnesty was to be 'held out to the people . . . in the most liberal sense of construction the proclamations admit of.'[112] Nevertheless, the amnesty was a success in the parts of the county where it was advertised which indicates that the Rathdrum area yeomanry and military may have been deliberately slow in offering terms to their enemies. 4,000 Wicklowmen received protections at Arklow by 13 July and a further 1,200 were quickly distributed by Moore's officers in Imaal. A government spy reported that only 'one in 1000' rebels had seen the proclamations and 'few of them' understood its significance and it was not until early August that Holt's men took stock of the implications of the amnesty.[113] Moore attempted to redress this problem by moving detachments of the 100th and 60th regiments under Huntley from Donard to Imaal in the last days of July 1798 with orders to 'promulgate the proclamation and grant protections'. It was hoped that their presence would discourage insurgent activity and enhance a more peaceful atmosphere in which demobilization could occur.[114]

The arrival of Moore's 89th regiment in Glenmalure from the direction of the Seven Churches while the 60th, 100th regiments and flank battalions approached from Fananierin and Rathdrum, did not strike a conciliatory note with the rebels. Holt's 500 or so men formed up in the valley as if they intended to stand and fight and opened fire on the advancing soldiers.[115] The fusillade stalled Moore's advance and while his troops assumed a defensive formation and prepared to return fire, the insurgents suddenly turned and made a dash for Imaal for the loss of only three or four men. They retreated northwards over Table Mountain into the King's River valley passing through Oakwood and Knocknadroose to Knockalt by which time they realized that the government was determined to frequent sanctuaries that had hitherto been virtually undisturbed. The object was clearly to force the insurgents to fight a general action which they had no prospect of winning. They consequently resolved 'not to stop long in any one place' and to tire the enemy troops by counter-marching in unfamiliar and difficult terrain.[116]

As it seemed likely that the rebels would be obliged to fight more often if the army persisted with its new tactics, the procurement of fresh supplies of munitions became urgent. After a brief halt in Imaal in the first week of August the insurgents moved south to Croghan Mountain straddling the Wexford border in a bid to establish contact with a rebel group in Killaughrim Woods. On 1 August the rebels were reported to be in great force around Tinahely intending to 'harass &

wear out the army'. Those who had already received protections were reputed to boast that they would 'unexpectedly take up the pike again'.[117] It was also hoped that stocks of gunpowder hidden in the barony of Arklow could be recovered. Dwyer, who was contemplating accepting amnesty terms at the time and was reluctant to fight outside his home area, refused to commit his company although they soon afterwards moved as far south as Ballymanus.[118]

When moving from Aghavannagh towards Croghan the main force sighted a military convoy on the Shillelagh-Arklow road lightly escorted by a party of dragoons. The rebels attacked them at Killballyowen over the Derry River and streamed down the slopes towards the startled soldiers on the road. The commissary officer's horse was shot under him and the panicked escort fled, pursued 'in all directions' by the insurgents.[119] Two of the drivers were quickly captured and a third was later found in a barn belonging to Sarah Graham. Patrick Kavanagh, of the disbanded Castlemacadam Cavalry, apparently prevented his rebel comrades burning Graham's house and executing a twelve-year-old boy named Ryan whom they believed was a driver. The boy, who was unharmed, was actually travelling to see his uncle in Wexford and remained with the rebels for 'some weeks'.[120] The convoy was burned and the prisoners taken to Croghan where two were piked upon being accused of being 'Orangemen . . . in the habit of informing against United Irishmen'.[121]

On Croghan the insurgents first learned of Moore's efforts in Imaal and those of General Hunter in Wexford to implement the amnesty and curtail the excesses of extreme loyalists. Moore's highlanders refrained from offensive operations and paid for all goods they obtained. This made a good impression on the few 'old men and terrified women' who had not fled Imaal in terror upon their arrival.[122] The moderate conduct of the troops quickly earned the respect of many local insurgents and when a number of officers from the 89th regiment were captured by the rebels after straying from Imaal they were neither injured nor detained. Huntley reciprocated the gesture shortly afterwards when James Doyle was arrested and then freed with a protection and assurances that the yeomen would be restrained from persecuting him.[123] From the outset Moore had exercised considerable pragmatism in giving out protections and did not insist on the surrender of arms as a prerequisite to granting the certificate. He reasoned, perhaps naively, that many insurgents had discarded or lost their weapons and without protections would have no choice but to take refuge with the rebels. A more serious and illegal deviation of Moore's was to grant protections to former yeomen who had become United Irishmen as all such defectors were deemed to hold 'leader' status in rebel formations and as such were ineligible for clemency. Many of Holt's men viewed the changed situation as an opportunity to take in the bumper harvest and the rebel force was consequently greatly reduced.[124]

Dwyer, who had remained in the vicinity of Imaal when the rebels departed for Croghan, was impressed by reports of Moore's integrity and seriously contemplated surrendering. He apparently visited Imaal camp on four or five occasions, received a protection and was urged to press Holt to obtain terms but his deliberations were curtailed when loyalists let it be known that they would not tolerate his return to their community. Rathdrum loyalist William Murray probably echoed wider opinion when he described Dwyer as 'one of General Moor[e]'s petts [sic]-who along with some more of our generals contributed to the ruin of this once happy country.'[125] A more explicit threat was delivered to Dwyer's father at his Camera home by Revd Edward Ryan of Donoughmore which informed him of the illegal resolution of local loyalists to kill his son. 'Rowley' Valentine of the Lower Talbotstown yeomanry also made threats which he reputedly retracted when confronted by the rebel leader. Yet despite grass-roots opposition to the clemency policy, Dwyer and other militant rebel officers in the mountains were of concern to Cornwallis. The Viceroy was even receptive to suggestions that they should be granted the same terms extended to the 'state prisoners' in Kilmainham on 28 July which amounted to banishment for life without trial, a concession which many conservatives deemed to be overly generous.[126]

The executions of the Sheares brothers, William Michael Byrne and John McCann between 14 and 26 July, and the imminent threat to the lives of Oliver Bond and Samuel Neilson, resulted in the negotiation of a pact between the remaining prisoners and the government whereby the United Irish leaders promised to produce a written account of the conspiracy in return for permission to go into exile. Byrne was executed at Green St Courthouse on 25 July 1798 having been convicted of high treason on the word of Thomas Reynolds and other reliable witnesses who included his former comrade Thomas Miller. A popular and stoic man, Byrne's death and the threat hanging over the highly respected Bond had much to do with garnering support for the pact. His loss was deemed particularly poignant as great efforts had been made to save his life if he would acknowledge regret at becoming a United Irishman and blame Lord Edward Fitzgerald for leading him astray. Byrne's execution brought to three the number of Wicklow county committee men killed between May and July 1798; William Young had been shot by the Antrim Militia in Carnew on or before 1 June and Thomas Kavanagh had been summarily executed after the battle of Stratford on 24 May.[127]

Wicklow's other imprisoned Leinster delelate, John Lynch, was one of those who could not be convicted of high treason due to lack of evidence. He became the first and perhaps the only state prisoner to receive formal permission to emigrate to America where many of his Kilmainham comrades followed from France in the early 1800s. Rufus King, the London-based American representative in Britain and Ireland in September 1798, had made clear the absolute opposition of President John Adams to the immigration of the Irish 'traitors' frustrating Cornwallis' plan to allow the most prominent United Irish prisoners settle on that continent.[128] Lynch was not deemed 'troublesome' and had American relatives of 'reputation and wealth' to answer for his good conduct.[129] Indeed, he had evidently received prior support for an American exile given that he petitioned as early as August 1798 for a month's liberty in Ireland in order to settle his affairs after which, 'health permitting', he would 'profit of the first opportunity of a vessell [sic] for New York'. In the event it was not until 17 December 1798 that Lynch was released from Kilmainham to embark for America via Liverpool, as per a request on his behalf lodged by his wife and supported to Revd Walter Blake Kirwan.[130]

His subsequent good behaviour in America proved that the gambit was justified although there was no way of knowing that he would not follow the seditious path of fellow committee member and pact signatory Richard O'Reilly who, along with the majority of state prisoners, was permitted to go to the continent after a period of internment in Fort George, Scotland. O'Reilly maintained contact with Arthur O'Connor in France from 1802 and in February 1806 travelled to Whitehall to present the newly instated Whig government with letters from the O'Connerites offering to assist in the overthrow of Napoleon whom they regarded as despotic. O'Reilly, treated frostily in London, was inexplicably permitted to travel to Dublin despite the prohibition of the Banishment Act and then to return to France. Elliott has surmised that this episode amounted to O'Connor testing the waters in London with a Foxite administration that was embarrassed by its former radicalism.[131]

When the pact was being negotiated in July 1798 Francis Dobbs, MP for Coleraine and a founder member of the pro-reform Northern Whig Club, organized a section of the agreement which involved sending rebel officers into Wicklow to 'put a stop to bloodshed and cruelty' in that county.[132] Expectations that the delegation might encounter suspicion if not hostility from the rebels led to the inclusion of three men 'whose character would give them credit with the insurgents'. The three were granted unconditional pardons and accompanied Dobbs and lawyer James Crawford to Moore's camp in Imaal. According to Samuel Neilson the mission 'had the desired effect; vast numbers came in, and the Orange persecution was completely put a stop to for that time in that country'.[133] William Putnam McCabe and James Farrell were two highly prominent representatives who used their status and reputations to request meetings with the outstanding rebel leaders. This took place before 5 August and their prime objective was evidently the surrender of Holt whom they reputedly wished to save along with his remaining followers.[134] It is unclear whether McCabe actually met Holt in person but his gesture exposed him to danger. When drinking with Farrell in Quinn's Hotel, Bray, some hours after their alleged meeting with Holt, the delegates came face-to-face with an unsuspecting man who claimed to be in search of them.[135]

McCabe also requested a meeting with Dwyer whom he knew from his previous trips to the county, probably with a view to enlisting his considerable influence in the Imaal district in support of the amnesty. Cullen learned:

> the people were very cautious of McCabe at this unexpected visit of his and particularly on account of his being in company with one or two strange gentlemen. In conversation with Dwyer he removed all suspicion as to the purity of his intention. Dwyer and mr McCabe and the other gentlemen went to Gen[eral] Moore's camp. They fell in with some people that were going to the camp to get protections. McCabe briefly addressed them. He told them that when he came amongst [them] on former occasions it was to encourage them to war but having tried that in vain he found it now to be his duty to endeavour to make peace. One of the [by]standers by name Dempsey interrupted him. It was your countrymen [i.e. Ulstermen] that prompted this affair and had they fought as they led us to believe they would we would not now be under the necessity of asking for pardon and begging protection from our enemies.[136]

As McCabe's circle later did their utmost to rededicate the Wicklow United Irishmen to future revolts it is clear that his ideological commitment to the republican cause had not diminished and his role in the pacification of the county was a short-term stratagem. Furthermore, when Farrell was arrested in Dublin by Major Sirr on 18 December he was found to have a dagger and seditious papers on his person.[137]

Garret Byrne of Ballymanus also spent some time in Imaal camp in early August having communicated his desire to Cornwallis to assist in 'restoring tranquillity' in Wicklow, just as Fitzgerald had offered to help General Hunter in Wexford.[138] Byrne had surrendered on 20 July under the same terms received by Aylmer and the Kildare leaders. It is not clear to whom he capitulated but he was free to visit Imaal on 7 August where he must have conversed with the scores of rebels that passed through the camp. Moore and Huntley found Byrne's presence moderately useful in convincing rank-and-file rebels that the rebellion should no longer be prosecuted and they were sufficiently impressed by his character to support his applications for preferential treatment in the subsequent years.[139] One of Byrne's less successful initiatives was to send a letter dated 14 July to his friend Murtough Byrne of Aughrim urging him to accept terms which the rebels in Glenmalure considered to be either forged or written under duress. Three months later Holt was to send a similar letter to his close associate Matthew Doyle and it seems that this type of overture was common in 1798–9. The reaction of the outstanding insurgents, however, suggests that they disapproved of their leaders seeking terms and some distrusted the programme of amnesty despite Moore's best efforts.[140]

Moore was highly critical of the many Wicklow landowners who had abandoned their property during the insurrection and had failed to take advantage of the presence of his troops to visit their tenants and ascertain their desire to return to a peaceful lifestyle. The county's hardline loyalists, for their part, were enraged at Moore for granting protections to the men who had destroyed their property. Moreover, a significant element within the yeomanry refused to recognize the legitimacy of protections and attempted to sabotage the policy by attacking pardoned rebels who had returned home as well as those going to Imaal to receive terms.[141] The popular Byrnes of Knocknamohill, a father and son, who had been in hiding since the Meath expedition, fell victims to the Rathdrum Infantry at this time who kept them overnight in the shell of a local chapel which they had recently burned and shot them the following morning at Crossleg. This was a provocative and possibly illegal act similar to another double killing around that time of two brothers named Byrne who had been pointed out to the Rathdrum Cavalry by the notorious informer and state's witness 'Croppy Biddy' Dolan of Carnew. The brothers had been wounded at Newtownmount-kennedy on 30 May and were concealed at great risk by Bryan Devlin of Cronebeg, father of Anne, and then by Thomas Halpin who worked as gardener for the loyalist Fawcett family near Rathdrum.[142]

The Rathdrum Infantry further demonstrated their contempt for the amnesty by shooting and robbing a young man employed by the former insurgent leader Michael Malone as he returned home over the Black Banks. If the yeomen realized that the money had just been gifted to their victim in Imaal by General Moore the attack would seem remarkably defiant and cold-blooded. Also killed around this time were one Timmon, who was shot by his employer James Chritchley, and protected rebel Morgan Toomey who was slain at Baravore by yeoman Billy Manning.[143] This calculated opposition to government policy was quite open as Captain Edwards of the Bray Infantry discovered on hearing that members of his own corps had 'declared their resolution to shoot anyone who might dare to return' home in consequence of the amnesty.[144] Later events in Wicklow proved that this outburst was not merely an isolated expression of loyalist frustration and on 5 August George Fenton of the generally tolerant Humewood corps killed an unarmed protectioned rebel named Andrew Doran. Moore promptly published a proclamation which offered 100 guineas for the apprehension of Fenton although the matter was never pursued.[145]

Wicklow loyalists were condemned by the general who was convinced that 'the county would again be quiet if the gentlemen and yeomen could behave themselves with tolerable decency and prudence.' He continued:

> I am constantly obliged to reprove their violence, which prompts them every instant, notwithstanding the orders and proclamations, to gratify their revenge and ill humour upon the poor inhabitants. I cannot but think that it was their harshness and ill-treatment that in a great measure drove the peasants and farmers to revolt . . . I foresee nothing but discontent and ferment in the country.[146]

Dobbs was present when the general had signed the Fenton document and on his return to the House of Commons at College Green spoke of Wicklowmen killed 'with protections in their pockets'. The casual violence of the yeomanry extended in at least one case in August 1798 to outright murder. Two yeomen brothers from the Donard area killed their former employer, John Metcalfe of Kilbaylet near Hollywood Glen, after pursuing him to Woodenboley. They then engaged in sheep stealing and when apprehended avoided the death sentence by going into the army.[147]

By the second week of August it became apparent that many rebels in the vicinity of Glenmalure, whether through militancy or fear of the loyalists, had no intention of surrendering. Moore consequently attempted to bring pressure to bear on them by moving his troops into their retreats simultaneously. Lieutenant-Colonel Stewart and the 89th went directly into Glenmalure from Imaal, Colonel Campbell with his First Flank battalion occupied the Seven Churches while the 100th on Toorboy mountain, the Dublin City Militia at Hacketstown and Colonel Skerret's Durham fencibles at Rathdrum converged on the district's rebels from their various approaches. Moore and Huntley left Imaal with the 500 soldiers of the 100th regiment and pursued the small parties of rebels they encountered towards other military columns.[148]

Dublin press reports of 13 August asserted that 'a decisive action' had taken place in Wicklow three days earlier in which 300 rebels had been killed near Wicklow Gap and while this was a gross exaggeration, the rebellion was temporarily suppressed in most of the county. It transpired that the fierce exchange of cannon fire heard in the surrounding district had not resulted from the clash of the rebels and the military but from two groups of disorientated soldiers who had mistaken each other for their quarry.[149]

Claims that 'there was not a rebel in arms throughout the counties of Wexford and Wicklow' by 10 August were also erroneous as they did not recognize the existence of Holt's vastly diminished hard core and several other smaller factions. It seems that at least one column had moved against Holt's positions on 6 or 7 August forcing the rebels to temporarily abandon their camp.[150] More ominous for the government was the failure of the senior rebels to respond to Moore's drive which indicated their ideological strength and militancy and also their confidence in withstanding the extremities and rigours of mountain campaigning. Elsewhere, the most important leaders had capitulated including Felix Rourke and his officers, Nicholas Lyons and Charles Rourke, who surrendered to General Dundas at Kilcullen on 8 August. Rourke claimed that the leaders of his faction had not sought protections as they understood that they were ineligible to receive them but had surrendered on the understanding that they would be considered State Prisoners. He was held initially in Naas gaol from where he kept in contact with fellow United Irishmen and after his release became involved in Robert Emmet's conspiracy in 1803. Edward Rattigan had capitulated some days before which left only Francis McMahon of the Dublin commanders still in the mountains.[151]

While Moore's Wicklow-based regiments and the troops in Wexford garrisons were available for deployment organized rebellion virtually ceased in Leinster. Many isolated incidents of no strategic significance occurred but while loyalists were undoubtedly intimidated and frequently robbed, relatively few were killed. Holt remained comparatively inactive until around 15 August when he and Dwyer 'with nearly the whole of their force' went towards Ballymurtagh to obtain ammunition.[152] They were only about 200 strong and moved in three divisions with Holt in overall command and Matthew Doyle acting as his senior officer. Elements of Dwyer's group encountered and captured Rathdrum Infantryman Joseph Tate whose unit had recently killed the Byrnes of Knocknamohill and burned a Catholic chapel in the area. After a brief deliberation Andrew Hackett and Dwyer pressed for Tate's execution and Holt, who did not mention the incident in his memoir, claimed some months later that the prisoner had been shot by the Antrim defectors. Once this was effected the rebels proceeded towards the coppermines.[153]

Hackett then drew off a party to seize some weapons near the Coppermines from the Johnson family of Millmount and as they approached the residence came under fire. Their lone assailant was discovered to be seventeen-year-old Christopher Cooper of Tinnehinch who then fled across the Aughrim river at Woodenbridge. He was pursued, apprehended and brought back to the main body of insurgents where an uncompromising element within the rebel force insisted that he be executed. Cooper was then shot, notwithstanding his youth and his failure to inflict casualties but his death was subsequently a matter of controversy for the rebels as he was related to Holt and his friends and family had expected the rebel leader to intervene. Those who opposed the measure were apparently powerless to reason with the violent and implacable element of the force who could not be challenged without risking factionalism and dissension. Holt was reputedly not 'very well liked' by some of his followers and it would have been imprudent for him to oppose the will of the majority of the insurgents under the circumstances.[154] The magnitude of the executions was immediately obvious and obliged the rebels to cancel their expedition and return to the safer ground of Glenmalure for the anticipated loyalist reaction. The press was generally slow to acknowledge successful rebel attacks on yeomen in Wicklow but in late August noted 'several atrocities . . . recently perpetrated on the persons and properties of those who distinguished themselves in putting down rebellion in that county.'[155]

A brief visit to Glenmalure was followed by rapid relocations to Knockalt and Whelp Rock, a district where they were to spend much time in the late summer and autumn of 1798. Holt there demonstrated his frustration at and personal disinterest in the administration of the amnesty in Imaal and elsewhere by issuing his own 'protections' to loyalists. Indemnity could by purchased by loyalist farmers who wished to leave the safety of garrison towns to harvest their crops without fear of rebel interference. Certificates were sold for 10s and the applicant was apparently obliged to swear an oath of secrecy to the United Irishmen, a measure which bound them not to divulge details of rebel activity or to prosecute them in courts.[156]

While the military were disinclined to attack the inaccessible Whelp Rock efforts were made to infiltrate the camp, possibly to gather intelligence that might facilitate a major assault. A boy named Murphy was unmasked as a spy who had been sent by Captain Roderick McDonald of the Glengarry Highlanders. Murphy was executed to send a strong signal to those who attempted to disturb the insurgents in the few districts in which they felt relatively secure. It was possibly as a result of this incident that the camp broke up and moved to Ballynabrocka near Athdown where Holt permitted his men to live at 'free quarters' in the community as its inhabitants were regarded as informers and thieves. It seems that this visit had been specifically occasioned to punish the villagers for their alleged misconduct and Holt asserted that he was 'gratified to have [had] the opportunity of inflicting punishment on so many sons of deception.'[157] Prior to leaving for Ballynabrocka Holt sent a message to the garrison at Russborough House concerning 'a large banditti' based at Ballynastockan who had used his name to steal. As a result of this information the army killed eleven men and took a further eight prisoner displaying their eagerness to crackdown on the burgeoning criminal factions in the county. The letter was addressed to his arch-enemy Lieutenant Thomas Hugo and on 17 August it was reported that eleven robbers had been arrested by the Rathdrum Infantry, probably the gang suspected of raiding homes near Rathfarnham.[158]

Wicklow's gentry were greatly troubled by the unhindered movements of rebels through the length and breadth of the Wicklow mountains whose capacity and will to kill perceived enemies had remained undiminished by the amnesty. On 21 August a high-profile deputation of concerned loyalists was granted an audience with Cornwallis in Dublin Castle. The noblemen and magistrates were headed by north Wicklow conservatives Powerscourt and Monck and made a case for abandoning Moore's generally reactive and passive anti-insurgent policy in favour of more vigorous methods.[159] They may have hoped to make an impression on the Viceroy in advance of the resumed but later cancelled Wicklow assizes which were to have been held on 25 August under Justices Kilwarden and Downes. Cornwallis was informed that 'the protestants would be obliged to leave the country' unless new steps were taken to which he gave 'a civil answer, that he would consider what was to be done'. Powerscourt, having received the freedom of the city in July 1798, increased his celebrity still further on 13 August by apprehending two fugitive rebel captains from south county Dublin. The timing of the deputation was unfortunate as the insurrection was transformed on 22 August by the landing of 1,099 French soldiers under General Joseph Humbert at Killala in Mayo.[160]

Humbert had sailed from La Rochelle on 6 August at which time 3,000 men under Hardy and Wolfe Tone were supposed to leave Brest with 4,000 more to follow. French mismanagement and unfavourable weather conditions ensured that only Humbert's ships put to sea and secured their preliminary objectives of landing and distributing arms to their Irish allies. 3,000 muskets and bayonets, 3,000 pouches, 400 swords, 200,000 cartridges, 1,000 uniforms and 3 cannon were landed at Killala alongside the hardened French veterans of the Italian and Vendean campaigns. This immediately heralded a state of emergency which sidelined actual and potential rebel activity in southern Leinster. It was unclear for several days that Humbert's relatively small contingent comprised only the advance party of approximately 7,000 soldiers embarking at Dunkirk and Brest under the overall command of General Jean Hardy. News of the development reached Dublin on 23 August whereupon the city yeomanry turned out as a precaution against internal unrest while General Francis Hely-Hutchinson prepared to contest French advances into Galway.[161]

Many Wicklow loyalists ignored the unduly optimistic pronouncements of some of their Leinster peers and correctly deduced that the emergency would necessitate the redeployment of troops out of the county.[162] Revd James McGhee was moved to claim, albeit with a view to retaining troops in Wicklow, that there were 6,000 rebels preparing to rise in the course of the week. He supported his argument with an exaggerated statement that 'not a night passes without one or two loyalists being murdered' and his claim that United Irishmen who had received protections were re-organizing their comrades in the Hacketstown district betrayed his political agenda. More plausible was McGhee's account of being 'waylaid' by twenty amnestied men until rescued by the 9th Dragoon bodyguards assigned to him by General Henniker.[163] The substance of his paranoid and transparent assertions was, however, largely endorsed by Major Peyton of the Leitrim regiment at Rathdrum who believed that notwithstanding 'the smallness' of the French force, which had then been ascertained, the landing would cause 'much trouble' in the county.[164] A deterioration in security was signalled on 24 or 25 August when a temporary army camp at Ballymanus was visited by rebels within an hour of its being abandoned and shots had been fired at General Eustace. Re-mobilization of rebel groups was also quickly in evidence, a Corporal Griffith, when being robbed of his ammunition, saw 200 men and was informed that there were 400 in all under 'Holt & another'. Yet the French crisis left Cornwallis in no position to comply with the wishes of nervous loyalists and on 24 August Moore was ordered to assemble his corps at Blessington and march for Clonmel the next day.[165]

Miles Byrne's associate Nick Murphy of Monaseed sent word from Dublin to Holt's group at Croghan on 26 August that the French had landed and the city rebels approved of his continued militancy. Any tactical support for the amnesty was cast aside and the resumption of large-scale offensive action was deemed necessary. The rebels were then attempting to revitalize the insurrection and augment their numbers to a level that would enable them to go onto the offensive and perhaps support a rising in the city. One method of gaining recruits was to antagonize the loyalists of a particular area to an extent that they retaliated against the locals and forced them to join the rebels for protection. Horse-stealing was a favourite tactic used for the purpose and it was reported that death threats were made.[166] Hackett was regarded as an adept recruiter and this may explain why it was he who is credited with accompanying Holt into the Blackwater area of Wexford in the last days of August where they allegedly used 'every means in their power to induce' the people in the district to join them in an attack on the capital.[167]

The Blackwater people were allegedly alarmed when the humane General Hunter left Wexford in consequence of the invasion as he had restrained the county's yeomanry. If Holt did enter the area to recruit, neither he nor Miles Byrne mentioned the fact, there were likely many who tempted to take refuge in their ranks. It is highly probable that Holt would have sent emissaries into north Wexford, particularly as he had gone to Croghan in early August to establish links with such men and his force contained native Wexfordians.

However, the prompt exertions of yeomanry Brigade-Major Fitzgerald reassured protectioned rebels that he would interest himself on their behalf and that they had much to lose by joining the Wicklow insurgents. Castle intelligence sources revealed that McMahon had undertaken the same mission and, given that a city assault had long been his objective, close co-operation with Holt seems likely. Reports of similar activities were also received from Kildare where Michael Foley was allegedly one of two pardoned captains endeavouring to 'set rebellion on foot again' in the Castletown area. Murphy's mission to the Wicklow mountains establishes that contact with Dublin-based rebels was feasible and the events of the last week of August suggest that Holt sought to take advantage of the invasion crisis.[168]

The great fear of loyalists was that the rebels who had surrendered would renounce their protections and 'take up the pike' while the vast majority of soldiers in Leinster were drawn to the western theatre to engage the French.[169] Robert Ross claimed on 24 August that the city was 'fuller of rascals ready to take up arms than it ever was, and all with protections in their pockets by order of his Excellency' and five days later alleged that 'the Croppies of Dublin are as alert as possible, and we are threatened with an insurrection if great care is not taken.'[170] Small uprisings in Longford and Westmeath illustrated the danger of the insurrection spreading to hitherto loyal or peaceable counties. There was speculation in Dublin that those city rebels who had not previously mobilized were 'determined to avail' of the emergency. William James' information was that they intended to act in concert with outstanding insurgents in the counties bordering on the capital who, as in the May 1798 plan, were to pin down what forces remained in the region.[171] Felix Rourke maintained that it had always been the intention of his Dublin insurgents who had fought in Wicklow and Meath to dishonour their terms of surrender at the 'first opportunity, as many have done, and take to the mountains'.[172]

Under the tense circumstances of late August it was understandably presumed that a large meeting of country people in the Bog of Allen had been called to organize the assault. No precise information was available to Dublin Castle but Alexander Marsden acknowledged that city defences had been 'seriously weakened & the disaffected were engaging in considerable activity'.[173] According to John Brown, the Bog of Allen meeting had taken place on 28 August and the city assault had been discussed the previous Sunday with one Dunne of Thomas Court. All the evidence from within and without the rebel networks pointed to a revival of the once close liaisons between city radicals and the most militant activists in the surrounding counties. It was believed that a propitious moment to rise would have been embraced and in Brown's opinion 'the mob of the county Kildare & Wicklow & Dublin were never worse incl[i]n[e]d then they are at this day'. Contingency plans were devised to cater for a possible attack including a provision to place the top United Irishmen imprisoned in the capital on ships in Dublin Harbour to facilitate their transportation abroad.[174]

Rumours of disturbances in nearby Blessington and Meath heightened loyalist anxiety as only those close to government sources were in a position to accurately assess the generally unfounded accounts in circulation. This was deemed a serious problem and General Asgill considered it necessary to issue a proclamation in early September which emphasized the criminality of rumour-mongering. Kildare magistrate Thomas Connolly blamed United Irish 'incendiaries' for a rash of false reports which had been spread in his sector and it seems that the rebels distributed thousands of copies of a 'manifesto' at Donnybrook fair on 28 August.[175]

Holt's faction, the largest in Ireland prior to the French invasion, may have established direct contact with their allies in the last days of August when a French soldier named Francois Joseph joined them. Joseph's 'levity and irreligion' did not endear him to some of the rebels but a less hostile eyewitness described him as a 'man of distinction'. In view of his reputedly expert sword-manship and ability to both speak and write English, it is likely that he was a junior officer in the French army rather than a Hessian deserter. Joseph claimed to have left Mayo on 25 August and could not, therefore, have given Holt anything other than general advice on interacting with Humbert or the other French forces then anticipated. It would have been imprudent for the French at Killala to make detailed plans so early in the campaign but they probably looked to the rebels in the Wicklow mountains to create disturbances in southern Leinster which would inhibit the transfer of the army reserves to the west. Menacing the capital clearly offered the best prospect of affecting the strategic picture in this way and, in the event of a French breakthrough, Holt's guerrillas would be well-poised to form the nucleus of a second attacking force. While the exact purpose of Joseph's mission is unknown he became a prominent, if unpopular, member of Holt's party.[176]

When posted with about forty men on Kilmaclone Hill near Ballymanus in late August, Dwyer observed a small column of the military advancing towards his position who were apparently unaware of their presence. This encouraged him to lay an ambush and he sent word to Holt's men at Aghavannagh and to Hackett's small group of south Wicklow insurgents in the Aughrim area seeking their co-operation. The Imaal leader was very disappointed when neither Hackett nor Holt responded in time to attack the enemy but his own group, nevertheless, showed themselves to the patrol in an unsuccessful effort to entice them from the road. Holt's inability to respond with sufficient speed to Dwyer's plan evidently led to tensions between the two factions although it could not have been a very serious breach given that they continued to co-operate.[177]

Once Moore had left Wicklow with the bulk of the government troops it fell to the county yeomanry to compensate for their absence. Yeomanry corps acted both singly and in groups of unprecedented size for the rebellion in Wicklow and operated without the restraint imposed on them by Moore and Huntley. Among the first to implement more aggressive patrolling was Lieutenant Thomas Hugo who led fifty-three Wicklow Town Cavalry in a brief foray into Glenmalure in the last days of August. They met with stiff opposition from Dwyer's followers and were quickly repulsed. A second incursion was attempted by the Stratford yeomanry a few days later and was similarly cut short by vigorous armed resistance. The vulnerability of the loyalists in this district was underscored within days of this clash when Dwyer reputedly fired upon Benjamin O'Neil Stratford and Morley Saunders upon catching sight of them in Imaal.[178]

Skirmishing also flared at this time in the south of the county. Holt, at the head of twenty-four mounted rebels, encountered a troop of Coolgreany or Arklow Northshire Cavalry near Kilcanor and made an unsuccessful attempt to prevent them reaching the safety of their barracks in Coolgreany. Luke McDermott received a mortal wound in the ensuring exchange of fire but Holt shot his assailant and Arklowman John Moore apparently killed two others before the remaining yeomen escaped. Holt retreated to Clone Hill and on 29 August fought a 'smart action' with the Rathdrum Infantry and Cavalry on the Arklow to Woodenbridge road in which his men killed another two yeomen. Captains King and Mills were again observed with their Rathdrum units the following day when crossing Mucklagh Hill towards Aghavannagh in search of the insurgents. Francois Joseph opened fire at great range wounding two yeomen while Holt, in a bizarre but corroborated act of bravado, challenged King to a duel. All was not as it seemed, however, as the sounding of trumpets alerted the rebels to the threat of encirclement by a large yeomanry force which consisted of the Rathdrum, Tinahely, Donard, Hacketstown and both Arklow corps.[179]

The rebels had no intention on fighting on ground chosen by their better armed adversaries and immediately attempted to pull back. Four insurgents were killed in the course of a fighting withdrawal to Aghavannagh where the yeomen were unwilling to follow and at least eight others wounded. A few rebels were taken prisoner and, according to one press report, they included Holt's sister Mary who was borne 'in triumph to Rathdrum'. It was incorrectly believed that Hackett was among the dead although it seems that quantities of weapons, horses and supplies had been dropped by the rebels during their retreat. The press also noted that Holt had 'not succeeded in producing any accession to their numbers amongst the repentant inhabitants of the county of Wicklow for the last six weeks.'[180] A garbled and very different version of these skirmishes appeared in the *Courier* of 5 September 1798 which commented on the 'most alarming progress' of Holt 'since he learned that the French had effected a landing'. It claimed that six yeomen had been killed on 24 August including two named Tate which suggests that the report also concerned the series of incidents in the Woodenbridge area the previous week. Holt was somewhat shaken by the unexpected ferocity of the skirmish and having provided for his wounded led his able-bodied men to Oakwood while Dwyer returned to Imaal.[181]

Dwyer left Knockadeery on 31 August in company with Holt's youngest brother Jonathan and Michael Dempsey of Bumbohall (Grangecon). They moved onto the Ballintruer road only to encounter Captain Hume at the head of a large number of yeomen. The surprised yeomen could not prevent the rebels escaping across a bog where the cavalry could not easily or safely pursue. Later that day, however, or on the following one, Hume's corps together with the Saundersgrove and Stratford Infantry and the Baltinglass Cavalry intercepted a large band of rebels who had been driven out of Imaal by the 89th regiment. The rebels had burned several houses in the valley and may have been surprised by troops responding to the smoke from the fires they had lit. Elements of the 89th regiment were then stationed at Blessington Camp and had been irritated by the theft of a horse that week. Soldiers under the command of Lieutenant Dorony, guided by Joseph Hawkins of the Stratford corps and Joseph Fenton of the Humewood Cavalry, flushed the rebels into the path of Hume's force.[182]

There was another skirmish shortly afterwards in which Dwyer's men seized prominent Colvinstown loyalist and Humewood yeoman William Hume Steel who was travelling from Talbotstown to Imaal. Dwyer and eight or nine rebels were forced to release Steel when challenged by a Humewood patrol which pursued them to Crosoona and Keadeen. Adam Magee of Greenan was shot dead at Keadeen Bog by the yeomen, prompting his comrades to halt and stand their ground. They had reputedly been angered on noticing that Magee's body was being robbed and 'vented their fury on the houses of several of the loyalist farmers that was particularly obnoxious to them'. The yeomen were first forced to abandon their pursuit when some of them were wounded including Sergeant Sandy Eager of the Humewood corps who was hit by Annamoe rebel Andrew Thomas. When the yeomen pulled back, the enraged rebels burned the empty homes of local yeomen Mark Weekes at Ballycarregan, Thomas Hawkins at Colvinstown and John Wilson at Fendecoyle before returning to Imaal.[183]

The resurgence in rebel activity and the presence of French troops in Ireland encouraged many prevaricating militiamen with republican sympathies to commit themselves to the insurrection. Twenty-one of the King's County Militia deserted from Arklow in the early hours of 2 September and killed a yeoman of the Wicklow Cavalry who had given chase. Militiaman Joseph Heffernan of Captain Palmer's company was also killed on the same night in unknown circumstances.[184] Their commander, Colonel L'Estrange, the victor of Newtownbarry, was so perturbed by the defections that he requested that his regiment be removed from the county and that the town's magazine be guarded by more reliable soldiers. General Eustace complied with his wishes and on 2 September sent fifty of the King's Countymen to Wicklow Town under the supervision of a detachment of 5th Dragoons. Two court-martialled deserters who had been captured in an earlier attempt were then executed in the county town. The fact that the Arklow defectors were accompanied by 'above one hundred' civilians from the town and its neighbourhood and that all seven Wicklow-based companies of the regiment lost members indicates that the incident was well-planned had involved local United Irishmen.[185] The Home Office in London was informed that the regiment had been affected by 'the religious party spirit' in Wicklow and that the men had joined Holt, 'a very notorious Rebel chief', at Seven Churches. Castlereagh may have been implying that the peculiarly Protestant and 'orange' character of the Wicklow yeomanry and similar sentiments of certain militia regiments had offended some of those who supported United Irish principles of religious tolerance.[186]

There was also a spate of desertions from the Leitrim Militia garrison at Rathdrum in late August and early September; two men went over to the rebels on 26 August, one on 3 September and a further nine absconded three days later. Major Peyton blamed Michael Dwyer's first cousin Hugh 'Vesty' Byrne of Kirikee, a hitherto inactive United Irishman, and women agents of the United Irishmen. Byrne was known to have been 'tampering with the men' and was mistakenly assumed to be a close relative of the much persecuted curate Fr Byrne of Greenan.[187] Holt claimed to have sixteen deserters from the regiment in his force which indicates that some or all those who deserted before and after the main defections had also joined the rebels. They were G. Flynn who deserted on 27 June, Phelim Croal and John Brown who deserted on 24 July and Phelim McDermott who left his post on 27 July 1798. At a Rathdrum courtmartial on 15 September Patrick Donnelly, who had attempted to defect on 2 September, was sentenced to death while the recaptured Croal and McDermot were sentenced to serve abroad for life. A cadre of Leitrim men who remained with their regiment in Rathdrum supplied Holt and later Dwyer with ammunition and intelligence. They also attempted to suborn members of other regiments which caused friction between them and the loyalist Fermanagh Militia.[188]

Disaffection on this scale and the perceived poor performance of the militia in action against the French was considered a grave problem by many loyalists who wrote of their fears to Dublin Castle and requested that reinforcements of regulars be sent to their areas.[189] The threat was taken seriously by the authorities who moved troops into the city from Lehaunstown to augment the garrison in the early days of September. The garrison was on alert on the night of the 5th when it was reported that 'the rebels in the environs and in the city of Dublin are very much up and impudent' and that the situation was 'more unpleasant than at any time of the rebellion'.[190] Two weeks later Ross made a near hysterical assessment of the situation in Wicklow when he incorrectly asserted that Holt had 700 militia deserters with him including 300 King's countymen who had defected *en masse*.[191]

Holt's force was camped at Knockananna in the Seven Churches area on 2 September when joined by the King's County deserters from Arklow. They were placed under the temporary authority of Andrew Hackett who was generally responsible for instructing new recruits in the ways of life in the mountains. Earlier that day the rebels had caused an incident in Knockananna chapel when a priest allegedly refused to celebrate Mass. The objection concerned the intimidating presence of armed insurgents who had brought their weapons into his service to guard against the possibility of being surprised by the yeomanry. Holt claimed that Antrim John, 'a violent tempered man', had threatened to shoot the priest if he did not proceed with the Mass. Their caution may have been inspired by a incident which had occurred the previous week when Dwyer, John Moore and one Kenny had a narrow escape from Davidstown chapel in Imaal. The rebels had fallen in with a group of soldiers from the 89th regiment who were going to church in Donard. On that occasion both parties had elected to refrain from fighting but no such truce could have been expected from the yeomen, many of whom viewed the rebellion as a bitter civil war.[192]

Soldiers reacted to the guerrilla tactics of the rebels by burning unoccupied houses to deny them shelter and by smashing the cooking utensils of those suspected of harbouring insurgents. This policy resulted in considerable hardship for many civilians and jeopardized the prospect of good relations between the army and uninvolved country people. In an effort to reduce the suffering of innocents, Holt made a proposal to Jones in early September, in which he offered to stem executions and house burnings by the insurgents if Jones would strive to prevent the 'wanton and barbarous acts' committed by pro-government agents.[193] This agreement may have been the 'terms' Major Hardy believed Holt and Dwyer had agreed with the yeomanry and the arrangement was honoured the following week when Holt's force went towards Aughrim for a rendezvous with his brother William and encountered a militia sergeant, eight soldiers of the Leitrim regiment and Jones' wife *en route* to her husband in Rathdrum. The soldiers were spared the fate which had befallen the commissary drivers at Kilballyowen and were released unharmed. This evidently influenced Jones' decision later that day to release William Holt from custody in Rathdrum where the Rathdrum corps, to which he had belonged in its Cronebane incarnation, had lodged him for attempting to contact his notorious brother.[194]

A constant feature of rebel activity in the Wicklow mountains was cattle- and sheep-stealing from loyalist farmers. As livestock could not easily or quickly negotiate the terrain covered by the insurgents during their frequent shifting of their camps, stolen herds had to be abandoned. Cattle raids were therefore one of the first signs that the rebels had moved into a district.[195] Upon arriving at Oakwood on 4

September the rebels were interested to learn of 'a great quantity of cattle' at Blessington which belonged to the Marquis of Downshire. They were short of food and set out for the town through Blackditches and Baltyboys. At Baltyboys Jonathan Eves, a Protestant friend of Holt's and a rebel harbourer, was killed owing to a misunderstanding by King's County defector Henry Downes. Eves was suspected of sheltering informers and was denounced to the rebels by a rival but had probably been confused with Benjamin Eves of Blessington who had received government money.[196]

This dismayed Holt who was advised against trying to punish the popular Downes for murder on the grounds that this would alienate and anger his comrades. Downes was from Blackditches but had lived in Dublin before the rebellion and joined the King's County Militia in late 1797 when it was stationed in Lehaunstown camp. He was moved with his detachment to Bray where he reputedly fought with a local orangeman who had jeered him and other Catholic militiamen going to attend Mass at Old Connaught chapel. Downes then decided to desert to the rebels which he did when the rebellion began. Downes left the rebel force after killing Eves and was arrested after a struggle in Dublin in early 1799 by Major Sirr whose chain-mail saved him from serious injury from the Wicklowman's knife. Downes and a Dublin City Militia deserter named Wall were hanged at Malahide in April 1799.[197]

The inactive and ineffective Blessington yeomanry offered little resistance to the rebels on their approach to the village and took refuge in the town's church. It seems that Captain Hornidge's thirty-strong corps used the church as a base, probably as no other suitable building had been left intact after repeated rebel raids. Revd Hill Benson's residence was also prudently 'barricaded against Mr. Holt's attempts'. They were trapped in the building while 400 head of cattle and 150 sheep were rounded up and driven off. That this was a far greater quantity of meat than the rebels could have hoped to butcher and consume indicates that there was a punitive aspect to their raid. A second attack was led by Matthew Doyle on 5 September during which the insurgents remained in Blessington for an hour while cattle from the surrounding area as far as Ballymore-Eustace were taken.[198] Most of the cattle was later recovered, however, by Lieutenant-Colonel Orde's Princess of Wales Light Dragoons and La Touche's Rathfarnham Cavalry. The troopers were determined to press home their attack and that evening closed with eighty mounted rebels at Ballynahound Hill in the act of burying men who had fallen that day. The rebels were not totally surprised and had little difficulty in escaping into the mountains where the military were unwilling to follow. A report in *Saunder's Newsletter* of 7 September that the insurgents 'could not possibly escape' the troops in pursuit of them is not credible and was probably an attempt by Blessington loyalists, the source of the information, to save face. In fact, within a few days of the Orde's operation one Rutherford, who had successfully defended his home against the rebels, and a man named Barker were robbed of cattle which they had just purchased at Blessington fair.[199]

After the Blessington raids the rebels relocated to Ballynabrocka and then to Imaal where they camped for three days. Francois Joseph and other minor leaders called to the homes of inactive and probably protectioned United Irishmen in the Glen whom they summoned to join the insurgents. James Byrne was shot dead by the Frenchman for giving evasive replies to queries as to the whereabouts of his sons. This act of brutality in a community generally sympathetic towards their cause resulted in a half-hearted trial of Joseph who was acquitted of murder by the rebel jury. To avoid further trouble with the inhabitants of Imaal, however, Holt crossed into Glenmalure and reestablished his headquarters at Pierse Harney's house at Baravore. It was probably here at 4.00 p.m. on 9 September that the rebels first learned of the defeat of Humbert's expeditionary force at Ballinamuck. This, according to leading loyalist James Chritchley, immediately threw 'a damp on their operations'. Chritchley maintained that the rebels had raided homes for arms the previous week on hearing positive reports of French progress in the West and was impressed by the 'rapidity of their movements and the uncommon secrecy which attends them'.[200]

Humbert's corps had easily captured Ballina and having distributed military equipment to several thousand enthusiastic Irish volunteers who rallied at Killala approached Castlebar on 27 August. Lake arrived to command the numerically superior army assembled by Major-General Hely-Hutchinson but was confounded when the French troops and their Irish allies attacked his positions from an unexpected direction causing confusion and panic.[201] Victory at Castlebar encouraged Humbert to establish a Provisional Government under John Moore of Moore Hall before advancing into Sligo where he easily defeated an attack on his column at Coloney. While the disaffected sections of the Irish population in the vicinity of the fighting were cautious and wary of committing themselves to a venture backed by so few French troops, the Longford and Westmeath United Irishmen rose on

4 September realizing Humbert's ambitions to spread the Rebellion. Successive defeats at Multifarnham, Granard and Mullingar, however, between 4 and 6 September contained these fresh outbreaks before they could gain momentum. The short campaign came to an abrupt halt on 8 September when Lake's overwhelmingly stronger forces defeated the French at Ballinamuck in Longford.[202]

Once the threat posed by Humbert had been eliminated Cornwallis resumed his policy of clemency towards outstanding insurgents whose belligerency threatened to attract further French invasions. Dispersed rebel bands in the counties through which the French had passed exacerbated the problem of the resurgent force in Wicklow and on 13 September a new proclamation was published demanding their surrender within the month. Disenchanted loyalists may have been appeased by the issuing of a second proclamation signed by Lieutenant-General Craig which offered £300 for Holt's capture. This followed the inclusion of the Wicklowman's name some weeks previously on the Fugitive Act, a provision which made him subject to the terms of the Banishment Act in the event of his capture. Holt countered the proclamation by offering a reward for Craig's arrest and the *Hibernian Telegraph* of 24 September 1798 reported that the 'insolent rebel' had offered £600.[203] In the short term the conditions affecting the security of Wicklow's loyalist population were not ameliorated by the improved national strategic developments. Loyalists in the Castlekelly district were reputedly obliged to abandon their homes on 12 September in the belief that Holt's 'maxim [was] to put all persons to death of that kind'. His provocative escalation of the rebellion in Wicklow had also elicited an increasingly hard-line military response of a kind not experienced in the county since before Moore's sojourn in Imaal. A fruitless search for 'the nefarious rebel leader' followed in the Dublin mountains.[204]

When in Glenmalure during the second week of September the rebels were notified that a quantity of gunpowder was being prepared for their use at Cronebane. This cache had, in all probability, been stolen from the mines by some of their many sympathizers who worked in the Avoca valley. The planned route of the rebels to Cronebane and the timing of their march was betrayed to the authorities by the girlfriend of Antrim defector Peter 'Goodpay' Kavanagh and around 300 insurgents were ambushed that night at Greenan bridge. According to Miles Byrne, the rebels had intended raiding townlands beyond Greenan for provisions and adopted the plan in preference to Holt's proposal to enter the Seven Churches. The insurgents allegedly insisted on this last minute route when Hester Holt, who was suspected of 'making terms for him [Holt] with the enemy at Rathdrum', had arrived unexpectedly in Glenmalure. The rebels resolved to march in the opposite direction to that suggested by Holt as a test of his loyalty and walked into the ambush in Greenan. The trap was sprung by the Rathdrum yeomanry who had taken up positions in the charred ruins of Henry Allen's factory complex and under the arches of the bridge.[205]

Lieutenant John Sutton ordered the yeomen under his command to open fire on the unsuspecting rebels as they approached the bridge but, owing perhaps to the darkness and the unprofessionalism of the loyalists, a potentially lethal volley was aimed high. A mere six or seven rebels were wounded in an ambush that might easily have claimed many lives. The situation remained dangerous for the exposed insurgents until Holt shouted orders to the pikemen, 'with the voice of a stentor', to cross the bridge and surround the enemy. The rebel gunmen were directed to simultaneously ford the Avonbeg but they had been disconcerted by the ambush and were reluctant to move forward. Fortunately for the rebels the yeomen had 'become terrified' on hearing Holt's bold commands and had hastily retreated to avoid close quarter battle with their enemies. Holt's decisiveness also allayed the fears of the Wexford contingent while the majority of the remainder were satisfied once the Wicklowman sent his wife out of their camp.[206]

On 14 September Holt stepped up the campaign against loyalists who had offered their property to the government. He led the rebels

GREENAN BRIDGE. Photography by Ruán O'Donnell

out of Glenmalure and descended from the mountains some hours later at Hollywood, the scene of Major Hardy's repressive actions from late 1797 until the outbreak of the rebellion. The focus of the attack was Lord Waterford's lodge which they decided to destroy on learning that it was to be converted into a block house for the military. Waterford (Henry de la Poer Beresford) had visited the ruins of Hollywood in company with a corps of Dublin yeomen cavalry on 11 August and then undertaken to provide his tenants with huts of the type used by soldiers until their homes were rebuilt at his expense. All the building materials collected for this purpose were razed by the rebels. This somewhat vindictive arson attack was a severe blow to the morale of loyalist families who were reportedly 'crouching for shelter amidst the naked walls' of their ruined homes. Sir Francis Hely Hutchinson, another major landlord whose tenants had suffered rebel attacks, remitted six months rent to those who had lost houses.[207]

That the rebels were capable of mounting repeated attacks with virtual impunity underlined the extreme vulnerability of Wicklow's fringe loyalist communities. The threat of sectarian massacre, never fulfilled if ever implied, may well have had a long-term demoralizing effect on pro-government elements. Moreover, while the rebels were undoubtedly convinced of the military justification of their actions, the intimidation of actual and potential enemies may also have been a factor underlying the use of such tactics. Specific individuals were targeted with unrelenting ruthlessness. The men who had wrecked Waterford's lodge seized the opportunity to mount their second or third attack on the home of Blessington landowner George Parvisol later that night. Parvisol only narrowly escaped to Rathfarnham to alert the yeomanry after an exchange of fire with insurgents who were attempting to break his door down.[208]

The following day a party of fifty mounted raiders burned the home of Revd Richard Symes at Ballybegg and drove off his livestock. Symes had been robbed by the rebels at least once before but a report that he had undertaken to put his home at the disposal of the yeomanry evidently sealed the fate of the property. Another politically active Protestant clergyman, Revd Edward Ryan of Donoughmore, was undeterred by these precedents and perhaps rendered desperate in his Imaal area home by their occurrence. On 'finding Holt's party daily growing more formidable' Ryan offered his fortified rectory to the military for their protection and his own. Ryan had made an enemy of Michael Dwyer in July 1798 by communicating loyalist threats to the Dwyer family at Camera but it was Holt's men who burned the rectory on 28 September. A secondary if not opportunist victim of the raid was Ryan's yeoman neighbour Richard Butler who also lost his house to rebel incendiaries.[209]

The intensity of this sudden onslaught on high-profile loyalists brought an inevitable reaction and on 15 September a large military force left Dublin to conduct anti-insurgent operations in Wicklow. Loyalist agents exploited the temporary reinforcement to step up their activities throughout the county. The troops brought 'cars laden with arms, ammunition, etc' but no cannon which were deemed to be useless against 'marauders skulking about the mountains and other recesses'.[210] An alarm was raised in Bray on the night of the 16th when it was rumoured that the rebels were approaching the town. This story proved to be unfounded and the true intentions and location of the rebels remained a discomfiting mystery. One report alleged that Holt and 400 well-armed men had gone to Carlow to recruit on or around 15 September leaving Francois Joseph in charge of the men.[211] Carlow magistrate Robert Cornwall discounted the possibility of Holt's presence in the county but believed that 'his colleague' Dogherty had been near Ballon 'to try the pulses of the people', a man referred to by Holt as 'the Carlow Dogherty' to distinguish him from other men bearing the same surname.[212] It was also inaccurately claimed that Holt was in the Celbridge area of Kildare on 16 September where his men robbed horses and perpetrated several murders. The Dublin leader, McMahon, who had realigned his corps with Holt's much larger faction, was thought to have gone to Wexford on a mission 'to raise all he can there [i.e. in Wexford] & if he succeeds is to make some attack near Dublin'.[213]

Holt and McMahon, or emissaries bearing their authority, were clearly endeavouring to replace men lost through attrition. McMahon was in Dublin city by 25 September at latest and Holt, if he did go to Carlow, was not more than a day away from his faction. McMahon apparently dispersed his force before going to Dublin telling them to 'meet no more till the French make a landing in force'. Confusion regarding short-term rebel intentions and their movements led to speculation in the press that a rupture had occurred in the rebel command whereas subsequent events suggest that they were co-operating to keep Leinster in ferment until the French returned. They may have been informed that Humbert's men were part of a much larger force that was still to land.[214]

Holt was in Wicklow on 16 September when the sympathizer known as the 'Moving Magazine' brought him 300 rounds of much needed ammunition which had been donated by friendly militiamen. The Wicklow leader also received word of an exceptionally violent loyalist backlash against insurgent activities and was appalled to learn that the yeomen had killed an eleven-year-old boy in Macreddin on the mistaken assumption that he was his son Joshua. It transpired that the victim was actually one Tom Howlett of Stamp Bridge near Avoca whose name was sufficiently similar to the rebel leader's to cost him his life when challenged. The yeomen were also alleged to have killed four men near Ballymanus and committed numerous 'petty plunders' with impunity.[215] Another four killings that week, those of William Jones, Henry Jackson and two children in the home of Mrs Mary Barker at Coolmana near Rathvilly in Carlow on 12 September, was blamed on the rebels. Initial suspicion centred on the Holt faction as the victims were Protestant and the suspected killer lived at Knocklashine in the home of Robert Sharp, a rebel fighting with the Wicklowman. The prime suspect, however, one Goss, claimed to have been acquainted with the Barkers and no political motive whether loyalist or republican emerged.[216]

The steady attrition arising from yeoman atrocities and brutal insurgent reprisals coincided with large-scale military-backed punitive patrols which turned tracts of the county into uninhabitable wastelands. A Dubliner who visited Roundwood on 16 September was confronted with 'a scene of desolation and misery' and for five miles around the village there was

> ... not a single cabin to be met with, all levelled to the ground ... here and there the elegant mansion of a nobleman or gentleman in ruins, the bare walls only standing; large groups of females, old and young, with numbers of children-want visibly depicted on their countenances, declaring they had no home-they were starving.[217]

Even more shocking was the discovery of Powerscourt yeoman John Blachford of Altidore, brother-in-law to Henry Grattan, that 'the houses of the peasantry [were] burning in all directions' in the countryside between his base near Enniskerry and Roundwood. His fellow Powerscourt yeomen had shot many of their occupants as they ran from their burning homes and Blachford did not see a single live person on his eight-mile ride through the district. When inquiring as to why the people had been killed his informant 'could assign no reason', although they may have been slaughtered on one of the rampages which frequently followed loyalist funerals in the county. Most loyalist and many republican protagonists of the Wicklow rebellion would have repudiated the notion that the Leinster rising had terminated in July or even in September, notwithstanding the failure of the French invasion.[218]

The aggression and clarity of purpose displayed by the rebels in the their September operations implied an ongoing awareness of yeomen depredations. No time was lost in mounting an ambitious raid on Aughrim once news had reached them in north-western Wicklow that two of the counties most violent yeomanry corps, Hunter Gowan's Wingfield Cavalry and Tom King's Rathdrum Cavalry, had taken up quarters in the village. Gowan had allegedly boasted on entering Aughrim that 'he would make a sixpenny loaf be a sufficient supper for Holt and his men.' Holt and Dwyer left Oakwood at nine in the morning of 19 September and halted five hours later at Ballygonnell near Aughrim having crossed very difficult terrain. Their approach had not been conducted with stealth and Gowan had sufficient warning of their movements to lead his garrison out of their base to meet them on Roddenagh Hill. When the opposing forces had closed within musket range the yeomen discharged an extremely accurate volley in their direction which might well have inflicted considerable casualties had not the battle-experienced John McVeigh warned his comrades to take cover.[219]

Around 150 rebels were sent through Roddenagh Wood in a bid to outflank the exposed yeomen but their ill-discipline and lack of training ruined the ploy when several men opened fire prematurely. The alerted yeomen fell back on Aughrim without loss but had evidently been unsettled by the encounter. Aughrim had survived the rebellion virtually unscathed and as such it was surprising that Gowan saw fit to abandon it to the encroaching rebels. This was a particularly unsound option as the insurgents were known to possess no cannon and were consequently unlikely to force them from the villages stone redoubts. Gowan was only outnumbered four to one which were not unfavourable odds for defending a town against lightly armed aggressors and his withdrawal was by no means 'unavoidable' as press accounts asserted.[220] The two corps retreated together over Aughrim bridge and Killacloran Hill with their unmounted enemies in close pursuit. Such was the desire of the rebels to come to grips with Gowan's men that forty rebel musketeers waded the Derry River to cut off his line of retreat while the main body gave chase to the fleeing yeomen. This stratagem obliged Gowan to hastily change his avenue of flight towards Whaley Abbey and they probably only escaped without loss as the rebels no longer had recourse to the accuracy and range hitherto offered by the skilled Shelmalier riflemen. Holt claimed, nevertheless, that Gowan had two horses shot under him as he fled Aughrim and that he was pursued as far as Clone.[221]

Dwyer received a minor leg wound in the action but rebel casualties were very slight in a sensational morale-boosting triumph. Rebel frustration at losing contact with one of their most hated adversaries was vented on Aughrim's yeomanry quarters and on the homes of several loyalists which were burned in the course of the night.[222] Holt recalled that his men were eager to 'burn all loyal houses' as they had done in Tinahely and Carnew and he had great difficulty protecting the home of his sister-in-law and that of a sympathizer named Boland. The successful attack on Aughrim was compounded the following day when seven Sligo militiamen joined their force. The men had deserted from Arklow on the previous night and one of them, Daniel Hunt of Major Robert Parke's company, had brought sixty rounds of ammunition to help replenish rebel stocks. Hunt was some time afterwards recaptured by the Fermanagh Militia and sentenced to death by a Rathdrum courtmartial in May 1799. Sergeant Michael Fenton, Dennis Cassidy and Richard Cunningham, who were all given the unusual designation of 'prisoner' in the muster lists, may have been implicated in the defections.[223]

The ignominious and politically embarrassing flight from Aughrim of the Rathdrum and Wingfield yeomen prompted General Eustace, a native of Naas, to personally led a cavalry patrol from Arklow on 21 September. A confidence-building gesture was evidently deemed necessary but the calming object the mission was entirely subverted. Eustace, 'to his infinite astonishment', was fired upon by a party of mowers whose protections he had just examined, an incident which underscored the precarious status of government ascendancy in Wicklow. The demonstrable failure to protect loyalist interests in the sector re-ignited long-standing recriminations concerning the amnesty program and fuelled a fresh bout of rumour-mongering.[224] In late September Holt was provocatively stated to be the 'master of the whole low country round Lord Carysfort's estate at Arklow' and he was falsely reputed to have burned Coolgreany. Wicklow Town was similarly threatened and Sarah Tighe, writing from her Ashford home, expressed her fears that the rebels were capable of capturing Rathdrum.[225] This unease and paranoia was evidently just the sort of the impression that Holt had striven to promote. On 23 September he allegedly sent a letter or a proclamation into Arklow 'to inform the inhabitants [that] he would speedily be among them, and that he would not spare a single orangeman'.[226] Such threats could not have been entirely dismissed by loyalists in the light of the spate of assassinations which occurred in late September. Holt was believed to be in the vicinity of Arklow with 400 men and was berated for 'shocking enormities . . . against the yeomanry, and the protestant orange families' in the county, a phrase which suggests rebel activists were successful in striking their local enemies.[227]

The disruptive influence of the rebels and the punitive sanctions elicited by their actions ensured that demobilized and hitherto inactive United Irishmen became combatants. On the night of 20 September twelve protectioned rebels from the Ballinacor district went to Ballinteskin to pike yeoman John Leeson. They buried Leeson's body on a nearby farm where it not discovered until three months later, a macabre and predictable resolution to what must have been an unsettling mystery. Leeson had been killed by a British United Irishman named 'English Will' who was renowned as a ferocious fighter. Will had worked at Revell's tanyard in Ballymoneen, where members of the Holt family lived, and had decided to assassinate Leeson for questioning him about his protection and activities.[228] The rebels rendezvoused with another group of twelve men who had stolen a gun from James Ellis and proceeded together to Laurence McGuirk's house in Ballinalea to drink. The rebels had first called to Thomas Booth's house where Henry Scully, one of Isaac Eccles' employees at Cronroe, urged them to steal his master's weapons. They consequently called to Cronroe in search of guns but while none was found a

'The Irish rebel who threatened to murder Mrs [Sarah] Tighe', Maria Spilsbury, *c.* 1798. Private Collection [Knight of Glin]

quantity of saddles, cloth and horses were carried off to the rebel camp at Oakwood. The raids and the resolution on 'going to Holt' had been carefully planned at a series of meetings in Nicholas Doyle's house at Ballynacuppogue and forced several other local men to go into hiding in the mountains to avoid the loyalist retaliation.[229]

The settling of scores with Leeson and the co-ordinated attempts to re-arm themselves indicated an intention to campaign indefinitely. This was a significant commitment as it implied that the men were optimistic about the ultimate outcome of the rebellion and were not intimidated by the hardships attending life in the mountains. The tortuous route to Oakwood and the precise location of the camp were also no impediment to the men who had probably spent time there when first mobilized. They were warmly greeted at Oakwood by Captain Michael Neil and the 100 rebels with him who were joined the following day by 400 with Holt. Leeson's killers did not remain long with the main force and returned to Ballinalea on 25 September with a view to killing the notorious Newtownmount-kennedy yeomen Ephraim Chapman and William Lively who had taken leading parts in the massacres of 31 May. Neither Lively nor Chapman were found in their usual haunts, however, and were fortunate to elude their determined enemies who proceeded to attack William Tighe's mansion at Rossana.[230]

The purpose of the Rossana raid was to procure arms but this changed once they realized that Isaac Eccles was one of several local loyalists who had taken refuge inside. Demands that Eccles be handed over to an uncertain but probably terminal fate only ceased when one of the raiders was shot and wounded as he attempted to break into the mansion.[231] This violent upsurge continued on the night of 26 September when some or all of the insurgents who attacked Rossana went to the Tighe's Ballynockan estate where they seized and exe-cuted Thomas, Joseph and James Bryan, two brothers and a son. All three were yeomen and an ex-rebel in their employ, Michael Wilkinson, was sentenced to death in 1799 for his complicity in the killings. This incident received a great deal of publicity and was regarded as sectarian when the early accounts omitted the fact that the victims were yeomen. Insurgent ruthlessness appalled moderate loyalists such as the Tighes who believed that not one 'house or protestant will be left in the county' and contemplated going to England to escape the 'war massacre'.[232]

This spate of killings owed much to the removal of the Wicklow yeomanry from permanent duty on 22 September. All the county's units were stood down, stripped of their salaries and entitlements to barracks accommodation. While the yeomen were not discharged or disarmed, they reverted to part-time duties and were obliged to either live at home or obtain private accommodation elsewhere. This cost-cutting and pacific measure was undoubtedly appropriate in the national context but it was highly injudicious in Wicklow and other disturbed parts of southern Leinster. Undefeated pockets of rebels were afforded unprecedented access and opportunity to act against their enemies.[233] Within hours of being stood down and sent home from Rathdrum's Flannel Hall barracks a yeoman named Jones of the Rathdrum corps was killed on his Ballikane farm and a private in the Wicklow Infantry suffered the same fate that night on venturing outside the protection of the garrison. The killers of Merginstown carpenter James Miley, who was shot three times in the head on 18 September, were not identified but it is possible that he had been mistaken for a yeoman. A more daring attack was made on a yeoman guarding Newtownmountkennedy who was shot and wounded on 24 September and two days later it was reported that three 'respectable farmers' named Byrne who lived near Roundwood had been attacked and killed by unknown assailants.[234]

While Byrne was probably given in error for Bryan and the losses were consequently double-counted, the uncorrected impression given by the report was that of numerous multiple killings in Wicklow. Such incidents ensured that the ongoing low intensity rebellion in the Wicklow mountains was in the news daily. Genuine and shocking yeomen losses gave credence to proliferating wild reports of engagements and massacres of loyalists in the county. One of the most dramatic accounts asserted that thirteen Humewood cavalrymen had been trapped in an Inn near Blessington and killed by the rebels. This was without foundation, as was a report that Captain Hume had been ambushed and captured near Baltinglass on 22 September.[235]

The herculean task of restoring order in Wicklow was entrusted to General Lake but command of the operation on the ground devolved upon Lieutenant-Colonel Robert Crawford. Crawford was an efficient leader who had distinguished himself at New Ross and against Humbert at Cloon. Almost 2,000 troops, including the Angus Fencibles and Fermanagh Militia, marched from Dublin to Wicklow on 22 September to reinforce a detachment which had been dispatched the previous week. The unreliable King's County Militia was also removed from Wicklow to barracks at Malahide, Balbriggan and other places in north County Dublin. The basic strategy in Wicklow recalled that adopted by Moore in July with heavily armed columns of infantry intersecting the mountains with a view to locating the elusive rebels and forcing them to a general action. A large body of cavalry was amassed from various units in the Kilcullen/Dunlavin region and based at Blessington in support of the operation and guards were placed on all major access routes to the city to prevent the rebels escaping into Dublin. One of these guard posts proved the merit of the initiative on 28 September when alert sentries seized a consignment of weapons and munitions at Macartney's Bridge being taken to the rebels.[236]

From 24 September 300 troops were stationed in the small but strategic village of Donard to hamper rebel communications in the Imaal district and to protect the area's principal loyalist settlement from rebel attacks. The Dorset and South Devon Fencibles in Waterford and Kilkenny also commenced operations against insurgent bands in the areas within their remit that week. Another important initiative was the recall of the Wicklow yeomanry to permanent duty several days after being stood down. In Wexford Brigade-Major Fitzgerald ordered the county's yeomanry back on permanent duty on 4 October owing to the 'present disturbed state of the country'. Province wide preparations led to speculation that southern Leinster military were positioned to contain the Wicklow rebels in their native mountains once Crawford's troops had flushed them out.[237]

The untypical aggression of several Wicklow yeoman officers evinced their newfound determination to prove their mettle to an administration that was sceptical of their capability and concerned by their extremism. The Earl of Meath sallied out with his Bray Cavalry and Edwards' Bray Infantry over Sorrel Mountain on 24 September. They patrolled as far as Blackmore Hill before returning to the town three or four days later without sighting a single rebel. The absence of the insurgents was not reassuring and gave rise to another round of fanciful reports that they had gone to Celbridge, Wexford and Monasterevan and were preparing to attack Dundrum (County Dublin) in the last days of the month.[238] The closest Lake's soldiers came to the rebels during the first week of the sweep was a minor skirmish near Luggela on 24 September between elements of the 89th regiment and a section of Holt's rebels. The report that Holt and eighty rebels had been killed or captured was greatly exaggerated, although several fatalities were sustained and a group of defectors from the King's County Militia and two Royal Irish Artillerymen were apprehended. Three of the deserters were brought into Dublin on 3 October to be court-martialled. Despite the massive increase in military forces in Wicklow a party of mounted and uniformed rebels stole the mails at Newrath Bridge on 25 September and plundered the local Inn. By 26 September, when Lake was obliged to leave Wicklow for Mallow, initial optimism that the insurgents would finally be rooted out had faded and only a few prisoners had been sent to the capital.[239]

Crawford received a detachment of extra troops in early October and streamlined his force by returning his 'useless' cannon to Dublin. The press sought to mitigate his failure by stating that 20,000 troops would be insufficient to form an effective cordon around the mountains but a breakthrough occurred on 27 September when Holt's position was discovered on Clone Hill near Aughrim. 900 troops moved from Carnew, Donard, Hacketstown, Rathdrum and Wicklow Gap and took up positions at Killaduff, Aughrim and Tinahely under Lieutenant-General Craig and the newly promoted hero of Arklow, Lieutenant-Colonel Skerret of the Durham fencibles. Holt's position was desperate and a conventional force might have contemplated surrendering. This was not an option open to the rebels, however, and they determined to attempt an escape that night through the army lines. Some 150 piles of furze were collected, positioned and fired to simulate the appearance of a large camp site and to lessen visibility. Under cover of darkness and acrid smoke, the rebels exploited their expert knowledge of the terrain and penetrated the cordon. They made their way through defiles and hedgerows towards Lugnaquillia and successfully evaded the soldiers encamped around Clone Hill.[240]

To prevent the loyalist residents of Sheilstown alerting the army and pointing out the direction they had taken, the inhabitants were sealed into their homes, probably by nailing wood across their doors and windows. By such precautions the absence of the rebels went unnoticed until the following morning when Craig and his yeoman guides reconnoitred Clone Hill in preparation for an attack. The general was disappointed to discover that the rebels had escaped but Skerret, however, learned shortly afterwards from a captured rebel officer named Byrne, possibly Murtagh Byrne of Aughrim, that his comrades were going to Oakwood.[241] The rebels were alert to the possibility of pursuit and did not stop until they had reached Knockalt near Oakwood in the King's River valley. Holt made his headquarters at Oliver Hoyle's house and began to ponder his options. Dwyer sought and effected contact with some of his many yeomen acquaintances in the area to ascertain the intentions of the army. He was apprised that rebel positions were known and that an attack was being planned from Blessington. It was with this warning in mind Holt that directed

Francois Joseph to supervise the digging of trenches at Knockalt which were used to confront 200–300 troops who approached the camp on or around 1 October.[242]

Sixteen Leitrim Militia defectors crossed the King's River to challenge the enemy while Dwyer manoeuvred sixty men to emerge unexpectedly on their flanks. When Dwyer's men were in position the remaining 300 or so rebels under Holt abandoned the trenches in which they had lain concealed and pursued the shaken soldiers for three miles. Dwyer's group were too fatigued to cut off their line of retreat but an estimated ten soldiers were killed and a considerable quantity of equipment captured. This timely accretion was further augmented by the 'Moving Magazine' who provided a further 300 rounds of ammunition. It was reported on 4 October that thirty-seven Fermanagh militiamen, some of whom were wounded, had arrived in Dublin. The militia claimed that their equipment had been taken by the insurgents but it is more likely that they had discarded their kits when fleeing from the Knockalt ambush. By October only the most determined and experienced rebels remained in the mountains. These were men who have proven themselves the equal of the local yeomanry and militia and capable of frustrating better trained British regulars. Moreover, the cadre of military defectors, which exceeded 110 men by September, provided the insurgents with a highly motivated and well-armed core force. This element did much to compensate for the diminishing numbers of Wicklow rebels during the final phase of the rebellion.[243]

The narrow escape of the insurgents from Clone and the evident willingness of the government to deploy large bodies of troops in the Wicklow mountains did not convince the surviving rebel forces that the time had come to capitulate. In early October 1798 there seemed, in fact, to be an increase in the intensity and geographic spread of insurgent activity. Paradoxically, this impression arose largely from the estrangement of Holt from a number of his more prominent officers which weakened his authority and lessened his ability to co-ordinate the rebel effort. The greater independence of rebel commanders such as Andrew Hackett, Michael Neil, John Harman and Dwyer, while superficially symptomatic of escalating violence, actually signified the death knell of organized rebellion. All four had distanced themselves from Holt's main faction and while it appears that none had completely separated from him, their fragile relationship was vulnerable to irreparable damage.[244]

On 2 October Michael Neil and his self-styled 'Roundwood Cavalry' held up the Cork mail coach near Redgap in Kildare. Mail coach robbery was considered a very serious and newsworthy crime as it interfered with the communications that the government was supposed to guarantee. Neil's veneer of political motivation was revealed when he forced the passengers to swear that they were not orangemen and limited the amount of cash stolen from each person to one guinea. He then issued his victims with safe conduct passes to protect them from further rebel attacks. That the raids undertaken by Neil's faction were not mounted for purely criminal purposes was indicated by their trial of mails robber Patrick Daly for keeping £300 for himself from a coach robbed at Redgap on 13 September. Daly only escaped a flogging by absconding from the insurgents but was seized by the military, court-martialled and hanged at Kilcullen Bridge on 21 October 1798.

It was initially believed in Dublin that the passengers had been 'made prisoners to General Holt' but while Neil was a close associate of his they were probably not in contact on this occasion. The name 'Roundwood Cavalry' was one of several adopted by the various mounted elements of the rebel forces; others were the 'Ballynastockan Cavalry' and 'liberty boys.' Neither the village of Roundwood nor the townland of Ballynastockan had actually fielded yeomanry corps which may have encouraged the rebels to use the terms in a sarcastic manner. Neil was credited with being a humane man who had formerly worked in Rathfarnham for Richard Frizell junior and when captured on 13 October near Baltinglass by the Dublin City Militia was dressed in the uniform coat of the coach's mail guard. Nearly twenty guineas in gold and three five-guinea notes were found on his person.[245]

A more brutal facet of insurgent activity was in evidence that week in the southern extremity of the county where 'Mad' Andrew Hackett's faction terrorized loyalists. Hackett, from Knockbawn, near Coolgreany, from a strong farming family, became 'reduced in his circumstances owing to the uncertainty of the years preceding the Insurrection'. This loss of status at a time when many prospered attuned the young Hackett to political concerns. Hackett consequently became an apprentice blacksmith on Arklow's Coach Rd and from 1797 was reputedly an industrious pikemaker. Having fought as one of the most active and aggressive rebel officers aligned to Holt the two were estranged by late September when the Coolgreany man returned to his home area of the south Wicklow/Wexford borderlands. On or around 28 September Hackett and Thomas Neil led a group of insurgents to rob John Gilbert of Coolgreany who promptly reported the crime to the local yeomanry. The rebels were consequently pursued towards Ballymanus and lost several of their number around Ballyfad.

These casualties resulted in a revenge raid on 7 October when Hackett returned to Coolgreany to kill Gilbert but upon failing to locate him attacked three members of the loyalist Hall family of Castletown. Henry, William and John Hall were all Castletown yeomen who had probably been involved in the Ballyfad killings and were killed before Sergeant Thomas Caulfield of the corps was taken prisoner and taken to the home of transported rebel leader Thady Bryan. Bryan's wife persuaded the insurgents not to kill him in her house and he was shortly afterwards taken out by Hackett who struck Caulfield on the head with his sword. Although also stabbed in the lungs and shot in the back the yeoman survived to testify against Thomas Neil. The killings intimidated opponents of the rebels and it was reported that 'every protestant farmer and yeoman, from Gorey to Arklow is obliged to quit his house and his industrous occupation, and to live in some town ever since the 2nd [sic] September when the yeomen were put off permanent duty.' In late October Hackett's men were unjustly blamed for a spate of chapel-burning in north Wexford which they supposedly carried out to turn local opinion against the yeomanry who were, in all probability, the actual perpetrators.[246]

One group of outstanding rebels who maintained contact with Holt were the so called 'babes in the woods' based in the Killaughrim and Monart woods to the east of Enniscorthy in Wexford. Hay asserted, and was in a position to know, that these men were 'occasionally visited by Holt and Hacket[t]', probably when the Wicklowmen were encamped on Croghan mountain.[247] Patrick Fitzsimmons of Ballindaggan, who belonged to the core group in the forests under Captain James Cody of Enniscorthy, stated on 6 October that they intended 'to keep themselves as quiet as possible until join[e]d by General Holt, and then to make a general attack' on the city. Fitzsimmons informed Carlow magistrate Robert Cornwall that Cody's men were all veterans of the battle of Vinegar Hill and had received protections without surrendering arms. His identification of James Corcoran is one of the first of a rebel leader who was to become notorious in the early 1800s.[248]

That a plan to attack Dublin was seriously contemplated at that time is doubtful, although all contingencies were necessarily shelved one week later when General Taylor mounted a major offensive against the Killaughrim rebels. The Cavan Militia and Ninth Dragoons from Newtownbarry were the principal troops employed but soldiers and yeomen from Enniscorthy and parts of Carlow were also drawn into the operation. The rebels were driven into the mountains after a sharp skirmish where the Carlow Militia, Killedmond yeomen and Cornwall's cavalry inflicted further casualties. A report that over 210 rebels had been killed was a vast overestimate but that seven of those captured and many of those killed were found to be in possession of protections was deemed serious. Some of the survivors relocated to the Wicklow mountains but a small number proved remarkably resilient to repeated efforts to expel them from the Killaughrim district and Carlow's barony of St Mullins. They held out with James Corcoran's faction until February 1804 at which time they were probably the last active insurgent force in Ireland.[249]

Despite the difficult climate facing the rebels Holt persisted with his efforts to spread disaffection to counties where it had been suppressed. There were reports of 'missionaries being sent by Holt' into Kilkenny and Carlow 'for the purpose of stirring up the deluded peasantry'. The *Courier* claimed that these efforts had 'but too well succeeded' but whatever level of co-operation was effected came to nothing when Holt proved incapable of fielding significant numbers of rebels to take to the field within and beyond Wicklow.[250] An extant proclamation dated 24 October 1798 was issued in Kilkenny in the name of 'General Holt' which warned people 'not to pay any rents or tythes or excessive taxes' nor to bid for goods sequestered from evicted tenants. Significantly, the notice invoked the authority of 'General Bonapart[e] to make and enact laws' which was calculated to appeal to the disaffected and gave the handwritten document a pseudo-legalistic aspect in keeping with its wording. While it is possible that the proclamation was issued by local malcontents who merely cited Holt's name the Wicklowman's penchant for sending threatening letters and notices to his enemies suggests that it is genuine. In early October 1798 Holt's promise to 'visit' Dundrum, County Dublin had been taken seriously. Holt was evidently impressed by the French associations of the United Irishmen and had a portrait painted in the uniform of a French officer.[251]

HOLT'S NEGOTIATIONS WITH THE GOVERNMENT

One issue which exacerbated the trend towards the dissolution of the main rebel force in Wicklow was Holt's negotiation of terms with the government. These became public knowledge as early as 4 October when it was claimed in the press that an offer by him to surrender in return for a pardon for himself and his deserter contingent had been rejected. These tenders were not entirely inconsistent with his bid to maintain a state of insurgency in the Wicklow mountains and may have been pursued as a safeguard against the non-arrival of the French. On 19 October the *Courier* reported that Holt had 'sent proposals of capitulation to government, for a pardon for himself and his gang' and eleven days later the *Hibernian Telegraph* specified that 'terms of transportation' had been demanded.[252]

The negotiations had apparently been initiated by Hester Holt who contacted the La Touche family of Bellvue (Delgany) through a relation whose husband was in their employment. Ann La Touche encouraged Holt to write a letter to Lord Powerscourt stating his desire to surrender which was used to interest Earl Meath and other powerful local noblemen on his behalf. This elicited a verbal undertaking from Powerscourt that Holt's life would be spared if he capitulated, which confirmed what he had heard from other sources; one Morne of Monamee informed him that Powerscourt would welcome his surrender. News of Mrs Holt's visit to Bellvue, where many ex-rebels worked, was not long kept from Dwyer's men and seemingly vindicated longstanding suspicions of her motives and to a lesser extent, those of their leader. Even Dwyer invoked the censure of his men shortly afterwards for allowing his new bride, Mary Doyle, join him in his quarters.[253] Warnings were also received from Dublin United Irishman William Hoey of Edgeworth Court and the contents of his letter of 11 October intercepted by Major Sirr were very incriminating. Hoey's note was addressed to 'Captain [Barney] Corragan' who led the King's County regiment deserters with Holt and made reference to Hester Holt's dealings in Powerscourt in the first week of October.[254]

Documentary proof of Holt's intriguing was obtained in Glenmalure just before Hoey's letter arrived which resulted in a confrontation at Harney's house at Baravore. According to Holt a miller from Whitestown named Keogh had delivered a letter to him from General Moore inviting him to inform the government of his terms for surrendering. Moore had previously attempted to enlist Dwyer's help in convincing Holt to surrender in August 1798 and it is clear that once the rebel leader's disposition was known, different channels were opened to encourage him to make the step. Holt claimed that Moore's letter was read aloud to the men by Matthew Doyle and that he was very surprised to be seized and required to explain his intentions. The version of events passed on to Luke Cullen by associates of the somewhat partisan Dwyer faction alleged that Holt had become confused when challenged and that his wife commenced an apology insisting that they had no intention of betraying the insurgents. The outcome of the dispute was the withdrawal of Holt from Glenmalure at the head of the main force over which he retained at least nominal command.[255]

Dwyer visited Holt's new camp shortly after the incident, conversed with him 'at a distance from the men [and] they met and parted . . . on very good terms'. Yet, even though the argument did not result in great acrimony, it is likely that it increased Holt's disillusionment with the course of the rebellion and thereby hastened the total disintegration of organized resistance in Wicklow. Holt's force went through Glenmacnass to Oakwood but had returned to Aghavannagh by 8 October where they numbered about 250 rebels. His younger brother Jonathan remained in west Wicklow and headed a mounted reconnaissance party which crossed into the Humewood area and fell in with elements of Dwyer's group operating out of Imaal. The rebels became dispersed in a heavy downpour of rain but one section encountered William Hume in advance of his corps who made the fatal mistake of assuming that the Antrim Militia defector John Moore was a yeoman.[256] Moore was wearing a scarlet cavalry cloak taken from a dead Briton or 5th Dragoon at Ballyellis and was in company with Jonathan Holt, Conway, Whitty, 'Big John' O'Neill and another man, possibly Andrew Byrne. They closely resembled a yeomanry patrol being all mounted, uniformed and in possession of military equipment. Conway, a King's County Militia deserter, was something of a celebrity among rebel sympathizers and in December 1798 Martin Kirwan of Athdown unwisely boasted of knowing him at William Troy's pub in Enniscorthy in the presence of a serving member of the regiment.[257]

The details of Hume's death were disputed by contemporaries but it appears that he sustained a fatal shot to the head and a less serious wound to the side from Moore, possibly while attempting to disarm the rebel. Daniel O'Brien of Talbotstown, who heard Moore's account of the killing shortly after it occurred, told Luke Cullen in the mid-1800s that the Arklowman had not intended to kill Hume which concurred with the opinion of Michael Kearns of Baltinglass who was one of about sixteen others riding behind Moore's advance party. Moore, a carpenter from Arklow before joining the Antrims, was apparently aggrieved that his father, a sheebeen keeper at Killalish near Humewood, had been put out of business and imprisoned in Baltinglass by Hume. He was court-martialled in Dublin barracks in June 1799, sentenced to death and afterwards gibbeted close to where the killing had taken place. In the course of the skirmishing which ensued Jonathan Holt was killed and several experienced rebels were taken prisoner; the 5th Royal Irish Dragoons were credited with taking 'some prisoners in a skirmish with some of Holt's daemons [sic]'.[258] This news greatly disheartened General Holt while the death of a member of parliament electrified the city loyalists. Hume, although a liberal member of the Fitzwilliam interest, was popular with the Wicklow yeomen on account of his family's service in their ranks. In 1795, when the Wicklow electorate was not as divided as it was in 1798, Fitzwilliam stated that Hume was 'indisputably the representative of my tenantry'. His death may well have spurred them to burn two Catholic chapels at Ballinvolagh and Kilpatrick on 11 October.[259]

Ill-health plagued Holt and with his movements dogged by informers anxious to claim the bounty offered by the government for his capture his role in the rebellion drew inexorably towards a close. After moving to Knockalt in early October Holt resolved to reduce his force to a more manageable number which effectively signalled an abandonment of his efforts to maintain a standing sizeable insurgent force as the rallying point for a new rising. He had another narrow escape from capture or death when visiting his family at Mullinaveigue which could have done little to bolster his resolve or health. Holt had been spotted by a patrol and was forced to take refuge in a small damp cave which had been cut into the bank of a stream to elude the military.[260]

Holt's efforts to revitalize the rebellion were unsuccessful and without massive French aid it must have seemed that it was only a matter of time before it petered out altogether. He rejoined his men at Quinns of Glenbride on 10 October where, according to King's County militia defector Mat Henzy, the rebels divided into smaller groups and went their separate ways. Henzy claimed that John O'Neil of Redwells went to Kildare with sixty men, Francois Joseph led a party towards Kilkenny in the unrealistic hope of making contact with survivors of Fr Murphy's June incursion while Dwyer's faction were already posted in Imaal. Joseph was associated with the militia deserters with Holt which may explain why Henzy believed he had succeeded him in command. The Frenchman, however, while corroborating Henzy on this point, claimed that he had only risen to this prominence when a Francis Street pawnbroker and United Irish captain named Greely urged him to return from Dublin to Wicklow. Holt apparently retained a bodyguard of about fifty men while the remainder went with his friend Matthew Doyle and 'others' who parted on amicable terms.[261]

Unfortunately for Holt, his harbourer had alerted the military at Russborough House to his presence at Glenbride and the house was attacked at dawn on 11 October. The Argyle fencibles under Major Meredith and Captain Richard Hornidge's Lower Talbotstown Cavalry took up positions surrounding the house but an excellent chance to kill or capture Holt was ruined when the troops manning the cordon abandoned their posts when the skirmish began. The rebels had heard the approach of the military and put up a fierce resistance in which English deserter Joseph Begly and James Donoghue from the Waterford Militia were shot dead along with several attacking soldiers. Holt killed the sergeant commanding the Scottish squad and escaped wounded into the darkness with three of his nine men. Four of those killed in the cottage were apparently members of Quinn family who had fallen victim to the indiscriminate gunfire of the army. Early press accounts misrepresented the affair and claimed that 'Holt and a large party' of insurgents had ambushed a small detachment of fencibles thereby transforming the army's bungled operation into an heroic stand. It was further claimed that nineteen rebels and one Scottish sergeant had been killed but *Saunder's newsletter* carried an account which lowered the figure to sixteen and emphasized that Holt was nearly captured in the 'terrible contest'.[262]

While Holt's activities were in terminal decline in October 1798, several former associates began to render themselves notorious. Naas-born west-Wicklow resident James Hughes, a one time officer in Holt's force, quickly became pre-eminent by mounting a series of vicious attacks on lone yeomen and soldiers. James Tattersdale of the Lower Talbotstown corps was piked in the face in mid-October when he encountered Hughes and a 'troop of rebels on horseback' at Coldwells. A similar incident occurred near Belan around that time when a member of the Upper Talbotstown corps, one Boyne, was shot at least once in the head by Hughes' men and left for dead in a bog hole. Boyne had been covered with foliage to conceal his body but remained conscious despite sustaining a pistol or musket wound to the face. He overheard his attackers discussing a rendezvous and later passed this information on to his comrades who captured four insurgents. Boyne also ascertained that the rebels had disposed of the body of another yeoman in a bog hole.[263] Attacks of this kind were not uncommon and the following week the body of an Ancient Briton who had been sent from Kildare to Athy was recovered from a shallow grave 'at a wild and lonely part of the Curragh'.[264] The Wicklow yeomanry used such incidents to justify their often illegal and brutal campaign waged against known and suspected rebels. There was little sympathy for protected rebels even in Dublin where it was alleged 'the protected rebels are as bad as ever in Wicklow and Wexford: loyal Protestants taken out of their beds and murdered every night.'[265]

In one of the most blatant yeoman reprisals Hugh Woolaghan of Middleton, a private in the Newtownmountkennedy corps, went to the Killincarrig home of an amnestied rebel Thomas Dogherty on 1 October and shot him dead without provocation. Woolaghan had given Thomas King some of the first details of United Irish infiltration of the Cronebane corps in January and prior to the rebellion had worked as a mason for the Thomas Archer of Mount John. He was accompanied by Charles and James Fox, probably the Foxs of Middleton, who did not act upon their threat to shoot other family members. The killing came just seven days after a member of their corps had been shot and wounded by rebels at Newtownmountkennedy and was probably envisaged as a calculated reprisal. Dogherty had been a prominent and popular rebel in the Delgany area and had fought from May 1798 until his arrest in the aftermath of the Meath expedition. Richard Byrne, a private in the Wallace Fencibles but previously a resident in Killincarrig, had observed him conducting pike drills in Johnson's Field at that place in the spring of 1798. His brother had been killed at Dunboyne but Thomas, although sentenced to death by a Slane court-martial on 18 July, was released from a Dublin Bay prison hulk on the intercession of his La Touche employers. It is possible that he was aware of a threat to his life as he generally worked as a shoemaker in Dublin but was recuperating from illness in his parents' Killincarrig home at the time of his death.[266]

Woolaghan was court-martialled in Dublin between 13 and 15 October for his flagrant affront to the amnesty legislation and the trial quickly took on national significance when its potential as a pivotal test case became apparent. This situation arose when the defence attempted to justify Woolaghan's actions by claiming he had been following standing orders to shoot suspected rebels on sight. Corporal George Kennedy testified that Captain John Warnford Armstrong of the King's County Militia, the man responsible for the conviction of the Sheares brothers, had ordered that rebels be shot on sight owing to 'the enormities' they had committed. This statement was supported by Sergeant Nathaniel Hayes who heard Armstrong declare his intention to 'shoot or hang any rebels whom he suspected'. Lieutenant William Tomlinson of the Rathdrum corps also admitted that orders had been given 'not to bring in prisoners'.[267]

The yeomen may have been encouraged to make such frank disclosures by the composition of the court-martial panel which drew its members from the Fermanagh Militia and Fifth Royal Irish Dragoons, two regiments noted for their extreme loyalty. Four of the panel, Major Brown, Captains Onge, Irwin and Carter, were from the Royal Irish Dragoons which had been commanded by the local landlord, Lord Rossmore, and stationed in Newtownmountkennedy for several years before the rebellion. It was reputedly 'peculiarly distinguished throughout the whole of the rebellion, for its unremitting and important services, and for the zeal and loyalty with which every man in it has emulated the bravery and spirit of their beloved and gallant officer the Hon. Col[onel Charles] Stewart', Castlereagh's brother.[268] The Fermanagh officers were the Earl of Enniskillen and Captain Leslie while the most junior officer on the panel, and presumably the most neutral, was Lieutenant Summers of the 68th [Devon] regiment. Lord Enniskillen of the Fermanagh Militia presided, a man who had fostered his regiment's identify as 'an ultra Orange body'. Their acquittal of Woolaghan was interpreted as a sign of their tacit approval of meeting out summary justice to protectioned rebels and as a rebuke to Cornwallis clemency policy.[269] Woolaghan took work as a builder in Dublin after his reprieve and in 1799 was mistaken for a United Irishman by Edward Holmes who invited him back to the house where the senior organizer James Hope was staying. Hope managed to escape the authorities but Holmes lost his job.[270]

The Viceroy could not countenance this naked repudiation of his legislation and took the extraordinary step of intervening to negate the verdict and to prevent the members of the court-martial from sitting on other cases. Extreme loyalists took 'great offence' at Cornwallis' comments and took to calling him 'Croppy Wallis' and other derogatory names.[271] Camden, the former conservative Viceroy, thought that the disbarment ruling was 'very severe' and feared that such explicit rebukes of ultra-loyalism would 'hurt the English interest in Ireland'.[272] Cornwallis began to assess all verdicts of reached in trials of rebels and mitigated the death sentences of hundreds of men to transportation and lesser terms during his time in office. This firmness impressed many nationalists although the ejection of Woolaghan from the yeomanry did not stem loyalist determination to conduct anti-insurgent operations as they saw fit. The liberal *Courier* exaggerated when it claimed that 'to be met on the road even with a protection . . . is inevitable death' but it is evident that many rebels shared Dogherty's fate in 1798 and 1799.[273]

The peculiar intensity of the late rebellion in Wicklow ensured that its yeomanry corps, more than that of any other county, were called to account for their actions in court. Captain Abraham Nixon of the Coolkenna Infantry was summoned before a Court of Inquiry at Dublin's Royal Exchange on 6 November to answer allegations that he had executed prisoners in Wicklow. Also charged were Robert Dowling, John Haskins, John Byrne and Thomas Codd of the Shillelagh corps. Their alleged victims included a protected rebel, James Granger, killed on 7 October, who had reputedly led the party which had killed Nixon's father at the battle of Ballyrahan Hill on 2 July. No disciplinary action was taken and Nixon had been, as Edward Cooke observed, 'most unlucky', but the public airing of such allegations was nonetheless significant. One of the primary reasons that no conviction had been possible was the utter refusal of Nixon's associates to testify and this, when coupled with the understandable unwillingness of rebel witnesses to give evidence, all but ensured his release.[274] The four Shillelagh yeomen were threatened with being tried as 'principles' and were detained for several days in Major Sandy's Provost Prison until Thomas Kemmis ordered their release in advance of anticipated habeas corpus proceedings. Nixon was bailed on 19 November to appear at the following Wicklow assizes where, if he did appear, he was not prosecuted.[275]

The Nixon case did not register any discernable reaction from the Wicklow rebels but Woolaghan's release elicited widespread outrage. Dwyer, on learning of the court's decision, led thirty to forty men on 16 October in the only attack carried out in the immediate vicinity of Rathdrum in 1798, the strongest garrison in north Wicklow. The raid occurred in broad daylight and was primarily directed against yeomen who had direct involvement in the trial, a circumstance which indicates that the rebels had noted the progress of the trial from various press accounts. Lieutenant Tomlinson, who had played a prominent part in the defence, was the main victim, losing his Ballinderry farm buildings to an unopposed incendiary attack. Tomlinson's home was also targeted but did not take fire. The rebels considered him to be a man 'of extreme orange principles and a terrorist to the core'. That the attack was intended to be more ambitious is suggested by the fact that Dwyer's cousin, Arthur Devlin, was left to guard the house of a Protestant friend, Jeremiah Smith, lest the detached Wexford rebels burn it or injure its owner by mistake.[276]

The loyalists were perhaps fortunate to be absent in the Oakwood district 'in pursuit of Holt' but the rebels, by the same token, did not have to contend with the bulk of the troops generally stationed at Rathdrum. County Coroner George Manning was burned out of his

Ballyteigue home as he and several of his sons and nephews were yeomen, notwithstanding the protestations of his wife who was acquainted with some of the attackers. The Mannings were held responsible for the burning of Bryan Devlin's home at Croneybeg early in the rebellion. Devlin was probably a United Irishman, his son 'Little' Arthur certainly was while Anne, his daughter, was to become one of the most famous heroines of the period. Bryan Devlin was also the uncle of 'Big' Arthur Devlin, Dwyer's cousin and companion.[277] William Magin's property was also destroyed and John Mills was robbed of arms before Dwyer's men withdrew into Glenmalure. John 'Kittagh' Byrne, described in 1803 as 'one of Dwyer's gang', allegedly burned the home of Thomas Cross on 31 October 1798 but this may well have actually taken place on the 16th.[278]

General Eustace was returning with troops and yeomen from the Oakwood expedition around three o'clock when they encountered the rebels at the head of Glenmalure. Insurgent gunfire drove off the cavalry elements who were incapable of acting with effect in that terrain and exposed the infantry to some peril. Eustace and his dismounted men were pursued to within a mile of Rathdrum by the lightly equipped and faster insurgents and the general's plight was deemed serious in hindsight. One commentator claimed that the rebels had 'burned all respectable houses for a mile & a half betwixt this [Rathdrum] & the mountains'.[279] James Chritchley asserted that the rebels had returned after nightfall and 'burnt Ballynaclash and almost all the Protestant houses', although there is no other record of this taking place. An extraordinary sequel to the events of 16 October was Dwyer's marriage to Mary Doyle of Knockandarragh that night at Knockgorragh.[280] The Rathdrum area was the following day 'covered with yeomen and military burning houses and shooting down such persons as they did not like' and arresting many suspects. One of those shot dead was John Coonan of Ballynockan, whose house was also burned along with that of one Ellis of Greenhills. Further excesses might well have taken place at the Devlin household at Croneybeg had not a tolerant Rathdrum cavalryman, Thomas Darby, intervened to protect the family. The Devlins had been jeopardized by their United Irish associations and had already lost one home in the rebellion.[281]

A more reasoned and effective response to the rebel outrages was scheduled for 20 October at the Eagle Tavern in Dublin's Eustace Street. The meeting was the most significant county gathering of the Rebellion and attracted magistrates, noblemen, landowners and yeoman officers concerned about the state of the county. That it was not held in Wicklow town is revealing and it seems that its siting reflected the angry mood of the participants who were eager to put the county's problems in the national context and to break with the failed anti-insurgent strategies of the past. A fund of £1,077 was established to locate and prosecute the men who had killed William Hume, an initiative which ultimately resulted in the execution of John Moore for the crime.[282] The creation of a system of 'small garrisons' or blockhouses was recommended by the Eagle Tavern delegates to impede rebel communications, an innovation which both Major Hardy and Colonel Skerret later claimed the honour of devising. This resolution may well have contributed to the building of the Military Road on which construction began in July 1800 and ceased in 1805 but it had no bearing on the rapidly diminishing insurgent forces in the Wicklow mountains.[283] Some action was taken in November 1798 when officers of the 89th regiment made initial surveys to locate suitable sites for 'a chain of telegraphic communication along the different heights' on which work later commenced in July 1802.[284] While it was reported that this and other 'salutary measures' devised by Powerscourt, Carysfort and other Wicklow and Wexford noblemen had received the approval of Cornwallis, there was in fact very little that could be done to contain the rebels in the short term.[285]

Military forces in Wicklow in October 1798 were close to their peak garrison strength at any time in the history of the county. They included the Leitrim Militia at Rathdrum, the Sligo Militia at Arklow, the Fermanagh Militia in Wicklow Town, the Fifth Dragoons at Newtownmountkennedy, the Duke of York's Highlanders or Argyle's at Russborough House, the Durham Fencibles at Knuckstown camp and the Princess of Wales Light Dragoons at Donard. There were also small detachments of these regiments and others stationed in Bray, Enniskerry, Blessington, Dunlavin, Baltinglass, Roundwood and in most settlements of village size. Additional regiments based at Lehaunstown and on the county borders were also available for temporary deployment in Wicklow in the event of an emergency or major operation. The various military stations were visited by a Lieutenant-Colonel in October who had been a foundling child nursed in Coolattin. He noted that the Hacketstown yeomanry were 'out night and day in search of Holt' while the Sligo Militia practised marksmanship and the Durhams held a field day at Knuckstown. On calling to his former nurse, a Mrs Toole in Coolattin, he found that her husband had been a rebel, three of her sons had been hanged in Wexford, two were killed at Vinegar Hill and three others at the

Battle Arklow. To compound her tragedy all four of her daughters had become diseased having gone 'with the mob'.[286]

The huge manpower resources at the disposal of the government ensured that large numbers of insurgents could no longer congregate with the relative impunity they had hitherto enjoyed under Holt. While the sweeps made by Moore, Lake and Craig were unsuccessful, it was evident that a decisive battle could not be avoided indefinitely as long as the government remained committed to and capable of mounting such large-scale drives. The advent of winter also posed grave problems for the insurgents with regard to subsistence and shelter, particularly as most had become undernourished and ill by the autumn. The three deserters formerly with Holt who were executed at Kilcullen on 3 November were reputedly 'barelegged, squalid and clad only with the ragged remnants of their military cloths'. The men, one Sligo and two Leitrim militiamen, declared that they had been

> . . . grievously punished by famine and misery of every kind for their treasons; that they had not during the whole absence been possessed of a single penny; that they had passed many days without food in the mountains and that even when a division of plunder took place amongst the rebels, they were not allowed any share.

While the claim about plunder was probably necessary to avoid incrimination in a crime that was in legal terms almost as serious as desertion, the remainder of the statement is plausible.[287] Banditry and minor raids could continue as long as there were small numbers of unreconciled or outlawed rebels but this in itself could not be considered as insurrectionary warfare. Indeed, the most famous die-hard, Michael Dwyer, rarely assembled more than fifteen men at a time after 1798 and was therefore incapable of mounting significant attacks on government forces.[288]

Holt's health deteriorated after the Glenbride ambush and his many wounds began to take their toll on his constitution. On escaping from the trap he passed through Shankhill and over Three Rock mountain, narrowly escaping capture by the Powerscourt yeomanry. His destination was Dundrum where he spent a short period recuperating. This respite was presented in his memoir as a minor event preceding his return to the mountains after a few days but this was not the case. Having temporarily eluded informers the mystery as to his whereabouts resulted in speculation that he had either been captured or had died. Holt had in fact entered Dublin city on 16 October and spent the night in a cellar on Francis St where his presence became known to government spies.[289] Sproule's contact, possibly Oliver Carlton, ascertained that Holt's 'wound and disappointment' had brought him to Dublin a day early and that he had determined that if he 'did not succeed' in some unspecified venture he 'would make to Dublin [and] from thence to England'. This had indeed been considered by Holt but had fallen through when Hester Holt was robbed of the funds they had raised by the auction of their assets. Holt had probably hoped to attend a meeting of the city's United Irish leadership at Surgeon Wright's home on 15 October where Francis McMahon, Shaw, Burke and other militants who had fought with him in Wicklow gathered to discuss strategy.[290]

The meeting may have been occasioned by news of the defeat of the French at the Battle of the Nile and Sir John Warren's destruction of the Brest fleet on 12 October. The prospect of more French assistance soon receded still further with news of the capture of Wolfe Tone on *L'Hoche* on 3 November. Such information was collected and assessed by the various Dublin-based factions who frequently issued instructions to rural rebel groups. On 14 October a Kevin St 'committee of active citizens' was discovered preparing letters of intelligence for the use of country-based insurgents.[291] The delegates at Wright's resolved that in view of the strategic picture 'all sh[oul]d be over & not to act without the French or [un]till the English troops are recalled'. They did, however, decide to make 'one desperate attempt' to seize the capital during the winter when it was anticipated that military patrols would be scaled down. This did not come to pass.[292]

Holt spent the night of 17 October in the Plunkett St home of a man name Neil who had fought with him in Wicklow and was visited there the following day by some of his friends. These men were very probably either protectioned United Irish migrants or fugitives hiding in the city, part of a burgeoning community in Dublin's newer southern districts. Neil had formerly served as a drill sergeant with the Liberty Rangers yeoman infantry and in the summer of 1799 Holt's rival Francis McMahon was living in Plunkett St when 'Neill a butcher' was identified as being 'a Capt[ain] of U[nited] I[rish]M[en]'.[293] They probably brought Holt news of the deliberations of the rebel leadership in the capital as on his return to Wicklow he confidently asserted that an insurgent victory was 'out of the question as the report of the French coming . . . [was] unfounded'.[294] Holt may also have received such information from his own contacts with the French Directory in the person of Leonard Bourdon, whose Kerry-born secretary, William Duckett, was a United Irish representative and in contact with the

Wicklowman. Sir James Crawford, British ambassador to the freeport of Hamburg and secret service controller on the continent, discovered this association in October 1798. Duckett, he alleged, had 'been in correspondence with Holt, the rebel chief, who through him, has been pressing the French for assistance.' An independent link with France emerged in late November when a vessel named the *Patrick and Fanny* was intercepted at sea. Its captain, one Doyle, claimed to know Holt and was found to be a courier of letters from Duckett.[295]

The authorities had brought increased pressure to bear on Holt to surrender during his absence and had detained one of his brothers at Russborough House, probably Thomas Holt, a United Irishman who lived near Ballinascorney.[296] Towards the end of October or in early November, Holt responded by sending a letter addressed to Lords Powerscourt and Monck through a neutral friend named William Keegan of Bahana. The communication was probably in furtherance of discussions initiated by Ann La Touche and Hester Holt in the first week of October and it set down his conditions for surrendering in a strident and defiant manner. Holt demanded a pardon, compensation for his losses and, while offering to become a loyal subject and fight for the Crown in the future, he flatly rejected consenting to transportation, indicating that this relatively mild sanction had been offered to him in return for capitulating.[297] The press received a copy of this or a very similar letter and referred on 7 November to the 'terrible rebel['s] . . . threats of increased depredation' with which he had ended his note.[298]

Holt returned to the city when his negotiations had reached an advanced stage and attended the 'great night of deliberation' on 4 November. It was probably at this meeting that Holt received positive information that the rebels could not expect French assistance in the short term, the object for which he had evidently prolonged the rebellion.[299] Holt had reportedly spent the night of 2 November in a house in Dirty Lane and moved the following day to Bridgefoot St where he was sighted by a police agent. The Castle authorities were informed that 'Holt's party' had met on 4 November in 'some street off Thomas Street', McMahon's at 'O'Hara's' and Shaw's at the 'Elephant' on Eustace Street. The United Irishmen had apparently discussed strategy in the light of recent events and laid plans for their most important leaders to be taken off the coast at Rush. These men were to be shipped out to join the 'determined enemy's' of Britain on the continent but none actually went at this time.[300] Despite this excellent and reliable intelligence, Major Sirr could not be contacted in time to act effectively. Sproule's agents, furthermore, were too timid to seize Holt or any of the other leading rebel on their own and the Castle was consequently deprived of a potential propaganda coup. Their caution may have been influenced by an embarrassing incident some weeks before when an English fencible officer had been mistaken for Holt at Dolphin's Barn and detained for a period.[301]

The meeting of 4 November transpired to be Holt's final act as an insurgent leader and he returned to his native county to surrender. He first assembled his few remaining adherents at Brady's of Ballylow and told them of the futility of further struggle and on the night of 9 November called to the Bahana home of his intermediary and friend, William Keegan, in whose company he surrendered to Lord Powerscourt the following day. It is clear that Holt had only taken this step when further resistance appeared futile and the will of the rebels to continue the insurrection had given way to disparate acts of terror and reprisal. An agenda that was more concerned with the imperatives of self-defence than revolution did not appeal to Holt. He was taken to Dublin Castle on 12 November by a 'formidable troop' of Powerscourt yeomanry where he remained until 1 January 1799 being questioned and receiving curious visitors.[302] His capitulation effectively ended the rebellion and while attempts were later made to resurrect the military aspect of the United Irish cause, the numbers of active insurgents in the field never equalled those commanded by Holt in September/October 1798. Holt's surrender was technically unconditional but the involvement of Monck, Powerscourt and the La Touches negated any possibility of bringing him to trial and he was ultimately permitted to exile himself with his family in New South Wales.[303]

Holt's long-anticipated capitulation was the subject of many speculative reports in the press. It was generally welcomed and optimism was expressed that this would lead to the total cessation of rebel activity in Wicklow and the recovery of stolen goods. One account claimed he had 'rioted in the blood and plunder of the loyal inhabitants of the counties of Wicklow, Wexford, Carlow and Kildare' and another looked forward to his 'full and minute disclosure of the whereabouts of looted goods and the retreats of his rebel comrades'.[304] When Dwyer read such accounts to his men, several were prompted to leave the county for fear of betrayal although others were satisfied that the reports were 'unjust allusions'.[305] Holt was obliged to co-operate with the authorities to a greater extent than most other compromised fighting rebel leaders as the circumstances in which he had found himself were quite different to that of the Wicklow/Wexford/Kildare group who had received terms in July 1798. He, unlike Garret Byrne, William Aylmer and Edward Fitzgerald, had prosecuted the rebellion after the watershed promulgation of the Amnesty Act, and the terms open to him were considerably harsher than those granted to his peers. Holt was the only senior fighting leader and one of very few United Irishman of high rank to set foot in New South Wales.[306] This was partly owing to his refusal to take direct action against his former associates.

Holt made at least one deposition in the Castle on 16 November which implicating nineteen robbers, some of whom were also rebels, and seventeen United Irishmen. He also referred to two rebels who had been killed and recommended two other people as sources of information. Virtually all those named had allegedly been involved in robberies, murders and lesser crimes but his information was unsworn and his unwillingness to appear in person to prosecute greatly lessened its importance. That only one man, James Kavanagh of Paddock, was not previously suspected of the activities detailed by Holt indicates that he had deliberately avoided compromising men and he generally confined his comments to incidents for which he was anxious to disclaim responsibility. It is also likely that the notes of Holt's deposition was a verbal response to questions about the individuals listed. This is suggested by his dwelling on details concerning Owen 'Kittagh' Byrne, a man whom he alleged had extorted goods in his name, who had been brought into Dublin on 5 November by the Bray Cavalry.[307] In keeping with general practice Holt was requested to urge his subordinates to seek terms and he wrote at least one ineffectual letter to his friend Matthew Doyle advising this course.[308]

From 23 January Holt was lodged on the *Lively* tender and then on the convict ship *Minerva* which conveyed him into exile on 24 August 1799. He was visited prior to sailing by several senior military officers and loyalists and was taken ashore in June to meet Major-General William Myers and Major Ross. According to Holt, Myers offered him command of a yeomanry corps in Wicklow if he would defect to the government which he flatly refused to do. He did, however, on 27 February 1799 divulge details, perhaps inventions, concerning a planned rising in Cork. That Holt was obliged to rely on the charity of the La Touche family to finance the passage of his family, expenses that he had been given to understand were to have been met by the government, indicates that the authorities were not overly pleased with his disclosures. Cornwallis for one queried 'what degree of credit' it merited.[309] The Holts arrived in Port Jackson, New South Wales on 11 January 1800 and returned to Ireland in

April 1814 at which time Holt had secured an absolute pardon and was possessed of some wealth accumulated by farming and property sales in the new colony.[310]

Wicklow in the aftermath of Holt's surrender remained disturbed as Michael Dalton, James Pluck, James Ryder and other rebel officers associated with his faction turned to robbery to survive. The emergence of these small bands instituted a period of lawlessness and banditry all over Wicklow, much of Wexford and parts of Kildare, Carlow and south County Dublin. John O'Neill from Redwells, Kildare, was arrested in Dublin and joined Major Sirr's staff of informers and agents who devoted much energy to hunting down rebel fugitives in the city. The few remaining Wexford men in Wicklow either returned home and attempted to resume pre-rebellion pursuits in the face of orange terrorism or like Miles Byrne, commenced new lives in Dublin. Byrne left Wicklow on 10 November 1798 and hid in Kevin Street until his half-brother Ned Kennedy brought him to a place of safety. At that time 'arrests of those coming from the counties of Wicklow and Wexford were every instant taking place throughout the city.' Byrne quickly slotted into the capital's United Irish network and dined with William Byrne of Ballymanus only days before the Wicklowman's arrest in 1799.[311] 'Antrim John' Mooney, James Doyle of Ballinacor, Francis Joseph and others also took refuge in the confusion of the metropolis but many of those who had spurned or could not obtain protections found it necessary to enlist in the British armed forces under assumed names to avoid detection and prosecution in 1799.[312] This option was especially favoured by the army and militia deserters whose legal predicament otherwise ensured that they comprised a disproportionately high number of outstanding rebels into the early 1800s. A Baltinglass court martial in November 1798 sentenced Roger O'Neil, Bernard McDonald and Charles Connor of the 89th regiment to death for defecting to the rebels and Daniel Reilly to serve abroad.[313]

Minor skirmishes, murders, robberies and revenge attacks continued in Wicklow and on its borders until the end of 1798 setting the pattern for the type of unrest which followed in the wake of the rebellion. In the last days of October two farmers named Redmond and Eagan were robbed of money on their way to the Dublin markets. A more serious skirmish occurred at that time at the home of Thomas Fisher near Donard. Two local insurgents armed with pikes were killed in the act of attacking Fisher's home by the Donard Infantry and the village's 89th regiment detachment. Another encounter in which the yeomen triumphed took place near Castledermot on 3

November when seventeen robbers led by one Lynch were seized at Widow Walsh's and conveyed to Baltinglass for courtmartial.[314] On that day or the following one the Ballaghkeen, Gorey and Wingfield yeomanry shot four rebels belonging to Andrew Hackett's faction at Ballyfad near Arklow for the loss of three men wounded. Hawtrey White had apparently received 'good information that the inhuman and sanguinary rebel Hacket[t]' would be at Ballyfad and he was initially thought to have died in the skirmish. The dead man transpired to be one 'Antrim Jack' Dogherty, not to be confused with 'Antrim John'.[315]

By far the most important coup for the authorities in this period was the killing of Hackett on 20 November when he was shot dead when attempting to rob Captain Thomas Atkins of the Arklow yeomanry of his firearm. His comrades attempted to carry off his mortally wounded or deceased body but were obliged to dump it when pursued by the yeomen. The death of the feared Hackett, the most daring and aggressive rebel leader in southern Wicklow, forestalled the emergence of his faction as a long-term source of instability in the mould of the Dwyer and Corcoran gangs. Successive blows to rebels on the Wicklow/Wexford border temporarily pacified the Arklow district where the insurgents reputedly became 'so few and feeble, that they never venture to appear without losing the greater part of their number'.[316]

No rebel groups of consequence were actively engaged in fighting government agencies for political ends outside of Wicklow and its immediate environs. Geography and the legacy of the bitter autumn clashes in the mountains had facilitated untypical militancy in the sector. The United Irishmen, nevertheless, did not regard the disastrous rebellion as a decisive defeat or the death, imprisonment and exile of virtually all their founding members as an insurmountable obstacle to ultimate victory. Indeed, 1799 witnessed a partial resurgence of the grass-roots organization in areas where heavy losses had been incurred the previous year. In addition the surprising longevity of the Dwyer and Corcoran factions ensured that national and international propaganda was available to United Irish agents attempting to interest their continental allies in renewing their commitment to liberate Ireland. While other counties were to experience deep unrest arising out of agrarian hardship and grievances, Wicklow remained the country's focal point of armed political struggle in the aftermath of the great rebellion.

Notes

CHAPTER ONE

1 See Robin Frame, *Colonial Ireland, 1139–1369* (Dublin, 1981), pp. 122–6.

2 Colm Lennon, *Sixteenth-century Ireland: the incomplete conquest* (Dublin, 1994), p. 43, Art Cosgrove, *Late medieval Ireland, 1370–1541* (Dublin, 1981), pp. 122–3 and Steven Ellis, *Tudor Ireland, crown, community and conflict of cultures, 1470–1603* (London, 1985), pp. 137–42, 270–1.

3 Ellis, *Tudor Ireland*, Chapters 7 and 8 and Lennon, *Incomplete conquest*, p. 193.

4 Lennon, *Incomplete conquest*, pp. 201–4, *The last county, the emergence of Wicklow as a county, 1606–1845* (Wicklow, 1993), pp. 9–11 and John Ryan, *The History and antiquities of the county of Carlow* (Dublin, 1833), pp. 110–111.

5 See B. Donnelly, 'From Grand Jury to County Council: an overview of local administration in Wicklow, 1605–1898' in Ken Hannigan and William Nolan (eds.), *Wicklow: history and society, interdisciplinary essays on the history of an Irish county* (Dublin, 1994), p. 855, Conor O'Brien, 'The Byrnes of Ballymanus' in Hannigan and Nolan (eds.), *Wicklow: history and society*, p. 306, and Ellis, *Tudor Ireland*, pp. 286, 303–6.

6 Ellis, *Tudor Ireland*, Chapter 9, Lennon, *Incomplete Conquest*, pp. 296–8, J. C. Beckett, *The making of modern Ireland, 1603–1923* (London, 1966), pp. 22–3 and *Last county*, pp. 11–12.

7 M. Perceval-Maxwell, *The outbreak of the Irish rebellion of 1641* (Dublin, 1991), p. 18, William F. Butler, *Confiscations in Irish History* (Dublin, 1917), pp. 90–1, 159–60 and Jane H. Ohlmeyer, 'The wars of religion, 1603–1660' in Thomas Bartlett and Keith Jeffrey (eds.), *A Military history of Ireland* (Cambridge, 1996), pp. 160–2.

8 Quoted in J. T. Gilbert, *History of the Irish Confederation and the war in Ireland, 1641–3*, 7 vols., (Dublin, 1882–91), III, p. 40. See also *The Irish Magazine, and monthly asylum for neglected biography*, July 1810, Perceval-Maxwell, *1641*, pp. 22, 225, 252, J. T. Gilbert (ed.), *A contemporary history of affairs in Ireland from 1641 to 1652* (Dublin, 1879), I, part 1, p. 16 and Patrick Francis Moran, *Historical Sketch of the persecutions suffered by the catholics of Ireland under the rule of Cromwell and the puritans* (Dublin, 1884), pp. 364–6 and *Last County*, pp. 14–15.

9 Moran, *Historical sketch*, pp. 364–6, Seamus O'Saothrai, 'Old Greystones and Ancient Rathdown' in *Journal of the Greystones Archaeological and Historical Society*, I, 1992, pp. 14–15 and Donnelly, 'overview of local administration', p. 856.

10 O'Brien, 'Byrnes of Ballymanus', p. 307, Nora M. Hickey, 'Cromwellian settlement in Balyna parish, 1641–1688' in *Journal of the Kildare Archaeological and Historical Society*, XVI, no. 5, 1985–6, p. 503 and Donnelly, 'overview of local administration', p. 856.

11 J. G. Simms, *The Williamite confiscations in Ireland, 1690–1703* (London, mcmlvi), pp. 177–92, Wall, *The Penal Laws, 1691–1760* (Dundalk, 1976), p. 43 and *Last county*, pp. 21–4.

12 Quoted in Marianne Elliott, *Wolfe Tone: Prophet of Irish Independence* (London, 1989), pp. 139–40.

13 See Thomas Bartlett, *The fall and rise of the Irish Nation: the Catholic question, 1690–1830* (Dublin, 1992) and R. B. McDowell, *Ireland in the age of imperialism and revolution, 1760–1801* (Oxford, 1979), Chapter 11.

14 Robert Day, 14 January 1794 in *Charges to Grand Juries*, Royal Irish Academy, MS 12. W. 11, II, p. 4, *FDJ*, 18–28 March and 15 April 1793 and *Hibernian Chronicle*, 11 March 1793.

15 Camden to [Downshire], 12 May 1795, Public Record Office of Northern Ireland, Downshire Papers, D.607/C/92A. See also *Faulkner's Dublin Journal*, 29 March and 8 April 1794.

16 James Smyth, *The Men of no property: Irish radicals and popular politics in the late eighteenth century* (Dublin, 1992), Chapter 7, *FDJ*, 24 January 1794 and 17 January 1795 and Deirdre Lindsay, 'The Fitzwilliam episode revisited' in David Dickson, Daire Keogh and Kevin Whelan (eds.), *The United Irishmen, republicanism, radicalism and rebellion* (Dublin, 1993), p. 199.

17 See David W. Miller, *Peep O'Day Boys and Defenders: selected documents on the County Armagh disturbances, 1784–96* (Belfast, 1990).

18 See 6 May 1798, National Archives, Rebellion Papers 620/37/29, ——, to Cooke, 7 May 1798, NA, 620/37/33, Ruan O'Donnell, 'General Joseph Holt and the rebellion of 1798 in County Wicklow', MA Thesis, University College Dublin, 1991, pp. 121–2 and L. M. Cullen, 'Politics and rebellion: Wicklow in the 1790s' in Dickson, Keogh and Whelan (eds.), *United Irishmen*, pp. 420–21.

19 Edward Wakefield, *An account of Ireland, statistical and political*, 2 vols., (London, 1812), II, p. 777 See also Ibid., p. 409.

20 Jacob Nevill, 'An actual survey of the county of Wicklow' (Dublin, 1760), *Last County*, pp. 26–33, 48–52, Kevin Whelan, 'The United Irishmen, the Enlightenment and Popular Culture' in Dickson, Keogh and Whelan (eds.), *The United Irishmen*, pp. 269–92 and Ruan O'Donnell, 'The Rebellion of 1798 in County Wicklow' in Hannigan and Nolan (eds.), *Wicklow: history and society*, pp. 341–78.

21 'An account of the several parts of the kingdom of Ireland that have been proclaimed' n.d., [c.late 1798], Public Record Office [England], Home Office 100/79/346–50, O'Donnell, 'Rebellion of 1798', pp. 346– 64, Daniel Gahan, *The people's rising, Wexford 1798* (Dublin, 1995), pp. 230–1, 10 May 1797, PRO, HO 100/70/247, 1 February 1798, PRO, HO 100/75/ 201–2 and Thomas Pakenham, *The Year of Liberty: The story of the great Irish rebellion of 1798* (London, 1969), pp. 123–40.

22 O'Donnell, 'Holt', pp. 106–7, Hereward Senior, *Orangeism in Ireland and Britain, 1795–1836* (London, 1966), pp. 97–8, J.F. Maurice, *The diary of Sir John Moore*, 2 vols., (London, 1904), I, pp. 309–10 and Luke Cullen, *Insurgent Wicklow*, edited by Myles V. Ronan, (Dublin, 1948), p. 75.

23 *Press*, 30 January 1798, Wakefield, *Ireland*, II, pp. 628, 632, William Shaw Mason, *A statistical account and parochial survey of Ireland* (Dublin, 1814–19), II, p. 40, T. Jones Hughes, 'A traverse of the coastlands of county Wicklow and east county Wexford' in *Baile*, 1983, pp. 6–7, Ken Hannigan, 'The Irish language in Co. Wicklow' in *Wicklow Historical Journal*, 1, no. 1, July 1988, p. 26 and W. E. Vaughan and A. J. Fitzpatrick, *Irish historical statistics, population, 1821–1971* (Dublin, 1978), pp. 33–60.

24 L. M. Cullen, *The emergence of modern Ireland, 1600–1900* (London, 1981), p. 37.

25 Wakefield, *Ireland*, I, pp. 349, 715–6 and II, p. 686 and Stewart, *Dublin Society Transactions*, 1799, p. 125. A breed of Wicklow sheep was often interbred with the South Down sheep although some farmers favoured the pure bred flock.

26 Curry to ——, 15 December 1838 in O'Donovan *et al.*, *Letters containing information relative to the Antiquities of the county of Wicklow collected during the progress of the Ordnance Survey in 1838* (Bray, 1928).

27 Miles Byrne, *The memoirs of Miles Byrne*, 2 vols. (Shannon, 1972), I, p. 11, *Irish Magazine*, August 1808 and R. R. Madden, *The United Irishmen, their lives and times*, 4 vols., 2nd ed., (Dublin, 1857–60), IV, p. 520.

28 Wakefield, *Ireland*, II, p. 632 and Cullen, 'Politics and rebellion', pp. 425–35.

29 *Walker's Hibernian Magazine*, May 1783, p. 278.

30 Robert Fraser, *General view of the co. Wicklow* (Dublin, 1801), p. 32, *Saunder's Newsletter*, 10 May 1793, *FDJ*, 11 May and 23 April 1793, L. Gilbert (ed.), *Calendar of ancient records of Dublin in the possession of the Munincipal Corporation* (Dublin, 1907), XIV, p. 371, GEC, *The Complete Peerage, or a history of the House of Lords and all its members from the earliest times* (London, 1936), XI, pp. 179–82, *WHM*, July 1789, p. 392 and November 1789, p. 616, *National Library Reports on the Private Collections*, no. 292, *Hibernian Journal*, 4 April 1787 and E. G. Evans, *An outline of the history of the county Wicklow regiment of militia* (1885) p. 49. Cunningham was MP for Monaghan 1769–96 where he owned an estate.

31 *FDJ*, 12 February 1795. See also Claude Chavasse, *The story of Baltinglass, a history of the parishes of Baltinglass, Ballynure and Rathbran in County Wicklow* (Kilkenny, 1970), pp. 44–6, A.K. Longfield, 'Linen and cotton printing at Stratford-on-Slaney, County Wicklow' in *Royal Society of Antiquities of Ireland Journal*, XV, 1945, pp. 24–5 and *WHM*, November 1786, p. 613.

32 *WHM*, August 1789, p. 448 and October 1789, p. 560, *FDJ*, 27 June 1789 and 9 October 1790, *Complete Peerage*, III, pp. 70–3, Wakefield, *Ireland*, I, p. 283, John Bateman, *The great landowners of Great Britain and Ireland* (London, 1876), p. 168 Fitzwilliam's income from his Wicklow estates was 20,488 pounds in 1787. W. A. Maguire, *The Downshire estates in Ireland, 1801–1845* (Oxford, 1972), pp. 68–70.

33 Maguire, *Downshire estates*, pp. 1–5, Elizabeth Maxwell, *country and town in Ireland under the Georges* (London, 1940), pp. 79, 82–3 and Maurice Craig, *The architecture of Ireland from the earliest times to 1880* (Dublin, 1982), pp. 188–90.

34 *WHM*, October 1782, p. 552 and February 1783, p. 163 *The official railway handbook to Bray, Kingston, the coast and the county of Wicklow*, p. 88, Bateman, *great landowners*, p. 314, *Complete Peerage*, IX, pp. 50–2, Cooke to Grenville, 28 August 1797, PRO, HO 100/72/174, Hardwicke to Pelham, 2 November 1801, PRO, HO 100/107/168, Elizabeth Batt, *The Moncks of Charleville House* (Dublin, 1979), pp. 7–15 and *National Library Reports on the Private Collections*, no. 107, p. 1073 La Touche purchased Ballydonough estate in 1753 for £30,000 and renamed it Bellvue. A.M. Fraser, 'David Digges La Touche, banker, and a few of his descendants' in *Dublin Historical Record*, V, 1942–3, p. 63.

35 *Complete Peerage*, VIII, pp. 616–7 and X, pp. 638–9, *FDJ*, 7 January 1790, *National Library Reports on the Private Collections*, no. 29, *WHM*, June 1789, pp. 333–4 and Rutland to Pitt, 20 July 1786 in *Correspondence between the Rt. Hon. William Pitt and Charles Duke of Rutland . . . 1781–1787* (London, 1890), p. 153. In March 1784 Lady Meath and two women of the Tottenham family who held land in Wicklow and Wexford attended a fancy dress ball in Dublin Castle dressed as 'a family of Quakers.' *WHM*, March 1784, p. 105.

36 Gilbert, *Calendar*, XIV, p. 304 and XV, p. 11, *FDJ*, 29 November 1794, *WHM*, November 1787, p. 613 and November 1791, *SNL*, 17 and 20 October 1798 and *Hibernian Telegraph*, 27 April 1798.

37 *WHM*, May 1789, p. 280 and July 1789, p. 391.

38 Maguire, *Downshire*, pp. 110, 237 and Wakefield, *Ireland*, I, pp. 98, 283–4 and II, p. 306.

39 Young, *Tour*, I, pp. 52, 96 and II, p. 8, Maguire, *Downshire*, pp. 37–9, Wakefield, *Ireland*, II, p. 306, Stewart, *Dublin Society Transactions*, 1799, pp. 118–20 and Cullen, *Modern Ireland*, p. 55. The Fitzwilliam estate was ably managed from Malton (Coolattin) by William Wainwright who diligently monitored the progress and industry of the tenants. The property was hailed by the generally reserved Wakefield as 'the best cultivated' in Ireland. Wakefield, *Ireland*, I, p. 283.

40 Byrne, *Memoirs*, I, pp. 1–3 and Young, *Ireland*, I, p. 95.

41 *SNL*, 2 and 11 January 1789.

42 *SNL*, 10 January 1795.

43 Fraser, *Guide*, p. 32 See also Wakefield, *Ireland*, I, p. 537.

44 W. McKenzie, *The Beauties of the County of Wicklow* (Dublin, 1794). *Beauties*, p. 10. Lord Chief Baron Edward Willes noted in August 1757 that the Wicklow mountains even then contained many 'country retirements for the inhabitants of Dublin.' Willes to the Earl of Warwick, 14 August 1757 in James Kelly (ed.), *The letters of Lord Chief Baron Edward Willes to the Earl of Warwick, 1752–62, an account of Ireland in the mid-eighteenth century* (Kilkenny, 1990), p. 23.

45 *SNL*, 12 March 1793.

46 *SNL*, 16 February and 25 May 1793, M.R. Quinn and Lord Monck, 'An account of cone wheat propagated in the county Wicklow' in *Dublin Society Transactions*, I, part 2, 1799, pp. 165–7, Abraham Mills, 'A mineralogist account of the native gold lately discovered in Ireland' in Ibid., II, 1801, pp. 454–63 and Mills, 'Second Report on the Goldmines in the county of Wicklow' in Ibid., III, 1802, pp. 81–7, 138.

47 *Beauties*, p. 16–18. In 1795 Avondale was left to Hayes' cousin and borough patron Sir John Parnell whom he greatly admired. See also Myles Tierney, *Cahill's Arklow and Wicklow County Guide and Directory* (Dublin, 1979), p. 31, F.S.L. Lyons, *Charles Stewart Parnell* (London, 1977), p. 20, J. Fraser, *Guide to the County Wicklow* (Dublin, 1842), p. 74, Wakefield, *Ireland*, I, p. 537 and *FDJ*, 3 April 1790.

48 *SNL*, 24 April 1789 See also Ibid., 3 February, 18 March and 6 October 1789 and *Dublin Gazette*, 28 October 1790.

49 *FDJ*, 11 June 1791, Eoin Neeson, *A History of Irish forestry* (Dublin, 1991), pp. 305–14, Mary Kelly Quinn, 'The evolution of forestry in county Wicklow from prehistory to the present' in Hannigan and Nolan (eds.), *Wicklow: history and society*, pp. 823–54, Wakefield, *Ireland*, I, pp. 569, 571 and Stewart, *Dublin Society Transactions*, 1799, pp. 119–20.

50 *FDJ*, 18 January 1790. See also Revd Beaver H. Blacker, *Brief sketches of the parishes of Booterstown and Donnybrook in the county of Dublin*, 2nd edn. (Dublin, 1861), p. 83, *Last County*, p. 52, Maxwell, *Country and Town*, p. 281 and 'They [sic] life and adventures of Joseph Holt . . . ', Mitchel Library, Sydney, MS A2024, pp. 16–19.

51 See M.R. Quinn and Lord Monck, 'An account of the cone wheat propagatel in the County of Wicklow' in *Dublin Society Transactions*, I, part 2, 1799, pp. 165–7, *FDJ*, 7 April 1791 and William Chapman, *Report on the improvement of the harbour of Arklow, and the practicability of a navigation from thence by the vales of the various branches of the Ovoca* (Dublin, 1792), pp. 3–14. By the end of the decade Pim was evidently aligned with the loyalist faction as his home was robbed by the rebels in 1798. Information of James Quinn, n.d. [June] 1799, NA, 620/47.

52 For smuggling around Bray see G. R. Powell, *Railway Handbook* (Dublin, 1860), pp. 29–30. In April 1794 a large English captained smuggling cutter with eighteen guns landed quantities of tobacco and gin, *SNL*, 11 April 1794.

53 *Last county*, p. 31, *FDJ*, 4 November 1790 and Young, *Tour in Ireland*, I, p. 98.

54 Chavasse, *The story of Baltinglass*, pp. 44–7, Longfield, 'Linen', pp. 24–7, Cullen, *Modern Ireland*, p. 77, *Dublin Evening Post*, 4 January 1785, 5 and 10 August 1786 and 11 September 1787 and 17 March 1795, Fraser, *General view*, pp. 87–88 and *SNL*, 11 March 1794. The Orrs may have been related to Thomas Orr of Henry Street, Dublin who kept a linen warehouse in the city and relinquished the business to his son James in 1793, *SNL*, 18 May 1793.

55 Wakefield, *Ireland*, II, pp. 706–7 and Cullen Papers, National Library of Ireland, MS 8339, p. 153.

56 [Revd Robinson] to Cooke, 9 May 1798, N.A., 620/37/43.

57 23 April 1798, NA, 620/36/228, Stephen Gwynn, *Henry Grattan and his times* (Connecticut, 1971), pp. 325–6, Cullen, *Insurgent*, p. 77 and *Dublin Evening Post*, 25 July 1799.

58 *FDJ*, 8 September 1791. See also Ibid., 10 December 1789, 9 October and 4 November 1790 and 25 October 1791, *HC*, 13 September 1791, Maxwell, *country and town*, p. 237 and L.M. Cullen, *Six generations, life and work in Ireland from 1780* (Cork, 1970), p. 55.

59 Fitzwilliam to Hardwicke, 15 September 1802, British Museum Library, MS 35736/152. See also *FDJ*, 14 October 1790, Rev. Edward Bayly to Lord Clonmore [Ralph Howard], 18 December 1787, NLI, MS 12, 149, p. 48 and W.E. Vandaleur, *Notes on the history of Killiskey Parish* (Dundalk, 1946), p. 11.

60 Des Cowman, 'The mining community at Avoca, 1780–1880' in Hannigan and Nolan (eds.), *Wicklow: history and society*, pp. 761–88, Anon., *The mines of Wicklow* (London, 1856), pp. 42–3, *FDJ*, 21 October 1790, Ernie Shepherd, 'Avoca Mines' in *Arklow Historical Society Journal*, 1986, p. 18 and *Wicklow Times*, 18 June 1997, p. 8.

61 *SNL*, 19 September 1789. The operation was also referred to as the Hibernian Mine Company.

62 Madden, *United*, IV, pp. 548–9 and Ibid., II, p. 6, Shepherd, 'Avoca Mines', p. 18 and *SNL*, 20 August 1789. The halfpenny's obverse was decorated with egalitarian images depicting mattocks and other mining tools in a traditional format of a quartered shield. *SNL*, 21 August 1789.

63 Sir John Parnell to T. Coke, 3 September 1796, NA, 620/18A/6. See also *Mines of Wicklow*, pp. 42–7, *Sydney Gazette*, 25 March 1804, Wakefield, *Ireland*, II, p. 301, Maguire, *Downshire*, p. 121 and Cullen, *Modern Ireland*, p. 217. Kyan's daughter, Mary Teresa, married Lieutenant Henry Ormsby of the staunchly loyalist Wicklow Militia in 1793. *SNL*, 16 November 1793.

64 Wakefield, *Ireland*, II, p. 688. Hearth tax collectors exempted 2,429 pauper households and 378 new homes which added to the 11,507 assessed gives a total of 14,314 homes in the county.

65 *Account of Delgany church, built by Peter La Touche Esq.*, *FDJ*, 19 February and 25 June 1791, *HC*, 12 September 1791, *HT*, 30 May 1798 and Gilbert, *Calender*, XII, pp. 346–7. Powell replaced the deceased Rev. Richard Strong in 1794 as Vicar of Rathdrum. Gilbert, Ibid., p. 431.

66 *SNL*, 2 September and 8 November 1794, Troy to Marshall, 12 October 1799 in Londonderry (ed.), *The memoirs and correspondence of Viscount Castlereagh*, 4 vols. (London, 1848), II, p. 421 and Fr. Kearns to [Troy?], 20 August 1801, Dublin Diocesan Archives, Troy Papers, 116/7/103 (iii).

67 Fraser, 'La Touche', p. 67. William Drennan visited the gardens in August 1796 and reported that he had seen 'a covered walk of glass and an Italian climate that must have cost an immense sum, as it extends several hundred yards, containing every rare flower and shrub that art can rear in a hot house.' Drennan to Mrs McTier, 12 August 1796 in D. A. Chart

(ed.), *The Drennan Letters, 1776–1819* (Belfast, 1931), p. 238. See also Stewart, *Dublin Society Transactions*, 1799, p. 130 and *HJ*, 11 August 1802.

68 *Freeman's Journal*, 30 May 1789.

69 *FDJ*, 1 May 1790. See also *WHM*, March 1785, p. 167, August 1785, p. 447 and January 1786, p. 54 and 28 June 1786, NLI, MS 15,303.

70 *SNL*, 18 April and 1 August 1789, 25 May 1793 and 9 April 1794.

71 *WHM*, June 1794, *Beauties*, p. 12, *Report on the private collections*, no. 182 and no. 51, p. 856, NLI, MS 5024, *FDJ*, 12 August 1790 and 4 June and 13 August 1791.

72 See 'Abstract of the effective men in the different Volunteer Corps, whose delegates met at Dungannon . . . 16th of April 1782' in *Miscellaneous works of the Right Honourable Henry Grattan* (Dublin, 1822), pp. 129–40, 235–8, *WHM*, April 1780, p. 231, June 1782, p. 335, July 1783, p. 390 and October 1783, p. 558, p. 181 and McDowell, *Ireland in the age*, pp. 252–4. See Appendix One for a list of Wicklow Volunteer units.

73 Robert Day, 'Two county Wicklow Volunteer medals' in *Cork Historical and Archaeological society journal*, 2nd series, IX, no. 60, 1903, pp. 226–8.

74 W. J. Fitzpatrick, *The life, times and contemporaries of Lord Cloncurry* (Dublin, 1855), p. 93 See also Gilbert, *History of Dublin*, III, p. 60, Rupert J. Coughlan, *Napper Tandy* (Dublin, 1976), p. 35 and *WHM*, April 1780, p. 231 and June 1785, p. 334.

75 *WHM*, July 1783, p. 390 and October 1783, p. 558.

76 Wexford Volunteer officers John Beauman of Coolgreany, Archibald Hamilton Jacob of Enniscorthy and Robert Hatton of Wexford Town all became notorious in 1798 for their extremist conduct. *WHM*, October 1781, p. 615 and September 1782, p. 503. For continuity in Carlow between the leading personalities of the volunteers, yeomanry and Orange Order, see Peter O'Snodaigh, '98 *and Carlow: a look at the historians* (Carlow, 1979), *FJ*, 11 September 1779 and McDowell, *Ireland in the age*, pp. 257–8.

77 *FDJ*, 13 February 1787 and *WHM*, June 1780, p. 349.

78 Fitzpatrick, *Cloncurry*, p. 93, *WHM*, November 1786, p. 612, April 1787, p. 223 and October 1787, p. 559 and *HC*, 7 June 1786. Whelan and two others were executed but John Mooney escaped from Dublin's New Prison and was re-arrested the following year at Primatestown in Meath. *HC*, 7 June 1786.

79 Young, *Tour in Ireland*, I, p. 99. See also Wakefield, *Ireland*, II, p. 483, *WHM*, April 1785, p. 221 and January 1786, p. 53, *HC*, 12 and 28 October 1786 and 14 July 1788 and J. S. Donnelly, 'The Whiteboy movement, 1761–5' in *IHS*, XXI, no. 81, 1978, pp. 20–54. Walter Read and Richard Maguaran were sentenced to death in July 1788 for murdering a French doctor and Pat Kelly received the same sentence at Wicklow assizes in May 1791 for killing Michael Hill at Coolawinnia. *FDJ*, 3 March and 6 May 1791.

80 *FDJ*, 25 October 1791, *HC*, 12 September 1791, Batt, *Moncks*, pp. 12–14 and *FDJ*, 25 October 1791.

81 Mills, 21 November 1795, *Dublin Society Transactions*, p. 459, Charles Coates to ——, 24 September 1795, NLI, MIC 5648, Camden to Portland, 8 October 1795 quoted in J. Buckley, 'Discovery of gold in Co. Wicklow' in *Royal Society of Antiquities of Ireland Journal*, III, 1913, 6th series, pp. 183–4, *The Celt*, I, no. 5, 1857, p. 75 and Richard Kirwan, 'Report of the Gold mines in the county of Wicklow with observations thereon, by R. Kirwan, esq.' in *Dublin Society Transactions*, II, part 2, 1801, pp. 132–43.

82 Fraser, *Guide*, p.14, Gwynn, *Grattan*, pp. 157, 323–6, 386–7.

83 Grattan to Day, 5 December 1788, RIA, MS 12. W. 9, *New Cork Evening Post*, 2 March 1796 and Wakefield, *Ireland*, II, pp. 384–5. William Brabazon Ponsonby was MP of Kilkenny in 1790 and George Ponsonby represented the Tighe family's Borough of Insitioge. *Dublin Gazette*, 20 May 1790.

84 *FDJ*, 3 April 1790 See also Ibid., 24 April 1790, *Dublin Gazette*, 23 May 1790 and *HC*, 22 April 1790.

85 *FDJ*, 24 April, 6, 8 and 28 May and 5 June 1790, 1, 12 and 15 March 1791, *Dublin Gazette*, 22 May 1790 and *Minutes of evidence taken before the select committee on the Baltinglass election, 10 November 1783* (Dublin, 1783), p. 5.

86 *FDJ*, 25 August 1792. See Kevin Whelan,'The religious factor in the 1798 rebellion in County Wexford' in Patrick O' Flanagan, Patrick Ferguson and Kevin Whelan (eds.), *Rural Ireland: modernisation and change, 1600–1900* (Cork, 1987), p. 65.

87 *FDJ*, 27 September, 25 August and 30 October 1792 and McDowell, *Ireland*, pp. 407–8.

88 Whelan, 'Religious factor', pp. 62–85, Thomas Bartlett, 'Religious rivalries in France and Ireland in the age of the French Revolution' in *Eighteenth-Century Ireland*, VI, 1991,

pp. 57–76, *FDJ*, 8 September 1792 and L. M. Cullen, 'The 1798 rebellion in its eighteenth century context' in Patrick Corish (ed.), *Radicals, rebels and establishments* (Belfast, 1985) p. 110.

89 Madden, *United*, IV, p. 542.

90 Thomas Cloney, *A personal narrative of those transactions in the county of Wexford in which the author was engaged, during the awful period of 1798* (Dublin, 1832), p. 81. Cloney claimed that Kyan 'ranked far above the plebian aristocracy of the county Wexford.' Ibid. See also Madden, *United*, I, pp. 415–6.

91 Francis Plowden, *An historical review of the state of Ireland . . .* , 2 vols. (London, 1803), II, pp. 389–94, O'Brien, 'Byrnes of Ballymanus', pp. 311, 325–6, 338 and *FDJ*, 3 January 1792.

92 See Cullen, 'Politics and Rebellion', pp. 438–9.

93 *HC*, 13 May 1793 and *FDJ*, 25 April 1793 and 18 September 1794.

94 *FDJ*, 6 November 1793 and 25 March and 18 September 1794.

95 *FDJ*, 1 August 1793. See also Ibid., 23 March and 30 July 1793 and Thomas Bartlett, 'An end to the moral economy: the Irish Militia disturbances of 1793' in *Past and Present*, no. 99, 1983, pp. 41–64.

96 *FDJ*, 6 May 1794. See also Ibid., 18 and 23 December 1794, *Cork Gazette*, 20 and 24 December 1794 and Brian Inglis, *The freedom of the press in Ireland, 1784–1841* (London, 1954), pp. 86–7.

97 *FDJ*, 20 May 1794. See also Ibid., 22 May and 1 November 1794 and *HC*, 3 October 1793.

98 *FDJ*, 15 July 1794. See also Ibid., 7 September and 1 August 1793.

99 *FDJ*, 15 July 1794. The coronation had been marked by a large gathering of nobility at Grierson's home at Seaview, Bray on 25 October 1790. *FDJ*, 2 November 1790.

100 *FDJ*, 6 May 1794. See Cullen, 'Politics and Rebellion', pp. 429–30 and Sir Edward Newenham to Pelham, 14 July 1795, NA, 620/22/16.

101 Newenham to Pelham, 14 July 1795, NA, 620/22/16. The pressures of the office of High Sheriff greatly taxed King who later commented that the county had not been 'much less agitated' in 1794 as it was in 1800 when the insurgent gangs of Michael Dwyer and Michael Dalton ranged across west Wicklow. King to Marsden, 23 February 1800, NA, Official Papers 78/10.

102 *SNL*, 15 May 1795.

103 *SNL*, 12 March, 14 April and 31 March 1795 and Madden, *United*, IV, p. 522–33.

104 *SNL*, 19 May 1795. See also Ibid., 3 and 17 June 1795.

100 Wakefield, *Ireland*, II, p. 20.

106 *A list of premiums paid for corn and flour brought from the county of Wicklow to the city of Dublin from 24 June to the 25th December 1791* republished in *Irish genealogical sources no. 2, Dun Laoghaire genealogical society*, 1997, pp. 16–27, D. A. Chart, *An economic history of Ireland* (Dublin, 1920), pp. 79–84, T. J. Kiernan, *History of the financial administration of Ireland to 1817* (London, 1930), pp. 278–82, Byrne, *Memoirs*, I, p. 28 and O'Brien, 'Byrnes of Ballymanus', p. 317.

107 Wakefield, *Ireland*, I, p. 411 and *DEP*, 29 March 1798.

CHAPTER TWO

1 O'Neil Stratford to ——, 19 May 1797, NA, 620/30/108.

2 McDowell, *Ireland in the age*, pp. 444–58 and Lindsay, 'The Fitzwilliam episode', pp. 197–208.

3 Camden to [Portland], 6 August 1796, NA, 620/18/11/1, Curtin, 'United Irish organization in Ulster: 1795–8' in Dickson, Keogh and Whelan (eds.), *United Irishmen*, pp. 212–3, Madden, *Antrim and Down*, pp. 98–9, *Commons' Journal Ireland*, XVII, pp. dcccxxii, McDowell, *Ireland*, pp. 471–2 and Roger Wells, *Insurrection: the British experience, 1795–1803* (Gloucester, 1986), pp. 62–3.

4 Curtin, 'United Irish organization in Ulster', pp. 211–3 and Graham, 'Union of power', pp. 246–7.

5 *Report of the committee of secrecy to the House of Commons* (London, 1797) Appendix II, p. 46. See also R. B. McDowell, 'The proceedings of the Dublin society of United Irishmen' in *Analecta Hibernia*, XVII, 1949, pp. 1–143.

6 United Irish constitution, 10 May 1795, PRO, HO 100/70/245 and NA, Frazer MS, 1/10.

7 1 February 1798, PRO, HO 100/75/199. See L. M. Cullen, 'The 1798 Rebellion in its eighteenth century context' in P. Corish (ed.), *Radicals, rebels and establishments* (Belfast, 1985), pp. 271–3 and 10 May 1795, PRO, HO 100/70/24.

8 Ashtown to Hardwicke, 4 July 1803, BM, MS 35740, p. 24 See also n.d., NA, 620/52/39.

9 Camden to [Portland], 6 August 1796, NA, 620/18/11/1.

10 10 May 1795, NA, Frazer MS 1/10.

11 R. R. Madden, *The United Irishmen, their lives and times* (rev. ed., 4 vols, London 1857–60), II, p. 14 and J. T. Gilbert (ed.) *Documents relating to Ireland, 1795–1804* (Dublin, 1893), p. 15.

12 Anon, n.d. 1798, PRO, H.O.100/76/11–4.

13 Cited in Elliott, 'Defenders', pp. 231–2. See also Curtin, 'The United Irish organization', p. 218. Elliott pointed out that James Hope made no reference to Defender-United Irish friction during the rebellion. Ibid., p. 230. The main authority for Defender dissension is Samuel McSkimmin, a United Irish informer and Government agent described by John A. Russell as a 'low fellow'. Russell to R. R. Madden, 27 February 1843, TCD, Madden Papers cited in W. E. Houghton (ed.), *The Wellesley index of Victorian periodicals, 1824–1900*, II, p. 354. See also Samuel McSkimmin, *Annals of Ulster: or Ireland fifty years ago* (Belfast, 1849), pp. 114–5. McSkimmin also collaborated with the noted folklorist Thomas Crofton Croker in 1836 whose integrity as an editor was highly suspect. O'Donnell and Reece, '"A clean beast": Crofton Croker's Fairy Tale of General Holt' in *Eighteenth-Century Ireland*, VII, 1992, pp. 11–12.

14 Elliott, *Partners in revolution*, pp. 245–6 and 'Defenders', p. 231.

15 Thomas Pelham to William Grenville, 17 December 1796, PRO, HO 100/62/368, anon., *French fleet in Bantry Bay* (Dublin, 1797) and Downshire to Reilly, 3 January 1797, PRONI, D.607/E/6, E. Jones, *An invasion that failed* (London, 1950) and *FDJ*, 20 December 1796 to 4 January 1797. See also the essays in John A. Murphy (ed.), *The French are in the Bay: the expedition to Bantry Bay, 1796* (Dublin, 1997).

16 Pelham to Lake, 3 March 1797, PRONI, D.607/E/148–9.

17 R. G. Morton, 'The rise of the yeomanry' in *Irish Sword*, VIII, 1967–8, pp. 58–64, William Richardson, *History of the origin of the Irish yeomanry with the steps taken to bring forward the measure previous to its final adoption* (Dublin, 1801) and *FDJ*, 20 October 1796.

18 Curtin, 'United Irish organization in Ulster', pp. 209–221.

19 A well-placed informer told Undersecretary of State Lord Castlereagh, that the 'military organization had no existence till towards the end of 1796, and was as near as could be engrafted on the civil.' ——, to Castlereagh, 7 August 1798, PRO, HO 100/78/34

20 Address of the Dublin County Committee of United Irishmen, 27 August 1797, NA, Frazer MS 1/17.

21 William MacNevin cited in Wells, *Insurrection*, p. 60 See also Cullen, 'The 1798 Rebellion' in Corish (ed.), *Radicals*, p. 272.

22 Ibid. See also Castlereagh to —— , 7 August 1798, PRO, HO 100/78/34, Anon., 16 February 1798, PRO, HO 100/75/132 and Gilbert, *Documents*, p.155.

23 1 February 1798, PRO, HO 100/75/201–2 and Madden, *United Irishmen*, II, pp. 14–5.

24 26 February 1798, PRO, HO 100/75/132.

25 Ormsby to Cornwallis, 11 June 1799, NA, State Prisoner's Petitions, 420.

26 26 February 1798, PRO, HO 100/75/132.

27 Byrne, *Memoirs*, I, pp. 68–71. Bugles were occasionally used by yeoman defectors from the yeomanry but whistles were used in the same role in Wicklow. See Luke Cullen, NLI, MS 8339, pp. 68–9 and Information of John Murray, 21 May 1798, NA, 620/3/32/6. See Appendix Two.

28 Anon., April 1798, PRO, HO 100/76/11–14.

29 John Beresford to —— , 4 September 1798, *The correspondence of the Right Hon. John Beresford* (edited by) William Beresford, 2 vols. (London,1854), II, p. 125 See also NCEP, 14 March 1796, Camden to [Portland], 15 November 1797, PRO, HO 100/66/60, NCEP, 13 April 1797 and Thomas Bartlett, 'Indiscipline', p. 123.

30 See Kevin Whelan,'The United Irishmen, the Enlightenment and popular culture' in Dickson, Keogh and Whelan (eds.), *United Irishmen*, pp. 256–68 and *The Tree of liberty: radicalism, catholicism and the construction of Irish identity, 1760–1830* (Cork, 1996), pp. 59–98.

31 Enniscorthy man Darby Kelly was threatened with transportation for 'being present when treasonable songs or expressions of a like tendency were uttered'. Petition of Darby Kelly,

10 April 1800, NA, Prisoners' Petitions and cases, 467. See also Pollock to Downshire, 21 March 1797, PRONI, D.607/E/214 and n.d., c.1797, NA, State of the Country Papers, 3167, pp. 2–5.

32 Memorandum of Major Sirr, 2 June 1803, NA, 620/67/2 and *Freeman's Journal*, 2 June and 17 December 1803. See also Wells, *Insurrection*, p. 159.

33 Camden to Portland, 7 May 1797, PRO, HO 100/69/251. See also Camden to Portland, 2 April 1798, PRO, HO 100/76/3 and Adjutant-General Hewitt to Lieutenant-General Dundas, 16 March 1798, PRO, HO 100/75/245.

34 See Kevin Whelan, 'The role of the Catholic priest in the 1798 rebellion in county Wexford' in Whelan (ed.), *Wexford; history and society* (Dublin, 1987), p. 299, Cullen, 'The 1798 rebellion', p. 275, Croker, *Researches in the South of Ireland*, pp. 347–8 and Grogan Knox to ——, 5 June 1797, NA, 620/31/38.

35 See Powell, 'economic factor', pp. 144–70.

36 See B. McEvoy, 'The Peep of Day Boys and Defenders in the County Armagh' in *Seanchas Ardmhacha*, 1986, pp. 123–63, Smyth, pp. 114–6 and Elliott,'Defenders', pp. 226–7.

37 *Union Star*, November 1797 in PRO, HO 100/70/236.

38 Camden to [Portland], 15 November 1797, PRO, HO 100/66/59.

39 See Ambrose Coleman, 'The oath of the early orangemen' in *Catholic Bulletin*, X, September 1920, no. 9, pp. 680–90 and Plowden, *Historical Review*, II, p. 537.

40 Camden to [Portland], 15 November 1797, PRO, HO 100/66/59.

41 Edward Hay, *History of the insurrection of the county of Wexford* (Dublin, 1803), p. 80.

42 Stowe MS, RIA, MS A. I. 3. See also Plowden, *Historical Review*, II, p. 661.

43 Byrne, *Memoirs*, I, pp. 8–9.

44 Information of John Mulligan, 21 May 1798, Trinity College Dublin, MS 871.

45 Ibid.

46 Information of Hugh Ollaghan [Woolaghan], 2 January 1798, NA, SOC, 1017/61.

47 Information of Pat Byrne, 4 January 1798, NA, SOC, 1017/61.

48 See Luke Cullen, *Insurgent Wicklow, 1798, the story as written by Revd Bro. Luke Cullen, O.D.C. (1793–1859) with additional material from other Mss*, edited by Myles V. Ronan (Dublin, 1948), p. 66 and Resolutions of special session of the peace, Wicklow, 20 February 1798, NA, 620/35/146.

49 Information of John Myrna [Mernagh], 23 May 1798, TCD, MS 871.

50 See 'They [sic] live and adventures of Joseph Holt, known by the title of General Holt in the Irish Rebellion of '98', Mitchel Library, Sydney, MS A2024 (hereafter cited as Holt MS), p.23.

51 Information of John Tyson, 17 January 1798, NA, SOC 1017/62.

52 Information of Pat Byrne, 4 January 1798, NA, SOC, 1017.

53 Cullen, NLI, MS 9762, p. 11.

54 Hanbidge, *Memories*, p. 54. See also 28 March 1799, NA, 620/17/30/33 and *SNL*, 20 June 1798.

55 Thomas King to ——, 8 April 1801, NA, 620/49/99 and Charles Dickson, *The life of Michael Dwyer with some account of his companions* (Dublin, 1944), pp. 294, 311–2, 338. Mrs. O'Toole of Ballycumber when interviewed in the 1930s recalled family traditions that the Byrnes of Blackrock (Aghavannagh), Birdthistles, Murphys and Heffernans of Roddenagh were all closely related and United Irishmen. Padraig O'Tuathial, 'Wicklow Traditions of 1798' in *Bealoideas*, V, 1935, pp. 154, 158, 161–7.

56 King to Stewart, 12 December 1802 cited in Dickson, *Dwyer*, pp. 207–8. See also Ibid., p. 60, King to Castlereagh, 22 May 1798, NA, 620/3/32/6, Mary Ann Byrne to Luke Cullen, 23 January, NA, MS 5892/7 and King to ——, 25 March 1798, NA, 620/3/51/1. For a detailed genealogy of the Byrnes and an assessment of their role in county affairs see Conor O'Brien, 'The Byrnes of Ballymanus' in Hannigan and Nolan (eds.), *Wicklow: History and Society*, pp. 305–39.

57 Revd P. Dempsey, *Avoca, A history of the Vale*, (Dublin, 1912), p. 27 and O'Brien, 'The Byrnes', p. 338.

58 King to Marsden, 16 January 1803, NA, 620/65/148. Michael Dwyer's cousin and right-hand man Hugh 'Vesty' Byrne of Kirikee was at one time employed by Byrne as a servant. 14 November 1799, NA, 620/17/ 30/62. See also John Edge to Edward Byrne, 20 September 1868, NA, MS 5892/7.

59 King to Marsden, 16 January 1803, NA, 620/65/148. See also Cullen, TCD, MS 1472, pp. 217–8, NLI, MS 8339, pp. 67–72, King to ——, 7 April 1799, NA, 620/10/116/12 and 28 July 1795, NLI, MS 5024.

60 John Joyce, *General Thomas Cloney, Wexford rebel of 1798* (Dublin, 1988), pp. 3, 12, 57–8, Byrne, *Memoirs*, I. p. 108–119, Cullen, '1798 rebellion', p. 271 and Thomas Pakenham, *The Year of Liberty: The story of the great Irish rebellion of 1798* (London, 1969), p. 314.

61 Information of John Murphy, 20 June 1798, NA, 620/38/188. See also Information of Owen Redmond, 23 May 1798, TCD, MS 871 and 'Address to the United Men of Ireland', n.d., [c.1798], NA, 620/52/39. For a full discussion of United Irish finances in Wicklow see O'Donnell, 'Holt', pp. 91–3.

62 R. B. McDowell, 'Proceedings of the Dublin Society of United Irishmen', *Analecta hibernica*, no. 17, p. 80. See also L. M. Cullen, 'Politics and Rebellion', pp. 426–8.

63 3 April 1798, NA, 620/32/228 and Camden to Portland, 13 March 1798, PRO, HO 100/75/218.

64 *FDJ*, 30 July 1793 and *SNL*, 7 April 1796. See also Bartlett, 'moral economy', pp. 41–64.

65 Richard Musgrave, *Memoirs of the Irish Rebellion of 1798*, fourth edition (Fort Wayne, 1995), p. 283 Cullen's sources, who may not have been in a position to comment, refuted this claim. Cullen, T.C.D., MS 1472, p. 175. See also Richard Musgrave, *Memoirs of the different rebellions in Ireland*, 2 vols., 2nd edn., (Dublin, 1802), I, p.372.

66 *FDJ*, 30 July and 1 August 1793. For the Cavan Militia see Seamus O'Loinsigh, 'The burning of Ballinagh' in *Breifne, Journal of Cumman Seanchas Bhreifne*, II, no.7, 1964, p. 361.

67 *NCEP*, 3 September 1795 and Camden to [Portland], 6 August 1796, NA, 620/18/11/1.

68 J. Winder to Cooke, [c.1796], NA, SOC, 3055, William Ridgeway, *A report of the trial of Michael William [sic] Byrne . . .* (Dublin, 1798), pp. 128–32 and Aldborough to Cooke, 9 August 1796, 620/24/97. For Kildare United Irishmen see 10 May 1797, NA, Frazer MS, 1/55, p. 12.

69 Nixon to Pelham, 20 December 1796, NA, SOC, 3053/1–2.

70 Thomas and Richard Dry of Weaver's Square, Dublin, sold a plot of land in Wicklow for £30 in 1791. See R. B. McDowell, 'The personnel of the Dublin Society of United Irishmen', *IHS*, 2, no.5, 1940, p. 32.

71 Thomas Hugo to Pelham, 30 December 1796, NA, 620/26/189. See also *FDJ*, 15 July 1794.

72 Information of Richard Turner, 9 July 1798, NA, 620/39/38. See also Edward Boyle n.d., 1798, NA, 620/52/45, 'B. Senior' to Cooke, 10 December 1796, NA, 620/18/1 and E. Black, 'James Hope (1764–1847), United Irishman' in *Irish Sword*, XIV, pp. 65–6.

73 'Autobiographical memoir of James Hope' in R. R. Madden, *Down and Antrim in '98* (Dublin, n.d.), pp. 104–11.

74 Turner, 9 July 1798, NA, 620/39/38.

75 Camden to Portland, 2 May 1797, PRO, HO 100/69/251. See also 22 May 1798, NA, 620/10/121/58.

76 J. Smith to ——, 15 May 1797, NA, 620/30/83.

77 Keating to ——, 16 April 1803, BM, MS 35378/266.

78 Smith to [Pelham], 16 June 1797, NA, SOC, 3086.

79 King to Castlereagh, 22 May 1798, NA, 620/3/32/6. See also L. M. Cullen, 'Politics and rebellion', pp. 427–8.

80 Smith to [Cooke], 16 May 1797, 620/30/89. See also Smith to Cooke, 15 May 1797, NA, 620/30/83.

81 Information of William Kelly, 3 November 1797, PRO, HO 100/70/237.

82 Nixon to Pelham, 30 May 1797, NA, 620/30/249. See also Captain William West to Pelham, 2 June 1797, NA, 620/31/11A, Smith to [Cooke], 16 May 1797, NA, 620/30/89 and Dickson, *Dwyer*, pp. 370–1. Noble was possibly Edward Noble of Donard who lost goods valued at £81 during the rebellion. June 1803, NA, OP 150/4 (5).

83 Smith to [Cooke], 16 May 1797, NA, 620/30/89. See also 16 May 1797, NA, 620/30/88.

84 Information of Eleanor Ryan, 7 June 1797, NA, 620/31/65. See also Dickson, *Dwyer*, pp. 96–7.

85 Information of James Byrne, 17 July 1804, NA, 620/50/38/78.

86 Benjamin O'Neil Stratford to ——, 22 May 1797, NA, 620/30/143 and 9 June 1797, NA, 620/31/65.

87 O'Neil Stratford to ——, 19 May 1797, NA, 620/30/108.

88 Chapman, *Report*, pp. 8, 9–14.

89 Report of staff surgeon R. M. Peile, 12 February 1802, PRO, HO 100/108/53 and *SNL*, 12 March 1793.

90 *DEP*, 6 November 1794.
91 *Hibernian Journal*, 10 November 1794. After the rebellion Miles O'Neil became the treasurer of the project to rebuild Arklow chapel (for the third time since 1794) and his son-in-law, Cornelius McLaughlin of Usher's Quay, Dublin, received the government grant to carry it out. Kearns to Troy, 8 September 1803, NA, 620/65/118.
92 Senior to Cooke, November 1797, NA, 620/18/3.
93 King to Castlereagh, 22 May 1798, NA, 620/3/32/6.
94 *A list of premiums paid for corn malt and flour from the County of Wicklow to the city of Dublin from 25th day December 1788 to the 24th day of June 1789* republished in *Irish Genealogical Sources, no. 2*, pp. 8–9, 12–13.
95 Hardy to [Cooke], 19 January 1798, NA, 620/35/48. He was later described as an 'extensive dealer reputed very rich'. King to Castlereagh, 22 May 1798, NA, 620/3/32/6. See also article from *WHM*, November 1790 reprinted in *The Irish Harp*, I, no. 1, January 1863, p.33.
96 Byrne, *Memoirs*, I, p. 28.
97 *SNL*, 5 November 1798.
98 King to Castlereagh, 22 May 1798, NA, 620/3/32/6. See also Information of Andrew Corcoran, n.d., 1798, SOC 3060.
99 King to Hardwicke, 7 November 1803, PRO, HO 100/114/172 and NA, 620/7/79/39. Another probable family member was Walter McDaniel who joined the Antrim Militia company stationed in his home town with two others bearing the surname on 1 April 1798 and deserted to the rebels in August 1798. April to August 1798, PRO, War Office 13/2574 and 23 February 1799, NA, 620/17/30/14. Emmet's rocket specialist was Michael McDaniel, 'a dyer by trade, who had some chemical knowledge' and was held responsible for the disastrous explosion in Patrick Street depot on 16 July 1803. Madden, *Emmet*, p. 85. See also Ibid., p. 88. A corroborating connection may be McDaniel's flight to Wicklow after the failure of the plot where he was later arrested. *FDJ*, 4 October 1803.
100 Information of John Sherwood, 5 October 1804, NA, 620/50/92 and Petition of John Byrne, June 1798, NA, 620/7/80/10.
101 'Sketch of the life of Mathew Doyle of Poolahoney [sic] near Arklow' in Cullen, NLI, MS8339. See also Byrne, *Memoirs*, I, pp. 96–7.
102 Byrne, *Memoirs*, I, p.96. See also Joseph Hardy to Cooke, 22 May 1798, NA, 620/37/127.
103 Perry Confession quoted in Dickson, *The Wexford Rising in 1798; its causes and its course* (Tralee, 1955), p. 46. See also Cloney, *Narrative*, p. 6 and Pakenham, *Liberty*, p. 162.
104 Byrne, *Memoirs*, I, p. 114, Joseph Holt to Matthew Doyle, 22 November 1798, NA, 620/57/157 and *The trial of William Byrne of Ballymanus county of Wicklow, esq.* (Dublin, 1799), p. 29. Murphy is listed as holding the rank of captain along with Murt Mernagh of Little Limerick and Nicholas Dixon of Castlebridge. Perry is listed as a colonel. Musgrave, *Rebellions*, II, p. 162.
105 Information of 'W.A.B.' [Thomas Murray], 21 May 1798, NA, 620/3 /32/6, Information of Simon Beakey, 25 May 1798, TCD, MS 871, Information of John Hall, 23 May 1798, TCD, MS 871, *SNL*, 5 November 1798, Dempsey, *Avoca*, pp. 26–7 and Caoimhin de Lion, *The Vale of Avoca* (Dublin, 1970), pp. 24–5. Fr Murray's first appointment following ordination in Salamanca was at St Paul's, Arran Quay, Dublin. He was apparently not a United Irishman and his claims to have dissuaded people from taking the oath was accepted by the bigoted Revd Bayly who remarked that Murray had 'exerted all his influence to preserve the tranquillity of that neighbourhood'. Petition of Revd Daniel Murray, 27 May 1798, (endorsed by Bayly) 19 June 1798, NA, 620/38/181. Dempsey's main source for Murray's experiences in 1798 was the Archbishop's grand-niece, Mrs Dargan. Murray's nephew, James Murray, became first bishop of Maitland, New South Wales, Australia. Patrick O'Farrell, *The Irish in Australia* (Sydney, 1987), p. 112.
106 King to Castlereagh, 22 May 1798, NA, 620/3/32/6. King signalled Murray's prominence in the organization in the phrase 'few others in the county had opportunity of knowing so much.' Murray is identified only as 'W.A.B.' in his statement but confirmation that he was in fact the informer is given in the information of Simon Beakey who explicitly admitted to succeeding 'Tho[ma]s Murray' which corresponds with the claim of 'W.A.B.' to have been 'succeeded by Simon Beakey'. Beakey, 25 May 1798, TCD, MS 871 and 'W.A.B.' [Murray], 21 May 1798, NA, 620/3/32/6.
107 [Murray], 21 May 1798, NA, 620/3/32/6. See also Information of Michael Donnelly, TCD, n.d., [c.May 1798] 869/5, ff. 13.

108 Beakey, 25 May 1798, TCD, MS 871 and 'list of premiums . . . 1791', p. 18. The Beakeys were evidently close to the Grahams and McDaniels as members of all three families supported the petition of fellow Arklow resident John Byrne in June 1799. NA, 620/7/80/10.

109 Beakey, 25 May 1798, TCD, MS 871. A D[avid?] Gilbert who had been arrested by the Antrim Militia was imprisoned on the hulk *John and Esther* in September 1798. This man was apparently released by March 1800 when Lawrence Toole was arrested for robbing him. See 'A Kalender [sic] of the prisoners now in the custody of Tho[ma]s Archer High Sheriff of the county of Wicklow, March 21st 1800.' NA, PPC, 382 and 21 September 1798, NA, 620/7/79/36.

110 [Murray], 21 May 1798, NA, 620/3/32/6.

111 Beakey, 25 May 1798, TCD, MS 871.

112 Mernagh, 23 May 1798, TCD, MS 871. See also Dempsey, *Avoca*, p. 27.

113 [Murray], 21 May 1798, NA, 620/3/32/6.

114 Tyson, 17 and 20 January 1798, NA, SOC, 1017/62.

115 Anon, *Mines Of Wicklow*, pp. 42–3.

116 See *A List of the counties of Ireland and the Yeomanry Corps in each county according to their precedence established by lost on the 1st June 1798* (Dublin, 1798), p. 91 and William Richardson, *History of the origin of the Irish Yeomanry with the steps taken to bring forward the measure previous to its final adoption* (Dublin, 1801).

117 Parnell to Coke, 3 September 1796, NA, 620/18A/6.

118 See King to Lieutenant-Colonel Stewart, 12 December 1802 cited in Dickson, *Dwyer*, pp. 204–5.

119 Ridgeway *Trial of William Michael Byrne*, p. 140.

120 Musgrave, *Rebellions*, 4th edn., p. 297.

121 28 March 1799, NA, 620/17/30/64 and Parnell to Coke, 20 August 1797, NA, 620/18A/6.

122 Cullen cited in Dickson, *Dwyer*, p. 26. For Brady see Petition of Catherine Brady, 9 March 1799, NA, SPP, 436 and Petition of Thomas Brady, 1810, Archives Office of New South Wales [Australia], 43/1846, p. 24.

123 Woolaghan, 2 January 1798, NA, SOC, 1017/62. One of the Traceys met William Kavanagh, Byrne and Martin Doyle at the home of one Hyland in Ballynapark around this time. 28 March 1799, NA, 620/17/30/64.

124 Hardy to Fitzwilliam, 15 March 1798, Wentworth Wodehouse Muniments, NLI, MIC 5641 and Tyson, 17 January 1798, NA, SOC, 1017/62. Woolaghan evidently transferred to the Newtownmountkennedy yeoman cavalry and became notorious in October 1798 when he was acquitted of murdering Thomas Dogherty, a pardoned rebel in Killincarrig. *The Genuine Trial of Hugh Woolaghan, yeoman, by a General Court Martial, held in the barracks of Dublin, on Saturday, October 13, 1798, for the murder of Thomas Dogherty* (Dublin, 1798).

125 Woolaghan, 2 January 1798, NA, SOC, 1017/62.

126 Cullen, NLI, MS 8339, pp. 189–90 and Holt MS, p. 117.

127 Ridgeway, *Trial of William Michael Byrne*, pp. 94–5 and Musgrave, *Rebellions*, 4th edn., p.626.

128 Cullen, NLI, MS 9762, p. 10 and Chavasse, *The story of Baltinglass*, pp. 44–9.

129 3 April 1798, NA, 620/36/228.

130 [Robinson?] to Cooke 9 May 1798, NA, 620/37/43, *DEP*, 25 July 1799, Cullen, *Insurgent*, p. 77 and Chavasse, *Baltinglass*, pp. 44–7.

131 [Robinson?] to Cooke, 19 May 1798, NA, 620/37/109. See also Cullen cited in Dickson, *Dwyer*, pp. 369–70.

132 Cullen, NLI, MS 8339, p. 153.

133 Quoted in Dickson, *Wexford rising*, p. 21.

134 Madden, *Down and Antrim*, pp. 115, 170–3. One of McCabe's most daring exploits was to impersonate a militia officer at Roscommon Spring Assizes and take Richard Dry, another important organizer, into his 'custody'. Dry was later recaptured and transported to New South Wales on the *Minerva* in 1800. Dry's son became the first premier of Tasmania. O'Farrell, *The Irish in Australia*, p. 36. See also Jim Smyth, 'Freemasonry and the United Irishmen' in Dickson, Keogh and Whelan (eds), *The United Irishmen*, pp. 167–75. The Belfast-based informer Smith claimed in August 1796 that the city's United Irishmen were all masons. Smith to Middleton, 17 August 1796, NA, Frazer MS, 2/31.

135 Cullen, NLI, MS 8339, p.153.

136 [Robinson?] to Cooke, 9 May 1798, NA,620/37/43.
137 O'Neil Stratford to ——, n.d., [c.7 August 1797], NA, SOC, 3099.
138 [Murray], 21 May 1798, NA, 620/3/32/6.
139 Information of Richard Bourke, 25 July 1797, NA, Frazer MS 1/44.
140 Muster Roll and Pay list of the Antrim Militia, PRO, WO, 13/2574, Holt, 22 November 1798, NA, 620/41/39A and Luke Cullen, *Personal recollections of Wexford and Wicklow insurgents of 1798* (Enniscorthy, 1959), p. 23.
141 [Robinson?] to Cooke, 19 May 1798, NA, 620/37/109. See also [Robinson?] to Cooke, 9 May 1798, NA, 620/37/43 and Dickson, *Dwyer*, p. 37. The Ballyhook man was very probably the Pierse Hayden employed as a slater on Donoughmore chapel in April 1802. Hanbidge, *Memories*, p. 100.
142 Senior to Cooke, n.d., NA, 620/18/2. See also [Robinson?] to Cooke, 9 May 1798, NA, 620/37/43B. An important connection clearly existed between the Coogan and Brophy families of west Wicklow: in January 1789 William Brophy of Rathmoon employed James Coogan to carry 336 stones of oats to Dublin. Brophy also used one John Bryan to cary a further 350 stone from Rathmoon on 24 January. 'List of premiums . . . 1789', pp. 10–11.
143 William Wickham to Castlereagh, 28 February 1799 in Londonderry (ed), *Memoirs and correspondence of Viscount Castlereagh*, 12 vols. (London, 1848), II, p. 185.
144 Senior to Cooke, n.d., NA, 620/18/2.
145 Cullen quoted in Dickson, *Dwyer*, p. 369. Imaal area yeomen John Hawkins of Muskaduff, Thomas Hawkins of Colvinstown and loyalist Maurice Hawkins of Mugduff all had their houses burned by the rebels in 1798. See 'A list of suffering loyalists', NLI, MIC 7665.
146 Burr's school was closed between 1798 and 1803 but re-opened in Donard where he taught until his death at a great age about 1820. O'Toole, *Clan O'Toole*, II, p. 516.
147 Cullen quoted in Dickson, *Dwyer*, pp. 369–70.
148 Cullen, NLI, MS 8339, p. 153. See also Cullen quoted in Dickson, *Dwyer*, p. 370.
149 O'Tuathail, 'Wicklow traditions of 1798', pp. 154–88.
150 See Dickson, *Dwyer*, p. 25.
151 Quoted in Cullen, *Insurgent*, p. 74. See also Cullen cited in Dickson, *Dwyer*, p. 370.
152 Cullen cited in Dickson, *Dwyer*, p. 26. See also Ruan O'Donnell, 'Michael Dwyer, The Wicklow Chief' in Bob Reece (ed.), *Irish Convict Lives* (Sydney, 1993), pp. 14–50.
153 [Murray], 21 May 1798, NA, 620/3/32/6.
154 Information of John Waters, 11 July 1798 NA, 620/39/51. See also James M'Ghee to ——, 11 July 1798, NA, 620/39/51 and Thomas King to General Sir Charles Asgill, 16 January 1803, NA, 620/65/148.
155 Waters and M'Ghee to ——, 11 July 1798, NA, 620/39/51.
156 Ridgeway, *Trial of William Michael Byrne*, pp. 116–7.
157 For Edward Byrne see O'Brien, 'Byrnes of Ballymanus', p. 320 and Dickson, *Dwyer*, p. 210.
158 Ridgeway, *Trial of William Michael Byrne*, pp. 116–7. Murray stated he that he 'did not know [the] *delegate* from Shillelagh'. emphasis added, 21 May 1798, NA, 620/3/32/6. Murray was either unable or unwilling to name every delegate in attendance and was evidently confused by which baronies some represented. From other sources it is possible to correct his errors and fill in the names of those who were in Annacurra. Of the three baronies not represented by two men, Arklow's second delegate (O'Neil) was merely absent, Ballinacor's second was John Lynch, who Murray neglected to mention, leaving only Shillelagh with a delegate unaccounted for.
159 Ridgeway, *Trial of William Michael Byrne*, pp. 94–5.
160 Wainwright to Fitzwilliam, 12 November 1797, NLI, MIC 5641.
161 Wainwright to Fitzwilliam, 27 January 1797, NLI, MIC 5641.
162 See 28 May 1799, NA, 620/17/30/57 and 14 November 1799, NA, 620/17/30/41.
163 Hardy to Fitzwilliam, 27 November 1797, NLI, MIC 5641.
164 Wainwright to Fitzwilliam, 9 November 1797, NLI, MIC 5641, 14 November 1799, NA, 620/17/30/42, Captain J. B. Beasley to Littlehales, 28 January 1800, NA, PPC, 411, Petition of John Fowler, 31 May 1800, NA, PPC, 409–10, 'List of premiums . . . 1791', p. 16 and Petition of Patrick Murray, June 1800, NA, 620/9/100/9. See also Ruan O' Donnell, 'Croppy Biddy' Dolan, "libidinous wretch" and informer of 1798' in *Cameos, women and history* (Dublin, 1990), pp. 26–9. Fowler's Christian name is incorrectly given as Robert in the official record of his court martial, 11 April 1799, NA, 620/17/30/19.

165 Ridgeway, *Trial of William Michael Byrne*, pp. 94–5.
166 Cullen cited in Dickson, *Dwyer*, p.56. See also Information of John Murphy, 20 June 1798, NA, 620/38/188.
167 [Murray], 21 May 1798, NA, 620/3/32/6.
168 King to Castlereagh, 22 May 1798, NA, 620/3/32/6.
169 27 November 1799, NA, 620/17/30/75.
170 Cullen quoted in Dickson, *Dwyer*, p. 56. William Michael Byrne and Garret Byrne had a common grandfather, Garret Byrne of Ballymanus, who had married Miss Colclough of Tintern and had three sons (Garret, John and Colclough). Colclough Byrne (who married Miss Galway of Cork, great-grandniece of James, first Duke of Ormond) was William Michael Byrne's father and uncle of Garret son of Garret. O'Hart, *Irish Pedigrees* (New York, 1923), I, p. 618.
171 Dickson, *Dwyer*, p. 56.
172 Luke Cullen greatly respected the Byrnes of Ballymanus and described them as 'the representatives of the first family in the Co. Wicklow and not inferior to any family in Europe.' NLI, MS 8339, p. 67. This admiration and knowledge of the leading roles played by Garret and 'the high blooded and gallant young gentleman' William Byrne influenced Cullen's assessment of their pre-rebellion status in the organization. Garret's role was inflated and William's diminished. Cullen, *Insurgent*, p. 66. When collecting folklore for the Ordnance Survey in 1838, Richard O'Donovan was informed at Ballymanus that Garret Byrne had been 'the senior representative of the Gaval Raghnuil [clan Ranelagh]' and a man of 'chieftain height, perfect symmetry of limbs, dauntless courage and–what is always an attribute of a true hero-universal benevolence'. O'Donovan *et al.*, *Letters*, p. 51. The Ballymanus estate had been granted to Garret Byrne by Sir Lawrence Esmond of Clonegal in January 1700 together with lands at Macreddin and Clogheenagh. O'Hart, *Pedigrees*, I, p. 619.
173 'A Milesian' [Luke Cullen], *Catholic Telegraph*, 29 September 1856. See also Dickson, *Dwyer*, p. 25.
174 See Gilbert, *Documents*, pp. 153–4.
175 Ridgeway, *Trial of William Michael Byrne*, pp. 95–5.
176 King to Castlereagh, 22 May 1798, NA, 620/3/32/6.
177 An even less convincing argument is the fact that two of his brothers, Colclough and John, were lieutenants in the Carlow Militia. Dickson, *Dwyer*, p. 58. See also King to Asgill, 16 January 1803, NA, 620/65/148.
178 Dickson, *Dwyer*, p. 60.
179 Musgrave, *Rebellions*, 4th edn., p. 823. A truncated version of this list is printed in Dickson's later work, *The Wexford Rising in 1798*, which omits all Wicklow and Kildare rebels. Dickson, *Wexford Rising*, pp. 187–8.
180 Cullen, *Recollections*, p. 36. For a dubious folk account of Byrne's exploits in 1798 see *Wicklow Star*, 28 November 1898. Byrne and several witnesses at his trial claimed that Daniel Kirwan had led the 'Ballymanus division' as the Wicklow contingent in the north Wexford rebel army was called. Kirwan probably only captained the rebels who formed the corps raised in the Ballymanus area. Miles Byrne recalled that when Kirwan was killed at Vinegar Hill on 21 June 1798 he was second-in-command to William Byrne. *The Tryal [sic] of William Byrne of Ballymanus*, pp. 29–30, 32, 42 and Byrne, *Memoirs*, I, p. 128.
181 See O'Brien, 'Byrnes of Ballymanus', pp. 314–5.
182 Caldwell to Cornwallis, 21 August 1799 in (Dublin, 1799), *Trial of William Byrne*, p. 79. An anonymous loyalist asserted that 'Mr Hugo was a most active magistrate of the Co. Wicklow in whose house Byrne was often hospitably treated.' n.d., [1800/1801], NA, S.P.P., 457.
183 Quoted in Dickson, *Dwyer*, pp. 58–9.
184 Cullen quoted in Dickson, *Dwyer*, p. 36.
185 23 April 1799, NA, 620/17/30/56 and O'Toole, *The O'Tooles*, p. cxviii.
186 Cullen, NLI, MS 8339, p. 70. See also Dickson, *Dwyer*, pp. 200, 306.
187 Cullen, NLI, MS 8339, p. 70. See also Cullen, TCD, MS 1472, p. 217 and O'Donnell, 'Holt', pp. 97–8.
188 O'Donnell, 'Holt', Chapter 2 and Ruan O'Donnell and Bob Reece, 'Clean Beast', pp. 7–42.
189 Holt MS, pp. 16–9.
190 King to —— , 16 January 1803, NA, 620/65/148.
191 *Wicklow Star*, 28 November 1898 and Holt MS, pp. 15–20.

192 Holt MS, p. 149 and Cullen, NLI, MS 8339, p. 41.
193 Cullen, NLI, MS 8339, p. 202, Madden, *Down and Antrim*, pp. 180–1 and O'Donnell, 'Holt', pp. 59–61.
194 Musgrave, *Rebellions*, 4th edn., p.823. List of Commissary John Brennan n.d., [4–5] June 1798, NA, 620/51/225.
195 Ridgeway, *Trial of William Michael Byrne*, p. 114.
196 [Murray], 21 May 1798, NA, 620/3/32/6 and Information of John Murphy, 20 June 1798, NA, 620/38/188.
197 Camden to Portland, 13 March 1798, PRO, HO 100/75/218.
198 Ridgeway, *Trial of William Michael Byrne*, pp. 120–2 and Cullen, *Insurgent*, p. 16.
199 W. Edmonds to ——, n.d. [1797], NA, 620/53/138. Edmonds also suspected that John McGuire and his brothers, weavers from the Scalp [Enniskerry], were United Irishmen and that one Horan who lived near Rathfarnham was a captain.
200 Ridgeway, *Trial of William Michael Byrne*, p. 115.
201 ——, to Castlereagh, 7 August 1798, PRO, HO 100/78/34.
202 1 February 1798, PRO, HO 100/75/199–202. Ryan and Miller were the key prosecution witnesses against Byrne when tried for treason in July 1798 and were held in Dublin Castle along with Maurice McCue while Lord Powerscourt and others prepared the case. In June 1798 Powerscourt reported that McCue had 'prevaricated in his evidence' against Byrne but that the others would be credible in court. Powerscourt to [Cooke], 30 June 1798, NA, 620/38/262.
203 Ridgeway, *Trial of William Michael Byrne*, pp. 128–32 and Delamere, 10 April 1800, NA, PPC, 346. The secretaries or sergeants included James Ryan, Maurice McCue, Edward Reilly, Charles Toole, William Booth (a treasurer from Glencree), John Sutton (Behana), Philip Byrne, Maurice Hanlon, Robert Parker, Christopher Reilly, John Kirwan, James Edwards, Pat Ward, Thomas Meagan, Francis Lamb, Christopher McMahon, Pat Brown, William Rutledge, Laurence McEnery, Michael McGuirk, Garret Quinn, Loughlin Sinnot, James Roach and Phil Byrne.
204 Information of George Coleman and John Mulligan, 21 May 1798, TCD, MS 871.
205 Coleman, 21 May 1798, TCD, MS 871. See also Cullen, *Insurgent*, p. 15 and Kelly, 24 May 1798, TCD, MS 871.
206 Mulligan, 21 May 1798, TCD, MS 871.
207 O'Hart, *Pedigrees*, I, p. 618 and Brennan list, n.d. [4–5 June 1798], NA, 620/51/225.
208 Ridgeway, *Trial of William Michael Byrne*, p. 128.
209 Delamere, 10 April 1800, NA, PPC, 346. Ordnance Surveyor Curry encountered the Revd Dr Delamere who kept a boarding school at Hollybrook near Powerscourt. O'Donovan *et al.*, *Letters*, p. 66.
210 See Daire Keogh, 'Fr John Martin's mission to the United Irishmen of Wicklow' in *Eighteenth-Century Ireland*, VII, 1992, p. 130.
211 See John Edwards to Cooke, 5 March 1798, NA, SOC, 3160.
212 Edwards to Meath, 2 December 1796, NA, 620/26/92A. For the Welsh origins of Edwards family see Chris Smal (ed.), *Ancient Rathdown and Saint Crispin's Cell, A uniquely historic Landscape* (Greystones, 1993), p. 21. Edwards married a Ms Wright of Nottingham in London on 14 February 1780 and led the 'Rathdown regiment of horse, together with the Rathdown infantry' the following April when they were reviewed in Dublin by the Duke of Leinster. *WHM*, February 1780, p. 170 and April 1780, p. 231.
213 Cullen, *Insurgent*, p. 15, Monck to Cooke, 19 March 1798, NA, 620/36/27 and *Catholic Telegraph*, 23 August 1856.
214 See NA, nd, [c. March 1798], 620/52/164 and 620/53/52 and Cullen, *Insurgent*, pp. 14–5.
215 See Muster list and pay rolls of the King's County Militia, 1798, PRO, WO 13/2961. C. H. Andfield to Lieutenant-Colonel Browne, 1 August 1798, NLI, MS 25,049. For an account of King's Countymen and 5th Dragoon defectors drilling the rebels in August 1798 see Information of Edward McLaughlin, 14 July 1798 and Bartholomew Connolly, 24 July 1798, NA, 620/37/73 and ——, to Lieutenant-General Peter Craig, 18 and 19 July 1798, PRO, HO 100/86/57–8.
216 Cullen TCD MS 1472, p. 197 and *Insurgent*, p. 25.
217 Cullen, *Insurgent*, pp. 25–7.
218 *SNL*, 17 April 1795.
219 King to ——, 25 March 1798, NA, 620/3/51/1, *SNL*, 19–20 May 1794 and *FDJ*, 20 May 1794.

220 Murphy, 20 June 1798, NA, 620/38/188.
221 Cullen, *Insurgent*, p. 29. See also 16 April 1796, NLI, MS 5024.
222 All 'Names of persons who have been arrested in the late rebellion and have fled from justice', August 1798, *Irish Statutes 30 Geo. III Chapter 80* and PRO, HO 100/66/340.
223 Cullen, *Insurgent*, p. 36.
224 The well-placed informer Boyle reported that this first meeting occurred '5 or 6 weeks back' but it is unclear whether this is to be backdated from his date of writing (6 December which would date the meeting towards the very end of October or beginning of November) or from 30 November 1797 when the meeting he described in that letter took place (implying a mid to late October first session). 'Senior' to [Cooke], 6 December 1797, NA, 620/18/3. The likelihood is that there were three meetings in McVeaghs as it is improbable that Boyle would have described the two-week interval between 16 and 30 November, when it seems that two meetings took place, as six weeks. This would have followed an earlier meeting in mid to late October 1797.
225 'Senior' to Cooke, 16 November 1797, NA, 620/18/3. See also 'Senior' to Cooke, 6 December 1797, NA, 620/18/3 and n.d., NA, 620/18/2.
226 'Senior' to Cooke, November and 14 December 1797, NA, 620/18/3.
227 Madden, *Down and Antrim*, p. 114.
228 'Senior' to Cooke, 14 December 1797, NA, 620/18/3.
229 'Senior' to Cooke, 6 December 1797, NA, 620/18/3.
230 Tyson, 20 January 1798, NA, SOC, 1017/6.
231 *Union Star* cited in Pakenham, *Liberty*, p. 47.
232 John Murphy, 20 June 1798, NA, 620/38/188.
233 27 August 1797, NA, Frazer MS 1/17.
234 King to Castlereagh, 22 May 1798, NA, 620/3/32/6.
235 *Wicklow Star*, 28 November 1898. The long article in this issue, 'Billy Byrne of Ballymanus, The history of the Wicklow Patriot', was written by Ms C. M. Doyle who was a direct descendant of John Loftus. Her great-grandmother, Mary Loftus, and that woman's daughter, Bridget, allegedly recovered Byrne's body after his execution in September 1799. Bridget Loftus appeared at Byrne's trial on 28 June and claimed that her father John and Byrne's father were 'cousin germans' and that both were related to Richard O'Reilly. She was aware of two meetings which had taken place in her father's house 'of United Irishmen, for the purpose of carrying on treasonable designs' but had given no information to the authorities.
236 Ridgeway, *Trial of William Michael Byrne*, pp. 115–6 and *Trial of William Byrne*, p. 39.
237 Murphy, 20 June 1798, NA, 620/38/188 and M'Ghee to ——, 11 July 1798, NA, 620/39/51. The County Committee of Wicklow, December 1797

Ballinacor	William Young, Ballinacor
	John Lynch, Roundwood
Talbotstown	Thomas Kavanagh, Talbotstown/Baltinglass
	John Dwyer, Seskin, Imaal
Shillelagh	John Waters, Johnstown
	[Edward?/Garret?] Byrne, Tinahely
Arklow	Philip O'Neil, Arklow Town
	John Lacey, Wicklow Town
Rathdown	William Michael Byrne, Parkhill
	Thomas Miller, Powerscourt
Newcastle	Richard O'Reilly, Newtownmountkennedy
	John Byrne, Cronroe

238 Murray further claimed that 'John Lacey and P. O'Neill attended the [Francis street] committee in Dublin as county representatives' and that 'Lac[e]y attended a Provincial meeting in January last but P. O'Neill did not attend.' However, it is unlikely that both Arklow baronial delegates monopolized the provincial slots leaving all other baronies unrepresented. Murray clearly meant that O'Neil and Lacey were the Arklow men on the county committee of Wicklow which had met several times in the city and, while Lacey may have attended a meeting of the provincial committee in Dublin, he was not one of the accredited delegates. The provincial men were elsewhere named by Murray as William Michael Byrne and O'Reilly. [Murray], 21 May 1798, NA, 620/3/32/6. Murray also divulged in May 1798 that 'Lacey was No. 2', an allusion to a coded reference to that post in the Report

of the County Committee dated 22 January 1798. This tallies with the statement of a lesser placed informer that Lacey was 'the head treasurer for the county Wicklow'. Murray, Ibid., Report of the Wicklow County Committee, 22 January 1798, NLI, MIC 5641 and Information of Andrew Corcoran, n.d., [late 1798] NA, SOC, 3060.

239 [Murray], 21 May 1798, NA, 620/3/32/6.
240 Ridgeway, *Trial of William Michael Byrne*, p. 116.
241 [Murray], 21 May 1798, NA, 620/3/32/6.
242 Ridgeway, *Trial of William Michael Byrne*, p. 116.
243 [Murray], 21 May 1798, NA, 620/3/32/6.
244 Ridgeway, *Trial of William Michael Byrne*, pp. 116–7.
245 *Trial of William Byrne*, p. 40.
246 Ridgeway, *Trial of William Michael Byrne*, pp. 116–7.
247 See Musgrave, *Rebellions*, 4th edn., pp. 625–7.
248 Ibid. Arklow barony had five of its members in prison, Shillelagh eight, Ballinacor fifteen, Talbotstown fifteen and Newcastle two.
249 Ibid. Lacey received £4 10s for the prisoners on 18 November 1797 from John Murphy of Knockrobbin, treasurer of a Newcastle company. Murphy claimed to have 'never received contributions' from more than 84 of its 160. If such irregular financial affairs were typical in Newcastle it would explain in part why the barony lacked armaments. Murphy, 20 June 1798, NA, 620/38/188.
250 Musgrave, *Rebellions*, 4th edn., p. 625. See also [Murray], 21 May 1798, NA, 620/3/32/6.
251 Musgrave, *Rebellions*, 4th edn., p. 625. For diagram of the structure adopted in Rathdown under the aegis of Miller, Ryan and Byrne of Parkhill see Ridgeway, *Trial of William Michael Byrne*, p. 128. This model provided for ten societies to form a company under a captain (120 men) and eight companies a regiment under a colonel (960). It is notable that Joseph Holt in his often disingenuous memoirs acknowledged that he only assumed 'the title of colonel' in June 1798 when he commanded '960 men' which points to the identification of the Wicklow rebel officers with the obsolete regimental format. The electoral irregularities caused by the disruptive impact of government coercion in April/May 1798 may well have given rise to the type of dispute regarding rank which dogged Holt and led to factionalism in the rebellion. Holt MS, p.30, Sproule to Cooke, 19 September 1798, NA, 620/40/76 and O'Donnell, 'Holt', pp. 165–6.
252 Musgrave, *Rebellion*, 4th edn., p. 825.
253 26 February 1798, PRO, HO 100/75/132.
254 Pakenham, *Liberty*, pp. 53–4 and Camden to Portland, 13 March 1798, PRO, HO 100/75/218.
255 Arthur Wolfe to Camden, 26 March 1798, PRO, HO 100/75/292 and William Ridgeway, *A report of the trial of John McCann upon an indictment for high treason* (Dublin, 1798), pp. 38–49.
256 [Murray], 21 May 1798, NA, 620/3/32/6.
257 Ibid.
258 Information of John Murray, n.d., Sirr Papers, TCD, MS 869/5, f.16.

CHAPTER THREE

1 Address to the inhabitants of the County of Wicklow, 3 April 1798 in Musgrave, *Rebellions*, 4th edn., p. 691.
2 John T. Gilbert, *Documents relating to Ireland, 1795–1804* (new ed., Dublin,1970), p. 154.
3 Cullen, *Insurgent*, p. 8. One report claimed that thirty prosecution witnesses had been killed by the United Irishmen. *FDJ*, 13 February 1798.
4 Information of Garret Quinn, 25 May 1798, TCD, MS 871.
5 Hardy to Cooke, 14 May 1798, NA, 620/3/32/5. See also [Robinson] to Cooke, 7 May 1798, NA, 620/37/39, Moreton to John Lees, 22 May 1798, NA,620/37/125 and Donnelly, 'overview of local administration', p. 863. In May 1798 500 shafts were found in Dublin's Bridgefoot Street. Mrs H. to Clarke, 23 May 1798, NLI, MS 13, 837. See also *FDJ*, 11 June 1791, Wakefield, *Ireland*, I, pp. 569–71, Eoin Neeson, *A history of Irish forestry* (Dublin, 1991), pp. 305–10 and Shaw Mason, *Statistical Survey*, II, p. 27.

6 Information of John Myrna [Mernagh], 23 May 1798, TCD, MS 871. For Mernagh of Glenmalure see Cullen, *Insurgent*, p. 51 and Dickson, *Dwyer*, pp. 290–3.

7 Information of Terence Kinselagh, 28 May 1798, TCD, MS 871. Musgrave's version of this document contains transcription errors. Musgrave, *Rebellions*, 4th edn., p. 693.

8 Quinn, 25 May 1798, TCD, MS 871. See also Hall, 23 May 1798, TCD, MS 871 and [Murray], 21 May 1798, NA, 620/3/32/6.

9 O'Neil Stratford to John Stratford, 1 April 1798, NA, S.O.C., 1017/66, Ridgeway, *Trial of William Michael Byrne*, pp. 94–5 and Dickson, *Dwyer*, p. 172.

10 Luke Cullen, *Personal recollections of Wexford and Wicklow insurgents of 1798* (Enniscorthy, 1959), p. 43, Edward Hay, *History of the insurrection of Wexford* (Dublin, 1803), pp. 215–7, Camden to Portland, 25 May 1798, PRO, HO 100/76/275 [Murray], 21 May 1798, NA, 620/3/32/6.

11 Quoted in Dickson, *Dwyer*, p. 409.

12 Information of Michael Dwyer, 11 January 1804, PRO, HO 100/ 124/26 and Bartlett, 'Masters of the Mountains', p. 407. A less accurate copy of the examination is printed in Dickson, *Dwyer*, pp. 253–7.

13 [Murray], 21 May 1798, NA, 620/3/32/6. See also John Byrne to Cornwallis, n.d., [c.July 1799], NA, 620/7/80/5 and 17 June 1799, NA, 620/7/80/10.

14 Byrne, n.d., [c.July] 1799, NA, 620/7/80/10. John's brother Michael was a master's mate with Sandwith and Robinson of Dublin from 1791–9 but afterwards associated with 'the most disaffected people in and about Wicklow'. He was suspected of smuggling in 1802 when tobacco and arms were thought to have been landed near the family farm. Michael Byrne owned a half share in a privateer valued at £2,200 which was captured briefly by the French in 1802. Having made his escape Byrne was detained on other vessels by both the Spanish and Danish navies who suspected him, apparently unjustly, of piracy. King to ——, 7 November 1802, PRO, HO 100/114/171 and Leigh to Wickham, 14 November 1803, PRO, HO 100/114/175.

15 Hardy to Cooke, 19 January 1798, NA, 620/35/48. See also King to ——, 7 November 1803, PRO, HO 100/114/172, King to ——, 25 March 1798, NA, 620/3/51/1, [Murray], 21 May 1798, NA, 620/3/32/6 and Beakey, 25 May 1798, TCD, MS 871.

16 Holt, 16 November 1798, NA, 620/41/39A. See also King to ——, 7 November 1803, PRO, HO 100/114/172, Hardy to Cooke, 19 January 1798, NA, 620/35/48, Hardy to Castlereagh, 22 May 1798, NA, 620/3/ 32/6 and 620/37/128, Hardy to Cooke, 27 May 1798, NA, 620/37/186 and Bayly to Parnell, n.d., [late] 1797, NA, 620/18A/6.

17 Cullen, NLI, MS 8339, pp. 70–1. See also O'Donnell, 'Holt', pp. 97–9.

18 William James to Cooke, 20 December 1798, NA, SOC, 3250. See also April 1797, NLI, MS 5024 and Charles Coates to Samuel Faulkner, 15 July 1797, Coates Correspondence, NLI, MIC, 1576.

19 *FDJ*, 10 August 1797 and *HC*, 18 August 1797. The *Journal* made political capital out of the incident on 12 August by condemning the *Dublin Evening Post, Hibernian Journal* and *Saunder's Newsletter* for 'attempting to palliate if not apologize for the authors of this bloody act' by pointing out that McCormick was an informer.

20 See Benson to Sirr, 26 July 1803, TCD, MS 869/7, f.25. For Benson's undistinguished career in Blessington until his resignation in 1809 see Maguire, *Downshire estates*, pp. 184, 255.

21 *FDJ*, 15 and 19 August 1797.

22 For a complete list see *FDJ*, 30 November 1797.

23 [Smith] to Pelham, 15 September 1797, NA, SOC, 3111.

24 [Smith] to [Cooke], 16 June 1797, NA, SOC, 3086.

25 Cullen, NLI, MS 8339, p. 193. See also Gilbert, *Documents*, pp. 10–12.

26 *FDJ*, 12 September 1797. See also *FDJ*, 12 August 1797 and *SNL*, 10 August 1797.

27 *FDJ*, 19, 22 and 29 August 1797 and 3 May 1798, *HC*, 24 August 1797 and Musgrave, *Rebellions*, 4th edn., pp. 287–8.

28 *HC*, 24 August 1797 See also *SNL*, 9 March 1795 and 31 March 1797, *FDJ*, 21 September 1797 and William Ridgeway, *A report of the trial of Robert Gore . . .* (Dublin, 1797).

29 See George Taylor, *An History of the rise, progress and suppression of the rebellion in the county of Wexford, in the year 1798* (Dublin, 1800), p. 24.

30 *FDJ*, 10 August 1797 and *WHM*, February 1784, p. 341.

31 Camden to Downshire, 4 January 1797, PRONI, D.607/E/7. See also L. M. Cullen, 'Politics and Rebellion', pp. 434–7.

32 *FDJ*, 30 September 1797 and *Dublin Gazette*, 1 December 1796.

33 [Henry Moreton] to —— , 26 September 1797, NA, SOC, 3120.

34 *FDJ*, 30 September 1797.

35 Stratford to [Pelham], 24 September 1797, NA, SOC, 3119/1.

36 [Robinson] to ——, 7 May 1798, NA, 620/37/35.

37 Mary Leadbeater, *The Leadbeater papers, the annals of Ballitore*, 2 vols. (London, 1862), I, p. 210. Deposition of William Cooke, 24 September 1797, NA, SOC, 3119/2 and *FDJ*, 1 October 1797.

38 [Robinson] to ——, 27 May 1798, NA, 620/37/35. Robinson was described by Leadbeater as 'an industrious intelligent little man . . . [of] very liberal sentiments, and rather more in the *new way* than one should expect from his cloth'. Leadbeater, *Papers*, I, p. 209.

39 Drennan to McTier, 29 September 1797 in *Letters*, p. 262. See also [Smith] to Pelham, 15 September 1797, NA, SOC, 3111.

40 *FDJ*, 30 September 1797.

41 *Press*, 5 October 1797.

42 *FDJ*, 9 and 27 May 1797.

43 Gilbert (ed.), *Calender*, XV, p. 34. This was a rare accolade for anti-insurgent services in the pre-Rebellion period and had last been awarded to a Wicklow resident in 1794 when Lord Rossmore, then simply General Cunningham, was honoured. It may be that Lord Mayor Thomas Fleming,who kept a house at Diamond Hill (Roundwood), influenced the bestowing of the honour on Stratford. Fleming's links to the Ballinacor conservative magistrates led to a rebel attack on his property in June 1798. *SNL*, 20 June 1798, Gilbert, *Calender*, XIV, pp. 371, 428 and XV, p. 11. Nicholas Doran, tried at Baltinglass on 22 September 1797 and dispatched to a Waterford convict depot where he spent up to four years before being transported on the Atlas II, was probably one of Stratford's successes. Archives Office of New South Wales [Australia], 4/4004, 1 May 1801, PRO, HO 100/106/41. Doran probably belonged to the Protestant innkeeping family who lived between Tuckmill and Baltinglass. Dickson, *Dwyer*, p. 97.

44 *FDJ*, 8 June 1797.

45 See Furlong, *Fr John Murphy*, p. 13 and *FDJ*, 9, 13 and 30 July 1793.

46 *FDJ*, 4 November 1797. See also Ibid., 19 April 1798.

47 Stratford had searched for the 4th Dragoons imposter with his yeomen and 'the remainder of the [North] Cork [militia].' Stratford to [Pelham], 24 September 1797, NA, SOC, 3119/1. Henry Moreton also mentioned that the Humewood United Irishman had been handed over to 'the Cork militia' to escort him to Wicklow Gaol. [Morton] to [Pelham?], 26 September 1797, NA, SOC, 3120. See also Hardy to Fitzwilliam, 24 December 1797, NLI, MIC 5641 and Leadbeater, *Papers*, I, p. 210.

48 Memo of Mr Connor, 11 November 1804, NA, OP 198/15 (12). See also Memorial of Major Hardy, [c. 1804], NA, OP 198/15 (10) and 'Lieut[enant] Col[onel] Hardy's charge for Brig[adie]r General allowances allowed by Government in 1797 & 1798', n.d., [c. 1798], NA, OP 198/15 (8).

49 'Major Hardy's Journal of the principal occurrences in Ireland and principally in the county of Wicklow between September 1797 and 1798 when the French landed and surrendered at Ballinamuck in which major Hardy was engaged' in Wentworth Wodehouse Muniments, Sheffield city library, F.30 and NLI, MIC, 5641, entry for 27 September 1797 (hereafter cited as 'Hardy Journal'). The 'journal' is not a day-by-day account of his experiences but rather an intermittent commentary written some time after the events described. Many of the references are vague and incorrect, e.g., Hardy records that the Battle of Newtownmoutkennedy occurred on 27 May 1798 when it was actually fought three days later. Hardy estimated that he suffered losses of £14,000 arising out of the rebellion and his account was probably written in order to obtain a pension or some other form of compensation, hence its collation with the Fitzwilliam papers.

50 Hardy Memorial, NLI, Melville MS.

51 Hardy Journal, September 1797.

52 PRO, WO 68/402/(i), pp. 218, 220. See also Hardy memorial, n.d., NLI, Melville MS and Dickson, *Dwyer*, Appendix, VIII, p. 373.

53 *Press*, 9 November 1797. This otherwise useful account erroneously stated that Henniker commanded the Fifth Dragoon Guards in Carlow.

54 See McDowell, *Ireland in the age*, pp. 552, 571–2, Blayney to —— , 26 April 1797, NA, 620/29/314 and *Press*, 9 November 1797.

55 —— , to Wilkinson, 14 July 1797, NA, SOC, 3097 and Giffard to Cooke, 5 June 1797, NA, 620/31/36.
56 Robert Cunningham to Cooke, 31 October 1795, NA, OP 46/2/3 and Ryan, *Antiquities of the county of Carlow*, p. 316.
57 Wainwright to Fitzwilliam, 28 November 1797, NLI, MIC 5641 and Bayly quoted in Mason, *Statistical Account*, II, pp. 63–4.
58 Hardy Journal, December 1797. See also n.d., [*c*.1799], NA, 620/52/9.
59 In February 1798 Hardy asserted that from 2 October 1797 he held an 'extensive command from Blessington to Enniscorthy & latterly to Wexford'. Hardy to Pelham, 27 February 1798, NLI, MIC 5641.
60 Hardy Journal, 29 May 1798.
61 Camden to Portland, 15 November 1797, PRO, HO 100/66/60.
62 Wainwright to Fitzwilliam, 9 November 1797, NLI, MIC 5641.
63 Mulligan, 21 May 1798, TCD, MS 871 and Musgrave, *Rebellions*, 4th edn., p. 287.
64 Musgrave, *Rebellions*, 4th edn., p. 287.
65 Camden to Portland,15 November 1797, PRO, HO 100/66/60. See also *FDJ*, 12 October 1797, Wainwright to Fitzwilliam, 9 November 1797, NLI, MIC 5641. Frazer, *Guide*, p. 32, Robert Ross to Downshire, 24 May 1798, PRONI, D.607/F/183, McDowell, *Ireland in the age*, p. 589 and *SNL*, 10 May 1793 and 15 May 1795.
66 Camden to Portland, 15 November 1797, PRO, HO 100/66/60
67 William Patrickson to Cooke, 27 October 1797, NA, SOC, 3126 See also Maguire, *Downshire estates*, p. 5 and *Dublin Gazette*, 11 February 1790.
68 John Bird [i.e., Smith] to Sirr, n.d. [*c*.1800] in Madden, *United*, I, p. 497. See also Patrickson to Cooke, 27 October 1797, NA, SOC, 3126, Wainwright to Fitzwilliam, 23 December 1797, NLI, MIC 5641 and *SNL*, 12 March 1795.
69 Dawes to [Smith], 31 October 1797 in Madden, *United*, IV, p. 47 and Gilbert, *Documents* , pp. 10–12.
70 Shannon to Boyle, 14 September [1798], PRONI, D.207/A3/3/118. Slighting allusions to Milltown continued into the early nineteenth century; *Finn's Leinster Journal* of 10 October 1801 took pains to point out that the 'notorious gaol breaker Captain Hughes had been arrested when 'in possession of a house near the Earl of Milltown's, at Russborough'.
71 John Patrickson to Downshire, 22 June 1798, PRONI, D.607/F/263.
72 Patrickson to Cooke, 27 October 1797, NA, SOC, 3126.
73 Patrickson to Downshire, 5 February 1799, PRONI, D.607/G/45.
74 See Maxwell, *Country and town*, pp. 79, 82–3 and Craig, *The architecture of Ireland*, pp. 188–90.
75 *FDJ*, 30 September 1797. See also Ibid., 11 November 1797.
76 Wainwright to Fitzwilliam, 9 November 1797, NLI, MIC 5641 and Address of Fr Purcell to his parishioners, 31 December 1797, NA, SOC, 3065/1. Cullen's informants confused him with his Tinahely magistrate relative William Nixon, 'one of the terrorists of the day'. Cullen, NLI, MS 9761, p. 162.
77 Wainwright to Fitzwilliam, 9 November and 28 November 1797, NLI, MIC 5641 and *SNL*, 20 November 1797.
78 Wainwright to Fitzwilliam, 28 November 1797, NLI, MIC 5641.
79 Wainwright to Fitzwilliam, 12 November 1797, MIC 5641.
80 A. Durdin to —— , 20 September 1797, NA, 620/34/20. Burton was probably the MP for Carlow in 1799. See also Ryan, *Antiquities of the county of Carlow*, pp. 323, 380.
81 *FDJ*, 10 January 1795, 'suffering loyalists', NLI, MIC 7665, *SNL*, 20 November 1797 and Wainwright to Fitzwilliam, 24 December 1797,NLI, MIC 5641. There was also a Captain Thomas Whelan in the Carlow Militia. Ryan, *Antiquities of the county of Carlow*, p. 312.
82 Furlong, *Murphy*, p. 178 and *FDJ*, 20 December 1796. James Symes of Coolboy lodged a claim with the suffering loyalist commissioners for clothes and potatoes in 1799. NLI, MIC 7665.
83 William Burton to —— , 2 November 1797, NA, 620/33/9 and Wainwright to Fitzwilliam, 12 and 28 November 1797, NLI, MIC 5641.
84 Wainwright to Fitzwilliam,9 November 1797, NLI, MIC 5641. See also Wainwright to Fitzwilliam, 12 November 1797, NLI, MIC 5641.
85 Wainwright to Fitzwilliam, 12 November 1797, NLI, MIC 5641.
86 Burton to Camden, 9 November 1797, NA, 620/33/29 and n.d., PRO, HO 100/78/348.

87 Wainwright to Fitzwilliam, 14 November 1797, NLI, MIC 5641. See also n.d., PRO, HO 100/78/348 and Cullen, NLI, MS 8339, p. 67.

88 Stratford to [Pelham], 9 November 1797, NA, 620/33/32. See also Stratford to [Pelham], 11 November 1797, NA, SOC, 3133/1 and *FDJ*, 23 November 1797.

89 *Press*, 19 October 1797. See also *FDJ*, 17 October 1797 and Leadbeater, *Papers*, I, p. 214.

90 Information of Edward Webb, 11 November 1797, NA, SOC, 3133/2.

91 Ibid., and Stratford to [Pelham], 11 November 1797, NA, SOC, 3133/1. For Orr and militia overtures see *FDJ*, 17–31 October 1797, *DEP*, 17 October 1797, Wolfe to Cooke, 19 September 1797, NA, 620/34/22 and McDowell, *Ireland in the age*, pp. 542–3.

92 Camden to Portland, 15 November 1797, PRO, HO 100/66/60.

93 Wainwright to Fitzwilliam, 28 November 1797, NLI, MIC 5641. See also Hardy to Fitzwilliam, 27 November 1797, NLI, MIC 5641 and *Press*, 9 November 1797 and 13 February 1798.

94 Hardy to Fitzwilliam, 27 November 1797, NLI, MIC 5641. See also Wainwright to Fitzwilliam, 28 November 1797, NLI, MIC 5641.

95 Hardy Journal, 19 November 1797.

96 —— , to Wilkinson, 14 July 1797, NA, SOC, 3097.

97 Hardy Journal, 19 November 1797. See also Report of the Medical Board, 12 February 1802, PRO, HO 100/108/44 and Lieutenant-Colonel Hodder to Tyrawley, 18 January 1800, NLI, Kilmainham Papers, CXXI, p. 28.

98 Hardy to Fitzwilliam, 24 December 1797, NLI, MIC 5641 and Hardy Journal, 29 May 1798 and Fitzwilliam to Hardwicke, 15 September 1802, BM, MS 35736/156.

99 Hardy Journal, 19 November 1797. See also Wainwright to Fitzwilliam, 28 November 1797, NLI, MIC 5641.

100 Wainwright to Fitzwilliam, 15 December 1797, NLI, MIC 5641. See also Hardy to Pelham, 22 February 1798 and Wainwright to Fitzwilliam, 28 November 1797, NLI, MIC 5641.

101 'Return of arms etc taken & surrendered . . . in Major Hardy's district in the counties of Wicklow & Carlow . . . Novemb[e]r 20th 1797', NA, OP 198/15 (1).

102 Carhampton to Hardy, 22 November 1797, NA, OP 198/15 (2), Wainwright to Fitzwilliam, 23 December 1797 and Hardy to Fitzwilliam, 24 December 1797, NLI, MIC 5641.

103 Hardy to Fitzwilliam, 24 December 1797, NLI, MIC 5641. The proposed depots and officers responsible for their security and maintenance were as follows: 1st district (Blessington)-Richard Hornidge, William Patrickson, J. Leeson, Rev. Hill Benson; 2nd district (Dunlavin)-William Ryves, Mr Fisher, George Heighington; 3rd district (Baltinglass)-Benjamin O'Neil Stratford, William King, Morley Saunders, Mr. Moore; 4th district (Belan)-Aldborough, Mr Yeats, Mr Francis Greene; 5th district (Hacketstown)-William Hume, William Hoare Hume, John [sic, Thomas?] Hardy; 6th district (Tullow), Archibald Rahilly, Edward Eustace, R. Eustace, Mr Drought; 7th district (Coolkenna)-Abraham Nixon, P. Whelan; 8th district (Tinahely)-Henry Moreton; 9th district-(Coolatin)-William Wainwright; 10th district-(Carnew)-Revd Charles Cope. Source: Wainwright to Fitzwilliam, 23 December 1797, NLI, MIC 5641.

104 Hardy to Pelham, 24 December 1797, NLI, MIC 5641. See also Hardy to Pelham, 27 February 1798 and Hardy to Fitzwilliam, 15 March 1797, NLI, MIC 5641.

105 Hardy to Fitzwilliam, 27 February 1798, NLI, MIC 5641.

106 Address of Fr Purcell, 31 December 1797, NA, SOC, 3065/1. Purcell is not to be confused with the priest of that name who succeeded Fr James Madden as parish priest of Kilbride and Barndarrig (Dunganstown, Wicklow) and survived an assassination attempt late in the Rebellion. Riordan, *Reportorium Novum*, I–II, 1961–4. See also Wainwright to Fitzwilliam, 28 November 1797, NLI, MIC 5641.

107 Hardy Journal, 19 November 1797 and Pelham to Lake, 3 March 1797, PRONI, D.607/E/149.

108 *FDJ*, 23 November 1797. When a sergeant of the New Romney fencible cavalry was murdered near Naas (Kildare) in early January it was claimed that 'more murders have taken place in the last year [in Kildare] . . . than have taken place throughout the whole kingdom before'. *FDJ*, 6 January 1798. Kildare's barony of Carbury was proclaimed in May 1797 in consequence of violent attacks on loyalists there and in parts of Meath. Wogan Browne to Pelham, 8 May 1797, NA, 620/30/46. On 28 April 1798 it was speculated that the county's disaffection was due to the lack of loyal magistrates and the 'rank and

property' of the leading United Irishmen who were often related to or landlords of magistrates.

109 *Press*, 9 November 1797. See also Hardy to Fitzwilliam, 27 February 1798, NLI, MIC 5641.

110 Cullen, NLI, MS 9761, pp. 161–2 and *Insurgent*, p. 20.

111 Wainwright to Fitzwilliam, 10 December 1797, NLI, MIC 5641. See also Hardy to Cooke, 4 February 1798, NA, 620/35/115.

112 See Wainwright to Fitzwilliam, 15 December 1797, NLI, MIC 5641, Hume to Hardy, 24 March 1798 and Hardy to Cooke, 28 March 1798, NA, SOC, 1017/63 and Senior to [Cooke], 6 December 1797, NA, 620/18/3.

113 Hardy to Cooke, 19 January 1798, NA, 620/35/48.

114 Hardy to Cooke, 19 January 1798, NA, 620/35/48, Cooke to La Touche, 16 January 1798, NA, SOC, 3152 and 22 January 1798, NLI, MIC 5641.

115 Petition of Laurence McGuirke, 10 June 1799, NA, SPP, 763 and Petition of Patrick Stanton, n.d., 1799, NA, SPP, 838. The memorials were supported by south Wicklow loyalists Thomas Acton, Alexander Carroll and Joseph Revell, possibly in view of Staunton's co-operation in the prosecution of Owen Byrne.

116 Hardy to Cooke, 19 January 1798, NA, 620/35/48. See also 20 February 1798, NA, 620/35/146.

117 Tyson, 17 January 1798, NA, SOC, 1017/61, Kavanagh, 20 January 1798, NA, SOC, 1017/62 and 2 and 4 January 1798, NA, SOC, 1017/61–2.

118 Wolfe to Camden, 26 March 1798, PRO, HO 100/75/295 22 January 1798. See also NLI, MIC 5641, and Musgrave, *Rebellions*, 4th edn., pp. 625–7, [Murray], 21 May 1798, NA, 620/3/32/6 and Hardy to Fitzwilliam, 27 February 1798, NLI, MIC 5641. Murray confirmed to King, Bayly and Atkins that the paper was 'the genuine report made on that day' and that he had seen Phil O'Neil's copy. This validation may have had bearing on the prosecution of William Michael Byrne as Joseph Thompson, one of Byrne's co-accused, had claimed that an incriminating list of names in his possession comprised persons intending to attend a charity ball. McDowell, *Ireland in the age*, p. 600.

119 *NCEP*, 26 October 1797 and *FDJ*, 22 January 1798. For proclaiming in Queen's County and Kildare see *FDJ*, 25 January 1798 and Patrickson to [Downshire], 5 February 1798, PRONI, D.607/F/45.

120 John Goddard to Downshire, 2 September 1796, PRONI, D.607/D/149. For the Viceroy's personal resigned attitude see Camden to Downshire, 4 January 1797, PRONI, D.607/E/7.

121 Senior, *Orangeism*, pp. 97–8, Whelan, 'Religious factor', pp. 68–9 and Luke Cullen to Madden, 27 July 1858, TCD, MS 1472/236. Cullen described Newtownmountkennedy as 'the chief seat of orangeism' and identified Armstrong's hotel as the venue for town's lodge meetings, a building burned on 31 May 1798 during the battle for the town but rebuilt. 'Suffering loyalists', NLI, MIC 7665.

122 *Press*, 7 October 1797.

123 Hardy to Fitzwilliam, 24 December 1797, NLI, MIC 5641 *Cork Gazette*, 26 November 1791 and 19 September 1792.

124 Matthews to Downshire, PRONI, D.607/D/372. See also *FDJ*, 19 April 1798. The political outlook of the North Corks was not uniform and, according to Hay, a drummer was lynched in the Enniscorthy lodgings of Revd Thomas Handcock for refusing to play the orange anthem 'The Boyne Water.' See also Hay, *History*, pp. 57, 150. On 11 July 1798 a serjeant and fifteen privates were discovered to be United Irishmen. *SNL*, 12 July 1798.

125 Caulfield to Troy, 23 August 1799, DDA, Troy Correspondence. See also Furlong, *Murphy*, pp. 38–40.

126 *Press*, 2 December 1797. See also Padraig O'Snodaigh, '98 *and Carlow, a look at the historians* (Carlow, 1979) and Seamus O'Loinsigh,' The rebellion of 1798 in Meath' in *Riocht na Midhe*, III, no. 4, 1966, pp. 342–7. United Irish returns in April 1798 gave Carlow's rebel strength as 11,300, Meath, 10,110, Kildare, 11,910 and Wicklow, 14,000. Robert Ross to Downshire, 25 April 1798, PRONI, D.607/F/150. For the myth of significant Orange Order presence in Wicklow prior to the rebellion and their role in sparking its outbreak see John Sherman, '*Donoughmore in omayle:*', *an historical sketch of the Glen of Imail, county of Wicklow, of the Ui Taidg and the O'Tooles of Imail* (Dublin, 1876).

127 C. Horton, 'The records of the Freemasons in Ireland' in *Familia, Ulster genealogical review*, II, no.2, 1986, p. 67, Batt, *The Moncks*, p. 9 and McPhail, *Guide*, p. 5.

128 Membership list of Grand Orange Lodge, Dublin, NLI, MS 5398, Cullen, *Insurgent*, pp. 13–14 and Stowe MS, RIA, A.I.E., pp. 51–3.

129 *Minutes of evidence . . . Baltinglass election*, pp. 4–25, Cullen, 'Rebellion in its eighteenth century context', p. 72 and Coleman, 'The Oath', pp. 685–8.

130 Hardy to Fitzwilliam, 24 December 1797 and 27 February 1798, NLI, MIC 5641. See also Petition of James McGhee, 22 April 1801, NA, OP 104/3 (1a), Camden to Portland, 25 June 1798, PRO, HO 100/81/199 and Lieutenant Gardiner to ——, 26 June 1798, NA, 620/38/239.

131 Cullen, *Insurgent*, p. 10. See also Archibald Nixon to Fitzwilliam, 19 January 1797, NLI, MIC 5641, 24 May 1798, NA, 620/37/139, Gordon, *History*, p. 162 and Byrne, *Memoirs*, I, p. 113.

132 n.d., 1801, NA, 620/10/116/1.

133 Madden considerably overstated the case in commenting 'the name of Orangeism had been made so detestable to the people [in Wexford that] . . . throughout the rebellion there was an abundant evidence of their frenzy being more the impulse of a wild resentment against Orangeism, than any spirit of hostility to the sovereign or the state.' Madden, *United*, II, pp. 348–9. See also Miles Byrne quoted in Cullen, *Insurgent*, pp. 8–11.

134 Hardy Journal, January 1798. See also *FDJ*, 3 August 1797 and 14 December 1797 and information of Gabriel Holles, 25 July 1797, NA, Frazer MS 1/44.

135 *Press*, 20 January 1798. See also *SNL*, 19 May 1795, 14 November 1799, NA, 620/17/30/42, Hay, *History*, pp. 57, 181 and Furlong, *Murphy*, pp. 39, 43. For colourful but unfounded Wicklow folklore of 'Tom the Devil' and the North Corks see O'Tuathial, 'Wicklow traditions', *Bealoideas*, V, 1935, pp. 161–2.

136 *Press*, 15 and 22 February 1798. See also Hardy to Cooke, 19 January 1798, NA, 620/35/48.

137 Hay, *History*, p. 76. See also Ibid., pp. 97–8.

138 Edwards to Camden, 14 January 1798, NA, 620/35/47. See also Cullen, *Insurgent*, p. 10 and Madden, *United*, I, p. 323.

139 31 December 1797, NA, SOC, 3065/1 and *FDJ*, 13 January 1798.

140 *FDJ*, 26 December 1797. See also Wainwright to Fitzwilliam, 10 December 1797, NLI, MIC 5641.

141 *FDJ*, 20 January 1798. See also Byrne, *Memoirs*, I, pp. 12–5, Musgrave, *Rebellions*, Appendix XVII, pp. 79–80.

142 Johnson to Downshire, 15 January 1798, PRONI, D.607/F/16.

143 Hardy to Cooke, 19 January 1798, NA, 620/35/48. See also *SNL*, 6 May 1793.

144 See Whelan, 'Religious factor', pp. 68–9, Byrne, *Memoirs*, I, pp. 10–11, 24, 84, 173, 234 and 246, Hay, *History*, p. 145 and Kavanagh, *Popular History*, p. 89.

145 Monck to Cooke, 17 May 1798, NA, 620/37/99. See also *SNL*, 6 October 1789, 27 March 1794, *Dublin Gazette*, 6 February 1790, *FDJ*, 30 July 1794 and 7 November 1797.

146 Monck to Marsden, 6 July 1801, NA, OP 104/3 (2).

147 Hardy to Cooke, 27 May 1798, NA, 620/37/184.

148 *SNL*, 31 March and 14 April 1795 and Dickson, *Wexford Rising*, p. 213.

149 Nixon to Fitzwilliam, 18 and 19 January 1797, NLI, MIC 5641 and Ryan, *Antiquities of the county of Carlow*, p. 381.

150 Plowden, *Historical Review*, II, pp. 714–5.

151 [Robinson] to Cooke, 9 May 1798, NA, 620/37/43.

152 Hardy to Cooke, 19 January 1798, NA, 620/35/48.

153 Hardy to Cooke, 4 February 1798, NA, 620/35/115. The death of his attorney in late 1798 or 1799 greatly hindered Byrne's attempts to settle his affairs in Ireland when in exile, not least in that the man held the only deeds and family papers not destroyed in the rebellion. Petition of Garret Byrne and Edward Fitzgerald, 18 April 1799, PRO, HO 100/66/ 411.

154 Hardy to Pelham, 22 February 1798, NLI, MIC 5641.
See also *FDJ*, 10 February 1798 and Hardy to Cooke, 4 February 1798, NA, 620/35/115. Those arrested were Bryan Sharkey, Pat Filsky, John Doyle, Maurice Burke, John Burke and James Cullen.

155 20 February 1798, NA, 620/35/146. This list is compiled from those present at a second meeting on 20 February which reconvened the earlier one.

156 Lieutenant Colonel Henry Howard commanded the Wicklow Militia and was considered as a candidate to replace the Fitzwilliamite William Hume in October 1798. *NCEP*, 16 January 1797 and Morley Saunders to Downshire, 27 October 1798, PRONI, D.607/F/495. For the Howards see NLI, MSS 9,582 and 12,146.

157 Sarah Tighe to ——, 21 April 1798, NLI, MS 4813.

158 20 February 1798, NA, 620/35/146.

159 *FDJ*, 20 December 1797.

160 Musgrave, *Rebellions*, 4th edn., p. 284 and Cullen, *Insurgent*, pp. 65–6. Cullen was informed that Thomas Lewins of Kilmacoo, one of Thomas King's tenants and a former member of the Cronebane Infantry, suggested the wording although it is by no means certain that there was a definitive text. Fr Meagher of Redcross parish told Cullen that Lewins was 'a snake from infancy', a comment which although typical of nationalist resentzment against informers may underestimate the character of Lewins. Cullen, NLI, MS 9761, p. 166. This accords with Musgrave's informant, probably King with whom he conferred when compiling his book. Musgrave credited 'a loyal papist' in the employ of King with devising the test. This man, clearly Lewins, afterwards became a convert to protestantism on learning that 'Fr.C[loney]', curate of Rathdrum, did not consider the oath of allegiance binding on Catholics and that Fr Meagher considered the test oath blasphemous. Musgrave, *Rebellions*, pp. 302–3. For links between King and Musgrave see *Catholic Telegraph*, 12 July 1858.

161 Monck to Cooke, 19 March 1798, NA, 620/36/27.

162 20 February 1798, NA, 620/35/146 and Musgrave, *Rebellions*, 4th edn., p.307.

163 Hardy to Pelham, 26 February 1798, NA, 620/35/159 and Byrne, *Memoirs*, I, pp. 12–15.

164 Musgrave, *Rebellions*, 4th edn., p. 282, *FDJ*, 24 November 1796, Newtownmountkennedy cavalry to Fitzwilliam, 2 December 1796, NLI, MIC 5641, NLI, MS 16,306 cited in Cowman, 'Mining community', p. 770 and Cullen, *Insurgent*, p. 37 For Catholic recruitment in the yeomanry see McDowell, *Ireland in the Age*, p. 559 and Blackstock, 'yeomanry', pp. 241–3.

165 Ridgeway, *Trial of William Michael Byrne*, p. 140.

166 Edwards to Cooke, 5 March 1798, NA, SOC, 3165.

167 Ridgeway, *Trial of William Byrne*, pp. 2–3. Lieutenant Thomas Hugo, son of the prominent Annamoe loyalist of that name, deposed that the oath 'was taken by the whole corps except the prisoner and four others who were expelled.' It is noteworthy that Hugo had heard that other Wicklow yeomen wanted to expel Byrne for disloyalty even before the test oath was put to the corps. This indicates that the information which came to light in late January and early February concerning Garret Byrne's disloyalty may also have implicated or tarnished his brother. Ibid., p. 3 and Hardy to Cooke, 4 February 1798, NA, 620/35/115.

168 Robinson to Cooke, 14 May 1798, NA, 620/3/32/5. See also Musgrave, *Rebellions*, 4th edn., p. 307 and *Trial of William Byrne*, p. 4.

169 Edwards to ——, 12 July 1798, NA, 620/39/63. See also Edwards to ——, 2 December 1796, NA, 620/26/92A, Edwards to Cooke, 2 April 1798, NA, 620/36/115, Cullen, *Insurgent*, pp. 15–16 and Edwards to Marsden, 13 August 1803, NA, 620/65/7.

170 19 March 1798, NA, 620/36/27.

171 Cullen, *Insurgent*, p. 16. See also Ibid., pp. 13–14.

172 Edwards to Cooke, 5 March 1798, NA, SOC, 3165. See also Edwards to Cooke, 2 April 1798, NA, 620/36/115.

173 Hardy to Fitzwilliam, 15 March 1798, NLI, MIC 5641, *FDJ*, 11 and 20 March 1798, Hardy Memorial, NLI, Melville MS and *HT*, 27 April 1798. Rossmore donated £2,000, Sir John Parnell £1,000 and Powerscourt £1,000. *FDJ*, 23 March 1798.

174 *FDJ*, 7 April 1798, [Robinson] to Cooke, 19 May 1798, NA, 620/37/109.

175 March 1798, NA, OP 198/15 (3).

176 John Craven to Rossmore, 15 February 1798, NA, 620/35/143 and Madden, *United*, IV, p. 45.

177 Hardy to Pelham, 26 February 1798, NA, 620/35/159. See also Hardy Journal, March 1798 and *FDJ*, 18 February 1798.

178 *FDJ*, 15 March 1798, O'Donovan *et al.*, *Letters*, p. 135, *Proceedings of a general court-martial held in the barracks of Dublin, on Friday the 12th of July, 1799 . . . upon charges brought against Capt[ain] John Giffard, of the city of Dublin regiment . . .* (Dublin, 1800), John Giffard to General Meadows, n.d. [1801], PRO, HO 100/102/187 and Musgrave, *Rebellions*, 4th edn., p. 413. Sherwood received compensation from the Government, possibly as early as April 1798, and was appointed overseer of the Martello tower construction site at Killiney in 1804. Martello Accounts, 13 June 1804, PRO, HO 100/119/381–3 and Deposition of John Sherwood, 5 October 1804, NA, 620/50/92 and 14 November 1799, NA, 620/17/30/42.

179 *FDJ*, 15 March 1798 and Camden to Portland, 7 April 1798, PRO, HO 100/76/46. Sherwood owned three houses in Arklow Town which were destroyed on 9 June 1798 and a Mary Sherwood lost property at Killahurler in Arklow barony. The Tomacork farm may have been the residence of his mother as it was referred to by Wainwright that of 'the widow Sherwood and her son'. Wainwright to Fitzwilliam, 13 March 1798, NLI, MIC 5641. See also 'suffering loyalists', MIC 7665. There was another Sherwood farm at Killinure with yeomanry members. George Sherwood to Marsden, 19 January 1803, NA, 620/67/51.

180 19 March 1798, NA, 620/36/27. See also *FDJ*, 24 March 1798, Richard Annesley to Downshire, 15 March 1798, PRONI, D.607/F/96, Pakenham, *Liberty*, pp. 53–4 and Camden to Portland, 13 March 1798, PRO, HO 100/75/218.

181 Musgrave, *Rebellions*, 4th edn., p. 250. See also L. M. Cullen,'Politics and Rebellion', p. 423.

182 McDowell, *Ireland in the age*, pp. 548–9, L. M. Cullen, '1798 Rebellion', p. 107 and Byrne, *Memoirs*, I, pp. 19–20.

183 *FDJ*, 7 April 1798, Hardy to Cooke, 4 April 1798, NA, 620/36/123, *BNL*, 1 February, 1798, O'Neil Stratford to John Stratford, 1 April 1798, NA, SOC, 1017/66, William Hume to Hardy, 24 March 1798, NA, SOC, 1017/63 and Hardy to Cooke, 28 March 1798, NA, SOC, 1017/63. According to Luke Cullen, who interviewed men who recalled the assizes, Cooper's information 'had the jails of Wexford and Wicklow crowded . . . but in striving too much, he spoiled the game.' Cullen, NLI, MS 9761, p. 162.

184 Moreton to John Lees, 24 May 1798, NA, 620/37/139. See also Wainwright to Fitzwilliam, 15 December 1797, NLI, MIC 5641 and *FDJ*, 10 January 1795. Contact between the southern Wicklow hardliners and Lees, whom along with Cooke was deeply involved in directing secret service activity, is indicative of relations between Wicklow's secret committee of magistrates and the Dublin Castle network. Lees, as controller of the post office was ideally placed to monitor and intercept the mail of those the government suspected of treason.

185 Cullen, NLI, MS 9761, p. 164 The predictably hostile Luke Cullen claimed that Cooper was 'broke down and was sent to an out farm to feed and fatten among the broken minded informers and perjurers'. Cullen, *Insurgent*, p. 20. See also Hume to ——, 24 March 1798 and Hardy to Cooke, 28 March 1798, NA, SOC, 1017/63.

186 Holt, *Rum Story*, pp. 32, 43 and 50, Ruán O'Donnell,'The Wicklow United Irishmen in New South Wales, part one' in *Wicklow Historical Journal*, no. 7, I, July 1994, pp. 46–52 and Archive Office of New South Wales, Memorials 1810, 4/1846, p. 35 and 4/1847, p. 159.

187 August 1798, PRO, H0 100/88/98, pp. 4–6, Cullen, NLI, MS 9762/II, p. 68, Tyson and Kavanagh, 19 and 20 January 1798, NA, SOC, 1017/62, Murphy, 20 June 1798, NA, 620/38/188, Thomas Archer to Marsden, 15 July 1804, NA, SOC, 1030/107 and Donnelly, 'overview of local administration', p. 863.

188 Hardy to Cooke, 4 April 1798, NA, 620/36/123. See also McDowell, *Ireland in the Age*, pp. 544–5.

189 *FDJ*, 5, 7 and 19 April 1798, Richard Johnson Smyth to Downshire, 13 April 1798 and Lane to Downshire, 14 April 1798, PRONI, D.607/F/ 142–3.

190 Kemmis to Cooke, 28 March 1798, NA, 620/36/92, Bird [Smith] to Sirr, n.d., [1798] quoted in Madden, *United*, I, p. 503, *A guide to West Wicklow* (Dublin, n.d.), p. 37, Musgrave to Lord Waterford, 17 March 1798, NA, 620/36/21, Camden to Portland, 22 April 1798, PRO, HO 100/79/123 and Buckingham to Grenville, *Fortescue*, IV, p. 217.

191 King to Cooke, 25 March 1798, NA, 620/3/51/1.

192 *FDJ*, 29 March 1798 and Madden, *United*, IV, pp. 46–7.

193 Cullen, *Insurgent*, p. 13 and *Catholic Telegraph*, 23 August 1856. See also J.W. Fowler to Downshire, 7 April 1798, PRONI, D.607/F/133, Colonel Sir Watkins Williams Wynne to ——, 25 May 1797, NA, 620/ 30/181, McDowell, *Ireland in the Age*, p. 576 and *Press*, 26 October, 18 November and 9 December 1797.

194 Cullen, *Insurgent*, p. 15.

195 Hardy Memorial, n.d. [c. 1804], NA, OP 198/15 (8), Evan Nepean to Camden, 17 December 1804, NA, OP 198/15 (13) and Chichester to Hardy, 20 November 1805, NA, OP 198/15 (14)

196 See March 1798, NA, OP. 198/15 (3).

197 *FDJ*, 29 and 31 March 1798.
198 Musgrave, *Rebellions*, 4th edn., p. 692 and Camden to Portland, April 1798, PRO, HO 100/76/44–6.
199 Hardy to Fitzwilliam, 15 March 1798, NLI, MIC 5641.
200 Camden to Portland, 2 April 1798, PRO, HO 100/76/7 See also Camden to Portland, n.d. [1798], PRO, HO 100/78/348, 30 March 1798, PRO, HO 100/80/161 and 7 April 1798, PRO, HO 100/76/44–6 and 2 April 1798, PRO, HO 100/76/3.
201 Castlereagh to Abercromby,30 March 1798, PRO, HO 100/75/351. The orders specified Kildare, Tipperary, Limerick, Cork, Queen's County and Kilkenny but not Wicklow which was probably covered by separate instructions of a similar if not identical nature issued on 26 March. See also Camden to Portland, 30 March 1798, PRO, HO 100/80/161.
202 Buckingham to Lord Grenville, 29 May 1798 in Fortescue, IV, p. 69. See also *Lieutenant-General Sir Ralph Abercromby KB, 1793–1801, a memoir by his son, James Lord Dunfermline* (Edinburgh, 1861), pp. 77–84 and *BNL*, 2 March 1798.
203 Castlereagh, *Memoirs*, I, pp. 169–70, 186–7 and Sir Henry McAnally, *The Irish militia, 1793–1816* (London, 1949), p. 116 and Pakenham, *Liberty*, p. 74.
204 Massey to Kemmis, 26 April 1798, NA, Frazer MS, II/68.
205 Asgill to Abercromby, 17 April 1798 in Castlereagh, *Memoirs*, I, pp. 184–5. See also Pakenham, *Liberty*, pp. 76–7, Lieutenant-General Sir Ralph Dundas to ——, 5 April 1798 in Castlereagh, *Memoirs*, I, p. 185.
206 Shannon to Boyle, 23 May 1798 in *Letters*, pp. 101–2. See also *FDJ*, 1 May 1798. Robert Ross thought freequarters too lenient and that the troops would find nothing to eat in their requisitioned lodgings. Ross to Downshire, 6 April 1798, PRONI, D.607/F/131A.
207 Musgrave, *Rebellions*, p. 691. See also Frederick Maitland, 3 April 1798 in Castlereagh, *Memoirs*, I, pp. 169–70.
208 Hardy Memorial, NLI, Melville MS.
209 Leadbeater, *Papers*, I, p. 213.
210 Hardy to Cooke, 4 April 1798, NA, 620/36/123. See also Edwards to Cooke, 2 April 1798, NA, 620/36/115, Cullen, TCD, MS 1472, p. 193.
211 [Robinson] to Cooke, 29 May 1798, NA, 620/37/211A. See also [Robinson] to Cooke, 16 May 1798, NA, 620/3/32/3 and 19 May 1798, NA, 620/37/109.
212 Hardy Journal, April 1798. See also Dempsey, *Avoca*, p. 27 and *SNL*, 5 November 1798.
213 Hay, *History*, pp. 96–7.
214 Byrne, *Memoirs*, I, p. 28, Terry Kavanagh, 'Arklow and the early Liverpool connection' in *Arklow Historical Society Journal*, 1996–7, pp. 46–9, Pakenham, *Liberty*, p. 166 and *FJ*, 3 July 1800. In 1799 Thomas Murray of Sheepwalk had the confidence to submit a claim for £537 damages to the 'Committee for the Relief of Suffering Loyalists'. See 'An account of the old claims in part heard and postponed for further evidence with such persons for postponement as can be given from the office', NA, OP 150/4 (2).
215 John Patrickson to Downshire, 5 April [1798], PRONI, D.607/F/130 and Cullen, *Insurgent*, p. 12.
216 H. Howard, *Reminiscences for my children* n.d. quoted in J. R. O'Flanagan, *The Irish Bar; comprising anecdote, bon-mots, and biographical sketches of the bench and bar of Ireland* (London, 1879), p. 131. This was the impression gained by Mrs Howard of Corby Castle, Cumberland who met Powerscourt in April 1799. Ibid.
217 Mac Suibhne, *Kildare in 1798*, p. 126.
218 Irish Folklore Commission, 654, cited in Fiachra Mac Gabhann, 'The Water was the Sheriff': the land beneath the Poulaphouca reservoir' in Hannigan and Nolan (eds.), *Wicklow: history and society*, p. 940.
219 Cullen, *Insurgent*, p. 18. See also Ibid., pp. 15–17, Cullen, TCD, MS 1472, p. 193 and *FDJ*, 12 October 1797 and 29 March 1798.
220 King to Cooke, 27 April 1798, NA, SOC, 3188/1 and Information of John Duff, 22 April 1798, NA, 620/36/194.
221 Cullen, *Insurgent*, p. 12.
222 PRO, WO 68/402/(i), pp. 257–8, 25 April 1799, NA, 620/17/30/78 and 12 and 24 April 1798, PRO, WO 68/422/257–8.
223 Cullen, *Insurgent*, p. 20. See also Ibid., p. 16 and *Press*, 26 October 1797.
224 Camden to Sir Laurence Parsons, 28 March 1798, NLI, MS 13,840/3. Laurence Parsons had been obliged to resign his command on 27 March 1798 in consequence of comments

which had blamed his 'mistaken lenity' for the allegedly undue level of disaffection in the King's County Militia. See Parsons to Camden, 27 March 1798, Ibid.

225 Thomas Parsons to Laurence Parsons, 17 April 1798, NLI, MS 13,840/3.

226 Holt, *Rum Story*, p. 71. The word 'eyes' in the printed text is a misrendering of 'thighs' and testifies to Holt's oral delivery to secretaries.

227 Edwards to Camden, 16 April 1798, NA, 620/36/176.

228 *Press*, 16 December 1797 and Leadbeater, *Papers*, I, p. 221.

229 Sproule to Lees, 22 June 1798, NA, 620/51/36.

230 Holt, *Rum Story*, p. 47. See also Ibid., pp. 117, 191.

231 Tighe to —— , 21 April 1798, NLI, MS 4813.

232 Cullen, *Insurgent*, p. 15 and Parsons to Thomas Parsons, 10 May 1798, NLI, MS 13,840/3.

233 Cullen, *Insurgent*, pp. 14–5 and List of Prisoners, n.d. [c. April 1798], NA, 620/52/164.

234 Cullen, *Insurgent*, p. 15, Coleman, 21 May 1798 and Information of William Kelly, 24 May 1798, TCD, MS 871.

235 *Press*, 13 February 1798. See also Cullen, *Insurgent*, p. 16.

236 Brownrigg to Grenville, 5 December 1797, PRO, HO 50/6.

237 5 May 1799, NA, 620/7/79/13, 16 and —— , to Craig, 20 September 1798, PRO, HO 100/86/65.

238 Monck to Marsden, 6 July 1801, NA, OP 104/3 (2).

239 Cullen, *Insurgent*, pp. 32–3. For the Longs see *FDJ*, 21 April 1798.

240 Cullen, NLI, MS 8339, pp. 8–9.

241 See Wicklow Militia Pay Roll and Muster List, 1798, PRO, WO 13/3531.

242 *Union Star*, November 1797 in PRO, HO 100/70/236 and Cullen, NLI, MS 8339, p. 9.

243 *Press*, 15 and 22 February 1798 and Cullen, NLI, MS 9762, p. 42. A Michael Fenton had his Ballinacloy house burned by the rebels and another Fenton home at Knockanarrigan (Imaal) was also destroyed. 'Suffering loyalists', NLI, MIC 7665. See also *FDJ*, 7 January 1797.

244 Musgrave, *Rebellions*, 4th edn., p. 283. Archbishop Troy, a bitter opponent of the United Irishmen, urged the same course of action in a pastoral of 27 May 1798. DDA, Troy Papers, II, 116/7/64.

245 Caulfield to Troy, 23 September 1799, DDA, Troy Correspondence. See also Musgrave, *Rebellions*, Appendix XVII, pp. 81–2. Musgrave believed that the efforts of the Wicklow clergy was a ploy intended to lure Government into a false sense of security so that the rebels could massacre the protestants. Without assessing the appeal of United Irish politics to Wicklow people he further stated that the insurrection in the county 'was purely religious; for there was no other motive to actuate the mass of the people, except the hope of plunder.' Ibid., pp. 304–5. See also Petition of Fr Daniel Murray, 27 May 1798, NA, 620/38/181.

246 Howard, *Reminiscences* cited in O'Flanagan, *Irish Bar*, p. 133. Powerscourt told Mrs Howard that Callaghan had been 'one of those whom the French had pushed off in a boat, by way of getting rid of him, and that he had got safely to Cannes.' See also Brendan O'Cathaoir (ed.), *Holy Redeemer Church, 1792–1992: a Bray parish* (Bray, 1992), p. 13 and William J. Fitzpatrick, *Memoirs of Fr Healy of Little Bray* (London, 1899), p. 51, Richard Hayes, *Ireland and Irishmen in the French Revolution* (London, 1932), p. 198 and 25 June 1796, PRO, WO 68/402/(i), p. 86. A very different and unfounded legend about the Powerscourt priest claimed that he had been accidentally shot and killed by loyalists in 1798 when remonstrating with rebels attacking the mansion. According to the story the priest 'laid a curse with his dying breath on the Powerscourt family, that no Lord P[owerscourt] should live to see his son come of age. There is a saying that no grass will grow on the spot where he was slain, and so the gravel pathway was widened to included this place.' NLI, MS 7665, p. 71.

247 Furlong, *Murphy*, pp. 23, 27–8.

248 Caulfield to Troy, 21 May 1798, DDA, Troy Correspondence, II, 6/7/134.

249 Bird [Smith] to Sirr, n.d., [1798] in Madden, *United*, I, p. 499. See also Musgrave, *Rebellions*, p. 308.

250 Comerford, *Collections* cited in Chavasse, *Baltinglass*, p. 52. See also Roger McHugh (ed.), *Carlow in '98; the autobiography of William Farrell of Carlow* (Dublin, 1949), pp. 169–7, *Observations on the state of Ireland* (Dublin, 1805), [Robinson] to Cooke, 7 May 1798, NA, 620/37/35 and *Irish Magazine*, 1811.

251 Holt, 16 November 1798, NA, 620/41/39A. See also *SNL*, 1 8 and 20 June 1798 and Information of Fr John Martin, 14 June 1798, NA, 620/38/160. Fr Ledwich also narrowly escaped assassination in February 1804, probably due to suspicions surrounding his relationship to Patrick Ledwidge who had been executed on 26 May 1798 for being a rebel leader. *FDJ*, 25 February and 28 June 1804 and Patrick Archer, 'Fingal in 1798' in DHR, XL, no. 2, March 1987, p. 70.

252 Fitzpatrick, *Fr Healy*, p. 98. See also Cullen, NLI, MS 9762, pp. 36–8 and Thomas Archer to Marsden, 7 July 1800, NA, 620/57/47.

253 Patterson to Downshire, 21 April 1798, PRONI, D.607/F/149. See also *FDJ*, 24 April 1798.

254 Ross to Downshire, 25 April 1798, PRONI, D.607/F/150 and Dundas to Castlereagh, 23 April 1798 in Castlereagh, *Memoirs*, I, pp. 187–9.

255 Castlereagh, 25 April 1798 in *Memoirs*, I, p. 189.

256 Lake to Downshire, 2 April 1798, PRONI, D.607/F/127. See also *FDJ*, 24 April 1798, Pakenham, *Liberty*, p. 76, Sir Jonah Barrington, *Rise and fall of the Irish nation* (Dublin, 1833), p. 211, John Patrickson to Downshire, 5 April 1798, PRONI, D.607/F/130, Ross to Downshire, 5 and 6 April, D.607/F/131A and —— , to Portland, 20 February 1798, PRO, HO 100/75/100.

257 Leadbeater, *Papers*, I, pp. 213–214.

258 [Robinson] to Cooke, 9 May 1798, NA, 620/37/43, William J. Fitzpatrick, *The Sham Squire and the informers of 1798* (Dublin, 1866), pp. 362–3, Leadbeater, *Papers*, I, pp. 216–7, Pakenham, *Liberty*, pp. 79, 84, Hardy to Cooke, 14 May 1798, NA, 620/3/32/3 and Seamus Cummins, 'Pike heads and the calico printer, Leixlip in '98' in *Journal of the Kildare Archaeological and Historical Society*, 1985–6, vol. XVI, no. 5.

259 [Robinson] to Cooke, 7 May 1798, NA, 620/37/33.

260 Hardy to Cooke, 14 May 1798, NA, 620/3/32/3. See also Cullen, NLI, MS 9762, pp. 17–8.

261 Patrickson to Downshire, 23 May 1798, PRONI, D.607/F/181. See also Cullen, NLI, MS 9762, p. 20 and Cullen, TCD, MS 1472, p. 205. A proclamation issued in July 1800 listed Denis Coogan of Englishtown and Patrick Coogan of Redwells; 'Brothers and farmers – were both captains in '98 and have much influence over the common men.' *SNL*, 26 July 1800. That the family was mentioned by Frazer points to their social prominence in the early 1800s. Frazer, *Guide*, p. 111.

262 O'Kelly, 'Historical notes', p. 330. See also Cullen, NLI, MS 9762, p. 18, Chavasse, *Baltinglass*, p. 52 and [Robinson] to Cooke, 7 May 1798, NA, 620/37/35.

263 Petition of Matthew McDaniel, 27 April 1798, NA, SPP, 237. King and Mills were clearly very close. King nominated Mills to defend him in the spring of 1800 when the Rathdrum attorney was embroiled in a pay dispute with yeomen under his command. A son, in fact, was named Daniel Mills King. King to Rev. Brownrigg, 25 April 1802, NA, OP 128/2 (3) and Daniel Mills King to —— , 12 May 1812, NA, OP 373/6.

264 Cullen, NLI, MS 9762, p. 20.

265 Cullen, NLI, MS 9762, p. 12 See also Ibid., p. 20, Leadbeater, *Papers*, I, p. 215 and Captain Alexander Taylor to Hardwicke, 20 June 1801, BM, MS 35729, p. 37.

266 Patrickson to Downshire, 7 May 1798, PRONI, D.607/F/163. Patrickson also notified Downshire of the defection of the prominent Kildare United Irishmen, Thomas Reynolds, the man alluded to in the *Journal* of the following day. *FDJ*, 8 May 1798.

267 Hardy to Cooke, 14 May 1798, NA, 620/3/32/3.

268 Edwards to Cooke, 17 May 1798, NA, 620/37/99. See also W. Cooper to William Cope, 13 May 1798, NA, 620/37/65 and Cullen, *Insurgent*, p. 39.

269 Hardy Journal, 15 [sic] May 1798, Holt MS, pp. 16–9 and O'Donnell, 'Holt', pp. 95–6, O'Donnell, 'Michael Dwyer', pp. 21–2 and Cullen, NLI, MS 9762, pp. 22–3.

270 Camden to Portland, 11 May 1798, PRO, HO 100/76/174.

271 See Musgrave, *Rebellions*, 4th edn., pp. 693–4.

272 Edwards to Cooke, 17 May 1798, NA, 620/37/99.

273 [Robinson] to Cooke, 16 May 1798, NA, 620/3/32/5. See also Hardy to Cooke, 16 May 1798, NA, 620/3/32/5 and Cullen quoted in Fitzpatrick, *The Sham Squire*, p. 335.

274 Hardy to Cooke, 16 May 1798, NA, 620//3/32/5.

275 [Robinson] to Cooke, 16 May 1798, NA, 620/3/32/5.

276 [Robinson] to Cooke, 19 May 1798, NA, 620/37/109. See also Cullen, NLI, MS 8339, p. 7 and [Robinson] to Cooke, 9 May 1798, NA, 620/37/43.

277　Hardy to Cooke, 14 May 1798, NA, 620/3/32/5.

278　Edwards to Cooke, 17 May 1798, NA, 620/37/99.

279　Ibid., and Edwards to Cooke, 6 June 1798, NA, 620/38/63.

280　Hardy to Cooke, 22 May 1798, NA, 620/37/270.

281　Quoted in Shaw Mason, *Statistical Survey*, II, p. 63–4. Henry Paget Bayly, nephew of the Lamberton magistrate, obtained a lieutenant's commission in the Wicklow Militia on 5 February 1801. *A list of the officers*, p. 48 and NA, MS 2464, p. 15.

282　John Kidd to John Lees, 22 May 1798, NA, 620/37/141. See also Hardy to Cooke, 22 May 1798, NA, 620/37/127.

283　Hardy Journal, May 1798. West had been the surgeon at Wicklow Infirmary in the county town until his resignation from that post in the first week of January. *FDJ*, 6 January 1798 and PRO, WO 68/402/(i), p. 217.

284　Byrne, *Memoirs*, I, p. 28.

285　McGhee to [Cooke], 7 May 1798, NA, 620/37/31. See also Fitzpatrick, *Sham Squire*, p. 335 and Garret Byrne and Edward Fitzgerald to Portland, 8 April 1799, PRO, HO 100/66/411. Some of McGhee's 'prompt and decided measures' during the rebellion years left him vulnerable to prosecution. Petition of James McGhee, 22 April 1801, NA, OP 104/3 (1a).

286　William Moreton to Lees, 22 May 1798, NA, 620/37/125. See also Hay, *History*, p. 76.

287　Catherine Carroll to Mrs Carroll, 29 May 1798 in *HMC, Report 3*, April 1872, p. 260. Carroll claimed that Paxton was a Lieutenant in the Antrim Militia but no such man is listed on their muster rolls. See PRO, WO 13/2574. There was, however, a Cornet Archibald Paxton in the Ancient Britons. *A list of the officers of the several regiments and corps of fencible cavalry and infantry . . . yeomanry . . . and volunteer infantry*, 5th edn., (London, 1797), p. 7.

288　See 28 March 1799, NA, 620/3/32/6.

289　Cullen, TCD, MS 1472, p. 203. See also Vandeleur, *Killiskey*, p. 12.

290　Campbell to ——, 14 May 1798, NA, 620/37/67. See also Campbell to ——, 15 May 1798, NA, 620/37/78 and McDowell, *Ireland in the age*, pp. 575–7.

291　Wainwright to Fitzwilliam, 6 February 1800, NLI, MIC 5641.

292　Hay, *History*, p. 97.

293　Shannon to Boyle, 19 May 1798 in *Letters*, pp. 97–8.

294　Byrne, *Memoirs*, I, p. 97. See also Ibid., p. 14.

295　Moreton to Lees, 24 May 1798, NA, 620/37/139, [Murray], 21 May 1798, NA, 620/3/32/6 and Beakey, 25 May 1798, TCD, MS 871. Mernagh, Hall, Kinselagh and the others who had made statements to Bayly between 21 and 28 May were predominately illiterate rank-and-file conspirators who endorsed their depositions with an 'x'. See TCD, MS 871 As their information was necessarily dictated, the emphasis on planned sectarian massacres of Protestants and non-United Irishmen, allegations absent from virtually every other surviving statement and all those of senior rebels, bear the imprint of Bayly. As early as September 1797 he had claimed that the United Irishmen considered 'all Protestants . . . proscribed'. It seems likely that if he did not interpolate the contentious sectarian elements of the statements of May 1798, the informers themselves tailored their almost formulaic claims to elicit more favourable treatment from him and the government. Bayly to Parnell, 21 September 1797, NA, 620/18A/6. Bayly was certainly aware of the propaganda value of such claims and sent copies of them to Musgrave for publication in his flawed account of the rebellion to bolster his assertions about United Irish sectarianism. Musgrave, *Rebellions*, Appendix XVI, pp. 70–1. Compromised and repentant United Irishmen often introduced hearsay and fabrications geared towards making their revelations more valuble to their captors. Isaac Harrison alleged in early May that once the French arrived, Monck, Powerscourt, Colthurst and Quinn 'and such gentlemen in the neighbourhood', were to be killed. He further claimed, in a bid to add heightened importance to his information, that this was to occur either on the day of his interview or the following one. Harrison, 5 May 1798, TCD, MS 871.

296　Musgrave, *Rebellions*, p. 310.

297　Hardy to Cooke, 22 May 1798, NA, 620/37/123. See also Hardy to Cooke, 4 February 1798, NA, 620/35/14.

298　Ridgeway, *Trial of William Michael Byrne*, pp. 94–5 and Beakey, 25 May 1798, TCD, MS 871.

299 Wickham to Grenville, 26 May 1798 in *Fortescue*, IV, p. 216. See also Hardy Journal, 31 May 1798, [Robinson] to Cooke, 7 May 1798, NA, 620/37/33, Hardy Memorial, NLI, Melville MS and Shannon to Boyle, 17 May 1798 in *Letters*, p. 96.

300 Hardy to Cooke, 22 May 1798, NA, 620/37/127.

301 Hardy to Castlereagh, 22 May 1798, NA, 620/37/128.

302 Moreton to Lees, 22 May 1798, NA, 620/37/125.

303 Ridgeway, *Trial of William Michael Byrne*, p. 122.

304 Ibid., p. 117.

305 Quoted in Plowden, *Historical Review*, II, p. 685.

306 Patrickson to Downshire, 19 May 1798, PRONI, D.607/F/173, Holt MS, p. 41, Information of Bartholomew Clarke, n.d., [July 1798], NA, 620/51/249 and n.d., 1799, NA, 620/17/30/64.

307 [Robinson] to Cooke, 9 May 1798, NA, 620/37/43. He was not an enthusiastic insurgent when the rebellion broke out, although republican sympathies may account for his decision to surrender the town of Narraghmore to the rebels rather than make a stand. Leadbeater, *Papers*, I, p. 219.

308 [Robinson] to Cooke, 9 May 1798, NA, 620/37/43. For Carlow units see Walter Kavanagh to General Floyd, 11 January 1804, NA, SOC, 1030/1.

309 Leadbeater, *Papers*, I, p. 217. See also Cullen, NLI, MS 9762, p. 30 and Dickson, *Dwyer*, p. 371, Carroll to Carroll, 29 May 1798 in HMC, Report 3, Appendix, 1872, p. 260 Aldborough's entry for 28 May in his sparse journal of 1798, 'the most unhappy year' of his life, is as follows: 'Dismissed soldiers as United Irishmen tho[ugh] yeomen on their own confession. Several of my corps dismissed as disaffected 2 of them shot for it'. NLI, MS 19,165.

310 [Robinson] to Cooke, 16 May 1798 in Dickson, *Dwyer*, p. 29. See also [Robinson] to Cooke, 19 May 1798, NA, 620/37/109.

311 Fitzpatrick, *Sham squire*, pp. 310–11, Musgrave, *Rebellions*, II, p. 383, Cullen, NLI, MS 9762, pp. 28–30 and Stratford to ——, 27 May 1798, NA, 620/37/133.

312 [Robinson] to Cooke, 9 May 1798, 620/37/43. See also Cullen, NLI, MS 8339, p. 7 and MS 9762, pp. 28, 45 and O'Kelly, 'Historical notes', p. 337.

313 Petition of James Dunne, July 1800, NA, PPC, 374. See also Dickson, *Dwyer*, pp. 370–1, Fitzpatrick, *Sham squire*, pp. 310–11 and Hay, *History*, p. 106.

314 Hardy to Wickham, 19 May 1798, NA, 620/37/93 and 25 May 1798, NA, 620/37/156, 28 May 1798, NLI, MS 19,165 and Fitzpatrick, *Sham squire*, p. 309.

315 Ridgeway, *Trial of William Michael Byrne*, pp. 94–5 and 'Senior' to [Cooke], 24 January 1798, NA, 620/18/13. For complete Leinster breakdown see Appendix Four.

316 [Murray], 21 May 1798, NA, 620/3/32/6. For weaponry of Wicklow United Irishmen see Tyson, 20 January 1798, NA, SOC, 1017/62 and Ridgeway, *Trial of William Michael Byrne*, p. 118. Arklow rebels were instructed to purchase pikes from recognized sympathisers rather than making their own in order to minimize risk of exposure. John Hall, 23 May 1798, TCD, MS 871.

317 Murray, nd[1798], TCD, MS 869/f.16.

318 6 May 1798, NA, 620/37/29 and [Robinson] to Cooke, 7 May 1798, NA, 620/37/33.

319 See O'Donnell, 'Michael Dwyer', pp. 17–22.

320 [Robinson] to Cooke, 19 May 1798, NA, 620/37/109. See also Hardy to Castlereagh, 27 May 1798, NA, 620/37/128.

321 Petition of Dennis Farrell, n.d. [1798/9], NA, 620/51/20. Farrell remained an untried prisoner on the prison hulk *Brunskill* in March 1799. See also 9 March 1799, NA, 620/7/79/40, Cullen, NLI, MS 8339, p. 125 and Fitzpatrick, *Sham squire*, p. 309.

322 Byrne, *Memoirs*, I, p. 22.

323 Sproule to Cooke, n.d. [late May 1798], NA, 620/51/25.

324 [Murray], 21 May 1798, NA, 620/3/32/6 See also PRO, WO, 13/2574 and McAnally, *Irish Militia*, pp. 153–9. For rebel expectations of militia defections in Wexford and Carlow see Byrne, *Memoirs*, I, pp. 155–6 and Farrell, *Carlow in '98*, p. 60.

325 *FDJ*, 8 and 10 June 1797.

326 27 October 1797, PRO, WO 68/402/(i), p. 208. See also *HJ*, 24 June 1795 and O'Cathaoir, *Holy Redeemer Church*, p. 13.

327 Cited in K. Murray,'Loughlinstown camp' in *DHR*, VII, no. 1, 1944, p. 25.

328 Fitzpatrick, *Cloncurry and his times*, pp. 93–4.

329 [Murray], 21 May 1798, NA, 620/3/32/6. See also Major-General George Nugent to Alexander Knox, 6 June 1798, NLI, MS 56, p. 178 and Musgrave, *Rebellions*, 4th edn., p. 213. The Kildare, Clare and Donegal Militia were all based in Lehaunstown during the winter of 1796/7 and afterwards. Also present were the Wexford and Limerick City Militia and the Inverness, Caithness and Rothsay Fencible Infantry. *NCEP*, 31 October 1796.

330 Pharis Martin to [Downshire], 8 April 1797, PRONI, D.607/E/245, Reamonn O'Muiri, 'Lt John Lindley St Leger, United Irishman' in *Seanchas Ard Mhaca*, II, no.1, 1985, pp. 133–98, Bartlett, 'Indiscipline', pp. 125–8, *FDJ*, 15 June 1797, Wells, *Insurrection*, Chapter 5 and McDowell, *Ireland in the age*, pp. 566–7.

331 Cullen, NLI, MS 9761, p. 155. See also Teeling, *Sequel*, p. 232, Lane to Downshire, 1 May 1797, PRONI, D.607/E/258, 21 May 1797, D.607/ E/262 PRO, WO 68/402/(i), p. 167.

332 Cullen, NLI, MS 9762, p. 10.

333 Sproule to Cooke, 17 May 1798, NA, 620/37/97.

334 Quoted in Madden, *United*, IV, pp. 348–9. See also, Ibid., pp. 255–6, McDowell, *Ireland in the age*, pp. 601–4, Sproule to Cooke, 19 May 1798, NA, 620/37/105, Sproule to Lees, 25 May 1798, NA, 620/51/20, Cullen, *Insurgent*, p. 15 and Parsons to Camden, 27 March 1798, NLI, MS 13,840. For early life and United Irish careers of the Sheares brothers see Madden, *United*, I, pp. 254–7, 415 and IV, pp. 200–390.

335 Graham, 'Union of Power', pp. 252–3.

336 Sproule to [Lees], 20 May 1798, PRO, HO 100/76/220.

337 Sproule's informant learned on 20 May that 'the two Shear[e]s & mr [William] Lawless were suspected of giving information to Government & therefore they had false information given to them in order that Government might be deluded'. Sproule to [Lees], 20 May 1798, PRO, HO 100/76/220. See also Graham, 'Union of Power', p. 252.

338 Sproule to Cooke, 17 May 1798, NA, 620/37/97. See also Musgrave, *Rebellions*, p. 202 and Appendix XIV.

339 McDowell, *Ireland*, p. 603.

340 Sproule to Cooke, 19 May 1798, NA, 620/51/27 and James Verner to ——, 24 May 1798, NA, 620/51/42.

341 Musgrave, *Rebellions*, p. 215.

342 Patrickson to Downshire, 23 May 1798, PRONI, D.607/F/181, Ridgeway, *Trial of William Michael Byrne*, pp. 113–6 and Delamere, 10 April 1800, NA, SPP, 346.

343 O'Neil Stratford to ——, 23 May 1798, NA, 620/37/133. See also 'J.W.' [Leonard McNally] to Cooke, 23 May 1798, NA, 620/51/23.

344 Sproule to Cooke, 23 May 1798, NA, 620/51/18. At that time Sproule believed that the city rising would follow within twenty four hours. Sproule to Lees, 23 May 1798, NA, 621/51/10.

345 Pakenham, *Liberty*, p. 113. Musgrave's sources claimed that only one hour's warning had been received. Musgrave, *Rebellions*, pp. 202–3, 214 and Hardy to Cooke, 22 May 1798, NA, 620/37/123.

346 Musgrave, *Rebellions*, p. 118.

347 Verner to J. W. Maxwell, 23 May 1798, PRONI, T.1023/146A. See also 'Senior' to Cooke, n.d. [May 1798], NA, 620/18/2 and Musgrave, *Rebellions*, p. 212.

348 Maria H to Helen Clarke, 23 May 1798, NLI, MS 13,839, Pakenham, *Liberty*, pp. 124, 131, Plowden, *Historical Account*, pp. 688–9 and Archer, 'Fingal in 1798', pp. 66–70. Musgrave's sources informed him that Holt 'was to have descended from the Wicklow mountains, as soon as he received intelligence that the rebels had risen in Dublin.' Musgrave, *Rebellions*, p. 218.

349 28 March 1799, NA, 620/17/30/18.

350 Camden to Portland, 24 May 1798, PRO, HO 100/76/258 and Pakenham, *Liberty*, p. 117.

351 *Irish Magazine*, July 1808, p. 323.

352 See Graham, 'Union of Power', p. 353 and Jonah Barrington, *Historic memoirs of Ireland* (Dublin, 1833), II, pp. 255–7.

353 Patrickson to Downshire, 23 May 1798, PRONI, D.607/F/181 and Mrs H. to Clarke, 23 May 1798, NLI, MS 13,837 Robert Ross supplied the following account of the rising to Downshire: 'Nine o'clock at night, government get a second information. Drums beat to arms. A rising in mass immediately expected. The army and yeomanry alerted spirited and in force, and the rising prevented ... much useful information obtained by their confessions

[i.e. prisoners] under the punishment'. Ross to Downshire, 24 May 1798, PRONI, D.607/F/183.

354 Ross to Downshire, n.d. [24 May 1798], PRONI, D.607/F/185. Wade and Ledwich were executed in Dublin on 26 May and their bodies thrown into the notorious 'croppies acre' or 'croppies hole' on the esplanade in front of what was then the Royal Barracks (Collins Barracks). J. Collins, *Life in old Dublin* (Dublin, 1913), pp. 57–61, Musgrave, *Rebellions*, p. 223–4 and Pakenham, *Liberty*, p. 131.

355 Camden to Portland, 24 May 1798, PRO, HO100/76/258.

356 Leadbeater, *Ballitore*, I, pp. 218. See also Pakenham, *Liberty*, p. 132. The Belfast coach was stopped by the rebels at Santry. Archer, 'Fingal in 1798', p. 66–7.

357 Ross to Downshire, 24 May 1798, PRONI, D.607/F/183.

358 Cullen quoted in Dickson, *Dwyer*, p. 30. See also Pakenham, *Liberty*, p. 138, Camden to Portland, 24 May 1798, PRO, HO 100/76/258 and Leadbeater, *Papers*, I, pp. 218–20.

CHAPTER FOUR

1 Patrickson to Downshire, 25 May 1798, PRONI, D.607/F/185. Patrickson learned of this from his son who was one of the senior officers in Ballymore during the attack. See also Pakenham, *Liberty*, p. 135, Aldborough to ——, 27 May 1798, NA, 670/37/182, Musgrave, *Rebellions*, 4th edn., pp. 243–4 and Fitzpatrick, *Sham squire*, p. 311.

2 Robinson to Cooke, 29 May 1798, NA, 620/37/211A.

3 Robinson to Aldborough, 24 May 1798, NA, 670/38/51 and Musgrave, *Rebellions*, Appendix XVI, p. 72. See also Pakenham, *Liberty*, pp. 114–6 and Shannon to Boyle, 24 May 1798, *Letters*, p. 103.

4 Lieutenant Macauley to Hardy, 24 May 1798 and Madden, *United*, IV, p. 392.

5 Camden to Portland, 25 May 1798, PRO, HO 100/76/271, Carroll to ——, 29 May 1798, HMC, Report 3, Appendix, 1872, p. 260 and Chavasse, *Baltinglass*, p. 5. Macauley claimed: 'We attacked the rebels on both sides, and completely routed them, leaving between one and two hundred killed, besides many wounded who made their escape . . . several of our men wounded, and one of the 9th dragoons very severely'. HT, 28 May 1798. Plowden was informed that 150 had been killed. Plowden, *Historical Review*, II, p. 150.

6 Dickson, *Dwyer*, p. 30–32, Cullen, *Insurgent*, pp. 76, 81, Cullen, NLI, MS 9762, p. 25. Valentine's death was wrongly attributed to Dwyer by the populist author J. T. Campion who also maintained the fiction that it was he who had placed Kavanagh in her care having fought at Stratford. J. T. Campion, *Michael Dwyer, or, the insurgent captain, a tale of '98* (Dublin, n.d.), pp. 58–60.

7 Cullen quoted in Dickson, *Dwyer*, p. 34. See also Petition of Hugh McClane, n.d., NA, 620/51/64 and 8 March 1799, NA, 620/17/30/11.

8 Cullen quoted in Dickson, *Dwyer*, p. 34. See also Musgrave, *Rebellions*, p. 242 and Fitzpatrick, *Sham Squire*, pp. 309–12.

9 Quoted in Fitzpatrick, *Sham squire*, pp. 260–1. For a list of those killed see Appendix Five. For differing and inaccurate accounts of Dunlavin see Kavanagh, *Popular History*, p. 39, Hanbidge, *Memories*, p. 84, Musgrave, *Rebellions*, 4th edn., p. 242, Hay, *History*, p. 79, O'Kelly, 'Historical note', p. 337 and Fitzpatrick, *Sham squire*, p. 262.

10 Musgrave, *Rebellions*, pp. 242–3. Fitzpatrick's account also erred in claiming that Saunders later persecuted Prendergast, the only survivor of the massacre. E. P. O'Kelly's researches revealed that Prendergast had 'completely recovered [from his wound] and entered Captain Morley Saunders' employment, and lived many years'. O'Kelly, 'Historical notes', p. 337. See also Fitzpatrick, *Sham squire*, pp. 261–2, 309.

11 Fitzpatrick, *Sham squire*, p. 309–10 and Cullen, NLI, MS 9762, p. 27 and MS 8339, p. 7. Cullen's source was probably Denis Griffin whose brother was one of those shot, apparently for venturing from Dublin to visit his aged father in Dunlavin. Fitzpatrick, *Sham squire*, p. 310.

12 ____ to Cooke, 19 May 1798, NA, 620/37/43, Cullen, *Insurgent*, p. 74, Cullen, NLI, MS 9762, p. 262 and MS 8339, p. 56. See also Kavanagh, *Popular History*, p. 39, Madden, *United*, IV, pp. 431, 473, Sherman, *Historical sketch*, p. 23, Plowden, *Historical Review*, II, pp. 732–3 and Gahan, *People's Rising*, p. 11.

13 Robinson to Cooke, 29 May 1798, NA, 620/37/211A.
14 Petition of Edward Byrne, 3 April 1799, NA, 620/49/110 Thomas King claimed 'Edward Byrne who lives as Glasscolman [i.e. Liscolman] near Tullow . . . headed the rebels at the first attack upon Hacketstown [25 May 1798] and fled, but being a freeholder obtained a protection through the influence, as is asserted, of Mr Hume'. King to Marsden, 16 January 1803, NA, 620/65/148.
15 *FJ*, 29 May 1798, Hardy Journal, 25 May 1798 and McGhee to ____, 25 May 1798 in Madden, *United*, IV, p. 400. Gardiner won great praise for his conduct at Hacketstown and in 1802 a printed document was compiled of notices and bulletins pertaining to his actions during the rebellion. n.d., 1802, BM, MS 35735, p. 211. Rossmore informed the Lord Lieutenant in June 1802 that 'Gardiner was for some time under my command at Hacketstown our situation was alarming . . . in those perilous days I did not meet a more loyal gentleman'. Rossmore to Hardwicke, 10 June 1802, BM, MS 35735, p. 149. Gardiner was a linen manufacturer who claimed to have received overtures from the United Irishmen to join them which obliged him to leave his home and work. He claimed somewhat cryptically in a petition to Hardwicke of having 'served Government more than is generally known which the attempts of the private assassin can tell'. Petition of Lieutenant Gardiner, 7 July 1802, BM, MS 35735, pp. 147–8.
16 McGhee to ——, 25 May 1798 in Madden, *United*, IV, p. 400. See also Ibid., p. 401, Camden to Portland, 26 May 1798, PRO, HO 100/80/330, King to Marsden, 16 January 1803, NA, 620/65/148 and Robinson to Cooke, 29 May 1798, NA, 620/37/211A.
17 R. Day, 'The medals of the Irish Volunteers' in *Cork Historical and Archaeological Society Journal,* 2nd series, IX, no. 60, 1906, pp. 167–8.
18 Fr P. Dunne to Troy, n.d., [c.1801] quoted in Madden, *United*, IV, p. 339. See also Pakenham, *Liberty*, pp. 135, 184, Patrickson to Downshire, 23 May 1798, PRONI, D.607/F/181 and Madden, *United*, IV, pp. 398–9.
19 Cooke to Wickham, 29 May 1798, HO 100/80/388 and Shannon to Boyle, 30 May 1798 in *Letters*, p. 107.
20 Pakenham, *Liberty*, pp. 160–3.
21 Cooke to Wickham, 29 May 1798, PRO, HO 100/80/338. See also O'Loinsigh, 'Rebellion in Meath', p. 64.
22 Major-General Morrison to Castlereagh, 26 June 1798, NA, 620/17/14.
23 Major General Nugent to General Knox, 26 May 1798, NLI MS 56, p. 165.
24 Castlereagh to ——, n.d., NA, 620/18/11/6.
25 See Ridgeway, *Trial of William Michael Byrne*, pp. 117–8. One of Boothman's brothers was a yeomen in Hornidge's Blessington Cavalry and his eponymous cousin who lived in Naas was an informer. Information of John Boothman, n.d. [c.May 1798], NA 620/51/60.
26 Johnson to Downshire, 6 June 1798, PRONI D.607/F/208. See also Cooke to Wickham, 28 May 1798, PRO, HO 100/80/336, E. Lynch to ——, 1 June 1798, NA, 620/38/15 and Hay, *History*, p. 103.
27 Parvisol to Cooke, 30 May 1798, NA, 620/37/218 and *SNL*, 21 September 1798.
28 Shannon to Boyle, 30 May 1798 in *Letters*, p. 105. See also Buckingham to Grenville, 31 May 1798 in *Fortescue*, IV, 1904, p. 225 and M.H. to ——, 31 May 1798, *Educational Facsimile*, no. 82.
29 Patrickson to Downshire, 1 June 1798, PRONI, D.607/F/190 and n.d., [30–31] May 1798, PRONI, D.607/F/185.
30 M.H. to ——, 31 May 1798, *Educational Facsimile*, no. 82. For the excesses of the Wicklow Militia see Liam Cox, 'Westmeath in the 1798 period' in *Irish Sword*, IX, 1969, pp. 6–7.
31 Patrickson to Downshire, 5 June 1798, PRONI, D.607/F/196.
32 R. Marshall to General Knox, 30 May 1798, NLI, MS 56, p. 170. See also Boothman, n.d. [c.May 1798], NA, 620/51/60.
33 Shannon to Boyle, 31 May 1798 in *Letters*, p. 107. See also Camden to Portland, 31 May 1798, PRO, HO 100/76/322 and Cooke to Wickham, 30 May 1798, PRO, HO 100/76/313.
34 E. Hinch to ——, 1 June 1798, NA 620/38/15.
35 Camden to Portland, 2 June 1798, PRO, HO 100/77/21 and Blayney to Lake, 31 May 1798, NA, 620/37/235.
36 Cullen, TCD, MS 1472, p. 202. See also Ridgeway, *Trial of William Michael Byrne*, p. 118.
37 Cooke understood that 'the force under Mich[ael] Reynolds which was driven from Blackmoor[e] Hill has much dispersed. Some [have] gone to Wexford, many sneaked home . . . many submitted'. Cooke to Wickham, 6 June 1798, PRO, HO 100/77/52.

38 Ann Tottenham to ——, 27 July 1798, NLI, MS 3531, p. 35 See also Hardy to Loftus, 29 May 1798, NA, 620/37/210 and Musgrave, *Rebellions*, I, pp. 386–7.

39 *HC*, 22 May 1788.

40 Holt MS, p. 15. See also *Irish Magazine*, May 1809, p. 24. Hugo's daughter Elizabeth married John Armstrong of the extremist Fermanagh Militia in 1800. See Ian Cantwell, 'Glendalough estate and the Hugos' in *Roundwood and district historical and folklore journal*, no. 4, 1991, pp. 32–4.

41 28 January 1801, NA, 620/10/113/5. See also 28 March 1799, NA, 620/17/30/33, Cullen, NLI, MS 8339, pp. 199–200 and Musgrave, *Rebellions*, 4th edn., p. 387.

42 Holt MS, pp. 21–2. See also Ibid., pp. 15–17. Musgrave, *Rebellions*, I, pp. 387–8, NA, MS 1017/6/10, Cullen, NLI, MS 8339, p. 57 and Hardy to Loftus, 29 May 1798, NA 620/37/210.

43 Ann Tottenham to ——, 27 July 1798, NLI, MS 3151, p. 35.

44 Cullen, *Insurgent*, p. 27.

45 Musgrave, *Rebellions*, I, p. 385. See also Ibid., p. 387, Marshall to Knox, 30 May 1798, NLI MS 56, p. 170, *HT*, 1 June 1798 and Cullen, *Insurgent*, p. 39.

46 Hardy Journal, 27 May 1798 and Musgrave, *Rebellions*, I, p. 386, Hardy to Loftus, 30 May 1798, NA, 620/37/224, 'Suffering loyalists', NLI, MIC 7665, Gilbert, *Documents*, p. 42 and Archer Papers, January 1801, NA, MS 1017/1/1.

47 Cullen, *Insurgent*, pp. 40–1, 28 March 1799, NA, 620/17/30/65 and Dickson, *Dwyer*, pp. 320, 347.

48 Musgrave, *Rebellions*, I, p. 386, *HT*, 1 June 1798 and Hardy to Loftus, 30 May, 1798, NA, 620/37/224. Gore's wound was deemed mortal and Edwards of Bray was not alone in considering him to be 'dying'. Edwards to Cooke, 30 May 1798, NA, 620/37/217. Holt was intrigued by Gore's scars when he viewed them in Dublin Castle in November 1798 and considered him an 'amiable gentleman'. Holt MS, p. 203.

49 Hardy Journal, 27 [sic] May 1798. See also Cullen, *Insurgent*, pp. 36–8, Musgrave, *Rebellions*, I, pp. 386–7, August 1798, PRO, HO 100/66/340 and Hardy to Loftus, 30 May 1798, NA, 620/37/224. Thomas McGuire was arrested by the Newtownmountkennedy yeomen in Dublin in July 1798 while attempting to flee the country on a ship. His Protestant cousins in the search party named Booth pretended not to recognize him in his sailor's uniform but he was seized by Corporal George Kennedy, courtmartialled and executed for killing Snell. Cullen, *Insurgent*, pp. 37–8. His brother John was probably the McGuire said in December 1798 to have succeeded Holt as the rebel commander and perpetrated 'several atrocious outrages'. *FJ*, 1 December 1798. This may have been the man of that name identified in October 1800 as an associate of Dwyer's who had escaped after capture in Santry, County Dublin. *FJ*, 25 October 1800.

50 Hardy to Loftus, 30 May 1798, NA 620/37/224.

51 Archibald McLaren, *A minute description of the battles of Vinegar Hill* . . . (1798), p. 9 and Hardy Journal, 27 [sic] May 1798. The muster rolls of the Britons show that they did not suffer fatalities other than Burganey, although it is possible that some of their wounded succumbed to their injuries. May 1798, PRO, WO, 13/2732. See also Camden to Portland, 30 May 1798, PRO, HO 100/80/348, *HT* of 1 June 1798, Shannon to Boyle, 30 May 1798 in *Letters*, p. 105 and Cullen, *Insurgent*, p. 41.

52 Shannon to Boyle, 30 May 1798 in *Letters*, p. 105. See also Taylor, *An History*, p. 115 and Musgrave, *Rebellions*, I, p. 396.

53 McLaren, *Minute description*, p. 9. See also Taylor, *An History*, p. 115 and Hardy to Loftus, 30 May 1798, NA, 620/37/224. Cullen mistakenly believed that this occurred about a week after the battle although his theory that some of those whose charred skeletons were recovered may have died of wounds is plausible. Cullen, *Insurgent*, p. 41.

54 Ann Tottenham to ——, 27 July 1798, NLI, MS 3151, p. 35. See also Hardy to Loftus, 30 May 1798, NA, 620/37/224 NLI, *Report on the private collections*, No. 51, p. 856.

55 Camden to Portland, 1 June 1798, PRO, HO 100/81/1.

56 Cullen, *Insurgent*, pp. 21–3. Cullen's highly detailed account was gleaned from interviews with surviving members of the affected families which he conducted in the early 1800s. His identification of some of the perpetrators is supported by the 1799 muster lists of the Newtownmountkennedy Cavalry and infantry which include M[ark?] Wickham, William Armstrong, Griffin Jones and several Foxs and Liveslys (aka Leasly). n.d., [July] 1799, NA, MS 1017/1/1 and 15 December 1799, 1017/6/5.

57 Cullen, *Insurgent*, pp. 23–5.

58 Ibid. pp. 24–7. There was an awareness in official circles that not all these killings could be justified and when John Farrell of the Delgany area was fatally 'assailed . . . with the utmost brutality' at Three Trout bridge William 'Smug Bill' Lively was confined in Wicklow Gaol for a period of several weeks. The censure may have arisen from the circumstance of Farrell being a wealthy man who had married into a 'very respectable protestant family'. At least one yeoman, McDonnell of Fairkelly, had opposed Bob Lively's actions and Cullen's sources maintained that Lively's brother William had been deliberately arrested to forestall a case being brought against the actual perpetrator. Cullen, TCD, MS 1472, p. 200.
59 Cullen, *Insurgent*, pp. 25–35. See also Fugitive Bill for Neil family members proscribed as United Irishmen, August 1798, PRO, HO 100/ 66/340.
60 See Information of John Murphy, 20 June 1798, NA, 620/38/188, Cullen TCD, MS 1472, p. 202 and Cullen, *Insurgent*, p. 29. Michael Niall is commemorated by a modern Irish language plaque in Newtownmountkennedy.
61 Memorial of William Steel, 14 October 1805 in Dickson, *Dwyer*, pp. 122–4. Dickson believed that Murphy was one of the Murphys of Spinians, which would explain why Michael Dwyer's men, who held him in high esteem, attacked Steel in late 1799. He may also be identified with the Murphy who led the insurgents at Ballitore on 24/25 May 1798. Ibid., pp. 126–7.
62 Richard Kirwan, 'Report of the gold mines in the county of Wicklow with observations thereon' in *DST*, II, part 2, 1801, p. 136. See also Edwards to Cooke, 30 May 1798, NA, 620/37/217.
63 NLI, MS 16,306 cited by Cowman, 'Mining community', pp. 770–71.
64 Lieutenant-Colonel Freeman to Tyrawley, 23 December 1799, NLI, *Kilmainham Papers*, CXI, p. 6.
65 *Proceeding of a general court martial . . . against capt. John Giffard . . .* , pp. 51–5. See also Ibid., p. 85.
66 Pakenham, *Liberty*, pp. 188–91.
67 Dickson, *Wexford Rising*, pp. 45–7, L. M. Cullen, '1798 Rebellion', pp. 290 and Cullen, *Recollections*, pp. 10–11.
68 Byrne, *Memoirs*, I, pp. 28–40, Hay, *History*, p. 106, Cullen, TCD, MS 1472, pp. 202–3, 214 and Madden, *United*, IV, pp. 431–2.
69 Cullen, *Recollections*, p. 17. A clash between the Camolin Cavalry and local insurgents led by Murphy at The Harrow was one of the first in the Wexford. Among the yeoman dead was Lieutenant Thomas Bookey whose brother Richard was a lieutenant in the Carnew Infantry. Furlong, *Murphy*, pp. 50–1 and Taylor, *An history*, p. 43.
70 Wainwright to Fitzwilliam, 6 February 1800, NLI, MIC 5641.
71 Hardy to Cooke, 28 May 1798, NA, 620/37/190.
72 Wainwright to Fitzwilliam, 6 February 1800, NLI, MIC 5641. See also Hay, *History*, p. 103.
73 Cullen, TCD, MS 1472, p. 204 and Madden, *United*, IV, pp. 432–3. See also Marshall to Knox, 30 May 1798, NLI, MS 56, p. 170 and Gahan, *People's Rising*, pp. 32–3.
74 Hay, *History*, pp. 102–3. See also Cullen, TCD, MS 1472, p. 204.
75 Hardy Journal, 28 May 1798. See also Richard Foote to ——, 27 May 1798, NA, 620/37/179, Croker, *Researches*, p. 348 and Brian Cleary, 'The battle of Oulart Hill' in *The Past*, no. 19, 1995, pp. 5–66.
76 Camden to Portland, 30 May 1798, PRO, HO 100/81/13. See also Plowden, *Historical Review*, II, p. 725, Gahan, *People's Rising*, pp. 36– 58 and Hay, *History*, p. 146.
77 Fawcett to Eustace, 31 May 1798, NA, 620/38/11. See also Cloney, *Narrative*, p. 21, Madden, *United*, IV, p. 436 and McDowell, *Ireland in the age*, p. 626.
78 Dickson, *Wexford rising*, p. 102 and Whelan, 'Religious factor', p. 68.
79 Byrne, *Memoirs*, I, pp. 28–48.
80 *Dublin Gazette*, 2 June 1798. See also Camden to Portland, 2 June 1798, PRO, HO 100/81/7.
81 L'Estrange to ——, 1 June 1798, NA, 620/38/4.
82 Wainwright to Fitzwilliam, 6 February 1800, NLI, MIC 5641. See also 14 November 1799, NA, 620/17/30/42 and 1 May 1800, NA, 620/17/ 30/19. Hay's published version of events was based on hearsay and, while more or less accurate in its general detail, confused the major 1 June incident with that of 28 May. Hay was apparently the first to misdate the more bloody massacre as 25 May, an error which has proven very influential. See Hay, *History*, pp. 97–8, Madden, *United*, I, p. 346, Gahan, *People's Rising*, pp. 10–11 and Pakenham, *Liberty*, pp. 135–6. Further evidence that the major massacre occurred in June

is contained within the MS notes compiled by Roundwood United Irishman James Kavanagh in 1801. Kavanagh stated that thirty-nine men had been killed 'at Carnew in June 1798'. n.d., NA 620/10/116/1.

83 Wainwright to Fitzwilliam, 6 February 1800, NLI, MIC 5641. See also n.d., 1801, NA, 620/10/116/1.

84 Quoted in Thomas Bartlett (ed.), 'An officer's memoir of 1798' in *Wexford Historical Society Journal*, no. 12, 1988–9, pp. 72–85, p. 76.

85 McLaren, *Minute Description*, pp. 9–10, Pakenham, *Liberty*, p. 206, Camden to Portland, 1 June 1798, PRO, HO 100/81/1 and Teeling, *Sequel*, pp. 91–2.

86 Patrickson to Downshire, 5 June [1798], PRONI, D.607/F/196.

87 Pakenham, *Liberty*, pp. 207–8, Castlereagh to Pelham, 6 June 1798 in Gilbert, *Documents*, p. 127 and Tighe to ——, 20 June 1798, NLI, MS 4813. Richard Johnson commented that Walpole had been 'out generalled and killed with about 100 men and the loss of his artillery', a remark indicative of the great unease his defeat aroused in loyalist circles. Johnson to Downshire, 6 June 1798, PRONI, D.607/F/202.

88 22 September 1798, PRO, HO 100/74/89–90. See also Castlereagh to Knox, 5 June 1798, NLI, MS 56, p. 176 and Camden to Portland, 5 June 1798 in Madden, *United*, IV, p. 40.

89 Tighe to [Ponsonby], 20 June 1798, NLI, MS 4813. Sarah Tighe criticized Walpole's 'vile generalship' in leading his men 'into the midst of the foe'.

90 Ancram, 'Officer's memoir', pp. 78–9.

91 McLaren, *Minute Description*, p. 10.

92 Castlereagh to Pelham, 6 June 1798 in Gilbert, *Documents*, p. 127 and Loftus to Bentinck, 3 July 1798 in *Irish official papers*, p. 185.

93 G. A. Hayes McCoy, *Irish battles*, (London, 1969), p. 285 and Furlong, *Murphy*, p. 101.

94 Loftus to Hardy, 4 June 1798, NA, OP 198/15 (5).

95 Hardy to Lake, 5 June 1798, NA, OP 198/15 (5).

96 Hardy Journal, 3–5 June 1798.

97 Hardy to Lake, Noon, 5 June 1798, NA, OP 198/15 (5). See also McCoy, *Battles*, p. 286.

98 Hardy to Castlereagh, 4 June 1798 quoted in Madden, *United*, IV, p. 404. When Revd Bayly met Hardy in Dublin on 15 June the major was anticipating an appointment to the army staff. Bayly to H. Bayly, 15 June 1798, NA MS 2426, p. 11.

99 Byrne, *Memoirs*, I, p. 28.

100 See *A list of the counties of Ireland and the respective yeomanry corps in each . . . 1st June 1798* (Dublin, 1798) and Nixon to Fitzwilliam, 18–19 January 1797, NLI, MIC 5641.

101 The lack of rebel activity in southern and eastern Wicklow influenced Henry Lambart Bayly's claim that this resulted from the failure of the United Irishmen to make an 'impression' in the district. This viewpoint did not take into account the exertions of large numbers of men from the region in the fighting in north Wexford and was primarily influenced by post-rebellion political concerns rather than historical ones. Mason, *Statistical Survey*, II, p. 63. The type of mobilization anticipated in Wicklow can be gleaned from what occurred in north Wexford where the rebel command structure was virtually intact on the eve of rebellion and vacancies were easily filled by substitutes and released prisoners once the fighting began.

102 Hardy to Castlereagh, 4 June 1798 in *Dublin Gazette*, 7 June 1798.

103 Byrne, *Memoirs*, I, p. 47.

104 Byrne, *Memoirs*, I, p. 95.

105 Leadbeater, *Ballitore*, I, p. 227.

106 Byrne, *Memoirs*, I, p. 114. See also 28 March 1799, NA, 620/17/30/64, *Trial of William Byrne*, pp. 7, 30–31, *Catholic Telegraph*, 29 September 1856 and Dickson, *Dwyer*, pp. 36–7, 256.

107 *Trial of William Byrne*, pp. 8–9.

108 *Trial of William Byrne*, pp. 19, 30.

109 McCoy, *Battles*, pp. 284–9 and Furlong, *Murphy*, pp. 104–5.

110 14 November 1799, NA, 620/17/30/42.

111 1 May 1800, NA, 620/17/30/19. See also Information of James Kenny, 8 July 1799 and Information of Mattew Fennell, 9 July 1799, NA, PPC, 411, Shannon to Boyle, 5 June 1798 in *Letters*, p. 160 and Furlong, *Murphy*, p. 107.

112 Castlereagh to [Knox], 5 June 1798, NLI, MS 56, p. 176.

113 McLaren, *Minute description*, p. 12. See also 14 November 1799, NA, 620/17/30/42 and Lake to Wickham, 7 June 1798, PRO, HO 100/81/31.

114 1 May 1800, NA, 620/17/30/19 and Information of Matthew Fennell, 9 July 1798, NA, PPC, 411.

115 Cullen, *Recollections*, p. 50 and Camden to Portland, PRO, HO 100/77/58. Rossmore told Shannon that 'large bodies [of rebels] are assembled on the confines of Wicklow and Wexford (Carnew I think) where he says they live in a riot,eating and drinking of the very best! Their cattle too live in the cornfields and meadows'. Shannon to Boyle, 5 June 1798 in *Letters*, p. 110.

116 Claims that Byrne had spent the whole rebellion prior to 8 June in hiding were based on hearsay which may have been falsified to obscure the true extent of his role in 1798 when on trial for his life. *Trial of William Byrne*, pp. 43–4. See also Dickson, *Dwyer*, p. 60.

117 *Trial of William Byrne*, pp. 6, 10.

118 Pakenham, *Liberty*, p. 214.

119 Madden, *United*, IV, pp. 533–7, 542–49, Cloney, *Narrative*, p. 81, Dickson, *Wexford Rising*, pp. 108, 200–1, Cullen, *Recollections*, p. 30, Byrne, *Memoirs*, I, pp. 95 and McCoy, *Battles*, pp. 288–9.

120 Elliott to Pelham, 4 June 1798 in Gilbert, *Documents*, p. 127 and Pakenham, *Liberty*, pp. 230–1.

121 Cloney, *Narrative*, p. 30. See also L. M. Cullen, '1798 rebellion', p. 287.

122 Cloney, *Narrative*, p. 35.

123 Teeling, *Sequel*, pp. 240–1. There was, however, some attempt to co-ordinate a second assault on New Ross. A Captain Michael Murphy of The Rower, Kilkenny, went from the insurgent camp at Glenmore to one in Wexford in June 1798, probably Lacken, to obtain a cannon and was told that 'he was to have notice when the rebels . . . were to attack Ross again from the Wexford side'. 20 July 1798, NA 620/6/70/1.

124 Pakenham, *Liberty*, pp. 230–2 and Camden to Portland, n.d., [June 1798], PRO, HO 100/71/127.

125 Tottenham to Anne Tottenham, 12 June 1798, Tottenham Papers, NLI, p. 4937. Lake to Wickham, 7 June 1798, PRO, HO 100/81/31, Major-General Johnson to Lake 5 or 9 June 1798 in Madden, *United*, IV, pp. 403–5 and Mrs Reed, 'Cursory remarks', p. 238.

126 Shannon to Boyle, 7 June 1798 in *Letters*, p. 112.

127 Camden to Portland, 6 and 8 June 1798 in Gilbert, *Documents*, pp. 128–32. Camden's successor, Lord Cornwallis, thought Johnson 'a wrong headed blockhead' but acknowledged that he was 'adored for his defence at New Ross.' Cornwallis to Ross, 15 July 1799 in *Correspondence*, III, p. 116.

128 Cloney, *Narrative*, p. 54.

129 n.d., [4–5 June 1798], NA, 620/51/225. See also Holt, MS, p. 21. For Brennan see *Enniscorthy Guardian*, 5 September 1936.

130 Cullen, *Recollections*, p. 30.

131 n.d., [4–5 June 1798], NA, 620/51/225. See also Cooke to Wickham, 6 June 1798, PRO, HO 100/77/52.

132 Dundas to Castlereagh, 8 August 1798, NA 620/39/158.

133 Sproule to Lees, 5 June 1798, NA, 620/38/57.

134 Byrne, *Memoirs*, I, p. 118.

135 Pakenham, *Liberty*, pp. 176–7, Tighe to ——, 12 June 1798, NLI, MS 4813 and Musgrave, *Rebellions*, p. 402.

136 Buckingham to Grenville, *Fortescue*, IV, p. 231. See also Tighe to ——, 9 October 1798, NLI, MS 4813.

137 Tighe to ——, 4 June 1798, NLI, MS 4813 and Abraham Chritchley to Castlereagh, 8 October 1800, NA 620/17/30/21.

138 McLaren, *Minute description*, p. 12. See also Pakenham, *Liberty*, p. 214.

139 Edwards to ——, 6 June 1798, NA, 620/38/63.

140 Cornwallis, *Correspondence*, II, p. 370, Maxwell, *County and town*, p. 83, Hanbidge, *Memories*, p. 84 and NLI, MS 7229, p. 71.

141 Steel memorial, 14 October 1805 in Dickson, *Dwyer*, p. 122. See also Ibid., pp. 121–3.

142 C.M. Drury, 'West county Wicklow notes' in *Kildare Archaeological and History Society Journal*, V, 1906–8, pp. 327–8.

143 Maxwell, *County and town*, pp. 79, 82–3, Shannon to Boyle, 6–7 June and 19 September 1798 in *Letters*, pp. 111, 159 and Information of Joseph Holt, 16 November 1798, NA, 620/40/39A.

144 Hardy Journal, 30 May 1798.

145 Camden to Portland, 5 June 1798, PRO, HO 100/77/50 McCoy, *Battles*, p. 285, Shannon to Boyle, 6 June 1798, *Letters*, p. 111, *HT*, 6 June 1798 and Camden to Pelham, 6 June 1798 in Gilbert, *Documents*, pp. 128–9. There was a marked reluctance in Britain to send regular troops to Ireland given the shortage of military personnel. One point of concern was that seven of the regiments available had been recruited in Ireland and were deemed unsuited to suppressing the rebellion. Dundas, when writing to the King, expressed his 'sincere reluctance . . . to consent to send[ing] so much of the small regular force in the country to Ireland, but considering the danger of the rebellion extending itself so far as to place the harbours or Cork & Waterford in the possession of the rebels, and consequently of France, mr Dundas does not feel it possible not to advise your Majesty to concur in the measure as now proposed and arranged'. Dundas to the King, 2 June 1798 in *The later correspondence of George III* (Cambridge, 1967), edited by A. Aspinall, 5 vols., III, pp. 68–9.

146 Castlereagh to Pelham, 8 June 1798 in Gilbert, *Documents*, pp. 131–2. See also Wickham to Castlereagh, 8 June 1798 in Castlereagh, *Memoirs*, I, p. 215.

147 Hardy to Lake, 11 June 1798, NA, 620/38/126, McLaren, *Minute description*, p. 12, Cooke to Wickham, 6 June 1798, PRO, HO 100/77/ 57. Hardy derived considerable respect for his conduct in the aftermath of Walpole's defeat and the *Annual Register* for 1798 singled him out for praise in its account of the rebellion. After a section detailing how the troops had fallen back on Wicklow Town it claimed; 'Major Hardy, its commander, had not been able to maintain [Wicklow Town] without considerable difficulty. This officer strongly remonstrated against the evacuation of Arklow, a position of great importance, and one which he thought might be defended successfully. Under his orders the garrison returned without halting even for refreshment'. *Annual Register*, 1798, p. 125. While this account compounded the first re-occupation of Gorey with that of Arklow and obscures the panic which had gripped the soldiery after Tubberneering, it attests to the significance placed on holding the town and Hardy's cool handling of the crisis.

148 Castlereagh to Pelham, 8 June 1798 in Gilbert, *Documents*, p. 131, McCoy, *Battles*, pp. 286–7, Camden to Pelham, 5 June 1798, PRO, HO 100/77/50 and Musgrave, *Rebellions*, 4th edn., p. 458.

149 *HT*, 6 June 1798. See also McCoy, *Battles*, pp. 288, 296.

150 Shannon to Boyle, 5 June 1798 in *Letters*, p. 110. Shannon further asserted that 'we do not seem to have ability equal to that of the rebels, and who, if they shall defeat our Wexford army, may march unmolested to Dublin'. Ibid., p. 108.

151 Castlereagh to Pelham, 8 June 1798 in Gilbert, *Documents*, p. 130.

152 Needham to Hardy, six a.m., 10 June 1798, NA, OP 198/15 (7), 'Murphy Papers', Notes of Lady Charlotte Mary, Countess of Carysfort (1838–1918) as transcribed by Georgina Murphy of Ferrybank, Arklow in 1877, pp. 49–50 and *Journal of the Society for Army Historical Research*, Spring 1974, LII, no. 209.

153 Needham to Littlehales, 18 December 1799, NA, 620/7/76/4 and Memorial of Owen Fawcett, 13 December 1799, NA, 620/7/76/9.

154 Musgrave, *Rebellions*, 4th edn., p. 403. See also Shannon to Boyle, 5 June 1798 in *Letters*, p. 110, Thomas Edwards to Cooke, 27 March 1800, NA, 670/57/94 and McLaren, *Minute description*, p. 12.

155 Musgrave, *Rebellions*, 4th edn., pp. 409–414. See also Plowden, *Historical Review*, II, p. 737.

156 *Trial of William Byrne*, p. 22. 'The different corps were drawn up, the gunsmen in the front, and the pikemen in the rear, and they were marched about'. Ibid., p. 10.

157 Dickson, *Dwyer*, p. 409. See also Cullen, *Recollections*, p. 23 and McCoy, *Battles*, p. 290. An attempt to account for the tardiness of the rebels en route to Arklow was made by Samuel Sproule who learned from one of his rebel informants that '[Revd Philip] Roach and [Fr Michael] Murphy said mass four times on the march from Gorey to Arklow'. This seems unlikely, not least in that Roche was in southern Wexford. Sproule to Hardwicke, 16 November 1801, BM, MS 35731, p. 219.

158 Cullen, *Recollections*, p. 23 and Furlong, *Murphy*, p. 113.

159 Murphy Papers, pp. 45, 52. Reuban Prole, a close relation of the Flight family, evidently had a narrow escape when local Catholics concealed his whereabouts from searching rebels.

160 Cullen, *Personal Recollections*, pp. 23–4.

161 McCoy, *Battles*, pp. 297–8, Musgrave, *Rebellions*, 4th edn., pp. 411–12 and Pat Power, 'The battle of Arklow, its cause and course, an illustrated lecture' (Arklow, 1997), pp. 20–21.

162 Henry Lambart Bayly to Edward Bayly, 9 June 1798, NA, MS 2464. Henry Bayly later misattributed the action to 'strangers during the heat of battle', probably in order to conceal the enmity in which his father had been held by local men and to shore up the myth of non-United Irish organization in Arklow. Shaw Mason, *Statistical Survey*, II, p. 62. In 1801 Bayly's friend Lord Proby was unequivocal in stating that the underlying reasons for the attack were that the reverend had exerted himself 'as much as it was possible'. Proby to Hardwicke, 22 July 1801, BM, MS 35729, p. 243.

163 Bayly to Henry Bayly,'Sunday' [9 June 1798?], NA, MS 2464, p. 8.

164 *Trial of William Byrne*, p. 80. Patrick Harold testified that he 'understood that it was burned by order of Perry and [the] prisoner [Byrne].' Ibid., p. 30. See also Byrne, *Memoirs*, I, p. 84 and John Hunter Gowan to Marsden, 22 October 1800, NA, 620/57/128.

165 Tighe to ——, 10 June 1798, NLI, MS 4813. See also Cullen, *Personal Recollections*, p. 23 and Gahan, *People's Rising*, p. 153.

166 Needham to Lake, 9 June 1798, PRO, HO 100/77/122.

167 *Trial of William Byrne*, pp. 8, 21 and Musgrave, *Rebellions*, 4th edn., p. 413.

168 See G. A. Hayes-McCoy, 'The Government Forces which opposed the Irish Insurgents at 1798' in *Irish Sword*, IV, no. 14, 1959–60, pp. 23–4 and H. Moore to Lake, 9 June 1798, NA, 620/38/112. According to Needham; 'About 3 o'clock . . . the rebel army presented itself at my outpost in very great numbers. They approached from Coolgreaney road and along the sand ditches on the shore in two immense columns about the whole of the intermediate space embracing my entire front was crowded by a rabble armed with pikes and fire arms and bearing down on me without any regular order'. Needham to [Camden], 10 June 1798, PRO, HO 100/73/219–21.

169 Bayly to Bayly, 9 June 1798, NA, MS 2464. Musgrave's claims that rebel and army cannon had begun exchanging fire around 11.00 and that the Durhams did not arrive until 1.00 are probably incorrect. Musgrave, *Rebellions*, p. 436.

170 Needham to Lake, 9 June 1798, PRO, HO 100/77/122. See also [Skerret] to [Moore], 16 July 1798, NLI, MS 21, 586. This officer,very probably Skerret of the Durhams,was dispatched from Dublin by Lake on 'every coach I could put my hands on' to reinforce Arklow and arrived at two a.m. on 9 June. Later in the afternoon '25,000 rabble with six pieces of cannon and 4000 stand of arms' attacked. He recalled that the rebels 'presented themselves in [a] column not unlike a large forrest of trees with pikes in their hands within a hundred yards of us with three pieces of cannon embracing a front of twenty yards. At this moment my cannon with grape shot and my *Brave Durhams* with small arms attacked them and threw in such a heavy fire in an hour and [a] half [that] we absolutely mowed down their ranks three times'.

171 Teeling, *Sequel*, pp. 250–1 and Cullen, *Recollections*, pp. 24, 45, Deposition of Andrew Sheppard, 23 September 1799 in Musgrave, *Rebellions*, 4th edn., pp. 768–70 and McLaren, *Minute description*, p. 18. Needham reported that the rebels had four pieces which were manned by two Antrim Militia and four Ancient Briton prisoners. Needham to Camden, 10 June 1798, NA, 620/38/114.

172 Cullen, *Recollections*, p. 24, Murphy Papers, p. 52 and *JSAHR*, Spring 1974, LII, no. 209, McLaren, *Minute description*, p. 18 and Byrne, *Memoirs*, I, p. 101.

173 McCoy, *Battles*, pp. 302–3, Musgrave, *Rebellions*, 4th edn., p. 414.

174 Murphy Papers, pp. 43–6 and *JSAHR* Spring 1974, LII, no. 209. Richard Kearon was a close business associate of Garret Graham. See Kavanagh, 'Liverpool connection', p. 46.

175 Murphy Papers, pp. 47–8. When the dying man expired, a man known as 'Gen[eral] O'Neill', probably Colonel Denis O'Neil of Enniscorthy, ordered that he be interred in the grounds of the Abbey. Murphy Papers, p. 48.

176 Moore to Lake, 9 June 1798, NA, 620/38/112.

177 *HT*, 18 June 1798. Property losses included the Arklow residences of George Heath, Thomas Bavister, Earl Carysfort, Charles Coates, Ralph Fairbrother, Thomas Gill, Thomas Graham, Ann Kearns, George Kearen, Thomas Kearen, Robert Kinch, Ann Marshall, William Moreton, Richard Price and John Sherwood. NLI, MIC 7665. Forty-nine persons had lost their homes in the battle. Musgrave, *Rebellions*, Appendix XVI, p. 72.

178 Power, 'Battle of Arklow', p. 26 and McLaren, *Minute description*, pp. 12–14.

179 *Trial of William Byrne*, p. 20.

180 [Skerret] to [Moore], 16 July 1798, NLI, MS 21, 586. See also Byrne, *Memoirs*, I, p. 103, Cullen, *Recollections*, p. 24 and William Maume to Sylvester Shea, 15 June 1798, NLI, MS 5006. Kirwan was related to the Byrnes of Ballymanus through his mother-in-law,

M. B. Meagher (nee Byrne) of Coolalugh. Kirwan's first wife, Mary Doyle of Ballintemple, died tragically in 1795 and his second, one Meagher, was related by marriage to the Byrnes of Monaseed. Byrne, *Memoirs*, I, pp. 117–20.

181 Needham to Hardy, 6.00 a.m., 10 June 1798, NA, OP 198/15 (7). See also Froude, *English in Ireland*, III, p. 422.

182 Needham to Hardy, 6.00 a.m., 10 June 1798, NA, OP 198/15 (7) Cullen, *Recollections*, p. 24. See also Madden, *United*, IV, p. 552.

183 Moore to Lake, 9 June 1798, NA, 620/38/100A. P. F. Kavanagh asserted that 'the English . . . [were] afraid to pursue' the retreating rebels when he unveiled George Smyth's statue of Fr Murphy in Arklow in July 1903. *Irish People*, 4 July 1903. See also *United Irishman*, 4 July 1903.

184 Cullen, *Recollections*, p. 25. See also Cullen, NA, M.5892(8), p. xii, Murphy Papers, p. 46 and *JSAHR*., Spring 1974, LII, no. 209.

185 Ibid., p. 25, Byrne, *Memoirs*, I, p. 108 and McCoy, *Battles*, pp. 305–6, Pakenham, *Liberty*, p. 246 and Furlong, *Murphy*, p. 116.

186 Johnson to Downshire, 12 June 1798, PRONI, D.607/F/231. Surgeon William Hartigan held a similar view stating 'there was no material advantage gained at Arklow, but merely repulsing them and killing 300 or 400. They keep their position, and are in great strength'. Hartigan to Downshire, 11 June 1798, PRONI, D.607/F/225. Many Wicklow inhabitants were pleased and the thirty-two ton ship built in the county town in 1798 was named *Needham*. Kavanagh, 'Liverpool connection', p. 47.

187 Hartigan to Downshire, 11 June 1798, PRONI, D.607/F/225. See also Mason, *Statistical Survey*, II, pp. 61–2.

188 *FDJ*, 3 December 1801. See also Hay, *History*, p. 182, Kavanagh, *History*, p. 188, Gordon, *Wexford*, pp. 258–60, Furlong, *Murphy*, p. 118 and *Irish People*, 4 July 1903.

189 Maitland to Lake, 9 June 1798, NA, 620/38/100A. See also Hardy Journal, 8 June 1798, Hardy to Lake, 9 June 1798, NA, 620/38/98a and Wheeler and Broadley, *War in Wexford*, pp. 120–1.

190 Wheeler and Broadley, *War in Wexford*, p. 120.

191 Dundas to Hardy, 10 June 1798, NA, OP 198/15 (6).

192 Murphy Papers, p. 51. See also Ibid., pp.44–6. See also *JSAHR*, Spring 1974, LII, no. 209.

193 Information of Fr John Martin, 16 June 1798, NA, 620/38/160. See also Hardy to Lake, 11 June 1798, NA 620/38/126. For an account of Fr Martin's career and relevant documents see Keogh, 'The most dangerous villain in society'; pp. 115–35, Richard Hayes 'Priests in the Independence Movement of '98' in *IER*, LXVI, 1945–6 and Daire Keogh 'Fr John Martin: An Augustinian friar and the Irish rebellion of 1798 in *Analecta Augustinia*, LI, Rome, 1988.

194 Quoted in Musgrave, *Rebellions*, 4th edn., p. 435.

195 Martin, 16 June 1798, NA, 620/38/160.

196 *HT*, 15 June 1798 See also Byrne, *Memoirs*, I, p. 118.

197 Martin, 16 June 1798, NA, 620/38/160. See also Martin, 16 June, NA, 620/38/126.

198 Martin, 16 June 1798, NA, 670/38/126, Petition of Fr John Martin, 24 March 1800, NA, PPC, 490, Information of Thomas Hawkins, n.d., [July 1798], NA, 620/52/127, 'Senior' to Cooke, n.d. [1798], NA, 620/17/32 and n.d., NA [1798], 620/18/1.

199 Holt MS, pp. 21–2. See also Sproule to Lees, 25 and 26 May 1798, NA, 620/51/25–6. See also Sirr papers, TCD, MS 869/8, f.92, f.98. McMahon of Aungier St is not to be confused with John McMahon, an ex-artillery officer and yeoman of New St, Phibsborough, who was also prominent in the city organization prior to his arrest in May 1798. McMahon of Phibsborough was well connected with the Kildare United Irishmen while Francis McMahon was 'a low set man.' Sproule to ——, n.d. [May 1798], NA, 620/51/38, Sproule to Lees, 19 May 1798, NA, 620/51/27, 17 May 1798, NA, 620/51/37 and 26 May 1798, NA, 620/51/26.

200 Sproule to Lees, 5 June 1798, NA, 620/38/57. See Camden to Pelham, 11 June 1798 in Gilbert, *Documents*, p. 132 and Connolly to Lees, n.d., [June? 1798], NA, 620/53/66.

201 Holt MS, p. 22. Holt derided McMahon as 'a little fellow . . . titled colonel McMahon'. For a fuller description of McMahon's activities and his relations with Holt see Information of Bartholomew Connolly, 24 July 1798, 620/37/73 and O'Donnell, 'Holt', pp. 159–60.

202 Holt MS, pp. 22–3.

203 Miley to Troy, 4 June 1798, DDA, Troy Correspondence, II, 116/7/91.

204 Senior to Cooke, n.d. [June 1798], NA, 620/18/1. Holt was apparently long considered the leader of the north Wicklowmen intending to attack the city and Musgrave was informed

that 'Holt was to have descended from the Wicklow mountains, as soon as he received intelligence that the rebels had risen in Dublin'. Musgrave, *Rebellions*, 4th edn., p. 218.

205 Giffard to Marsden, 14 June 1798, NA, 620/38/145.

206 NLI, MS.5398 and Madden, *United Irishmen*, II, pp. 181–9, 290–6. Giffard's comments may well have influenced the Downshire circle's notions of the Catholic nature of 1798 as they were privy to the contents his later correspondence from Wicklow and Wexford. Hartigan to Downshire, 20 June 1798, PRONI, D.607/F/258.

207 Tighe to ——, 16 June 1798, NLI, MS 4813.

208 *SNL*, 30 June 1798.

209 Musgrave, *Rebellions*, Appendix XVI, p. 73. See also NLI, MIC 7665, 28 March 1799, NA, 620/17/30/33, 66 and Dickson, *Dwyer*, p. 320. The following were robbed of arms or lost their houses; Thomas Hugo (Drumeen), Cornelius Chritchley (Derrybawn), John Chritchley (Laragh), Henry Harding, Joseph Harding, Robert Scarf, Alexander Scarf, Robert Freeman (all Tomriland), Christopher Wybrants, Charles Frizell and John Rochfort (all Castlekevin), John Freeman (Willmont), Francis Synge (Roundwood), Peter La Touche (Luggelaw), Revd Ambrose Weekes and William Weekes (Annamoe), Thomas Fleming (Diamond Hill), Andrew Price (Fairview/Mullinaveigue) and Frances Beresford, Andrew Keegan, George Coaly and Charles Burbidge (all Ballinastow). *SNL*, 14, 20 and 30 June, 4 July, 7 and 8 August 1798.

210 *SNL*, 20 June 1798, Archer to Marsden, 7 July 1800, NA, 620/57/44 and Cullen, NLI, MS 8339, p. 349.

211 Martin, 11 June 1798, NA, 620/38/126. Cullen, *Insurgent*, pp. 42–3. A few nights before this attack members of the corps had tried to assassinate Fr Andrew O'Toole, parish priest of Wicklow, who they lured under false pretences to dine with them. 'Big' John Gilbert of Blainroe allegedly attempted to strangle O'Toole at the table and might have succeeded had not a servant girl intervened. Ibid., p. 44.

212 *SNL*, 14 June 1798, King to Cooke, 10 January 1801, NA, 620/10/119/2 and Fitzpatrick, *Sham Squire*, p. 35.

213 See Ruan O'Donnell, 'Roundwood in 1798' in *Roundwood and district historical and folklore journal*, no.3, 1990, pp. 6–9.

214 Revd F. Lascelles to Downshire, 4 June 1798, PRONI, D.607/F/195 and Patrickson to Downshire, 6 June 1798, PRONI, D.607/F/199.

215 Stephenson to Downshire, 8 June 1798, PRONI, D.607/F/208, J. McKey to Downshire, 10 June 1798, PRONI, D.607/F/219, Pakenham, *Liberty*, pp. 170–3, 216–8 and McDowell, *Ireland in the Age*, pp. 636–8.

216 Stephenson to Downshire, 12 June 1798, PRONI, D.607/F/226. Stephenson related how on the approach of the military the rebels 'ran in all directions. They were pursued, and 25, or thereabouts, all that could be found [were] killed'. Nugent's assessment of the battle was more sober and put rebel losses at 300–400. Nugent to Lake, 10 June 1798, NA, 620/38/121.

217 Pakenham, *Liberty*, pp. 170–1, 215. One loyalist who described Munro as 'a little, hot headed fellow, who kept a shop in Lisburn' was satisfied that 'for some years past there was something brooding in the minds of the Republicans, and now it has broke out, and that they could not succeed, they will become loyal subjects'. J. McKey to Downshire, 14 June 1798, P.R.O.N.I., D.607/F/224.

218 28 March 1799, NA, 620/17/30/64 and Plowden, *Historical Review*, II, pp. 751–2 and Dwyer, 11 January 1804, PRO, HO 100/124/30.

219 28 March 1799, NA, 620/17/30/64, Cullen, *Personal Recollections*, p. 29, *Trial of William Byrne*, pp. 31–2, Furlong, *Murphy*, p. 123 and Byrne, *Memoirs*, I, p. 118.

220 Cullen, TCD, MS 1472, p. 211.

221 *Trial of William Byrne*, p. 14. See also Byrne, *Memoirs*, I, pp. 115–16 and Cullen, *Recollections*, pp. 28–30.

222 Byrne, *Memoirs*, I, p. 115. See also 14 November 1799, NA, 620/17/ 30/41 and Musgrave, *Rebellions*, Appendix XVI, pp. 72–3.

223 *Trial of William Byrne*, pp. 22, 31–2.

224 Byrne, *Memoirs*, I, pp. 111–12.

225 Camolin Duty Book cited in Wheeler and Broadley, *War in Wexford*, p. 140. See also Castlereagh to Pelham, 13 and 16 June 1798 in Gilbert, *Documents*, pp. 133, 140 and Pakenham, *Liberty*, pp. 282–5.

226 Byrne, *Memoirs*, I, pp. 114–5, Cullen, *Recollections*, pp. 29–30, *SNL*, 20 June 1798 and Gahan, *People's Rising*, pp. 184–5.

227 Cullen, *Recollections*, pp. 29–30.

228 Quoted in Madden, *United*, III, p. 242. The story that the rebels ordered Catholic houses, of which there were very few in Tinahely of the 1790s, to illuminate so that they might be distinguished from Protestant dwellings and protected is as improbable as it is impractical. Musgrave, *Rebellions*, p. 524.

229 *Trial of William Byrne*, pp. 13, 26. See also Camolin Duty Book cited in Wheeler and Broadley, *War in Wexford*, p. 142 and NLI, MIC 7665. Charles Coates, probably the eponymous son of William Byrne's friend, was an ensign in the Reay Fencibles prior to 1802. July 1802, PRO, HO 100/111/122. In March 1802, 500 acres of the Clone property was advertised for rent by Charles Coates who was then one of many loyalist farmers suffering from the loss of livestock to marauding rebel bands and thieves. *FDJ*, 25 March 1802. For a folk account of the persecution of Tinahely Catholics see O'Toole, *Clan O'Toole*, II, pp. 517–8.

230 Hardy Journal, 17–18 June 1798. See also Needham to Craig, 18 June 1798, NA, 620/38/174 and Ancram, 'Officers memoir', pp. 79–80.

231 Ancram, 'Officers memoir', pp. 80–81. See also Dickson, *Wexford Rising*, pp. 135–6.

232 Lake to Castlereagh, 19 June 1798 in Castlereagh, *Memoirs*, I, p. 271 and *SNL*, 20 June 1798.

233 Giffard to Marsden, 14 June 1798, NA, 620/38/143. See also Byrne, *Memoirs*, I, pp. 120–1, Gahan, *People's Rising*, pp. 187–90, *Trial of William Byrne*, pp. 5–6, Cullen, *Recollections*, p. 30 and 'Camolin Detail Book' in Wheeler and Broadley, *War in Wexford*, p. 148. Ancram's body moved cautiously towards Monaseed where he spent the night in the home of Miles Byrne's comrade, Captain Nick Murphy. Ancram found it 'a tolerably good house where we found plenty of good meat . . . a very considerable quantity of bullets of different sizes, some bullet moulds, pikes . . . in consequence of which we determined to burn the house next morning on our departure'. Ancram, 'Officers memoir', p. 82.

234 Moore, *Diary*, I, pp. 290–302, J. W. D. Ennis, 'The battle of Fook's Mill' in *The Past*, no. 6, 1950, pp. 104–17, Gordon, *History*, p. 258 and Furlong, *Murphy*, p. 130.

235 Lake to Castlereagh, 21 June 1798 in Madden, *United*, IV, p. 408, Castlereagh to Elliot, 15 June 1798 in Gilbert, *Documents*, p. 136, Ancram, 'Officer's memoir', p. 82, Byrne, *Memoirs*, I, pp. 126–8 and Camolin Detail Book cited in Wheeler and Broadley, *War in Wexford*, p. 148.

236 Ancram, 'Officer's memoir', p. 82. See also Madden, *United*, IV, p. 416 and Lake to Castlereagh, 21 June 1798 in Madden, *United*, IV, pp. 409–10.

237 Teeling, *Sequel*, pp. 259–60 and Gahan, *People's Rising*, p. 210.

238 Cullen, *Recollections*, pp. 35–6 and 28 March 1799, NA, 670/17/30/40. The notorious perjurer 'Croppy' Biddy Dolan claimed to have seen Garret Byrne in the camp on the 21st and alleged that a group of men had protested that 'they would not march without being led by Garret Byrne, and others that they would not go without their captain William Byrne.' *Trial of William Byrne*, p. 6. See also Ibid., p. 10. The reliable James Doyle of Ballinacor was adamant that neither 'that witch Biddy Dolan' nor Garret Byrne was amongst the Ballymanus men. Quoted in Cullen, *Recollections*, pp. 36–7. Dolan further alleged that William Byrne had a dispute with another Wicklow officer who accused him of 'cowardice' at Vinegar Hill as he had 'ran away'. This supposedly led to Daniel Kirwan being appointed in his place after Byrne had offered to duel with his accuser. *Tryal of William Byrne*, p. 39. See also Ibid., pp. 6, 34. This story is belied by eyewitness accounts of Byrne's bravery at Enniscorthy and may have been concocted by Dolan or her handlers to blacken his name during the 1799 trial. The kernel of truth may have been the incident in which Doyle of Ballinacor had deposed Charles Byrne of Ballyrogan as commander of the Redcross company owing to his apparent incompetence. 28 March 1799, NA, 620/17/30/64.

239 Cullen, *Recollections*, p. 37. See also Dickson, *Wexford Rising*, pp. 200–1.

240 Byrne, *Memoirs*, I, p. 128. See also 23 November 1799, NA, 620/17/ 30/17.

241 Quoted in Cullen, *Recollections*, p. 36.

242 Camolin Detail Book in Wheeler and Broadley, *War in Wexford*, p. 148 and Moore, *Diary*, I, p. 304. Needham gained the nickname 'needless Needham' or the 'late General Needham' in some quarters for this and other actions in which his performance was inadequate and was held responsible for Vinegar Hill not being the decisive encounter

both rebel and government forces wanted. Loftus to Bentinck, 3 July 1798, PRONI, T.2905/21/90.

243 Lake to Castlereagh, 21 June 1798 in Castlereagh, *Memoirs*, I, p. 233. See also Hay, *History*, p. 105, Teeling, *Sequel*, pp. 261–2, Pakenham, *Liberty*, p. 294 and Cullen, TCD, MS 1472, pp. 211–2. The rebels had also commandeered Revd Nunn's home when he left Enniscorthy and used it as a 'hospital'. 'Mrs Pounden's experiences during the 1798 rising in co. Wexford' in *The Irish Ancestor*, VIII, no. 1, 1976, p. 6.

244 Dickson, *Dwyer*, p. 57, Hay, *History*, pp. 215–7 and Cullen, TCD, MS 1472, p. 211, Cloney, *Narrative*, p. 81 and Pakenham, *Liberty*, p. 306.

245 Teeling, *Sequel*, pp. 263–4, Wheeler and Broadley, *War in Wexford*, p. 153, Lake to Castlereagh, 21 June 1798, *Memoirs*, I, p. 233, Ennis, 'Fook's Mill', pp. 104–17, Lake to Castlereagh, 22 June 1798, PRO, HO 100/81/161, Moore to Johnson, 23 June 1798, PRO, HO 100/81/166 and Moore, *Diary*, I, p. 300.

246 Anon to J[ohn McMurray], n.d., [June 1798] Clarke Papers, private collection, Shropshire, England. See also 'Mrs Pounden's experiences', pp. 4–8. Alice Pounden of Daphne (Monart), whose husband Captain John Pounden of the Enniscorthy yeoman infantry was killed in the defence of that town, moved in the same social circles as the author of the letter which reached Wicklow. The two women were evidently confined together on the Wexford coal ship. Ibid., p. 6. See also Gahan, *People's rising*, pp. 46–8.

247 Cullen, *Recollections*, p. 37.

248 Cullen, *Recollections*, pp. 37, 46, Byrne, *Memoirs*, p. 151, Memorial of Denis O'Neill, 30 January 1799 in Castlereagh, *Memoirs*, II, p. 233, Pakenham, *Liberty*, pp. 309–10 and Cloney, *Narrative*, p. 81.

249 Cullen, *Personal Recollections*, pp. 42, 51. See also Hay, *History*, p. 238.

250 Madden, *United*, IV, p. 554 and Teeling, *Sequel*, pp. 270–1.

251 Madden, *United*, II, pp. 329–30, IV, pp. 553–4, Hay, *History*, pp. 105, 153–8, 236–7 and Cullen, *Recollections*, p. 42.

252 Lett Diary, NLI, MS 4472. West Wicklow loyalists hated the 'arrogance, avarice and impudence' of the Hessians. Hanbidge, *Memories*, p. 57.

253 Camolin Duty Book cited in Wheeler and Broadley, *War in Wexford*, pp. 142, 205.

254 Moore, *Diary*, I, p. 303.

255 Camolin Detail Book in Wheeler and Broadley, *War in Wexford*, pp. 202–3 and Cullen, *Recollections*, p. 42.

256 Plowden, *Historical Review*, II, p. 782, Byrne, *Memoirs*, I, p.195 and Dickson, *Dwyer*, p. 38. Madden recorded that nine men and three women were 'shot by the yeomanry in the village of Aughrim'. Madden, *United*, I, p. 323.

257 Quoted in Madden, *United*, IV, p. 554, Cullen, TCD, MS 1472, p. 202 and Gilbert, *Documents*, p. 13.

258 Giffard to Marsden, 14 June 1798, NA, 620/38/143.

259 Cullen, *Recollections*, p. 42. See also Ibid., p. 51.

260 Byrne and Fitzgerald to Portland, 8 April 1799, PRO, HO 100/66/411. The family were for some time 'reduced to great poverty' in consequence as they were ineligible for compensation. Cullen, TCD, MS 1472, p. 229.

261 Cullen, *Personal Recollections*, p. 42 and Hay, *History*, p. 247.

262 19 August 1799, NA, 620/17/30/85. See also Holt MS, p. 23, 28 March 1799, NA, 620/17/30/58, 28 March 1799, NA, 620/17/30/33 and NLI, MS 8282.

263 19 August 1799, NA, 620/17/30/13, 22 August 1794, NLI, MS 5024, 30 May 1799, NA, 620/17/30/52, Holt MS, pp. 3, 23 and 28 March 1799, NA, 620/17/30/33.

264 Information of Joseph Thompson, 27 June 1798, NA, 620/38/243.

265 Holt, MS, p. 23.

266 Ibid., p. 24.

267 Thompson, 27 June 1798, NA, 620/38/243.

268 Captain H. Morrison to Rossmore, 20 June 1798, NA, 620/38/192. See also Camden to Portland, 21 June 1798, NA, 620/18/9/1.

269 Holt MS, pp. 25–6. See also 25 March 1799, NA, 620/17/30/66, Morrison to Rossmore, 20 June 1798, NA, 620/38/192 and Madden, *United*, IV, p. 412.

270 Patrickson to Downshire, 24 June 1798, PRONI, D.607/F/275. See also Thompson, 27 June 1798, NA, 620/38/243 and 19 August 1799, NA, 620/17/30/85.

271 Thompson, 27 June 1798, NA, 620/38/243. See also Holt MS, pp. 26–7, TCD, MS 869/8, f.98, Information of Daniel Doyne, 15 July 1798, NA, 620/51/48 and Sproule to Cooke, 19 September 1798, N.A., 620/40/76.

272 Holt, MS., p. 26. This woman was identified by Thomas Crofton Croker as Susy O'Toole of Annamoe although the name does not appear in Holt's original manuscript. Joseph Holt, *Memoirs of Joseph Holt, General of the Irish rebels in 1798, edited from his original manuscript, in the possession of Sir William Betham . . . by T. Crofton Croker, Esq.*, 2 vols. (London, 1838), I, p. 217. For Croker's treatment of O'Toole and Holt's autobiography see O'Donnell and Reece, 'A clean beast', pp. 24–5. As Croker had visited Roundwood in the 1830s, and very probably other parts of Wicklow, it is possible that he then gleaned some inkling of the identity of the 'Moving Magazine' which Holt had suppressed. Yet his penchant for fictional interpolations raises doubts as to the credibility of his overblown description of 'O' Toole'. Cullen, NLI, MS 9762, p. 26.

273 Thompson, 27 June 1798, NA, 620/38/243 and 19 August 1799, NA, 620/17/30/85.

274 19 August 1799, NA, 620/17/30/85.

275 Information of Joseph Thompson, 20 June 1799, TCD, MS. 871.

276 19 August 1799, NA, 670/17/30/85. See also Kavanagh, *Popular History*, p. 332.

277 Holt MS, p. 23. In March 1799 Pat Connor wandered drunk into the guardhouse of the Fermanagh Militia at Roundwood and attempted to purchase a bayonet to 'stick the Edges, the Hardens [Hardings?] and the Hattons'. 25 April 1799, NA, 620/17/30/51 Members of the Edge family were long serving Churchwardens of Glendalough. H. Rooke, *Glendalough from the past: Diocese of Glendalough, parish of Wicklow, town of Wicklow* (Dublin, 1895), p. 25.

278 Tighe to ——, 20 October 1798, NLI, MS 4813.

279 Hanbidge, *Memories*, p. 57, Gordon, *History*, p. 206, Thompson, 27 June 1798, NA, 620/38/243, Hardy Journal, 22 Junes 1798, *Dublin Gazette*, 28 June 1798 and Musgrave, *Rebellions*, 4th edn., pp. 480– 82. The husbands of Ann Cahoe and Mary Saunders of Kiltegan and Margaret Ellison of Hacketstown were killed on 25 June 1798 in unknown circumstances. Musgrave, Ibid., p. 695.

280 Dickson, *Dwyer*, p. 39 and R. R. Madden, *The life and times of Robert Emmet* (Glasgow, n.d.), p. 129. Hugh Dwyer, brother of Michael, was also present and estimated that the rebels numbered 15,000 men. See also Musgrave, *Rebellions*, p. 50, Thompson, 27 June 1798, NA, 620/ 38/243 and Madden, *United Irishmen*, IV, p. 554.

281 Hay, *History*, p. 247 and 29 May 1798, NA, 620/38/243.

282 Cullen, *Personal Recollections*, p.43, Dickson, *Dwyer*, pp. 176–9 and 25 June 1798, NA, 670/38/239.

283 Madden, *United*, IV, p. 555, Musgrave, *Rebellions*, 4th edn., pp. 480– 81, Hardy Memorial, n.d., NLI, Melville MS and *Wicklow People*, 9, 16, 23 and 30 July 1938. For compensation paid to Hardy's widow and children see n.d., [1799], NA, 620/52/9. On 25 June 1829 Captain Hardy's sons Lieutenant-Colonel Henry Hardy and Revd John Hardy erected a memorial to their father in Hacketstown which read: 'Sacred to the memory of Thomas Hardy, Esq., who was killed in action when fighting for his King and Country against the rebels, at the battle of Hacketstown, on the 25 of June, 1798'. *Letters containing information relative to the antiquities of the county of Carlow collected during the progress of the ordnance survey in 1839* (Bray, 1934).

284 Musgrave, *Rebellions*, 4th edn., p. 481. See also *SNL*, 6 July 1798, Cullen, *Recollections*, p. 43 and Dickson, *Dwyer*, p. 40. A 1766 survey listed fifty-four Protestant families in Donoughmore parish. O'Toole, *Clan O'Toole*, II, p. 510.

285 Hanbidge, *Memories*, p. 57. See also Ibid., p. 84, Leadbeater quoted in Mac Suibhne, *Kildare in 1798*, p. 119, Duffy, 'West County Wicklow notes', p. 326 and Cornwallis to Portland, 26 June 1798, NA, 620/38/239.

286 Musgrave, *Rebellions*, 4th edn., p. 481. See also NLI, MIC 7665 and Dickson, *Dwyer*, pp. 40–1.

287 Thompson, 27 June 1798, NA, 620/38/243. See also n.d., TCD, MS. 869/8, f.193, Dickson, *Dwyer*, p. 176, Wheeler and Broadley, *War in Wexford*, p. 205, Madden, *United*, IV, pp. 409, 555 and Sproule to Lees, 18 October 1798, NA, 620/40/170.

288 n.d., TCD, MS 869/8, f. 133.

289 Madden, *United*, IV, p. 556. See also Teeling, *Sequel*, p. 272.

290 McGhee to Castlereagh, 5 July 1798 in Dickson, *Dwyer*, p. 42. One of Cullen's informants also heard that Reynolds had 'received a ball through the body' and died but was also mistaken. Quoted in Madden, *United*, p. 555. Some months later a spy reported that 'Mich[ae]l Reynolds frequents the Cherry Tree [on] Tho[ma]s St' and implied that he was in contact with other veterans of the Wicklow campaign, including McMahon, who lodged in that part of the city. n.d. [1799], TCD, MS 869/8, f. 92. See also Patrickson to Downshire, 23 May 1798, PRONI, D.607/F/181. Reynolds, 'much recovered from his wound', had made his way to London by 1802 and was mentioned in a letter sent by Wicklowman Robert Walsh to Holt, then an exile in New South Wales. Walsh to Holt, 5 November 1803 quoted in George William Rusden, *Curiosities of Colonization* (London, 1874), p. 80.

291 Thompson, 27 June 1798, NA, 620/38/243 See also Madden, *United*, IV, pp. 555–6, Hardy Journal, 25 June 1798, *SNL*, 6 July 1798 and Cullen, *Recollections*, p. 43.

292 Cornwallis to Portland, 26 June 1798, PRONI, HO 100/81/199, Thompson, 27 June 1798, NA, 620/38/243 and Dickson, *Dwyer*, p. 41.

293 *SNL*, 6 July 1798. See also *Dublin Gazette*, 28 June 1798, Madden, *United*, IV, p. 556, 14 November 1799, NA, 620/17/30/41, Cullen, *Recollections*, p. 43, Dickson, *Dwyer*, p. 43 and Hay, *History*, p. 248. Patrickson's opinion that the battle was a 'complete triumph' is likely to have been a minority one. Patrickson to Downshire, 26 June 1798, PRONI, D.607/F/276.

294 Hanbidge, *Memories*, pp. 56–7.

295 Ross to Downshire, 24 June 1798, PRONI, D.607/F/271. See also Taylor to Wickham, 25 June 1798, PRO, HO 100/81/171–2.

296 Parsons to Parsons, 25 June 1798, NLI, MS 13,840 (4).

297 *FDJ*, 28 June 1798.

298 Ross to Downshire, 24 June 1798, PRONI, D.607/F/271, Taylor to Wickham, 25 June 1798, PRO, HO 100/81/171–2, Parsons to Parsons, 26 June 1798, NLI, MS 13,840 (4) and *FDJ*, 28 June 1798.

299 Sproule to Lees, 25 June 1798, NA, 620/38.

300 Thompson, 27 June 1798, NA, 670/38/243. See also Holt MS, p. 27 and Madden, *United*, IV, p. 556.

301 Holt MS, pp. 27–9.

302 Holt MS, p. 30. See also Ridgeway, *Trial of William Michael Byrne*, p. 128.

303 Sproule to Cooke, 19 September 1798, NA, 620/40/76.

304 Holt MS, pp. 30–1 and *SNL*, 4 July 1798. A controversy arose over the alleged maltreatment of John Arnold by Roche which, resulted in Holt removing his men to a nearby camp. Cullen's informants doubted the truth of a claim in the memoirs that a duel had been proposed by Holt but declined by Roche. Holt MS, pp. 33–4.

305 Moore, *Diary*, I, p. 300, Madden, *United*, IV, pp. 416–9, *Catholic Telegraph*, 29 September 1856, Wheeler and Broadley, *War in Wexford*, pp. 212–3, Teeling, *Sequel*, p. 265, Cloney, *Narrative*, p. 87 and Asgill to Castlereagh, 27 June 1798, PRO, HO 100/81/201 and 26 June 1798, PRO, HO 100/81/81–2.

306 *HT*,4 July 1798. See also Musgrave, *Rebellions*, p. 54, Holt MS, p. 33, Cullen, *Recollections*, p. 43 and Trembath to Musgrave, 22 April 1799, NLI, MS 4156. Musgrave believed that White's mansion was burned after the Battles of Ballyellis and Carnew.

307 Musgrave, *Rebellions*, 4th edn., p. 516. See also Byrne, *Memoirs*, I, p. 140 and Camolin Detail Book, 28 July–9 June 1798 in Wheeler and Broadley, *War in Wexford*, pp. 209–9.

308 Taylor, *An history*, pp. 212–3. See also Byrne, *Memoirs*, I, p. 198, Gordon, *History*, pp. 209–10 and Plowden, *Historical Review*, V, p. 43. For composition of Puleston's force see also Camolin Detail Book, 30 June 1798 in Wheeler and Broadley, *War in Wexford*, p. 210 and Musgrave, *Rebellions*, p. 516. Miles Byrne, who did not fight at Ballyellis, was probably incorrect in placing the Arklow and Coolgreany yeomanry at the battle which he misdated as occurring on 29 June. Byrne, *Memoirs*, I, p. 197. This error misled Luke Cullen as to the date of Ballyellis and has proven durable with the unfortunate result that it is inscribed on the otherwise impressive 1798 memorial near Ballyellis crossroads and on Carnew's commemorative plaque. Cullen, *Recollections*, p. 42.

309 Cullen, NLI, MS 8339, p. 74. See also Byrne, *Memoirs*, I, p. 199, Taylor, *An History*, p. 213, Holt MS, p. 35 and Cullen, *Recollections*, p. 45.

310 Holt MS, p. 34 and Dickson, *Dwyer*, p. 44. For a fuller discussion of Holt's role in the affair and the weak rival claims of Fr Taaffe, McCabe, Fitzgerald and others, see O'Donnell, 'Holt', pp. 183–5.

311 Musgrave, *Rebellions*, p. 516. See also Holt MS, pp. 34–5, Cullen, *Recollections*, p. 45, Byrne, *Memoirs*, I, p. 199, Taylor, *An History*, p. 214, 14 November 1799, NA, 620/17/30/41, 7 December 1799, NA 620/17/30/44 and Cullen, NLI, MS 8339, p. 74.

312 Camolin Detail Book, 30 June 1798 in Wheeler and Broadley, *War in Wexford*, pp. 210–11. See also Byrne, *Memoirs*, I, p. 199, Holt MS, p. 35 and *HT*, 4 July 1798.

313 June/July 1798, PRO, WO 13/3732.

314 Holt MS, p. 35, Cullen, *Personal Recollections*, pp. 44–5, Cullen, NLI, MS 8339, p. 65, Musgrave, *Rebellions*, II, p. 54, Castlereagh to Wickham, 3 July 1798, PRO, HO 100/81/223, Madden, *United*, IV, pp. 557–8.

315 Cullen, NLI, MS 8339, p. 66. Matthew Kearns of Baltinglass related to Cullen how Dwyer had 'snapped up' a Briton's sword on the road and 'slung it to his side'. He then saw Dwyer enter a derelict cabin and had just discharged his musket at a trooper in the fields whereupon another dashed into the small room. The Welshman had 'his sword in one hand and a pistol or carbine in the other . . . and he looked frightfully wild. He was a very large man much heavier than Dwyer . . . they closed but spoke not a word and the contest was soon over.' Dwyer informed Kearns that he had 'no time for reflection when I turned round and saw such a powerful man with his sword drawn and sufficiently near to cut me down I had nothing to do but to strike as soon as I could. Had the unfortunate fellow called for quarter he should have had it although it is said that they used the most blasphemous language at the killing of an idiot named Byrne in the field when they met him at Newtownmount-kennedy.' *Ibid*. See also Cullen, *Recollections*, p. 45 and Madden, *United*, p. 557.

316 Holt MS, p. 36.

317 Quoted in Madden, *United*, IV, p. 557. See also PRO, WO 13/3732, 19 June 1798, PRO, HO 100/73/327 and Holt MS, pp. 36–7.

318 14 November 1799, NA, 620/17/30/41. See also *The tri-coloured ribbon* (Cork, 1966), pp. 7, 13, O'Toole, *The O'Tooles*, p. cxvii and Sproule to Lees, 22 June 1798, NA, 620/51/36.

319 Cullen, *Insurgent*, p. 71, *Catholic Telegraph*, 9 October 1858 and Cullen, TCD, MS 1472, p. 200. Inman had been pursued into Stone's field by Pat Delaney and was later found dead. He was buried by James Bolger and Jeremiah Reilly but his body was shortly afterwards recovered by his brother-in-law, William Green. Other dead yeomen included Peter Standford and George and William Butler of Clough and John Buttle. 7 December 1799, NA, 620/17/30/44 and Musgrave, *Rebellions*, 4th edn., pp. 749, 751.

320 Camolin Detail Book, 1 July 1798 in Wheeler and Broadley, *War in Wexford*, p. 216. See also 7 December 1799, NA, 620/17/30/42, PRO, WO 13/3732, Gordon, *History*, p. 210 and Taylor, *An history*, p. 214. The Dublin press was initially unwilling or incapable of presenting its readership with authentic details of the defeat. *Hibernian Telegraph* of 4 July 1798 stated that only a 'small party' had been killed while the more reliable *Saunder's Newsletter* of that date disclosed that 'nearly 40 men' had died. Shannon was apprised on 2 July that '13 of the Ancient Britons were surprised and murdered' at Ballyellis. Shannon to Boyle, 2 July 1798 in *Letters*, p.136. On 6 July the official Castle bulletin had mentioned only that 'some loss in men and horses' had been sustained on 30 June, even though Castlereagh had sent details to London on 3 July of the 'loss of 49 men and horses'. Madden, *United*, IV, p. 419 and Castlereagh to Wickham, 3 July 1798, PRO, HO 100/81/223. For details of the controversy in Westminster arising from the suppression of information regarding Ballyellis, see O'Donnell, 'Holt', pp. 185–6.

321 *Annual Register*, 1798, p. 139 and Musgrave, *Rebellions*, 4th edn., p. 516. See also Lake to Roden, 3 July 1798, NLI, MS 25,049, Cullen, NLI, MS 8339, p. 75, Hay, *History*, p. 248, Cornwallis to Portland, 6 July 1798, PRO, HO 100/81/227 and Byrne, *Memoirs*, I, p. 200.

322 Musgrave, *Rebellions*, 4th edn., p. 517 and Taylor, *An history*, p. 214. See also Hay, *History*, p. 262 and Cullen, *Recollections*, p. 47. Hunter Gowan's son Ogle claimed that the Wingfields had been meeting as an Orange Lodge in Mount Nebo to initiate Lt George Smith of Cummer when they heard that 200 troops had passed by from Gorey to Carnew and were 'reported to be advancing of Kilkelvin [sic] Hill'. Puleston had allegedly retreated towards Carnew before they arrived at Ballyellis whereupon; 'the rebels were deceived by the costume, and cheered what they believed to be a reinforcement. Soon, however, the cheering subsided. The Wingfield men reserved their fire till they got within ten or twelve yards of the enemy, and then they went to work with zeal and precision . . . the rebels sought safety in flight.' *The formation of the Orange Order, 1795–1798, the edited papers of colonel William Blacker and Colonel Robert H. Wallace* (Belfast, 1994), pp. 99–100.

323 Byrne, *Memoirs*, I, p. 201. See also Ibid., p. 197 and III, p. 352 and Cullen, NLI, MS 8339, p. 67.
324 Byrne, *Memoirs*, I, p. 199. See also Dickson, Dwyer, p. 389.
325 19 April 1800, NA, 620/17/30/28. See also *Catholic Telegraph*, 9 October 1856, Cullen, *Insurgent*, p. 35 and Teeling, *Sequel*, p. 273. Surprisingly, the *Annual Register* also pointed out that the insurgents had won their victory at Ballyellis 'without the loss of a man'. Ibid., 1798, p. 139. These assertions were contradicted by Musgrave who insisted that Gowan's Wingfield corps, misidentified in the 1801 edition of his book as the Tinahely yeomanry, had killed twenty to thirty from a vantage of rising ground and in so doing prevented even heavier government losses. Musgrave, *Rebellions*, 4th edn., p. 516. This claim is unconvincing and while Gowan's men may indeed have enjoyed success against a rebel patrol earlier that day it is likely that Musgrave's support the reputation of his fellow orangeman Gowan was an attempt to redress the magnitude of the government defeat. Holt, who played a leading role in the action, also claimed that while four rebels were wounded none died although his tally of 370 enemy losses is a wild exaggeration. Holt MS, p. 36.
326 Hewitt to ——, 21 June 1798, J. Lewis Higgins to ——, 26 June 1798 in Madden, *United*, IV, pp. 417–9 and 7 December 1799, NA, 620/17/ 30/44.
327 John McMurray to Mary McMurray, n.d., [2 July 1798], Clarke Papers.
328 Camolin Detail Book, 30 June 1798 in Wheeler and Broadley, *War in Wexford*, p. 211. See also Taylor, *An History*, p. 214 and Byrne, *Memoirs*, I, pp. 197–201.
329 Holt MS, pp. 36–7. Kelly later defected to Holt's force and was accepted into its ranks. He was by no means the only native Irishman in the Welsh regiment and Fr Meehan recorded that some years after the rebellion a Rathdrum orangeman was 'styled the Briton, because he belonged to a regiment so called, that [had] perpetrated the most unheard of barbarities in this county [Wicklow] in [17]98.' O'Toole, *The O'Tooles*, p. xvii. An Arklow tradition recorded that 'One party [of Britons] at Bally Ellis [sic] on the way to Carnew, got caught up in a sand pit, a wall ten f[ee]t high and bushes at the top, cars turned up across the road, the Rebels fired into them and all but two were killed. One jumped his horse from between the shafts of a car over the backs and escaped'. Murphy Papers, p. 47.
330 Byrne, *Memoirs*, I, p. 200. See also 14 November 1799, NA, 620/17/ 30/42.
331 *SNL*, 6 July 1798. See also Holt MS, p. 37, Cullen, *Recollections*, p. 46 and Musgrave, *Rebellions*, 4th edn., p. 517.
332 Holt MS, pp. 38–40.
333 John McMurray to Mary McMurray, n.d., [2 July 1798], Clarke Papers.
334 28 May 1799, NA, 620/17/30/57. See also 14 November 1799, NA, 620/17/30/41 and Musgrave, *Rebellions*, 4th edn., pp. 484, 637–8.
335 Cullen, *Recollections*, p. 47. See also Maxwell, *History*, p. 174, Cullen, NLI, MS 8339, p. 80, Musgrave, *Rebellions*, 4th edn., p. 484 and 28 May 1799, NA, 620/17/30/57.
336 McDonald MS. A short privately owned MS entitled 'The battle of Ballyrahan and after' was compiled by John McDonald of Clonmore from folk accounts preserved by Thomas Donnelly of Knockatomcoyle. Donnelly, whose grand-uncle had fought at the second battle of Hacketstown, interviewed many 'old neighbours' in the Ballyrahan locality.
337 Cullen, *Recollections*, p. 47.
338 Musgrave, *Rebellions*, 4th edn., p. 484, Holt MS, p. 11 and Wheeler and Broadley, *War in Wexford*, p. 217. Cullen's sources overestimated loyalist losses at Ballyrahan at 'above eighty'. Cullen, *Recollections*, p. 47. Musgrave included the names of most, if not all, the yeoman losses at Ballyrahan in his list of 'Protestants massacred in the county of Wicklow'. Certainly killed in the action were Joseph Chamney, his eponymous nephew, Abraham Nixon sr, James and Charles Twamley of Nurney, Michael Leonard of Nurney, James Bardon of Coolakenny, George Davison and Thomas Carleton of Coolkenna, William Myers of Crownalay, William Rice and Annesley Green of Tinahely, Charlton of Kilquiggan and James Smith and John Waters of Crosspatrick. William Waters was killed that day in cold blood but the fate of the Halfpenny brothers, Driver and Restly is unclear. Musgrave, *Rebellions*, 4th edn., pp. 695–8.
339 McDonald MS.
340 McDonald MS and Hay, *History*, p. 250.
341 Cullen, *Recollections*, pp. 47–8, 52 and Cloney, *Narrative*, pp. 88–91.
342 Cullen, NLI, MS 8339, p. 79. See also Camolin Detail Book, 1–4 July 1798 in Wheeler and Broadley, *War in Wexford*, pp. 216–8, Cullen, *Recollections*, p. 48, Castlereagh to

Wickham, 3 July 1798, NA, 620/ 39/9 and Castlereagh to Wickham, 4 July 1798, PRO, HO 100/81/225, Cornwallis to Portland, 5 July 1798, PRO, HO100/81/223, *DEP*, 7 July 1798 and *Dublin Gazette*, July 1798.

343 Hay, *History*, p. 250, Cullen, *Recollections*, p. 48, Madden, *United*, IV, p. 538, Cullen, NLI, MS 8339, pp. 79–80 and *HT*, 9 July 1798. Shannon commentated that 'this Needham is always late'. Shannon to Boyle, 6 July 1798 in *Letters*, p. 137.

344 See Cullen, *Recollections*, pp. 49–50, Musgrave, *Rebellions*, 4th edn., pp. 486–7, Cornwallis to Portland, 5 July 1798, PRO, HO 100/81/227, Camolin Detail Book, 5 July 1798 in Wheeler and Broadley, *War in Wexford*, pp. 218–9 and Hay, *History*, p. 251. Duff's forces lost five or six men killed and sixteen wounded. *SNL*, 7 July 1798 and *Dublin Gazette*, 6 July 1798. Cullen's sources made the unlikely claim that over a hundred government troops had been killed but admitted that their losses had not been properly estimated. See Dickson, *Dwyer*, pp. 375–6.

345 Hunter to Hewitt, 8 July 1798, NA, 620/39/35. See also *SNL*, 6 July 1798 and Camolin Detail Book, 29 June–5 July 1798 in Wheeler and Broadley, *War in Wexford*, pp. 209–19.

CHAPTER FIVE

1 Moore, *Diary*, I, p. 304.

2 28 May 1799, NA, 620/17/30/57 and 14 November 1799, NA, 620/17/30/41. See also Musgrave, *Rebellions*, 4th edn., p. 696.

3 *HT*, 9 July 1798. The women also 'asked them with feigned anxiety, whether they had lost many?-they replied, that they had lost thousands: that General Duff and his flying guns had destroyed them while they were separated from the main body by a fog; "then", said they, "the petticoat men (highlanders) from Arklow, and Hunter Gowan's Corps from Wexford, fell on us while we were retreating, and cut us all *to ribbands*, except the few that are here. The main body got to Carrigrua in the Co[unty] of Wexford'.

4 Holt MS, p. 41. See also Information of Bartholomew Clarke, n.d., NA, 620/51/249, *A list of the officers of the several regiments and battalions of militia* (Dublin, 1801), p. 48 and Turner, 9 July 1798, NA, 620/39/38. The Finnamores remained at Ballyward in the 1840s. Fraser, *Guide*, p. 109.

5 PRO, WO, 8/9, PRO, HO 30/2/34–6, Henry Dundas to the King, 2 June 1798 and the King to York, 3 June 1798 in Aspinall (ed.), *Later Correspondence*, III, pp. 70–3.

6 Cornwallis to Ross, 13 July 1798, *Correspondence*, II, p. 363 and Teeling, *History*, p. 95.

7 Patrick Power, 'A survey: some Wicklow maps 1500–1888' in Hannigan and Nolan (eds.), *Wicklow: history and society*, pp. 731, 734–5, 758.

8 Sproule to Lees, n.d. [July 1798], NA, 620/39/70. See also Prince Bouillon to Dundas, 16 July 1798, NA, 620/30/2/119.

9 Information of Edward McLaughlin, 14 July 1798, NA, 620/39/73. See also Clarke, n.d., NA, 620/31/249.

10 Sproule to Lees, 12 July 1798, NA, 620/39/60.

11 —— to Craig, 18 and 19 July 1798, PRO, HO 100/86/56. All but two of the sentences were commuted to service abroad for life. See also Hartigan to Downshire, 12 July 1798, PRONI, D.607/F/315.

12 *SNL*, 12 July 1798.

13 Cullen, *Recollections*, p. 53 and Teeling, *Sequel*, p. 274. One rebel plan was to mass forces in the hills near Naas and attack it for its cannon and ammunition which would be used on a city assault. Releasing the senior United Irish prisoners whose trials were underway was apparently an objective; 'chiefly [Oliver] Bond whose name they say if they had to send to the north that whole quarter of the kingdom would rise'. Sproule to Lees, 10 July 1798, NA, 620/39/44.

14 *SNL*, 11 July 1798, Cooke to Wickham, 11 July 1798, PRO, HO 100/ 81/243, Hartigan to Downshire, 9 July 1798, PRONI, D.607/F/310 and Shannon to Boyle, 9 July 1798, *Letters*, p. 138.

15 —— to Cooke, 6 July 1798, NA, 620/37/28 See also Cooke to Wickham, 11 July 1798, PRO, HO 100/81/243, Cullen, NLI, MS 9762, p. 77 and *SNL*, 11–13 July 1798.

16 Turner, 9 July 1798, NA, 620/39/38. See also *SNL*, 11 July 1798, Sproule to ——, n.d., NA, 620/52/210–212, Shannon to Boyle, 9 July 1798 in *Letters*, p. 138 and Connolly, 24 July 1798, NA, 620/37/73.

17 Turner, 9 July 1798, NA, 620/39/38. See also James to Castlereagh, 7 July 1798, NA, 620/3/51/8 and Enniskillen to ——, 6 July 1798, NA, 620/39/25.

18 Connolly, 24 July 1798, NA, 620/39/73.

19 McLaughlin, 14 July 1798, NA, 620/39/73.

20 Beresford, *Memoirs*, II, p. 156. See also 'Senior' to Cooke, n.d., NA, 620/18/1 and *SNL*, 11 July 1798. Sproule's agents forewarned that the rebels were 'to be joyned by friends from the White Rock & Tallaght-1000 men if the reinforcements come in equal to their expectations, they will pour into Dublin at that side'. Sproule also alleged that diversionary attacks on Tallaght and Naas would occur. Sproule to [Lees?], 12 July 1798, NA, 620/39/60.

21 Cooke to Wickham, 9 July 1798, PRO, HO 100/81/239. Two days later Cooke reported 'they send out foraging parties & parties to terrify the country people to join them and they succeed a little in both.' Cooke to Wickham, 11 July 1798, PRO, HO 100/81/243. See also Turner, 9 July 1798, N.A.,620/39/38 and *SNL*, 11 July 1798.

22 Shannon to Boyle, 10 July 1798, *Letters*, p. 140. See also Beresford, *Correspondence*, II, p. 156.

23 *SNL*, 10 July 1798 and Shannon to Boyle, 11 July 1798 in *Letters*, p. 140. Robert Ross was informed that the rebels had only received the 'passes and protections' on 8 July. Ross to Downshire, 9 July 1798, PRONI, D.607/F/309.

24 Edwards to ——, 12 July 1798, NA, 620/39/63.

25 Cooke to Wickham, 9 July 1798, PRO, HO 100/81/243 and SNL, 12 and 13 July 1798.

26 Cooke to Wickham, 11 July 1798, PRO, HO 100/81/243. Cooke was angered by the wild speculations of some 'men who ought to know better' as he knew 'pretty well' the true strength of the rebels whom he castigated as a 'miserable flying or exhausted banditti'. Cooke to Wickham, 12 July 1798, PRO, HO 100/81/247.

27 Warburton to Berwick, 11 July 1798 in *Official Papers*, p. 189, Shannon to Boyle, 9 July 1798 in *Letters*, p. 138, Beresford, *Correspondence*, II, p. 156 and McLaughlin, 14 July 1798, NA, 620/37/73.

28 Moore, *Diary*, I, p. 304. See also Cooke to Wickham, 9 July 1798, PRO, HO 100/81/239 and 12 July 1798, PRO, HO 100/81/247.

29 Cullen, NLI, MS 9762, p. 94. See also Cullen, *Recollections*, p. 53, *SNL*, 13 July 1798, Deposition of Ponsonby Pillsworth, 18 December 1798, NA, 620/41/90 and John Hayden, 18 December 1798, NA, 620/41/91. For a fuller account of this incident see O'Donnell, 'Holt', pp. 181–2.

30 Moore, *Diary*, I, p. 308.

31 Ibid. pp. 304–5. See also SNL, 11–12 July 1798.

32 John McMurray to Mary McMurray, 12 July 1798, Clarke Papers.

33 Moore, *Diary*, I, p. 307. They were probably the 'two hessians' piked with a black soldier on Lugnaquilla to whom reference was made during a courtmartial in 1799. 28 March 1799, NA, 620/17/30/27. See also McLaren, *Minute Description*, p. 36, Cornwallis to Portland, 31 April 1798, PRO, HO 100/73/141–4 and Pakenham, *Liberty*, p. 266.

34 William Pole to Downshire, 17 July 1798, PRONI, D.607/F/326. See also Cooke to Wickham, 12 July 1798, PRO, HO 100/81/247, Moore, Diary, I, pp. 308–9, Cooke to Cornwallis, 14 July 1798, PRO, HO 100/81/248, *Dublin Gazette*, 16 July 1798 and *SNL*, 14 July 1798.

35 Cullen, *Recollections*, p. 53 and Holt MS, p. 48.

36 Holt MS, pp. 42–3, Shannon to Boyle, 9 July 1798, *Letters*, p. 138, Captain William Griffin to ——, 7 July 1798, NA, 620/3/32/10, Whelan, 'Religious factor', p. 68 and John Jones, *An impartial narrative* cited in Madden, *United*, IV, pp. 539–40.

37 [Rourke] to Mary Finnerty, 27 July 1798 in Madden, *United*, IV, p. 546 Bartholomew Connolly understood that they were 'to meet [Bryan] McDermot and his party in ye North'. Connolly, 24 July 1798, NA, 620/39/73. See also George Lambert to Cooke, 15 July 1798, NA, 620/51/49, Sir Fenton Aylmer to Castlereagh, 4 July 1798, NA, 620/ 39/18 and Teeling, *Sequel*, p. 287.

38 Griffin to ——, 17 July 1798, NA, 620/3/32/10. See also *SNL*, 9, 11 and 13 July 1798 and Byrne, *Memoirs*, I p. 220.

39 Holt MS, pp. 43–4, Cullen, *Recollections*, p. 54, Cooke to Wickham, 11 July 1798, PRO, HO 100/81/243, *SNL*, 18 July 1798 and Pakenham, *Liberty*, p. 315.

40 Holt MS, p. 44. See also Cullen, *Recollections*, p. 54.

41 [Rourke] to Finnerty, 27 July 1798 in Madden, *United*, IV, p. 546.

42 Cullen, *Recollections*, p. 54 and Madden, *United*, IV, p. 539. Madden, drawing on Jones, put rebel losses at 150 but Holt's figure of sixty men seems more likely as it tallies closely with the '65 rebels' of which the well-informed William Hartigan was apprised. Hartigan to Downshire, 12 July 1798, PRONI, D.606/F/315 and Holt MS, pp. 44–5. See also Seamus O'Loinsigh, 'The rebellion of 1798 in Meath' in *Riocht na Midhe*, IV, 1967–9, pp. 63–4.

43 [Rourke] to Finnerty, 27 July 1798 in Madden, *United*, IV, p. 547. See also *Dublin Gazette*, 16 July 1798 and Cooke to Wickham, 12 July 1798, PRO, HO 100/81/243.

44 Cullen, *Recollections*, p. 56. See also Holt MS, p. 44, Musgrave, *Rebellions*, 4th edn., pp. 495–6 and Hay, *History*, p. 251. Myles V. Ronan, one of Cullen's editors, erroneously claimed that Holt was 'amongst those who deserted'. Cullen, *Recollections*, p. 60.

45 Gough to Colonel Verecher, 12 July 1798, NA, 620/4/36/1.

46 [Rourke] to Finnerty, 27 July 1798 in Madden, *United*, IV, p. 547 and Holt MS, p. 46.

47 Holt MS, pp. 47, 54–5, 61 and O'Donnell, 'Holt', pp. 186–7.

48 [Rourke] to Finnerty, 27 July 1798 in Madden, *United Irishmen*, IV, p. 547, Information of Oliver Nelson, 15 July 1798, NA, 620/39/75, Connolly, 24 July 1798, NA, 620/39/73, Byrne, *Memoirs*, I, p. 220 and Dickson, *Dwyer*, pp. 62, 85.

49 *SNL*, 13 July 1798. See also Cullen, NLI, MS 8339, p. 84.

50 Lambart to Cooke, 15 July 1798, NA, 620/51/49.

51 Cooke to Wickham, 15 July 1798, PRO, HO 100/77/248.

52 Information of Stephen Murray and Daniel Doyne, 15 July 1798, NA, 620/51/48.

53 Connolly, 24 July 1798, NA, 620/39/73. See also [Rourke] to Finnerty, 27 July 1798 in Madden, *United*, IV, pp. 546–7.

54 [Rourke] to Finnerty, 27 July 1798 in Madden, *United*, IV, p. 546. Luke Cullen was informed that 'Holt made himself remarkably useful' in the campaign in the role of commissary general 'although not particularly appointed to the office . . . there was no other man in the army so well qualified.' Cullen, *Recollections*, p. 53.

55 Cooke to Wickham, 17 July 1798, PRO, HO 100/81/248.

56 Cullen, *Recollections*, pp. 65–6, Meyrick to Fingal, 17 July 1798, NLI, MS 8029 (4) and *Dublin Gazette*, 16 July 1798.

57 Weyms to Taylor, 15 July 1798, NA,620/39/85. See also Myers to Hewitt, 15 July 1798, NA, 620/39/83, Captain Archibald Gordon to ——, 15 July 1798, NA, 620/39/87, Johnson to Pelham, 15 July 1798, NA, 620/ 39/77 and Teeling, *Sequel*, pp. 276–81.

58 *Trial of Hugh Woolaghan*, p. 26.

59 Johnson to ——, 15 July 1798, NA 620/39/77. See also Petition of John Byrne, 23 February 1799, NA, SPP, 449, NA, 620/7/79/36, 40, Cullen, *Recollections*, pp. 58–9, Campbell to Cooke, 19 August 1798, NA, 620/ 39/186, 19 March 1799, NA, 620/7/79/40, Petition of Daniel Fogarty, n.d., [1799], NA, 620/51/70 and *Trial of Hugh Woolaghan*, p. 26. The fourteen were Anthony Kavanagh, Peter Kirwan, Mathew Byrne, Luke Reilly, Peter Flynn, Thomas Magreene, Thomas Farrell, James Tongue, Daniel Hanlon, Charles Byrne, Patrick Byrne, Michael Byrne, Michael O' Neil and Philip Carney. 18 July 1798, TCD, MS 872, p. 16.

60 Cullen, *Recollections*, p. 59. See also, ibid., pp. 74–5, Cornwallis to Portland, 15 July 1798, NA, 620/39/80, Gordon to ——, 15 July 1798, NA, 620/39/87, Teeling, *Sequel*, pp. 173–4 and *Catholic Telegraph*, 22 December 1856.

61 Madden, *United*, IV, pp. 540–3, Wickham to Portland, 28 July 1798, *NA*, 620/39/113, *HT*, 27 July and 9 August 1798, Byrne, *Memoirs*, I, p. 223 and Annesley Brownrigg to Castlereagh, 29 July 1798, NA, 620/ 39/127.

62 Sir Fenton Aylmer to Castlereagh, 4 July 1798, NA, 620/39/18 and 16 July 1798, NA, 620/4/36/2, Cornwallis to Pitt, 20 July 1798 in *Correspondence*, II, p. 367, Cloney, *Narrative*, pp. 206–7, *Dublin Gazette*, 3 July 1798, n.d., NLI MS 8029 (3), *SNL*, 31 July 1798, Moore, *Diary*, I, p. 310 and Byrne, *Memoirs*, I, p. 226.

63 Cooke to Wickham, 20 July 1798, PRO, HO 100/77/256.

64 Cooke to Wickham, 24 July 1798 in *Correspondence*, II, pp. 371–2.

65 Castlereagh to Wilford, 19 July 1798, NA, 620/3/47/4. See also Cullen, *Recollections*, p. 88, Wilford to Cornwallis, 18 July 1798 in *Correspondence*, II, p. 368 and Charlemont to Parsons, 30 July 1798, NLI, MS 13, 840 (4).

66 Cooke to Wickham, 21 July 1798, PRO, HO 100/77/268. See also Teeling, *Sequel*, p 237, Cornwallis to Wilford, 24 July 1798 in *Correspondence*, II, pp. 371–2 and *SNL*, 25 July 1798.

67 Ross to Downshire, 26 July 1798, PRONI, D.607/F/339 Ross claimed 'every many in Dublin that is loyal is extremely angry at this business.' Downshire's other Dublin-based

informant William Hartigan condemned the 'lenity, nay, the kindness, that the rebels are treated with, causes great murmurings and discontent-even *notorious, wicked leaders*, as Fitzgerald (of Wexford), etc.'. Hartigan to Downshire, 26 July 1798, PRONI, D.607/F/340.

68   Chritchley to Parnell, 21 July 1798, NA, 620/51/198. See also Holt MS, p. 61, O'Donnell, 'Holt', pp. 190–1, Byrne, *Memoirs*, I, p. 220, Dickson, *Dwyer*, pp. 65, 82 and Musgrave, *Rebellions*, I, p. 305.

69   William James to Cooke, 16 July 1798, NA, 620/39/90 See also Holt MS, pp. 62–5 and *Catholic Telegraph*, 29 September 1856. In 1799 Mary Scott of Imaal deposed that after the Boyne expedition 'sev[era]l scattered parties returned to the mountain from the county of Meath side, where they rem[aine]d until the prot[ectio]ns were given'. 14 November 1799, NA, 620/17/30/41.

70   27 November 1799, NA, 620/17/30/73.

71   28 March 1799, NA, 620/17/30/27, Dickson, *Dwyer*, p.332, Musgrave, *Rebellions*, p. 313 and 29 April 1800, NA, 620/17/30/92. Chritchley, according to Bryan Farrell of Baltyboys, 'was a cruel hearted tyrant, and shot some of them [i.e. other rebels] in cold blood . . . [and] handed them over to the Ancient Britons, who had a camp in the glen'. O'Toole, *O'Tooles*, p. lxxvi.

72   1 May 1800, NA, 620/17/30/55, 11 October 1799, NA, 620/17/30/97, Dickson, *Dwyer*, p. 331 and Cullen, *Insurgent*, pp. 75–6. Musgrave accidentally listed Bolton twice on his 'list of protestants murdered in Wicklow' and in his first entry recorded that he was a weaver in Clara and Rathdrum. Musgrave, *Rebellions*, 4th edn., pp. 695–6.

73   Chritchely to Parnell, 11 September 1798, NA, 620/40/36.

74   27 November 1799, NA, 620/17/30/73. See also 28 March 1799, NA, 620/17/30/27, 1 May 1800, NA, 620/17/30/55 and Cullen, *Insurgent*, p. 77.

75   27 November 1799, NA, 620/17/30/73 and Dickson, *Dwyer*, p. 319.

76   27 November 1799, NA, 620/17/30/77, 11 October 1799, NA, 620/17/30/97 and Cullen, NLI, MS 8339, pp. 23–4.

77   Holt MS, p. 62. See also Cullen, NLI, MS 8339, pp. 101, 112.

78   Holt MS, p. 78, Sproule to Lees, 19 October 1798, N.A., 620/40/172, Holt to William Colthurst, 18 May 1799, NA, 620/47/38, Cornwallis, *Correspondence*, III, p. 85, Dickson, *Dwyer*, p. 325, 15 February 1799, NA, 620/17/30/3, 13 June 1800, NA, 620/59/43, 27 November 1799, NA, 620/17/30/73, Cullen, TCD, MS 1472, p. 203 and *Insurgent*, p. 45.

79   McKenzie, *Beauties*, p. 27.

80   O'Neil Stratford to ——, 28 July 1798, NA, 620/37/123. See also Holt MS, p. 63.

81   Holt MS, p. 64. See also Castlereagh to Wickham, 7 August 1798, PRO, HO 100/78/23 and Appendix Six.

82   July 1798, PRO, WO 13/2574. In February 1799 when the House of Commons discussed the high desertion rates of the Antrim, Longford and King's County regiments the member for Antrim asserted that those of the county he represented 'had been enlisted in Co. Wicklow . . . prior to 1797 in which year extra-county enlisting had been prohibited, though it might have occurred'. Cited in McNally, *Irish Militia*, pp. 153–4. In actuality, all almost those who joined Holt in July 1798 had enlisted in April 1798, the same month in which the regiment's officers donated 300 pounds to the Treasury Defence Fund. *HT*, 27 April 1798.

83   *Courier*, 11 October 1798. See also Ibid, 30 October 1798, Cullen, NLI, MS 9762, pp. 35, 10 and NLI, MS 8339, p. 25 and Byrne, *Memoirs*, I, pp. 71–2, 222.

84   Holt, 22 November 1798, NA, 620/41/39A. See also Holt MS, p. 74. In 1798 he recalled the units as the Cavan Militia (5), Hessians (3), King's County (30), Leitrim (16), Sligo (9), Kildare (5), Dublin [City?] (5), Antrim (28), Durham fencibles (2) and an English soldier named Joseph Begly. Holt's November list, which he acknowledged as incomplete, omitted mention of ten to fifteen Royal Irish Artillery and 5th Royal Irish Dragoons with his force.

85   June 1798, PRO, WO 13/2574. See also Holt MS, pp. 90, 111, Holt, 16 November 1798, NA, 620/41/39A and n.d., NA, 620/52/60. Dickson, following Miles Byrne, asserted that Mooney was a sergeant but at the time of his defection to the insurgents he was a private. Dickson, *Dwyer*, p. 273.

86   Cullen, NLI, MS 8339, p. 170. See also Cullen, *Recollections*, pp. 102–5 and Byrne, *Memoirs*, I, pp. 156, 227.

87   Byrne, *Memoirs*, I, p. 227. See also Holt MS, p. 74.

88   27 November 1798, NA, 620/17/30/73. See also Byrne, *Memoirs*, I, p. 276.

89 Holt MS, p. 90 and Cullen, NLI, MS 8339, p. 122. This gave rise to accusations of sectarianism on the part of the insurgents who viewed their actions as pre-emptive strikes against known loyalists. Beresford to Auckland, 9 August 1798 in *Correspondence*, II, p. 171, Castlereagh, *Memoirs*, II, p. 421 and Byrne, *Memoirs*, I, p. 222.

90 Byrne, *Memoirs*, I, p. 203.

91 Holt MS, p. 93.

92 28 March 1799, NA, 620/17/30/27. See also Cullen, *Insurgent*, p. 77 and Henry Allen to Wainwright, 14 March 1807, NLI, MS 4951.

93 n.d., NA, 620/52/60, 2 October 1799, NA, 620/17/30/6, Cullen, NLI, MS 8339, p. 123 and 27 November 1799, NA, 620/17/30/73.

94 Holt MS, pp. 90–91. See also 28 March 1799, NA, 620/17/30/2. One of Cullen's informants refuted Holt's account of rescuing Allen's daughter from threat and killing the man that menaced her in an orchard near Greenan. The woman in question was apparently a Miss Collins and her assailant was not severely punished. Cullen, NLI, MS 8339, pp. 112–3 and Cullen, NLI, MS 9762, p. 73. The Collins family lived at Ballinaclash and in 1760 were reputedly involved in the attack led by Buck 'Jerusalem' Whaley on Greenan Chapel in which Whaley and his friends were reputed to have discharged their pistols at a picture of the 'Blessed Virgin and Child'. Cullen, *Insurgent*, p. 76. See also Ibid., pp. 77–8.

95 28 March 1799, NA, 620/17/30/24. See also 27 November 1799, NA, 620/17/30/73 and Cullen, *Insurgent*, pp. 76–7.

96 O'Neil Stratford to ——, 28 July 1798, NA, 620/39/127, *SNL*, 30 July 1798 and Ross to Downshire, 23 July 1798, PRONI, D.607/F/334A.

97 *SNL*, 30 July 1798. It may have been this encounter which prompted Hartigan's statement that 'houses are still burned every night in the Co. Wicklow'. Hartigan to Downshire, 27 July 1798, PRONI, D.607/F/340.

98 *SNL*, 30 July 1798. See also Ibid., 28–29 July and 1 August 1798 and *HT*, 30 July 1798.

99 Leadbeater, *Papers*, I, p. 250. See also *SNL*, 23 October and 8 November 1798. Rebel groups were frequently referred to as 'plunderers' due their activities. Cornwallis to Ross, 28 July 1798, *Correspondence*, II, p. 379.

100 9 May 1800, NA, 620/17/30/93, 19 August 1799, NA, 620/17/30/85, Cullen, NLI, MS 9762, pp. 13–14 and Dickson, *Dwyer*, p. 270.

101 Byrne, *Memoirs*, I, p. 230. See also Holt MS, p.64.

102 11 April 1800, NA, 620/17/30/77, Holt, 16 November 1798, NA, 620/41/39A and May 1800, NA, 620/9/57/7.

103 Cullen, NLI, MS 8339, p. 128. See also Holt MS, p. 20 and King to Marsden, 12 December 1802 cited in Dickson, *Dwyer*, p. 203. Holt claimed that Marks was brought to him by reinforcements in company with another yeoman named Chapman and that his men killed them both. However, no other extant source mentions Chapman. Holt MS, p. 99.

104 Hardy Journal, 17 and 20 July [sic?] 1798, NLI, MIC 5641.

105 Cornwallis to Ross, 24 July 1798, *Correspondence*, II, p. 371 Robert Johnson imputed sinister motives to the excursion and alleged that its purpose was 'as dark as all the rest of his government'. Johnson to Downshire, 24 July 1798, PRONI, D.607/F/335. See also Ross to Downshire, 24 July 1798, PRONI, D.607/F/334B.

106 Cornwallis to Portland, 8 July 1798 in *Correspondence*, II, p. 358.

107 Moore, 19 July 1798, *Diary*, I p. 309.

108 Hartigan to Downshire, 23 July 1798, PRONI, D.607/F/334A.

109 Cornwallis to Ross, 28 July 1798 in *Correspondence*, II, p. 379. See also Cornwallis to Portland, 28 July 1798, PRO, HO 100/81/283.

110 Moore, *Diary*, I, pp. 309–10.

111 Colonel Walter Jones to ——, 19 July 1798, NA, 620/39/78.

112 Castlereagh to Parsons, 12 July 1798, NLI, MS 13,840/4.

113 Sproule to Lees, 21 July 1798, NA, 620/39/102. See also Moore, *Diary*, I, p. 309, 11 October 1799, 620/17/30/97 and *SNL*, 13 July 1798.

114 Moore, *Diary*, I, p. 309.

115 Byrne, *Memoirs*, I, p. 231, Moore, *Diary*, I, pp. 309–10, *Wicklow People*, 12 August 1939 and Cullen, NLI, MS 8339, p. 128.

116 Byrne, *Memoirs*, I, p. 233. See also Holt MS, pp. 64–5 and Cullen, NLI, MS 8339, p. 128.

117 Sproule to Lees, 1 August 1798, NA, 620/39/134.

118 Cullen, *Insurgent*, p. 81 and Holt, 16 November 1798, NA, 620/41/39A.

119 Byrne, *Memoirs*, I, p. 233. See also Holt MS, p. 108. Holt believed there were fourteen carts going to Tinahely to collect wheat but other sources confirm that the convoy attacked on 7 or 8 August consisted of several cars 'laden with provision' destined for the garrison at Arklow. He had probably confused two incidents which is suggested by his relation of the episode out of chronological order in his memoir. *SNL*, 8 and 13 August 1798.

120 Holt, *Memoirs*, I, p. 202. See also Tyson, 17 January 1798, NA, SOC, 1017/62 and 28 March 1799, NA 620/17/30/24.

121 Holt MS, pp. 109–10. See also Cullen, NLI, MS 8339, p. 167. Byrne claimed that the 'drivers or conductors were soon captured and unluckily some of them were killed in the fray', a comment which suggests that he either did not actually witness their fate or wished to represent it in a less cold blooded light. Byrne, *Memoirs*, I, p. 233.

122 Moore to Cornwallis, 20 August 1798, NA, SOC, 1017/64.

123 Cullen, NLI, MS 8339, pp. 137–8 and *Catholic Telegraph*, 22 September 1856.

124 Moore to Cooke, 17 August 1798, NA, 620/39/87, Moore to Cornwallis, 20 August 1798, NA, SOC, 1017/64, Castlereagh to Wickham, 24 July 1798, PRO, HO 100/81/275 and Byrne, *Memoirs*, I, pp. 223–4. Byrne recalled Holt declaring that 'all those who could not remain at their houses might return to us' and how their 'small corps' was reduced to a 'mere band'. Ibid., p. 236. See also *HJ*, 10 August 1798.

125 Murray to Lees, 16 October 1798, NA, 620/40/156. Cullen implausibly asserted that Dwyer was offered a commission in the British army if he surrendered. Cullen, NLI, MS 8339, p. 138.

126 Cullen, NLI, MS 8339, pp. 137–8.

127 Madden, *United Irishmen*, I, p. 461 and IV, pp. 64–8, 161–3, 259, O'Brien, 'The Byrnes of Ballymanus', p. 317, William MacNeven, *An account of the treaty between the United Irishmen and the Anglo-Irish government in 1798* cited in Gilbert, *Documents*, p. 211, Cooke to Wickham, 21 July 1798, PRO, HO 100/77/268, Beresford, *Correspondence*, II, pp. 163–5, MacNeven, *Pieces of Irish History*, p. 149, Cullen, *Insurgent*, p. 76, Wainwright to Fitzwilliam, 6 February 1800, NLI, MIC 5641 and Hay, *History*, pp. 97–8.

128 King to Portland, 13 September 1798, PRO, HO 100/79/328, Madden, *United Irishmen*, II, pp. 166–80 and Martin Burke, 'Piecing together a shattered past: the historical writings of the United Irish exiles in America' in Dickson, Keogh and Whelan (eds), *United Irishmen*, p. 303.

129 Portland to Cornwallis, 26 November 1798, PRO, HO 100/82/297.

130 Petition of John Lynch, 27 August 1798, NA, 620/4/29/217. See also September 1799, NA, 620/7/79/31, Petition of John Lynch, 6 December 1798 and Petition of Frances Lynch, 1 September 1798, NA, SPP, 200.

131 See n.d., [August 1798], PRO, HO 100/78/338 and Elliott, *Partners in Revolution*, pp. 347–9.

132 Madden, *United*, IV, p. 68. See also James Crawford to Francis Dobbs, 3 August 1798, NA, 620/3/51/6 and Dickson, *Revolt*, p. 245.

133 Madden, *United*, IV, p. 68. See also Cullen, NLI, MS 8339, p. 202 and Thomas A. Emmet, *Memoirs of Thomas Addis and Robert Emmet with their ancestors and immediate family* (New York, 1915), 2 vols, I, p. 253. The rebel delegates were not located until 5 August at which time they were 'anxious to take the benefit of the terms' of pardon promised to Dobbs by Castlereagh. Dobbs to Castlereagh, 5 August 1798, NA, 620/3/51/18.

134 Madden, *Antrim and Down*, pp. 180–1. See also Cullen, NLI, MS 8339, pp. 138, 153, Dobbs to Castlereagh, 5 August 1798, NA, 620/3/ 51/8 and Cooke to Castlereagh, 18 December 1798, *Memoirs*, II, p. 47.

135 According to Madden 'a gentleman unknown to either, joined the conversation, and in the course of it, stated, that he had come down to that village, for the purpose of arresting the notorious McCabe the friend of Lord Edward Fitzgerald. Both McCabe and Farrell, eagerly offered their assistance to the stranger, to attain so "desirable an object". The conversation was carried on with great spirit for some time, when the strangers separated from each other. McCabe and his friend, walked to the end of the town, ordered a post-chaise, and whilst the government messenger was on the watch, for any rebels coming from the mountains of Wicklow, they were travelling with all speed for Dublin, where both arrived, in perfect safety.' Madden, *Antrim and Down*, p. 181. See also Cullen, NLI, MS 8339, pp. 138, 202.

136 Cullen, NLI, MS 8339, pp. 153–4.

137 Cooke to Castlereagh, 18 December 1798 in Castlereagh, *Memoirs*, II, p. 47.

138 Moore, *Diary*, I, p. 310. See also Cornwallis to Portland, 7 August 1798, PRO, HO 100/78/20 and Hardy Journal, 7 August 1798. It seems unlikely that Byrne could have been

a member of Dobbs' delegation as contemporaries claimed it consisted of 'strange gentlemen' and it is highly probable Byrne would have been recognized by some of the officers. Cullen, NLI, MS 8339, p. 153. See also Cullen, *Recollections*, p. 76, Byrne to ——, 24 March 1799, PRO, HO 100/66/413, Byrne and Fitzgerald to Portland, 8 April 1799, PRO, HO 100/66/411, Cornwallis to Portland, 26 July 1798, *Correspondence*, II, p. 374 and *SNL*, 31 July 1798.

139 Moore, *Diary*, I, p. 310. Moore recalled that while Byrne's exertions were helpful they were 'not of so much as he himself had expected'. Five years later Moore claimed 'it was thought from his connection with the disaffected he might be of use in making them surrender. His conduct there was very good . . . Lord Huntley and me made him live with us, and paid him some attention for which he has ever expressed himself very grateful.' Moore to Cornwallis, 1 September 1803, PRO, HO 100/119/40. Byrne was no doubt partially motivated to render such 'essential services' by secret assurances and on the 'express condition' that he and Fitzgerald would be permitted to live in England. Hardwicke to Pelham, 26 September 1802, NA, 620/61/111. This arrangement went beyond that granted to most others and seems to have been the basis of repeated attempts between 1799 and 1804 to have the two men pardoned. As early as April 1799 Byrne revealed that Cornwallis had assented to allow them live in Britain and further stated that Cooke had informed him that an absolute pardon would be granted if Ireland 'was tranquil at the expiration of a year'. Byrne and Fitzgerald to Portland, 8 April 1799, PRO, HO 100/66/411. Matters came to a head the following month when Lieutenant-General James Rooke objected to their presence in Bath and Bristol leading to their arrest on 22 March, deportation to Hamburg and residence in Altona. Rooke to ——, 23 March 1799, PRO, HO 100/66/421. The temporary halt in the French War in March 1802 led to intercessions by both Cornwallis and Hardwicke in support of pardoning the rebel leaders. Cornwallis to Marsden, 5 September 1802, PRO, HO 100/119/36, Hardwicke to Portland, 27 September 1802, PRO, HO 100/119/38 and Cornwallis to Pelham, 18 October 1802, PRO, HO 100/110/314. In January 1803 permission was granted for Byrne and an ailing Fitzgerald to go to England but this was rescinded the following month and legal difficulties surrounding the issue of pardon and the precedent it would set for other exiles ultimately prevented their return to their native country. Pelham to Hardwicke, 28 January 1803, PRO, HO 100/119/48 and Alexander to Shee, 20 February 1803, PRO, HO 100/112/72.

140 Byrne, *Memoirs*, I, p. 226 and Holt to Matthew Doyle, 22 November 1798, NA, 620/57/157.

141 Moore to Cornwallis, 20 August 1798, NA, SOC, 1017/64, Cullen, NLI, MS 8339, p. 139 and Chritchley to Parnell, 11 September 1798, NA, 620/40/11.

142 Cullen, NLI, MS 9761, pp. 9, 141–2 and Cullen, NLI, MS 8339, p. 145.

143 Cullen, NLI MS 8339, p. 139 and Cullen, *Insurgent*, p. 75.

144 Edwards cited in Cullen, NLI, MS 1472, pp. 200–201. See also *Insurgent*, p. 75.

145 *SNL*, 11 and 15 August 1798 and Cullen, NLI, MS 8339, p. 139.

146 Moore, *Diary*, I, p. 309.

147 Quoted in Teeling, *Sequel*, pp. 287–8. See also Fitzpatrick, *Sham Squire,* p. 513.

148 Moore, *Diary*, I, p. 311, Moore to Cornwallis, 20 August 1798, NA, SOC, 1017/64, Cornwallis to Portland, 7 August 1798, PRO, HO 100/ 78/70 and *SNL*, 13 August 1798.

149 *SNL*, 13 August 1798. See also *HJ*, 17 August 1798.

150 *SNL*, 13–14 August 1798 and *HJ*, 17 August 1798. The report was based on a letter from Tinahely dated 7 August which misidentified him as 'Hall, the famous rebel General'.

151 Rourke to Dundas, 9 September 1798, NA, 620/40/46, Madden, *United*, I, pp. 329–30, Dundas to Castlereagh, 8 August 1798, NA, 620/39/158, McAllister to ——, 21 August 1798, NA, 620/40/46, *HJ*, 6 August 1798 and Sproule to Lees, 19 September 1798, NA, 620/40/76. Rattigan later went to France where he enlisted in the army and died at the battle of Marengo. Madden, *United*, II, p. 409.

152 Cullen, NLI, MS 8339, p. 143. Cullen understood that this expedition began 'about the 17' of August but it was evidently some days earlier than this as the killings which ensued occurred shortly before that date. See also Sproule to Lees, 1 August 1798, NA, 620/39/139, Beresford, *Memoirs*, II, p. 169, *SNL*, 15 August 1798, 3 March 1799, NA, 620/17/ 30/86 and 28 March 1799, NA, 620/17/30/24.

153 Cullen, TCD, MS 1472, p. 218 and NLI, MS 8339, pp. 120, 149, 204 and Holt, 16 November 1798, NA, 620/41/39A.

154 Sproule to Cooke, 19 September 1798, NA, 620/40/76 See also Cullen, NLI, MS 8339, pp. 145–7. Cullen gave Cooper's Christian name as Fred in error for Christopher which is noted in the Castlemacadam Church of Ireland parish register entry for 30 August 1798. A document of June 1799 also refers to the death of Christopher Cooper of Newbridge (Avoca) on 28 August 1798 while another contemporary report dated the killings as occurring prior to 24 August. 1 June 1799, PRO, HO 100/84/7 and *Courier*, 5 September 1798.

155 *HT*, 24 August 1798.

156 Holt MS, pp. 71–9. It was widely reported that Holt's men did 'levy contributions' of specific sums. *FDJ*, 21 September 1798 See also *Courier*, 11 October 1798.

157 Holt MS, p. 82. See also Ibid., pp. 79–81.

158 Holt MS, p. 83. See also *Courier*, 16 August 1798 and *HJ*, 10 and 17 August 1798.

159 The Wicklowmen apparently informed Cornwallis of the 'melancholy state of the county, and the dangerous circumstances to which they are exposed from his Majesty's troops not contriving to act as heretofore'. *HT*, 24 August 1798.

160 Richard Annesley to Downshire, 22 August 1798, PRONI, D.607/F/388. See also *SNL*, 15–17 August 1798 and Gilbert, *Calender*, xv, p. 60.

161 Pakenham, *Liberty*, pp. 298–301, 341, Wheeler and Broadley, *War in Wexford*, pp. 247, McDowell, *Ireland in the Age*, p. 646 and Elliott, *Wolfe Tone*, pp. 381–3. On 24 June loyalist estimates of French strength at Killala ranged from a surprisingly accurate 1,500 to 18,000 while 'some', apparently claimed there were only 800. Hartigan to Downshire, 24 August 1798, PRONI, D.607/F/360.

162 Musgrave to Bishop of Dromore, 28 August 1798, NLI, MS 4157. Musgrave wrote: 'four French frigates had entered the Bay of Killala . . . this intelligence has not created the smallest alarm here nor is it expected that it will occasion an insurrection in any part of the Kingdom, Wicklow & Wexford are very quiet & there is not a stir in Munster'.

163 M'Ghee to ——, 22 August 1798, NA, SOC 1017/3.

164 Peyton to ——, 26 August 1798, NA, 620/3/31/2.

165 Peyton to ——, 26 August 1798, NA, 620/3/31/2. See also Moore, *Diary*, I, p. 312, 27 March 1799, NA, 620/17/30/43 and Camolin Detail Book, 2 September 1798 in Wheeler and Broadley, *War in Wexford*, p. 267.

166 Byrne, *Memoirs*, I, p. 235, Holt MS, p. 126 and *Courier*, 27 September 1798.

167 Hay, *History*, p. 266. See also Ibid., pp. 326–7 and *Courier*, 30 October 1798.

168 Thomas Connolly to ——, 29 August 1798, NA, SOC, 1017/25. See also Hay, *History*, p. 265 and Sproule to Lees, 19 September 1798, NA, 620/40/76.

169 Sproule to Lees, 1 August 1798, NA, 620/39/134.

170 Ross to Downshire, 24 and 29 August 1798, PRONI, D.607/F/361, 373. There were only 500 soldiers in the city according to Ross protecting a 'much threatened' population. Ross to Downshire, 30 August 1798, PRONI, D.607/F/375.

171 James to ——, 28 August 1798, NA, 620/39/273. James alleged that city rebels had recovered pikes hidden in children's graves and were hopeful of success if aided by their comrades in the surrounding counties. See also McDowell, *Ireland*, p. 650.

172 [Rourke] to Finnerty, 27 July 1798 in Madden, *United*, IV, p. 543.

173 Marsden to Portland, 30 August 1798, PRO, HO 100/66/399. See also Shannon to Boyle, 6 September 1798 in *Letters*, p. 146, *SNL*, 7 September 1798, Dundas to Castlereagh, 27 August 1798, PRO, HO. 100/78/213 and Thomas Roche to Alex Hamilton, 6 September 1798, NA, 620/40/25.

174 Brown to ——, 29 August 1798, NA, 620/39/227.

175 Connolly to ——, 19 August 1798, NA, SOC 1017/25. See also Hartigan to Downshire, 29 August 1798, PRONI, D.607/F/371 and *SNL*, 7 and 18 September 1798.

176 Cullen, NLI, MS 8339, p. 78 and Sproule to Lees, 19 September 1798, NA, 620/40/76. See also Cullen, NLI, MS 8339, p. 78, 28 March 1799, NA, 620/17/30/24, Sirr to ——, n.d., NA, 620/51/278, Information of Francois Joseph, 5 July 1799, NA, 620/56/100 and Petition of Francois Joseph, 29 June 1799 quoted in Dickson, *Dwyer*, p. 37. Writing years later Holt claimed that Joseph was 'a French (deserter) man from a Hessian regiment who lay in Imaal' and which marched west with Moore on 25 August. Holt MS, p. 74. Cullen, following Holt, also referred to him as 'Francois the Hessian', although weight of evidence makes this unlikely. Quoted in Fitzpatrick, *Sham squire*, p. 333 and Cullen, NLI, MS 8339, p. 119. See also O'Donnell, 'Holt', pp. 209–10.

177 Cullen, NLI MS 8339, pp. 129–32 and Cullen, NLI, MS 9762, pp. 20–21. When the troops were out of range, Holt joined Dwyer's men and began 'indulging in his loquacious

habit' and was allegedly rebuked by a Dublin bricklayer named John Reilly for failing to assist. Cullen, NLI, MS 9762, p. 22.

178 Dickson, *Dwyer*, pp. 69–70 and Cullen, NLI, MS 8339, pp. 156–7.

179 Cullen, NLI, MS 8339, p. 114, Holt MS, pp.65–7, August 1798, PRO, WO 13/2574, Madden, *United*, IV, p. 421 and *SNL*, 5 September 1798. In his memoir Holt compounded his account of the encounter with a second clash which occurred the following day against the same units. Holt MS, pp. 121–2, 203.

180 *SNL*, 5 September 1798. See also Holt MS, p. 124, Cullen, NLI, MS 8339, pp. 58, 190–91 and MS 9761, p. 272.

181 Holt MS, p. 127 and Cullen, NLI, MS 8339, p. 191.

182 *SNL*, 5 September 1798. Madden, *United*, IV, p. 421 and Dickson, *Dwyer*, p. 76, 13 March 1799, NA, 620/17/30/15 and *SNL*, 30 August 1798.

183 Cullen, NLI, MS 8339, p. 187. See also Ibid., pp. 151–3, 'Suffering loyalists', NLI, MIC 7665, Steel Memorial, 14 October 1805 quoted in Dickson, *Dwyer*, pp. 121–2 and Ibid., pp. 78–9.

184 L'Estrange to Eustace, 1 September 1798, NA, 620/40/10, Eustace to Castlereagh, 2 September 1798, NA, 620/40/10 and L'Estrange to Castlereagh, 2 September 1798, NA, 620/40/11.

185 L'Estrange to Castlereagh, 2 September 1798, NA, 620/40/11. See also Appendix Six. It was rumoured in Dublin that there were 600 rebels in Wicklow with 'above 200 of the King's county militia' with them. Annesley to Downshire, 14 September 1798, PRONI, D.607/F/408.

186 Castlereagh to Wickham, 3 September 1798, PRO, HO 100/82/74.

187 Thomas King to Sirr, 17 January 1803, NA, 620/65/147. See also Peyton to Jones, 6 September 1798, NA, 620/40/27, Cullen, *Insurgent*, pp. 76–7, 27 November 1799, NA, 620/17/30/73, 14 November 1799, NA, 620/17/30/62 and 8 April 1801, NA, 620/49/99. Cullen was informed that Byrne had made 'a large breach in the company of the Leitrims on his first turn[ing] out'. Cullen, *Insurgent*, p. 92.

188 PRO, WO 13/2980, 15 September 1798, PRO, HO 100/86/62, 26 November 1800, NA, 620/17/30/47, 6 December 1800, NA, 620/17/ 30/48, 3 December 1799, NA, 620/17/30/86 and 3 April 1799, NA, 620/17/30/31.

189 —— to Castlereagh, 3 September 1798, NA, 620/3/32/14, Richard Frizell to ——, 4 September 1798, NA, 620/3/32/15 and Beresford, *Memoirs*, II, p. 128.

190 Ross to Downshire, 5 September 1798, PRONI, D.607/F/386. See also Shannon to Boyle, 3 September 1798 in *Letters*, p. 141.

191 Ross to Downshire, 20 September 1798, PRONI, D.607/F/420.

192 Holt MS, pp. 111–2, Cullen, NLI, MS 8339, pp. 159, 172 and *Catholic Telegraph*, 29 September 1856. A folk account of the incident related in 1934 misidentified Dwyer and Samuel McAllister as the main protagonists. Mrs O'Toole was also in error in compounding this incident with one which occurred at Rathdangan over a year later when Dwyer was compromised when attending Mass. O'Tuathail, 'Wicklow traditions', pp. 175–6 and Campion, *Insurgent*, p. 51.

193 Holt MS, pp. 112–4. See also Abraham Chritchley to Castlereagh, 14 June 1800, NA, 620/57/72.

194 Hardy Journal, 4 August 1798. See also Holt, MS, pp. 115–7 and Cullen, NLI, MS 8339, p. 190. Tom King noted in January 1803 that William Holt lived at Cornelscourt and 'went out late in the rebellion . . . is a very dangerous fellow'. King to ——, 17 January 1803 in Dickson, *Dwyer*, p. 212. Cullen was informed he was 'clever and a fine looking young man affable and generous to the hearts core without one particle of malice to a human being'. Cullen, NLI, MS 8339, f.3, p. 188.

195 *SNL*, 14 September 1798 and *HT*, 24 September 1798. A Wicklow farmer named Coogan who lost thirty-eight bullocks recovered two of them offered for sale in Smithfield market in late September. *SNL*, 1 October 1798.

196 Holt MS, pp. 127–31, Cullen, NLI, MS 8339, pp. 190–2, Madden, *United*, II, p. 77, Gilbert, *Documents*, p. 8 and *Catholic Telegraph*, 23 August 1856.

197 *Catholic Telegraph*, 23 August 1856, Cullen, NLI, MS 8339, p. 362 and Dickson, *Dwyer*, p. 326.

198 Ross to Downshire, 14 September 1798, PRONI, D.607/F/405. He was probably related to Stawell Benson of Blessington who died before his claim for £50 damages from the

government could be paid. NA, OP 150/4/3. See also *Courier*, 10 September 1798, *HJ*, 7 September 1798 and *SNL*, 12, 14 and 21 September 1798.

199	*Courier*, 12 September 1798 and *SNL*, 12 and 15 September 1798.
200	Chritchley to Parnell, 11 September 1798, NA, 620/40/36. See also Holt MS, pp. 84–5.
201	Pakenham, *Liberty*, pp. 298–314, Madden, *United*, IV, pp. 422–3 and Henry McAnally, 'The Government forces engaged at Castlebar in 1798' in *Irish Historical Studies*, IV, pp. 316–31.
202	*Dublin Gazette*, 8 September 1798, Shannon to Boyle, 5 September 1798 in *Letters*, p.143, Madden, *United*, IV, pp. 420–1 and Pakenham, *Liberty*, pp. 319–335.
203	See also *DEP*, 24 September 1798, Ross to Downshire, 14 September 1798, PRONI, D.607/F/405, *DEP*, 11 September 1798, *SNL*, 12 September 1798 and August 1798, PRO, HO 100/66/342.
204	*FJ*, 15 September 1798.
205	Byrne, *Memoirs*, I, pp. 220–21. See also Cullen, NLI, MS 8339, p. 199, NLI, MS 9762, pp. 20–21 and Holt MS, p. 86.
206	Byrne, *Memoirs*, I, p. 222. See also Ibid., pp. 123, 220–23, Cullen, NLI, MS 8339, p. 121 and Holt MS, p. 87. Cullen's informant, who was not at Greenan, claimed that Dwyer was present and the men did not await Holt's order to charge the yeomen but is contradicted on both points by the eyewitness Byrne who specified that Dwyer had remained in Glenmalure that night and that the panicked rebels were rallied by Holt's 'brilliant conduct'. Cullen, NLI, MS 8339, p. 122.
207	*SNL*, 15 August 1798. See also *SNL*, 3 October 1798, *DEP*, 4 October 1798, Holt MS, p. 131, Cullen, NLI, MS 8339, p. 196 and Shannon to Boyle, 14 September 1798 in *Letters*, p. 153. Shannon wrote: 'General Holt is laying waste the county of Wicklow'. For the Beresfords see Fitzpatrick, *Sham Squire*, pp. 205–6, *HT*, 27 April 1798 and Cloney, *Narrative*, p. 273.
208	*SNL*, 21 September 1798. Two rebels named Highland and Loughlin were arrested in a follow-up search. For the first attack in late May see Parvisol to Cooke, 30 May 1798, NA, 620/37/218.
209	*FJ*, 4 October 1798. See also *Courier*, 9 October 1798, *SNL*, 14 September 1798 and *DEP*, 4 October 1798.
210	*SNL*, 17 September 1798.
211	Sproule to Lees, 19 September 1798, NA, 620/40/76. One of Sproule's agents left Holt's group at this time 'in disgust from want of subordination & robbing being the object'.
212	Cornwall to William Jones, 25 September 1798, NA, 620/40/105 and Holt, 16 November 1798, 620/41/39A.
213	Sproule to Lees, 25 September 1798, NA, 620/40/76 and *SNL*, 19 September 1798.
214	Sproule to Lees, 25 September 1798, NA, 620/51/270. See also *Courier*, 15 and 22 September 1798.
215	Holt MS, pp. 103–4 and Cullen, NLI, MS 8339, p. 163.
216	Captain Thomas Aylmer to ——, 15 September 1798 and Aylmer to Cooke, 13 September 1798, NA, 620/40/57.
217	*Courier*, 26 September 1798.
218	*Memoir of the life and times of the Rt. Hon. Henry Grattan, by his son* (London, 1847), IV, pp. 392–3.
219	Holt MS, pp. 101–2. See also Ibid., pp. 103–5 and Cullen, NLI, MS 8339, pp. 41, 163.
220	*SNL*, 24 September 1798 and *Courier*, 26 September 1798.
221	Holt MS, pp. 105–6 and Cullen, NLI, MS 8339, p. 165. The precipitate flight of Gowan repeated an earlier incident when 'Mad [Andrew] Hacket[t]' with a few rebels had frightened his corps out of the town. Cullen, TCD, MS 1472, p. 226.
222	Cullen, NLI, MS 8339, p. 41 and Holt MS, p. 107.
223	September 1798, PRO, WO 13/3220, Kidd to Lees, 20 September 1798, NA, 620/40/80, 29 May 1799, NA, 620/17/30/39, 50 and Holt, 16 November 1798, NA, 620/41/39A. See Appendix Six.
224	*SNL*, 26 September 1798.
225	*FDJ*, 21 September 1798 See also *Courier*, 1 October 1798 and Tighe to ——, 9 October 1798, NLI, MS 4813.
226	*Courier*, 1 October 1798.
227	*Courier*, 8 October 1798.

228 Cullen, NLI, MS 8339, p. 204. William Kerfoot was alleged to have boasted at Oakwood rebel camp that the piking of Leeson 'afforded fine sport'. 23 March 1799, NA, 620/17/30/90. See also 28 March 1799, NA, 620/17/30/17, 1 June 1799, NA, 620/17/30/81 and 1 April 1799, NA, 620/17/30/59.

229 23 April 1799, NA, 620/17/30/30. See also 23 April 1799, NA, 620/17/30/31.

230 23 April 1799, NA, 620/17/30/56, Cullen, TCD, MS 1472, p. 200 and Cullen, *Insurgent*, pp. 25, 38, 42.

231 Tighe to ——, 9 October 1798, NLI, MS 4813. Other prominent families suffered rebel attacks at this time. On 20 September Caesar Colclough's Mohurry mansion was destroyed by rebel fugitives based in the Killaughrim woods and *Saunder's Newsletter* of 26 September reported that 'some of the gang from the Co. Wicklow were joined with the perpetrators'. See also *DEP*, 27 September 1798. Milltown's Russborough House was also, albeit erroneously, reported as having been destroyed. Shannon to Boyle, 19 September 1798 in *Letters*, p. 159.

232 Tighe to ——, 9 October 1798, NLI, MS 4813. See also NLI, *Report on the private collections*, no. 181, p. 193, 23 April 1799, NA, 620/17/ 30/56, Information of James Quinn, n.d., NA, 620/47/4, *SNL*, 1 and 3 October 1798, *DEP*, 29 September 1798 and *Courier*, 3 October 1798.

233 See Camolin Detail Book, 23 September 1798 in Wheeler and Broadley, *War in Wexford*, pp. 275–6.

234 *SNL*, 24–6 and 29 September 1798, *Courier*, 8 October 1798 and *DEP*, 29 September 1798.

235 *HJ*, 3 October 1798, *SNL*, 1 October 1798, *DEP*, 29 September 1798 and *Courier*, 24 September and 9 November 1798. The rebels continued to be described as 'strong' despite many accounts of them sustaining heavy losses to the yeomen, the majority of which were exaggerated or unfounded. Shannon to Boyle, 17 September 1798 in *Letters*, p. 156. See also *Courier*, 25 September 1798 and *SNL*, 14 September 1798.

236 *SNL*, 16, 21 and 24 September and 3 October 1798, *HJ*, 26 September 1798, *FDJ*, 21 September 1798, Lake to Taylor, 8 September 1798 in Madden, *United*, IV, pp. 424–5, Shannon to Boyle, 24 September 1798 in *Letters*, p. 162. Shannon thought they left the city 'with rather too much parade to be able to surprise' the insurgents.

237 Camolin Detail Book, 4 October 1798 in Wheeler and Broadley, *War in Wexford*, p. 276. See also Arthur Connolly to ——, 6 October 1798, NA, 620/40/132, *HJ*, 1 October 1798 and *SNL*, 29 September 1798.

238 *SNL*, 1 October 1798 and *Courier*, 5 October 1798. Meath reputedly travelled 'very safe ground'. Cullen, NLI, MS 8339, p. 41. See also *Courier*, 2 October 1798 and *SNL*, 24 September 1798.

239 *HT*, 28 September 1798 and 8 October 1798, *SNL*, 28 September and 5 October 1798, Johnson to Downshire, 28 September 1798, PRONI, D.607/F/435 and Shannon to Boyle, 24 September 1798 in *Letters*, p. 162. The frustration of Dublin loyalists was expressed by Richard Annesley who wrote 'nothing has yet been done with Holt who is in force about 400, plundering away. Mrs Tighe, the member's mother, had her house plundered this week. Newry Bridge [sic] burned. And in the county of Kildare it is as bad'. Annesley to Downshire, 27 September 1798, PRONI, D.607/F/433.

240 *DEP*, 9 October 1798. See also *SNL*, 29 September and 3 and 8 October 1798 and Holt MS, pp. 66–69. One of Cullen's sources gave a different account of the ruse: 'Dwyer and a few of his friends knew every valley and defile whereby the army at night with a good guide could unperceived take possession of the open space that lay between the fugitives and that important place the mountain [Lugnaquillia]. They represented to Holt and the rest of their companions in arms the necessity of promptly falling back on Lugnacoille [sic] and of setting fire to the furze'. Cullen, NLI, MS 8339, p. 115.

241 Cullen, NLI, MS 8339, p. 115. Skerret's informant claimed that Holt led only 'about seventy of his wretched followers' of whom twenty were mounted. This was a considerable underestimate which was probably intended to lessen the army's urgency in closing with them again. *SNL*, 3 October 1798.

242 Holt MS, pp. 74–5 and Madden, *Robert Emmet*, p. 123.

243 *Courier*, 4 and 6 October 1798. See also Dickson, *Dwyer*, p. 68 and Holt MS, p. 76.

244 Cullen, NLI, MS 8339, p. 197, Holt MS, p. 137 and Cullen, *Recollections*, p. 102.

245 Shannon to Boyle, 2 October 1798 in *Letters*, p. 168. See also 29 April 1800, NA, 620/17/30/72, *Courier*, 11 October 1798, *DEP*, 4 October 1798, and *SNL*, 8, 17 and 23 October 1798 and 3 June 1799, NA, 620/5/61/1.

246 *HT*, 15 October 1798. See also 29 April 1800, NA, 620/17/30/72 and *HT*, 29 October 1798.

247 Hay, *History*, pp. 278–9. The 'whole tract' of country along the Wexford/ Carlow border was reputedly so 'completely in the power of the fugitives who refuge in the woods of Kiloughram [sic] that not a Protestant gentleman or farmer can venture to reside between the Slaney and the Barrow; and even the Roman Catholics are now so frequently attacked by the rebels as to render their residence extremely dangerous.' *SNL*, 10 October 1798.

248 Information of Patrick Fitzsimmons, 6 October 1798, TCD, MS 471.

249 *SNL*, 17 October 1798, Mountnorris to Lieutenant-Colonel Finlay, 10 August 1798 in Wheeler and Broadley, *War in Wexford*, p. 238, 10 February 1804, NA, SOC, 3030/111 and Cullen, *Recollections*, pp. 110–11.

250 *Courier*, 4 October 1798.

251 24 October 1798, PRO, HO 100/76/281. See also *DEP*, 4 October 1798, *Courier*, 7 November 1798 and O'Donnell, 'Holt', pp. 58–9. For the full text of the document see Appendix Seven.

252 *Courier*, 19 October 1798. See also *HT*, 30 October 1798, *SNL*, 4 and 10 October 1798, *Courier,* 10 September and 19 October 1798.

253 Holt MS, pp. 159, 171–2, Cullen, NLI, MS 9762, pp.21–2, 35–43 and Dickson, *Dwyer,* pp. 86–7.

254 Hoey to Captain Corrigan, 11 October 1798, NA, 620/51/238; See also *SNL*, 17 October 1798 and PRO, WO 13/2961 Luke Cullen suggested that the name was 'Corcoran' but there was no such deserter with Holt and he is probably also mistaken in assuming that this particular note of Hoey's, dated 11 October, was the immediate cause of Holt being challenged in Glenmalure. That incident had apparently occurred prior to 8 October. Cullen, NLI, MS 8339, p. 187. Wicklow rebel Andrew Corcoran implicated Corrigan in the killing of county MP William Hume on 8 October. n.d., [c.December 1798], NA, SOC, 3060. Hoey wrote: 'Captain Corragan [sic] I take this opportunity to let you know that Mrs Holt has been in Pourscourt [sic] this week past & has General Holt's pardon from Lord Pourscourt & Lord Monck & Doctor Quin[n] with out dou[b]t & if you & captain Dwier [sic] do[e]s not mind her & him you are all lost. Sir you may depend on this as the most certain truth'. 11 October 1798, NA, 620/51/278.

255 Madden, *Robert Emmet*, pp. 121–2. Belfast United Irishman, James Hope learned of the incident from Dwyer's men when visiting Wicklow in 1803 to liaise with them in connection with Robert Emmet's coup attempt. Dwyer and Hugh 'Vesty' Byrne had gone from Imaal to Holt's camp at Baravore to contact friends and relatives and became suspicious of Hester Holt's presence. They stopped a man at the Black Banks bringing a letter to Holt which was found to be a communication from the Government when John Harman stole it from Holt's billet. Harman's violent tendencies were restrained by Protestant rebel James Richardson, Holt's neighbour, 'intimate friend' and best man in 1782. The story that Dwyer settled the issue by declaring 'you are a protestant and that alone shall save you go from us you shall not be molested' is not credible and is belied by their future co-operation. Cullen, NLI, MS 8339, p. 201. See also Ibid., pp. 199–202 and Holt MS, p. 134.

256 Cullen, NLI, MS 8339, pp. 206–7. See also Ibid., p. 41, Holt MS, pp. 147–150 and *SNL*, 10 October 1798.

257 Information of Edward Comerford, 10 December 1798, NA, 620/41/76. Kirwan was probably the man who was committed to Kilmainham on 11 December by Enniskerry district magistrate William Colthurst. He had allegedly been caught 'in the very act of seducing a private of the King's County militia' which indicates that he had been set up for arrest by the soldier. *HT*, 12 December 1798.

258 *SNL*, 12 October 1798. See also Dickson, *Dwyer*, pp. 132–4, 389–91, Campion, *Dwyer,* pp. 31–3, *DEP*, 11 October 1798 and *SNL*, 12 October 1798, 3 June 1799, NA, 620/5/61/1 and *HJ*, 5 November 1798.

259 Fitzwilliam to ——, 6 October 1795, NLI, MIC 5641. See also Holt MS, p. 149, Maxwell, *History*, p. 446 and Cullen, NLI, MS 8339, p. 27.

260 Holt MS, pp. 146, 152–9, 166. See also *Irish Times*, 23 July 1938.

261 Sirr to ——, n.d., [October 1798], NA, 620/51/278. Internal evidence suggests that Henzy was referring to either 3 or 10 October but the latter is more likely. James Doyle of Ballinacor affirmed that the final split occurred 'at the beginning of the month of October', although he may have had the Glenmalure parting in mind. Cullen, *Recollections*, p. 102. See also Joseph, 5 July 1799, NA, 620/56/110 and Holt MS, p. 151.

262 *SNL*, 15 October 1798. See also *Courier*, 18 and 22 October 1798, Holt MS, pp. 161–4 and *HT*, 15 October 1798. One report estimated the strength of Holt's men at Glenbride at 'about 40'. Ross to Downshire, 12 October 1798, PRONI, D.607/F/459.

263 3 April 1799, NA, 620/17/30/7. See also *HJ*, 31 October 1798

264 *SNL*, 7 November 1798.

265 Hartigan to Downshire, 18 October 1798, PRONI, D.607/F/470.

266 *Trial of Hugh Woolaghan*, p. 26, 16 April 1796, NLI, MS 5024, *SNL*, 1 October 1798, Cullen, *NLI*, MS 8339, p. 27, 2 January 1798, *NA*, SOC, 1017/62, Teeling, *History*, p. 146–52, *DEP*, 23 October 1798. Doherty was misidentified as 'one Toole, a noted rebel' in the *Hibernian Telegraph* of 19 October 1798.

267 *SNL*, 11 October 1798 and *HT*, 19 October 1798.

268 Charles Handfield to Lieutenant-Colonel Vandeleur, 10 April 1797, NLI, MS 25,049 See also Fortescue, *British Army*, IV, p. 596 and *SNL*, 12 October 1798.

269 Fitzpatrick, *Sham squire*, pp. 250–51. See also 23 April 1799, NA, 620/17/30/51 and *The formation of the Orange Order*, pp. 71–2.

270 Madden, *Down and Antrim*, p. 137.

271 Ross to Downshire, 29 October 1798, PRONI, D.607/F/502. See also Taylor to Craig, 18 October 1798 in Teeling, *History*, p. 152, Cloney, *Narrative*, p. 230, *Catholic Telegraph*, 15 September 1858, Annesley to Downshire, 24 October 1798, PRONI, D.607/F/487 and Ross to Downshire, 31 October 1798, PRONI, D.607/F/506.

272 Camden to Castlereagh, 4 November 1798 in Castlereagh, *Memoirs*, II, pp. 424–6.

273 *Courier*, 31 October 1798.

274 Cooke to Castlereagh, 9 November 1798 in Castlereagh, *Memoirs*, II, pp. 431–2. See also *FDJ*, 10 November 1798 and *SNL*, 7 November 1798. An examining committee consisting of Captains Annesley, Cavendish, Dunn, Blackwood, Abbot, Greene and White heard statements from various concerned parties including General Moore and Rossmore. *SNL*, 7 November 1798.

275 Taylor to Craig, 18 November 1798, PRO, HO 100/86/43. Kemmis conceded the Shillelagh men 'appear as if they never w[oul]d give any testimony.' Kemmis to Marsden, 20 November 1798, NA, SOC, 3235/1. See also *FJ*, 20 November 1798 and *FDJ*, 10 November 1798.

276 Cullen, NLI, MS 9762, p. 11. See also Cullen, NLI, MS 8339, p.178, 8 April 1801, NA, 620/49/99 and 28 March 1799, NA, 620/17/30/77, *SNL*, 27 October 1798 and Cullen, NLI, MS 9762, p. 95. One traditional account misdated the raid as occurring on 15 October and has it that the motivation was Dwyer's desire to protect prominent Ballintombay rebel Michael Malone from persecution from the yeomen. Cullen cited in Dickson, *Dwyer*, p. 381.

277 *HJ*, 21 October 1798. See also *Courier*, 27 October 1798 Cullen, NLI, MS 8339, pp. 54–6, 177.

278 *FJ*, 31 March 1803. See also *HJ*, 19 October 1798 and 14 November 1799, NA, 620/17 /30/62.

279 Murray to Lees, 16 October 1798, NA, 620/40/156.

280 Chritchley to Abraham Chritchley, 18 October 1798, NA, SOC, 3224/3. See also Dickson, *Dwyer*, pp. 85–7.

281 Cullen, NLI, MS 9761, p. 12. See also Dickson, *Dwyer*, pp. 83–4 and Cullen, Ibid., p. 381.

282 *FDJ*, 10 November 1798. The subscribers were Meath, Carysfort, Aldborough, Wicklow, Powerscourt, Monck, Rossmore, Benjamin O'Neil Stratford, Peter La Touche, Nicholas Westby, Morley Saunders and William Hoey who each donated fifty pounds. Twenty pounds was given to the fund by William Ryves, Hugh Howard, Thomas Acton, George Putland, Isaac Eccles, William Eccles, Edward Westby, John Hunt, Revd James Symes, John Blachford, Tramers Hunt, Ulick Allen and Thomas Hugo while eleven pounds, seven shillings and sixpence was donated by Francis Greene, Henry Humphrey, Edward Fisher, John Coates, Isaac Coates, John Edwards, Revd Edward Bayly, John Fisher, Thomas Quinn, R. Saunders, James Symes, Owen Saunders, Henry Harrington, Crowe Greene, William Colthurst, Henry Bunbury, Laurence Pearson, Cuthbert Hornidge and George Heighington. James McClatchly gave ten pounds while Revd Edward Ryan, Vaughan Pendred and John Parr each gave £5 13s 9d. *SNL*, 18 and 23 October 1798 An advertisement appeared in the paper's 18 October edition dated 17 October which gave interested parties only two days notice.

283 *DEP*, 3 November 1798. See also Cullen, NLI, MS 9762, p. 80, *HJ*, 11 August 1798 and *SNL*, 3 October 1798, Wright, *Wicklow*, p.64 and Dickson, *Dwyer*, pp. 187–9.

284 *Courier*, 13 November 1798.

285 *HT*, 5 November 1798.

286 *HT*, 19 October 1798. See also Ibid., 5 November 1798. On 9 November an English regiment, probably based at Lehaunstown camp, requisitioned horses and carts at Bray to carry their baggage to the north of Ireland where they had orders to march. Miles Byrne and some comrades making for Dublin city from Wicklow had reached the outskirts of Bray without incident that day and witnessed 'numbers of carmen escaping in every direction out of the town' to avoid losing their possessions. Byrne, *Memoirs*, I, p. 239.

287 *SNL*, 7 November 1798.

288 Cullen, NLI, MS 8339, p. 201.

289 Holt MS, pp. 166–7. One report specified that Holt had 'died of a fever'. *Courier*, 27 October 1798. For spurious reports of his arrest see *HT*, 22 October 1798 and *SNL*, 23 October 1798.

290 Sproule to Lees, 18 October 1798, NA, 620/40/139. See also Holt MS, pp. 145, 152–3 and Sproule to Lees, 18 October 1798, NA, 620/40/170.

291 *SNL*, 17 October 1798. See also Pakenham, *Liberty*, pp. 386–7, *DEP*, 9 October 1798 and *HT*, 7 and 9 November 1798. Another committee was seized in Sth Earl St on 7 October on the premises of a publican named Dwyer. It consisted of thirty United Irishmen described as 'journeymen, slaters, plasterers, shoemakers and ribbon weavers'. Among those arrested were many bearing common Wicklow and Wexford surnames such as Byrne, Kavanagh, Carty, Dunn, Connor, Roe and Moore which suggests that this committee may have included rebel refugees and protectioned men from those counties. *SNL*, 10 October 1798. Such networks were exploited by Dwyer's men who received money, shelter, employment, munitions, information and moral support from them between 1798 and 1803. Information of Thomas Halpin, 4 April 1800, TCD, MS 869/5, f. 59 and King to ——, 12 December 1801 in Dickson, *Dwyer*, p. 208.

292 Sproule to Lees, 18 October 1798, NA, 620/40/176.

293 Joseph, 5 July 1799, NA, 620/56/110. See also Sproule to Lees, 19 October 1798, NA, 620/40/172.

294 Holt MS, p. 173.

295 Crawford to Grenville, 23 October 1798 in Castlereagh, *Memoirs*, II, pp. 263–4. See also Wickham to Castlereagh, 20 November 1798, PRO, HO 100/179/192 and 25 November 1798 in Castlereagh, *Memoirs*, II, p. 103, Richard Hayes, *Biographical dictionary of Irishmen in France*, (Dublin, 1949), pp. 75–6, Elliott, *Partners*, pp. 59–60, *Courier*, 6 June 1797 and [Samuel Turner] to Richardson, 27 September 1798, PRONI, D.607/F/432.

296 *Courier*, 8 November 1798 and King to Marsden, 17 January 1801 NA, 620/63/147.

297 Holt to Powerscourt, n.d. [*c*.October 1798], NLI, MS 4720. For the full text see Appendix Six.

298 *Courier*, 7 November 1798.

299 Sproule to Lees, 4 November 1798, NA, 620/41/12.

300 Ibid. On 3 November what was taken to be Holt's horse was found in Wicklow and his escape from the military reputedly 'impossible'. *Courier*, 8 November 1798. See also *Courier*, *HT* and *SNL*, 7 November 1798.

301 *Courier*, 3 October 1798.

302 *Courier*, 19 November 1798. Holt's arrival in the Bermingham Tower was just two days after that of Wolfe Tone who was briefly interviewed in the Castle before being sent to the Provost Marshalsea where he committed suicide. *HT*, 9 November 1798. Among the first to see Holt was Sarah Tighe who claimed that 'Tone being dead the reigning topic is "General Holt" and various are the inventions about what he is to disclose.' Tighe to Ponsonby?, 20 November 1798, NLI, MS 4813.

303 See O'Donnell, 'Holt', pp. 244–8 and same author, 'General Joseph Holt' in Bob Reece (ed.), *Exiles from Erin, convict lives in Ireland and Australia* (Dublin, 1991), pp. 27–56. Edward Cooke was displeased that Holt had been encouraged to surrender and informed Castlereagh: 'Lord Monck was with Lord Cornwallis on the subject. Lord Cornwallis said he could promise no terms but if he surrenders after any [such] conversation . . . how can he be executed?' Cooke to Castlereagh, 9 November 1798 in Castlereagh, *Memoirs*, II, p. 433 See also Holt, *Rum Story*, p. 33. The *Hibernian Telegraph*'s claim that 'Holt . . . had surrendered himself a prisoner to Lord Powerscourt on condition of a pardon with

transportation for life' proved to be one of the paper's more accurate statements. *HT*, 14 November 1798.

304 *Courier*, 19 October 1798 and *DEP*, 15 November 1798. See also *HT*, 26 November 1798, *HJ*, 17 November 1798 and *Courier*, 20–22 November 1798.

305 Cullen, NLI, MS 8339, pp. 211–2.

306 Holt's *Minerva* shipmate in 1799, Peter Ivers, was also a very senior figure having served as the provincial delegate for the Carlow organization. Ivers kept a low profile in New South Wales and probably adopted an alias but was seen there in the early 1800s assisting fellow United Irish exile Fr James Harold of Rathcoole at Mass. *Irish Magazine*, V, February 1812, p. 59.

307 Holt, 16 November 1798, NA, 620/41/39A, King to Marsden, 13 March 1801, NA, 620/60/16, 27 February 1801, NA, 620/9/95/4 and *SNL*, 7 November 1798. Holt named Owen 'Kittagh' Byrne of Bonavally, Daniel Carberry (Byrne's son-in-law), Matthew Byrne (brother of Owen), Thomas Harris and John Harris (brothers), Valentine Brown, William Repton, one Byrne, Michael and Francis Wafer, William Brady of Roundwood, James Kavanagh of Paddock, Charles Nowlan, Andrew Byrne, John Bryan, Garret Nowlan, one Classon of Roundwood, Thomas Smith (deceased), John Walsh of Bonavalley, William McQuirk of Ballysmutten, 'the two Harmans' (probably John and Laurence), John Healy of Seven Churches, Andrew Thomas of Drummin, John 'Kittagh' Byrne, Andrew Hackett, John Porter (given in error by Holt as 'Peter'), Patrick Warder of Moneystown, James Butler of Ballymoneen, Walter Butler, one Smullen, Katty Kinsella, Val Browne, Fr Christopher Lowe and Joseph Begly (deceased). Also named in passing were Terence 'Kittagh' Byrne, 'Long Peter Nowlan' and his wife, Andrew Kavanagh, Samuel Wallis of Oldcourt near Blessington, McQuirk of Glenbride, 'Carlow' Doherty (deceased). The Wicklow loyalists referred to were John Smith of Roundwood, Thomas Hugo, John Hatton (deceased), John Burbidge (deceased), Freeman (deceased), Christopher Cooper (deceased), [Henry?] Marks (deceased) and Joseph Tate (deceased). See also Bartlett, 'Masters of the mountains', pp. 397–400.

308 Holt informed Doyle that he was 'never so happy for anything' he had done. Holt to Doyle, 22 November 1798, NA, 620/57/157. When Doyle was apprehended and in no position to strike a deal, Holt asserted that he 'was the only man of his purfession [sic] that always strove to save the lives of protestants'. Holt to Colthurst, 18 May 1799, NA, 620/47/38. Carysfort also appealed for clemency for Doyle but he was obliged to join the 87th regiment (aka the Royal Irish Fusiliers) in New Geneva barracks in which he fought as a private in Egypt and elsewhere until the Peace of Amiens in 1802. Once demobilized he became involved in Robert Emmet's conspiracy. Carysfort also sought clemency for the Doyles of Polahoney and in October 1798 recommended the release of John Doyle as well as that of John and Thomas Doyle of Ballygriffen, probably relatives, who were confined in Wicklow gaol and on the hulks. Carysfort to Cornwallis, 30 October 1798, NA, 620/4/29/43, Byrne, *Memoirs*, I, pp. 97–8, 226, Edward Fitzgerald to Cornwallis, 18 August 1798, NA, 620/51/3/23 and Dickson, *Dwyer*, p. 317.

309 Cornwallis to Portland, 4 March 1799, PRO, HO 100/86/19. See also Castlereagh to John King, 8 September 1798, PRO, HO 100/81/265, Holt MS, pp. 201–2, Holt, *Rum Story*, pp. 33–48, Castlereagh, *Memoirs*, II, pp. 186–7 and Holt to Peter La Touche, 15 January 1799, NA, 620/ 56/97.

310 O'Donnell, 'General Joseph Holt', pp. 39–51. He died in Dun Laoghaire, then Kingstown, in May 1826 and was buried in Carrickbrennan cemetery where a plaque was unveiled to his memory by the National Graves Association on 9 October 1994. *Saoirse*, Deireadh Fomhair 1994, p. 12

311 Byrne, *Memoirs*, I, pp. 240–1 See also 17 December 1799, T.C.D, MS 869/5, f. 36, Cornwallis, *Cornwallis*, III, p. 85, Cullen, NLI, MS 8339, p. 208, and 15 February 1799, NA, 620/17/30/3. A Castle document marked 'retained in the service of Major Sirr' listed O'Neil, Thomas Jackson, John Hanlon, James Kain and James [Jemmy] O'Brien. n.d., [c.1799], NA, 620/52/7.

312 Ennis, 'Fook's Mill', pp. 114–7, Byrne, *Memoirs*, I, pp. 237–40, Cullen, NLI, MS 8339, pp. 390–91 and *Catholic Telegraph*, 22 September 1856. Dennis O' Neil of Enniscorthy, a United Irish 'colonel of the Insurgents during the late attempt for the recovery of liberty in Ireland', escaped to France on 2 December 1798 and sought a commission in the Irish Legion. Memorial of Dennis O'Neil, 30 January 1799 in Castlereagh, *Memoirs*, II, p. 230.

Joseph claimed in June 1799 that he had married an Irishwoman and became a prominent member of the United Irishmen in Dublin. Joseph, 5 July 1799, NA, 620/56/110 and 29 June 1799 in Dickson, *Dwyer*, p. 377. Mooney, in whom Major Sirr had taken a special interest, was sometime after October 1798 reported to be 'in Dublin and a silk weaver to trade'. Corcoran, n.d. [1798], NA, SOC, 3060. See also TCD, n.d., [c.1799], MS 869/8, f. 55.

313 15 November 1798, PRO, HO 100/86/86.
314 *SNL*, 29 October and 2 and 8 November 1798 and *HJ*, 5 November 1798.
315 *SNL*, 9 November 1798. See also Holt, 16 November 1798, NA, 620/41/39A. Hackett's death had been predicted on 26 October and prematurely reported on 5 November and afterwards. *HT*, 26 October 1798 and *SNL*, 5, 7 and 9 November 1798.
316 *DEP*, 22 November 1798. See also *Courier*, 28 November 1798 and 1 December 1798, 13 June 1800, NA, 620/57/43, 15 February 1799, NA, 620/17/30/3, Colonel King to ——, 21 November 1798, NA, 620/41/55, Cullen, TCD, MS 1472, p. 226 and O'Donnell, 'Holt', pp. 219–20.

Appendices

APPENDIX ONE
THE WICKLOW VOLUNTEERS, *c*.1779–85

Mounted

The Rathdown Cavalry/Rathdown Association/Rathdown Regiment of Horse
Rathdown Light Dragoons
Rathdown Carbineers
Wicklow Foresters
Independent Wicklow Horse
Dunlavin Light Dragoons

Infantry

Arklow Volunteers (Captain Ryan)
Aldborough Volunteers (Colonel Morley Saunders)
Dunlavin Volunteers (Colonel Sir John Stratford)
Rathdown Infantry
Wicklow Foresters (Colonel Samuel Hayes)
Talbotstown Invincibles (Colonel Nicholas Westby)

Artillery

Wicklow Artillery
Aldborough Artillery

APPENDIX TWO
MILITARY INSTRUCTIONS TO THE UNITED IRISHMEN,
19 APRIL 1798

A return of muskets in each regiment.

Ten good flints is sufficient quantity of powder for each musket to be got directly.
  A man to be got in each regiment or barony, who understands making ball cartridges & a cartridge stick to be got for each company, the man to instruct others in making cartridges.
  One bullet mould must be had for each company at least.
  Powder of each regiment to be kept, if possible by the colonel or someone shopkeeper who can be depended on the powder by no means to be buried.
  Each reg[imen]t to find a person who has served in the army or militia, to act as adjutant to go thro[ugh] the companies by rotation & to be paid by the baronial committee.

A standard to be got for each company 10 feet long, with a pike in the end the flag to be green stuff about two feet square.

Each company to provide a horn a buglehorn if possible, if not a cows horn the persons appointed to have them, to learn three sounds, 1st an assembly 2nd a charge 3rd a call to captains to assemble.

Every man to provide himself with a haversack, & if possible to have constantly by him at least a week's provisions.

Every man to have kettles or pots in readiness.

Every serjeants division to be provided with one shovel, Every 2nd division with one fork, every 3rd with one pick, every division with one billhook, & every company with one axe.

Every company to have one good carr [sic] & horse, both in good & perfect order for work.

Every man to provide himself with straps to carry his greatcoat or blanket, also small straps for his can or spoon. A bit of green stuff, or any other colour, to be fastened at the end of each pike, as it has a great effect in frightening the horses of cavalry.

PRO, HO 100/76/138–9.

APPENDIX THREE
THE WICKLOW YEOMANRY, 1796–98

Cavalry

Bray Cavalry: (Captain Earl Meath)

Castlemacadam Cavalry: (Captain John Camac, First Lieutenant Burgess Camac, Second Lieutenant Benjamin Coates; disbanded March 1798)

Powerscourt Cavalry: (Captain Charles Stanley Monck, First Lieutenant William Colthurst, Second Lieutenant Charles William Quinn)

Wingfield Cavalry: (June/July 1798, First Captain Lord Powerscourt, Second Captain Hunter Gowan, First Lieutenant George Smith, Second Lieutenant Robert Hatton)

Newtownmountkennedy Cavalry: (Captain Robert Gore, First Lieutenant Thomas Archer, Second Lieutenant Richard Gore)

Wicklow Town Cavalry: (Captain Alexander Carroll, First Lieutenant John Revell, Second Lieutenant Thomas Hugo junior)

Rathdrum Cavalry: (Captain Thomas King, First Lieutenant William Tomlinson, Second Lieutenant Richard Bestall)

Arklow Northshire: (Captain Lord Viscount Wicklow, Second Captain Robert Howard junior, First Lieutenant Richard Manifold, Second Lieutenant Robert Darlington)

Arklow Southshire: (Captain Thomas Jones Atkins, First Lieutenant Abraham Coates, Second Lieutenant John Sherwood)

Baltinglass Cavalry: (Captain Benjamin O'Neil Stratford, First Lieutenant William King, Second Lieutenant Humphrey Johnson)

Aldborough Cavalry: (Captain Earl Aldborough)

Dunlavin Cavalry: (aka Rathsallagh Cavalry; Captain William Ryves, First Lieutenant John Fisher, Second Lieutenant John Ryves)

Upper Talbotstown: (aka Humewood Cavalry; Captain William Hume, First Lieutenant William Pendred, Second Lieutenant Michael Fenton)

Lower Talbotstown Cavalry: (aka Blessington Cavalry; Captain Richard Hornidge, First Lieutenant William Patrickson, Second Lieutenant William Hemsworth)

Shillelagh Cavalry: (Captain William Wainwright, First Lieutenant Solomon Scott, Second Lieutenant Joseph Braddell)

Infantry

Bray Infantry: (Captain John Edwards, Lieutenant James Edwards, Second Lieutenant Isaac Litton)

Wicklow Town Infantry: (Captain William West, First Lieutenant Thomas Keogh, Second Lieutenant Thomas Halbert)

Rathdrum Infantry: (see Cronebane Infantry)

Saundersgrove Infantry: (aka Ballynacrow and Tuckmill Infantry/ Imaal Infantry; Captain Morley Saunders, First Lieutenant Thomas Jones, Second Lieutenant James Wall)

Castlemacadam Infantry: (aka Ballymurtagh Infantry; Captain Turner Camac, First Lieutenant John Maxwell Templeton)

Cronebane Infantry: (aka Rathdrum Infantry after March 1798; Captain Abraham Mills, First Lieutenant Thomas Weaver, Second Lieutenant George Blood)

Hacketstown Infantry: (Thomas Hardy, Lieutenant William Saul, Second Lieutenant Francis Thomas)

Donard Infantry: (Captain George Heighington, First Lieutenant Henry Cheney, Second Lieutenant Arthur Connolly)

Stratford-on-Slaney Infantry: (aka Aldborough Infantry/ Stratford Lodge Infantry; Captain Paul Stratford)

Coolattin Infantry: (Captain Joseph Chamney, First Lieutenant Thomas Chamney, Second Lieutenant George Binks)

Coolkenna Infantry: (Captain Abraham Nixon, First Lieutenant Abraham Nixon junior, Second Lieutenant John Revell)

Carnew Infantry: (Captain Thomas Swan, First Lieutenant Richard Bookey, Second Lieutenant Robert Blaney)

Tinahely Infantry: (Captain James Moreton, First Lieutenant George Coates, Second Lieutenant Henry Dowse)

Supplementaries

Tinahely 'True Blues': (Captain William Moreton)

Powerscourt Infantry: (Captain Viscount Powerscourt)

Newtownmountkennedy Supplementary Infantry

Arklow Supplementary Infantry

March 1798, NA, OP 198/15 (3), *List of yeomanry corps on county basis* (Dublin, n.d., [1798]), Ryan, *County of Carlow*, p. 381, *Dublin Gazette*, 12 and 28 June and 28 July 1798.

APPENDIX FOUR
UNITED IRISH FORCES, LEINSTER, APRIL/MAY 1798

April/May 1798			January 1798
Wicklow	14,000	12	9,666
Carlow	11,300	12	1,100
Kildare	11,910	12	6,505
Meath	10,110	4	——
Kilkenny	6,700	4	1,200
Dublin (county)	7,412	3	1,000
Dublin (city)	8,595	6	1,500
King's County	6,500	6	——
Westmeath	5,250	3	5,500

Ross to Downshire, 25 April 1798, PRONI, D.607/F/150, Senior to [Cooke], 24 January 1798, NA, 620/18/13, n.d. [spring 1798], NA, 620/52/105 and Senior to Cooke, 24 January 1798, NA, 620/18/3.

APPENDIX FIVE
THE DUNLAVIN MASSACRE, 24 MAY 1798

Saundersgrove yeomen and locals:

James Mara (Maher), (Uppertown, Dunlavin)
John Reeravan
Daniel Reeravan
John Williams
Andrew Ryan
Patrick Duffy
James Duffy (Baltinglass)
John Webb (Baltinglass)
Patrick Curran
David Lee
Matt Kavanagh
Michael Neil (Dunlavin)
Richard Kelly
Morgan Doyle
Thomas Doyle (Tuckmill)
John Doyle (Scruckawn)
Matthew Farrell (Stratford)
James Moran
Charles Evers
William Dwyer
Andrew Prendergast (Ballinacrow)
Thomas Brien (Ballinacrow Hill)

Narraghmore yeomen and locals

James Keating
Thomas Keating
John Wickham (Eadestown)
Martin Walsh
Edward Shaughnessy
Andrew Carty
Edward Slalleny
Darby Byrne
John Dunne
Martin Griffin
Daniel Kirwan
Thomas Kirwan
Laurence Doyle
Thomas Neil,
Two brothers named Bermingham
Costello

Non-yeomen United Irish officers

John Dwyer (Seskin, Imaal),
Peter Hayden (Killabeg, Imaal)
Peter Kearney (Donard)
Laurence Doyle (Dunlavin)

Cullen papers, Dickson, *Dwyer*, pp. 370–1 and Fitzpatrick, *Sham squire*, pp. 310–11. Note: David Prendergast is included on Dickson's list but survived the rebellion.

APPENDIX SIX
MILITIA DEFECTORS

1. Antrim Militia, July 1798

Darby Dunne, James Keegan, Peter Murphy, Edward Dogherty, John Savage, Patrick Whitty, Thomas Barrett, Thomas Grant, Edward McDonald, Walter McDonald, Patrick Brannagh, David Campbell, John McVeigh, Samuel McAllister, Peter McLaughlin, Farrell O'Reilly, James Spence, Peter Ward, John Moore, Luke McDermott, Charles Neeson, Edward Summers, William Grant, Felix McGuinness, Bernard Dogherty, Dennis McDonald and John Connor.

Antrim Militia Payroll and Muster Lists, July 1798. PRO, WO 13/2574.

2. King's County Militia Defectors, 1–2 September 1798

James Mooney, John Connolly, John Egan junior, William Killfide, Hugh McLauchlan, Hugh Phelan, Michael Caine, Barney Corrigan, James Carroll, James Connors, Thomas Dolan, Tim Daley, Jim Dale, Thomas Davis, Corporal Matthew Henzie, William Parsons, Christopher Guynam, Patrick Connors, Martin Dunne, James McLauchlan and John Rourke.

King's County Militia Payroll and Muster Lists, September 1798. PRO, WO 13/2961.

3. Leitrim Militia Defectors, June–September 1798

G. Flynn, John Brown, Phelim Croal, Patrick Donnelly, Phelim McDermott, Loughlin Confrey, Peter Dogherty, Francis Sullivan, Thomas Duffy, Patrick Devine, Conor Rourke, David Little, Andrew McLee, Luke Mullaney, William Keegan, Jeremiah Donovan and James Foley.

Leitrim Militia Payroll and Muster List, August/September 1798. PRO, WO 13/2980.

4. Sligo Militia Defectors, September 1798

Patrick Foley, Mark Doyle, Daniel Hunt, Thady Rooney, Daniel Smyth, Charles Tighe, Michael Calvey, John Fullerty, John Furey, Patrick Gilligan, Patrick Loughlin, Martin Graham and Augustine Kerr.

Sligo Militia Payroll and Muster List, September 1798. PRO, WO 13/3220.

APPENDIX SEVEN
HOLT DOCUMENTS

1. Holt proclamation, 24 October 1798

Whereas I am empowered and Authorized by General Bonapart [sic] to make and enact laws and statutes in this realm I do hearby [sic] caution all undertenant[s] or tenants in the county Kilkenny not to pay any rents or tythes [sic] or excessive taxes but [for] the making of roads or repairing of roads in s[ai]d county to any lord or landlord in s[ai]d county Barony, or parish or parishes provide [?] any good member residing in s[ai]d county to give unto s[ai]d landlord so much and lies in your power to give him a decent lively hood. I also caution on pain of death any person or persons concerned in bidding for the goods or chattels of any tenant or tenants in s[ai]d county, barony or parish if seize[d] or dist[r]ained for rent or rents by any lord or landlord if found to be concerned & acting contrary to my laws shall be taken and hanged at his own door and his worl[dly] substance consumed to ashes as I expect to pay those tyrant gentlemen of s[ai]d county a visit shortly. I also forbid that no person or persons shall take down this paper for the space of six clear days or if found to be concerned shall meet with severe punishment or any person or persons that don't abide by my laws given under my hand and seal this 24 of October 1798. General Holt.

PRO, HO 100/76/281.

2. Holt to Powerscourt, n.d., [c.October 1798]

This is to let the Gentle men know of my intention present and the cause of my being so headstrong. The[y] burned my house and substance and in c[o]urse I c[o]u[l]d not help but turn out to fight for my life. I never would only for such usage but im ti[re]d of fighting against the Crown I would manfully [have] faught [sic] for it and if my wife was paid about half my loss which is 30 Guineas and the Lord Liftennat [sic] signs my pardon I am able & willing to sarve my king and Contry and I know very well how to Do it but as to give myself up and be transported I never will I wo[u]ld suffer to be shot in pieces first for I am not afraid to Die of Either sid[e]s. I make no doubt but my plans would be very useful at any time to my country because I know as much as is necessary in all points pray don't believe that me or any of my men are the people that robs for be god I would put a robber to death in one minute[s] worning [sic] let my wife know as soon as possible and if the Contents of this will not be done let us all mind ourselves I wish my Country men wel[l] no more G[ene]r[a]l Holt.

NLI, MS 4720.

Bibliography

1. PRIMARY SOURCES

National Library of Ireland

Coates Papers	MIC 5648
Cullen Papers	MSS 9760–2, 8339
Fitzwilliam Papers	MIC 5641–3
Hardwicke Papers	MIC 942, 959–7, 984, 990–2
Holt Letters	MS 4770–1
Kilcoole Sessions	MS 5024
Kilmainham Papers	MS vols. 121–2, 193–8, 254–6
Lake Letters	MS 56, MIC 1588
La Touche Papers	MSS 3151, 12705
Maume Letters	MS 5006
Melville Papers	MS 54A–55, 135
Musgrave Letters	MSS 4156–7
Parsons Letters	MSS 13840/3–4
Powerscourt Papers	MS 7229
Shannon Letters	MSS 13295–13306
Stratford Papers	MSS 13837, 19163–5
Tighe Papers	MSS 4813–4, 13615
Wicklow Papers	MSS 1725, 4239, 12149
General MSS	MS 82029/3, 21586

Trinity College Dublin

Beresford Letters	MS 2319
Courtmartials	MSS 871–2
Croker Papers	MSS 2455–8
Cullen Papers	MS 1472
Madden Papers	MS 1471
Sirr Papers	MS 869

Royal Irish Academy

Burrowes Papers	MSS 23. K. 53, 62
Day Journals	MSS 12. W. 11, 14–17
Stowe Papers	MS A. I. 3
General MSS	MSS 24. K. 14–15 and 23. G. 33 (c)

National Archives

Archer Papers	MS 1017
Bayly Papers	MS 2464
Byrne Papers	MS 5892A
Frazer Papers	MSS 1–4
Rebellion Papers	MSS 620/1–67

State of the Country Papers   MSS 1017–31, 3053–3522
Prisoners Petitions and Cases/
  State Prisoners Petitions
  (1798–1805)
Official Papers   MS 1–400

Dublin Diocesan Archives

Troy Correspondence 1796–1804

Public Record Office, Northern Ireland

Downshire   MS D.607/C–G
Bentinck   MS T.2905/21

Public Record Office, England

Home Office   MSS 30/2, 38, 42/40–8, 50/6–8, 50/29–32,
                                51/128, 150–3, 100/66–124, 148/120–24,
                                171/18–45

War Office   MSS 1/778, 1/1101, 2/79, 3/18–20,
                                13/2574–5, 13/28612, 13/2961, 13/2980,
                                13/3220, 13/3351, 13/3732–3, 68/402

British Museum Library, London

Hardwicke Papers   MSS 35711–2, 35729–42

Mitchel Library, Sydney

Bonwick Collection   MSS A2000–4
Byrne Letters   MS 5471
Holt Autobiography   MS A2024

Archives Office of New South Wales, Sydney

Pardons   MSS 4/3490a–c, SZ 758–9
Petitions   MSS 4/1821–4, 4/1833–6, 4/1840–53,
                         4/1862

2. NEWSPAPERS AND PERIODICALS

Annual Register
Belfast Newsletter
Catholic Bulletin
Catholic Telegraph
Cork Gazette
Cork Mercantile Chronicle
Courier
Dublin Evening Post
Dublin Gazette
Faulkner's Dublin Journal
Finn's Leinster Journal
Freeman's Journal
Hibernian Chronicle

Hibernian Journal
Hibernian Telegraph
Irish Times
Press
New Cork Evening Post
Saunder's Newsletter
Sydney Gazette
*The Irish magazine and monthly asylum
    for neglected biography*
Walker's Hibernian Magazine
Wicklow People
Wicklow Star

3. PRINTED PRIMARY SOURCES

Bayly, Henry Lambart, 'Statistical account of the parish of Arklow' in William Shaw Mason, (ed.), *Statistical account or parochial survey of Ireland*, 2 vols. (Dublin, 1816)

Beresford, Rt. Hon. W. (ed.), *The correspondence of the Rt. Hon. John Beresford*, 2 vols. (London, 1854)

Byrne, Miles, *Memoirs of Miles Byrne*, 2 vols. (Paris, 1863)

Cantwell, B. J., *Memorials of the dead in county Wicklow*, 4 vols. (1974–8)

Chart, D. A. (ed.), *The Drennan letters, 1776–1819* (Belfast, 1931)

Cloncurry, V. B., *Lawless, personal recollections of the life and times of Lord Cloncurry* (1849)

Cloney, Thomas, *A personal narrative of those transactions in the county of Wexford . . . 1798* (Dublin, 1832)

Correspondence between the Rt. Hon. William Pitt and Charles Duke of Rutland . . . 1781–1787 (London, 1890)

Croker, Thomas Crofton (ed.), *Memoirs of Joseph Holt, General of the Irish rebels in 1798, edited from his original manuscript in the possession of Sir William Betham . . .* 2 vols. (London, 1838)

Cullen, Luke, *Personal recollections of Wexford and Wicklow insurgents of 1798* (Enniscorthy, 1959)

Davis, Thomas (ed.), *The speeches of the Right Honourable John Philpot Curran edited with memoir and historical notes* (Dublin, n.d.)

Day, Robert, *A charge delivered to the Grand Jury of the county of Dublin . . . 15th January 1793* (Dublin, 1793)

de Monfort, Simon L. M., 'Mrs Pounden's experiences during the 1798 rising in Co. Wexford' in *Irish Ancestor*, VIII, no. 1, 1976

Finegan, John J. (ed.), *The Anne Devlin gaol journal, faithfully written down by Luke Cullen* (Cork, 1968)

Fraser, Robert, *General view of the Co. Wicklow* (Dublin, 1801)

Gilbert, J. T. (ed.), *Documents relating to Ireland, 1795–1804* (Dublin, 1970)

Gilbert, Lady (ed.), *Calendar of ancient records of Dublin in the possession of the Municipal Corporation of that city* (Dublin, 1907)

Grattan, Henry, *Memoirs of the life and times of the Rt. Hon. Henry Grattan* edited by his son, 5 vols. (London, 1839–46)

Grimes, Seamus (ed.), *Ireland in 1804* (Dublin, 1980)

Hanbidge, Mary, *The memories of William Hanbidge, aged 93, 1906, An Autobiography with appendices and chronicles of his family by his daughter Mary Hanbidge* (St Albans, 1939)

Hewitt, Esther (ed.), *Lord Shannon's letters to his son, a calendar of the letters written by the 2nd Earl of Shannon to his son, Viscount Boyle, 1790–1802* (Belfast, 1982)

Holland, Lord, *Memoirs of the Whig party*, 2 vols. (London, 1852)

Irish genealogical sources no. 2, corn growers, carriers & traders, County Wicklow, 1788, 1789 & 1790 (Dun Laoghaire, 1997)

Kelly, James (ed.), *The letters of Lord Chief Baron Edward Willes to the Earl of Warwick, 1752–62, an account of Ireland in the mid-eighteenth-century* (Kilkenny, 1990)

O'Shaughnessy, Peter (ed.), *A rum story, the adventures of Joseph Holt, thirteen years in New South Wales (1800–12)* (Sydney, 1988)

———, (ed.), 'General Joseph Holt, extracts of his memoirs' in *Roundwood and district History and Folklore Journal*, no. 6, 1994, pp. 3–56

Letters containing information relating to . . . the county of Carlow collected during the progress of the ordnance survey in 1838 (Bray, 1934)

Leadbeater, Mary, *The Leadbeater papers*, 2 vols. (London, 1862)

List of the officers of the several regiments and corps of fencible cavalry and infantry of the . . . yeomanry and . . . volunteer infantry 5th edn. (London, 1797)

Lists of the officers of the several regiments and corps of militia . . . raised since the first of January, 1793 (London, 1794)

Londonderry (ed.), *Memoirs and correspondence of Viscount Castlereagh*, 4 vols. (London, 1848)

MacDermot, Brian (ed.), *The Catholic question in Ireland and England, 1798–1822; the papers of Denys Scully* (Dublin, 1988)

MacDonagh, Michael (ed.), *The Viceroy's post bag, correspondence hitherto unpublished of the Earl of Hardwicke, first Lord Lieutenant of Ireland after the Union* (London, 1904)

McHugh, Roger (ed.), *Carlow in '98: the autobiography of William Farrell of Carlow* (Dublin, 1949)

MacLaren, Archibald, *A minute description of the battles of Gorey, Arklow and Vinegar Hill: together with the movements of the army through the Wicklow mountains . . .* (1798)

McNeven, William, *Pieces of Irish History* (New York, 1807)

Maurice, J. F. (ed.), *Diary of Sir John Moore* (London, 1904)

Minutes of evidence taken before the select committee on the Baltinglass election, 10 November 1783 (Dublin, 1783)

O'Donovan, *et al.*, *Letters containing information relative to the antiquities of the county of Wicklow collected during the progress of the ordnance survey in 1838* (Bray, 1928)

——, *Letters containing information relative to the antiquities of the county of Wexford collected during the progress of the ordnance survey in 1840*, 2 vols. (Bray, 1933)

Reed, Mrs Hugh, 'Cursory remarks on the voyage of the Friendship' in *The Asiatic Journal and monthly register for British India and its dependencies*, VIII, 1819

Ridgeway, William, *The trial of William Michael Byrne* (Dublin, 1799)

Ridgeway, William, *A report on the trial of John McCann* (Dublin, 1798)

Ross, Charles (ed.), *Correspondence of Charles 1st Marquess Cornwallis*, 3 vols. (London, 1849)

Teeling, Charles, *The history of the Irish rebellion of 1798 and sequel to the history of the Irish rebellion of 1798* (new edn., Shannon, 1972)

The tryal of William Byrne of Ballymanus . . . (Dublin, 1799)

The genuine trial of Hugh Woolaghan . . . (Dublin, 1798)

Wakefield, Edward, *An account of Ireland, statistical and political*, 2 vols. (London, 1812) *Wilson's Dublin Directory 1794* (Dublin, 1794)

Woods, C. J. (ed.), *Journals & memoirs of Thomas Russell* (Dublin, 1991)

Young, Arthur, *A tour in Ireland, 1777–1779* (London, 1780) new edn., 2 vols. (Shannon, 1970)

4. SECONDARY SOURCES

'A noble minded rebel' in *The Celt*, August 1857, pp. 238–9

Archer, Patrick, 'Fingal in 1798' in *Dublin Historical Record*, XL, no. 2, March 1987

Argall, P. H., 'Notes on the ancient and recent mining operations in the East Ovoca district' in *Journal of the Royal Geological Society of Ireland*, V, part 3, 1879, pp. 150–64

Bartlett, Thomas and Jeffrey (eds.), *A Military history of Ireland* (Cambridge, 1996)

Bartlett, Thomas and Jeffrey (eds.), 'Defence, counter-insurgency and rebellion: Ireland, 1793– 1803' in Bartlett and Keith Jeffrey (eds.), *military history*, pp. 247–93

——, 'Indiscipline and disaffection in the armed forces in Ireland in the 1790s' in Corish (ed.), *Radicals*, pp. 115–35

——, 'An end to the moral economy: the Irish militia disturbances of 1793' in *Past and Present*, no. 99, 1983, pp. 41–64

——, 'Masters of the Mountains', the insurgent careers of Joseph Holt and Michael Dwyer' in Hannigan and Nolan (eds.), *Wicklow: history and society*, pp. 379–410

Bateman, John, *The great landowners of Great Britain and Ireland* (London, 1876) new ed. (Leicester, 1971)

Batt, Elizabeth, *The Moncks of Charleville House* (Dublin, 1979)

Beames, M. R., *Peasants and power, the Whiteboy movements and their control in pre-Famine Ireland* (Brighton, 1983)

Beckett, J. C., *The making of modern Ireland, 1603–1923* (London, 1966)

'Bishop Joseph Stock of Killala and Achonry, 1798 to 1810' in *North Mayo Historical and Archaeological society journal*, I, no. 2, 1983, pp. 12–15

Blacker, Revd Beaver H., *Brief sketches of the parishes of Booterstown and Donnybrook in the county of Dublin* (Dublin, 1861)

Blackstock, Alan, 'The social and political implications of the raising of the yeomanry in Ulster: 1796–9' in Dickson, Keogh and Whelan (eds.), *United Irishmen*, pp. 234–43

Boake, Rev. Henry Vaux, 'Tinahely over the centuries' in *Journal of the West Wicklow Historical Society*, 1989, pp. 41–2

Brims, John, 'Scottish radicalism and the United Irishmen' in Dickson, Keogh and Whelan (eds.), *United Irishmen*, pp. 151–66

Brynn, Edward, *Crown and Castle, British rule in Ireland, 1800–1830* (Dublin, 1978)

Buckley, James, 'Discovery of gold in Co. Wicklow' in *Royal Society of Antiquities of Ireland Journal*, III, 1913, pp. 183–5

Butler, William, F., *Confiscations in Irish History* (Dublin, 1917)

Campion, John Thomas, *Michael Dwyer, or, the insurgent captain of the Wicklow mountains, a tale of the rising in '98* (Dublin, n.d.)

Cantwell, Ian, 'Glendalough estate and the Hugos' in *Roundwood and District History and Folklore Journal*, no. 4, 1991, pp. 32–4

Cantwell, Ian, 'The trial of Patrick Murray' in *Roundwood and District History and Folklore Journal*, no. 2, 1989

Chandler, David, *The campaigns of Napoleon* (New York, 1966)

Chart, D. A., *An economic history of Ireland* (Dublin, 1920)

Chavasse, Claude, *The story of Baltinglass: a history of the parishes of Baltinglass, Ballynure and Rathbran in County Wicklow* (Kilkenny, 1970)

Childs, John, 'The Williamite war, 1689–1691' in Bartlett and Jeffrey (eds.), *Military History*, pp. 188–210

Corish, Patrick (ed.), *Radicals, rebels and establishments* (Belfast, 1985)

Coughlan, Rupert J., *Napper Tandy* (Dublin, 1976)

Cowman, Des, 'The Mining community at Avoca, 1780 to 1880' in Hannigan and Nolan (eds.), *Wicklow: history and society*, pp. 761–88

Croker, Thomas Crofton, *Researches in the South of Ireland* (London, 1824)

Culhane, Thomas F., 'Traditions of Glin and its neighbourhood' in *Journal of the Kerry Archaeological and Historical Society*, no. 2, 1969, pp. 74–101

Cullen, Luke, '98 in Wicklow (ed.), Myles V. Ronan (Wexford, 1938)

——, *Insurgent Wicklow, 1798* (ed.), Myles V. Ronan (Dublin, 1948)

Cullen, L. M., *The formation of the Irish economy* (Cork, 1969)

——, *Six generations of life and work in Ireland from 1780* (Cork, 1970)

Cullen, L. M., 'The 1798 rebellion in its eighteenth-century context' in Corish (ed.), *Radicals*, pp. 91–113

——, 'The 1798 rebellion in Wexford: United Irishman organisation, membership, leadership' in Whelan (ed.), *Wexford; history and society*, pp. 248–95

——, 'Politics and Rebellion: Wicklow in the 1790s' in Hannigan and Nolan (eds.), *Wicklow: history and society*, pp. 411–502

Curtin, Nancy, 'The United Irish organization in Ulster: 1795–8' in Dickson, Keogh and Whelan (eds.), *United Irishmen*, pp. 209–221

Day, Robert, 'Two county Wicklow volunteer medals' in *Cork History and Archaeological Society Journal*, 2nd series, IX, no. 60, 1903, pp. 226–8

de Brun, Padraig, 'A song relative to a fight between the Kerry militia and some yeomen at Stewartstown, Co. of Tyrone' in *Kerry Archaeological and Historical Journal*, VI–VIII, 1973–5, pp. 101–30

Dempsey, Fr P., *Avoca, a history of the vale* (Dublin, 1912)

Dickson, Charles, *The Wexford Rising in 1798: its causes and its course* (Tralee, 1955)

Dickson, Charles, *The life of Michael Dwyer with some account of his companions* (Dublin, 1944)

——, *Revolt in the North: Antrim and Down in 1798* (Dublin, 1960)

Dickson, David, Keogh, Dáire and Whelan, Kevin (eds.), *The United Irishmen, Republicanism, Radicalism and Rebellion* (Dublin, 1993)

——, 'Paine and Ireland' in Dickson, Keogh and Whelan, (eds.), *United Irishmen*, pp. 135–50

Donnelly, Brian 'From Grand Jury to County Council: an overview of local administration in Wicklow 1605–1898' in Hannigan and Nolan (eds.), *Wicklow: history and society*, pp. 855–94

Donnelly, J. S., 'The Whiteboy movement, 1761–5' in *Irish Historical Studies*, XXI, no. 81, 1978, pp. 20–54

Dunfermline, James Lord, *Lieutenant-General Sir Ralph Abercromby KB, 1793–1801, a memoir by his son, James Lord Dunfermline* (Edinburgh, 1861)

Ekirch, Roger, *Bound for America, the transportation of British convicts to the colonies, 1718–1775* (Oxford, 1987)

Elliott, Marianne, *Wolfe Tone: prophet of Irish independence* (Yale, 1990)

——, *Partners in Revolution, the United Irishmen and France* (London, 1988)

——, 'The Defenders in Ulster' in Dickson, Keogh and Whelan (eds.) *United Irishmen*, pp. 222–32

Evans, E. G., *An outline of the history of the county Wicklow regiment of militia* (1885)

Fagan, Patrick, 'The population of Dublin in the eighteenth-century with particular reference to the proportions of protestants and catholics' in *Eighteenth-Century Ireland*, VI, 1991, pp. 121–59

Fitzpatrick, William J., *The life, times and contemporaries of Lord Cloncurry* (Dublin, 1855)

——, *The Sham squire and the informers of 1798* (Dublin, 1866)

——, *The Secret Service under Pitt* (Dublin, 1892)

——, *Memoirs of Fr Healy of Little Bray* (London, 1899)

Ffolliott, Rosemary, 'Some Irish militia movements during the Napoleonic wars' in *Irish ancestor*, I, no. 2, 1969, pp. 109–113

Ford, F., *Maritime Arklow* (Arklow, 1988)

Foster, Roy, *Modern Ireland, 1600–1972* (London, 1988)

Fortescue, Sir John, *History of the British army*, 13 vols. (London, 1899)

Fraser, A. M., 'David Digges La Touche, Banker, and a few of his descendants' in *Dublin Historical Record*, V, 1942–3

Fraser, J., *Guide to the county of Wicklow* (Dublin, 1842)

Fraser, Robert, *General view of the agriculture and mineralogy, present state and circumstances of the county Wicklow* (Dublin, 1801)

Froude, James Anthony, *The English in Ireland in the eighteenth-century*, 3 vols. (London, 1874)

Furlong, Nicholas, *Fr John Murphy of Boolavogue, 1753–1798* (Dublin, 1991)

Gahan, Daniel J., 'The 'Black Mob' and the 'Babes in the Wood': Wexford in the wake of the rebellion, 1798–1806' in *Journal of the Wexford Historical Society*, VI, no. 13, 1990, pp. 92–110

——, *The people's rising, Wexford 1798* (Dublin, 1995)

G.E.C., *The complete peerage, or a history of the House of Lords and all its members from the earliest times* (London, 1936)

Gwynn, Stephen, *Henry Grattan and his times* (London, 1939)

Hale, Leslie, *John Philpot Curran, his life and times* (London, 1958)

Hammond, Joseph W., 'Behind the scenes of the Emmet Insurrection' in *Dublin Historical Record*, VI, no. 4, 1944, pp. 91–106

Hannigan, Ken and Nolan, William (eds.), *Wicklow: history and society, interdisciplinary essays on the history of an Irish County* (Wicklow, 1994)

Hannigan, Ken, 'The Irish language in Co.Wicklow' in *Wicklow Historical Journal*, I, no. 1, July 1988

Hay, Edward, *History of the Insurrection of Wexford* (Dublin, 1803)

Hayes, Richard, *Biographical dictionary of Irishmen in France* (Dublin, 1949)

——, *The last invasion of Ireland* (Dublin, 1937)

Hayes-McCoy, G. A., 'The topography of a battlefield: Arklow 1798' in *Irish Sword*, I, no. 1, pp. 50–56

——, *Irish Battles, a military history of Ireland* (London, 1969)

Henry, Brian, *Dublin hanged: crime, law enforcement and punishment in late eighteenth-century Dublin* (Dublin, 1994)

Hickey, Nora M., 'Cromwellian settlement in Balyna parish, 1641– 1699' in *Journal of the Kildare Archaeological and Historical Society*, XVI, no. 5, 1985–6

Joyce, John, *General Thomas Cloney, a Wexford rebel of 1798* (Dublin, 1988)

Kavanagh, P. F. Revd, *A popular history of the insurrection of 1798* (Dublin, 1874)

Kavanagh, Joan, 'Wicklow county gaol' in *Roundwood and District Historical Journal*, no. 4, 1991, pp. 21–5

Keogh, Daire, 'Archbishop Troy, the Catholic Church and Irish radicalism' in Keogh, Dickson and Whelan (eds.) *United Irishmen*, pp. 124–34

——, "The most dangerous villian in society", Fr John Martin's mission to the United Irishmen of Wicklow in 1798' in *eighteenth-Century Ireland*, VII, 1992, pp. 115–32

Landreth, Helen, *The pursuit of Robert Emmet* (Dublin, 1949)

Latimer, W. T., *A history of the Irish Presbyterians* (Belfast, 1902)

Lennon, Colm, *Sixteenth-century Ireland: the incomplete conquest* (Dublin, 1994)

Lyons, F. S. L., *Charles Stewart Parnell* (London, 1977)

Longfield, A. K., 'Linen and cotton printing at Stratford-on-Slaney, County Wicklow' in *Royal Society of Antiquities of Ireland Journal*, XV, 1945, pp. 24–5

Longmate, Norman, *Island Fortress, the defence of Great Britain 1603–1945* (London, 1993)

McAnally, Sir Henry, *The Irish Militia, 1793–1816, a social and military study* (London, 1949)

McCarthy, J. F., 'The Beresford family' in *Clonmel History and Archaeological Society Journal*, I, no. 3, 1955, pp. 61–3

McD[. . .], 'Anecdotes and reminiscences of the celebrated captain Michael Dwyer, of the Wicklow mountains' in *The Celt*, August 1858, pp. 261–9

McDowell, R. B., *Ireland in the age of imperialism and revolution, 1760–1801* (London, 1979)

____, 'The personnel of the Dublin Society of United Irishmen', *Irish Historical Studies*, II, no. 5, 1940

Mac Gabhann, Fiachra, 'The Water was the Sheriff': the land beneath the Poulaphouca reservoir' in Hannigan and Nolan (eds.), *Wicklow: history and society*, pp. 927–52

McKenzie, W., *The beauties of the County of Wicklow* (Dublin, 1794)

Macken, James, *Martin Burke, the father of Pittwater* (Sydney, 1994)

Mac Suibhne, Peadar, *Kildare in 1798* (Naas, 1978)

Madden, R. R., *Down and Antrim in '98* (Dublin, n.d.)

____, *The life and times of Robert Emmet* (Dublin, 1847)

____, *The United Irishmen, their lives and times*, 4 vols., 2nd edn. (Dublin, 1857–60)

Maguire, W. A., *The Downshire estates in Ireland, 1801–1845* (Oxford, 1972)

Mason, William Shaw, *A statistical account and parochial survey of Ireland*, 2 vols. (1814–19)

Maxwell, W. H., *History of the Irish rebellion in 1798* (London, 1845)

Maxwell, Elizabeth, *Country and town in Ireland under the Georges* (London, 1940)

Mills, Abraham, 'A mineralogist account of the native gold lately discovered in Ireland' in *Dublin Society Transactions*, II, 1801, pp. 454–63

____, 'Second Report', *Dublin Society Transactions*, III, 1802, pp. 81–7

Mitchell, Brian, *A new genealogical atlas of Ireland* (Baltimore, 1986)

Moran, Patrick Francis, *Historical sketch of the persecutions suffered by the catholics of Ireland under the rule of Cromwell and the puritans* (Dublin, 1884)

Murphy, John A. (ed.) *The French are in the bay: the expedition to Bantry Bay, 1796* (Cork, 1997)

Musgrave, Sir Richard, *Memoirs of the different rebellions in Ireland* (Dublin, 1801) and 4th edn., (Fort Wayne, 1995)

Neeson, Eoin, *A history of Irish Forestry* (Dublin, 1991)

Neville, Jacob, *An actual survey of the county of Wicklow* (Dublin, 1760)

O'Brien, Conor, 'The Byrnes of Ballymanus' in Hannigan and Nolan (eds.), *Wicklow: history and society*, pp. 305–40

O'Brien, Gerard, *Anglo-Irish politics in the age of Grattan and Pitt* (Dublin, 1987)

O'Coindealbhain, Sean, 'The United Irishmen in Cork County' in *Journal of the Cork Historical and Archaeological Society*, LIV–LVI, 1949–51

O'Donnell, Ruan, 'The Rebellion of 1798 in County Wicklow' in Hannigan and Nolan (eds.), *Wicklow: history and society*, pp. 341–78

____, 'General Joseph Holt and the Rebellion of 1798 in County Wicklow', MA thesis, University College Dublin, 1991

____, 'Croppy Biddy' Dolan' in Eimear Burke (ed.), *Cameos* (Dublin, 1990), pp. 26–30

____, 'General Joseph Holt' in Bob Reece (ed.) *Exiles from Erin, convict lives in Ireland and Australia* (London, 1991), pp. 27–56

____, 'The Wicklow United Irishmen in New South Wales, part 2' in *Wicklow Historical Society, Cumann Seanda Chill Mhantain*, II, no. 1, (July 1995), pp. 10–17

____, 'Michael Dwyer: The Wicklow Chief' in Reece (ed.), *Irish convict lives*, pp. 13–50

O'Flanagan, J. R., *The Munster Circuit, tales, trials and traditions* (London, 1880)

Ohlmeyer, Jane H. (ed.), *Ireland from independence to occupation, 1641–1660* (Cambridge, 1995)

____, 'The wars of religion, 1603–1660' in Bartlett and Jeffrey (eds.), *Military history*, pp. 160–87

O'Loinsigh, Seamus, 'The burning of Ballinagh', *Breifne, Journal of Cumman Seanchais Bhreifne*, II, no. 7, 1964, pp. 359–64

——, 'The Rebellion of 1798 in Meath', part 1 in *Riocht na Midhe*, III, no. 4, 1966, pp. 338–50, part 1 continued in IV, no. 1, 1967, pp. 33–40, part 2, IV, no. 2, 1968, pp. 33–50

O'Muiri, Reamonn, 'Lt John Lindley St Leger, United Irishman' in *Seanchas Ard Mhaca*, II, no. 1, 1988, pp. 133–201

O'Reilly, Stan, 'Wicklow rebels of 1798, no. 1, William Michael Byrne' in *Wicklow Historical Society Journal*, I, no. 7, July 1994, pp. 16–18

O'Snodaigh, Peter, '*98 and Carlow: a look at the historians* (Carlow, 1979)

O'Toole, J., *The O'Tooles, Ancient Lords of Powerscourt* (Dublin, n.d.)

O'Toole, Revd P. L. [pseud. Fr Meagher], *History of the Clan O'Toole (Ui Tuatail) and other Leinster septs* 2 vols. [vol. II incorporates *The history of the clan O'Byrne*] (Dublin, 1890)

O'Tuathail, P., 'Wicklow traditions of 1798' in *Bealoideas*, V, no. 2 (1935)

Pakenham, Thomas, *The Year of Liberty: the story of the great Irish Rebellion of 1798* (London, 1969)

Percival-Maxwell, M., *The outbreak of the Irish rebellion of 1641* (Dublin, 1994)

Platt, Hester, 'Anne Devlin: an outline of her story' in *The Catholic Bulletin*, VII, 1917, pp. 498–503

Plowden, Francis, *An historical review of the state of Ireland, from the invasion of that country under Henry II to its Union with Great Britian*, 2 vols. (London, 1803)

Powell, G. R., *The official railway handbook to Bray, Kingstown, the coast and the county of wicklow* (Dublin, 1860)

Power, Patrick, 'A survey: some Wicklow maps 1500–1888' in Hannigan and Nolan (eds.), *Wicklow: history and society*, pp. 723–60

Power, Thomas, *Land, politics and society in eighteenth-century Tipperary* (Oxford, 1993)

Price, Liam, *The place names of county Wicklow: the Irish form and meaning of parish, townland and local names* (Wexford, 1935)

Quinn, M. R. and Lord Monck, 'An account of the cone wheat propagated in the county Wicklow' in *Dublin Society Transactions*, I, part 2, 1799, pp. 165–7

Reece, Bob, *Irish Convict Lives* (Sydney, 1993)

Robinson, Portia, *The women of Botany Bay, a reinterpretation of the role of women in the origins of Australian society* (Sydney, 1988)

H. Rooke, *Glendalough from the past: diocese of Glendalough, parish of Wicklow, town of Wicklow* (Dublin, 1895)

Rusden, George William, *Curiosities of Colonization* (London, 1874)

Ryan, John, *The history and antiquities of the county of Carlow* (Dublin, 1833)

Sadlier, T. U., 'The manor of Blessington' in *Royal Society of Antiquities of Ireland Journal*, XVIII, 1928, pp. 128–31

Senior, Hereward, *Orangeism in Ireland and Britain, 1795–1836* (London, 1966)

Shaw, A. G. L., *Convicts and the Colonies, a study of penal transportation from Great Britain and Ireland to Australia and other parts of the British Empire* (London, 1966)

Sheedy, Kieran, *Upon the mercy of government, the story of the surrender, transportation and imprisonment of Michael Dwyer and his Wicklow comrades, and their subsequent lives in New South Wales* (Dublin, 1988)

Shepard, Ernie, 'Avoca mines' in *Arklow Historical Society Journal*, 1986, pp. 18–20

Sherman, John, 'Donoughmore in omayle': an historical sketch of the Glen of Imail, county of Wicklow, of the Ui Taidg and the O'Tooles of Imail* (Dublin, 1876)

Simms, J. G., *The Williamite confiscation in Ireland, 1690–1703* (London, 1956)

Smyth, James, *The men of no property, Irish radicals and popular politics in the late eighteenth-century* (Dublin, 1992)

Stewart, A. T. Q., *A deeper silence: the hidden origins of the United Irishmen* (London, 1993)

Stewart, Donald, 'The report of Donald Stewart, itinerant mineralogist to the Dublin Society' in *Transactions of the Dublin Society*, I, part 2, 1799, pp. 1–42

Swords, Liam, *The Green cockade, the Irish in the French Revolution, 1789–1815* (Dublin, 1989)

The formation of the Orange Order, 1795–1798: the edited papers of colonel William Blacker and Colonel Robert H. Wallace (Belfast, 1994)

The last county, the emergence of Wicklow as a county, 1606–1845 (Wicklow, 1993)

The life and glorious achievements of the gallant general Sir John Moore, KB, who fell at the memorable battle of Corunna, January 16, 1809 . . . (London, n.d.)

Turner, Larry, 'Andrew Byrne: "intelligent, honest, sober, and industrious"' in Reece (ed.), *Irish Convict Lives*, pp. 80–108

Vandeleur, W. E., *Notes on the history of Killiskey parish* (Dundalk, 1946)

Vaughan, W. E. and Fitzpatrick, A. J., *Irish historical statistics, population, 1821–1971* (Dublin, 1978)

Wall, Maureen, *The penal laws, 1691–1760* (Dundalk, 1976)

Waters, Ormonde D. P., 'The Revd James Porter, Dissenting minister of Greyabbey, 1753–1798' in *Seanchas Ard Mhacha*, XIV, no. 1, 1990, pp. 80–101

Wells, Roger, *Insurrection: the British experience, 1795–1803* (Gloucester, 1986)

Wheeler, H. and Broadley, A. M., *The war in Wexford: an account of the rebellion in the south of Ireland in 1798* (London, 1910)

Whelan, Kevin, *The tree of liberty: radicalism, catholicism and the construction of Irish identity, 1760–1830* (Cork, 1996)

____, 'The role of the Catholic priest in the 1798 rebellion in County Wexford' in Whelan (ed.), *Wexford: history and society* (Dublin, 1987)

____, 'The religious factor in the 1798 rebellion in County Wexford' in P. O'Flanagan and Kevin Whelan (eds.), *Rural Ireland, 1600–1900* (Cork, 1987)

Whitaker, Anne-Maree, *Unfinished Revolution, the United Irishmen in New South Wales, 1800–1810* (Sydney, 1994)

Wright, G. N., *An historical guide to the city of Dublin* (London, 1823)

____, *A guide to the County of Wicklow* (London, 1822)

Zimmerman, George Denis, *Songs of Irish rebellion* (Dublin, 1967)

Index